VITAS

Author:

Tom Barnes
Master of Arts in History—Northern Colorado University, 1966
History Instructor—Santa Ana College, 1969-1973
AP and IB Teacher—Laguna Hills High School, Laguna Hills, California, 1987-2005
Co-Author with Gordon Utz of the 5th Edition of *Multiple-Choice & Free-Response Questions with DBQ in Preparation for the AP United States History Examination*, 2006
Author of *Casablanca Film Trivia: Here's Looking at You, Kid!* 2009

Editorial Consultants:

Richard Neffson
Master of Arts in Political Science—U.C. Davis, 1978
AP US History Teacher at Rancho Cotate High School, Rohnert Park, California, 2004-2013
Exam Reader in AP US History for the College Board, 2008-2014

Tim Vargish
Master of Arts in American History—Cal State Long Beach, 1974
AP US History Teacher at Mission Viejo High School, Mission Viejo, California, 1990-2014
Instructor at Long Beach City College, 1977-1979
Instructor at Saddleback College, 1983-2014

DEDICATION

To my wife Vonne
for her forbearance,
assistance and love.

PREFACE

The 6th edition of D&S Marketing's AP U.S. History Prep Book (*Multiple-Choice and Essay Questions with Review Material in Preparation for the AP United States History Examination*) is designed to prepare students for the "new" curriculum starting with the May, 2015 AP U.S. History Exam. The multiple-choice questions are based on the College Board's new testing format, as are all of the essay questions. The 6th edition includes extensive "review material," 730 new multiple-choice questions, and 4 complete sets of new short answer, long essay, and DBQ (Document Based Question) questions.

Much of the extensive "review material" from the 18 chapters of the 5th Edition has been rewritten and reorganized into 34 distinct units, making it much easier to locate material on specific subjects. Each of the 34 units consists of review material and 15 document based multiple-choice questions. It is an ideal supplement to the class textbooks and weekly lessons. The lengths of the chapters vary slightly, and are organized around commonly taught U.S. History subjects and themes. At approximately 626 pages, the overall length of the 6th edition is significantly longer than the 5th edition and can be used not only as a prep book but also as a complementary textbook so more time can be spent examining and analyzing primary source documents.

As always, in D&S books, there is a Teacher's Manual. Answers and complete explanations for all of the 730 multiple-choice questions are in the Teacher's Manual. The 6th edition of the Teacher's Manual also includes suggested historic information with sample answers that can be used in answering the short answer, long essay, and DBQ sections of the new test.

The 5th edition was a joint endeavor with my colleague and co-author, Gordon Utz. I will always be grateful to him for the collegiality we shared in writing the 5th edition and his passing is a great loss to the AP U.S. History community. All of the material for the 6th edition is my work.

As the purpose of the AP U.S. History Prep Book is to assist the student in preparing for the 2015 examination, the 6th edition has been structured to complement the new curriculum framework with questions that are similar to the sample questions that have been provided by the College Board.

The most significant change in both the AP curriculum framework and the 6th edition are the multiple-choice questions. For the most part these are based on a wide variety of primary and secondary source documents that also include songs, poems, cartoons, posters, speeches, charts, graphs, maps, and other visuals. Some of these are familiar documents like the Mayflower Compact, Declaration of Independence, Declaration of Sentiments, Gettysburg Address and the Gulf of Tonkin Resolution. Others like the Old Deluder Satan Act, "Follow the Drinking Gourd," Ostend Manifesto, Cable Act of 1922, and the Port Huron Statement, are not as well known.

More than 25% of the documents and questions are on, about, or by underrepresented groups of minorities and women. Students should find many of the documents engaging, and the variety of sources they come from will lead to a wider understanding of the breadth and depth of U.S. history. Two to five questions are written on each document, and the 730 multiple-choice questions (510 chapter questions and 220 on the sample tests) are based on more than 240 different documents. All of the MC questions have 4-option answers instead of 5 on previous tests that mirror the new AP Exam. Each of the four sample AP tests include: 55 MC Questions, four Short Answer, two Long Essay (formerly FRQ or Free Response Questions), and one document based question (DBQ).

No test preparation book can substitute for the hard work that is required of each student to be successful. However, this preparation book can serve as a resource to guide students in their quest to know and understand U.S. History. Along with the teacher and textbook, the 6th edition of the AP U.S. History Prep Book will be an invaluable asset to accomplish the task of preparing for the new AP U.S. History Examination.

I would like to thank Richard Neffson of Rancho Cotate High School and Tim Vargish of Mission Viejo High School for editing the entire 6th edition. Any flaws that remain in the book are mine alone. Hopefully, the 6th edition will be as successful as its predecessor the 5th edition and reflect the changes that have been made in the U.S. History curriculum for the upcoming 2015 examination. The new test will be a challenge for students, teachers and authors of AP U.S Test Prep books; I trust that we will all be up to the task.

Tom Barnes
Teacher Emeritus, AP U.S History

TABLE OF CONTENTS

HISTORICAL PERIODS/CHAPTER TITLES
MULTIPLE-CHOICE DOCUMENTS

Period 1—1491 to 1607: Early Contacts Among Groups in North America

Period 2—1607-1754—North American Societies in the Context of the Atlantic World

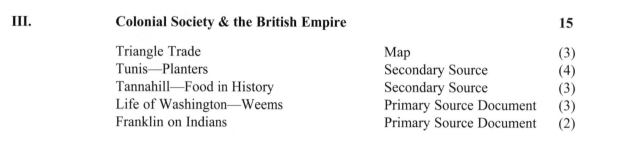

Period 5—1844-1877: Expansion, Regional Separation, the Civil War and its Aftermath

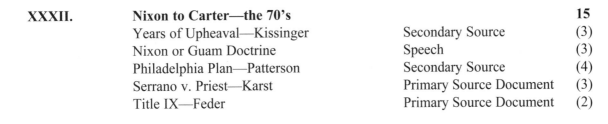

Multiple-Choice Tests ONE, TWO, THREE, FOUR

TEST ONE Multiple-Choice

TEST TWO Multiple-Choice

TEST THREE Multiple-Choice

TEST FOUR Multiple-Choice

UNIT I
NATIVE AMERICANS &
EUROPEAN EXPLORATION

Prior to the arrival of the Europeans a varied indigenous culture existed in the New World. Originally coming from the Siberian part of Asia these people's contact with the Europeans would decimate their populations and lead to the demise of many of the cultures. After adapting to their new surroundings in the Americas they practiced a wide variety of lifestyles and spoke several thousand different languages. These indigenous people would be misnamed by Europeans as Indians because Columbus thought he had reached the outskirts of the East Indies.

Characteristics of Native Americans (Indians)

· Asia Origins
It is believed by many anthropologists and archaeologists that the first people arrived during the last ice-age, approximately 20,000-30,000 years ago. The sea level was lower and glaciers formed a thousand mile passageway between the continents of Asia and North America crossing the land-bridge at the Bering Sound, from northeastern Siberia into Alaska.

· Hunter-Gatherers
What were to become the indigenous people were predominately hunter-gatherers who followed herds across the land bridge of Berengia between Siberia and Alaska stalking large game like bison and the now extinct wooly mammoth. Most experts believe these nomadic people migrated in search of food. These people were on the continent before the mammoth, wild horse, and ground sloth had become extinct.

· Anatomical Types
Native Americans were of a common ancestry which is the same general type that has been called Asiatic or Mongoloid.

1

·Uneven Population

Distribution was dense along the coasts but sparse in the interior. Modern scholarship has estimated that the population was somewhere between 12 million and 90 million in all of the Americas at the time of the arrival of the Europeans. Much of this population was in Mexico and South America.

Native American (Indian) Political and Social Organization

·Tribe

The primary form of organization was an independent, self contained, social and political unit called the tribe by Europeans. The estimated number of tribes that existed when the Europeans arrived was 1,000–2,000.

·Extended families

These existed within the tribes and tied the people together in a closely knit social fabric. Frequently parents, children, grandparents, aunts, uncles, and cousins would exist in one household.

·Council

The basic tribal ruling unit of government for many tribes was the council.
1. Tribal councils could consist of males over 30.
2. Often matters of importance had to be approved by this body, and not by the chief alone.
3. The chief did not have absolute power or inherent power as was the case with many European monarchs.
4. A chief's personality and accomplishments enhanced his credibility and power among his people.

·Meeting of the Council

The chief usually notified members of the time of the meeting. When the adult males assembled, he presented with clarity the questions at issue. Members then spoke on the issue and there was absolute silence while this was going on. Discussions ensued that might be completed in one sitting or might go on for days. Women would bring in food at appropriate times. As the meeting went on there was a great deal of smoking and pipe passing. Anyone could observe the proceedings but there could be no noise. At the end of the meeting one of the councilors summed up and formulated the prevailing opinion that had been arrived at by consensus and that was the course of action that was taken. The chief spoke for the tribe but did not make decisions for the tribe, the council did.

·Religion

Like all other cultures, the Indian societies of North America hoped to enlist the aid of the supernatural in controlling the natural and social world. Each tribe had its own set of religious observances devoted to that goal. Individuals tried to woo or appease powerful spiritual entities with private prayers or sacrifices of valuable items (e.g., furs, tobacco, food), but when entire communities sought divine assistance to ensure a successful hunt, a good harvest, or victory in warfare, they called upon shamans and priests whom they believed to have acquired supernatural powers through visions. These abilities included predicting the future and influencing the weather. Shamans might also assist individuals by interpreting dreams and curing or causing outbreaks of witchcraft. With the arrival of the Europeans the Indians to varying degrees melded many of their religious practices into the religion of the conquerors, especially Catholicism.

Confederations and Alliances

·Loose alliances

These were exceptions, not the rule, as most tribes were wary or even hostile toward each other as they competed over the use of land. The tribes that were able to combine into confederations were usually more powerful than individual tribes.

·Abenaki Confederacy
1. Algonquin-speaking Native American tribes in the Northeast included the Maliseet, Norridgewock, and Penobscot among others.
2. Extending across most of northern New England into the southern part of the Canadian Maritime Provinces, the Abenaki called their homeland *Ndakinna* meaning "our land."
3. This Confederation was formed after 1670 to ward off European exploitation, but it failed to achieve its goal as epidemics killed most of the people.

·Iroquois League
This confederation was founded by the legendary leader Hiawatha, along with his half brother, the Prophet.
1. Five tribes controlled territory from the Great Lakes to the Adirondacks including Pennsylvania and up-state New York. These were the Mohawk, Oneida, Onondaga, Cayuga, and Seneca (Tuscaroras were added later).
2. Native American name was *Ganonsyoni* or *Haudenosaunee*–which describes the extension of the Longhouses where as many as 20 families would share the lodging.
3. The social structure of the longhouse was controlled by women; they owned the house and all its belongings.
4. Iroquois controlled their Indian neighbors through skillful diplomacy. Because of their strategic location between the French and other Indian colonies, they played a principal role in dominating the beaver trade.

·Civilized Tribes of the Southeastern Woodlands
1. This group included among others the Creek, Cherokee, Choctaw, Chickasaw, and Seminole.
2. They built a complex political alliance, which united native peoples in what became Georgia, Alabama, and South Carolina.
3. Although they spoke a variety of languages, including Muskogee, Alabama, and Hitchiti, these tribes were united in their wish to remain at peace with one another.
4. Creeks and the European colonists exchanged slaves (capturing other Native Americans in Florida until the supply ran out) and deerskins for textiles, kettles, and other European goods.

Native American (Indian) Languages

·51 Independent Language Families
Each tribe had its own language peculiarities that were unintelligible to Europeans and often to other tribes. This lack of a common language made it difficult for tribes to unite against the incursion of the Europeans.

·Language Families
These occupied the largest land areas.
1. **Algonquin** –Located in the Northeast United States and Canada.
2. **Sioun**—Dominated the Upper Mississippi and Missouri area.
3. **Uto-Aztecan**—Predominated on the Plains and Great Basin.
4. There were 30 distinct language families west of the Cascades or on the Pacific Coast.

Native Americans Concept of Land

·Concept of Land
Land was unique as it could not be owned, sold or transferred; it could only be used.

·Part of Nature

Land was an integral, inseparable part of nature. Tecumseh said, "… sell a country! Why not sell the air, the clouds, the great sea as well as the land."

·Sustenance

Land existed to sustain the beings that lived upon it and used it.

·Tribes

Each one had a right to use the land but no one could own it. Disputes between tribes were over land use, not ownership.

·Problems

This differing concept of land would cause great problems between the Native Americans (Indians) and the Europeans.

Europeans Concept of Land and Treaties

·English

All Europeans based their land claims on discovery, exploration, or settlement.

·Colonial Policy

Each colony could deal with the Indians as they wished.

·Extinguishing Occupation

Most Europeans felt Indians had a right to occupy land, but that this could be extinguished by purchase or treaty.
1. Land could not be legally occupied by the Europeans until it had been purchased from the tribes.
2. Individuals could not purchase lands directly from Indians without the approval of colonial authorities.
3. Negotiations were often with the chief, who did not have the power to decide for the Council, but sometimes did so anyway as in the case of Major Ridge who signed the treaty that led to the removal of the Cherokee in what became the "Trail of Tears."
4. Europeans saw the chief as the sovereign equivalent of a European monarch.

·Treaties by Colonial Agents

Custom developed that required treaties of any kind to be negotiated by agents of the colonial government.

·Misunderstandings

In what should have been an orderly process the early treaties were haphazard and chaotic.
1. Boundaries were often vague and indefinite.
2. Many "walking" and "riding" treaties and overlapping treaties.
3. Treaties were used to justify existing conditions of illegal squatting.
4. "Squatter sovereignty" was accepted by those on the frontier—especially the Scots-Irish.

·Compensation

This included livestock, beads, cloth, manufactured goods (including guns) and sometimes an annual payment of money. The most famous of these transactions was Peter Minuet's purchase of Manhattan Island for 60 Dutch Guilders (about $24) in trade goods.

Economic Activities

·Hunters and Gatherers
They sought out wild foods including game, fruits, and nuts.

·Agriculture
Secondary means of support was agriculture—primarily maize (corn).

·New Mexico and Arizona
Agriculture was intensive and productive and consisted of maize, beans, squashes, and sunflowers.

·Great Lakes
Wild rice often replaced maize as the staple in this region.

·California
The plentiful acorn was the predominate food.

·Deer
It was the chief food animal except for the prairie where the bison dominated. After the Spanish introduced the horse to the Plains Native Americans (Indians) it became the basis of their lifestyle.

·Turkey
It was somewhat domesticated (other common farm animals were not domesticated).

·Textile Arts
Were usually primitive except for the tribes of the lower Mississippi who wove fine cloth from vegetable fiber.

·Basswood
It was used for bark fiber, nettle, Indian hemp cordage and cloth.

·Skin/Fur-Weaving
This was the dominant handicraft or domestic enterprise especially for the hunter-gatherer tribes.

Tribes and Nations

·Dynamic Cultures
The tribes were at different stages of cultural development and were not static.

·Around 100 A.D. Meso-American
From Honduras to Mexico City its influence began to spread to the North and this brought about dramatic progress in the cultures of North America.

·Ohio River Valley and Southeast Mississippi
Early mound builders were in Ohio River Valley and their structures meant a high degree of cooperation and powerful leaders. Features like earthen mounds and wood and thatch temples predominate until 500 AD when the culture began to die out. Later mound builders in the Cahokia area of Illinois near St. Louis where a city of 35,000 may have existed in 1100 AD, constructed buildings that had many similarities to Meso-American pyramids. Metal work and sculpture were of high quality. When Europeans came the culture was less sophisticated than during earlier times. People were predominately farmers who would move when the land wore out. They had an elaborate social structure with class distinctions and Europeans called their settlements towns. They traded goods from Yellowstone in Wyoming, to the Great Lakes and the Gulf of Mexico. Some

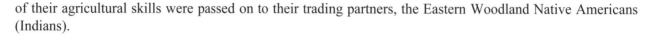

of their agricultural skills were passed on to their trading partners, the Eastern Woodland Native Americans (Indians).

· Eastern Woodlands

They hunted, fished, and cultivated corn, beans, and squash in the same plots and cleared areas for agriculture by girdling trees and slashing the bark. Building styles included the wigwam and the longhouse of the Iroquois. The heaviest population concentrations were near or along the seacoast, lakes, ponds, marshes, creeks, and rivers where animals could be hunted, fish caught, birds taken, leaves, seeds, and roots of wild plants could be gathered, shellfish collected, and crops grown. In certain parts of the upper Great Lakes area, wild rice grew in abundance and the Menominee especially depended on it.

· Great Plains

An inhospitable area where Native Americans did not arrive until 1600. Plains Indians needed a horse and rifle to hunt the buffalo and these were provided by the Spanish. The Chippewa drove the Dakota and Sioux tribes out of the Minnesota region to the Great Plains. The Cheyenne migrated from the Minnesota farming areas to the Great Plains. Kiowas, Commanches, Arapahoes, Crows, and Blackfoot all abandoned farming for the buffalo. The teepee, feathered war bonnet, war paint, and nomadic existence were all elements of the culture of the Plains Indians. Sioux refers to a large group of Native Americans speaking a common or similar languages. The buffalo provided them with food, clothing, fuel, covering for their dwellings, and the raw material for many of their tools.

· The Southwest

Also influenced by Meso-American culture, the cultures of the Hopis, Pimas, and Pueblos were very similar. Tribes were sedentary farmers with an agricultural tradition. Pueblos had a classless society with a theocracy and the power of the theocracy was immense but based on the consent of the governed. The Southwest Indians were skilled in the arts of pottery, weaving, and working with shells. The Athabascan tribes—Navaho and Apache—made a business out of war.

· Pacific Northwest Coast

There was little Meso-American influence or farming in this area. Hunting, fishing, and gathering were relatively easy to do because the area was rich in natural products. Because of their relative wealth there was a great deal of spare time to engage in activities. Their woodworking was elaborate and demonstrated by the high quality of their totem poles that told their history and beliefs. Houses, dishes, nets, clothing, boats, chests, and wooden masks were important features in their lives. Acquisition of metal tools brought about an artistic outburst. Three social classes predominated which featured chiefs, commoners, and slaves. The elaborate Potlatch ceremony as practiced by the Kwakiutl showed their emphasis on wealth, status, and conspicuous consumption.

· Mesoamerica

They were the people of Central America and southern Mexico including the present day countries of Belize, Guatemala, El Salvador and some sections of Honduras and Nicaragua. These pre-Columbian societies dominated this region before the Spanish colonization in the 15th and 16th centuries resulted in the decimation of these cultures. Starting in 7000 BC the domestication of maize, beans, squash and chili brought about a transition from hunter-gatherer tribal groupings to sedentary agricultural villages. These cultures created complex mythological and religious practices, a numeric and calendar system, distinct architectural styles, and a tradition of ball playing. Society became highly stratified and developed into complex chiefdoms. A system of trade routes developed for the exchange of luxury goods including obsidian, jade, cacao, cinnabar, shells, and ceramics. The wheel, except as a children's toy, and metallurgy were absent from these cultures. The main tribes included the Olmec, Maya, Mixtec, Toltec, and Aztec.

European Exploration

·Norseman

These Vikings explored different parts of the North Atlantic and North America from the 9th to 11th centuries. They left a great deal of physical evidence in North America and oral descriptions told of their explorations; but the information was never disseminated to the rest of Europe.

1. **Eric the Red**—He first colonized Iceland and Greenland around 982.
2. **Bjarni Herjulfsson**—The first European to see the North American coast in 986 after being blown off course by a storm, but he did not land.
3. **Leif Erickson**—Explored Labrador, Newfoundland, Nova Scotia, and Massachusetts in 996 and called the area Vinland for the grapes he saw growing.

·Portugal

Led the way in exploration in order to reach India by going around Africa.

1. **John I**—Crusades were conducted against the Moors in Northern Africa to open up that area.
2. **Prince Henry**—John's son who was called the Navigator because of his interest in nautical exploration. Portugal would explore the Azores, Madera, and Cape Verde Islands as it began to work its way around Africa.
3. **Bartholomew Diaz**—In 1486, he reached the Cape of Storms in South Africa and renamed it Cape of Good Hope in what might be the first example of political correctness or at least a euphemism.
4. **Vasco de Gama**—Sailed around Africa and reached India in 1498. Profits from the voyage were more than 600% as he brought back spices and other valuable products.
5. **Pedro Cabral**—On his way to India around Africa he was blown off course and touched down in Brazil in 1500 claiming that area for Portugal.
6. **Alfonso de Albuquerque**—Established a Portuguese colony in India at Goa and cleared the Muslims from the Arabian Sea and Indian Ocean.

·Spain

After Castile and Aragon were united by the marriage of Isabella of Aragon to Ferdinand of Castille, the Moors were driven out or driven underground in Spain in 1492. The major explorations of Spain included:

1. **Christopher Columbus**—Genoan sailor who tried but failed to get Portugal to back a voyage as he was convinced that India was 4,000 miles to the west of Europe. With Spain's financial backing he made his first voyage in 1492 and landed on San Salvador Island in the Bahamas where he erroneously called the indigenous Taino people Indians because he thought he was on the outskirts of India. He would make three subsequent voyages and explore Haiti (where he left a colony after his first voyage), Puerto Rico, Cuba, Trinidad, as well as Central America and the Venezuelan coast. Columbus died believing he had explored the outskirts of Asia.
2. **Amerigo Vespucci**—Controversial figure who may have made 4 voyages to the New World between 1497-1503. He realized the New World was not India.
3. **Vasco de Balboa**—Sighted and named the Pacific Ocean as he traversed Panama in 1513.
4. **Ponce de Leon** –Explored Florida in 1513 while looking for the mythical fountain of youth but ended up being killed by the Native Americans.
5. **Ferdinand Magellan**—His expedition circumnavigated the globe from 1519-1522 for Spain and he was killed in the Philippines but the voyage was completed under Sebastian Cano.
6. **Hernando Cortez**—Most notable of the Spanish conquistadores who conquered the Aztec Empire from 1519-1522, gaining precious metal riches for Spain in the process.
7. **Francisco Pizarro**—He and his brothers conquered the Inca Empire in Peru from 1531-1534 and gained riches in silver for Spain and themselves.

8. **Francisco Coronado**—With an expedition of almost a thousand including conquistadores and enslaved natives, he searched for the fabled seven Golden Cities of Cibola in northern Mexico and the southwestern U.S. (including Arizona, New Mexico, Texas, Oklahoma, and Kansas) from 1540-42. His expedition found only Zuñi, Hopi, and Pueblo Indians who repelled Coronado when he demanded that they convert to Christianity. Coronado killed many Native Americans during this expedition but did not find gold, silver, or other treasures. His expedition was considered a failure by the Spanish leaders.

9. **Hernando De Soto**—Leaving from Cuba he explored the Southeast crossing the Mississippi from 1539-1542. His expedition brutally mistreated the Native Americans with iron-collars and attack dogs but he would die from fever and wounds, which symbolized his "bloody" expedition.

10. **Bartholomew de las Casas**—A Spanish colonist, priest, and explorer who was the founder of a utopian community and first Bishop of Chiapas. As a scholar, historian and 16th century human rights advocate las Casas has been called the "father" of anti-imperialism and anti-racism and an early and energetic advocate and activist for the rights of native peoples. He was in part responsible for the repeal of laws which allowed the Indians to be used in what amounted to slave labor gangs in the *econmienda* system. The repeal did not last because of pressure from the colonials and the *encomienda* system was restored.

·Papal Bull and Treaty of Tordesillas

In 1493, Pope Alexander VI (Spanish born) decreed after Columbus' voyage that all lands west of a meridian 100 leagues west of the Cape Verde Islands should belong to Spain while new lands discovered east of that line would belong to Portugal. Portugal was unhappy with this arrangement so the line was moved in the Treaty of Tordesillas in 1494 to 1770 km. west of the Cape Verde islands and extended to Asia. It divided the world between the two Catholic countries. The rest of Europe, primarily France and England, were excluded from the agreement causing them to reject it.

·Waldesmuller

He was the German geographer who named the New World after the Italian explorer and fellow cartographer Amerigo Vespucci.

·Mercator

In drawing the first maps showing the discoveries Mercator wrote America across both North and South America in honor of a fellow cartographer and explorer Amerigo Vespucci.

·England

1. **John Cabot**—Another mariner from Genoa he explored the North American coast for England in two voyages in 1497 and 1498 but the English made little use of his discoveries.
2. **Sebastian Cabot**—Son of John who explored North America in 1509.
3. **Francis Drake**—One of the English "sea dogs" who preyed on Spanish shipping in the Caribbean, Drake sailed around South America to California and on a later voyage was the 2nd to circumnavigate the globe.
4. **Humphrey Gilbert**—Took possession of Newfoundland in 1583 but was lost at sea on the voyage back to England.
5. **Walter Raleigh**—Took over the Gilbert patent for all of North America and established a colony at Roanoke in 1587 that became the "Lost Colony." The 90 men, 17 women and 9 children, were discovered to be missing in 1590, and the only evidence of their departure was the word "Croatan" carved on a post.

6. **Martin Frobisher**—Made a number of expeditions to the region of Northern Canada in search of a Northwest Passage to Asia.

·France

1. **Giovanni de Verrazano**—In 1524 he attempted to find a passage through North America and sailed up the entire east coast entering New York Harbor and Narragansett Bay.
2. **Jacque Cartier**—Originally tried to find a Northwest Passage but discovered the St. Lawrence and founded a colony at Quebec in 1541.
3. **Samuel de Champlain**—Made a total of 11 voyages to Canada establishing the fur trade in the process.
4. **Marquette and Joliet**—Jacques Marquette, a Jesuit missionary, and Louis Joliet, a fur trader began their trip in Quebec and traveled through Michigan's upper peninsula taking canoes across Lake Michigan in order to find the Northwest Passage. They entered the Mississippi River in 1673 but soon realized it was not the Northwest Passage as it flowed south. After exploring the Mississippi to the Arkansas River they returned to Canada.

·Netherlands

Henry Hudson—English explorer who sailed for the Muscovy and the Dutch East India Companies and explored Newfoundland, the Carolina coast, Delaware Bay, and ultimately Hudson and James Bay. As he tried to return to Europe he was set adrift by his own men and perished.

·Columbian Exchange

This phrase is used to describe the biological and cultural exchanges that took place between Europe, the Americas, and Africa. The most significant change was the dispossession of Native Americans from most of their land, yet not their total disappearance. The exchange of specific things is the tangible evidence of the exchange and can be narrowed down to the most important five items in terms of their biological and cultural impact—corn (maize), potato, horses, disease, and sugar.

1. **Food**—The increase and improvement of the food supply is clearly the most important factor in population explosions since the beginning of the Columbian Exchange. It is also clear that the addition of Native American food plants is the most significant change for the world food supply. In addition to maize and the potato, some of the most important plants from America were: beans, squash, chili peppers, sunflowers, peanuts, tomatoes, manioc (cassava), avocado, pineapple, and cocoa.
2. **Horses**—The role of the horse in conquest, with new pastoral tribes, and in economics for breeding and labor, makes the horse the greatest influence of all the animals in the Columbian Exchange. For the Plains Indians, who were mainly displaced from the Eastern Woodlands, horses would provide an edge in bison hunting, economics, and warfare from about 1750 to 1890.
3. **Disease**—Infectious disease was the most effective weapon that Europeans brought to America. The devastating effect of disease on native peoples was mostly due to the biological isolation and the limited intrusion of infectious diseases in America before 1492. Native peoples suffered 80-90% population losses in much of America with influenza, typhoid, measles and smallpox taking the greatest toll in devastating epidemics.
4. **Sugar**—Sugarcane was a major component of the Columbian Exchange and unfortunately the principal commodity for stimulating the American slave trade. The initial labor for sugarcane plantations in America would fall on Native Americans, but by 1600, 95 % of Native Americans in the Caribbean and Atlantic Coast populations would be dead, primarily due to disease and hard labor. African slavery would replace Native American slave labor.

·Popé's Revolt

The Pueblo people of New Mexico felt hostility toward the Spanish primarily due to the fact that the Spanish belittled their traditional religion and tried to prohibit its practice. Economic difficulties also resulted from actions of the Spanish in forcing the Indians to labor on the *encomiendas* as well as the mines of Chihuahua. When drought came to the area in the 1670s, famine resulted as well as increased attacks on the Pueblo from nomadic tribes, which the Spanish did little to quell. In 1675 Governor Juan Francisco Treviño arrested 47 medicine men and accused them of practicing witchcraft. After publicly whipping them he hung four of them, in the plaza of Santa Fe. One of the survivors was Popé, a medicine man who devised a plan of revolt. Popé and his allies surprised the Spanish and killed 21 of the province's forty Franciscans and 380 other Spaniards were killed. Popé made himself governor of the Pueblos and became an autocratic ruler. He ordered the Indians to burn or destroy crosses and other Catholic religious imagery. Spanish culture was disavowed, including the keeping of Spanish livestock and fruit trees. He would not allow the Indians to grow wheat and barley, two European crops. Popé went too far when he ordered Indians who had been married according to the rites of the Catholic Church to dismiss their wives and to take others after the old native tradition. Popé set himself up in the Governor's Palace as ruler of the Pueblos and collected tribute from each Pueblo until his death in 1688. A drought paved the way for the "bloodless reconquest" in 1692. Diego de Vargas returned to Santa Fe and surrounded the city and promised clemency if the Indians would swear allegiance to the King of Spain and return to the Christian faith. The Indian leaders gathered in Santa Fe, met with de Vargas, and agreed to peace; thus ending the 12 years of independence under their own leaders.

UNIT I
MULTIPLE-CHOICE QUESTIONS

Questions 1–3 refer to the following:

"... differences in food production constituted a major ultimate cause of disparities between Eurasian and Native American societies... the... proximate factors behind the conquest, the most important included differences in germs, technology, political organization, and writing. Of these, the one linked most directly to the difference in food production was germs. The infectious diseases that regularly visited crowded Eurasian societies, and to which many Eurasians consequently immune or genetic resistance, included all of history's lethal killers: smallpox, measles, influenza, plague, tuberculosis, typhus, cholera, malaria and others. Against that grim list the sole crowd [of] infectious diseases...attributed ... to pre-Columbian Native American societies were non-syphilitic treponemas [bacterial genus]."

Jared Diamond, *Guns, Germs, and Steel: The Fates of Human Societies*, 1999

1. The interpretation in the passage above can best be supported historically by which of the following statements?

   (A) The drop in Native American population in North and South America from 25 million to under 250,000 after the arrival of the Europeans
   (B) The forced relocation of Native Americans that disrupted their normal patterns of procreation
   (C) Bringing tobacco products from Eurasia to the Native Americans which would ruin the health of the indigenous people
   (D) The importation of African slaves forced the Indians out of the labor force so they could no longer earn a living

2. The arrival of the Europeans brought about the decimation of the Native American population primarily because

   (A) there was not enough land to support both the Native Americans and the Europeans
   (B) of the spread of highly contagious diseases to which they had no immunity
   (C) most of the Indians were not prepared to give up the nomadic life of the hunter for the sedentary life of the farmer
   (D) the prevalence of converting the Indians to the European religions which destroyed their noble character and will to live

3. The factor that brought about the difference in food production from the Eurasians to the Native Americans was

   (A) technology
   (B) writing
   (C) political organization
   (D) germs

11

Questions 4–6 refer to the following:

"Columbus's ships,... short-circuited millions of years of divergent evolution in the two hemispheres by rapidly introducing Old World plants, animals, and micro-organisms into New World environments, and vice versa.... The New World happened to be much a healthier place than the Old before 1492, hosting few or none of the devastating diseases... Thus, when Europeans arrived, they generally found life in the Americas to be... healthy.... By contrast, American Indians—never before exposed to vicious Old World pathogens like smallpox... began dying at apocalyptic rates.... new diseases ... killed off as much as 90% or more of the indigenous population.... The adoption of efficient, carbohydrate-rich [Indian] crops such as corn, potatoes, and cassava allowed Europeans and Africans to overcome chronic food shortages.... while Native American populations were decimated by Old World diseases, European and African populations swelled as American crops helped to overcome Old World famine."

Anonymous, "Columbian Exchange"

4. The primary European disease that decimated the Indian population as well as playing havoc with the European settlers was

   (A) polio
   (B) influenza
   (C) measles
   (D) smallpox

5. Which of the following is the best statement of what both parties received as a result of the "Columbian Exchange" in the passage above?

   (A) Europeans gained jobs, Indians gained goods
   (B) Europeans acquired land, Indians gold and silver
   (C) Europeans got crops, Indians got diseases
   (D) Both Europeans and Indians became healthier

6. Which of the following statements is the clearest interpretation of the above passage?

   (A) Many historians now believe that diseases introduced after Columbus's arrival killed off as much as 90% or more of the indigenous population of the Americas
   (B) Historian Alfred Crosby called the introduction of Old World plants, animals, and micro-organisms into the New World the Columbian Exchange
   (C) The Indians received germs from Europe into their healthy environment while the Europeans gained food stuffs to overcome famine in what amounted to an unequal exchange that benefitted one party over the other
   (D) Millions of years of evolution were short-circuited by Columbus's ships and the European ships that followed by bringing together plants, animals, and micro-organisms from the Old World into the New World environments

Questions 7–10 refer to the following:

"The oldest... is the myth of the Noble Red man or the Child of Nature, who is credited either with a habit of flowery oratory of implacable dullness or else with an imbecilic inability to converse in anything more than grunts and monosyllables. That first myth was inconvenient. White men soon found their purposes better served by the myth of ruthless, faithless, savages, and later when the 'savages' had been broken, of drunken, lazy, good-for-nothings. All three myths coexist today, sometimes curiously blended in a schizophrenic confusion such as one often sees in moving pictures.... Part of the myth of the first Americans is that all of them... had one culture and were at the same stage of advancement. The tribes and nations that occupied North America varied enormously, and their condition was anything but static."

Oliver La Farge, "Myths that Hide the American Indian," October, 1956

7. The ideas of which French philosopher popularized the myth of the Noble Red man or Child of Nature in the 19th century?

   (A) Jean Jacques Rousseau
   (B) Voltaire
   (C) Marquis de Lafayette
   (D) Jean Paul Sartre

8. Which of the following is NOT a myth about the Native Americans

   (A) glorification of the natural life as personified by the noble savage
   (B) canny, astute, businessmen as demonstrated by Indian casinos
   (C) ruthless, blood-thirsty savages as depicted in films
   (D) simultaneous cultures amongst all the Indians when the Europeans arrived

9. The image of the Indian as the noble child of nature predominated in much of the mid-19th century as a part of which artistic, literary, and cultural movement?

   (A) Feudalism
   (B) Gothic Revival
   (C) Classicism
   (D) Romanticism

10. A revival of Indian mores and culture was a significant part of which 20th century social and cultural movement

   (A) lost Generation
   (B) progressivism
   (C) counterculture
   (D) yuppies

For **Questions 11–12** refer to the following image:

Moundbuilders

11. The relics above indicate which of the following?

   (A) These Indians were likely to be exclusively sedentary agriculturalists
   (B) These relics suggest that the Moundbuilders were hunter-gatherers and farmers
   (C) The tribes used the horse to help in the acquisition of food
   (D) Fish was a major source of protein for the Moundbuilders

12. It is clear that the Moundbuilders were skilled

   (A) equestrians
   (B) buffalo hunters
   (C) pottery makers
   (D) home builders

Questions 13–15 refer to the following document:

"1609...as for corn provision and contribution from the savages, we had nothing but mortal wounds with clubs and arrows; as for our hogs, hens, goats, sheep, horse...our commanders, officers, and savages daily consumed them,... then swords, arms, pieces, or anything, we traded with the savages, whose cruel fingers were so often imbrewed [stained] in our bloods...after Captain Smiths departure, there remained not past 60 men, women, and children,...preserved for the most part by roots, herbs, acorns,...so great was our famine that a savage we slew and buried the poorer sort took him up again and eat him;...one amongst the rest did kill his wife, powdered (salted) her, and had eaten part of her before it was known, for which he was executed, as he well deserved. Now whether she was better roasted, boiled, or carbonadoed [broiled] I know not, but such a dish as powdered wife I never heard of.... This was that time, which still to this day we called the starving time...."

Captain John Smith, *The General Historie of Virginia*, 1624

13. The description of the indigenous people is contrary to which 19th century view of the Indians?

   (A) Idealization by the Romantics
   (B) Eradication by the industrialists
   (C) Toleration by the homesteaders
   (D) Racism by the Know-Nothings

14. Smith's description of the relations between the colonist and the indigenous people is similar to

   (A) Jeffersonian views on nature
   (B) those southerners who favored outlawing slavery
   (C) the attitude of the Jackonians as demonstrated by the Trail of Tears
   (D) advocates of the Dawes Act

15. Which statement in the above passage could be viewed as an attempt by Smith to invoke "gallows" humor?

   (A) "...as for corn provision and contribution from the savages, we had nothing but mortal wounds with clubs and arrows"
   (B) "Now whether she was better roasted, boiled, or carbonadoed I know not, but such a dish as powdered wife I never heard of...."
   (C) "so great was our famine that a savage we slew and buried the poorer sort took him up again and eat him
   (D) "...one amongst the rest did kill his wife, powdered (salted) her, and had eaten part of her before it was known, for which he was executed, as he well deserved

UNIT II
EUROPEAN COLONIZATION

The time period of European colonization is the longest in United States history. Lasting from the first permanent English colony in Jamestown in 1607 (although the Spanish colony of St. Augustine, Florida in 1565 is the oldest permanent settlement in the present U.S.) through the colonial period and up to the end of the Seven Years War (French and Indian War) in 1763, each European colonizer made their own contributions to the development of culture in the New World.

Spain

The primary holdings of Spain were in Mexico, Central and South America, as well the Caribbean islands but significant colonies were also established in the Spanish borderlands—the northern areas of Mexico that are now a part of the United States.

·St. Augustine (Florida)
Established in 1565 it was never much more than a military outpost which originated when a French corsair intercepted a Spanish galleon that started the new trade of pirating from the Spanish. An unsuccessful missionary campaign among the North American natives was abandoned. It has the distinction of being the oldest city in the present day United States.

·Pensacola (Florida)
It was originally founded in 1559 to make it the oldest outpost in the continental United States. A hurricane destroyed the original colony and the first of three presidios was established in 1698. The area was continually traded back and forth between Spain and France and ultimately the British gained control until it went back to Spain during the American Revolution. It became permanently a part of the United States as a result of the Adams-Onis Treaty of 1819.

•Santa Fe (New Mexico)

Became a colony in 1609 as a buffer against the advances of other European countries and established the *encomienda* system, which caused tension with the Pueblo Indians. Apache, Navajo, and Comanche Indians continually threatened the colony. Its economy was based on cattle and sheep raising along with trade with the Indians. Popé led a revolt of the Pueblo in 1680 that killed 400 Spanish settlers before Spain re-established control by 1697. Santa Fe is the oldest city in the U.S. west of the Mississippi river and the oldest capital city.

•San Antonio (Texas)

The leading town established in Texas in 1718 and along with 30 missions, it acted as a barrier against the incursions of the French. It became the largest Spanish settlement in Texas. After the failure of Spanish missions to the north of the city, San Antonio became the farthest northeastern extension of the culture of Mexico.

•San Francisco and Los Angeles

Pueblo settlements in California in 1776 and 1781 were begun in response to the Russian advance in the north, and a desire to settle new land by eleven families coming from the Mission San Gabriel in the South.

•Spanish Borderlands

The term Spanish borderlands refers to the Spanish colonial frontier in the land area that later became the United States. By the late 18th century, the Spanish land claims extended west along the southern rim of North America from Florida to California and north to Alaska. Once Mexico became independent from Spain in 1821, the Spanish claim to the borderlands was ended and over the next 33 years these areas would become a part of the U.S. Despite the loss of this territory to the U.S., their cultural legacy endured, and much of the American Southwest has a strong Spanish and Mexican influence.

Colonization (Spain)

Following the exploits of the conquistadors, the Spanish method of colonization was highly centralized and autocratic. The following are some of the instruments of colonization that were used.

•*Encomienda*

A Spanish system of land tenure in their New World colonies which became one of serfdom for the Native Americans (Indians). They were required to work the land under the tutelage of their landlords by farming, ranching or mining. Despite promises of treating them fairly, the landlords (usually the missionaries), often abused their charges and the system resulted in depopulation of the Native Americans (Indians).

•Hacienda

In time, it replaced the *encomienda* and was originally a land grant made to minor nobles in order to get them to come to the New World. It became an extensive system of land ownership where the Native American (Indians) became peons who worked for the owner of the hacienda. Although not as harsh as the *encomienda* it was still an institution of exploitation.

•Mission

The mission served to introduce Native Americans (Indians) into Spanish society. Catholicism, the foundation of Spanish culture, was a nationalistic religion controlled and subsidized by the Crown. The mission was both an arm of the church and an agent of the state. Twenty-one of these were established in California under Junipero Serra and Firmin Lasuen and more than 100 others in Texas and New Mexico. Religious orders like the Jesuits, Franciscans, and Dominicans established most of the missions.

·*Presidio*

As an agent of the state the *presidio* or fort were garrisons where military officers commanded the soldiers to keep order and keep in check hostile Native Americans (Indians). *Presidios* existed throughout the frontier areas of Spain's colonies with prominent ones in California (San Diego, Monterey, San Francisco), and Texas. In all more than 100 *presidios* were established in the Spanish borderlands.

·*Pueblo*

These towns were to complement the mission and the *presidio* but never reached the importance of those two institutions. They were to be comprised of families recruited from Mexico who would provide agricultural support for the *presidios* as well as centers of expanding population and military reserves. New Mexico led the way with nineteen but only three were ever established in California.

·*Ranchos*

They covered much of the most fertile land in California. The *Alcaldes* (municipal magistrates) of the *pueblos* were given the authority to grant lots of land within their jurisdiction and this evolved to the granting of lands outside of these jurisdictions—hence the ranchos. These were granted in order to encourage agriculture and industry, reward soldiers, and provide land for settlers who held no property. These *rancho* land grants were limited to a maximum size of eleven square leagues with most being considerably smaller. Of the 800-plus *rancho* grants made, the Spanish government granted approximately thirty and the rest were by the Mexican government.

New France

At one time the holdings of New France were so extensive they hemmed in the British to the eastern seaboard and rivaled those of Spain. However, this would not last, and France would be removed from the North American mainland in 1763 as a result of the Seven Years War (known as the French and Indian War in North America).

·Fort Caroline

This was a French attempt to settle Huguenots in Florida near present day Jacksonville in 1564. Spain became incensed at this and established St. Augustine where it launched an attack that wiped out the French by killing 500 of their colonists.

·Port Royal

One of a series of fur trading outposts established by the French in Acadia (Nova Scotia), it lasted from 1598 to 1604.

·Quebec

Founded by Samuel de Champlain in 1608, this colony's economic viability was based on good relations with the Hurons and the fur trade with them, as well as a French and Huron alliance against the powerful Iroquois Confederation.

Colonization

Although New France was removed by the British at the conclusion of the French and Indian War (1763) it left a rich history in the North American continent.

·Fishing

The Grand Banks off of Newfoundland in the North Atlantic where plentiful catches of cod and haddock were supplied to "fish starved" Catholic Europe.

·**Forts and places**

From Detroit to Cadillac to Terre Haute to New Orleans to Des Moines, to St. Louis to New Orleans to the Grand Tetons; remnants of French culture and place names remain in the United States.

·**Fur trading**

This became the mainstay of the economy in New France. The posts and forts were designed to protect this valuable economic activity.

·*Coureurs de bois* **(runners of the woods)**

They emerged as the chief supplier of beaver furs after the early monopoly to licensed traders was ended. They roamed far and wide in the interior to supply the fur and were rugged individuals who often lived amongst the Native Americans (Indians) and took native women as their wives.

·*Filles de Roy*

Between 1663 and 1673, Louis XIV personally contributed to the recruitment of approximately 775 of these women who were destined to marry settlers in the colony of New France where there were very few women of marriageable age. These "King's Daughters" were considered wards of the king.

·*Seigneurs*

Feudal system adapted to New France in which the large landholders become an agent of the state in promoting colonization. In actuality they lived little better than the habitants who tilled the soil for them. Instead of promoting agriculture much of their time was spent hunting and fishing.

·*Habitants*

This is the name given for the hired hands of the *seigneurs* who tilled the soil. Most of these agricultural workers were soldiers, workmen, or servants from northern France who came in very small numbers to work for the *seigneurs*.

·*Huguenots*

France would not let these hard working Protestants colonize New France which could have given the colony a population base to help support its vast size. The colony of New France had a total population of 65,000 at the time of French and Indian War and it would face a population of 2.5 million in the British colonies.

·*Voyageurs*

A system devised by Champlain where young men would live among the Indians. This led to good relations between the Indians, especially the Huron and Algonquin. In time these men often married Indian women and became the middle-men in transporting furs in the fur trade. The French did not have the fear of miscegenation that the English colonies had.

England

By establishing 13 colonies in what would later become the United States, the English had the greatest and most varied impact on North American colonization. Despite some similarities there were a number of difference to make the colonies and regions distinct. The differences in the colonies added to their strength and they became a magnet for population growth.

New England

· Plymouth (Massachusetts)

English Separatists founded (1620) the Plymouth Colony in New England. Most of these Separatists (also known as Pilgrims) were farmers, poorly educated and without social or political standing. They originally moved to the Netherlands because they had broken away from the Church of England. In 1617, discouraged by economic difficulties, the pervasive Dutch influence on their children, and their inability to secure civil autonomy, the congregation voted to emigrate to America. Fewer than half the 102 passengers on the *Mayflower* were Separatists. After first landing at Provincetown they soon discovered Plymouth Harbor, on the western side of Cape Cod Bay, and made their historic landing on December 21, 1620. They were able to survive the first winter with the help of the friendly Native Americans (Indians) Squanto and Samoset. William Bradford served as governor for 30 years and his published journal *Of Plymouth Plantation* provides a rich history of the colony.

· Massachusetts Bay

Unlike the other colonies who were sparse in number, the Puritan community at Massachusetts Bay were part of a "Great Migration" that sent 185,000 from England to New England (25,000), Chesapeake (50,000), and the West Indies (110,000) from 1629 to 1660. Of these it was the Puritans who had the greatest impact. With 11 ships and 700 passengers arriving in 1630 the Puritans were to establish according to John Winthrop, their leader and governor, "a city upon a hill, the eyes of all people are upon us." They attempted to build a godly community that would inspire those in England to reform the church. These middle class burghers in their "errand into the wilderness in this new world" would focus on bringing a new sense of community out of their religious idealism. Their contribution to the development of the American character was greater than any other colonial group and much of it still exists today.

· Connecticut

Primarily for economic reasons, different groups left Massachusetts Bay to settle the fertile lands of the Connecticut Valley. The most important of these was led by Thomas Hooker who established a colony at Hartford in 1636." His democratic views as well as those of others were incorporated into the "Fundamental Orders" that provided a framework for government.

· New Haven

John Davenport and Theophilus Eaton founded the colony of New Haven in 1638 on Long Island Sound. The colony was dominated by Puritan church officials and was somewhat less democratic than the Connecticut colony. New Haven was absorbed, against its wishes, by the Connecticut colony in 1662.

· Rhode Island

Four towns were established by buying land from Native Americans by dissenters from the Bay colony. Roger Williams secured a charter for Providence Plantations (1636) that would unite the towns as well as instilling the concept of freedom of conscience in the colonies. This self governing colony became a haven for the "otherwise minded" including Williams, Anne Hutchinson (who later migrated to Long Island and was killed in an Indian attack), and William Coddington. It was the contrarian colony of New England going against the Puritan dominated colonies.

· Maine and New Hampshire

These colonies were created by land grants given to John Mason and Ferdinando Gorges for land between the Merrimack and Kennebec rivers in 1622. They further divided it in 1629 as Gorgas received the north (Maine) and Mason the south (New Hampshire). Maine would be absorbed into Massachusetts Bay as well as New Hampshire for a time, until it was made independent in 1680.

Characteristics of English Colonization

Because religion was so important to New England much of the colonial history of this region revolves around issues of faith.

· Mayflower Compact

While on board the ship *Mayflower*, the Separatists signed an agreement establishing a "body politic " and a basic legal system for the colony. This agreement created a legal authority and an assembly, and it also asserted that the government's power derived from the consent of the governed and not from God. It started the road to democracy in the colonies.

· "blue laws"

Passed by the Puritans, these laws were aimed at limiting simple pleasures and suppressing some human instincts. Connecticut enforced these laws to such an extent that it became known as the "Blue Law State." The name was coined because of the blue paper on which these repressive or "sumptury" laws were printed on. For example, in New Haven a couple was fined twenty shillings for kissing in public. These laws also forbade stage plays, playing cards, dice, and "May games." Doing almost anything on the Sabbath was forbidden as well as "excessive hilarity."

· bundling

Courting practice of the Puritans which allowed young, courting couples to share the same bed separated by a bundling board. This was done to save wood but still allow social interaction among young people.

· education

Schooling was a mainstay in New England primarily for religious reasons. Harvard College (1636) was established six years after the Puritans arrived to train ministers. Because parents were not teaching enough about religion and the civil government according to a 1642 law, the Old Deluder Satan Act was passed in 1647 that required towns of 50 families to hire a school master to teach reading and writing. Student's could read the Bible to ward off the devil.

· Fundamental Orders of Connecticut

Adopted in 1639 by the Connecticut council to state their principles. Some of the main ideas of the document are that the government is based on an individual's rights, free men elect magistrates by secret ballot, and that there are limits on the government's powers. The principle of individual rights in this document was applied later to the Constitution.

· Great Awakening

The First Great Awakening occurred in the 1730s and 1740s. Protestants in the colonies, first stirred up by Jonathan Edwards and his call for a return to strict Calvinism and God-fearing in his most famous sermon, "Sinners in the Hands of an Angry God," became emotionally involved in their convictions. They displayed a new passion that greatly contrasted with the former method of worship of passive listening. People began reading the Bible in their homes, resulting in the decentralization of the church and a greater emphasis on individual worship. New colleges were founded in the spirit of this "new light" preaching. George Whitefield, the best known of the revivalist preachers, carried the movement into the South.

· Half-Way Covenant

This was a decision made by the Congregational churches in New England in the 1650's. There was a concern about the lack of newcomers to the religion. Even more alarming was the decline of conversions (people's testimonial that they had received God's grace), which was the only way to be admitted to the church and become part of the elect. To deal with the decline in new membership the Congregational churches proposed the Half-Way Covenant. This offered partial membership rights to those believers who had not yet gone through regeneration.

· Hutchinson, Ann

She was a difficult woman who gained a following by criticizing the ministers and began practicing and advocating antinomianism—the belief that faith and God's grace alone was enough to earn a place among the "elect." Her criticism of the clergy for being deficient in grace got her into "hot water" with the government officials. She was eventually tried for heresy, convicted, and banished from Puritan society and exiled to Rhode Island. Her contrarian views were accepted in this most "contrary" colony.

· King Philip's War (1675–76)

This was a devastating war between the colonists and the Native Americans in New England. Led by King Philip (Metacom), chief of the Wampanoag, the Indians maintained peace with the colonists for a number of years. Hostility eventually developed over the steady succession of land sales forced on the Native Americans because of their growing dependence on English goods. In the two-year conflict about 600 colonists and 3,000 Native Americans were killed. The war resulted in the virtual extermination of the Native American's tribal life in New England and the disappearance of the fur trade.

· Puritan (Protestant) Ethic

Business was a calling and success a sign of regeneration (God's grace) according to this fundamental Puritan belief. Hard work was considered character building and morally good. A distrust of leisure, which is a sign of the ungodly, would help to create a capitalist mentality that would contribute to making the U.S. a nation of hard working people. Many aphorisms contain these sentiments such as the ones in Benjamin Franklin's *Poor Richard's Almanack.*

· Regeneration

This was the concept of salvation in the Puritan religion where man faced God directly without an intermediary and became one of the elect (this had been predestined by God) through a concrete religious experience. Sometimes it is referred to as conversion or being "born again."

Middle Colonies

· New Netherlands

After explorations of Henry Hudson for the Netherlands a group of Walloons became the first settlers. New Netherlands was established on Manhattan and other islands in 1624, as well as on land along the Hudson River. Peter Minuet purchased Manhattan Island for 60 guilders ($24) in trade goods from the Indians and changed its name to New Amsterdam. It became a cosmopolitan mixture of Walloons, Huguenots, Swedes, Dutch and Africans. Its unique system of landholding into *patroonships* established an aristocratic class of feudal lords along the Hudson River. England's defeat of the Netherlands in the Wars of Devolution or 2nd & 3rd Anglo-Dutch wars resulted in New Netherlands being absorbed into England and being renamed New York after the king's brother the Duke of York in 1673.

· New Sweden

Founded by a trading company financed by Dutch and Swedish investors in 1638 along the Delaware River. Dutch investors were bought out which increased hostilities between the two, leading to skirmishes ultimately resulting in a Dutch takeover.

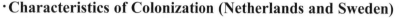

·Characteristics of Colonization (Netherlands and Sweden)

Although they did not last long as colonies, both New Netherlands and New Sweden made positive cultural contributions to the United States.

·Leisler's Rebellion

During the Glorious Revolution Jacob Leisler led a rebellion that took control of New York from 1689-1691. Backed by Dutch laborers and artisans who resented the English ruling elite, he enacted a government of popular representation. There was also a move to redistribute wealth to the poor. He earned the scorn of New York's predominantly Anglican merchant and aristocratic classes. The new king William of Orange (William III), sent a new governor in 1691 and after Leisler refused to give up his authority, English troops entered the city arrested Leisler for treason, tried and found him guilty, and had him hung and drawn and quartered. So-much for popular representation.

·Hudson River Settlements

The Dutch established a series of trading posts, towns, and forts up and down the Hudson River. Fort Orange (Albany) was the northernmost of the Dutch outposts.

·Gambrel roof

A main feature of what is often called the Dutch Colonial style that was popular in all of the colonies is the gambrel roof. The idea of the slanted pitches came from Dutch windmill designs. This style would later be revived in the late 1800s and early 1900s.

·Knickerbocker literature

Written in the 19th century, but the themes were based on the 40 year Dutch experience in the New World in such works by Washington Irving as *Rip Van Winkle* and the *Legend of Sleepy Hollow*.

·Log cabin

This innovation was Sweden's original contribution to America that would become the standard home in frontier life.

·*Patroonships*

In order to encourage settlement these large tracts of land (16 miles on a navigable river) were offered to anyone who would transport 50 people across the Atlantic to the colony. A few were established but the only partially successful one was owned by the Amsterdam jeweler Van Rensselaer. All the *patroonships* suffered from absentee management, quarrels with the Dutch West India Company, and conflict with the Indians.

·Pennsylvania

In payment for a debt, the crown granted to William Penn a large section of land west of the Delaware River. He was made absolute proprietor and extensively publicized his colonial venture to attract Welshmen, Quakers (from the Palatinate and England), Irish, Dutch and other immigrants. Unlike most other colonizers he signed treaties with the Indians to gain legal title to the land. From its inception in 1682, Pennsylvania's population dramatically increased and the liberal government made it an attractive haven for settlers from Europe. Penn's enlightened policy toward the Native Americans (Indians) insured an interval of peace that lasted for 75 years. The pacifism of the Quakers contributed to the peace and harmony that existed. The Scots-Irish immigrants on the western frontier with their anti-Indian sentiments would disrupt this tranquility.

·New Jersey

After the Duke of York acquired his large holdings in the New World in 1665 he gave land already inhabited by Dutch settlers and New Englanders to George Carteret and Lord John Berkeley. The proprietors promised colonists religious liberty, land acquisition on easy terms, and the right to democratically elect the legislature. For a number of years the colony was in turmoil because ownership vacillated between the Dutch, Quakers, and ultimately, the Crown.

Characteristics of Colonization (Pennsylvania and New Jersey)

These Middle Colonies had the greatest degree of economic, social, and religious diversity. This made them attractive to immigrants from Europe and settlers from other colonies. For example, in Pennsylvania a third of the population were Germans.

·"Bread Colonies"

Name given to the Middle Colonies because of their agricultural surplus in wheat, oats, rye, barley, corn, and other grain crops. Exports went to Europe and the West Indies.

·Chief Tammany

His settlement with William Penn on behalf of the Delaware tribe symbolized the good relations between Penn's settlers and the Native Americans (Indians). By the time of the revolution his name would symbolize the spirit of independence and a New York political club would later adopt his name for their organization.

·Pennsylvania Dutch

Name erroneously given to the German pietistic farmers (e.g. Amish and Mennonites) who emigrated in significant numbers from the Palatinate and settled in Pennsylvania where they spoke *Deutch* (German). The inability of Americans to pronounce *Deutch* led to their misnaming it as Dutch.

·Scots-Irish

Immigrant ethnic group who originated in the lowlands of Scotland, left that area for economic reasons to settle in Northern Ireland (Ulster), and ultimately came to Pennsylvania during the 17th and 18th centuries. Many also illegally "squatted" on land in the frontier along the "great wagon road" that went to the Carolinas. They incessantly quarreled with the Indians and movements like the Paxton Boys and Regulators kept the frontier in constant turmoil. These settlers were mobile, frequently illegally squatted on land they did not own, and tended to wear out the land. Many ended up going South along the Appalachian frontier interior of Virginia, the Carolinas and Georgia.

·Society of Friends

Protestant sect commonly known as the Quakers who were founded in England by George Fox but many of its members moved to America because of being persecuted in England. They favored direct communication with God with no intermediaries such as priests or ministers between them and the deity. Many moved to Pennsylvania after Quaker William Penn founded that colony as a sanctuary for persecuted people. They were industrious, pacifistic people who became the first abolitionist. Politically they tended to dominate the colony, especially in Philadelphia or the "city of brotherly love."

Chesapeake Colonies

·Jamestown (Virginia)

This 1607 venture was a joint stock company's settlement that was named for King James I. Many English settlers were the younger sons of aristocrats, who were not entitled to their parent's fortunes. These sons came to the New World to strike it rich and squandered their time searching for gold. In the short run, John Smith saved the colony made up of "slackers" by his dictum of "he who does not work, shall not eat." John Rolfe assured the long-term economic viability of the colony, when he perfected methods of cultivating tobacco that he had learned from the Indians. In 1619, the first Africans were purchased in Jamestown from a Dutch ship that had taken them off of a Portuguese ship. They became indentured servants.

·Maryland

Founded by the first Lord Baltimore (George Calvert) in 1634 as a refuge for Catholics, this colony became profitable almost immediately. Wise Indian policy and the introduction of tobacco assured its economic success. A social hierarchy was established by the quit rent system of land tax that had long passed away in England. After Puritans from Virginia became the Protestant majority, the Toleration Act of 1649 was passed granting liberty of conscience for all who believed in the divinity of Jesus.

Southern Colonies

·Roanoke Island

Colony founded by Sir Walter Raleigh in 1585 off the coast of Virginia. 114 settlers arrived in 1587. Here, Virginia Dare was born, the first child to be born in the English colonies, but the colony was found mysteriously deserted with no sign of the colonists in 1590. Raleigh was forced to abandon the idea due to inadequate financial resources.

·North Carolina

Originally a part of South Carolina called Albemarle, it was an outpost that attracted malcontents from Virginia even before it was chartered in 1663. Like Rhode Island in New England it was known as a place for those who did not fit in—a place for runaway slaves, debtors, fugitives and other "riff raff." Political turmoil ensued and later it became known as a center for paper-money agitation and other economic heresies. Its location between its two haughty neighbors of Virginia and South Carolina made it a natural abode for those who were uncomfortable with the aristocratic ways of those two colonies.

·South Carolina

Founded by eight proprietors in 1670, they received their grant from Charles II during the Restoration. It was modeled after Maryland with a constitution drawn up by John Locke that was quickly abandoned. The proprietors established an aristocratic tone to Carolina society and helped to create a plantation based gentry in Charleston that became the cosmopolitan center of the South with settlers from Barbados, French Huguenots, and other colonies. Huge rice plantations made it a colony that resembled more the sugar plantations of the West Indies than the other North American colonies. Trade from the West Indies came to Charleston and it became the center of slave dispersal to the other southern colonies.

·Georgia

It was a unique colony subsidized by the crown when it was founded in 1732 as a buffer against attacks on South Carolina by Spanish Florida and as a refuge for bankrupt debtors. Its leader James Oglethorpe tried to keep out slavery and alcohol to no avail. Few debtors actually arrived and immigrants from Germany, Switzerland, and Scotland, along with some Jews made it the least English of all of the colonies except for Pennsylvania.

Characteristics of Colonization

The mainstay of the mercantilist system were these southern colonies that developed unique social institutions of which slavery would become the most important.

·Cash Crops

In accordance with the mercantilist system the southern colonies relied upon cash crops that were exported to England. Tobacco in Virginia, Maryland, and North Carolina, and rice and later indigo in South Carolina and Georgia were the main products.

·Indentured Servants

They provided a solution to the shortage of labor especially in the Chesapeake colonies. Immigrants paid for their passage by selling their future labor (four to seven years) to individuals who would use this credit as a way of obtaining 50 acre grants of land or "headrights" for importing the labor. About 50% of the immigrants came to the colonies as a result of indentured servitude.

·Joint Stock Companies

Joint Stock Companies were the modern corporations of the early 1600's. Younger sons of wealthy aristocrats, hoping to make their fortune, chartered investors (called "adventurers") to pool their capital. The companies were supposed to cultivate in the New World, and then dissipate after a few years when the investors liquidated their profits. The colonists were encouraged to become successful before the companies liquidated.

·Headright System

The Europeans who settled Jamestown were employees of the Virginia Company, whose stockholders controlled all the English claims to land in the colony. Once the English recognized that the colony's value was based on tobacco, and tobacco required large tracts of land, the company began encouraging immigration by promising land to settlers. The Virginia Company encouraged wealthy individuals to establish settlements by the "headright" system. It authorized the grant of 50 acres for every individual brought to Virginia. The colony had an excess of land and a shortage of people, so it was public policy to encourage population growth through immigration. In theory, the servants would work 5-7 years clearing new land. The indentured servants did not acquire title to land through their work during their term of service. At the end of their term of indenture, they were given some basic clothing and equipment, and expected to move to the unsettled frontier. They could purchase unimproved land, and "improve" it by cutting down the trees and preparing fields suitable for growing crops such as corn and tobacco. They frequently moved to virgin land and did not purchase it but lived off it as "squatters."

UNIT II
MULTIPLE-CHOICE QUESTIONS

Questions 1-3 refers to the following document:

"First, that the blood of so many hundred thousand souls... is not required nor accepted by Jesus Christ the Prince of Peace.

Secondly, pregnant scriptures and arguments are throughout the work proposed against the doctrine of persecution for cause of conscience

Thirdly, satisfactory answers are given to scriptures....

Fourthly, the doctrine of persecution for cause of conscience is proved guilty of all the blood of the souls crying for vengeance under the altar.

Fifthly, all civil states with their officers of justice in their respective constitutions and administrations are proved essentially civil,...

Sixthly, it is the will and command of God that (since the coming of his Son the Lord Jesus) a permission of the most paganish, Jewish, Turkish, or antichristian consciences and worships, be granted to all men in all nations and countries;...

Seventhly, the state of the Land of Israel, is proved figurative and ceremonial, and no pattern nor precedent for any kingdom or civil state in the world to follow.

Eighthly, God requireth [sic] not a uniformity of religion to be enacted and enforced in any civil state; which enforced uniformity (sooner or later) is the greatest occasion of civil war...

Ninthly, in holding an enforced uniformity of religion in a civil state, we must necessarily disclaim our desires and hopes of the Jew's conversion to Christ.

Tenthly, an enforced uniformity of religion throughout a nation or civil state, confounds the civil and religious, denies the principles of Christianity...

Eleventhly, the permission of other consciences and worships than a state professeth only can (according to God) procure a firm and lasting peace....

Twelfthly, lastly, true civility and Christianity may both flourish in a state or kingdom, notwithstanding the permission of divers and contrary consciences, either of Jew or Gentile...."

Roger Williams, "*The Bloody Tenant of Persecution*," 1644

28

1. Liberty of conscience was defended by Roger Williams on the grounds that

   (A) the signers of the Mayflower Compact had guaranteed it in the original document governing the colony
   (B) Puritan ideas about sin and salvation were outmoded
   (C) theological truths would emerge from the clash of ideas
   (D) colonial governments were an improper and ineffectual agency in matters of the spirit

2. Which of the following statement would Roger Williams agree with?

   (A) The doctrine of persecution for the cause of conscience is justified by the Bible
   (B) All religions were equal in the eyes of God
   (C) Forced uniformity of religion in a civil state denies both the principles of civility and Christianity
   (D) Civility and Christianity cannot flourish in a state or kingdom of diverse Jews and Gentiles

3. The document could be interpreted to be the beginning of which subsequent tradition in American religious culture?

   (A) Great Awakening
   (B) Social Gospel
   (C) Anti-semitism
   (D) Evangelicalism

Questions 4-7 refer to the following:

"...adjectives used by historians to describe Americans of the nineteenth and early twentieth centuries—optimistic, self confident, buoyant, pragmatic—are the same as those applied to provincial Americans, and, before them...English yeoman. [They] reflected the immense success of the English colonies; they were not the product of a preconceived philosophy. The ideas of progress and perfectibility in American thought did not arise out of the Enlightenment, rather the Enlightenment supplied words and concepts for expressing an attitude of mind to which Americans had, in fact, subscribed for several centuries. A clergyman and his parish might hold the doctrinal position that humanity is forever condemned and doomed...but their daily lives revealed a commitment to the ideal of progress and betterment that belied their expressed views."

Clarence Ver Steeg, *The Formative Years*, 1607-1763, 1964

4. The observations made in the passage above tends to contradict the commonly accepted views of which group?

   (A) Puritans
   (B) Separatist
   (C) Frontiersmen
   (D) Pioneers

5. The ideas of progress, perfectibility, and betterment as expressed in the Ver Steeg interpretation influenced which late 19th and early 20th century movement?

   (A) Gospel of Wealth
   (B) Settlement House
   (C) Social Darwinism
   (D) Nativism

6. The buoyant, self confident, optimistic view of the colonial Americans led to the 19th century belief in

   (A) religious conformity
   (B) original sin
   (C) secularism
   (D) pragmatism

7. The two concepts that dominated the daily lives of the colonials were

   (A) condemned and doomed
   (B) economic hardship
   (C) progress and betterment
   (D) enlightenment philosophy

Questions 8-11 refer to the following:

"The aristocracy or planter class which emerged in Virginia, Maryland, and South Carolina during the seventeenth century had its basis in extensive private landowning and in a labor system which exempted the wealthy planter from physical toil. Prior to 1680 the labor force consisted chiefly of indentured servants, afterward increasingly of Negro slaves. How deep was the social gulf between owner and worker appeared in the layout of the plantation, where the owner's house stood apart amidst shrubs, while the workers occupied cabins at a distance, not far from the pens and barns, which housed the livestock.... Since many of the planters were descended from well-to-do members of the English middle class they were able to establish themselves in the colonies by virtue of inheritance and family assistance."

Curtis P. Nettles, *The Roots of American Civilization: A History of American Colonial Life*, 1963

8. The event that led to the end of the labor system of indentured servitude was

   (A) Salem Witch Trials
   (B) King Phillips War
   (C) Bacon's rebellion
   (D) passage of the Navigation Act

9. By the location of their dwellings the passage is comparing the workers on the plantations with

   (A) Native Americans
   (B) European immigrants
   (C) forest animals
   (D) farm animals

10. The planter class rose to a position to be free from physical toil as a result of

   (A) legislation from the colonial assemblies
   (B) inheritance from their well off middle class families
   (C) grants of land from the ruling monarchs of Great Britain
   (D) hard work in acquiring the lands of the plantation

11. In terms of the development of the American character the planter class did **NOT** have what characteristic that is considered to be an essential ingredient in its development?

   (A) Puritan (Protestant) ethic
   (B) Respect for liberty
   (C) Constitutionalism
   (D) Principles of Republicanism

Questions 12-13 refer to the following:

"[white Indians] stayed because they found Indian life to possess a strong sense of community, abundant love, and uncommon integrity, values that the English colonists also honored, if less successfully. But Indian life was attractive for other values for social equality, mobility, adventure, and, as two adult converts acknowledged, "the most perfect freedom, the ease of living, [and] the absence of those cares and corroding solicitudes which so often prevail with us." As we have learned recently, these were values that were not being realized in the older, increasingly crowded, fragmented, and contentious communities of the Atlantic seaboard, or even in the newer frontier settlements.... Whatever it was, its power had no better measure than the large number of English colonists who became, contrary to the "civilized" assumptions of their countrymen, white Indians."

John Axtell, "The White Indians of Colonial America," 1975

12. The terms uncivilized and savage are not accurate one for describing Indian culture because

   (A) whites were brutally treated by their Indian captors
   (B) whites voluntarily stayed with the tribes because they preferred the Indian life style and culture
   (C) whites were grateful for being rescued from their captivity by other English colonists
   (D) whites welcomed being reintroduced into crowded, fragmented, and contentious communities of the Atlantic seaboard and the frontier

13. The interpretation in this passage indicates that which subsequent view of the Indians was in error?

   (A) Rousseau's "noble savage"
   (B) Helen Hunt Jackson's, *A Century of Dishonor*
   (C) Drunken, uncivilized, heathens
   (D) Story of the "Trail of Tears"

Questions **14-15** refer to the following:

"Our traditional picture of the earliest New England communities is essentially a still life... the themes of steadfast piety,... old fashioned virtues, measured forms of civil government, and a closely ordered social life, suggest a placid, almost static kind of existence. We take for granted the moral and religious aims which inspired the founding of many of these communities, and we accept the assumption of the colonists themselves, that success in these aims depended on maintaining a high degree of compactness and closeness of settlement. Yet, in the case of the Plymouth Colony at least, this picture is seriously misleading.... Individuals frequently transferred their residence from one house or one town to another. Land titles changed hands with astonishing rapidity. Families were rearranged by a wide variety of circumstances."

John Demos, "Notes on Life in Plymouth Colony," 1965

14. A characterisitc of American culture in the 20th century that is a continuity with the Plymouth colony is

(A) dominance of moral and religious ideas
(B) the development of an individualistic sense of help
(C) geographic mobility
(D) economic liberty

15. One of the reasons why the Plymouth colony differed from the other New England colonies is

(A) the occupation of those in Plymouth was different from those in the other New England colonies
(B) those at Plymouth were Separatists and were used to moving around while the other New Englanders were Puritans and were stable
(C) Plymouth was overrun with Quakers and other sects which caused a great deal of instability compared to the monolithic Puritans
(D) reliance upon the fishing and whaling industries contributed to the mobility of those living in Plymouth compared to those in Massachusetts Bay

UNIT III

COLONIAL SOCIETY &
THE BRITISH EMPIRE

As colonial society developed in the late 17th & the 18th century, American institutions evolved and often came into conflict with British imperial policy. The British were occupied by a series of wars with their European rivals that contributed to leaving their American colonies alone in what became known as the policy of "salutary neglect." During this time the British and American colonials never worked out an agreement on the precise extent of the mother country's control over the colonies. Failure to do so would ultimately result in the colonies breaking away from British rule.

Social and Political Systems

· Salutary Neglect
Initiated by Sir Robert Walpole, first British Prime Minister, it was a system where the actual enforcement of external trade relations was lax. He believed that this enhanced economic freedom for the colonists would stimulate commerce. The colonies were not at the top of Britain's list of priorities, and therefore, were ignored for a time; however, the result was ultimately positive for the colonials. The American people discovered that they were capable of governing themselves and did not need Britain to rule over them. This policy from 1690 to 1763 allowed the colonies to govern themselves politically and economically. These essentially autonomous colonies soon became accustomed to the idea of self-rule. The effects of such prolonged period of isolation eventually resulted in the emergence of a collective identity for the colonies that considered themselves separate from England. Ending "salutary neglect" was one of the causes for the impending American Revolution as the British abandoned it after the Seven Years War (French and Indian War) and the colonies ultimately revolted.

· Political Development
Although the British crown chose the governor of each colony, his authority was often curtailed by the colonial assembly that held the "power of the purse." By controlling revenues and expenditures the assembly held the ultimate political power in the colonies and could bend the Governor's wishes to their will. Moreover,

many of the governors were incompetent and inept political "hacks" and this contributed to their own undoing. Colonial leaders developed a strong sense of political efficacy as they often dueled with and controlled the crown appointed officials. The colonies learned to govern themselves without interference from the "mother country."

·Zenger Case

In 1733, printer and editor John Peter Zenger of *The Weekly Journal* published numerous articles critical of New York Governor Cosby who retaliated by having Zenger arrested and jailed for ten months. Zenger was brought to trial and charged with seditious libel. The prosecution argued that the sole fact of publication was sufficient to convict and excluded the truth as relevent evidence. Alexander Hamilton (not the one who became Secretary of the Treasury in Washington's administration) Zenger's attorney, admitted that Zenger published the offending stories, but denied that it was libel unless it was false. By arguing both the facts and the law Hamilton gained an acquittal. This finding of not guilty established truth as a defense against libel that still stands today and was a landmark victory for freedom of the press. It also set a precedent against judicial tyranny in libel suits.

·Tidewater and Piedmont

The Tidewater is the area along the Atlantic coast east of where the rivers first reach the tides. It became the richest area often associated with an aristocracy that controlled the colonies politically, especially in Virginia. The Piedmont was the interior region that was at the foot of the Appalachian Mountains and sometimes called the upcountry or backcountry. Featuring small farmers, often Scots-Irish, they were politically at odds with the ruling Tidewater elite.

·Dominion of New England

After James II came to the throne in 1685 an attempt at colonial unification was tried as the Middle Colonies of New York and New Jersey were combined with New England in what became known as the Dominion of New England. This attempt was short-lived as the governor sent from England, Sir Edmund Andros, alienated the colonies by his taxation, land title, and town meeting limitation policies. With the removal of James II in the Glorious Revolution, the Dominion also fell apart and the colonies were once again governed according to their individual colonial charters.

Rebellions

·Gloucester Rebellion

Following earlier attempted uprisings in Mexico, Brazil, and the island of St. Kitts, the first documented slave uprising in the English colonies occurred in 1663 at Gloucester Virginia. This uprising was a combination of black slaves and indentured servants, and one account depicted the "White servants" as being Irish slaves who had been captured and sold during the heyday of the Irish slave trade (1649-1657) under Cromwell. In any case, as would often happen with slave revolts, the conspiracy was betrayed from within. The betrayer was an informant, who received a reward of five thousand pounds of tobacco plus his freedom for his efforts on behalf of the slave owners. An unfriendly account states that the "uprising was led by mutinous and rebellious followers of Oliver Cromwell, 'soldiers that were sent thither as servants' when King Charles II was restored to the throne in 1660." One account says the conspirators were beheaded while another says the heads of the ringleaders were impaled in the public square. In either case the rebellion was short-lived but would pave the way for numerous other rebellions by slaves leading up to the Civil War.

·Stono Rebellion

After the Gloucester rebellion of 1663 the first major slave uprising occurred in 1739 at the Stono River area in South Carolina. Several factors contributed to this uprising including a yellow fever epidemic that had weakened the power of slaveholders, talk of a war between Britain and Spain, and accounts of slaves who had obtained their freedom by escaping to Spanish-controlled Florida. About 20 slaves led by Jemmy or Cato, a literate slave described as Angolan (i.e. Kongo Empire in Central Africa) met near the Stono River 20 miles south of Charleston and marched down the roadway holding a banner that said "Liberty" and chanted that word as they marched. Their goal was to reach Florida as the Spanish governor had allegedly promised liberty to all fugitive English slaves. At the Stono Bridge they seized weapons from a store, killing the two storekeepers and raising their banner flag as they headed towards St. Augustine. Along the way they burned the houses of slave owners as more recruits joined them. Their number grew close to 100. According to one account "the rebels destroyed everything in their path, killing about 30 whites" along the way. Plantation owners and other slave-holders formed a posse to seek out Jemmy/Cato and his liberty-seeking followers. Planters on horseback caught up with the procession and a battle ensued in which 20 white Carolinians and 40 of the slaves were killed before the rebellion was suppressed. A few of the slaves managed to escape but the captured ones were decapitated. The Stono Rebellion resulted in South Carolina enacting a harsher slave code, which banned slaves from earning money and receiving an education. A 10-year moratorium on slave imports through Charleston was also passed, removing it as the main depository of slaves coming in from the West Indies for a time.

· Bacon's Rebellion

Farmers of the Piedmont, stressed by economic factors beyond their control which included declining tobacco prices, growing commercial competition from Maryland and the Carolinas, an increasingly restricted English market, and the rising prices from English manufactured goods because of the Navigation Acts and mercantilism, took it upon themselves to make the local Indians their scapegoat. Nathaniel Bacon led the popular uprising against the Tidewater gentry and the Governor Sir William Berkeley. Berkeley had refused to do anything about claims that the Indians were committing murder and theft on the frontier. The colonial governor was making a good profit from trading with the Indians, and was not willing to disrupt that business by triggering open war. Bacon took command of two unauthorized but successful expeditions against the tribes, often attacking friendly tribes like the Susquehanna instead of the alleged enemies. Bacon triggered the civil war in 1676 by demanding a military commission that would authorize him to further attack the Indians. Berkeley refused and Bacon threatened to act without authorization. Trying to restore some order, Berkeley declared him a rebel. The response was a public wave of support for Bacon, frightening Berkeley enough to force him to finally schedule an election for a new House of Burgesses. Bacon was elected, and Berkeley let him briefly take his seat on the Council. Bacon quickly left Jamestown, rallied a mob, and attacked innocent Occaneechi, Tutelo, and Saponi Indians. The Baconites marched back to the capital forcing the governor into exile on the eastern shore (across the Chesapeake Bay). The House of Burgesses, intimidated by the mob, passed election reform laws demanded by Bacon. Berkeley returned to the capital at Jamestown but was forced to flee again as Bacon's forces captured and burned the town. Both men marshaled their forces but before they could meet in battle Bacon abruptly died of the "Bloodie Flux (dysentery)" and "Lousey Disease (body lice)." This later gave rise to a ditty by the anti-Bacon group:

> Bacon is Dead I am sorry at my hart
> That lice and flux should take the hangman's part

Shortly after Bacon's death, Berkeley regained complete control and hanged the major leaders of the rebellion. He also seized rebel property without going to court. Overall, 23 were hung for their part in the rebellion. Later, after an investigating committee from England issued its report to King Charles II, Berkeley was relieved of the Governorship and returned to England where he died in July 1677.

· Culpepper's Rebellion

Bacon's Rebellion in Virginia had reverberations in Albemarle (North Carolina) as some of Albemarle's residents had been active in the Virginia revolt. In Albemarle disagreement between the early settlers who bought their lands from the Indians and those who had received land patents from the Lord Proprietors was one underlying cause of the dispute. In addition, there were conflicts between Quakers and non-Quakers. The government's attempts to restrict the export of tobacco by enforcement of the Navigation Acts sparked the uprising. The newly elected Anti-proprietary Parliament chose John Culpepper as Governor and Customs Collector. He went to London and was arrested upon his arrival and tried for treason. In his defense, Culpepper was aided by an address by Lord Shaftesbury; his testimony resulted in the acquittal of Culpepper on charges of rebellion. He was found guilty only of rioting. He pleaded for mercy from King Charles after admitting committing the crime of custom's embezzlement and King Charles II freed him. This event was the first of many popular uprising against what was considered to be unfair taxation, especially in regard to the mercantilist provisions of the Navigation Acts. Most accounts call Culpepper a minor figure in the revolt, which was really masterminded by George Durant and other more prominent individuals.

Colonial Economic Policy

· Mercantilism

This system of political/economic thought dominated Western Europe in the 17th and 18th centuries. It was essentially an effort to achieve economic unity and political control to keep the state prosperous by economic regulation. The leading powers relied on strong central governments in order to direct their economies. This philosophy of economic nationalism had its goal of acquiring gold and silver by exporting more than was imported so the trading partner would have to make up the difference in hard money (gold & silver). The British system was not as strict as Spain or France but the goal was to have the colonies provide raw materials (e.g. lumber and naval stores) or products that did not compete with British products (tobacco) in order to bring about self- sufficiency of the "mother country." On the other hand, the colonists were expected to buy surplus British manufactured goods. Features of mercantilism included: a nation's wealth was measured by the amount of gold and silver it possessed (bullionism); economic self-sufficiency; a favorable balance of trade (selling more than was bought); tariffs should be high on imported manufactured goods and low on imported raw materials; colonies would provide captive markets for manufactured goods and sources of raw material; sea power was necessary to control foreign markets and a powerful merchant fleet would keep a state from becoming dependent on foreign shipping; and state action was needed to regulate and enforce the policies of mercantilism although England relied on it less than other nations.

· Navigation Acts

British implementation of mercantilism was through a series of laws starting in 1651 that required all goods in colonial trade be carried on English ships and that certain goods (enumerated goods such as sugar, tobacco, indigo, and rice) had to be shipped directly to England. English and colonial ships were given a monopoly on trade and British merchants a monopoly on selling colonial products. Other acts extended these restrictions to include the principle that required all foreign goods be shipped to the American colonies through English ports. In return for restrictions on manufacturing and the regulation of trade, colonial commodities were often given a monopoly of the English market and preferential tariff treatment. The Molasses Act of 1733, which raised duties on French West Indian sugar, angered Americans by forcing them to buy the more expensive British West Indian sugar. Extensive smuggling and loopholes meant the laws were not rigidly enforced (the policy of "salutary neglect") but were an annoyance and the antithesis of free trade.

·Woolen Act

It was passed by Parliament in 1699 to prohibit the export and inter-colonial sale of certain textiles in an attempt to protect the British wool industry from colonial manufacturers. Colonists were only supposed to supply raw materials and the British would make the woolen finished products.

·Iron Act

A 1750 mercantile law to stop the development of colonial manufacturing in competition with the British home industry by restricting the growth of the American iron industry to the supply of raw metals. To meet British needs, pig iron and iron bar made in the colonies were permitted to enter England duty free, but any finished iron product was prohibited.

·Hat Act

A British law of 1732 restricting colonial manufacturing and export of hats (primarily beaver) in direct competition with English hat makers. As a result of this part of the mercantile system, London hatters were able to capture markets in other colonies and southern Europe formerly supplied by New England and New York manufacturers. The hat industry would revive after the Revolution.

·Triangle Trade

This term is used to describe international trade primarily between Africa, the West Indies, and New England during the 17th and 18th century. New England ships carrying rum and guns went to Africa where slaves were captured and brought to the West Indies. The West Indies sent sugar and molasses back to New England to make rum. The rum was then shipped to Africa for the slaves as the process repeated itself. Other variations of the trade were manufactured goods from England for colonial tobacco, fish, grain, and naval stores (mast, rosen, pitch, tar, and turpentine); and foodstuffs and lumber traded from the colonies for sugar, molasses, and slaves from the West Indies.

International Relations and Wars

·Political Conflicts

From 1689 to 1763 four major wars were fought between England and the other European powers including France, Spain, Prussia, Austria and others. For the most part these wars were fought throughout the world from Europe to the Americas and to Asia. All of these wars were fought, in part, over who would rule North America. At the end of these wars England reigned supreme in North America and was the most powerful country in the world. England usually names the wars after their ruling monarch (in parentheses)—a different name is used by other countries.

·War of the League of Augsburg (King William's War), 1689-1697

A coalition of European countries worked to stop Louis XIV designs in Europe. In the Americas, the French disrupted trade, combined with Indians to harass English settlements on the frontier and turned back an assault on Quebec led by Governor Phips of Massachusetts. The Iroquois, wary of the French, strengthened their alliance with the British and this would be important in future wars. In the New World the French got the best of most of the battles. The Peace of Ryswick ended the conflict to give the combatants a breathing spell before the next outbreak of war.

·War of Spanish Succession (Queen Anne's War), 1702-1713

Taking advantage of unsettled politics in Spain, Louis XIV put his grandson on the throne and this move was opposed by England under King William III and Queen Anne. The war played havoc on Massachusetts and the Carolinas but ultimately France and Spain were defeated which weakened their hold in the New World. At the Peace of Utrecht, France had to recognize the Iroquois as British subjects, give up Acadia (Nova Scotia),

and lose prized Caribbean islands like St. Christopher (St. Kitts). Britain received commercial concessions from France and Spain that enhanced both American and English trade.

·War of Austrian Succession (King George's War), 1739-1748
A third war, also over dynastic succession resulted in the colonies capturing the mighty fortress Louisburg that France had constructed at the entrance to the Gulf of St. Lawrence on Cape Breton Island. At the Peace of Aix–la-Chapelle the fortress was returned to France so the British could receive Madras in India. Colonials who had fought and died for the mother England were incensed at this giveaway.

·Seven Years War (French and Indian War), 1754/1756-1763
The final of four wars fought between the French and British in the late 17th and 18th century is known as the Seven Years War in Europe and French and Indian War in North America.

1. **American Beginnings**—Unlike the others this war actually started in North America as General Braddock with George Washington as his aide was sent to halt the French entry into the Ohio River Valley where they were defeated at Ft. Necessity just south of Ft. Duquesne (Pittsburgh).
2. **Albany Plan**—Under the leadership of the Crown and drawn up by Benjamin Franklin this Albany Plan of inter-colonial union was an attempt to unite the colonies under a grand council for the purpose of making peace with the Indians and gain support from the Iroquois in the coming war with France. It would also administer the western lands and frontier territories and levy taxes for a colonial army.
3. **Plan Defeated**—Both the crown and the colonial governments opposed it and land speculators, especially in Virginia, would not allow the distribution of the Ohio lands to an inter-colonial congress. Also, every colonial assembly jealously guarded its own right to tax.
4. **British Defeats**—In both North America and the West Indies (Caribbean) the French were victorious which exposed the western frontier to Indian and French attacks in Pennsylvania, Maryland, and Virginia.
5. **New Leadership**—After William Pitt became leader of Great Britain a new strategy was tried. Emphasizing sea power to bottle up the French fleet, and by moving the war from the Caribbean to Canada, this resulted in a series of victories. Once again Louisburg was captured and Wolfe defeated Montcalm at Quebec on the Plains of Abraham, which resulted in the British taking all of Canada.
6. **Treaty of Paris (1763)**—It gave all of North America east of the Mississippi except New Orleans, to the British. The French also turned over their claims of New Orleans and the lands west of the Mississippi to Spain, as compensation for Spain's surrendering Florida to the British. Primarily for military reasons the British chose to keep Canada instead of the two captured French islands of Guadalupe and Martinique. France gave Spain all of its North American Territory west of the Mississippi including the Isle of Orleans. France retained fishing rights on the banks of Newfoundland and the small islands of Saint Pierre and Miquelon in Canada.
7. **Results and Implications**—The removal of both the French and Spanish threats resulted in the colonials no longer having a need for British protection. This would lead to the movement toward independence.

Political Issues

·Writs of Assistance
In 1761, James Otis resigned as Advocate General of the Vice-Admiralty court in opposition to the issuing of writs of assistance (general search warrants) by the Superior Court of Massachusetts, which authorized customs officials to search for smuggled goods. New England merchants were trading with the French in Canada while the war was on. Arguing before the court, Otis claimed that the writs violated the natural rights

of the colonials as Englishmen and that any act of Parliament violating those rights was void. Otis lost the case but soon became a leader of the radical wing of the colonial opposition to British measures and the enemy of the Hutcheson political machine in Massachusetts.

·Pontiac's Rebellion

With the change in power from the French to the British, the Ottawa Chief Pontiac with his allies led a rebellion that lasted from 1763-1766. The cause was colonial encroachment on Indian lands and it was eventually put down by the British after the frontier had become inflamed. A treaty was concluded in 1766 with Pontiac receiving a pardon from the British.

·Proclamation of 1763

In order to lessen tensions between colonial settlers and Native Americans this British proclamation forbid settlement west of the Appalachians and was bitterly resented by colonial land speculators, squatters, frontiersman, and others wanting to settle in the west.

·Parson's Cause

The colony of Virginia traditionally paid the Anglican clergy in tobacco, but when the price of tobacco increased, they switched to paying them in currency at about 1/3rd of the market price of tobacco. The crown vetoed this act by the House of Burgesses and James Maury, a clergyman, sued for back wages. Patrick Henry first emerged as notable figure in fighting for the rights of the colonists in defending Virginia against Maury in court. He argued for the vetoed Two-Penny Act, saying "that a King, by disallowing Acts of this salutary nature, from being the father of his people, degenerated into a Tyrant and forfeits all right to his subjects' obedience." The court found in favor of Maury, but he was awarded one penny in damages effectively nullifying actions of the crown.

·Paxton Boys

During the Pontiac rebellion, warfare on the frontier inflamed the Scots-Irish against all Native Americans, peaceful or warlike. In 1763, 20 peaceful and defenseless Conestoga Indians, who lived by selling handicrafts, were massacred by 57 rangers from Paxton. Proclamations were issued to bring the culprits to trial but were not served as justices and juries were sympathetic to their cause. Much of this sympathy stemmed from the fact that the East controlled the government due to a system of unequal representation and the government was blamed for allowing the frontier to become inflamed. Six hundred backcountry armed inhabitants marched on Philadelphia intent on destroying their political opponents and violence was only averted by the skillful diplomacy of Ben Franklin and others.

·Regulator Movement

From 1764 to 1771 a long struggle took place in North Carolina between the back county settlers and the oppressive administration of the laws by the ruling officials in the coastal areas. This Piedmont animosity toward the Tidewater government was particularly strong in Anson, Granville, Halifax, Orange and Rowan counties. Efforts to reform the assessment of taxes and fees were unsuccessful; the courts and assembly were not responsive and seemed to favor the causes of the wealthy Tidewater elements. Regulator groups arose to close down local courts (county commissions) and suppress tax payments; rioting broke out in several counties. In 1771, Governor William Tryon led a militia force of 1200 against the 2,000 Regulators (many of whom were unarmed) and defeated them at Alamance Creek. Most of the rebels were pardoned, but seven of the leaders were hanged. Sixty five hundred Piedmont settlers were forced to take an oath of allegiance to the government. The movement was over but tensions between east and west remained.

·Financial Problems & Revenue Needs

Although the British won the Seven Years War and acquired an even larger empire, the country added 58 million pounds of debt for a total British debt of 130 million pounds. British landowners were paying a third of their incomes in taxes and the cost of the new expanded empire would be even greater. Naturally, the British thought that the American colonials should pay part of the cost of the new expanded empire.

·Enlightenment

European thinkers and writers, primarily in London and Paris believed that human reason could be used to combat ignorance, superstition, and tyranny to build a better world. In their reliance upon both thought and science they attacked what they saw as the twin evils of the Catholic religion and a hereditary aristocracy. The intellectual leaders of the American colonies were drawn to the Enlightenment rationalist way of thinking. Many of the most distinguished leaders of the American Revolution—Thomas Jefferson, George Washington, Benjamin Franklin, and Thomas Paine—held strongly to the concept of separation of church and state. The God in the Declaration of Independence is the same deist God Rousseau worshipped, not the one venerated in the traditional churches that still supported and defended monarchies all over Europe. Jefferson and Franklin both spent time in France absorbing the influence of the French *philosophes*. The language of natural law, inherent freedoms, and self-determination, which all became a part of the American belief system was the language of the Enlightenment. Of all the ideas of the Enlightenment the natural rights doctrine was most important to the Americans. They readily used these ideas to support their views in their quarrel with Great Britain.

UNIT III
MULTIPLE-CHOICE QUESTIONS

Questions 1-3 refer to the following map:

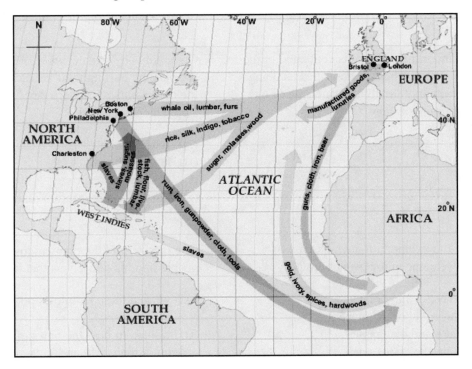

1. This map reflects which of the following?

    (A) Bilateral trade
    (B) Common market
    (C) Spice trade
    (D) Triangle trade

2. This map depicts economic activites that are often called the

    (A) Mercantile system
    (B) Peculiar institution
    (C) Columbian Exchange
    (D) "middle passage"

3. The greatest degree of bilateral trade occurred between

    (A) North America and Europe
    (B) West Indies and North America
    (C) Europe and West Indies
    (D) Africa and North America

43

Questions 4-7 refer to the following:

"The...hospitality of the plantation houses, where great and mean (unimportant people) were always welcome and no limit was set on the length of the visits, isn't merely a romantic story. Isolated as he was, and by nature gregarious, the planter was hungry for company and news. There were no newspapers. He could find out what was going on in the world and in the Colony only by letters and by word of mouth. So, if a strange boat beat up the river, it was hailed ashore and its passengers were invited up to the house. If a road ran near his place, the planter was likely to keep a slave posted at the entrance to his mile-long lane to invite all travelers to come in and rest a spell. The custom was so universal that innkeepers bitterly complained that it hurt their business..."

Edwin Tunis, *Colonial Living* (abridged), nd

4. The type or kind of history that is contained in the above document could best be described as being written from which of the following frame of reference (aka point of view)?

   (A) Economic
   (B) Diplomatic
   (C) Political
   (D) Social

5. According to the interpretation which type of people were welcome in the plantations?

   (A) Fellow slave owning planters
   (B) The social equal of the owners
   (C) Upper class and the masses
   (D) Spiritual and religious ones

6. Complaints by innkeepers about the hospitality of the planters hurting their business are similar to the complaints of modern day hotels who try to stop which enterprise

   (A) roadside motels
   (B) bed and breakfast
   (C) destination resorts
   (D) private home vacation rentals

7. One reason why the planters invited all types of people into his house was that he

   (A) viewed these people as potential investors in his business
   (B) wanted to hear the news of what was going on in the world and in the colony
   (C) believed that all people, regardless of their race, were equal in the eyes of God
   (D) hoped to run for political office in the future and was trying to get their support

Questions 8-10 refer to the following:

"Competition over sugar brought an end to the first phase of imperialism, which had begin with competition over spices. At the beginning sugar had been of little importance, a minor luxury.... [as] supplies of Europe's traditional sweetener, honey, begin to fall off...sugar became readily available, it also became popular...it was discovered (1600) that fruit could be preserved in it and (1730) jam made with it. By the 1670s sugar was a trading commodity of such importance that the Dutch yielded New York to England in exchange of the sugar lands of Surinam, while in 1763 France abandoned the whole of Canada to the British for the sake of Guadalupe. But not even the most optimistic eighteenth-century sugar merchant could ever have foreseen that by the 1980s the British would be consuming 80 pounds of it per head per year, or the North Americans 126 pounds."

Reay Tannahill, *Food in History*, 1988

8. Sugar became a major product in going from the Caribbean to Europe in what is now usually called the

   (A) market revolution
   (B) commercial revitalization of Europe
   (C) Columbian Exchange
   (D) Triangle Trade

9. According to the passage above sugar became so important that European countries

   (A) used it as a form of money
   (B) gave up larger land areas for smaller ones that produced it
   (C) made alliances to fight the British to keep them from gaining a sugar monopoly
   (D) went into debt producing it

10. A historical continuity that started in the 17th century and continued into the 20th century is that

   (A) the amount of sugar consumption was more than 1/3rd of a pound a day per person among North Americans
   (B) countries with the largest amount of sugar production became the richest countries in the world
   (C) the final ending of slavery in Brazil in 1888 brought an end to sugar production in Latin America
   (D) in order to curb sugar consumption laws were passed in the United States to curtail its production

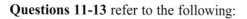

Questions 11-13 refer to the following:

"the following story [was] related to me twenty years ago by an aged lady, who was a distant relative. 'When George,' she said,' was about six years old he was made the wealthy master of a hatchet... and was constantly going about chopping,... he unluckily tried the... hatchet... on an English cherry tree, which he barked so terribly, I don't believe the tree ever got the better of it. The next morning, the old gentleman, finding out what had happened to his tree... came into the house.... Presently George and his hatchet made their appearance. George, said his father, do you know who killed that beautiful little cherry tree.... I cannot tell a lie, Pa! You know I can't tell a lie. I did cut it with my hatchet. Run to my arms you dearest boy, cried his father in transports of joy—run to my arms; glad am I, George, that you killed my tree; for you have paid for it a thousand fold. Such a set of heroism in my son is worth more than a thousand trees.'"

Mason Locke Weems, *The Life of George Washington*, 1832

11. The aged lady, a distant relative of Washington who related the story to Weems about the Cherry tree, could be challenged on the historical accuracy of her account

   (A) because she was a Federalist partisan
   (B) due to advanced age and family relationship to Washington
   (C) her lack of historical training to make judgments about facts
   (D) as a newspaper reporter she was inherently biased

12. Regarding the cherry tree incident the evidence seems to suggest that the

   (A) tree was chopped down by George Washington
   (B) incident never happened
   (C) tree was damaged and would die but was not chopped down
   (D) tree was replaced by a new tree

13. The moral of the story that Weems was trying to convey was based on which Ben Franklin saying from Poor Richards' Almanac?

   (A) Honesty is the best policy
   (B) Fools make feast and wise men eat them
   (C) A small leak will sink a great ship
   (D) Make haste slowly

Questions 14-15 refer to the following:

"When an Indian Child has been brought up among us, taught our language and habituated to our Customs, yet if he goes to see his relations and makes one Indian Ramble with them, there is no perswading [sic] him ever to return. [But] when white persons of either sex have been taken prisoners young by the Indians, and lived a while among them, tho' ransomed by their Friends, and treated with all imaginable tenderness to prevail with them to stay among the English, yet in a Short time they become disgusted with our manner of life, and the care and pains that are necessary to support it, and take the first good Opportunity of escaping again into the Woods, from whence there is no reclaiming them."

Benjamin Franklin, *The Papers of Benjamin Franklin*, IV, 1961

14. The observation that Franklin expressed in the above passage is contrary to the English belief about the Indians that

    (A) Indians had an obligation to learn European ways and become a part of European culture
    (B) the superiority of British civilization meant that no person in possession of his faculties or free from undue restraint would choose to become an Indian
    (C) they were to remain economic allies but would not mix with the British colonials socially
    (D) they were the custodians of the earth who could teach the colonials to preserve the environment intact for future generations

15. The point of view in the above document makes all of the following conclusions EXCEPT

    (A) Indian children raised by the English will return to the Indian ways at the first opportunity
    (B) Whites raised by the Indians and then returned to English culture take the first opportunity to return to Indian culture
    (C) Whites after living with Indians, when returned to the English culture soon become disgusted with the manner of life and the pains that are necessary to support it and return to the Woods
    (D) If an Indian is taught the English language he will remain with his English captors even if the opportunity arises for him to escape back to his Indian culture

UNIT IV

REVOLUTIONARY WAR

Dramatic changes would take place between 1763 and 1788 when 13 of Great Britain's 33 colonies broke away and established their own independence. With the help of the French the American colonist would achieve independence from Great Britain and double the size of the country by a successful peace treaty. The results of this war would start a movement toward independence of subject peoples that would dominate the history of the 19th and 20th centuries throughout the world.

Greenville's Program

·Sugar Act (Revenue Act of 1764)

The new British Prime Minister replacing William Pitt after the French and Indian War was George Greenville. He devised a system for having the colonies pay the administrative cost of the new expanded empire in North America. Abandoning "salutary neglect," the Revenue Act attempted to put teeth in the 1733 Molasses Act by actually lowering the duty on sugar by cutting it in half but insisting on its enforcement. Long accustomed to evading the duty by buying off officials or smuggling, colonial merchants led the protest against this Act. Other parts of it were equally onerous as new and higher duties were placed on non-British textiles, coffee, and indigo; Madeira and Canary wines were taxed for the first time; foreign rum and French wines were prohibited; it doubled the duties of foreign goods reshipped in England to the colonies; and added iron, hides, whale fins, raw silk, potash, and pearl ash to the enumerated (goods forbidden to be shipped to any country except England) list. The worst aspects were the increase in "red tape" including the requirement that a bond had to be posted before any item could be loaded on a ship. The paperwork in getting the bond was extensive and both John Hancock's ship the *Liberty*, and Henry Laurens' *Anne*, were seized by customs officials for technical violations of the bonding provisions. The customs service was reformed by setting up Vice-Admiralty Courts in Halifax where those accused of smuggling would be tried. Also, the right of the accused to sue for illegal seizure was annulled and the accused had to post bond for the trial costs. The

objective of these laws was to raise 45,000 pounds of the 300,000 pounds needed to pay for the administrative and military costs in the colonies.

·Currency Act (1765)

Aimed primarily at chronically in debt Virginia, the Currency Act forbid the paying of debts with paper money. This ban had been in effect in New England since 1751. It had a deleterious economic effect on the colonies as this deflationary policy (forcing prices down) at a time of post-war business decline contributed greatly to the colonial negative reaction against these new policies.

·Quartering Acts (1765-1766)

Requested by General Gage the law required colonial governments to supply barracks and supplies for British troops at prices according to a schedule. The soldiers would be barracked in inns, alehouses, and other public or unoccupied buildings.

·Stamp Act (1765)

The Stamp Act was the first direct tax ever levied by Parliament and was designed to raise 60,000 pounds and it was the cornerstone of the Greenville program. The new tax was imposed on all American colonists and required them to pay a tax on every piece of printed paper or document they used. Ship's papers, legal documents, licenses, newspapers, diplomas, other publications, and even playing cards were taxed. The money collected by the Stamp Act was to be used to help pay the costs of defending and protecting the American frontier near the Appalachian Mountains (10,000 troops were to be stationed on the frontier). What made the law so offensive was the precedent it established. In the past, taxes and duties on colonial trade had always been viewed as measures to regulate commerce, not to raise money. The Stamp Act, however, was viewed as a direct attempt by England to raise revenue in the colonies without the approval of the colonial legislatures.

·Virginia Resolves

Seven resolutions were drawn up by Patrick Henry on the last day of the legislative session in the House of Burgesses in 1765 when 77 of the 116 members were absent. The first four resolutions were accepted by a close vote of 22-17 and were vague statements regarding the natural rights of the colonists that were being violated by the Stamp Act. The 5th one said only Virginia could lay taxes on the colonists and it was rejected. The 6th and 7th which were much more radical were not submitted to a vote and they said Virginians did not have to obey any laws except their own legislatures and anyone denying the sole right of the power of the legislature was an enemy of the colony. In introducing the resolutions Henry made an inflammatory speech that included the lines "Caesar had his Brutus, Charles the First his Cromwell and George the Third may profit by their example. If this be treason, make the most of it." The next day all seven resolutions were printed in the newspapers and it was assumed all had passed the House of Burgesses. Because of Henry's careful maneuvering the newspaper reports made it seem like the Burgesses had taken a more radical position than it had.

·Committees of Correspondence

First proposed by the colonial legislature in Boston in 1764 these "extra-legal" organizations would play an important role in the coordination of anti-British propaganda throughout the colonies. Many correspondents were members of the colonial assemblies and also were active in the secret Sons of Liberty organizations.

·Sons of Liberty

These arose out of the union of the two major gangs of Boston by Alexander McIntosh. Sam Adams helped form the "Sons of Liberty" from these gangs. Sam Adams used the Caucus Club, an influential and popular political club that had been started by his father, as the mechanism to recruit the gangs for his cause. At around the same time a similar group started in New York. The actual name for these former gang members came from a speech given by a pro-colonial British Member of Parliament Issac Barre calling them, "these Sons of Liberty."

·Stamp Act Congress
James Otis spearheaded the meeting of delegates from nine colonies in New York who adopted a 14 point document of protest called the Declaration of Rights and Grievances that was to be sent to George III and Parliament in the form of a moderate petition written by John Dickinson.

·Non-Importation and Violence
This policy was adopted to ban the purchase of European goods and to actively resist the use of the stamps. The protests were largely effective through the enforcement mechanism of the Sons of Liberty and frequently resulted in violence directed at the appointed Stamp Tax Agents (who all resigned) along with the destruction of the stamps and other property. Business and the judicial system came to a halt as they could not legally function without the stamps. Before the end of the year business was renewed without the stamps in open violation of the act on the grounds that the stamps no longer existed because they had been destroyed by "person's unknown."

New Ministries

·Parliament's Repeal (1766)
Greenville's ministry fell over his clumsy handling of the Regency Act of 1765 and a group of merchants in London worked for the Stamp Act repeal with the new government under the Marquis of Rockingham. As Parliament debated repeal Greenville called for military action to enforce it and William Pitt praised the colonials for opposing a tax adopted by a body in which that they were not represented. Pitt fully accepted the American argument of "no taxation without representation." Early in 1766 the repeal bill passed the House of Commons 275-167 and was accepted by the House of Lords after George III applied pressure to that body. Colonial reaction included the abandonment of non-importation and erecting statues in New York honoring the King and Pitt.

·Declaratory Act (1766)
Passed the same day as the repeal of the Stamp Act this face saving measure asserted that Parliament had full authority to make laws binding on the colonists "in all cases whatsoever."

·Non-Compliance with Quartering Act
New York voted insufficient money to provide barracks and provisions and the assembly's governing power was suspended by Parliament.

·Townshend Acts (1767)
Taking advantage of the colonial argument that said external taxes (those regulating trade) were acceptable but internal taxes (raising revenue) were not, Chancellor of the Exchequer Charles Townshend, running the ministry for Pitt (replacing the Rockingham ministry) who was ill, proposed new external taxes on paints, lead, glass, paper, and tea.

·*"Letters from a Pennsylvania Farmer"*
In 14 essays written for the *Pennsylvania Chronicle* and republished throughout the colonies, John Dickinson declared the Townshend Acts unconstitutional because they were disguised as trade regulations but their intent was to raise revenue. This made them an illegal internal tax that was disguised to look like an external tax. This argument by a Philadelphia lawyer gave the colonists the legal justification to oppose the Townshend

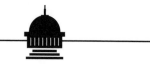

duties. He also assailed the suspension of the colonial assembly of New York as an attack on the liberties in all the colonies.

·Non-Importation
This policy was instituted again in response to the Townshend duties especially against British luxury goods.

·Massachusetts Circular Letter (1768)
Written by Sam Adams, endorsed by the Massachusetts assembly and sent to other colonies, the letter was denounced as seditious by the governor and Secretary of State for the Colonies Lord Hillsborough who ordered it rescinded. By then New Hampshire, New Jersey, and Connecticut had endorsed it and Virginia had written its own letter in support of Massachusetts. Governor Bernard ordered the Massachusetts assembly to rescind the letter and it refused by a vote of 92-17. The 17 rescinders came under attack by the Caucus Club and Sons of Liberty and all of them would be defeated when they stood for reelection. The radicals would gain complete control of Massachusetts politics.

·*Liberty* Seizure (1768)
The seizure of John Hancock's sloop on the grounds that it had illegally landed Madeira wine without paying the duty resulted in a riot by the Sons of Liberty that forced customs officials to retreat to an island and brought about the stationing of troops in Boston.

·Associations Formed
George Mason introduced resolutions by George Washington in the Virginia House of Burgesses asserting the sole right of Virginia to tax itself and condemned the British ministry for its denunciation of the Massachusetts and Virginia Circular Letters. This action brought about the dissolution of the Burgesses by the governor. They met informally at Raleigh's Tavern in Williamsburg and adopted the Virginia Association. This led to other Associations being formed in most of the other colonies that gave non-importation the force of the colonial assemblies. Colonial imports from England fell by more than 60% in most colonies.

·Townshend Duties Repealed (1770)
A new ministry headed by Lord North had Parliament do away with all the duties except for the one on tea that was kept as a symbol of Parliament's right to tax. Despite Boston's attempt to hold the line until the one on tea was removed, non-importation collapsed and trade resumed.

·Battle of Golden Hill (1770)
Alexander McDougall's broadside criticizing the new assembly for caving in on Quartering led to clashes between citizens and soldiers in New York. On Golden Hill, 30-40 soldiers with bayonets clashed with the Sons of Liberty armed with cutlasses and clubs with several on both sides being seriously wounded. McDougall was subsequently arrested and imprisoned for his authorship of the broadside.

·Boston Massacre (1770)
With 4,000 troops in a city of 16,000 frequent clashes occurred between citizen and soldier. After an argument broke out between a soldier and merchant a crowd assembled and began pelting a single sentry with a variety of materials—stones, oyster shells, ice, and chunks of coal. Reinforcements under Captain Thomas Preston were rushed in to relieve the beleaguered sentry. The mob taunted the soldiers by calling them lobster backs (a derogatory term) and daring them to fire. After a soldier was hit with a wooden club someone yelled, "Fire!" The soldiers did so and Preston, who clearly had not given the order, ended the firing and tried to restore order. Five colonials would die with six others being wounded. An uprising was averted when Sam Adams convinced Lt. Gov. Hutchinson to withdraw the troops to the islands in the harbor away from the town. John Adams and Josiah Quincy defended the soldiers in court who were acquitted except for two, who were found

guilty of manslaughter, pleaded clergy, and were released after being branded on the hand. The engraving by Paul Revere called the "Boston Massacre" showed the British troops lined up like a firing squad—it was an effective work of propaganda that definitely stretched the truth. The most notable fatality was Crispis Attucks, a mulatto, and one of the leaders of the mob.

· *Gaspee* (1772)

After running aground in Narragansett Bay while chasing smugglers, the British customs ship *Gaspee* was boarded, the captain Dudingston wounded, the crew set ashore, and the ship was burned. Led by merchant John Brown none of the Rhode Islanders responsible was ever prosecuted despite the British offer of generous rewards. The British were going to invoke extraterritoriality by holding the trials in England, which alarmed even political moderates in the colonies.

· Tea Act (1773)

In order to stave off the bankruptcy of the East India Company, Parliament passed a bill allowing the company to sell tea in the colonies without paying taxes or going through a middleman. This would enable the company to sell its tea cheaper than smuggled tea from Holland that was already in the colonies. Colonial opposition was based on the establishment of a monopoly and the Sons of Liberty branded tea importers as enemies to America while advocating non-importation.

· Boston Tea Party (1773)

Hutchinson refused to send the tea back and as 8,000 people gathered in protest. The Sons of Liberty disguised as Mohawk Indians, boarded the ship and dumped the tea into the harbor without damaging the chests or the ships. Further tea disorders followed with tea being dumped into the harbor in New York, destroyed by fire including the ship in Annapolis Maryland, and a warehouse of tea burned in New Jersey. Tea landed at Charleston harbor, but it was not allowed to be sold by the Sons of Liberty and the Association. Later the revolutionary government auctioned the tea off in 1776.

· Coercive Acts (Intolerable Acts) (1774)

Parliament passed the Boston Port Bill closing the harbor for any shipment of goods, which would not be reopened until the tea was paid for. The Administration of Justice Act protected governmental officials from prosecution and stipulated that trials would be held in England. The Massachusetts Government Act gave the Governor (who was appointed by the crown) the power over all appointments and town meetings could not be held without his written approval of time, place, and agenda. A new Quartering Act legalized the quartering of troops in private residences.

· Quebec Act

This law had been in preparation for a long period of time and by chance it was passed at the same time as the Coercive Acts and was considered to be another intolerable act. After the Treaty of Paris ended the French and Indian War the French citizens of Canada had not been integrated into the British Empire. This act attempted to accomplish that goal by appointing a separate governor and council for Quebec; officially recognizing the French civil code for use in Quebec; continue English law in criminal matters; give recognition to the Roman Catholic Church in Quebec which allowed Catholics to run for public office after taking a loyalty oath; and extend the administrative boundaries of Quebec south to the Ohio and west to the Mississippi rivers which was an admission that the Proclamation of 1763 had been a failure.

· Suffolk Resolves

Written by Sam Adams and Joseph Warren and adopted by Suffolk County Massachusetts these resolutions denounced the Coercive Acts; declared 10 Parliamentary acts void and would not be obeyed; and, advised the people to elect their own militia and learn the art of war as soon as possible. When these were adopted by the First Continental Congress John Adams said, "America will support Massachusetts or perish with her."

·1st Continental Congress (1774)

Except for Georgia all the colonies sent delegates to meet in Philadelphia at Carpenter's Hall where the political moderates were a majority. News about events in Massachusetts were accompanied by the Suffolk Resolves. After a fierce debate these were endorsed by the Continental Congress. Conservative Joseph Galloway proposed a plan to create a Grand Council of Legislatures for the colonies which would jointly govern them along with Parliament. This plan was tabled 6-5. Radicals had carried the day with their endorsement of the Suffolk Resolves. This would the be the position taken by the Congress.

·North's Conciliation Plan

After the rejection of Pitt's plan of conciliation which would have granted sovereignty to the colonies in something similar to dominion status, North's plan promised to not lay taxes except to regulate trade and the colonial assemblies would be responsible for raising revenue to support the civil government, judiciary, and provide for defense. Along with this Parliament also passed laws to forbid New England from trading with anyone except Britain and the British West Indies and these laws barred New Englanders from fishing in the North Atlantic.

·"Give me Liberty"

As New England prepared for war, Patrick Henry of Virginia gave a speech in which he said, "The war is actually begun! … Why stand we here idle? … Is life so dear, or peace so sweet, as to be purchased at the price of chains and slavery? Forbid it, Almighty God! I know not what course others may take; but as for me, give me liberty or give me death!"

·Minutemen

These were the younger (under 30), more mobile members of the state militia who could gather in a moments notice and take action. Some were Sons of Liberty but most of them were yeoman farmers. Their officers were elected by popular vote and decisions were made by consultation and consensus. They were most effective in irregular (almost guerilla) fighting as sharpshooters. For the most part they used their own equipment and would go back to their job when the immediate fighting ended.

Revolutionary War

·Lexington and Concord (1775)

Following orders, General Gage had 700 men march to Concord to capture supplies. Paul Revere, William Dawes, and Samuel Prescott went to warn Sam Adams and John Hancock who were in Lexington of the British movement. After issuing the warning they went on toward Concord. Revere was captured and detained, Dawes turned back, and only Prescott got through to issue the warning. Upon reaching Lexington, 70 Minutemen opposed the British on the Village Green but shots were fired and 8 were killed and 10 wounded. The British reached Concord where they destroyed some gun carriages, trenching tools, and a liberty pole. After being attacked at Concord's North Bridge by Minutemen, the British forces retreated back to Boston where they were continually fired upon by about 4,000 Americans in the field with 73 being killed and 174 being wounded compared to the American's 93 casualties who were dead, wounded or missing.

·Ticonderoga and Crown Point

Cannon from the colonial capture of these two forts in Massachusetts was transported to Boston on sleds (the brainchild of Henry Knox) to give the colonist a commanding position on the heights to force the British out of Boston.

·2nd Continental Congress

It met again in Philadelphia at the State House where many of the conservatives who had been at the first Congress were not present. It resolved to put the colonies into a state of defense and at the urging of John Adams appointed Virginian George Washington to command the Continental Army that consisted of the troops in Boston.

·Battle of Bunker Hill

With instructions to establish a defensive positions on Bunker Hill, the Patriots constructed a redoubt on nearby Breed's Hill instead. The British were surprised to see the rebel fortifications upon the hill that they had intended to occupy. General Howe led two costly and ineffective charges against the Patriot's fortifications without inflicting significant casualties on his opponents. After obtaining 400 reinforcements Howe ordered a bayonet charge to seize Breed's Hill. In this third attempt, the British were finally able to breach the breastworks of the American redoubt and the Patriots were forced to retreat back to the mainland. This battle, though victorious, proved costly for the British. Of the 2,400 British soldiers in Howe's command, the 1,054 casualties accounted for nearly forty percent of their ranks. The American casualties were 441 and the battle convinced Americans that the British were not as invincible in the field as they had been portrayed.

·Olive Branch Petition

Written by John Dickinson and adopted by the 2nd Continental Congress it professed loyalty to George III and asked him to cease hostilities until reconciliation could be worked out.

·Actions of the Continental Congress

Dickinson and Thomas Jefferson wrote a "Declaration of the Causes and Necessities of Taking Up Arms" that rejected independence but said they were ready to die rather than be enslaved. It also mentioned the idea of receiving foreign aid against Great Britain. Lord North's plan of reconciliation was rejected and commissioner's were appointed to negotiate treaties with the Native American tribes.

·Failure to Take Canada

Two expeditions invaded Canada, had some success in taking Montreal but trying to take Quebec was a disaster. Commander Richard Montgomery was killed, Benedict Arnold was wounded and more than 100 men were killed. Out of an invasion force of 950, 300 were captured.

·*Common Sense* (1776)

By attacking the King directly as a "Royal Brute" Thomas Paine's pamphlet issued the first call for independence. His arguments convinced many that separation was the only course to take. Published in 1776, *Common Sense* challenged the authority of the British government and the royal monarchy. The plain language that Paine used spoke to the common people of America.

·Declaration of Independence (1776)

Written as a justification for passing Richard Henry Lee's resolution that said that these United Colonies are and ought to be independent states. A committee consisting of Thomas Jefferson, Benjamin Franklin, John Adams, Robert Livingston, and Roger Sherman was formed with Jefferson given the responsibility of writing the document. Borrowing heavily from the natural rights ideas of Enlightenment thinkers and especially John Locke, Jefferson wrote a justification for revolution that listed a long list of abuses the King had committed (there was no mention of Parliament). This was done to make sure the document reflected a complete and total break not with just the government of England but the sovereign himself. The document was adopted unanimously by 12 colonies of the Continental Congress, New York abstained.

·Military Battles in the Middle Colonies (1776)

After the initial fighting in New England the next phase of the war was fought in the Middle Colonies as the main British force left Boston and landed unopposed on Staten Island. Washington moved to New York where the British dislodged him. First, they drove Washington off Long Island, then, from lower Harlem. After this initiative, Washington retreated to White Plains, where for the first time, he was able to hold off the British forces. However, the British out maneuvered Washington on Manhattan Island and he was forced to retreat to New Jersey. Despite these losses he retreated in good order keeping his army intact to fight another day.

·Victories at Trenton and Princeton

By surprising a Hessian (German mercenaries hired by the British) force on Christmas Eve, Washington captured 918 of them after killing 30, and only suffered 5 casualties. This move was made possible by crossing the ice-choked Delaware River in secrecy with 2,400 troops. Outmaneuvering his opponent Washington gained a victory at Trenton and established winter quarters in the hills around Morristown.

·British Capture Philadelphia

Defeating Washington's entrenched position at Brandywine Creek, Howe captured Philadelphia which sent the Continental Congress to Lancaster and then York. After Washington's counter attack at Germantown failed, he retired to winter at Valley Forge. It was a winter of hardship and suffering for the troops but it was also a winter of training, in which the American troops were taught how to be professional soldiers. This process was helped by the recruitment of foreign officers including 20 year old Marquis de Lafayette from France, Johann De Kalb and Friedrich von Steuben from Prussia, and Thaddeus Kosciusko from Poland.

·Crisis Papers

Published between 1776 and 1783 by Tom Paine these essays were about issues such as how to treat Tories, what to do with the western lands, and the need for federal taxation. The first one opened with the words, "These are the times that try men's souls. The summer soldier and the sunshine patriot will, in this crisis, shrink from the service of their country; but he that stands it now, deserves the love and thanks of man and woman."

·Saratoga (1777)

In what became a turning point in the war the British launched a three-pronged attack to try to split New England from the other colonies that ended in disaster.

1. The 1st prong was Barry St. Leger with a force of 1800 Loyalists and Native Americans who left from Lake Ontario toward the interior of New York where they laid siege to Fort Stanwix. An American relief force sent to relieve the siege was ambushed at Oriskany by British and Native Americans, led by the Mohawk leader, Joseph Brant. The Americans managed to fight out of the ambush, severely depleting the British forces and opening the way for Arnold's relief of the fort. St. Leger returned to Lake Ontario without meeting up with the other two armies. His force was intact but he had accomplished very little.

2. The 2nd prong was John Burgoyne's force of 7,700 that marched from St. Johns with a huge baggage train and 138 pieces of artillery where his forces became bogged down because of the forested terrain as the Americans blocked the way with felled trees. After failing to get supplies with the defeat at Bennington by John Stark and the Green Mountain Boys with the loss of 1,000 troops, Burgoyne was stopped from advancing to Albany at Bemis Heights by American forces. He retreated to Saratoga where he was surrounded by Horatio Gates's army and militiamen and surrendered his remaining force of 5,700 on October 13, 1777. One quarter of the British forces in North America were marched to Boston and returned to England with a pledge not to serve in the war again against America.

3. The 3rd prong—General William Howe was to leave Philadelphia and join up with the other two forces around Albany where they would crush any army opposing them. Instead, Howe stayed in the New York, Philadelphia, and New Jersey area enjoying the attention of his mistress Elizabeth Loring, wife of a prominent Loyalist, and he never reached Albany to help Burgoyne.

· French Alliance (1778)

Two months after the battle of Saratoga, France recognized the United States. On January 7, 1778, the French royal council declared unanimously in favor of a treaty of amity and commerce with the United States. It was followed on February 6th with a treaty of alliance. France consented to the American conquest of Canada and Bermuda and the U.S. promised to accept the French conquest of the West Indies. After a clash between British and French naval forces the two rival countries were at war.

· Carlisle Peace Proposal

Lord North had a commissioner present a peace proposal to the Continental Congress, but it fell well short of recognizing colonial independence and was rejected.

· Molly Pitcher

During the battle of Monmouth in 1778 lasting through "one of the hottest days ever known" when soldiers were dying of heat and thirst, Mary Hays McCauly, the wife of John Hays, a sergeant of artillery, was carrying water in a pitcher to the thirsty soldiers who called her Molly Pitcher for this service. Her husband was struck down and his artillery piece was ordered to be withdrawn. She took over for him using the rammer in helping to fire the gun until the end of the battle. The nickname was subsequently used to describe all women who helped in the actual fighting of the Revolution.

· Culper Ring

Name for a group that spied for George Washington during the American Revolution. Included in the group were its organizer Benjamin Tallmadge, Abraham Woodhull, Robert Townsend, and agent 355 that was the code name for a woman. The group worked throughout the war, mainly in the New York and New England area and were so well disguised that their true identities were not unearthed until the twentieth century.

· State Constitutions

Connecticut and Rhode Island kept their colonial charters while all other states adopted new constitutions. These governments featured: bicameral legislatures except for Pennsylvania's unicameral; weak executives except for Massachusetts and New York where an executive was elected by the people; strong legislatures with frequent elections; property qualifications for office holding and voting; and an appointive judiciary. Most of the states adopted Bills of Rights.

· Primogeniture and Entail

Starting with Georgia in 1777 laws abolishing these Medieval and anti-democratic practices were generally abolished. These were two British legal doctrines governing the inheritance of property. Primogeniture required that a man's real property pass in its entirety to his oldest son. Entail required that property could only be left to direct descendants (usually sons), and not to persons outside of the family.

· John Paul Jones

He successfully raided British commercial ships from bases in France. His most daring raid occurred when he captured the British warship *Serapis* while his own ship the *Bonhomme Richard* sank. At the onset of the battle when the *Serapis*' guns were destroying Jones's ship, his reply to the British when they asked him to surrender was, "I have not yet begun to fight."

· Loyalist and Native American Raids

A series of raids took place in the Wyoming Valley area in Pennsylvania that culminated at Cherry Valley in New York when 40 patriots were massacred after their surrender.

· Clinton Replaces Howe

After dawdling in Philadelphia while Washington's army was freezing at Valley Forge less than 20 miles away, Howe was replaced by Henry Clinton who evacuated Philadelphia moving his base to New York. After a skirmish at Monmouth, Washington took a position at White Plains above New York City as the British force occupied the city.

· Kaskaskia, Vincennes, Cahokia (1778)

George Rogers Clark with a small force of 172 frontier fighters defeated Loyalist and Native American forces as he captured these three forts in Indiana and Illinois. This would give the colonists a claim to this area in the west.

· Arnold's Treason

A controversial figure who had figured prominently in many early colonial battles including Saratoga, Benedict Arnold, while recovering from his wounds in Philadelphia, fell in love with the Loyalist Peggy Shippen. High living in Loyalist society put him in debt and in 1780, he obtained command of West Point in order to surrender it to the British. When his scheme was detected by the timely capture of Major John Andre, he fled to the British at New York, a disgraced and hated traitor. Receiving a brigadier-general's place in the British army and a paltry amount of money, he conducted military operations in Virginia and would move to England with his wife after the war.

· Final Battles in the South

1. **Savannah**—In 1778, British forces captured this major Georgia port city and from this base brought all of Georgia under British control. A combined colonial and French siege of the city failed to retake it and it would be the launching pad to subdue the rest of the South.
2. **Charleston**—A British siege ended in 1780 with the capture of the city and the surrender of 5,000 patriot troops to Clinton and the British.
3. **Camden**—Lord Cornwallis with 3,000 men defeated Horatio Gates at this battle, which gave the British complete control of South Carolina.
4. **King's Mountain**—The British move north was stopped at this battle in North Carolina when 1,200 militia men defeated a Loyalist force of about 1,000 killing 157, severely wounding 163 and capturing 698. The patriot militia lost only 28 killed and 62 wounded.
5. **Cowpens**—Colonial troops under Daniel Morgan captured the entire British force under Tarleton at this battle on the border of the Carolinas. The British had lost 910 men, 110 killed and 800 taken prisoner, as well as all of their supplies. The American lost only 12 killed and 61 wounded.
6. **Guilford Courthouse**—Nathaniel Greene who had replaced Gates forced Cornwallis out of North Carolina by inflicting heavy casualties despite the British holding the field at the end. The British had no supplies, and it had begun to rain heavily. With 550 already dead and wounded compared to the American loses of 250, Cornwallis moved first to Wilmington and then to Virginia, abandoning the Carolinas to the Patriots.

7. **Yorktown (1781)**—Settled in on a Virginia peninsula with the British navy protecting them, Cornwallis was confident his position was secure. A large French fleet had set sail from the West Indies under Admiral de Grasse with 3,000 troops. Joined by Comte de Rochambeau's 5,000 troops from Newport R.I. Washington moved his army of 9,000 to encircle Yorktown. De Grasse's fleet, after skirmishing with the British fleet and sending it to New York added another 3,000 troops to join the existing forces. After a short siege Cornwallis surrendered his 8,000 troops while the military band played "The World Turned Upside Down." A week after the surrender Clinton arrived with 7,000 troops to end the siege but went back to New York when he learned of the surrender. Yorktown was the last significant battle of the war as the North ministry fell and a peace ministry under Rockingham and Shelburne of the Whigs took over the government.

·Pact of Paris, (1783)

Along with Great Britain recognizing the independence of the U.S. the treaty granted the United States territory as far west as the Mississippi River, but reserved Canada to Great Britain. Fisheries in Newfoundland remained available to Americans and navigation of the Mississippi River was open to both countries. Congress promised to recommend that states return confiscated Loyalist property, but they had no power to enforce this demand. Creditors in both countries were free to pursue the collection of debts. This was agreed to without the approval of the French who criticized the favorable terms for the Americans but went along with it. Benjamin Franklin, John Jay, and John Adams used leverage to achieve this windfall and they worked with the British against the interest of Spain (it had joined the war late) and its ally France. In other parts of the Treaty, Spain received Florida and the island of Minorca from Great Britain but did not get what it was after which was Gibraltar. France received Tobago, two islands in the St. Lawrence, and trading posts in India and Senegal. The treaty was a tremendous windfall for the U.S. as it doubled the size of the country.

UNIT IV
MULTIPLE-CHOICE QUESTIONS

Questions 1-3 refer to the following:

"...effigies of Andrew Oliver [stamp master] and Lord Bute were hung on a tree...the council labeled such actions 'boyish sport.' [the governor]...ordered the sheriff to take down the effigies but the sheriff did not dare. After sunset the effigies were carried to a new building erected by Andrew Oliver, which the mob tore down.... When Governor Bernard asked the colonel of the militia to out his men, the colonel said it was useless, since probably all his drummers were in the mob. Thomas Hutchinson [Lieutenant Governor] and the sheriff went to the riot only to have rocks thrown at them and they ran from the scene. The forces of law and order in Boston were helpless and the riot ended about midnight, probably because after eighteen hours of activity, the members of the mob were worn out. The next day a frightened Andrew Oliver resigned as stamp distributor."

Merrill Jensen, *The Founding of a Nation: A History of the American Revolution* 1763-1776, 1968

1. The colonial response to the Stamp Act was to

   (A) comply with the law as good British subjects
   (B) rely upon petitions to get the law repealed by Parliament
   (C) riot and intimidate officials to stop the distribution of the stamps
   (D) file legal action against the act so the British courts could nullify the act

2. The action of the colonials in this 1765 incident would ultimately lead to the

   (A) American Revolution
   (B) writing of the Constitution
   (C) abolition of the Navigation Acts
   (D) jailing of the mob leaders

3. In order to improve their image, after this incident against the Stamp Act the Boston mob began to call themselves

   (A) Minutemen
   (B) Committees of Correspondence
   (C) Colonial Militias
   (D) Sons of Liberty

Questions 4-8 refer to the following quotation:

"Sir, we have done everything that could be done to avert the storm which is now coming on. We have petitioned;...we have prostrated ourselves before the throne,...

Our petitions have been slighted;... There is no longer any room for hope. If we wish to be free—.... we must fight!...They tell us, sir, that we are weak—unable to cope with so formidable an adversary. But when shall we be stronger?... Shall we gather strength by... inaction? Sir, we are not weak,... Three millions people,...are invincible.... There is a just God who presides over the destinies of nations, and who will raise up friends to fight our battles for us.... There is no retreat but in submission and slavery! The war is inevitable—and let it come!... Gentlemen may cry, "Peace! Peace!"—but there is no peace. The war is actually begun!... Our brethren are already in the field!... Is life so dear, or peace so sweet, as to be purchased at the price of chains and slavery? Forbid it, Almighty God! I know not what course others may take; but as for me, give me liberty, or give me death!"

Patrick Henry – March 23, 1775

4. The conflict that Patrick Henry is referring to eventually became the

   (A) French and Indian War
   (B) War Between the States
   (C) Revolutionary War
   (D) American-British War

5. When Henry refers to "our petitions have been slighted" which of the following is a subsequent petition that was spurned by the British?

   (A) Petition of Rights
   (B) Olive Branch
   (C) Petition to the Courts
   (D) Laurel Wreath

6. The idea of God raising up friends to fight our battles for us became a major part of what 19th century movement that saw providence as guiding the country?

   (A) Great Awakening
   (B) Abolitionism
   (C) Social Gospel
   (D) Manifest Destiny

7. Henry's statement of "give me liberty or give me death" was put into practice by Nathan Hale when he was being put to death by the British and said,

   (A) I only regret that I have but one life to give for my country
   (B) we have met the enemy and they are ours
   (C) the end may justify the means as long as there is something to justify the end
   (D) it is better to die on your feet than live on your knees

8. Henry's statement of a British guard will be stationed in every house was a reference to which British practice of quatering that was detested by the colonials and was later outlawed in the

   (A) Articles of Confederation
   (B) Suffolk Resolves
   (C) Washington's Farewell Address
   (D) Bill of Rights

Questions 9-11 refer to the following:

Nathaniel Currier, "The Destruction of Tea at Boston Harbor," 1846

9. This 1773 event captured in the lithograph directly led to

   (A) the death of Crispis Attucks and four others
   (B) the establishment of "home rule" for Massachusetts
   (C) British issuing the "writs of assistance"
   (D) convening of the First Continental Congress

10. As a consequence of this event the British took which subsequent action?

   (A) Passed the Coercive Acts that the colonials called the Intolerable Acts
   (B) Petitioned the colonial legislature asking them to pay for the tea
   (C) Rescinded the Tea Act because of the success of the Sons of Liberty
   (D) Blamed the Mohawk Indians for the destruction of the tea

11. A modern day protest by groups calling themselves the "Tea Party" movement oppose

   (A) an extension of the New Deal programs under President Clinton
   (B) undeclared and unpaid for wars in Afghanistan and Iraq
   (C) the Emergency Economic Stabilization Act, American Recovery and Reinvestment Act & Affordable Care Act
   (D) Great Society overreaches including the War on Poverty, the War on Drugs, and Aid to Families with Dependent Children

For Questions 12-13 refer to the following quote:

Historian Carl Becker has written, "...the American Revolution was fought not only over home rule, but who should rule at home."

12 Which of the following statements could be used to support this interpretation?

(A) The Revolution was two-sided, on one hand a struggle between the colonists and England and on the other hand a struggle between the colonists themselves

(B) These are the times that try men's souls. The summer soldier and the sunshine patriot will, in this crisis, shrink from the service of their country; but he that stands by it now, deserves the love and thanks of man and woman

(C) Americans, although having political disagreements, some of which sparked violence, had nonetheless always operated within a framework of agreement on basic principles, namely political and economic liberalism

(D) Throughout American history there has been a wide consensus about which policies to follow and the colonists were no exception to this as they comprised a homogeneous group that engaged in a unified battle against the English as a common enemy

13. All of the following are factual or interpretive statements that support the Becker interpretation EXCEPT

(A) the North-end mob clashed with the South–end mob over the political control of the streets of Boston

(B) James Otis' motivation in arguing against the "writs of assistance" had as much to do with his opposition to the Hutchinson machine that controlled the politics of Massachusetts as it did over any issue of "natural rights"

(C) class conflict between the merchants and the artisans characterized the internal revolution in the cities of the colonies

(D) The Revolution was effected [sic] before the War commenced. The Revolution was in the minds and hearts of the people, a change in their religious sentiments of their duties and obligations

Questions 14-15 refer to the following excerpt:

"That religion, or the duty which we owe to our Creator and the manner of discharging it, can be directed by reason and conviction, not by force or violence; and therefore, all men are equally entitled to the free exercise of religion, according to the dictates of conscience; and that it is the mutual duty of all to practice Christian forbearance, love, and charity towards each other."

Virginia Declaration of Rights, June 12, 1776

14. The ideas expressed in this document were later incorporated into

   (A) the U.S. Constitution
   (B) Declaration of Independence
   (C) First Amendment
   (D) Gettysburg Address

15. Most modern day neo-conservatives and conservatives would object to which of the following:

   (A) the Christian practice of love and charity
   (B) freedom of religion
   (C) reason directing man's action
   (D) absence of the word God

UNIT V

CONFEDERATION & CONSTITUTION

Although the Articles of Confederation were written and went into effect as the first government in 1777; they did not become the official government until 1781. The time period from the end of the American Revolution to the adoption of the new government under the Constitution is called the Confederation Era. It lasted from 1781 to 1789. The writing of the new government, the Constitution, would take place at the end of the Confederation Era in 1787. The new nation would be transformed in 1787 when the Constitution was written to replace the first government—the Articles of Confederation. The decade after the ratification of the Constitution would consolidate power in the hands of the central government and establish a number of precedents that would be followed by subsequent generations.

Articles of Confederation

·Articles of Confederation and Perpetual Union
Written by John Dickinson it was adopted by the 2nd Continental Congress after a long debate over taxation and representation on November 15, 1777. They were not ratified until 1781 when the 13th state Maryland finally agreed to them once Virginia dropped its claims to western lands. The essential features of this first government of the United States that lasted from 1777 to 1789 were:
1. A firm league of friendship amongst sovereign and independent states;
2. Powers not given to it were reserved to the states or localities;
3. Amendments had to be approved unanimously;
4. Major bills needed a 2/3rd vote to pass;
5. Taxes to be determined by the legislatures of the several states;
6. No executive or judicial branch—to be left up to the states;
7. It could make treaties, declare war and peace, borrow money, print paper currency, fix weights and measures, establish and operate post offices and handle affairs with Native Americans;
8. Annual elections of representatives by the state governments;

9. Term limits were imposed allowing representatives to serve three out of six consecutive years;
10. Settle disputes between the states over western land claims;

This government was a weak central government that reflected the philosophy of the Declaration of Independence. The original founders were opposed to the strong central government as represented by the British model.

·Newburgh Address

After Yorktown, complaints by Washington's army that bordered on mutiny were: arrears in pay, failure to settle food and clothing accounts, and Congress' lack of action in making provisions for the life pension of half-pay. These issues were contained in a letter that circulated among officers. Washington issued General Orders denouncing it and at a meeting of his officers he finished a letter to his officers that ended by him saying, "Gentlemen, you must pardon me. I have grown gray in your service and now find my self growing blind." This ended the incident as his loyal officers took over once he left the meeting and assured that there would be no mutiny. The speech also reinforced the concept of civilian control of the military.

·Loyalists

Somewhere between 65,000 and 100,000 left the colonies and settled in Europe, Canada, and the Caribbean. This exodus was due, in part, to repressive legislation passed by the states that included: laws in 9 states exiling prominent Loyalist; 5 states disenfranchised all Loyalists; in most states they were expelled from all offices; they were generally barred from the professions and had to pay double or treble taxes; and, by 1782, all states passed confiscation acts. New York would receive $3.5 million and Maryland $2 million from the sale of Loyalist property. About 50,000 went to Canada. Of these, 34,000 went to Nova Scotia, 2,000 to Prince Edward Island and 10,000 to Ontario (a part of Quebec at this time). 7,000 went to Great Britain (usually the wealthiest and most prominent), and 9,000 to the Bahamas and British colonies in the Caribbean. The 34,000 who went to Nova Scotia were not welcomed by Nova Scotians, who were mostly descendants of New Englanders and had settled there before the Revolution. The colony of New Brunswick, a part of Nova Scotia until 1784, was created for the 14,000 of those Loyalist who had settled in Nova Scotia.

·Princeton Retreat

Mutineers from Lancaster and Philadelphia forced the Congress to retreat to Princeton and later to Trenton to conduct its business when state authorities were unwilling or unable to deal with them or pay them money they were owed.

·Society of Cincinnati

A patriotic, benevolent, and historic association in the United States and France formed by officers in 1783 that had served in the Revolution. Membership eligibility was inherited through primogeniture, it excluded enlisted men, and in most cases militia officers. Washington was its first President and some were critical of it for creating a hereditary elite.

·New York

The Continental Congress moved to New York from Trenton in 1784, as commissioners planned (later abandoned) a permanent capital on the banks of the Delaware River.

·China Trade

With the closing of the British West Indies to trade from the U.S. a lucrative trade with China for tea, silks, and other luxury goods was established by the clipper ship *Empress of China* in 1784. Great Britain still remained the main trading partner as most U.S. manufactured goods could be imported on the same favorable terms as in the colonial days.

·Commerce

Congress appointed James Monroe to head a committee to deal with the problem of states enacting their own tariffs against foreign commerce. The recommendation of an amendment to the Articles to give the government the power to regulate interstate commerce was not approved.

·Post-War Depression

A business boom had occurred during the Revolution caused by not only increased demand but also by the printing of paper money and borrowing large amounts to finance the War. This was followed by extensive importation of British goods immediately after the war that created an economic downturn and sharp deflation in the U.S. imports. Exports dropped by 50%, farm wages suffered a 20% decline, and this would lead to unrest that would eventually topple the government. A recovery would start in 1787 but it would be too late to save the Articles of Confederation government.

·Treaties

1. **Jay-Gardoqui (1785)**—When Spain closed the port of New Orleans to American commerce in 1784, Congress sent John Jay to Madrid to get an agreement to open up the Mississippi to Americans. Instead, Jay signed an agreement that ignored the problem of the Mississippi in exchange for commercial advantages benefiting the Northeast (the Jay-Gardoqui Treaty). Congress rejected the treaty and the issue was not solved until the Pinckney Treaty of 1795 was passed by the new government.
2. **Prussia Treaty (1785)**—Negotiated by both John Adams, Minister to Great Britain and Ambassador to France, and Thomas Jefferson's secretary William Short, it outlawed privateering and endorsed the principle of "free-ships free goods."
3. **Morocco Treaty (1786)**—With no more protection from the British fleet U.S. commerce suffered at the hands of the pirate states of North Africa, Tunis, Algiers, Tripoli, and Morocco. Jefferson proposed a plan for an international expedition against the Barbary states that was voted down. Instead the U.S. gave the Emperor of Morocco $10,000 in exchange for an agreement; thus starting the tradition of payments to the "Barbary Pirate" states.

·Virginia Statue for Religious Freedom

Jefferson drafted it but it was Madison who secured its adoption by the Virginia legislature in 1786. It was copied by other states and was also the basis for the religion clauses in the Constitution's Bill of Rights. It's chief tenant was "…no man shall be compelled to frequent or support any religious worship, place, or ministry whatsoever, nor shall be enforced, restrained, molested, or burdened in his body or goods, nor shall otherwise suffer on account of his religious opinions or belief; but that all men shall be free to profess, and by argument to maintain, their opinion in matters of religion…"

·Land Ordinance of 1785

To solve the problem of western lands this law was a modification of a plan submitted by Thomas Jefferson a year earlier. It provided for the creation of a rectangular system of land survey. The basic unit of ownership was to be the township—six-mile square or 36 square miles. Each township was to be divided into 36 sections, each a one-mile square or 640 acres. The law also provided that Section 16 in each township, the New England practice, was to be reserved for the benefit of public education. All other sections were to be made available to the public at auction at one dollar an acre for a minimum price of $640 for a section.

·Northwest Ordinance of 1787

Along with the Land Ordinance of 1785, this law decided how the western lands north of the Ohio River and east of the Mississippi River would be settled and become states on an equal basis with existing ones. It provided for: no fewer than three or more than five states would be formed; admission to the Union would be available when the number of free inhabitants reached 60,000; a territorial system of government would be established when the population reached 30,000; civil rights and liberties would be guaranteed; education would be encouraged; and slavery and involuntary servitude would be prohibited. This law would provide a precedent for the admission of future states and it settled once and for all the question of ownership of western lands.

·Annapolis Convention (1786)

Nine states accepted Virginia's call for a conference at Annapolis to deal with items of commerce and the earlier failure to amend the Articles. Only five states were present (the condition of the roads slowed the arrival of other delegates). At the urging of Alexander Hamilton, a subsequent convention was called for in Philadelphia in May of the next year to discuss commercial problems, effective government, and revision of the Articles.

·Shay's Rebellion

Daniel Shays, a war veteran, led a rebellion by debt-ridden farmers, upset with economic conditions in Massachusetts, against the eastern politicians who refused to inflate the currency. They also protested against excessive taxes on property, poll taxes, unfair actions by the court of common pleas in its foreclosures, the high cost of lawsuits, and excessive salaries for court and government officials. They demanded the government issue paper money. Their actions included mobbing the court buildings in Northampton, Great Barrington, Worcester and Concord to prevent the courts, whose actions had been grossly unfair to working people, from functioning. Shays led 2000 rebels to Springfield to storm the arsenal, but government forces of 1200 soldiers led by General Shepard quelled the uprising. Some rebels were captured and sentenced to death for treason in February 1787, but were later pardoned.

·Constitutional Convention

It was held in Philadelphia in the summer of 1787 where the members met in secrecy and created a new government with a written constitution.

·Assemblage of Demi-Gods

Jefferson's (he was absent as Ambassador to France) term could apply to the writers of the Constitution. The most influential were the oldest Franklin at 81 and Washington (presiding officer elected unanimously). Leaders in the floor discussions were Madison (whose diary of the Convention would be released in 1840), Roger Sherman, George Mason, Gouverneur Morris (who wrote the document), Elbridge Gerry, Alexander Hamilton, and James Wilson. Radical leaders of the Revolution like Sam Adams, John Hancock, Patrick Henry, Tom Paine and Christopher Gadsden were either not chosen as delegates or refused to go. Henry refused and said, "he smelled a rat." Thomas Jefferson and John Adams were out of the country. The men were primarily lawyers, planters, and merchants with no representation from the agrarian classes. The average age was 42 (younger than any man every elected President), and most were college graduates. Only 8 of the 39 final signers had signed the Declaration of Independence 11 years earlier.

·Virginia Plan

Introduced by Edmund Randolph at the urging of Madison, it called for a bicameral legislature based on population, an executive chosen by the legislature, and an independent judiciary. This plan favored by the large states (population) was dissected and debated for almost a month.

·New Jersey Plan

Small state New Jersey countered the Virginia Plan with its own plan introduced by William Patterson that called for proportional rather than equal representation. His plan did grant Congress the power to regulate foreign and interstate commerce but was too similar to the Articles to be accepted.

·Connecticut Compromise
Proposed by Roger Sherman, population would be proportional in the lower house and each state would have an equal vote in the upper house. After first being rejected it was eventually accepted in what would be called the "Great Compromise."

·3/5th Compromise
Before the Sherman plan could be accepted the issue of what constituted population that was eligible for representation had to be resolved. Delegates agreed to count slaves as 3/5ths of a person when apportioning representation and taxation. This fraction was chosen to equalize the amount of representation that both the North and the South had in the House of Represenatives.

·Electoral College
Another compromise to pacify the small states who would be guaranteed 3 electors to choose the President (2 for each Senator and 1 minimum for the House of Representatives) regardless of their population. By having the state legislatures choose the electors it both decentralized the process as well as making the chief executive independently elected.

·Slave Trade
Sectional divisions also showed up with the adoption of a clause that the U.S. could abolish the foreign slave trade after 20 years (1808).

·Commerce
Both foreign and interstate commerce could be regulated by the national government. A compromise was reached that allowed tariffs on imports (favored by the North) but none on exports (favored by the South).

·Other Debatable Issues
Two-year terms for the members of the lower legislative body, the House of Representatives was established. It would be the only part of the government that was democratically elected. Six-year terms for the upper house, the Senate, which was seen as a careful deliberative body, chosen by the state legislatures, that could check democratic excesses was established. A four year term for the President who was indirectly chosen by a group of electors selected by the states was established. Life-time tenure for the judiciary would put their decisions beyond the reach of popular opinion. Checks on both the President and the Judiciary, had to start in the House through the impeachment process. Removal from office was put in the hands of the more deliberative Senate. As with the colonial assemblies, all money bills had to originate in the House while all treaties had to be approved by a 2/3rd vote of the Senate. Cabinet and Supreme Court nominees required a majority vote of the Senate.

·Philosophical Influences
John Locke's ideas on natural rights was apparent as the Constitution was based on the concept of consent of the governed as well as being an agreement amongst the people ("We the People"). A distrust of human nature came from Thomas Hobbes and John Calvin and is in the document with the overlapping powers of checks and balances that would keep any single group from plundering or even dominating other groups. Montesquieu's reverence for liberty would be protected through the implementation of federalism with its basic division of power between the states and the national government as well as the divisions of the three branches of the national government. The "founding fathers" may not have trusted man but they did trust a government that could control men.

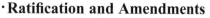

·Ratification and Amendments

With only 12 states attending (Rhode Island did not send delegates) it would go into effect with the approval of 9 states. The states would ratify it by special state conventions. Unlike the Articles, the amending process did not require unanimity but would be difficult to achieve by requiring a 2/3rds vote of both houses as well as ratification by 3/4ths of the states.

·Final Product

Surprisingly short (Article I dealing with Congress was over 50% of the Constitution), the documents 7 Articles were a mere 12 pages in length. Compared to many state constitutions which can run hundreds of pages it was a model of brevity. After nearly 4 months of work it was approved by 39 delegates (Gerry, Randolph, and Mason refused to sign) on September 17, 1787 and submitted to the states for ratification.

Ratification by the States

·Federalist and Antifederalist

The group supporting the new government called themselves Federalist—although they actually favored a more centralized government than the Articles had been—and the group opposing became the Antifederalists, a less attractive name. Propaganda by both sides was widely disseminated throughout the states.

·Federalist Papers

These were 77 essays that appeared in New York newspapers under the pseudonym *Publius*. These pro-Constitution writings by Alexander Hamilton (51), James Madison (29) and John Jay (5) explained the principles of republicanism contained in the Constitution as well as attacking the weaknesses of the Articles of Confederation.

·Delaware

Became the first state to ratify which it did so unanimously on December 7, 1787 thus earning the honor of being called "the Constitution State."

·Pennsylvania

A spirited battle over ratification took place in Pennsylvania where the commercial interests battled the agrarians who attempted a series of amendments and delays but were defeated when it was ratified 46-23 on December 12, 1787.

·New Jersey

Unanimously ratified after a week of debate on December 18, 1787.

·Georgia

Unanimously ratified it on January 2nd, 1788.

·Connecticut

Voted 128-40 for ratification on January 9, 1788.

·Massachusetts

With the Anti-Federalists having strong leadership, an estimate gave them 192 votes to 144 for the Federalist, a battle over ratification took place. The Anti-Federalist argument voiced the fear that ordinary men would become subject to the rich who would control the federal government. Their argument was that lawyers, college educated, and men of wealth with leisure time would swallow up the "little folks just as the whale swallowed up Jonah." In order to win over the opposition, a series of amendments were proposed for adoption. Sam Adams and some of the Anti-Federalist leaders were won over and it was unconditionally approved 187-

168 on February 6, 1788. Nine recommended amendments were sent along with the approval with the most important amendment being one that would reserve all powers not delegated to the Constitution, to the states.

·Maryland
It became the 7th state to ratify 63-11 on May 12, 1788.

·South Carolina
After barely carrying the call for a convention by 1 vote, the Anti-Federalist sentiment seemed to melt away and ratification was carried 149-73 on May 23rd 1788.

·New Hampshire
This states delegates to the Constitutional Convention arrived two months after it convened because money was not allocated by its legislature for their journey. Finally, two delegates paid their own way to give it representation. The first attempt at ratification failed in February. On June 21st the Federalists put together enough votes to ratify it 57-47. Along with ratification 12 amendments were proposed.

·Constitution Adopted
With New Hampshire's vote 9 states had ratified which put the Constitution in place. However, 4 states had not adopted and two of them Virginia and New York were large, significant states. Without them the new government could scarcely go into effect.

·Virginia
The issue was in doubt in the largest state with a population more than 12 times that of Delaware. Patrick Henry, Edmund Randolph and George Mason who made formidable charges against the Constitution led the Anti-Federalist forces. Madison made the case for the Federalist and it was ratified on June 25, 1788 by a narrow margin of 89-79.

·New York
When the convention met in Poughkeepsie on June 17, the Anti-Federalists led by Governor George Clinton were still in the majority. Hamilton achieved a delay in the voting until results from New Hampshire and Virginia came in. This ploy seemed to work as New York did not want to stand alone with North Carolina and Rhode Island, and ratified it on June 26, 1788 by a close vote of 30-27.

·North Carolina
Its convention adjourned (August 2, 1788, by a vote of 185-84) without voting on the Constitution. With the first Congress's proposal of amendments in 1789, the hold-out state of North Carolina ratified the Constitution November 21, 1789 (195-77).

·Rhode Island
While failing to send a delegation to Philadelphia the commercial classes tried to get a state convention called. Instead, the agrarian leaders called for a popular referendum, which the Federalist boycotted and it rejected the new Constitution by a vote of 2708 to 237 on March 24, 1788. It took two more years to finally win ratification—well after the new government was launched—by the close vote of 34-32 on May 29, 1790.

UNIT V
MULTIPLE-CHOICE QUESTIONS

For Questions 1-3 refer to the chart below:

The Township System

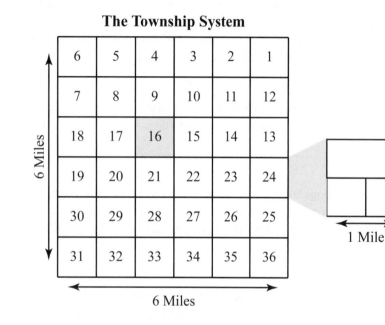

Full Section = 640 acres
Half Section = 320 acres
Quarter Section = 160 acres

1. Use the image above to figure out how many square miles would be contained in a township according to the Land Ordinance of 1785?

   (A) 6
   (B) 36
   (C) 360
   (D) 640

2. According to the Land Ordinance of 1785 the 16th section was going to be reserved for

   (A) a religious meeting house
   (B) government buildings
   (C) a village green
   (D) schools

3. A further subdivision of the land into 40 acres would logically be called a (an)

   (A) 80 acre section
   (B) half-quarter section
   (C) quarter-quarter section
   (D) partial section

Questions 4-7 refer to the following:

"We like to think in America that we are a democratic people. We point to our Declaration of Independence as a great democratic document, as it is; yet our weakness as a nation is that we have allowed the Declaration to remain a mere declaration, while we have operated our nation under a constitution that puts checks upon democracy at every turn... Each of these innovations, the secret ballot, the primary, and the reformed party is a step toward democracy—a step toward the Declaration of Independence and away from the Constitution, which so feared majority rule that the majority was hedged about with checks and balances at every possible point."

William Allen White, *The Old Order Changeth*, 1910

4. According to the passage above which of the following could be an anti-democratic measure in the Constitution?

    (A) The fact that Congress could make all laws that are necessary and proper
    (B) The full faith and credit clause
    (C) Choosing the House of Representatives
    (D) Selection of a President by the Electoral College rather than popular vote

5. Amendments 15, 19, 26 made changes to the Constitution to allow for more

    (A) liberty
    (B) democracy
    (C) property
    (D) equal protection of the laws

6. Which of the following ways of selecting government officials could be considered the most democratic in the un-amended Constitution?

    (A) Choosing the Supreme Court
    (B) Choosing the United States Senate
    (C) Choosing the House of Representatives
    (D) Choosing the President

7. The White thesis sees what document as the protector of democracy?

    (A) Declaration of Independence
    (B) Constitution
    (C) Bill of Rights
    (D) Federalist Papers

Questions 8-11 refer to the following:

"The term 'well born' implied a hereditary aristocracy, and it is true that by the 1780s such a thing did exist in America, but its basis was pecuniary [relating to money], property, not birth, was the major factor in determining class structure. Phrases such as 'the rich,' 'men of wealth and ability,' 'men of Sense and Property' describe the upper class as the Revolutionary generation saw it.... Such men were frequently termed 'gentlemen,' a word which usually implied superior wealth as well as superior status as the phrase "gentlemen of property" suggests. Indeed, wealth was essential in order to acquire the attributes of a gentleman: to dress fashionably, become educated, patronize arts, purchase luxuries, and conduct oneself in society as gentlemen were supposed to do. The distinction between gentlemen and other sorts of men existed everywhere..."

Jackson Turner Main, *The Anti-Federalists; Critics of the Constitution 1781-1788*, 1961

8. Class structure in America existed in the 1780s but was based on all of the following EXCEPT

(A) birth
(B) wealth
(C) property
(D) ability

9. Those who had the attributes of superior wealth and status in the 1780s in America were given the descriptive title of

(A) aristocracy
(B) the rich
(C) Mr.
(D) Gentlemen

10. The change that occurred between the 1780s and the 1880s regarding men of wealth is that the men of wealth of the latter period, the so-called, *nouveaux riche*, or new rich were primarily men of

(A) property
(B) commerce/manufacturing
(C) high social status
(D) hereditary wealth

11. Fashionable dress, education, art patronage and buying luxuries were all attributes of

(A) men of hereditary wealth
(B) the well born
(C) gentlemen
(D) self-made me

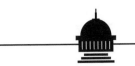

Questions 12-15 refer to the following:

"We the People of the United States, in Order to form a more perfect Union, establish Justice, insure domestic Tranquility, provide for the common defence, promote the general Welfare, and secure the Blessings of Liberty to ourselves and our Posterity, do ordain and establish this Constitution for the United States of America."

Preamble to the United States Constitution, 1789

12. This government established in 1789 replaced which of following governments?

   (A) Articles of Confederation
   (B) Parliament
   (C) Continental Congress
   (D) Declaration of Independence

13. The phrase "do ordain" in this document has what kind of connotation?

   (A) Secular
   (B) Religious
   (C) Intellectual
   (D) Economic

14. This document was based on the idea of which theory of government?

   (A) compact
   (B) divine right
   (C) sovereignty of the people
   (D) hereditary

15. The U.S. Constitution primarily represents a

   (A) statement of philosophy
   (B) propaganda document
   (C) law or ordinance
   (D) change of government

NO TESTING MATERIAL ON THIS PAGE

UNIT VI

FEDERALIST ERA (1788–1800)

After the adoption of the new government under the Constitution those who favored a stronger central government were in ascendancy. The time period between 1788 and 1800 is known as the Federalist Era or decade. This group of political nationalist would eventually became the Federalist political party. They built a strong governmental structure that even their political opponents the Jeffersonians did not try to tear down. The 12 years the Federalists were in power they established a governmental system as well as many precedents that would last long beyond their political control of the nation.

Federalist Domestic Policy

·First Congress
It was comprised of 59 members in the House and 22 in the Senate when it convened in March of 1789. With the addition of North Carolina and Rhode Island these numbers would rise to 64 and 26. Strong Federalist majorities existed in all the delegations except for Virginia. Fifty five members had been members of the Constitutional Convention or the state ratifying conventions. An example of the changing of the guard from the older revolutionaries to the younger Federalists occurred in Massachusetts when Fisher Ames was elected to Congress by defeating Sam Adams.

·"Mr. President"
With many grave problems facing the nation, Congress wasted most of the first three weeks it met with debates over what to call the president. A Senate committee recommended that his title be: "His Highness, the President of the United States and Protector of the Rights of the Same." Washington preferred, "His Mightiness" and other suggestions included "His Elective Highness" and "His Excellency." Because the House and Senate could not agree on a given title no title was chosen and the chief executive was simply called, Mr. President.

77

·Tariff and Tonnage

The first revenue bill, a tariff that originated in the House according to the Constitution, was steered through that body by Madison but failed to pass the Senate. It contained provisions that greatly favored American ships at the expense of England and other foreign nations. These discriminatory features were scaled down and in the final version the tariff averaged 8.5% with a range of 5% to 50% (e.g. steel, ships, tobacco). American shippers were still favored and paid 10% less than foreigners. Tonnage duties followed which were 6 cents a ton for American ships and 50 cents a ton for foreign ships.

·Judiciary Act of 1789

Established the federal court system of thirteen district courts with one judge each, three circuit courts with three judges each (one district and two federal supreme court judges) and a Supreme Court with a Chief Justice and five associate justices.

·First Cabinet

Unanimously elected by the Electoral College, Washington chose as his first cabinet, Thomas Jefferson, Secretary of State, Alexander Hamilton, Secretary of the Treasury, and Henry Knox, Secretary of War. Although not provided for in the Constitution these department heads begin to meet informally and Washington would soon join them in what became a permanent fixture of the federal government.

·Bill of Rights

These were pieced together by James Madison and George Washington urged their passage in his inaugural address. States like Virginia, New York, Massachusetts and New Hampshire had ratified the Constitution because of the promise of a bill of rights. 12 amendments passed Congress and were submitted to the states which quickly ratified 10 of them. The first 8 guaranteed the unalienable rights of man and 9 and 10 were a strategic retreat from the nationalism of the Constitution by guaranteeing powers not in the Constitution to the people and the states. The Amendments in the Bill of Rights:

1. Freedom of Religion, Speech, the Press, Assembly, & Petition
2. Right to keep and bear arms
3. Restrictions on the Quartering of solders
4. Freedom from unreasonable search and seizure
5. Protection from imprisonment unless indicted by a Grand Jury, freedom from double jeopardy, right to remain silent, right to due process, private property cannot be taken without just compensation
6. Right to speedy & public trial, impartial jury, know the charges against you, right to confront the witnesses, and have the right to counsel
7. Right to trial by jury in Civil Proceedings
8. Freedom from excessive bail, fines, and cruel and unusual punishment
9. Other rights not in the Constitution are retained by the people
10. Reserve powers to the States

·North Carolina and Rhode Island

With the adoption of the Bill of Rights these two states quit trying to go it alone and joined the Union. North Carolina did it in November of 1789 and Rhode Island in May of 1790. There were now 13 states in the United States.

·Hamilton's Fiscal Program

As Secretary of the Treasury Hamilton had a unique relationship with Congress as the Constitution allowed him to submit reports directly to them. He did this in a number of areas: foreign, domestic, and state debts; a national bank; and an excise tax. Controversy over Hamilton's proposals would ultimately lead to the development of two distinct political parties—Federalist and Jeffersonians (Democratic-Republicans).

· Report on the Public Credit

The foreign debt borrowed primarily from the French and Dutch was nearly $12 million; the domestic debt was $40 million; and the state debts were approximately $25 million. Hamilton recommended funding the foreign and domestic debt at par (face value) and having the new federal government assume the state debt. Philosophically he favored this because he wanted to assure future buyers of government debt that America was a credit worthy nation. Also, the most influential people, who held most of the debt, would have a stake in the new government so they would support it. Hamilton believed that the people looked to the moneyed class for their natural leaders. There was no opposition to funding the foreign debt left over from the Confederation government as it was considered sacred and must be repaid. Debtors and agrarians strongly opposed funding the domestic debt at par, as they had sold off their securities at steep discounts to meet their own debts. Taking over or assuming the state debts was another controversial issue as some states had no debts and others had retired their debts.

· Funding and Assumption

Madison's idea of distinguishing between current and original securities holders failed to pass Congress primarily because of the cost. Hamilton's assistant William Duer had given out inside information of the plan to fund at par to speculators before it became public. They proceeded to get to the "backwater" areas of the country to buy up the securities for 5% to 10% of their value before the news of funding at par reached the hinterland. The South was particularly opposed to Assumption as Virginia had paid its debts by issuing paper money. Georgia, North Carolina, and Maryland had few debts and did not want to pay for other states that had run up a debt. New England strongly favored Assumption as they had done almost nothing to pay off their state debts. The only Southern state with a high debt was South Carolina. Funding of the national debt passed Congress while Assumption of the state debts was defeated four straight times when it came to a vote.

· Funding-Assumption Compromise

When Jefferson returned from France to take up his job as Secretary of State Hamilton approached him to use his influence to intervene to get votes changed to pass Assumption. Jefferson agreed to do this in return for having the permanent capital moved to the South on the Potomac River. To further clinch the deal states with small debts like Delaware and North Carolina received subsidies from the government. With passage of Funding and Assumption the national debt would soar past $80 million; the capital would be in Philadelphia for ten years and then be moved to a future "Federal City" in the South to be named after the first President.

· First Bank of the United States

Hamilton proposed that a national bank be formed capitalized at $10 million with government ownership at 20% and private capital at 80%. This commercial bank would supply notes for businesses transactions, it would assist the government by lending money to meet financial obligations, it would be a place of deposits for government revenues, and, it would provide loans to individuals so they could pay their taxes. It passed Congress with strong southern opposition. Madison argued that it was unconstitutional because the Constitutional Convention had rejected the idea that the federal government could charter companies. Washington heard arguments by Hamilton in favor of the bank based on the "implied powers" clause of Article 1, Section 4, and ones against the bank by Jefferson based on the reserve powers of Amendment 10. Washington ultimately gave his support to Hamilton, whose political views were Federalist, as well as his office was most closely involved with the institution in question. The bank was established in Philadelphia with a twenty year charter.

· Excise Tax

To pay for Funding and Assumption, Hamilton asked Congress to pass the Revenue Act of 1791 that established tariffs on selected imported goods and imposed excise taxes on a variety of goods including horse-drawn carriages, distilled liquor, snuff, and refined sugar. It was commonly called the Whiskey Tax. Hamilton hoped it would raise $800,000 annually. The tax on whiskey brought widespread protest resulting in violence against the Act especially in North Carolina and western Pennsylvania. Western farmers found it was much more profitable and avoided high transportation cost by converting grain into whiskey; moreover, the scarcity of hard currency meant that whiskey was used for that purpose so the tax on it seemed to be a tax on money itself.

· Whiskey Rebellion

Although strongly opposed in the South, it was the Scots-Irish farmers of western Pennsylvania who turned violently against the act. Whiskey poles were erected similar to the Liberty poles of the Revolution and organized mobs kept the tax from being collected. Finally a 13,000 man army was raised and 100 men were arrested of which two were convicted of treason but were pardoned by Washington. In the end little was collected, the tax was lowered on small stills, and the tradition of "moonshine" or illegal whiskey was established that still exists today in the U.S.

· Report on Manufactures

This was Hamilton's plan to turn the U.S. into a powerful industrial state through a system of tariffs, bounties (subsidies), and internal improvements. He felt the U.S. needed a sound policy of encouraging the growth of manufacturing. He argued this could be achieved through bounties or subsidies to industry, regulation of trade with moderate tariffs (not intended to discourage imports) to raise revenue to support American manufacturing through subsidies, and other government encouragement. These policies would not only promote the growth of manufacturing but provide for diversified employment opportunities and promote immigration into the young United States. Much of his program was not adopted by Congress but would resurface later as a part of Henry Clay's American System.

· Washington's Reelection

No one contested Washington and once again he was unanimously elected President with three electors abstaining. The growing political division of the nation into separate political parties was shown by the Vice-Presidential vote as John Adams received 77 electors and George Clinton 50.

· Vermont

This cantankerous area finally became the 14th state added to the Union in 1791 after a turbulent history. The Green Mountain Boy's had been formed prior to the Revolution by Ethan Allen and his brothers to keep the area known as the New Hampshire Grants from becoming part of New York. Land speculators and settlers banded together in armed groups to defend their lands by threat, intimidation, and violence against the New Yorkers who had been awarded the area by the British. Vermont eventually declared itself an independent country in 1777. Although it initially supported the American Revolutionary War and sent troops to fight at Ticonderoga and Bennington, Vermont eventually adopted a more neutral stance and became a haven for deserters from both the British and American armies.

· *Chisholm v. Georgia*

Heirs of Alexander Chisholm of South Carolina sued the state of Georgia for compensation for property that had been confiscated during the Revolution (Chisholm was a Loyalist). Chief Justice John Jay ruled that the suit was lawful but Georgia refused to comply with the decision. The idea of defying Supreme Court decisions was prevalent in the early republic, as the court did not have the prestige it now enjoys and the Executive department was reluctant to enforce the court's decision.

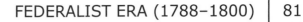

·11th Amendment

In the wake of the Chisholm decision, however, howls of protest arose throughout the country and Congress proposed and the states ratified the Eleventh Amendment, which overturned the principle of the *Chisholm* decision by providing that "the Judicial power of the United States shall not be construed to extend to any suit in law or equity, commenced or prosecuted against one of the United States by Citizens of another State."

Foreign Policy

The French Revolution had a dramatic impact on politics in the U.S. and would eventually lead to the formation of two distinct political parties.

·French Revolution

During the early liberal stage most Americans applauded the French for getting rid of absolutism and feudalism. This changed when France guillotined the king and queen, adopted the Republic and the "reign of terror" that went with it, and declared war on Great Britain, Spain, and the Netherlands.

·Neutrality Proclamation

Washington issued this document to declare that the U.S. was at peace with Britain and France and that we should abstain from acts of hostility against the belligerents. He did not use the word neutrality in the proclamation.

·Citizen Genet

Representative of the *Girondist* faction who came to the U.S. as a foreign minister from France, Edmund Charles Genet commissioned privateers and tried to organize American expeditions against Spanish and British territories. When chastised for this conduct by Washington he threatened to go over the head of the President to the American people. Even Madison and Jefferson turned against him as the Cabinet ordered his recall. However, his faction fell out of favor in France to the *Jacobins* and the new government ordered his arrest. Washington refused to extradite Genet and magnanimously offered him asylum. He became an American citizen and married New York Governor George Clinton's daughter.

·Treaty of Greenville, 1795

Two disastrous defeats by General Harmar (1,500 men routed) and Governor St. Clair (2,000 men defeated and forced to flee) led to General "Mad Anthony" Wayne's victory over the Northwest tribes at Fallen Timbers, in 1794. The tribes gave up most of their land in Ohio, which opened that area up for extensive settlement.

·Federalists vs. Jeffersonians

Two distinct political parties emerged in the 1790s despite the efforts of Washington and others to stop the growth of "factions." There were no constitutional provisions for these institutions but they developed in spite of this.

1. **Federalists**—Comprised of most of the rich and well born they had a clear, coherent program (Hamilton's), and were supported by most of the newspapers, clergymen, and other makers of public opinion. They controlled the army and made use of it in the Whiskey Rebellion, and, had local political operatives through the Society of Cincinnati. Washington's policies reflected the philosophy of the Federalist although he eschewed political parties.

2. **Jeffersonians** (Democratic Republicans/or Republicans)—Led by Jefferson and Madison they preferred the power of the states over the national government. They saw Hamilton's program as one that benefited the Northeast at the expense of the South and the new emerging West. They tended to be Anglophobes as compared to the Federalist Anglophiles and began to use propaganda (called education) to sway the voters.

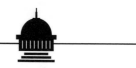

3. **Fenno vs. Freneau**—John Fenno was the editor of the Hamiltonian newspaper the *United States Gazette*, the unofficial spokesman for the Federalist cause. In 1791, the poet Philip Freneau started publishing the *National Gazette* that stated the Jeffersonian position and soon outdistanced Fenno's paper in circulation.

4. **Jeffersonian Supporters**—Governor Clinton in New York helped Aaron Burr defeat General Schuyler (Hamilton's father-in-law) for the Senate in New York to politically take control of that state with the help of the Society of Tammany, a drinking club and benevolent society. Various other individuals including the Swiss immigrant Albert Gallatin of western Pennsylvania, John Taylor of the Carolinas, Benjamin Rush the noted scientist from Philadelphia, all supported the new emerging party.

·Jay's Treaty

In 1794, the Chief Justice of the Supreme Court was sent to England to seek solutions over long standing problems left over from the Revolutionary War as well as issues of "freedom of the seas" over the existing conflict between Great Britain and France. The resulting agreement stirred up heated passions within the cabinet with Hamilton supporting the agreement and Jefferson opposing it. The treaty called for the withdrawal of British soldiers from posts in the American West. A commission would be established to settle border issues between the U.S. and Canada and to resolve issues over American losses in British ship seizures and Loyalist losses during the War for Independence. British admission of U.S. vessels to East Indian ports and the British West Indian trade was opened to U.S. ships of less than 70 tons who were not carrying cotton, sugar, cocoa, coffee and molasses. Not mentioned in the treaty were issues regarding the detaining of American ships and impressment of American seamen. The treaty was also silent on the Native American question and slaves removed during the Revolution.

·Reaction to Jay's Treaty

The public reaction was intense with Hamilton being stoned in New York, Jay resigning as Chief Justice, and the remaining members of Washington's cabinet resigning (Jefferson had resigned earlier). The Senate with its strong Federalist majority approved it by the bare 2/3rd s vote, the minimum that was required. The House voted for the appropriations to implement it by 51-48 that resulted in Congressman Muhlenberg being stabbed by his brother-in-law a rabid Jeffersonian.

·Pinckney's Treaty

Disputes with Spain left over from the Revolution led to the Treaty of San Lorenzo or Pinckney's Treaty. Agreement was finally made possible as a result of the European wars. Spain agreed to the 31st parallel as the boundary between its colonies and the U.S.; promised to quit inciting the Indians; gave the U.S. full rights of navigation on the Mississippi River; and, agreed to allow Americans the right to deposit goods at New Orleans before sending them on ocean going ships. This right was good for three years but it was renewable.

·Washington's Farewell Address

Written by Hamilton and never delivered but published in the newspapers it warned the nation against the formation of parties or factions. In foreign affairs he urged good commercial relations with all but warned the nation to steer clear of permanent alliances (the word entangling was never used).

John Adams' Presidency

·Election of 1796

After considering John Jay, who was unelectable due to the discord over his treaty, the Federalists chose Vice-President John Adams as their candidate although Hamilton tried to gain the nomination for Thomas

Pinckney. The results of the election gave Adams 71 votes while Jefferson received 68, which made him Vice-President under the electoral rules in place.

·Cabinet Government

Adams kept in place the second rate cabinet that Washington had appointed and they were frequently in charge of the government as he was absent for 385 days in one term compared to Washington's 181 days in two terms. Sometimes he was gone for months at a time spending it in Quincy, Massachusetts with his books.

·XYZ Affair

While still President, Washington replaced the Francophile James Monroe with Charles Pinckney as Ambassador to France. France refused to accept him and he fled to Amsterdam when threatened with arrest. News of this incident reached Adams (who was now President) and he tried to stave off the clamor in his own Federalist Party for war by sending John Marshall and Elbridge Gerry to join Pinckney in securing a treaty with France. Three French go-betweens (called X, Y, & Z in the diplomatic dispatches of the Americans) asked for a $250,000 bribe before the Americans could see the French Foreign Minister Talleyrand. The Americans refused and Pinckney and Marshall returned to the U.S. Gerry dallied in France until Adams ordered him to return. Adams submitted the XYZ correspondence to Congress and when it became public there was a clamor for war. The cry became "Millions for defense but not one cent for tribute" and Congress unilaterally terminated the existing treaty with France.

·Undeclared War

A naval war with France from 1798-1800 in the West Indies resulted in the U.S. capturing almost 100 French ships while suffering numerous losses themselves. The pro-war faction of the Federalist Party led by Hamilton and Secretary of War Timothy Pickering pressured Adams for all out war but he resisted and resorted to diplomacy instead.

·Logan Act

A Quaker, Dr. George Logan traveled to France to try to preserve the peace between the U.S. and France in 1798. This law made it a high misdemeanor subject to fine and imprisonment for any private citizen to carry on correspondence with a foreign government that was engaged in a controversy with the U.S. The law is still on the books but never enforced.

·Fries Uprising or Window Tax

Congress levied a direct tax on houses, land, and slaves—sometimes called the Direct House Tax of 1798. The tax in Pennsylvania was determined by the number and size of the windows in the dwellings. It aroused strong opposition among the Germans and many of them refused to pay it. John Fries, assumed leadership of a movement, organized an armed band of about 60 men, a force that grew to about 400, who marched about the country intimidating the assessors and encouraging the people to resist. The governor called out the militia and the leaders were arrested. Fries and two others were twice tried for treason and were sentenced to be hanged, but were pardoned by Adams.

·Convention of 1800

After Talleyrand offered the U.S. assurance that ministers would be treated with respect, Adams appointed a commission of Vans Murray, Oliver Ellsworth, and William Davie to negotiate with France. The Treaty of Morfontaine commonly called the "Convention of 1800" released the U.S. from its 1778 defensive alliance with France. In return the U.S. gave up its demand for $20 million for French seizures of ships and cargo.

•Alien and Sedition Acts

In an attempt to stifle political opposition, especially of leading Jeffersonian journalists and publicists who were European nationals, these laws were passed by Congress and signed by John Adams in 1798.

1. **Naturalization Act**—Extended the period of residence required to become a citizen from 5 to 14 years. It would be repealed in 1802 when the 1795 law (5 years) was reinstated.
2. **Alien Act**—It gave the President the power to deport from the U.S. any alien regarded as dangerous to the public peace and safety or if they were suspected of "treasonable or secret" inclinations. It expired in 1800.
3. **Alien Enemies Act**—During a time of declared war the President could arrest, imprison, or banish aliens that were under an enemies power.
4. **Sedition Act**—It made it a high misdemeanor punishable by severe fines and jail penalties for anyone speaking, writing, or publishing with intent to defame the U.S. government, Congress, or the President. The fine could not be for more than $2,000 or more than two years in jail. It succeeded in repressing political opposition as 25 prosecutions and 10 convictions of Jeffersonian editors and printers took place including Ben Franklin's grandson.
5. **Matthew Lyon**—A Jeffersonian congressman from Vermont was imprisoned for 4 months and fined $1,000 (while his constituents reelected him).
6. **James Callender**—Went before Salmon Chase, the most notorious of the Federalist judges who fined him $200 and sentenced him to prison for 6 months.
7. **Thomas Cooper**—Also appearing before Chase he was sentenced to 9 months in prison.
8. **Pardons**—When he became President, Jefferson pardoned all the men and Congress restored their fines with interest.

•Kentucky and Virginia Resolutions

Written anonymously by Jefferson and Madison these statements reflected the compact or states right theory of government and maintained that the Alien and Sedition Acts were unconstitutional. Jefferson, in the Kentucky Resolutions went further than Madison when he maintained that the legislature of each state had the right to check unauthorized power by the federal government. When measures went beyond the agreement, the states had a right to declare them "unauthoritive, void, and of no force" and to decide the appropriate remedies. The essence of the theory of nullification was introduced in these resolutions.

•Election of 1800

The Jeffersonians emerged victorious by defeating John Adams 73-65 but Thomas Jefferson and Aaron Burr received the same number of electoral votes. Under the Constitution at that time, each elector was to vote for two candidates without specifying who was to be president or vice president. The election went to the House of Representatives, where each state had one vote. Burr refused to step aside, and the election was deadlocked for almost a week. Hamilton, giving his support to his arch political enemy Jefferson, used his influence to help him win election on the 36th ballot because he believed Burr was a scoundrel. In 1804, the Twelfth Amendment corrected this problem by requiring electors to vote separately for president and vice president.

•Revolution of 1800

This term has been used to describe the election because power was transferred peacefully from one political party, the Federalist, to the other, the Democratic-Republicans or Jeffersonians. In what was considered an inherent weakness of a republic form of government, the transfer of power, was smoothly accomplished.

•Midnight Appointments

In an attempt to prolong their power before Adams left office, the Federalists enacted the Judiciary Act of 1801. This law gave courts increased jurisdiction over land and bankruptcy cases; it added six new federal circuit courts with sixteen new judges; and, it added dozens of new justices of the peace to the District of Columbia. During the lame duck period, Adams, with the approval of the Senate, appointed Federalists right up to the time he was leaving office at the "proverbial stroke of midnight." The enraged Jeffersonians, once in power, quickly repealed the 1801 Act; thus, restoring the original jurisdictional authority of the federal courts. However, removing the midnight judges presented a difficult constitutional question because it provided that federal judges were to hold office as long as they demonstrated good behavior—in effect, for life. Many of those whom Adams appointed refused to serve, but the most important of these was John Marshall, appointed Chief Justice of the Supreme Court by Adams as one of his midnight appointments. He would keep the Federalist philosophy alive for 35 years, long after the party was dead politically. Of all these appointments the one that would cause the most difficulty for the incoming Jeffersonians was the appointment of William Marbury, Justice of the Peace.

UNIT VI
MULTIPLE-CHOICE QUESTIONS

Questions 1-3 refer to the following:

"Opponents of the Federalists... calling themselves 'Republicans,'... hoped to convince the voters that the Federalists were monarchists. In fact, both agreed that republicanism was best for America, just as both agreed that federalism was right.... Federalists were republicans, but for them the adjective 'aristocratic' had to modify the noun 'republican.' They believed in government by the few who were the best; and, the best, in Hamilton's view were the rich, the well-born, and the able. They comprised an economic, a social, and an intellectual elite. The Jeffersonians opposition to Federalists believed in a broader base. The adjective 'democratic' ought to modify 'republican.' Not all Jeffersonians liked the democratic emphasis; they feared the consequences of Federalist claims that tyranny of mobs was a threat to the ordered life of a good republic... Federalists often preferred to speak of their opponents as democrats rather than as republicans for that reason."

Raymond H. Robinson, *The Growing of America: 1789-1848*, 1973

1. Which modern day political party is often perceived as being the party of the rich, well-born, and the able?

   (A) Republican
   (B) Democrat
   (C) Libertarian
   (D) Federalist

2. What term was seen as a negative one by the Federalist and some of the Jeffersonians?

   (A) Republican
   (B) Aristocratic
   (C) Democratic
   (D) Federalism

3. The first time a political party could use the term democrat openly without trepidation was under which man's Presidency?

   (A) George Washington
   (B) Andrew Jackson
   (C) Martin Van Buren
   (D) Abraham Lincoln

Questions 4-8 refer to the following quotation:

"Congress shall make no law respecting an establishment of religion, or prohibiting the free exercise thereof; or abridging the freedom of speech, or of the press; or the right of the people peaceably to assemble, and to petition the Government for a redress of grievances."

Bill of Rights, 1789

4. This statement is from which document in United States History?

(A) Preamble to the U.S. Constitution
(B) Declaration of Independence
(C) 1st Amendment to the U.S. Constitution
(D) Articles of Confederation

5. Which of the following institutions does the document refer to in prohibiting certain actions?

(A) State Governments
(B) Senate and House of Representatives
(C) Supreme Court
(D) President and Cabinet

6. The freedoms mentioned in the quotation above are usually known collectively as

(A) civil liberties
(B) rights of passage
(C) democracy
(D) liberal rights

7. The phrase "respecting an establishment of religion, or prohibiting the free exercise thereof" means

(A) tax money can be used to support churches
(B) established churches can be supported by the government
(C) private religious schools are exempt from constitutional limitations
(D) people have the right to found a religion and worship as they please

8. All of the following are rights or freedoms guaranteed in this document EXCEPT

(A) speech
(B) petition
(C) voting
(D) assembly

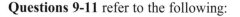

Questions 9-11 refer to the following:

"It was the French Revolution, and... the war... that made the party breech un-negotiable and almost irreconcilable.... From the spring of 1793, when the provocative French Minister Citizen Genet arrived... there came a series of events which rapidly polarized the leaders and their followers, and finally inflamed them to the point at which the entire political system was threatened: the Whiskey Insurrection of 1794, the scourging of the Democratic Societies by Washington, the heated debate over Jay's Treaty in 1795, the frenzy over the conduct of the French in the XYZ affair in 1798, the undeclared naval war with France, the Alien and Sedition Acts... [causing] each side to doubt the legitimacy and Americanism of the other.... Each party saw the other has having a foreign allegiance, British or French, that approached... treason."

Richard Hofstadter, *The Idea of a Party System:
The Rise of Legitimate Opposition in the United States, 1780-1840*, 1969

9. The development of political parties into the Federalists and Jeffersonians came primarily because of discord over

(A) Religion
(B) Economics
(C) Social structure
(D) Foreign policy

10. The reference to foreign allegiance to the British was a reference to which political party?

(A) Federalist
(B) Republican
(C) Whig
(D) Democratic

11. The Jeffersonians or Democratic Republicans were most opposed to which of the following Federalist sponsored measures that attempted to stifle the Jeffersonians dissent?

(A) Undeclared naval war with France in the Caribbean
(B) Conduct of the French in the XYZ affair
(C) Passage of the Alien and Sedition Acts
(D) Whiskey Tax

Questions 12-15 refer to the following:

"Some Federalist, ...wished to honor President Washington with a title... The stronghold of this 'monarchical faction' was the Senate,... this body... proposed to address the President as 'His Excellency' or 'His Elective Highness,' and a committee... reported in favor of 'His Highness the President of the United States and Protector of the Rights of the Same'.... Since the House of Representatives refused to concur with the Senate in the matter of a title... a joint committee was appointed. But the committee was unable to reach an agreement, and in the end the Senate was obliged to accept defeat... [and} as a last gesture of defiance, the Senate put itself on record in favor of annexing a title to the office of President from a decent respect for the opinion and practice of civilized nations."

John C. Miller, *The Federalist Era, 1789-1801*, 1960

12. The reason the that the President of the United States was not given a title is because

    (A) the Constitution forbid it
    (B) Washington was not in favor of a title
    (C) House and Senate could not agree
    (D) a title was foreign to the American political experience

13. The failure to provide the President with a formal title resulted in what subsequent title that emerged out of practice and experience?

    (A) Mr. President
    (B) Citizen President
    (C) Hail to the Chief
    (D) Honorable President

14. The reference the Senate made of "a decent respect for the opinion and practice of civilized nations" was likely referring to

    (A) the democratic nations of the world
    (B) economic trading partners of the U.S.
    (C) an international alliance system
    (D) European monarchies

15. What later 19th century political movement dealt the death knell to the trappings of monarchy that the Federalist flirted with?

    (A) Manifest destiny and western expansion
    (B) Jacksonian democracy
    (C) Mid-century immigration of Irish and Germans
    (D) The Whig Party's American System

NO TESTING MATERIAL ON THIS PAGE

UNIT VII

JEFFERSONIANISM & NATIONALISM

The years from 1800 to 1824 are known as the Jeffersonian era. The Virginia dynasty of Jefferson, Madison, and Monroe held the presidency, each elected to two full terms. The ideals of Thomas Jefferson replaced the philosophy of the Federalist to dominate the U.S. political scene. One irony is that when they gained power, the Jeffersonians did little to dismantle the political structure that had been created by the Federalists. In fact, a group of Jeffersonians actually opposed the Virginia dynasty's programs because they felt it was not pure Jeffersonian principles. They became known as the "Old Republicans" or *Tertium Quids*. The Federalist Party would disappear and Jeffersonians would have single party rule for a period of time, but this too would end as the Jeffersonians split into two groups—National Republicans (later the Whigs) and Democrats.

Jefferson's Administration

·Jeffersonianism
Fundamental principles of Jeffersonianism included a view of a limited government, strict adherence to the U.S. Constitution, belief in an agrarian economy, states' rights, and the good sense of the ordinary citizens to make political decisions as long as they were educated. It stood for democratic principles at a time when Federalism had been dominant.

·Jefferson's Inaugural
Was conciliatory in tone as he called for unity when he said, "We are all Republicans, we are all Federalists." He also asked for a wise and frugal government that would restrain men from injuring each other but should leave them free "to regulate their own pursuits of industry and improvement, and shall not take from the mouth of labor the bread it has earned." This is what he saw as the sum of good government.

·Tripolitan War (1801-1804)
Unlike his Federalist predecessors who had continued the custom started by the British of paying tribute to the Barbary States (Algiers, Morocco, Tunis and Tripoli), Jefferson refused to increase the amounts to the

Pasha of Tripoli. As early as 1784, he had recommended that the U.S. go to war with them and he had tried unsuccessfully to put together a coalition of maritime powers to blockade the pirates. The war was indecisive with one positive note when Stephen Decatur boarded and burned the frigate *Philadelphia*, which had been captured by Tripoli. A blockade led to a peace treaty where the U.S. still paid tribute until 1816, but at a much lower rate than before. This war was fought without a formal declaration of war by Congress.

·Gallatin's Financial Program

Secretary of the Treasury, Albert Gallatin carried out Jefferson's policy of frugality and retrenchment by pairing expenses in the War and Navy Departments, repealing internal (excise tax on whiskey) taxes, and creating a system of appropriations for specific purposes. Despite expenditures for Louisiana and the Tripolitan War, the debt was reduced from $83 million to $57 million when Jefferson left office. He did not attempt to dismantle Hamilton's Federalist financial program.

·Louisiana Purchase

Spain had received this large area from France in 1763 at the Treaty of Paris as a result of losses in the French and Indian War, but gave it back to France in 1802. Napoleon wanted Louisiana as a granary for its Caribbean sugar islands especially Santo Domingo (Haiti). He also wanted to revive French nationalism and its empire in North America. Before the transfer, Spain suspended the "right of deposit" at New Orleans and did not name another site as required by Pinckney's Treaty. Those in the West were talking secession or war unless Spain restored the "right of deposit." James Monroe, a pro-West representative land speculator was sent as a special envoy by Jefferson to assist Robert Livingston with instruction to offer France $10 million for New Orleans and West Florida. Napoleon was forced to abandon Santo Domingo after his army of 70,000 suffered horrendous losses and could not put down the slave rebellion of the native people led by Toussaint L'Ouverture. American diplomats were offered all of Louisiana for $15 million (about 3 cents an acre) with the stipulation that they buy all of it or none. The envoys took the deal but Jefferson was upset because he questioned the constitutionality of acquiring an empire. As a political realist he had to accept it and the Senate overwhelmingly confirmed the treaty 24-7. Spain felt betrayed for they would not have sold the Louisiana territory to France if they had known the U.S. would end up with it. European distress worked to the advantage of the U.S. Although the boundaries were left vague by Napoleon, a problem that would have to be solved in the future, the U.S. was immensely enriched by this acquisition.

·*Essex Junto*

Starting in 1778 a number of men gathered in Essex County, Massachusetts, to oppose the new state constitution. Composed of lawyers and merchants the group included politicians George Cabot and Timothy Pickering, as well as jurist Theophilus Parsons. The *Essex Junto* began as a small, independent faction of prominent, educated men that developed into a strong faction of the Federalist Party. During Adams' presidency there was talk of forming a Northern Confederacy of New England, New Jersey and New York. Hamilton opposed this scheme that was predicated on Aaron Burr being elected governor of New York. The *junto* staunchly opposed the policies and ideologies of Jefferson including the Louisiana Purchase, the Embargo Act of 1807, and the War of 1812. It's influence ended after the failure of the Hartford Convention in 1814.

·Marshall Court

As Chief Justice of the Supreme Court his decisions would keep the philosophy of Federalism alive and strengthen the national government from 1801 to 1836.

·*Marbury v. Madison* (1803)

William Marbury had been promised a justice of the peace commission by John Adams but it had not been properly sealed and delivered to him by the outgoing Secretary of State John Marshall. He filed suit against Jefferson's Secretary of State James Madison to receive the commission asking the court to issue a *writ of mandamus* compelling the handing over of the commission. The Jeffersonians used obstructionist tactics by having Attorney General Levi Lincoln take the 5th Amendment rather than admit he had destroyed the commission, making clerks unavailable to testify, and boycotting the proceedings. Marshall's dilemma was that he felt Marbury had been wronged and deserved the commission but if he made that ruling the Jeffersonians would not honor it and this would harm the power and prestige of the court. Using logic, rather than legal reasoning, Marshall ruled that Marbury was entitled to the commission; Madison was violating the law by withholding it; but the Supreme Court could not issue the *writ of mandamu*s because the Judiciary Act of 1789 which gave it that power was unconstitutional. His legal reasoning for the unconstitutionality was that writs could be issued only in certain cases specified in the Constitution and these cases must come on appeal. Because the Marbury case originated in the Supreme Court the court could not act. By denying the power of the court to issue the writ, Marshall was increasing its power by having the court declare a federal law unconstitutional for the first time. This concept of judicial review once established was not used again until the Dred Scott case more than 50 years later.

·*McCulloch v. Maryland* (1819)

The case arose when Maryland placed a tax on the 2nd Bank of the U. S.'s Baltimore branch and the cashier of the bank James McCulloch refused to pay it. The two legal issues to be determined as the case was appealed to the Supreme Court was the bank constitutional and was the tax on the bank constitutional. Speaking for a unanimous court Marshall argued that the bank was constitutional based on the loose construction argument that the power granting it was "implied" in the Constitution. Furthermore, the state of Maryland could not tax the bank because the "power to tax is the power to destroy" and that the state could not destroy an agency of the federal government. This would violate the supremacy clause of the Constitution. This case established the "elastic clause" (necessary and proper clause) as a powerful instrument that would allow the national government expansive legislative power. Many laws passed by Congress would be based on this part of the Constitution (Article 1, Section 4).

·**Lewis and Clark (1804-1806)**

At Jefferson's request Congress appropriated money for an expedition to explore the Missouri and Columbia rivers and tell the western Indian tribes that traders would soon come to buy their furs and that the Louisiana area was now owned by the U.S. Led by Meriwether Lewis, Jefferson's secretary, and William Clark, the party of 45 explorers was able to make a detailed report on western geography, climate, plants, animals, and to study the customs and languages of the Indians. With the help of Sacagawea, a Shoshoni they encountered along with way, the explorers explored 8,000 miles of territory over a period of almost 2 1/2 years. Their records contributed important new information concerning the land, its natural resources, and its native peoples. Lewis and Clark learned that the surprising width of the Rocky Mountain chain effectively destroyed Jefferson's hoped-for easy connection between the Missouri and Columbia River systems. Congress rewarded the officers and men of the military enterprise, including Toussaint Charbonneau (Sacagawea's French trapper husband), with grants of land. Sacagawea received no compensation for her invaluable services.

·**Judiciary Impeachments (1804)**

Federal Judge John Pickering of New Hampshire was impeached and removed for high crimes and misdemeanors although the trial showed he was merely insane. Samuel Chase, Associate Justice of the Supreme Court was impeached for his biased conduct in the Fries and Callander trials but the Senate failed to remove him. This ended the Jeffersonian's attack on the federal judiciary and discouraged future administrations from using impeachment to remove obnoxious judges.

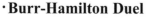

·Burr-Hamilton Duel

In 1804, Aaron Burr killed Alexander Hamilton in a duel in New Jersey (where it was legal). The dispute arose because Hamilton had helped to defeat Burr for governor of New York and had called him a "dangerous man…who ought not to be trusted with the reins of government."

·Burr Conspiracy (1805-1807)

Discredited by his duel with Hamilton as well as his political defeat for governor of New York, Aaron Burr became involved in an effort to capture Spanish possessions in the Southwest or to engineer the secession of western states from the Union, or both. Working with the shady governor of Indiana territory, James Wilkinson, and Irish immigrant Harmar Blennerhasset, who provided funding for the outfitting of a small fleet of flatboats, the Burr plot unfolded in 1806. The assemblage began a cruise down the Ohio River, headed for the Mississippi and eventually to New Orleans. Realizing the expedition was doomed to failure, Wilkinson reported Burr's actions to Jefferson, and the President ordered Burr's arrest where he was taken to Richmond for trial on charges of treason. Burr's trial was presided over by Chief Justice John Marshall, always anxious to spite his distant cousin and political opponent Jefferson. Marshall insisted upon the narrowest possible interpretation of treason, requiring an overt act to prove treason as witnessed by two people and not just a conspiracy to do so. Despite Jefferson's stage management, the prosecution's case was badly mishandled and Burr was acquitted. Burr went into exile in Europe to escape his creditors.

·Freedom of the Seas

At the beginning of Jefferson's second term (he won re-election over his Federalist opponent Charles C. Pinckney 162-14) the peace in Europe ended and France and England were once again at war. As it controlled the seas the British policy of destroying American commerce with French and Spanish colonies in the Caribbean was at odds with the traditional U.S. concept of "freedom of the seas." The British "Rule of 1756" stated that trade forbidden in times of peace shall not be open in time of war. The U.S. circumvented this law by use of the "broken voyage" which was upheld by British courts in 1800 but reversed in 1805. Along with seizures of ships the U.S. protested the impressment of American sailors into the British navy. Both the British and French declared blockades and the U.S. was hard pressed to continue its trading with nations at war.

·*Chesapeake-Leopold*

When the U.S. frigate *Chesapeake* refused the British HMS *Leopold's* request to board it in search of British deserters, the Leopold fired on the Chesapeake, killing 3 and wounding 18, and boarded it and took off 4 alleged deserters. As the crippled U.S. ship returned to Norfolk Virginia, anti British feeling intensified and the demand for reparations would last from 1807-1811.

·Embargo

When the Non-Importation Act adopted in 1807 failed to bring about a change in policy, Jefferson recommended and Congress passed the Embargo Act that stopped all land and seaborne trade with foreign nations. Smuggling to Canada became common and the act had a minor effect on the British economy as it created a monopoly for British shippers who used this to open up new markets in South America to replace the U.S. ones. The French used it as an excuse to seize all vessels in French ports or areas in Europe that France controlled. Opposition to the embargo was intense especially in New York and New England. Despite legal challenges, the embargo was upheld by John Marshall's Supreme Court in the case of *Peters v. US* sustaining the power of the national government over the states.

·*Tertium Quids*

This group was a states' rights faction of Jeffersonian Republicans in Congress led by John Randolph of Virginia who felt that Jefferson and Madison had retreated from the states' rights position they had taken in the Kentucky and Virginia Resolutions and had become nationalists. Along with the Federalist, their political opposites, they led the opposition against Jefferson's embargo. Politically the *Quids* tried to deprive Madison of the presidential nomination in 1808 as Jefferson's successor, but their candidate, James Monroe, received support only in Virginia. This group was also called the "Old Republicans" because they stood for the original Jeffersonian republican values that they felt Jefferson had abandoned once becoming President.

Madison's Presidency

· Election of 1808
Following the precedent set by Washington, Jefferson refused to run for a third term. Madison defeated the Federalist Charles C. Pinckney 122-47, although the Federalist did gain some seats in Congress but not a majority.

· Non Intercourse Act
At the end of Jefferson's term Congress replaced the Embargo Act of 1807 with the equally unenforceable and ineffective Non-Intercourse Act (March 1809). This law lifted embargoes on American shipping except those going to British or French ports. The intent was to damage the economies of the England and France. It contributed to the coming of the War of 1812 and seriously damaged the economy of the United States.

· Macon's Bill #2
Passed in 1810 it said that if either Britain or France removed its trade restrictions and the other country did not follow suit, non-intercourse would be implemented against the non-removing nation. Napoleon claimed he had complied, he had not, and Madison issued a proclamation opening trade with France and cutting it off from Great Britain.

· Annexation of West Florida
The land along the Gulf of Mexico that today comprises the southeastern part of Louisiana, Alabama, Mississippi and a small section of Georgia was an area of contention between Spain and the U.S. Settlers from the U.S. established a foothold in the area and resisted Spanish control. British settlers who had remained also resented Spanish rule. The rebellion of 1810 resulted in the capture of Baton Rouge and the establishment of the Free and Independent Republic of West Florida with its capital at St. Francisville. Congress incorporated the area into the Mississippi territory and during the War of 1812 the Spanish fort at Mobile was captured and would remain a part of the U.S.

· Yazoo Land Fraud
After bribing the legislature of Georgia, four companies received 35 million acres of land for $500,000. A new Georgia legislature rescinded the deal. Georgia ceded to the U.S. its western lands and the U.S. awarded 5 million acres to the holders of Yazoo land warrants. The bill was blocked in Congress by John Randolph and the *Quids* for three years and finally passed when he was removed as majority leader. Georgia refunded the money paid for the land, but some of the land had been resold to people who refused the money, preferring the land instead. The state did not recognize these claims and the matter ended up in court. In 1810 the Supreme Court struck down the reform act as unconstitutional in the case of *Fletcher vs. Peck* ruling the state had infringed on a valid contract, even if fraudulently obtained.

· Bank Recharter
Despite being favored by Secretary of the Treasury Albert Gallatin, the re-charter of the U.S. bank failed when its opponents united in Congress to defeat it. These included the "Old Republicans" who opposed it on constitutional grounds, anglophobes who saw it as aiding the enemy as 2/3rds of the stock was owned by the British, and State chartered banks that wanted the bank's business for themselves.

·Battle of Tippecanoe

Shawnee war leader Tecumseh with his brother the Prophet formed a confederacy to stop the expansion of pioneers into their homeland in Indiana. While Tecumseh was absent, territorial governor William Henry Harrison attacked and scattered the confederacy at the Battle of Tippecanoe although the actual fighting had been inconclusive. Tecumseh would ally with the British during the War of 1812 and die at the Battle of Thames in 1813.

War of 1812

·"War Hawks"

Name given by John Randolph to a group of young congressmen from the south and the west, who, despite being a numerical minority, took control of the House of Representatives in 1811 and elected 34 year old Kentuckian Henry Clay as Speaker of the House. They supported a war with the British as a way to achieve territorial expansion by taking Canada and Florida.

·Madison's War Message

In asking for war, Madison cited as the reasons: impressments, violation of neutral rights, the British blockade, and, the British refusal to revoke its orders in council (these would be rescinded by the British two days before the U.S. declared war but the U.S. would not know about it until two weeks passed). It passed the Senate 19-13 with the Federalist and *Quids* opposing it and passed in the House 79-49.

·Election of 1812

By now the Federalist were strictly a regional party and they gave their support to anti-war Republican DeWitt Clinton of New York. The Republicans (Jeffersonians) unanimously re-nominated Madison. Madison won 128-89 in the Electoral College although Clinton carried all of the Northern states except Vermont and Pennsylvania. The Federalists doubled their strength in the new Congress but were still in the minority.

·Military Battles

Three different attempts to take Canada ended in failure. The U.S. had some naval success, the most notable was the *Constitution's* dismantling of the British *Guerriere* and the *Java* which earned it the nickname "Old Ironsides." Overall, the British blockade was highly effective. The USS *Chesapeake* was captured by the British despite the dying captain's rallying cry," Don't Give Up the Ship." A number of battles took place in and around the Great Lakes with neither side able to gain an advantage. Despite being outnumbered, a British force routed U.S. defenders and captured Washington D. C. They burned the White House and the Capital. The British attempt to take Baltimore failed as its bombardment of Fort McHenry in the harbor inspired Francis Scott Key to write words to an old drinking song that became the "Star Spangled Banner." The final battle was fought two weeks after the peace treaty was signed and resulted in Andrew Jackson becoming a national hero by defeating the British forces at the Battle of New Orleans. The British lost 2,036 men to the Americans 21 and it helped to convince the U.S. that it had won the war.

·Treaty of Ghent (1814)

Both countries agreed to end hostilities by returning to the exact same conditions that had existed before the war. The United States, though it achieved none of its stated war aims, did achieve the goal of pushing the Native Americans off their traditional lands that were now open for white settlement. The settlement resulted in a condition of *status quo ante-bellum*.

·Hartford Convention

This was a gathering of New England Federalists who met in secrecy at Hartford and drafted proposals for constitutional amendments that would challenge what they saw as President James Madison's military despotism and would force him to resign. Their recommendations would have been more separatist if the *Essex Junto*, a group of extremist Federalists, had not been restrained by the moderation of delegate Harrison Gray Otis. By the time the Hartford delegation of five New England states arrived in Washington to make their recommendations, the War of 1812 was over. The Treaty of Ghent had already been signed and news of Andrew Jackson's victory at New Orleans had reached the capital. "Their position," according to a French diplomat, "was awkward, embarrassing, and lent itself to cruel ridicule," and they swiftly withdrew their recommendations.

Post-War Nationalism—Monroe's Presidency

·Defeat of the Barbary States (1815)
Stephen Decatur with 10 ships defeated the Dey of Algiers and exacted a treaty where the Barbary State would give up both its attacks on U.S. commerce as well as the "tribute" it had been receiving. Similar treaties were signed with Tunis and Tripoli and compensation was given to the U.S. for ships that had been seized by the British with the cooperation of the Barbary States. This ended the problem with the Barbary States after 31 years of paying tribute.

·Demographic Changes
With a post-war economic boom European demand for cotton and tobacco increased as well as demand for corn, wheat, and beef. By 1820 the West had more than 2 million settlers and was now larger than New England. Ohio now had more people than Massachusetts. With this demographic change came an increase in land speculation funded by $100 million in paper money issued by wildcat state banks.

·2nd Bank of the U.S. (1816)
A bill was introduced to create a 2nd Bank because the state banks were unable to stabilize the currency during the War of 1812. Supported by Clay (who had opposed it in 1811) and John C. Calhoun and opposed by Daniel Webster, it passed the House 80-71 (38 Federalist and 33 Republicans opposed) and the Senate 22-12. It was capitalized at $35 million, had a 20- year charter, and most of its provision followed the 1st Bank of the U.S.

·Election of 1816
Some of the younger Republicans supported William Crawford for the nomination, but the nomination of James Monroe continued the Virginia dynasty" by winning the vote in the caucus 65-54. The discredited Federalists, due to their opposition to the war, fielded their last candidate for President, Rufus King. Monroe carried all the states except Massachusetts, Connecticut and Delaware and won 183-34 in the Electoral College.

·Era of Good Feelings
This phrase was first used in Boston's *Columbia Centinel* (1817) to describe the time period that corresponded to Monroe's two administrations. The fact that there was only one political party contributed to this belief as the Federalist Party had become moribund.

·Rush-Bagot Agreement
Unanimously approved by the Senate in 1818 it called for demilitarization of the Great Lakes by both Great Britain and the U.S. It also paved the way for settling the border between U.S. and Canada that would be finalized in the Convention of 1818.

·First Seminole War
After defeating the Creek Confederation during the War of 1812 at the Battle of Horseshoe Bend, Andrew Jackson marched into Spanish Florida, took the forts at St. Marks and Pensacola, captured and executed two

British traders Alexander Arbuthnot and Robert Ambrister who were accused of being spies, and routed the Seminole's who had protected runaway slaves and other hostile Native Americans. This met with the approval of the American public and made Jackson and even greater hero than before, although he probably went beyond his instructions which made his actions questionable.

·Convention of 1818

The U.S. and Great Britain agreed to the 49th parallel as the boundary between the U.S. and Canada; joint occupation of the Oregon country for 10 years; and U.S. fishing privileges off the coast of Newfoundland and Labrador.

·Panic of 1819

A primary cause of this economic downturn (Panic was the term used for a Depression until 1893) seems to have been a change toward more conservative credit policies by the 2nd Bank of the U.S. The directors viewed with scorn the unconventional practices of many western wildcat banks. The Bank of the United States called in its loans, forcing the state banks to do the same. State bank loans had been made to land speculators who were unable to repay; banks failed and depositors were wiped out. Post- war economic expansion ended when banks throughout the country failed; mortgages were foreclosed; falling prices characterized agriculture and manufacturing; and widespread unemployment ensued. All regions of the country were affected and prosperity did not return until 1824. Conditions were exacerbated by the influx of large quantities of foreign goods into the American market and the slumping cotton market in the South. The Bank became known as "The Monster," an epithet originated by Senator Thomas Hart Benton and became a scapegoat for all of the countries economic ills.

·Tallmadge Amendment, 1819

The enabling act for Missouri statehood was derailed when New York Congressman James Tallmadge introduced an amendment that would have freed all slaves in Missouri when they reached 25 and prohibited the further introduction of slaves into Missouri. It passed in a close vote in the House but failed in the Senate which had a number of members representing the 11 free states who had been born in the 10 slave states.

·Missouri Compromise, 1820

After a great deal of political discord it was decided to allow Missouri to enter the union as a slave state and Maine (now severed from Massachusetts) to enter as a free state. This kept the U.S. equal with the same number of free and slave states. A final provision prohibited slavery in the Louisiana territory north of the 36 degree 30 minute line. When he heard of the compromise Jefferson said, "like a fire bell in the night, [it] awakened and filled me with terror. I considered it at once as the knell (sound of a mourning bell) of the Union."

·Election of 1820

With only one unopposed candidate, Monroe was reelected with 231 votes (one elector voted for John Quincy Adams and there were 3 abstentions).

·Cumberland Road

Often called the National Road or Turnpike its construction had been stopped by the Panic of 1819. A bill authorizing repairs, establishing toll-gates, and the collection of tolls, was vetoed by Monroe because he felt it was unconstitutional. He favored a constitutional amendment for a national system of internal improvements.

·Foreign Policy

At the urging of Henry Clay resolutions were passed that called for the recognition and establishment of diplomatic relations with Latin American countries who had established their independence from Spain.

Furthermore, Russia's claim to the Pacific coast all the way to California conflicted with the U.S. claim to the joint occupation of Oregon and Secretary of State John Quincy Adams warned the Czar that the American continents were no longer subjects for any new European colonies.

·Monroe Doctrine

Stated during Monroe's seventh annual message to Congress in December of 1823, it contained the concepts of separate spheres of influence for the Americas and Europe, non-colonization, and non-intervention. The doctrine was intended to signify a clear break between the New World and the autocratic governments of Europe. Monroe forewarned the European powers against interfering in the affairs of the newly independent Latin American states or potential United States territories. While Americans generally objected to European colonies in the New World, they also desired to increase United States influence and trading ties in Latin America. European mercantilism posed the greatest obstacle to economic expansion. In particular, Americans feared that Spain and France might reassert colonialism over the Latin American peoples who had just overthrown European rule. Signs that Russia was expanding its presence southward from Alaska toward the Oregon Territory were also disconcerting. For its part, the British also had a strong interest in ensuring the end of mercantilist Spanish colonialism. Earlier in 1823, British Foreign Minister George Canning suggested to the Americans that the two nations issue a joint declaration to deter any other power from intervening in Central and South America. Secretary of State, John Quincy Adams, however, vigorously opposed cooperation with Great Britain, contending that a statement of bilateral nature could limit United States expansion in the future. He also argued that the British were not committed to recognizing the Latin American republics and may have had imperial motivations themselves. Because it was in the British interest, they used their powerful navy to support the Monroe Doctrine in the 19th century. For the most part, other European countries ignored what they considered to be a declaration from an upstart nation. To make the document more palatable the U.S. said it would refrain from interfering in the affairs of Europe.

·American System

Henry Clay first proposed the American System in a speech defending the protective tariff of 1824. It was an economic philosophy intended to allow the U.S. to become economically independent and nationally self-sufficient. High protective tariffs, internal improvements, and support for a national banking system were its chief features. It was built on the policies of Hamilton, and was supported by J.Q. Adams as well as Clay.

·End of King Caucus

The system of having the congressional caucus nominate a candidate for President came to an end. Dissension in Monroe's cabinet between the John C. Calhoun forces and the William Crawford forces led to candidates being nominated by state legislatures. J.Q. Adams was nominated by Massachusetts, Henry Clay by Kentucky, and Andrew Jackson by Tennessee and Pennsylvania. John C. Calhoun after first announcing for the Presidency withdrew and became the Vice-Presidential candidate of both Jackson and Adams. A rump caucus of only 66 of the 216 Republicans in Congress nominated Crawford as the last caucus candidate.

·Election of 1824

With no incumbent or rival political parties and four strong candidates, the election results found no candidate with a majority of the electoral votes. Jackson had 99, Adams 84, Crawford 41, and Clay 37 (he had more popular votes than Crawford but fewer electoral votes). As provided for in the Constitution the three top candidates were submitted to the House of Representatives who, voting by states, would have the final say. Clay advised his supporters to support Adams although some of them had been instructed by their state legislatures to vote for Jackson. The final vote found 13 states for Adams, 7 for Jackson, and 4 for Crawford. After Henry Clay was appointed Secretary of State by Adams, Pennsylvania Representative George Kremer leveled the charge of "corrupt bargain" between Adams and Clay in an unsigned letter to a newspaper. The charge stuck and tarnished the Adams presidency.

· Political Divisions

The Republican Party of the "Virginia dynasty" of Jefferson, Madison, and Monroe now became divided into the Adams-Clay National Republicans and the Jacksonian Democrats. This realignment would last until the Whig Party replaced the National Republicans after the election of 1832. The Democratic Party of Jackson remains a major political party today.

· Rise of Democracy

As six new states entered the union between 1800 and 1820 they did so with no property qualifications for voting. By 1841, Rhode Island—under the charter of 1663—was the only state that had not accepted universal white male suffrage. The era from 1816 to 1830 also saw the liberalizing of existing state constitutions by the removal of both religious and property qualifications for voting. The selection of electors was transferred from the state legislatures to the people and by 1828 only two states still chose their electors through their legislatures.

John Quincy Adams' Presidency

· J. Q. Adams' Program

His nationalism was against the state's rights advocates who coalesced against him. He recommended internal improvements (roads and canals), a national university, astronomical observatories, standardization of weights and measures, interior and Pacific coast exploration, promotion of agriculture, commerce, and manufacturing, and encouragement for the arts and sciences. The country was not ready for all of this visionary nationalism.

· Civil Service and Patronage

Adams attempted to be non-partisan and failed to build a party when he would not appoint his own supporters to political office. He would only remove an officeholder (12 in all) who had committed official misconduct or who was incompetent. Many of those who held these jobs supported other candidates and they used their influence against the President.

· Panama Conference

Adams attempted to send representation to this conference called by Simon Bolivar to create a union of Latin American republics to counter any Spanish attempt to regain their colonies. He was rebuffed by Congress who saw it as being counter to the traditional U.S. policy of neutrality. During the debate in the Senate, John Randolph made his infamous reference that the administration was "the coalition of Blifil and Black George" the combination of a puritan and a black-leg (taken from Henry Fielding's novel *Tom Jones*). Clay challenged Randolph to a duel; it took place in Virginia and both shots missed leaving the challengers unharmed.

· Like Father, Like Son

Faced throughout his term with organized opposition from the Jacksonian Democrats—who were committed to limiting Adams to a single term—Adams was reluctant and unable to forge the political alliances necessary to push his ideas into policy. Like his father, John Adams, who had also ignored the political side of the office, he served only one term. J. Q. Adams lost his reelection bid to Jackson in 1828. The only two of the first seven presidents to not win reelection were Adams father and son.

UNIT VII
MULTIPLE-CHOICE QUESTIONS

Questions 1-3 refer to the following document:

".... But every difference of opinion is not a difference of principle. We have called by different names brethren of the same principle. We are all Republicans, we are all Federalists.... I know, indeed, that some honest men fear that a republican government can not be strong, that this Government is not strong enough; but would the honest patriot, in the full tide of successful experiment, abandon a government which has so far kept us free and firm on the theoretic and visionary fear that this Government, the world's best hope, may by possibility want energy to preserve itself? I trust not. I believe this, on the contrary, the strongest Government on earth.... Sometimes it is said that man cannot be trusted with the government of himself. Can he, then, be trusted with the government of others? Or have we found angels in the forms of kings to govern him? Let history answer this question."

Thomas Jefferson, *First Inaugural Address*, 1801

1. Jefferson's statement "We are all Republicans, we are all Federalist" was meant to

   (A) reassure a divided country that we all shared the same American values
   (B) keep political parties or factions from forming
   (C) send a message to the world to not be involved in the affairs of the U.S.
   (D) pave the way for the territorial expansion into the West

2. The statement "Or have we found angels in the forms of kings to govern him" was directed at

   (A) Europeans who wanted to impose a monarchy on the United States
   (B) uniting those who favored a hereditary system with those who favored a theocracy
   (C) those who did not believe man could govern himself (a representative government) but felt they could govern others
   (D) Federalist supporters of John Adams

3. The phrase "brethren of the same principle" is used by Jefferson to mean

   (A) a belief in the ideals expressed in the Declaration of Independence
   (B) Republicans and Federalist are alike in their political ideology
   (C) the brotherhood of mankind is akin to belonging to the same church
   (D) support for constitutional protections for freedom of religion

101

Questions 4-7 refer to the following:

"Jeffersonianism seemed to be a comprehensive social philosophy... [that] offered a practical and humane program of national development... It had not yet been distorted by the caprice of circumstance into a somewhat nebulous idealism, nor confined within the narrower limits of political equalitarianism and states rights theory. By later generations Jefferson has been interpreted too exclusively in terms of the Declaration of Independence, the glowing idealism of which has proved curiously elastic and has been stretched by later libertarian movements to meet their special and particular ends: by the Jacksonian democracy in their struggle for manhood suffrage; by the Abolitionists in their attack upon a slave-sanctioning Constitution; by other idealists in their various crusades... Jefferson,... has come to be commonly associated with the conception of democracy and the ideal of social justice. But to his young Virginia followers... he embodied for them the many-sided liberalism of French revolutionary thought... the strongest creative influence on the mature Jefferson came from the Physiocratic group,... the brilliant founders of an economy that was primarily social rather than narrowly industrial or financial. Historically the Physiocratic school is as sharply aligned with idealistic agrarianism as the Manchester school is aligned with capitalistic industrialism."

Vernon L. Parrington, *Main Currents in American Thought*

4. According to the document the name of Jefferson in 1800 has been commonly associated with

    (A) a strong central government imposing order on the republic
    (B) concepts of democracy and ideals of social justice
    (C) the Manchester school of capitalistic industrialism
    (D) narrow limits of political equalitarianism and states rights theory

5. Idealistic agrarianism had all of the following features EXCEPT

    (A) it was the polar opposite of the capitalist industrial school in England
    (B) it was the Physiocratic school of economics that originated in France
    (C) an economy was primarily social rather than narrowly industrial or financial
    (D) it supported the mercantilist ideology characterized by the Navigation Act

6. Libertarian, Jacksonian, and Abolitionist movements have all

    (A) used Jefferson to support their causes
    (B) returned to Federalism for political ideology
    (C) supported the Physiocratic school of economics
    (D) were all supporters of the concept of manifest destiny

7. The continuity of the idealism of Jeffersonianism of 1800 can best be seen in the ideology of which 20th century President?

    (A) Theodore Roosevelt
    (B) William Howard Taft
    (C) Woodrow Wilson
    (D) Franklin Delano Roosevelt

Questions 8-10 refer to the following:

".... No tribe has the right to sell, even to each other, much less to strangers [the land]... Sell a country! Why not sell the air, the great sea, as well as the earth? Didn't the Great Spirit make them all for the use of his children?... The white people,... want us to be... "assimilated,..." destroying our own way of life and our own cultural patterns. They believe we should be contented like those whose concept of happiness is materialistic and greedy.... We want freedom from the white man rather than to be integrated. We don't want any part of the establishment, we want to be free to raise our children in our religion,... to be able to hunt and fish and live in peace. We don't want power, we don't want to be congressmen, or bankers.... we want to be ourselves. We want to have our heritage, because we are the owners of this land and because we belong here. The white man says, there is freedom and justice for all. We have had "freedom and justice," and that is why we have been almost exterminated. We shall not forget this."

Tecumseh, "Speech to the Governor of the Indiana Territory, William Harrison," 1810

8. In the passage above Tecumseh points out an important philosophical difference between the Indians and the whites over which issue that the Dawes and Wheelor-Howard Act would try to solve?

(A) Role of the Chief
(B) Decisions of the council
(C) Land ownership
(D) Religion

9. A subsequent decision by U.S. politicians to impose assimilation by making the Indians into yeoman farmers was passage of the

(A) Homestead Act
(B) Morrill Act
(C) Newlands Act
(D) Dawes Severalty Act

10. In what would prove to be the ultimate indignity for the Indians, the civilized tribes of the southeast would be forced to leave their land to travel thousand of miles west in what became known as the

(A) Great Trek
(B) Trail of Tears
(C) Mass Migration
(D) Native American Exodus

Questions 11-12 refer to the following:

".... *BE it enacted.* That...no British or French armed vessel shall be permitted to enter the harbor or waters under the jurisdiction of the United States. . . . except when they shall be forced in by distress.... That all pacific intercourse with any interdicted foreign armed vessels, the officers or crew thereof, is hereby forbidden, Sec. 4. That in case either Great Britain or France shall, ... revoke or modify her edicts as that they shall cease to violate the neutral commerce of the United States,... and if the other nation shall not within three months thereafter so revoke or modify her edicts in like manner, then....[the act] shall, ... have full force and effect, ... of the nation thus refusing or neglecting to revoke or modify her edicts in the manner aforesaid. And the restrictions imposed by this act shall... cease and be discontinued in relation to the nation revoking... her decrees..."

Macon's Bill #2, 1810

11. The failure of the European countries to adhere to this bill would result in the

(A) Spanish American War
(B) Mexican War
(C) Tripolitan War
(D) War of 1812

12. A common understanding of Macon's Bill #2 is

(A) if either France or the British lifted their trade restrictions the U.S. would trade with them and not the other country
(B) if the two countries continued to violate the neutral commerce of the U.S. then the U.S. would not trade with either country
(C) it was tilted in favor of France and which meant there would be a war between the United States and Great Britain.
(D) Great Britain tended to be favored in the bill because of the common language and culture

Questions 13-15 refer to the following:

"... as far as the west, the articulate war maker was concerned, the freedom of the seas played only a minor part in the precipitation of the conflict... it must be understood that the war of 1812 was really meant to be a land war, advocated and fought by a section of the country that had no contact with or interest in the things of the sea..., the war of 1812 was ordered by an agricultural people... to have at its goal the acquisition of Canada not so much because that meant cutting off of the living threat of England, as because Canada stood for great reserves of agricultural land. In short, the west desired Canada and therefore sought war with England."

Louis M. Hacker, "Western Land Hunger and the War of 1812," 1924

13. The passage above could be considered an early example of what important concept in U.S. history that would dominate in the mid-nineteenth century?

    (A) "We shall be as a City upon a Hill, the eyes of all people are upon us"
    (B) It was the manifest destiny of the U.S. to expand its territory over North America
    (C) Social reform movements to transform American society
    (D) Development of a market economy to transfer goods throughout the continent

14. The interpretation stated by Hacker runs contrary to the dominate historical interpretation that sees the War of 1812 being fought primarily over

    (A) subduing Native Americans on the frontier
    (B) British intrigues with foreign powers to weaken the U.S. hold on the West
    (C) Maritime rights including freedom of the seas
    (D) French and British ideological conflicts

15. The Treaty of Ghent ending the War of 1812 proved the total failure of which war aim of the U.S. that had also been a failed war aim of the Revolutionary War?

    (A) Establishing neutral rights for shipping
    (B) Proving the U.S. could stand up to the British with an overwhelming victory at New Orleans
    (C) Establishing a setting for a post-war sense of nationalism
    (D) Expanding U.S. territory by acquiring Canada

NO TESTING MATERIAL ON THIS PAGE

UNIT VIII

JACKSONIAN ERA

Andrew Jackson's election as President in 1828 brought a new era in American politics and government. More than any of the other early presidents, Jackson's actions transformed the office creating many of its modern features. Democracy has often been associated with the Jacksonian era as the franchise was extended to include all white males. Fierce sectional struggles between the North, South, and West took place over issues like the tariff, 2nd Bank of U.S, and internal improvements. The time period from 1824 to 1848 is roughly considered to be the "Age of Jackson" because of his dominating influence.

· Tariff of 1828

During the political campaign of 1828 some of Jackson's supporters came up with a plan to discredit the Adams-Clay "American System." Different groups wanted an upward revision of the 1824 tariff. New England textile manufacturers pressed Congress and the administration for higher protective measures, arguing that British woolens were being dumped on American markets at artificially low prices. The Jacksonians hoped this tariff would fail so they put high duties on raw materials, which would gain support in the West but be hated in New England. The South under any circumstance was opposed to protectionism. No one was pleased with the 1828 tariff that John Randolph said was to encourage "manufactures of no sort or kind except the manufacture of a President of the United States." To the surprise of everyone the tariff passed despite its odorous features. Adams reluctantly signed the tariff that would ultimately result in his political downfall. He did not consider a Presidential veto as these, in his mind, were reserved for laws that were thought to be unconstitutional. The Tariff of 1828 had been purposely drafted to make Andrew Jackson appear as a free trade advocate in the South and as a protectionist in the North. Daniel Webster said about the tariff, "Its enemies spiced it with whatever they thought would render it distasteful; its friends took it, drugged as it was." The tariff became known as the "Tariff of Abominations."

Election of 1828

In what became a re-match of the two leading candidates of 1824, Jackson—aided by the corrupt bargain charge—defeated Adams 171 to 83. Calhoun who ran with Jackson this time was reelected Vice-President. Jackson carried heavily populated New York by 5,000 votes due to the support of the powerful political machine of Martin Van Buren and William Marcy, the Albany Regency.

Jackson's Presidency

Inaugural Address

With no clear statement of policy on the leading issues of the day—the tariff, internal improvements, the Bank of the U.S. and currency issues—it was unclear just where Jackson stood. He seemed to favor state's rights, revamping the civil service, economy in government, and what he called a "just and liberal" policy toward Native Americans.

Peggy Eaton Affair

Despite some criticism Jackson appointed his friend Senator John Eaton to be his Secretary of War. Eaton had married a widowed daughter of a Washington innkeeper Margaret (Peggy) O'Neill while the rumor mill ground out gossip that O'Neill and Eaton had had an affair prior to her husband's death. The Cabinet wives, led by Mrs. John C. Calhoun were scandalized by these rumors and refused to attend events when Peggy Eaton was present. Jackson, who knew and liked Peggy, was not pleased with this snub, remembering how deeply his late wife had been hurt by scandals and she died during the election of 1828. He resented Calhoun's inability to control his wife and was disappointed when only widower Martin Van Buren among the Cabinet officers defended Peggy Eaton. While the scandal was going on his Cabinet was dysfunctional. In 1831, Eaton and Van Buren resigned their offices, putting pressure on the other Cabinet members to do likewise. These resignations gave Jackson the opportunity to appoint Cabinet officers who were loyal to him rather than Calhoun. The final result was to elevate Van Buren who became Vice President in 1833 as Jackson's chosen successor instead of Calhoun.

Spoils System

Sometimes called "rotation in office," the phrase "to the victor belong the spoils" was first used by the Albany Regency's William Marcy. Patronage for party purposes had been used sparingly by Jefferson, but the Jacksonians elevated it to a party building apparatus as 10% of officeholders were removed in his first year and 20% during his two terms as President. Jackson defended the Spoils System (called rotation in office by its defenders) as a reform measure and a positive good as he felt the jobs of government service were so basic that anyone could do them—no expertise was required.

Kitchen Cabinet

Because of the rancor over the Eaton affair, Jackson ceased holding cabinet meetings and relied on a small group of friends for political advice that opponents called his "kitchen cabinet." This was the beginning of a White House staff and Jackson's "kitchen cabinet" included among others Amos Kendall, Duff Green, Francis Blair and Andrew Donelson.

Foot Resolution

In 1829, Senator Samuel Foot of Connecticut proposed that the committee on public lands study the feasibility of limiting the sale of western lands. This innocuous suggestion led to sectional debates over the nature of the union itself. Land speculation had become an important part of the American character. Foot represented the New England view that cheap land encouraged westward migration, which robbed the factories of a captive labor supply. The Democrats in the West opposed the resolution since they favored cheap land in their region.

The states' rights forces in the South took advantage of this situation and tried to forge an alliance with the West, hoping that this would lead to reworking such issues as the tariff.

· Webster-Hayne Debate (1830)
Robert Hayne of South Carolina in a speech invoking strict constructionism, the compact theory, and states' rights views attacked the Foot Resolution and labeled Northeasterners as selfish and unprincipled for their support of protectionism and restricted land policies. Daniel Webster changed the debate by examining the Southern positions on states' rights in general and nullification in particular. He concluded his reply to Haine with the words, "Liberty and Union, now and forever, one and inseparable!"

· Battle of the Toasts (1830)
At a Jefferson day dinner after listening to 24 prepared toasts, most with themes supporting state sovereignty and nullification, Jackson delivered a toast that said, "Our Union: it must be preserved." Calhoun responded with his toast, "The Union, next to our liberty, the most dear. May we always remember that it can only be preserved by distributing equally the benefits and burdens of the union." It was clear that Jackson did not stand with Southern supporters of nullification although he did agree to amend his toast for publication to read "Our Federal Union...."

· Maysville Road Veto (1830)
Following Van Buren's advice with the purpose of weakening Clay's American System, Jackson vetoed a 60 mile road in Kentucky on strict constructionist grounds. He opposed the road because it was in a single state and felt that a constitutional amendment was needed for federally subsidized roads and canals. He did support the Cumberland Road Bill.

· Anti-Masonic Party
It originated in New York after the disappearance of William Morgan, who had written an exposè of Freemasonry. This movement opposed all secret societies and it was anti-Jackson as he and many other prominent politicians were Masons. A state Anti-Masonic party was formed in 1828 and was successful in electing local and statewide candidates. . It nominated its candidate for President, William Wirt, by a national nominating convention (first party to do so). Wirt had been the U.S. Attorney General and, possibly, a Mason. Wirt only carried Vermont in the election of 1832 but his did make a strong showing in New York. The parties prime impact had been to drain votes away from Henry Clay, the candidate of the National Republicans who opposed Jackson. Around 1834, the Anti-Masonic Party began a rapid disintegration with some of its members helping to establish the new Whig Party while others migrated to the Democratic Party.

· *Cherokee Nation v. Georgia*
The Cherokee Nation sought a federal injunction against laws that were passed by the state of Georgia discriminating against them. In *Cherokee Nation v. Georgia*, former Attorney General William Wirt argued that the Cherokee Nation was a separate foreign nation according to the United States Constitution. According to this belief, Wirt felt that the Cherokee nation should not be subject to the state's jurisdiction. The Supreme Court refused to hear the suit on the grounds that the Cherokee Nation did not possess original jurisdiction because the tribe was not a state. Despite this claim the Supreme Court labeled the Cherokee Nation tribe as a "denominated domestic dependent nation."

· Indian Removal Policy (1830)
After four months of debate Andrew Jackson signed the bill into law removing the Indians to the West. This desire for Indian lands was also abetted by a negative attitude toward the Indians by many frontiersmen. Jackson had played a major role in earlier removal with his defeat of the Creek Confederation. This period of forcible removal first started with the Cherokee Indians in Georgia. In 1802, the Georgia legislature signed

a compact giving the federal government all of its claims to western lands in exchange for the government's pledge to extinguish all Indian titles to land within the state. The Cherokee Constitution proclaimed that the Cherokee nation had complete jurisdiction over its own territory. When the Cherokee nation sought aid from newly elected president Andrew Jackson, he informed them that he would not interfere with the lawful prerogatives of the state of Georgia. Jackson saw the solution of the problem with the removal of the Cherokee tribes to lands west. This would keep contact between Indians and Americans minimal. When President Jackson began to negotiate with the Indians, he gave them a guarantee of perpetual autonomy in the West as the strongest incentive to emigrate. To ensure peace the government forced these five tribes, called the Five Civilized Tribes (Creek, Cherokee, Choctaw, Chickasaw, and Seminole) to move out of the lands they had lived on for generations and move to land given to them in Oklahoma. In Jackson's mind this as a way of protecting them from the white culture.

Worcester v. Georgia
Chief Justice John Marshall ruled in favor of the Cherokees in 1832 when the state of Georgia took their land away. However, President Andrew Jackson refused to enforce the verdict allegedly saying, "John Marshall made the decision let him enforce it." Jackson argued that the Indians were not an independent nation: the court ruled that they were. The case did set an important precedent as far as the rights of Native Americans were concerned laying out the relationship between tribes and the state and federal governments, and building a foundation for the doctrine of tribal sovereignty in the United States.

"Trail of Tears"
Term given to the period of years (1831-1839) in which over 70,000 Indians had to give up their homes and move to certain areas assigned to tribes in Oklahoma. The tribes were given a right to all of Oklahoma except the panhandle. The government promised this land to them "as long as grass shall grow and rivers run." Unfortunately, the land that they were given only lasted until white settlers wanted the land and then they were forced to move to other reservations. The "Trails of Tears" were several trails that the Five Civilized Tribes traveled on their way to their new lands. Many Indians died because of famine or disease. The tribes had to walk all day long and got very little rest. All this was done in order to free more land for white settlers. The period of forced removal started when Andrew Jackson became President in 1829. At that time there was reported to be sightings of gold in the Cherokee territory in Georgia. This caused prospectors to rush in, tear down fences and destroy crops and cause mayhem with Indian owned lands.

Nullification Controversy
In his 1831 message to Congress Jackson recommended a downward revision of the 1828 Tariff of Abominations. Some revision was accomplished in the Tariff of 1832 but not enough to satisfy the South. With the nullification party now in control after the elections of 1832 in South Carolina, and supported by Vice President John C. Calhoun, a special convention called by Governor James Hamilton nullified the tariffs of 1828 and 1832. Jackson issued his "Proclamation to the People of South Carolina" that declared nullification an "impractical absurdity" and asserted the supremacy of the federal government. Hayne became the governor of South Carolina and Calhoun resigned the Vice-Presidency and took Hayne's place in the Senate. An attempt to rally other states to South Carolina's cause resulted in replies that condemned both nullification and secession. Jackson asked Congress for authority to force South Carolina to comply with the revenue laws (tariffs) and to use force if necessary. Webster and Calhoun debated nationalism and states rights in the Senate while Henry Clay worked on a compromise tariff lowering rates. This compromise passed along with the Force Act. South Carolina rescinded the ordinance of nullification, but as a face saving measure nullified the Force Act.

· "South Carolina Exposition and Protest"

Drafted secretly by Vice-President John C. Calhoun, this document was presented to the state's House of Representatives in 1828 by a special committee charged with formulating a response to the federal protective tariff passed earlier that year. The theory of the right of nullification was established by Calhoun in this document. Although not adopted by the South Carolina legislature, 4,000 copies of this states' rights manifesto were printed and distributed at state expense.

· War on the Bank

A prosperous 2nd Bank of the U.S. under the guidance of Nicolas Biddle became a target of Jackson as he questioned whether the bank was constitutional. In 1832, Jackson vetoed a bill for the early re-charter of the bank before its 20-year term was up. Attacking the bank for its monopoly and special privilege it became the leading issue in the campaign for the Presidency in 1832.

· Election of 1832

Henry Clay made his second run for President becoming the candidate of the National Republicans in 1832. Jackson was re-nominated by the Democrats at their first national convention with Martin Van Buren as his running mate The convention adopted the 2/3rds rule for nomination, which would be in place for the next 104 years. Van Buren's rise to the Vice-Presidency was somewhat of a surprise as he had previously failed to win confirmation as Ambassador to England 24-23 in the Senate with Calhoun casting the deciding vote against him. Many thought this had finished him politically. A third party, the Anti-Masonic Party, nominated William Wirt for President. Jackson won 219-49 with Wirt carrying Vermont's 7 electoral votes.

· Deposit Removal

Interpreting his reelection as a mandate to proceed against the Bank, Jackson took the federal deposits out of the 2nd Bank of the U.S. and had them re-deposited in state banks (called "pet banks" by his opponents). Clay introduced two censuring resolutions in the Senate, attacking Jackson for exceeding his constitutional authority, and both passed 26-20. The House passed resolutions supporting his bank policy. Through the efforts of Senator Thomas Hart Benton the censuring of Jackson was removed in 1837.

· Whig Party

A general coalition of groups opposed to what they saw as the tyranny of "King Andrew I" formed the Whig Party. It consisted of National Republicans, supporters of Clay and Adams' American System, administration officials opposed to Jackson's bank policy, states' rights groups opposed to Jackson's stand on nullification, Southern Planters, Northern Industrialists, and the remains of the Anti-Masonic Party. Led by Clay and Webster with the independent Calhoun often supporting the Whigs for a time, it would become the 2nd political party for the next 20 years and contest with the Democrats for political power. Twice it would elect Presidents, both were generals, but they would both die in office to be succeeded by nominal Whigs.

· Specie Circular

With the end of the 2nd Bank of the U.S. Jackson's pet banks (many with "wildcat" tendencies) issued paper money that fueled land speculation in the West. Jackson tried to check the inflation and speculation by requiring that land payments be made with hard currency. He also wanted to limit the quantity of land sales and confine it to actual settlers. The economic consequences of his action would be seen in the Panic of 1837 that would take place after he left office.

· Election of 1836

The newly formed Whig Party hoped to throw the election into the House of Representatives by nominating candidates with regional appeal—Daniel Webster, Hugh White, and William Henry Harrison (also nominated by the Anti-Masonic Party). Martin Van Buren the Democratic nominee would carry 15 of the 26 states and

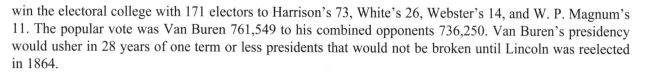

win the electoral college with 171 electors to Harrison's 73, White's 26, Webster's 14, and W. P. Magnum's 11. The popular vote was Van Buren 761,549 to his combined opponents 736,250. Van Buren's presidency would usher in 28 years of one term or less presidents that would not be broken until Lincoln was reelected in 1864.

Political Party Factions

·Locofocos (Equal Rights Party)

Opposed to banks in general and especially paper money, this group, which was a remnant from the Workingman's Party formed earlier in Philadelphia, asked for free public education and protection against convict labor. The radical Locofocos gained control of the Democratic Party in New York. Their name came from the new self-igniting friction matches they used to light candles in order to conduct a meeting after the Tammany Hall regulars turned out the gas lights. Also called the Equal Rights party, the name Locofoco would be subsequently used to describe any radical group. In the main they were strict constructionist, "Old Republican," *Quid* like Jeffersonians who in Ralph Waldo Emerson's words were opposed to "tools, taxes, turnpikes, banks, hierarchies, governors,...laws."

·Barnburners

This group was a radical wing of the Democratic Party faction in New York led by former president Martin Van Buren and Silas Wright. Use of the term Barnburners was based on its members' willingness to burn down the barn (the party) to rid it of its rats (its enemies the Hunkers). The Barnburners favored balanced budgets, hard money, and opposed state funding for canals, roads, a national bank, and the speculative lending of wildcat state banks. After the Panic of 1837, they fiercely resisted Whig governor William H. Seward's successful plans, supported by the Hunkers, to use state funds for spending policies, especially on canals. After Martin Van Buren's failed to be nominated for President in 1844 tensions within the Democratic Party increased. The new Democratic President James Polk failed to recognize the Barnburners' election efforts on his behalf, including Wright's successful run for governor, which helped Polk win New York state. He favored the avowed opponents of the Barnburners, the Hunkers by rewarding them with patronage. In the late 1840s the Barnburners antagonized their Democratic opponents by supporting the Wilmot Proviso (forbidding slavery in territory acquired in the Mexican War), which challenged Polk's attempt to add new slave territory in the West. The state Democratic Party formally split in 1847; thereafter two Democratic organizations fought each other as well as the Whigs. In 1848 the Barnburners joined with antislavery Whigs to form the national Free Soil Party, with Martin Van Buren as its presidential candidate. They opposed the Democrats and Whigs, or anyone who favored the expansion of slavery, and many would ultimately join the antislavery Republican Party later in the 1850s.

·Hunkers

Unlike their party opponents, the Barnburners, the conservative faction of the Democratic party in New York state in the 1840s, the Hunkers, favored internal improvements the liberal chartering of state banks, and opposed the antislavery movement. There name came because they were supposed to "hanker" or "hunker" after office at all cost. They usually controlled the party machinery and the patronage in New York and in the 1846 gubernatorial nomination they turned against the Barnburner Democratic candidate, Gov. Silas Wright. The Barnburners responded by voting for the Free-Soil ticket in the 1848 presidential election, won by the Whig candidate, Zachary Taylor. The Barnburners who did not persist in their antislavery views were welcomed back to the party fold in 1850. The Hunkers later divided themselves between pro and anti Pierce factions in the Democratic Party in the1850s.

·Doughfaces

In the years leading up to the Civil War, "doughface" was used to describe Northerners who had Southern sympathies. The expression was coined by John Randolph of Roanoke, Virginia during the Missouri Compromise debates. Randolph had no respect for northerners who voted with the South, considering them, "weak men, timid men, half-baked men." In 1820, seventeen doughfaces voted for the Missouri Compromise. In 1836, sixty northern congressmen voted with the South in passing the gag rule to prevent anti-slavery petitions from being received in the House of Representatives. In 1847 twenty-seven northerners joined with the South in opposing the Wilmot Proviso, and in 1850 thirty-five supported a stronger fugitive slave law. By 1854 the South had changed its position on the Missouri Compromise and fifty-eight northerners supported its repeal in the Kansas-Nebraska Act. Doughfaces eventually had their greatest influence in the Senate. In the House the growth of the northern population gave it a greater proportion of votes, but in the Senate the even balance of slave and free states required that only a few northerners needed to support the South in order to hold the House in check. The clearest case came in the Wilmot Proviso votes of 1846 and 1847 when the Senate rejected the Proviso after its passage in the House. There were 320 Congressional doughfaces in the period from 1820 to 1860; many of them had originally lived in the South and had migrated north. Franklin Pierce and James Buchanan were both commonly referred to as doughface presidents. Southerners split with the doughfaces over the issue of popular sovereignty. By the late 1850s Southerners were no longer content to simply rely on preventing the Federal government from interfering with slavery in the territories, they now insisted on Federal intervention to protect slavery and prevent any decision on slavery until a territory prepared a constitution as part of an application for statehood. Northern Democrats and Stephen A. Douglas could not go that far. This southern failure to support popular sovereignty ended the influence of doughfaces as an agent for sectional compromise.

Martin Van Buren's Presidency

·Panic of 1837

In part, as a result of the specie circular, banks restricted credit and called in loans; depositors rushed to their local institutions and attempted to withdraw their funds causing a run on the banks. Unemployment touched every part of the nation and food riots occurred in a number of large cities. Construction companies were unable to meet their obligations, sparking the failure of railroad and canal projects, and the hardest hit were thousands of land speculators who were ruined.

·Conflicts with Great Britain

1. **Copyright Laws**—56 British authors asked for copyright protection from U.S. "piracy," but the Congress ignored them. Writers traveling to the U.S. were quick to point out that the U.S. was made up of "boors, blusterers, and cheats." American authors replied attacking England as well in this war of the words.
2. **Debt Default**—During the hard times following the Panic of 1837 that would last until 1843, state governments and private corporations defaulted to their British creditors on loans that had been made.
3. *Caroline* **Affair**—The *Caroline* Affair began in 1837 when Canadian authorities seized and burned the American vessel *Caroline*, on the U.S. shore of the Niagara River near Buffalo. The ship was leased to run troops to Navy Island for the support of Canadian revolutionaries led by William MacKenzie. A Canadian militiaman killed an American but ultimately the Canadian was acquitted. Hard feelings ensued between the U.S. and Canada but diplomacy kept hostilities to a minimum.

4. **Aroostook War**—Left over from the Treaty of Paris ending the Revolutionary War was a boundary dispute between Maine and New Brunswick. By the 1830s rival gangs of lumberjacks inhabited the area near the Aroostook River and were preparing for conflict. Hostilities were averted when Winfield Scott accompanied by Federal soldiers arranged a truce and both Maine and New Brunswick withdrew their militia. The dispute was referred to a boundary commission and eventually settled with the Webster-Ashburton Treaty of 1842.

Independent Treasury

Van Buren's plan to solve the currency problem that had resulted from the destruction of the 2nd Bank of the U.S. was the Independent Treasury. His 1837 proposal for this system did not pass until 1840. It gave the Treasury control of all federal funds and had a legal tender clause that required by 1843 that all payments to be made in legal tender rather than in state bank notes. The act was short-lived, had little impact, and was repealed in 1843.

Preemption Act

Law passed in 1841 by Congress in response to the demands of the Western states that squatters would be allowed to preempt lands—that is, own the lands that they had illegally occupied. Pioneers and frontiersmen often settled on public lands before they could be surveyed and auctioned by the government. At first, the squatter claims were not recognized, but in 1830 the first of a series of temporary preemption laws was passed by Congress. Eastern states opposed preemption primarily because they saw the encouragement of western migration as a threat to their labor supply. They also saw it as wrong to reward illegal behavior.

UNIT VIII
MULTIPLE-CHOICE QUESTIONS

Questions 1-3 refer to the following political cartoon:

BORN TO COMMAND.

OF VETO MEMORY.

HAD I BEEN CONSULTED.

KING ANDREW THE FIRST.

1. Which of the following is the best interpretation of the meaning of the above political cartoon?

(A) Jackson wanted to have the same prestige that European monarchs had
(B) His imperious nature included trampling the Constitution and use of the veto to create one-man rule
(C) The throne and scepter symbolized a republics equality with the royalty of Europe
(D) Political opponents depicted him as a weakling and a coward

2. Which of the following could be a considered to be a continuity in United States History similar to the depiction of Jackson?

(A) Expansionist presidencies of Polk and Taylor
(B) Progressive presidencies of Roosevelt and Wilson
(C) Conservative presidencies of Coolidge and Hoover
(D) Imperial presidencies of Johnson and Nixon

3. Which of the following actions by President Andrew Jackson best supports the interpretation of his presidency in the cartoon shown above?

(A) Expulsion of the Cherokee nation from Georgia and Tennessee
(B) Refusal to support the admission of Texas to the union as a slave state
(C) Veto of the re-charter bill for the 2nd Bank of the United States
(D) Adoption of the Independent Treasury plan

115

Questions 4-7 refer to the following:

"...voting became more widespread and more important, thus competition between candidates increased, manifested in less concern for issues than for character assassinations of opponents.... a new party system [developed], which required money, people, and organizations to run campaigns and get out the vote. Jackson, a firm believer in the "common man," used all of this to gain the presidency... Jackson's supporters...came from all regions of the country; they were united by suspicion of special privilege and large business corporations, belief in freedom of economic opportunity and political freedom (for white males), the conviction that ordinary citizens could perform the tasks of government, and support for states' rights. Jackson ran his administration according to such principles, as he employed the spoils system..., killed the second Bank of the United States, and preferred to leave local improvement projects to the states."

John Garraty, *The American Nation: A History of the United States*, 1995

4. The political term frequently associated with the Jacksonian era is

   (A) democracy
   (B) republic
   (C) confederation
   (D) popular sovereignty

5. Although the two movements differed the Jacksonians liked to trace their origins back to the

   (A) anti-federalist
   (B) federalist
   (C) Jeffersonians
   (D) Whigs

6. From 1828 to 1860 the Jacksonians became the dominant political party and were called which Party?

   (A) National Republicans
   (B) Federalist
   (C) Democratic-Republicans
   (D) Democrats

7. The issues the Jacksonians believed in included

   (A) support for the national bank, a protective tariff, and internal improvements
   (B) distrust of privilege and large businesses, belief in rotation in office, support for states' rights
   (C) reforms like temperance, abolitionism, mental health, prisons, schools, vegetarianism, peace
   (D) Homestead Act, Wilmot Proviso, Preemption, Nativism, Sabbatarianism

Questions 8-10 refer to the following:

"No man in this country has ever been subjected to such a torrent of applause, and few men have been less prepared to withstand it by education, reflection, and experience.... The country expected great things of the victor of New Orleans.... He swept down into the province [Florida] like a tornado, and drove the poor remnant of the Seminoles into the Everglades. He assumed, he exercised all the prerogatives of an absolute sovereign. He raised troops... invaded a foreign territory, made war on his brother sovereign, the King of Spain, put his subjects to death without trial; shot [Robert C.] Ambrister, and permitted the murder of [Alexander] Arbuthnot, both British subjects. He came home, not in chains...but in triumph, to receive the approval of the President...and the applause of the people. What an effect such an experience as this was likely have upon such a mind as his, we need not say.... He reappeared in Florida as its Governor...his conduct there in 1821...[was] violent, arrogant and disgraceful to the civilization of his country.... [he was] like a madman."

James Parton, *Life of Andrew Jackson*, 1860

8. Parton's description of Andrew Jackson's activities in Florida from 1816-1821 formed the basis of the Whig Schoolof historiography that saw Jackson as

   (A) a strict constitutionalist
   (B) a benign stward of the presidency
   (C) unqualified by background, breeding, and temperment to tbe president
   (D) a warrior who saved the nation in a time of distress

9. Which later action by Andrew Jackson after he became President in 1829 was foreshadowed by Parton's interpretation of his activities in Florida from 1816-1821?

   (A) Trail of Tears
   (B) Bank re-charter veto
   (C) Battle of the Toasts with John C. Calhoun
   (D) Adoption of the Force Bill

10. Parton accuses Jackson of all of the following offences EXCEPT

   (A) illegally invading a foreign country
   (B) being unprepared by education, reflection, and experience for the adulation he received
   (C) acting like a King
   (D) going against the wishes of the people

Questions 11-13 refer to the following:

"Even in those states and territories where suffrage was broadly exercised, men who owned and speculated in land and had money in the bank were often accepted as natural leaders... Such beneficiaries of popular confidence developed a stronger faith and wisdom and justice of popular decisions than did the gentlemen of the older seaboard states, where class lines were no longer fluid.... A man like Jackson who had been on the conservative side of economic issues in Tennessee could become the leader of a national democratic movement without feeling guilty of inconsistency. When we find a planter aristocrat of this breed expressing absolute confidence in popular judgment, it is unfair to dismiss him as a demagogue. He became a favorite of the people, and might easily come to believe that the people chose well."

Richard Hofstadter, *The American Political Tradition: And the Men Who Made It*, 1948

11. In the passage above, Hofstadter attempts to bridge the gap between

(A) those who see Jackson as a conservative aristocrat or as a popular democratic leader
(B) a natural leader that Jackson represents and a developed leader of the upper class
(C) the rigidity of the class lines of older seaboard states and the fluidity of the planter aristocracy
(D) Jackson's absolute confidence in popular judgment and his leadership of a democratic movement

12. The Preemption Act of 1841 that allowed "squatters" to purchase up to 160 acres of land they were illegally occupying is based on which concept presented by Hofstadter

(A) American Plan
(B) popular democratic judgement
(C) conservative economic principles
(D) popular sovereignty

13. Some historian's interpretation of Jackson and his relationship with the people is that

(A) Jackson represented an elite position of authority because of his superior wisdom and knowledge
(B) he followed the leadership of the gentlemen of the older seaboard states
(C) his inconsistent position as a conservative land speculator and as well as a leader of the masses greatly troubled him
(D) there was reciprocity of trust between Jackson and the people—they had their faith in each other

Questions 14-15 refer to the following:

"Whigs tended to respond more favorably than Democrats to the 'church and state' concept. Moreover, the Whig political philosophy postulated an activist, positive state, responsible for improving the material and moral well being of society and capable of wielding broad national powers. In contrast the Democratic philosophy postulated a negative, passive state in general, and a restricted, passive federal government in particular. [Abolitionist were] originally attracted to the Whig Party... because its active political doctrine closely corresponded to their activist religious doctrine... the state must act to purge society of moral evils... men convinced that organized collective action contributed to human progress tended more to vote Whig than Democrat.... Whigs tended toward collectivism, Democrats toward individualism."

Lee Benson, *The Concept of Jacksonian Democracy: New York as a Test Case*, 1961

14. The driving force behind the Abolitionist's attraction to the Whig Party was that its political doctrine fit with their religious beliefs, which is similar to the ideas and actions of

(A) the moral majority and the Republican Party of the 1980s
(B) the Populist movement
(C) liberalism of the Great Society
(D) optimism of the reformers at the beginning of the 20th century

15. Ultimately, the Whig Party as a national force disappeared after the election of 1852 primarily because it

(A) could not reconcile the inherent conflict between church and state
(B) fell apart because they did not have an answer over the issue of slavery in the territories
(C) lacked the ideas to compete in politics at the national level
(D) its leaders were men of second rate qualities who could not match the intellectualism of the Democrats

UNIT IX

ANTEBELLUM ERA: ECONOMIC & SOCIAL

The time period after the War of 1812 and up to the Civil War brought forth many economic and social changes including, in the words of historian Charles Sellers, the "market revolution." America was transformed from local and regional markets to a world market. As a society it threw off its dependence from Europe and developed its own cultural institutions in areas like art and literature. During this antebellum period a great many things were going on that were not a part of the political climate of sectionalism and slavery that dominated the political scene.

Economics

· Westward Migration
Americans moved to the west in large numbers as they frequently despoiled the land by over-planting (especially tobacco) and needed new land to farm. Some did this legally by purchasing the new land while others squatted on land that they did not own, thus, establishing the principle of "squatter sovereignty."

· Primitive Agriculture
Pioneers moving into the Ohio River Valley and the areas of the Old Northwest in the early 19th century went with a minimum of capital and equipment. Rifle, axe and a few household and farm implements including a two-wheel wooden cart, crude plow, sickle, cradle, and some hoes and shovels, along with a cow, a team of oxen, and maybe a horse was all that he needed to plant corn and garden vegetables. It was a type of farming that had not changed since the colonial times. It would be replaced by the market revolution.

· Transportation Revolution, 1800-1840
1. **National Road (Cumberland)**—Built in stages with federal money it stretched from Cumberland Maryland to Vandalia Illinois. This would provide the important infrastructure for economic development although it would become less important after 1850 with the advent of canals, railroads, and the telegraph.

2. **Steamboats**—Starting in 1807 with Robert Fulton's successful commercial launching of the *Clermont*, steamboats enabled freight and passengers to move up-river as well as down. Over time they became larger and more opulent with a tremendous increase in tonnage as well as ornate cabins, private staterooms, bars, gambling casinos, and bands. Steamboat racing would take place later in the century.

3. **Erie Canal**—Begin in 1817 and completed in 1825 under the leadership of Governor Dewitt Clinton, this 40 foot wide, 4 foot deep ditch was 363 miles long and included 83 locks to lift boats over 600 feet. Yankee ingenuity in the form of stump pullers, new mortar replacing expensive English cement, aqueducts, and the use of Dupont blasting powder showed the world how enterprising Americans could be. Its success in cutting transportation charges, raising land values, and capturing for New York most of the western trade that would now go up-river in steamboats to the Great Lakes through the canal to New York city led to canal "mania" in other states. Its importance would be supplanted in the 1850s by railroads.

4. **Railroads**—Starting in 1830 with the Baltimore and Ohio laying 13 miles of track, by 1860 there were more than 31,000 miles as the railroad surpassed all earlier forms of transportation in importance. Railroad "mania" would surpass canal mania and much of the funding for its growth came from foreign, usually British, investors. As with the canals, much of the labor was supplied by Irish immigrants (later Chinese immigrants would build the railroads in the west).

5. **Turnpikes**—Starting in the 1790s with the building of a private road in Lancaster Pennsylvania these turnpikes or toll roads would aid both commerce and westward expansion, as a number of them would be built in the early 19th century.

·Inventions & Innovations

1. **Cotton Gin**—It's invention by Ely Whitney transformed the economy of the South from tobacco, indigo, rice, and sugar cane to one that was based strictly on short-staple, upland, cotton. Most of the production was in the new lands in the South and Southwest.

2. **Interchangeable Parts**—This concept taken from clockmakers was developed by Eli Whitney in 1803 in the manufacture of muskets and would lead to mass production and later the assembly line process.

3. **Reaper**—A 1834 invention by Cyrus McCormick that enabled farmers to use a horse drawn machine to cut 12 acres of wheat a day instead of the two or three acres that a man could do with a cradle-scythe.

4. **Steel Plow**—Invented by John Deere in 1837 it enabled the farmer to double his productivity in the labor of plowing his field which made the cultivation of more acreage possible. It replaced the iron plow that often broke when tilling the soil.

5. **Telegraph**—Samuel F. B. Morse's 1844 invention enabled people to instantly communicate with each other over distance; it was a boon to business decision making and was the first of many inventions in communications.

6. **Sewing Machine**—Invented by Elias Howe in 1846, and perfected by Isaac Singer, it gave another boost to northern industrialization especially in the textile industry.

·Commercial Agriculture

The combination of the transportation revolution and scientific inventions brought about a change in agricultural production in the Old Northwest. The need for cash to purchase land along with capital for the new machines changed farming from subsistence agriculture to production for sale. This would become a major component in the development of a market economy in the Antebellum period.

·Samuel Slater

This 21 year old factory worker evaded British law against emigration of textile workers in coming to the U.S. with the plans for the Arkwright machine system in his head. With funding from Rhode Island businessman Moses Brown, Slater built a mill that was the first American factory to successfully produce cotton yarn with water-powered machines.

·Lowell Factory System

In 1823, a fully mechanized complex of new textile mills was built by Francis Lowell. With the production process fully mechanized the company recruited young farm girls from the surrounding countryside for their labor supply. In order to attract these women and to reassure their families, the owners developed a paternalistic approach to management that became known as the Lowell system. The mill workers were housed in clean, well-run boardinghouses, were strictly supervised both at work and at home, and were paid decent wages. The farm girls became excellent employees, and their self-improvement program (including a literary magazine) drew international attention. Most of the women worked for a few years and then returned home to marry. Despite its success, in 1834 an economic downturn led to the mills' first wage cuts. In the 1840s, managers instituted a speedup, requiring higher and higher output for the same hourly wage which led to the women going on strike. The women formed the Lowell Female Labor Reform Association and tried to appeal to their employers, and then to the state legislature through petitions, for relief. These attempts failed to bring any action. After 1848, conditions deteriorated further, as New England's textile industry began to suffer from overexpansion. Seeking cheaper labor, the mill owners turned increasingly to Irish immigrants and in the process discontinued the management policies they had devised to attract female workers from the farms. By the 1850s, the Lowell system had been abandoned and replaced by a more exploitive system based on cheap labor and poorer working conditions.

·Clipper Ships

Beginning in the late 1840's American shipbuilders started to build a new kind of merchant vessel—the Clipper ship. A Clipper ship was technically a sailing ship with three masts on which sat a large expanse of square sails. It was designed to carry a small, highly profitable cargo over long distances at high speeds. The clipper's masts could reach as high as a twenty story building and they carried more sails and more kinds of sails than any other ship. The long lines of the ship combined with the enormous driving power of the sails allowed the ships to "*clip*" along at speeds that earlier generations of sailors never dreamed of and later generations never matched. The best of the Clipper ships could cover more than 400 miles a day and speed meant big profits for the owners and captains. Thousands of people were eager to get to the California gold fields and would pay premium prices to get there by the fastest clipper ship. Tea from China brought a good price in New York and London, but it had to be delivered before it lost its taste. In time Clipper ships could not compete with steamships with their larger carrying capacity and reliability (not dependent on the winds) and soon went out of business.

·Pony Express

This short-lived method of carrying the mail to the west and back lasted for 1 1/2 (1860-61) years but consistently lost money and was rendered obsolete by the building of the transcontinental railroad.

·Stagecoach

Another form of transportation, immortalized by Mark Twain in *Roughing It*, was the stagecoach. The California gold fields and mail contracts from the government kept it going for while but even with the merger of the two main companies Wells Fargo and Butterfield in 1861, it could not compete with the railroad.

·Conestoga Wagon

This heavy freight-carrying vehicle originated in the Conestoga region of Pennsylvania and was first used by farmers to carry heavy loads long distances before there were railroads to convey produce to markets. It was also used to carry manufactured goods across the Alleghenies to frontier stores and settlements and to bring back the frontier produce. The transportation of goods by wagon train developed into a major business employing thousands of wagons before the railroads crossed the mountains. It became the favored mode of transportation for those going west along the Oregon and California trails before the transcontinental railroad supplanted it.

·Legal Protections

The Marshall Court was responsible for a number of decisions that encouraged commercial enterprise. In a series of cases it asserted federal power over state governments by striking down state laws that hindered commerce.

1. *Fletcher v. Peck*—Attempt by a subsequent legislature to rescind a contract by its predecessors who were bribed was stopped by the Supreme Court when they ruled it was not within their province to inquire into the motives of a legislature and the subsequent rescinding act impaired the "obligation of contracts" clause of the Constitution. This 1810 (Yazoo land) case was the first time the Court ruled that a state law was unconstitutional.

2. *Dartmouth College v. Woodward*—In 1816, the New Hampshire legislature attempted to change Dartmouth College—a privately funded institution—into a state university by altering its royal charter. The court in a 6-1 decision declared that the original charter, even though it was with the Crown, was a private contract that could not be broken by the democratic majority of the state legislature. This decision encouraged business growth by placing charters of existing private corporations outside the scope of control by the states that chartered them.

3. *Gibbons v. Ogden*—In this 1824 case the court kept the state of New York from giving a monopoly over a steamboat line to Robert Fulton inventor of the steamboat. His invention was protected by a patent but its commercial application was not. This curb on state authority freed transportation from state restraints and invalidated many similar monopoly privileges that other states had granted. It reinforced the constitutional principle that the national government had jurisdiction over interstate commerce.

4. *Charles River Bridge v. Warren Bridge*—In this 1837 case new Chief Justice Roger Taney supported economic opportunity by ruling against the claims of the bridge company asking for a monopoly. He asserted that ambiguous clauses must operate against the corporation and in favor of the public. The decision challenged the Marshall court's earlier interpretation of the contract clause established in *Dartmouth College v. Woodward* as it attempted to balance states rights and private property rights.

·Market Revolution

Term used to describe the dramatic change in the economy that took place in the first half of the 19th century. Reaching its peak in the Jacksonian era it also gave rise to new forms of social life, consciousness, politics, and reform. Along with nationalizing the economy through the inter-dependence of the various regions of the country, the market economy also changed the individual from the independent, self-reliant, yeoman farmer, artisan, or shop-owner to one who was dependent on market forces far beyond his ability to control or even have much say over. The earlier transportation and scientific revolutions made this transformation possible and the market revolution in the antebellum period would continue into the post Civil War period as the Industrial Revolution.

Social and Cultural

·Religious Movements

A great deal of religious ferment and change occurred during time period from 1800 to 1860. Just as Deism had challenged the earlier Calvinist based religions, the new religious movements would challenge both traditional Puritanism as well as Deism.

1. **Western Revivalism**—Started by James Mc Gready in Kentucky around 1800 the best known of the circuit rider preachers was Peter Cartwright, an unschooled master of the stump speech and the polemics of religious revivalism. To Easterners, the jiggling, baying, and howling that accompanied the service seemed more like the work of Satan than God. But these physical manifestations of worship had a certain appeal in the frontier environment.

2. **Unitarianism**—Although Deism was in retreat, many rationalists thinkers turned to Unitarianism which denied the divinity of Jesus and held that God existed in only one person, not the orthodox trinity. Founded by William Ellery Channing, this intellectual form of Protestantism with its emphasis on the essential goodness of human nature, free will and salvation by good works, appealed to many intellectuals.

3. **2nd Great Awakening**—This was another movement that grew out of the opposition to Deism. By the end of the 18th century, many educated Americans no longer professed traditional Christian beliefs. In part, it was a reaction to the secularism of the age. This religious revival spread westward in the first half of the 19th century and it strengthened the Methodists and the Baptists, as well as bringing about a new form of religious expression—the camp meeting.

4. **"They Gathered at the River"**—Term used to describe the great revival meetings that were started by Charles Grandison Finney, a charismatic lawyer-turned-itinerant preacher, who argued against the belief that a Calvinist God controlled the destiny of human beings. He told congregations throughout the northern United States that they were "moral free agents" who could obtain salvation through their own efforts—but they must hurry because time was short. Success was achieved in the up-state New York "burned-over district" where prayer meetings, conversions, and confessions of sin were frequent. Finney and other preachers tried to be entertaining and to appeal to the average citizen. Their approach and the new techniques of evangelizing—protracted meetings, communitywide campaigns, the "anxious bench" for those wrestling with the decision to convert, testimony meetings for the converted—all worked and in one year church membership grew nationally by 100,000 souls.

5. **Impact of Revivalism and 2nd Great Awakening**—The revival movement also inspired or contributed to many secular reform movements, including sabbatarianism, temperance, peace movement, abolitionism, anti-dueling, moral reform, public education, philanthropic endeavors, and utopian socialism. It especially appealed to women, many of whom were encouraged to become missionaries and lay preachers and others who would become active in the women's rights movement.

6. **Transcendentalism**—Much of this philosophical-religious movement came from dissatisfaction with Calvinist orthodoxy and Unitarian rationalism. The formation of the movement took place in 1836 with the establishment of the Transcendental Club of Boston. The early transcendentalists included the essayist and poet Ralph Waldo Emerson, the feminist, social reformer, and author Margaret Fuller, minister Theodore Parker, and the naturalist and author Henry David Thoreau. German, Oriental, and Romantic ideas influenced the movement's emphasis on God in nature and a vision of the universe in which God, the world, spirit, and matter, existed in an intimate symbolic relationship. Transcendentalists maintained that truth transcended the senses and it could not be found by observation alone. Every individual possessed an inner-light (borrowed from the Quakers) that could illuminate the highest truth and put individuals in direct touch with God or the "Oversoul." The movement was short-lived, a bit too mystical for most Americans, and it died out in the 1850s. Its influence lived on far beyond the movement as it had an impact on many subsequent individuals and movements.

·Immigration

A major change occurred after 1832 as the population of immigrants went from 1.5 % in the 1820s to more than 11% by 1860. Encouraged by industrialists who needed unskilled workers and western states who needed population this would be the first of many waves of immigrants to the United States. Two groups would dominate this early immigration.

1. **Irish**—Because of the potato blight a famine devastated Ireland in the 1840s killing a million people. More than 1.5 million Irish would migrate to the U.S. settling in the large east coast cities like New York and Boston. They established the Catholic Church in America, parochial schools, and the men did the grunt labor of digging the canals and laying the track for railroads. The women replaced the New England farm girls in the textile mills and became the live-in domestic servants for the rich. The Irish faced a great deal of xenophobia as signs were common that said, "Help Wanted: No Irish Need Apply." Despite this discrimination they flourished and soon took to politics, law enforcement, and the priesthood.

2. **Germans**—Coming for a variety of reasons after 1848, political, economic, and social, German immigrants became more numerous than the Irish after 1854. German immigrants tended to move to farms or frontier towns in the Midwest and were less active politically than the Irish. Many were skilled artisans who found good paying jobs in the developing market economy. In Cincinnati and St. Louis, they sought to reestablish old German lifestyles, setting up German fraternal lodges, coffee circles, and educational and music societies. German immigrants carried important aspects of German culture with them, which quickly became integral parts of American culture, including the Christmas tree, Christmas gift giving, kindergarten, and the gymnasium. Comprising a middle class group they fit into American society without being discriminated against compared to other immigrant groups.

·Communitarianism

The 1820s to the 1850s was the great age of American communitarianism, a form of utopian socialism that existed in America because it had been relatively easy to establish in a generally tolerant, prosperous nation with abundant land. These social organizations in small cooperative, partially collectivist communities, reached their greatest peak of activity during periods of religious and social ferment like the 2nd Great Awakening. A reaction to the changes brought forth by the market revolution also contributed to the growth of the movement. One of the ironies of utopian communities—and a source of their recurring strength—is that of all forms of social action, they presented an all-encompassing alternative to the way things were; yet, did so by withdrawing from, rather than directly confronting, the existing social order. Many of these movements originated in the "burned-over" district of up-state New York and subsequently would move further west. Their economic success was often based on land values going up.

1. **Shakers**—This sect founded by an Englishwoman, Mother Ann Lee (the female side of God), was established in North America in 1774 and by the 1840s it had approximately six thousand members scattered in 20 communities. They were bound together by their shared faith and a commitment to common property, celibacy, confession of sins, equality of men and women, pacifism and separation from the world. Their name came from the fact that they partook of the physical manifestations of worship as they shook and trembled to rid themselves of evil. First called Shaking Quakers, this was shortened to Shakers. As they sought to create their vision of "heaven on earth," they applied the virtues of simplicity, purity and perfection to their work and to themselves. Function and quality was emphasized in their products designs and they were known for the high quality of their handicraft work, especially their furniture. Because of their policies of celibacy and not proselytizing it was not surprising the movement died out after the Civil War. Their rustic furniture is prized by antique collectors today.

2. **Mormons**—Started by Joseph Smith after he had a number of charismatic experiences in the "burned-over" district of upstate New York, the movement called the Church of Jesus Christ of Latter Day Saints moved to Kirtland Ohio, Missouri, and then Nauvoo Illinois. Opposition from neighbors who resented the cooperation which contributed to the economic success of the movement, suspicion that Mormon bloc voting would lead to a theocracy, and rumors that Smith was practicing polygamy (he called it plural marriage), led to his arrest. A mob stormed the jail and killed Smith and his brother. Brigham Young led the remaining Mormons on an exodus to the far reaches of Mexican territory and established a community at Great Salt Lake in what was to be called Deseret (later Utah). After this area became part of the U.S., Federal troops and the Mormons fought a guerilla war in 1857-1858 before working out a tenuous truce. The movement survived many schisms but continued to flourish and after it abandoned polygamy it gained statehood as Utah.

3. **Millerites**—Led by William Miller this "burned-over" district group interpreted the Bible to mean Christ would return to earth on March 22, 1844. Thousands of followers gave away their possessions in anticipation of the event and dressed in white robes as they climbed up on roofs and hilltops to be closer to Jesus when he came down from the heavens. When nothing happened Miller, undeterred, set a new date of October 22. When nothing happened this time it became known as the "Great Disappointment." After Miller's death in 1849, the movement splintered over doctrinal differences. This fragmentation ultimately gave rise to a variety of denominations, including the Jehovah Witnesses and the Seventh-Day Adventists.

4. **Oneida**—The most radical experiment in social and religious thinking was the Oneida community founded by John Humphrey Noyes and called Perfectionism or Bible Communism. It's most controversial belief was "complex marriage," the idea that every man was married to every woman and vice versa. Forced to flee from Putney, Vermont the movement moved to Oneida, N.Y. (burned over district) where communal living was established. The community was successful economically (known for their silverware) but by 1879, internal dissension had arisen and outside hostility became so strong that Noyes went to Canada after being accused of statutory rape. After adopting monogamy the community continued its commercial success but became socially conventional.

5. **Fourierism**—Philosophy of social reform developed by the French social theorist Charles Fourier that advocated the transformation of society into self-sufficient, independent "phalanges" (phalanxes) of 1620 people. Albert Brisbane, who renamed it Associationism, transplanted Fourierism to the United States. He lectured and launched a Fourier community and his book explaining it, *Social Destiny of Man* (1840), attracted widespread attention when Horace Greeley offered Brisbane space in the "New York Tribune" to spread his views. Ultimately, all the Fourier

communities (approximately 40 of them) failed as was generally true of most utopian socialist communitarian movements that were secular and had no religious base.

6. **New Harmony**—Founded by English industrialist-philanthropist Robert Owen who addressed Congress in 1824 and invited the industrious and well disposed to join his settlement. In reality, New Harmony attracted crackpots and slackers along with the hard working and serious minded. This secular utopian commune in Indiana attracted a great deal of fanfare in 1825 built on land purchased from another utopian socialist group, the Rappites. Putting into practice Owen's theories of socialism and human betterment, the constitution provided for absolute equality of property, labor, and opportunity along with freedom of speech and action. The absence of authority brought about a state of anarchy amongst the 1,000 in the community and Owen had to admit to failure in 1827 and withdrew his economic support.

7. **Brook Farm**—Founded by George Ripley and other Transcendentalists in 1841 as a communal cooperative society in which members shared manual and intellectual labor as men and women living in a simple environment of a cultivated society. In 1845, Ripley attempted to bring more organization to the enterprise by adopting the Fourier model of phalanx organization. A fire destroyed the new building and the commune could not pay the 5% interest agreed to by its investors and it failed. Ripley worked for 20 years to pay off the debt. A failure economically, the commune was a social success as entertainment, music, culture, spirited conversation, and a successful progressive educational program gave it *cachet*. Nathaniel Hawthorne was one of many who visited and he later wrote a satire of it called the *Blythdale Romance*.

·Hudson River School

The most important painters of the antebellum period were this group of landscape artists who became the first native school of "American Art." Dating from the 1820s, it was a loosely organized group of painters who took as their subject the unique naturalness of the American continent, starting with the Hudson River Valley region in New York, but eventually extending in time and space all the way to California in the 1870s. Their time period was one of momentous social, political and economic change in American history, and the work of the Hudson River School artists represents part of the process of nationalization. Prominent artists included Thomas Cole, George Innes, Asher Durand, and Jasper Cropsey.

·Literature

After the War of 1812, a wave of nationalism contributed to the development of an indigenous American literature, separate and distinct from Europe.

1. **Washington Irving**—His *Knickerbocker History of New York* and *Sketch Book* and individual short tales like "Rip Van Winkle," and the "Legend of Sleepy Hollow" described the Dutch experience in New York which made him the first American writer to achieve world wide fame.

2. **James Fenimore Cooper**—Created an original American literature with his *Leatherstocking Tales* and the frontier character of Natty Bumppo. His depiction of the contrasting values of the rugged men of the wilderness with artificiality of modern civilization became a reoccurring theme in American literature.

3. **Nathaniel Hawthorne**—Puritanism and its heavy hand were dominant themes in his works like *The Scarlett Letter* and *The Fall of the House of Usher*.

4. **Herman Melville**—Went to sea at a young age and captured the experience in works such as *Typee* and *Billy Budd*. His major work *Moby Dick*, a symbolic and allegorical tale of good and evil was ignored by both critics and the general public until decades later.

·Phrenology

At a time when conventional medicine was sorely lacking, the idea that the mind and human behavior could be examined by analyzing the bumps and depressions of the human skull gained wide popularity in the antebellum period. Businesses would use phrenology charts to choose suitable employees and young women would subject their fiancés to phrenology analysis before agreeing to marriage. Drawing phrenology charts became a popular parlor pastime during the 1840s and 1850s as Americans attempted to better themselves by understanding science—even pseudo-science.

·Dueling

Dueling imported from Europe lost favor in the North at the time of Burr-Hamilton duel but remained a part of the social code of the South until the Civil War. For the most part, only gentlemen dueled and southerners required that only men of the same social class could duel. The smoothbore flintlocks used often misfired. Button Gwinnet, who had signed the Declaration of Independence, was shot down by General Lachlan McIntosh and Commodore Stephen Decatur of the United States Navy, an experienced duelist, died at the hands of another commodore. Even Abraham Lincoln narrowly averted a battle with swords by apologizing. Benjamin Franklin and George Washington were among the most prominent Americans to condemn dueling. Religious and civic officials worked hard to stop duels. Due to the partisan nature of their work, politicians frequently received challenges—as did newspaper editors and attorneys. Andrew Jackson, future president of the United States, earned a reputation as a formidable duelist. His honor suffered, however, after a duel against Charles Dickinson in 1806. Dickinson fired his pistol, slightly wounding Jackson. Jackson's weapon misfired —which according to dueling rules counted as a shot. Technically, the duel should have ended there. But Jackson pulled his hammer back again and fired, this time killing Dickinson. In the eyes of many, Jackson's behavior amounted to murder. In the South, where the chivalrous novels of Walter Scott held sway, dueling remained the preferred way to defend one's honor—or even to commit murder. For every man who gloried in the duel, there were many others who feared it. Particularly in the South, where men who refused to duel would be "posted." A statement accusing them of cowardice would be hung in public areas or published in a newspaper or pamphlet. By the time of the Civil War, dueling was in decline, even in the South.

UNIT IX
MULTIPLE-CHOICE QUESTIONS

Questions 1-4 refer to the following chart:

Value of Leading United States Exports for Selected Periods 1815-1860				
Article	1816-1820		1856-1860	
	Value in millions	% of total	Value in millions	% of total
Cotton	121.5	39	744.6	54
Wheat and flour	50.6	16	157.7	11
Tobacco	47.5	15	86.5	6
Manufactured goods	21.1	7	167.3	12
Lumber	15.5	5	29.3	2
Rice	13.1	4	11.3	1
Corn and corn meal	7.6	2	24.7	2
Fish	6.8	2	3.9	0.3
Pork	4.2	1	53.9	4
Beef and beef products	3.7	1	21.8	2

1. The above chart supports which interpretation of the South on the eve of the Civil War?

    (A) Diversified agriculture
    (B) Grain crops dominate
    (C) Cotton is king
    (D) Manufacturing rules

2. Exports between 1816 and 1860 had which of the following characteristics?

    (A) The product with the greatest % increase in value from 1816-1820 to 1856- 1860 was manufactured goods
    (B) Tobacco suffered the greatest loss in % terms from 1816-1820 to 1856-1860 and also suffered an monetary loss in the value of the product
    (C) Beef and beef products tripled in value from 1816 to 1860
    (D) Tobacco went from 15% of total exports to 9% which was a 40% loss, the greatest loss of any product

3. As a percentage of total exports the only product that remained the same between 1815 and 1860 was

    (A) corn and corn meal
    (B) beef and beef products
    (C) wheat and flour
    (D) lumber

4. A number of products decreased their market share between 1815 and 1860 but the two who produced fewer products in absolute terms were

    (A) wheat & flour and tobacco
    (B) manufactured goods and cotton
    (C) pork and lumber
    (D) rice and fish

130

Questions 5-8 refer to the following:

"During the years from 1830 to 1860 the nation witnessed the rise—and also, happily, the fall—of a great anti-Catholic crusade. It took various forms. Some anti-Catholics were content to issue moderate propaganda arguing that the Bible proved Protestantism right and Romanism wrong. Others... described the Church as the 'whore of Babylon' and the 'abomination of abominations,' they attached priests and nuns for imaginary sexual perversions, they portrayed the pope as the Antichrist.... Occasionally anti-Catholics turned violent, as did the mob which burned an Ursuline convent... both local and national political organizations tried to restrict the power of Catholics and other immigrants as well; their efforts culminated in the American, or Know-Nothing, party which acquired amazing strength by 1855."

C. S. Griffin, *The Ferment of Reform*, 1830-1860, 1967

5. The great anti-Catholic crusade from 1830 to 1860 was caused primarily by which of the following events in United States history?

   (A) Immigration of the Irish and the southern Germans
   (B) Manifest destiny bringing in large areas of Mexican territory
   (C) Development of a national economy through the market revolution
   (D) Sectionalism becoming the dominant characteristic of political life

6. To a certain extent anti-Catholicism was put to rest in the mid-20th century with the

   (A) merger of the Roman Catholic and mainstream Protestant churches
   (B) inter-marriage of Catholics with non-Catholics
   (C) election of John F. Kennedy, a practicing Catholic as President
   (D) acceptance by the Church of modern religious practices like the non-Latin mass

7. The American or Know-Nothing Party became the second largest political party in the House of Representatives with 52 members to the Democrats 82 in 1854 but their numbers would plummet in 1856 as which new party took most of their membership?

   (A) Democrats
   (B) Republicans
   (C) Whigs
   (D) Free Soil

8. A primary reason for the anti-Catholic crusade was the large number of immigrants who were arriving from

   (A) the Balkans
   (B) Scandinavia
   (C) Mediterranean countries
   (D) Ireland

Questions 9-10 refer to the following chart:

Estimated Gross Tonnage and Value of Domestic Commerce in 1852				
	Millions of Tons		Billions of Dollars	
	Amount	%	Amount	%
Coastal Trade	41	59	3.3	60
Canal	18	26	1.2	21
Railway	11	15	1.1	19

9. From the chart above all of the following statements are true regarding domestic commerce in 1852 EXCEPT

   (A) canal and railroad commerce comprised 40% of the total amount of commerce in monetary value
   (B) moving products by navigable rivers and protected inland waterways was the most important part of domestic commerce in both tonnage and dollar amounts
   (C) the man made movement of goods exceeded the natural movement of goods by 1852
   (D) the railroads trailed both canals and coastal waterways in economic importance in 1852

10. Which of the following interpretations best fits with the above chart?

   (A) Although canal commerce was more than 20% greater than railroad commerce in tonnage it only exceeded railroad tonnage by 2% in the amount of money earned
   (B) Compared to its tonnage the $ value for Railroad was increasing while Canal was decreasing and Coastal trade (shipping) was staying the same
   (C) Canal and Railroad production were just about equal to shipping in 1852
   (D) The movement of goods was equally divided between shipping, canals, and the railroads

Questions 11-13 refer to the following:

"The strong desire for material well-being is an important factor in the economic development of the United States... the habit of hard work and the desire to 'get ahead' became imbedded in the American character.... In the Virginia colony, John Smith insisted a man must work if he expected to eat. Some colonies passed laws requiring that people be engaged in some kind of work, and in many frontier settlements it was a matter of working for survival or perishing... the habit and custom of hard toil [was] considered not only honorable but righteous.... Americans tended to [seek] as much worldly wealth as possible... financial success was... a [sign] of social superiority. Edward Dicey said, 'money making is the chief object of the nation;... 'The poor struggle to be rich, the rich to be richer... Americans... love money.'"

Gilbert Fite and Jim Reese, *An Economic History of the United States*, 1959

11. The ideas expressed in this passage had its origins primarily in which group or movement

   (A) Puritanism
   (B) Enlightenment thinkers
   (C) Expansionist
   (D) Pioneers

13. The idea of hard work became a central factor in the development of the

   (A) institution of slavery
   (B) welfare state
   (C) republican ideal
   (D) national character

12. The Americans attitude toward work is that it is

   (A) a necessary evil
   (B) a positive good
   (C) to be avoided at all cost
   (D) a luxury

Questions 14-15 refer to the following:

"We have laws for the body... by giving to each its proper food and exercise, we keep that harmony which is health. If we break these laws we incur pain and disease ensues. The same is true of the other part of our nature. It may be strengthened by use weakened by abuse.... Nothing can deprive man of the sense of what is right. This is the law of nature—the same in all—the only foundation of practical religion.... This, then is the doctrine of Transcendentalism—the substantive, independent existence of the soul of man, the reality of conscience,... the inner light, of man's religious affections, his knowledge of right and truth, his sense of duty— [honor]... apart from the [useful]...—his love for beauty and holiness, his religious aspirations—with this it starts as something not dependent on education or anything beyond man himself."

Charles Mayo Ellis, "An Essay on Transcendentalism," 1957

14. As a religious philosophy transcendentalism could be closely tied to the

   (A) charasmatic religious movements of the burned-over district
   (B) religious revival of the First Great Awakening
   (C) ecumenical unity movement of the Christian Churches
   (D) spirituality and mysticism of easter religions

15. The religion in New England most connected to transcendentalism was

   (A) Unitarianism
   (B) Catholicism
   (C) Episcopelian
   (D) Congregationalism

UNIT X

REFORM MOVEMENTS & ABOLITIONISM

The antebellum period was a great age of reform movements. Some would achieve success and others would be short-lived. Part of the reason for the spread of these reforms was that the usual public institutions seemed incapable with dealing with all of the issues facing the U.S. After a time, Abolitionism would become the pre-eminent reform and drew almost all of the others movements into it. Reform types who first gravitated to other movements would ultimately become abolitionists.

Reform Movements

·School Reform
Horace Mann brought about a doubling of appropriations for schools in Massachusetts, extended the school year to 6 months, raised teachers salaries, modernized the curriculum, based teacher training on the European model, established the age-grade system for organizing classes, and established normal schools for teacher training. Other states in the North and Northeast followed his example.

·Ten Hour Workday
Workers pushed for this in the 1830s and President Van Buren decreed a 10–hour work-day for all labor on federal contracts in 1840. An attempt to extend this to the private sector did not succeed until much later.

·Temperance
Founded in 1826, the American Society for the Promotion of Temperance had 200,000 members who were trying to address a serious problem among men who consumed large quantities of whiskey, rum, bourbon, and hard cider. Success first came with Neil Dow's Maine law in 1851, as it became the first state to outlaw intoxicating liquor. The campaign would continue into the next century when all alcoholic beverages would be banned with passage of the 18th (Prohibition) Amendment. At times, the temperance movement actually merged with the women's movement as supporters of one tended to be supporters of the other.

Peace Movement

William Ladd founded the American Peace Society in 1828. He devoted his life to this society and during the Aroostook War between Maine and Canadian lumberjacks, he showed the need for an international tribunal to mediate the dispute.

Vegetarianism

Sylvester Graham was an American Presbyterian minister who preached temperance and stressed using whole-wheat flour instead of the chemically laden flower that was used by most bakers. Graham achieved fame for his touting of un-sifted, coarsely ground, wheat flour that he used in creating the graham cracker. He compared people physiologically to orangutans and concluded that vegetarian food was natural for both primates. Graham had many devoted followers, known as "Grahamites," who slavishly followed his principles that included temperance, sexual restraint, and baths, in addition to vegetarianism.

Mental Illness

Dorothea Dix worked for 20 years (1840-1860) to improve the treatment of mentally ill patients as she encouraged legislatures to build institutions to treat them instead of housing them with criminals or even in mental asylums confining them in cages bound with ropes and chains.

Prison Reform

The structural pattern of outside cells, with a central corridor, was the chief architectural feature of the Pennsylvania system of prison construction. For the first time imprisonment through solitary confinement was used as the usual method of combating crime. A different system was the Auburn model where the emphasis was on individual cell block architecture to create an environment to rehabilitate and reform the prisoners. By separating the criminals from all contact with corruption and then teach them moral habits of order and regularity by means of severe discipline and contract labor was the goal of this system. It influenced the emergence of reform schools and workhouses. The word "penitentiary" came from the Pennsylvania Quakers and their belief in penitence and self-examination as a means to salvation.

Legal Code Reforms

These included a reduction in crimes punishable by death; abolishing public hangings in many states; and abandoning flogging and other cruel punishments that violated the 8th Amendment.

Lyceum Movement

Started by Josiah Holbrook, these adult education and self-improvement traveling lecture programs numbered 3,000 by 1835. Notable intellectuals like Ralph Waldo Emerson often spoke for a fee at these gatherings. The Lyceums were voluntary local associations that sponsored lectures and debates on topics of current interest. The interest they brought to their topics helped to contribute to the broadening of the curriculum in schools and the public's interest in expanding museums and libraries.

Lane Seminary

Founded in Cincinnati in 1830 this seminary was affiliated with the Presbyterian Church and between 1832 and 1850, Reverend Lyman Beecher served as the head of the school. In the 1830s the seminary was divided over the issue of slavery as the school's board of directors tried to prohibit students from supporting abolitionism. In 1834, Theodore Weld and other students left the school and many of them enrolled at Oberlin College.

Oberlin College

Became the first university to admit African Americans and followed this up by admitting women in 1837. After the enrollment of the Lane students the school became a hot-bed of abolitionist sentiment.

·McGuffey's Readers

These eclectic readers, first published in 1836, became primers for grades 1-6 and featured oratory, literature, and elocution all revolving around themes of nationalism, patriotism, and moral precepts. The series consisted of stories, poems, essays and speeches. The advanced readers contained excerpts from the works of great writers such as John Milton, Daniel Webster and Lord Byron. The McGuffey Readers reflect their author's personal philosophy, as well as his rough and tumble experiences as a frontier schoolteacher. The books were far more than a group of textbooks; they helped frame the country's morals, attitudes and tastes, as well as shaping the American character. The lessons in the Readers set standards of morality throughout the U.S. for more than a century. Geared to the natural curiosity of children they emphasized the values of work and an independent spirit, encouraged love of country and an understanding of the importance of the values of religion. Filled with stories of strength, character, goodness and truth, the books drew moral conclusions against lying and inculcated children with the values of the19th century.

·Noah Webster

He believed in promoting the cultural independence of the United States. This could be done best by adopting a distinctive American language with its own idioms, pronunciations, and style. In 1806, Webster published *A Compendious Dictionary of the English Language*, the first truly American dictionary. For the next two decades he worked on his *magnum opus*, *An American Dictionary of the English Language*, for which he learned 26 languages, including Anglo-Saxon and Sanskrit, in order to research the origins of his own country's language. This 1828 publication with 70,000 entries became a new standard of lexicography and fully established the uniqueness of the American language.

Women's Rights Movement

1. **Seneca Falls Convention**—Organized by Lucretia Mott and Elizabeth Cady Stanton in 1848, the convention issued a "Declaration of Sentiments," stating, "all men and women were created equal." It took a more radical position when it said "the history of mankind is a history of repeated injuries and usurpations on the part of man toward woman, having in direct object the establishment of an absolute tyranny over her." The convention attracted many abolitionists, but also advocates of moral reform, temperance, peace, religious reform, and married women's property rights. The delegates passed 12 resolutions, all unanimously except the one dealing with women's right to vote, which passed in a close vote and almost split the convention.

2. **Elizabeth Cady Stanton**—Fiery women's rights organizer who had the word obey dropped from her wedding ceremony. As an abolitionist she became enraged when the 1840 World's Anti-Slavery Convention in London denied official standing to women delegates, including Lucretia Mott. In 1848, she and Mott called for a women's rights convention near her home in Seneca Falls, New York. After 1851, Stanton worked in close partnership with Susan B. Anthony and they focused on female suffrage and founded the National Woman Suffrage Association with Stanton as president.

3. **Lucretia Mott**—Involved in both the anti-slavery movement as well as the women's movement, this Quaker refused to use cotton cloth, cane sugar, and other slave produced goods. She worked with Elizabeth Cady Stanton with the idea of the holding a mass meeting to address women's rights. After the Seneca Falls Convention she was a key organizer in the broader-based convention for women's rights held in Rochester, New York in 1850 at the Unitarian Church. She became the first president of the American Equal Rights Convention after the end of the Civil War. She worked hard to reconcile the two factions that split over the issue of women's suffrage or black male suffrage.

4. **Amelia Bloomer**—She is best known for her support for an outfit of attire of tunic and full "pantaloons" (also called Turkish Trousers). This clothing style was initially worn by actress Fanny Kemble, and women's rights advocate Elizabeth Cady Stanton. Bloomer defended the attire in her newspaper *The Lily*, and her articles were picked up in *The New York Tribune*. Soon the outfit was

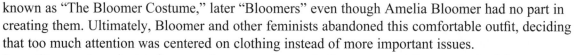

known as "The Bloomer Costume," later "Bloomers" even though Amelia Bloomer had no part in creating them. Ultimately, Bloomer and other feminists abandoned this comfortable outfit, deciding that too much attention was centered on clothing instead of more important issues.

5. **Lucy Stone**—American reformer, who was a pioneer in the movement for women's rights. Disagreeing with her father's belief that men should be dominant over women, Lucy undertook to educate herself and graduated from Oberlin College in 1847. She toured the country, lecturing against slavery for the Anti-Slavery Society and also advocated equality for women. In 1855, she married Henry Blackwell, a crusader for women's suffrage, and by mutual agreement with her husband she retained her maiden name. Women who followed this practice of keeping their maiden name were called "Lucy Stoners."

6. **Margaret Fuller**—Classically educated author, journalist, teacher, and literary critic who conducted "conversations" (similar to the salons of 18th century Paris) amongst leading Transcendentalist intellectuals. Served as co-editor of *The Dial* with Ralph Waldo Emerson and her book, *Woman in the Nineteenth Century*, expressed her belief in the intellectual equality of women. After traveling to Italy as the *Tribune's* foreign correspondent, and supporting the romantic nationalist Mazzini in the Revolutions of 1848, she married a Roman nobleman, had a child, and the family tragically perished in a shipwreck when they returned to the United States.

7. **Catherine Beecher**—Daughter of Lyman Beecher and sister of Harriet Beecher Stowe and Lyman Beecher Jr., she succeeded in feminizing public education by getting women to leave the home and become public school teachers.

8. **Susan B. Anthony**—A social reformer for temperance and other causes she achieved world-wide fame as a crusader for women's rights. She often collaborated with Elizabeth Cady Stanton. Many of her accomplishments took place after the Civil War.

9. **Emma (Hart) Willard**—In 1807 she went to Middlebury, Vermont to head a female academy. After marrying doctor John Willard she opened her own school, the Middlebury Female Seminary to provide advanced education that young women were denied by colleges. Emma moved to Troy, New York, in 1821, where she opened the Troy Female Seminary. With both boarding and day students it was the first U.S. institution of serious, academic learning for young women.

10. **Mary Lyon**—Mary Lyon was the founder of the first women's college. One of seven children, she lost her father when she only five years old and attended school until the customary age of 13. Besides helping with the family farm, she got her first job as a teacher while still in her teens. Mary Lyon taught and managed schools in Massachusetts and New Hampshire before establishing one of her own. Despite a great deal of criticism, she worked hard to create a place that would provide women with the opportunity to obtain higher education. Lyon was able to raise enough funds for her new school. In 1837, the Mount Holyoke Female Seminary opened in South Hadley, Massachusetts, with 80 students. The school's reputation grew when its alumni went out into the world taking with them the educational philosophies and teaching methods learned at Mount Holyoke.

11. **Elizabeth Blackwell**—Became the first woman doctor in the U.S. after graduating from Geneva College in New York in 1849. Barred from practicing in most hospitals, she founded her own infirmary, the New York Infirmary for indigent women and children.

Abolitionism

·Quakers

Starting with Benjamin Say's book condemning slavery in 1737, the Quakers from 1755 to 1776 became the first community in history to ban slaveholding. From at least the 1750s, Anthony Benezet became the leading opponent of slavery. His solitary campaign took two forms: first, he worked to convince his Quaker brethren in Philadelphia that slave owning was not consistent with Christian doctrine; second, he wrote and published at his own expense a number of anti-slavery tracts and pamphlets that led to the establishment of the anti-slavery movement in America.

·Colonization

This attempt to deal with the issue of the free blacks who were discriminated against throughout the U.S. started with the formation of the American Colonization Society founded by Robert Finley in 1816. Its purpose was to send "free Negroes" back to Africa by colonizing areas along the west coast. Congress in 1819 supported the effort with a grant of $100,000 and President Monroe, Henry Clay, Daniel Webster, Abraham Lincoln and other prominent individuals were supportive of the movement. Over time colonies were founded in Liberia (its capital was named Monrovia after the President) and by 1865 an estimated 13,000 free blacks had been sent to that country. The colonization movement came under the bitter attack by the abolitionists, who charged that in the South it strengthened slavery by removing the free blacks. The blacks themselves were not enthusiastic about abandoning their native land for the African coast and generally opposed the movement. Eventually twelve state legislatures including border states Maryland, Virginia, and Kentucky approved the society.

·Benjamin Lunde

Wrote the "*Genius of Universal Emancipation*" in 1821 which called for the national government to have sole authority to abolish slavery in the territories; the further prohibition of slave states into the union; abolition of the internal slave trade; giving free blacks the same legal status as whites; government aid for colonization; repeal of the 3/5ths compromise; and the gradual emancipation of slaves in the South.

·William Lloyd Garrison

Although influenced by both colonization and Lunde, Garrison took the radical position of immediate emancipation in his newspaper *The Liberator*, first published in 1831. He said, "I do not wish to think, or speak, or write, with moderation. . . . I am in earnest – I will not equivocate – I will not excuse – I will not retreat a single inch – AND I WILL BE HEARD." His was an unpopular view during the 1830s, even with northerners who were against slavery. Unlike the vast majority of Americans, Garrison believed that freed slaves could assimilate into society. Garrison went so far as to advocate northern secession because he could not support the Constitution which sanctified slavery.

·Wendell Philips

Phillips was converted to abolitionism when he heard William Lloyd Garrison speak at the Boston Female Anti-Slavery Society in 1835. He was particularly impressed by the bravery of these people and during the meeting a white mob attempted to lynch Garrison. Phillips was so outraged by what he saw that he decided to give up law and devote his life to obtaining the freedom of all slaves. Phillips became a leading figure in the anti-slavery movement and was the society's most popular public speaker. He also contributed to Garrison's newspaper and wrote numerous pamphlets on slavery.

·Theodore Dwight Weld

Influenced by Charles Finney and the "Great Awakening," Weld organized the American Anti-Slavery Society with its mid-western base. Training 70 agents to resist mob violence in speaking out against slavery, his group came from the Lane Theological Seminary where the famous antislavery debates he organized in 1834 among the students led to his dismissal. Almost the entire student body then requested dismissal, and it was from these theological students that Weld and Henry B. Stanton selected agents for the American Anti-Slavery Society. He anonymously compiled and wrote *American Slavery As It Is: Testimony of a Thousand Witnesses* (1839), on which Harriet Beecher Stowe partly based *Uncle Tom's Cabin*. It was a record of facts and statements taken from Southern newspapers that showed the inhumanity of the southern slave system. Both Sarah and Angelina Grimke became important agents in the Weld system and Weld married Angelina.

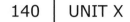

Other prominent abolitionists that Weld worked with included New York philanthropists Arthur and Lewis Tappan, and James Birney, Presidential candidate of the Liberty Party in 1844.

·Frederick Douglass

He was the son of a Negro slave and white slaveholder. He secretly taught himself to read and write which was a serious crime in the antebellum South. His book, *Narrative of the Life of Frederick Douglass* published in 1845, recounted the harsh life in the pre-Civil War plantations in which he lived and worked before escaping to New York. He described the senseless cruelty of the masters and the debased lives of slaves. His contribution to the emancipation cause included recruiting Negro volunteers during the Civil War and he was also instrumental in safeguarding and preserving the rights of the freedmen during Reconstruction.

·Grimke Sisters

The Grimke sisters, Sarah and Angelina, originally of South Carolina, were two early female abolitionists and women's rights activists. After leaving the South they converted to the Quaker faith and traveled throughout the North lecturing about their first-hand experiences with slavery on their family plantation. They were among the first women to act and speak out publicly in the social reform movements. As abolitionist and women they received abuse and ridicule for their activities. They became early activists in the women's rights movement and Angelina married the abolitionist leader Theodore Dwight Weld.

·Harriet Tubman

A runaway slave from Maryland she became known as the "Moses" of her people for leading them out of slavery. Over a 10-year period and at great personal risk in 19 dangerous trips to the South, she led 300 slaves to freedom along the Underground Railroad. She later became a leader in the abolitionist movement and during the Civil War she acted as a spy for the federal forces in South Carolina.

·Sojourner Truth

Sojourner Truth was born Isabella Bomefree (later spelled Baumfree) about 1797 in Ulster County, New York. She was bought and sold four times finally gaining her freedom in 1823 when Van Wagener bought her and her daughter in order to give them freedom. In 1843, Isabella changed her name to *Sojourner Truth* and told her friends, "The Spirit calls me, and I must go." She became a Methodist and left to make her way traveling and preaching about abolitionism. For the next 60 years Sojourner spoke out for womens rights, abolition, prison reform, and addressed the Michigan legislature speaking against capital punishment. She was ahead of her time and took women to task for the way they dressed, trussing themselves up in corsets and wearing high-heeled shoes and adorned hats.

·Underground Railroad

The Underground Railroad refers to the effort—sometimes spontaneous, sometimes highly organized—to assist persons held in bondage to escape from slavery to Canada. The system used terms from railroading: the homes and businesses where fugitives would rest and eat were called "stations," and "depots" and were run by "stationmasters;" those who contributed money or goods were "stockholders;" and the "conductor" was responsible for moving fugitives from one station to the next. Stations were usually about twenty miles apart and conductors used covered wagons or carts with false bottoms to carry slaves from one station to another. By the middle of the 19th century it was estimated that 50,000-100,000 slaves had escaped from the South using the Underground Railroad. One of the most notable participants was Levi Coffin, a Quaker who assisted more than 3,000 slaves to freedom.

UNIT X
MULTIPLE-CHOICE QUESTIONS

Questions 1-3 refer to the following:

"Here, then, is the philosophy of *School Discipline*. Authority, Force, Fear, Pain! The ideas of Childhood and Punishment indissolubly associated together... these motives... are to be inscribed on the lintels [header] and door posts of our schoolhouses... conscience is nowhere referred to, as one of the motive-powers in the conduct of children... one of the grand objects of our schools [is] to bring these children under humanizing and refining influences; to show them that there is something besides wrath... and suffering, in God's world; to lift these outcast and forlorn beings from their degradation, by gentle hands, and to fold them to warm and cherishing bosoms."

Horace Mann, "Education and the Child," 1844

1. Mann's critique of the book *School Discipline* indicates that he was opposed to

    (A) Progressive education
    (B) McGuffey's Readers
    (C) corporal punishment
    (D) whole language reading instruction

2. From the comments in the passage above which of the following sayings would Mann be most opposed to?

    (A) Seeing is different than being told
    (B) As the twig is bent, so inclines the tree
    (C) Bad company corrupts good character
    (D) Spare the rod, spoil the children

3. The ideas expressed by Horace Mann paved the way for which late 19th century and early 20th century school of learning often called Progressive Education which featured

    (A) cognitive—focuses on informational processing (how we take in, store, and retrieve information) and meaningful learning (to organize, structure and teach information so that it might be used best)
    (B) humanistic—focus on social and emotional learning and development . Make children feel better about themselves and accepting others
    (C) behavioral—attempts to explain why we behave the way we do primarily through operant conditioning
    (D) classical—learning as set forth in the "Great Books" of Western civilization within a framework to teach all human knowledge

Questions 4-6 refer to the following:

"In the 1820's, when the Temperance movement began its organization and initiated its doctrine, the drive toward abstinence from distilled spirits (beer, wine, and cider were still permitted) functioned as a means to restore a superior position to the declining Federalist elite. As decline in moral behavior symbolized the sad facts of a waning social power, the old aristocracy sought to retain their prestige and power.... It was not an effort to reform the habits and behavior of those who made up its membership. The lowly, the small farmer, the wage earner, the craftsman—these were the objects of reform. This is not to maintain that there was no conviction of sin among the responsible citizens who made up the Temperance associations... such associations sought to disseminate and strengthen the norms of life which were part of the style of the old elite."

Joseph R. Gusfield, *Symbolic Crusade: Status, Politics and the American Temperance Movement*, 1963

4. In the passage above the most important motivating factor behind those involved in the Temperance movement was

    (A) the loss of status of the displaced Federalist elite
    (B) concern for the betterment of mankind through social reform
    (C) concentrating on moral changes of the individual
    (D) an attempt to get people back into the churches of the old time religion

5. The elites of the Temperance movement were trying to control which political group that was emerging as a power force in politics?

    (A) Federalist
    (B) Jacksonian Democrats
    (C) National Republicans
    (D) Whigs

6. The Temperance movement would ultimately have its greatest victory in 1919 with

    (A) outlawing all liquor sales except for beer and wine
    (B) Protestant and Catholic churches uniting in their opposition to the consumption of alcohol
    (C) passage of anti-immigrant laws that would keep liquor imbibing southern and eastern Europeans from entering the U.S.
    (D) ratification of the 18th Amendment

Questions 7-9 refer to the following:

"We will prove that slaves in the United States are treated with barbarous inhumanity; that they are overworked, underfed, wretchedly clad and lodged, and have insufficient sleep;... [they] wear round their necks iron collars armed with prongs, to drag heavy chains...while working in the field; and to wear yokes;... they are often confined in the stocks day and night... made to wear gags in their mouths for hours and days, have some of their front teeth torn out or broken off, that they be easily detected when they run away; ... they are flogged... have red pepper rubbed into their lacerated flesh... they are often stripped naked, their backs and limbs cut with knives... their ears are cut off, their eyes knocked out, their bones broken, their flesh branded with red hot irons.... We will establish all these facts by the testimony of scores and hundreds of eye-witnesses, [and] by the testimony of slaveholders...."

Theodore Dwight Weld, *Slavery As it Is: Testimony of a Thousand Witnesses*, 1839

7. Which popular novel against slavery was inspired by Weld's book?

   (A) *Gone With the Wind*
   (B) *Red Badge of Courage*
   (C) *Uncle Tom's Cabin*
   (D) *The Impending Crisis of the South*

8. The sentiments expressed in the above passage were a part of which movement to get rid of slavery?

   (A) Colonization
   (B) Emancipation
   (C) Eradication
   (D) Abolition

9. The Weld book proved the inhumanity of the institution of slavery in the South primarily by

   (A) running newspaper advertisements in the South condemning slavery
   (B) the words of the slave owners themselves
   (C) comparing it to slavery in Africa and the Middle East
   (D) analyzing laws in the South that defended and protected slavery

Questions 10-11 refer to the following excerpt:

"...thou art blind to the danger of marrying a woman who feels and acts out the principle of equal rights.... Hitherto, instead of being a helpmate to man, in the highest, noblest sense of the term, as a companion, a co-worker, an equal; she has been a mere appendage of his being, an instrument of his convenience and pleasure, the pretty toy with which he whiled away his leisure moments, or the pet animal whom he humored into playfulness and submission."

Angelina E. Grimke, "Letters to Catherine Beecher," 1838

10. Grimke's ideas in the above document helped to inspire

   (A) feminism
   (B) Republican motherhood
   (C) cult of domesticity
   (D) "Rosie the Riveter"

11. Angelina Grimke, along with her sister Sarah, were both leading advocates of which two reform causes in the antebellum period?

   (A) Women's rights and abolitionism
   (B) Education and prison reform
   (C) Temperance and worker's rights
   (D) Peace movement and vegetarianism

Questions 12-15 refer to the following:

"... Christian zeal... lay in the work of the Evangelicals.... He was distinguished by a determination to make Christian morality a vital part of the everyday life of all Americans and in doing so bring under judgment all the vices and injustices that disfigured the Republic. The center of the Evangelical movement... was the experience of conversion, of being 'born again' from infidelity or merely formal Christianity to an ecstatic devoutness to the Lord... both by faith and by works. Charles Grandison Finney was the virtual inventor of this form of Christianity, which he adopted from the frontier revival, lessoning the extreme emotionalism of that experience and adding generous amounts of social conscience...."

Paige Smith, *The Nation Comes of Age: A People's History of the Ante-Bellum Years*, 1981

12. The Evangelicalism referred to in the above passage was a part of which mid 19th-century movement

(A) Transcendentalism
(B) Enlightenment
(C) 2nd Great Awakening
(D) Progressivism

13. The only one of the following religions that did not engage in evangelicalism was

(A) Catholic
(B) Methodist
(C) Baptist
(D) Congregational

14. Finney's social conscience form of evangelism resulted in inspiring what reform movement that would eventually dominate all reform movements in the antebellum period?

(A) Temperance
(B) Mental Health
(C) Communitarianism
(D) Abolitionism

15. The evangelical belief of conversion or being "born again" was similar to regeneration that originally came from the

(A) Cavaliers
(B) Puritans
(C) Quakers
(D) Anabaptist

UNIT XI

MANIFEST DESTINY & THE MEXICAN WAR

Manifest Destiny was John O'Sullivan's catch phrase coined in 1845 to explain and justify the continental expansion by the United States from ocean to ocean by acquiring contiguous territory. It revitalized a sense of "mission" or national destiny for many Americans who believed providence had ordained the U.S. for imperialistic expansion. This policy would be carried out in the 1840s with the acquisition of Texas, Oregon, and the Mexican Cession as a result of a war with Mexico. When diplomacy failed, war would be used to achieve the objective of territorial acquisition.

Background:

·Louisiana Purchase
This vast area was bought from France in 1803 for $15 million or less than 3 cents an acre. It gave rise to exploration by Lewis and Clark and later settlements by pioneers.

·Pike's Peak
Zebulon Pike, a soldier and explorer for the U.S. government, led two expeditions into the West, one to find the source of the Mississippi River, and the other to the headwaters of the Arkansas and Red Rivers in 1806-1807. During this expedition, Pike came within the vicinity of the Rocky Mountain peak that now bears his name. He and his men were captured by Spanish authorities north of Santa Fe, and later released.

·Santa Fe Trail
In 1821, William Becknell had three wagons loaded with merchandise, 24 oxen, and twenty-one men and proceeded to open up the newly independent country of Mexico to trade. The 3,000 people in Santa Fe, the center of a population 40,000 in New Mexico were starved for Mississippi Valley trade goods like textiles, hardware, and gimcracks (geegaws). Soon, other American traders followed Becknell's route and traders returned with wagons filled with exported merchandise from New Mexico such as hides, blankets, pottery,

147

jewelry, gold, silver, copper, and livestock. The trail served as an international road between Missouri and Mexico for 25 years until relations soured between Mexico and the U.S. in the 1840s over the Texas issue.

·Great American Desert

The "Great American Desert" was the term applied to the land west of the Missouri River and east of the Rocky Mountains. The landscape had no trees, little rainfall and tough prairie sod. This land seemed like a desert to the many who passed through this unexplored area on their way to the Pacific Coast. This area is mostly semi-arid grassland that is today extensively cultivated for agriculture. In the 19th century, the area was relatively unexplored and the belief was that it was almost uninhabitable. In 1823, Stephen Long, a government surveyor and cartographer, produced a map labeling the area the Great American Desert and the name persisted

·Colonizing Texas

Between 1800 and 1820, traders and military adventurers filtered into Texas and established commercial relations with the people of the Spanish borderlands. In 1820, a charter from New Spain granted land to Moses Austin for the settlement of 200 families. Moses died before he could commence the development. After Mexico became independent from Spain in 1821, Moses' son, Stephen, carried out the grant and renewed it under subsequent Mexican governments. Other promoters received similar grants. By making these grants Mexico thought the settlement of white Americans would protect their country from Indians and possibly incursions by the U.S. In the next decade 20, 000 settlers along with 2, 000 slaves moved into Texas which was a part of, and governed by, the Mexican state of Coahuila. By 1830 relations between the white settlers and Mexican officials had deteriorated, in part, because the Texans had failed to convert to Catholicism, brought in slaves illegally, and settled in lands along the coast reserved for Mexicans. A short-lived revolt by a Haden Edwards led group established the Republic of Fredonia that was put down by Mexico in 1826.

·Republic of Texas

When Mexico refused to allow further colonization in 1830, this change in policy angered the Texans who tried to get Mexico to sever Texas from the corrupt Coahuila government. After a revolution in Mexico in 1832 when General Santa Ana came to power, the Texans revolted. After a series of battles (including two instances where the Texans were annihilated at the Alamo Mission in San Antonio and at Goliad) the Texans under Sam Houston defeated the Mexicans at San Jacinto and captured their President Santa Anna. For nine years from 1836 to 1845, Texas remained an independent republic until it was annexed to the U.S in 1845.

·Oregon Territory

The Oregon area in the Pacific Northwest had long been claimed by both the U.S. and Great Britain as well as Russia and Mexico at various times. The U.S. claim was based on explorations of Robert Gray in 1792, the Lewis and Clark exploration, treaties with Spain and Russia, and a fur trading post at Astoria on the Columbia river established in 1811. British claims were based on a voyage of Captain Cook in 1778, Nootka Sound Treaty with Spain in 1790, explorations of George Vancouver in the Columbia river area in 1792, and fur trading posts of the Hudson Bay Co. Both countries had strong claims to the area.

·Mountain Men

These rugged individualist proved to be a key element in opening up the west to migration as they paved the way for future settlers. Most were both adventurous and practical; they came to the wilderness to turn a profit. This desire to make a living and their ability to survive in the wilderness made them ideal trappers during the heyday of the fur trade from 1820 to 1840 and kept them in the mountains long after the beaver were gone. They became explorers, guides and even government officials. The Mountain Men had a great deal of first hand experience in dealing with Native Americans, and though they were not always sympathetic, they at least understood the Indian. Like the French *coer de bois* before them, they were willing to take Indian women as their wives. Their experience proved invaluable to settlement in the west as they helped military and emigrant parties to try to avoid conflict and survive in a hostile environment.

·Rendezvous
William Ashley, head of the Rocky Mountain Fur Company, established the first Rendezvous in 1824. A French word meaning "appointed place of meeting" it was a place where trappers, both white and Indian, could sell their furs, and trade for needed supplies (which could include Indian wives), meet with old friends, get drunk, engage in storytelling, gambling, gun duels and contests such as horse racing, wrestling, and shooting. It was generally a time to socialize after the long solitude of being a "Mountain Man." Alcohol was abundant and the festivities could last for weeks. Sites in Wyoming, Idaho and Utah were chosen where there was enough space for up to 500 mountain men and 3,000 Indians. All of these gatherings were held in Shoshone territory, rather than farther east or north where the hostile Sioux, Blackfoot, and Crow ruled. The Rendezvous came to an end in 1840 because of over-trapping and the changes in fashion from beaver hats to those of silk from China.

Political Events

·Election of 1840
The Whigs, ignoring their political leaders Clay and Webster and wanting a winner, nominated General William Henry Harrison an "Old Republican," Jeffersonian from Virginia and John Tyler, who was not a Whig but had broken with Jackson and the Democrats over nullification. Running on the campaign slogan of "Tippecanoe and Tyler Too" the Whigs embraced the image of "log cabin and hard cider" that the Democrats had labeled their candidate as favoring. The Whigs overwhelmed the discredited Van Buren 234-60 in the Electoral College. Ho joined the two Adams' as the only Presidents up to that time to not win reelection. For the unlucky Whigs, Harrison gave a long-winded inaugural speech (the longest on record) in a cold March rain, caught pneumonia, and died exactly one month later after having served the shortest time of any President before or since.

·Tyler's Administration
Ridiculed and called "his Accidency," the Whigs were now stuck with Tyler, the first President ever to come to office by constitutional succession, and who had not exhibited any deep allegiance to Whig principles. His core belief in states' rights led him to veto a bill for another federal Bank of the United States, that the Whig majority in Congress favored. Every member of Tyler's original Cabinet (the Harrison Cabinet) except Secretary of State Daniel Webster resigned in protest (Webster was negotiating a boundary dispute with Great Britain). He also alienated the Whigs by repudiating the spoils system and refusing to appoint Whigs to replace certain Democrat ministers serving abroad. Clearly, Tyler was no "party man," and believed in making decisions based on an idea's merit and impact on what he perceived to be the nation's best interests, without regard to politics.

·Webster-Ashburton Treaty
The Aroostook War had spotlighted the problems of the U.S. and Canadian border boundary that had not been spelled out in the 1783 Treaty of Paris. In 1842, Secretary of State Daniel Webster met with the British Foreign Minister, Lord Ashburton (Alexander Baring). The resulting Webster-Ashburton Treaty reached agreement by clearly defining boundaries between Maine and New Brunswick, and also an area in the Mesabi range in the Great Lakes area would be given to the U.S. and later would prove to be an invaluable source of iron-ore. The United States received control of 7,015 square miles of the disputed territory and Great Britain 5,012 square miles. The issue of extradition, which had become politically sensitive following the Caroline Affair was discussed but not acted on. Finally, the U.S. agreed to station ships off the African coast in an effort

to detect Americans engaged in the slave trade. Webster rejected a request to allow boarding of American ships by the British navy. The Oregon boundary issue was not dealt with in this agreement.

·O'Sullivan's Newspaper Article

In 1845, John O'Sullivan, editor of the influential *Democratic Review*, coined the phrase "Manifest Destiny" to describe a vision of a United States stretching from Atlantic to Pacific. This became a catch phrase to justify the nation's expansionism "to over spread and to possess" the whole continent. In the eyes of the Americans, it meant that it was God's will that Americans expand their territory from coast to coast and develop liberty and self-government for all.

·Annexation of Texas

From the onset of breaking away from Mexico, Texas, under the leadership of Sam Houston, wanted to become part of the U.S. This was delayed because anti-slavery groups did not want to add more slave territory and Mexico would consider U.S. annexation to be the equivalent of a declaration of war on Mexico. Both Jackson and Van Buren saw it as a political issue that was too hot to handle and they did not want to antagonize Northern Democrats.

·Joint Resolution

On Tyler's last day in office in 1845 Texas was made a part of the U.S. by a majority vote of a Joint Resolution of Congress since a 2/3rds vote could not be achieved in the Senate for ratification of a treaty.

·Conestoga Wagon

The major mode of transportation to California and Oregon was the Conestoga wagon. It was expensive to travel to the West, as a typical family might need $1,000 in addition to a wagon that could cost $400. The wagons were skillfully made in Pennsylvania mainly of wood, but iron was sparingly used to reinforce it at crucial points. The wagons were packed with food, supplies, cooking equipment, water kegs, and other essentials needed for the journey. These wagons could carry loads of more than a ton, but the recommended maximum was 1,600 pounds. A typical family of four carried 800 pounds of flour, 200 pounds of lard, 700 pounds of bacon, 200 pounds of beans, 100 pounds of fruit, 75 pounds of coffee and 25 pounds of salt. Furniture when taken was often abandoned or used for firewood on the trip. There was little room in the wagon for people and so most of the family walked beside the slow moving vehicle or rode on the back of a horse. The wagon train would travel at around two miles an hour, the speed of walking oxen, which enabled the emigrants to average 10-12 miles a day. With good weather the 2,000 mile journey from Missouri to California and Oregon would take about five months, often longer because of bad weather. The emigrants used horses, oxen and mules to pull their wagons with the most practical being the ox. The oxen were cheaper, stronger and easier to work with than horses or mules and they were able to exist on sparse vegetation along the way.

·Oregon Trail

On the 2,000 mile trek from Missouri, the Oregon Trail (the Oregon-California Trail) generally followed the Platte River to its headwaters; it then crossed the Rocky Mountains. In southern Idaho, the California Trail split off (until this point, the Oregon Trail and the California Trail were one and the same) and became its own separate trail. The Oregon Trail then followed the Snake River until it reached the Columbia River, which flowed into the Pacific. In the years between 1840 and 1848 an estimated 11,512 settlers migrated overland to Oregon and another 2,735 to California.

·Oregon Settlements

Through the efforts of Methodists missionaries like Jason Lee and Marcus & Narcissa Whitman, large numbers of settlers arrived in the Willamette Valley during the 1830s and 1840s. This rapid increase in population gave the Americans the edge over the British in the allocation of the Oregon area.

·Election of 1844

The frontrunners for the nominations in both parties, Henry Clay (Whig) and Martin Van Buren (Democrat), feared the issue of the annexation of Texas.. They agreed to duck the issue in the hope of keeping it off center stage. They said they would support annexation if Mexico would agree, although they knew there was absolutely no chance that this would happen. Incumbent President Tyler, a nominal Whig who was actually an "Old Republican" Jeffersonian used this situation to advance his remote hopes for a second term by backing the annexation of Texas. Clay easily won the Whig nomination, but Van Buren ran into trouble at the Democratic convention. The delegates reinstituted an old rule that required a two-thirds majority for nomination, rendering it impossible for Van Buren's anti-annexation campaign to succeed. For the first time a true "dark horse" candidate (one who had received little notice before the convention) was able to secure the nomination. James K. Polk of Tennessee appealed to the delegates because he was a protégé of Andrew Jackson (called "Young Hickory"), had initially supported the frontrunner Van Buren, and was an outspoken expansionist. Polk won the nomination on the ninth ballot. The campaign was a bitter one. Clay was confident and believed the pro-annexation vote would be split between Polk and Tyler. However, Tyler recognized the hopelessness of his cause and pulled out of the race. With Van Buren out of the way Polk and the Democrats were ardent expansionist, calling for the "reoccupation of Oregon" and the "re-annexation of Texas." The slogan of "Fifty-four Forty or Fight!" condemned the British presence in the Northwest. Clay belatedly switched his position on annexation. Polk's margin in the Electoral College was substantial, but the popular vote was close. His boisterous expansionism played very well in the West and he lost just Ohio and Tennessee. The anti-slavery campaign of James G. Birney of the Liberty Party drew away sufficient votes in New York to deny Clay the presidency.

·Polk Presidency

Accomplishing almost everything that he had promised to do Polk was able to lower the tariff (Walker tariff of 1846); settle the Oregon question; reestablish an Independent Treasury; and embark on an expansionist program that added a million square miles to the U.S. adding the future states of Arizona, Utah, Nevada, California, Oregon, Idaho, Washington, much of New Mexico, and portions of Wyoming, Montana, and Colorado.

·Oregon Settlement

In spite of the Democratic platform cry of "54° 40' or fight" Polk was willing to settle the boundary with the British at the 49° parallel. With the war with Mexico just starting it was more prudent to fight just one war at a time.

War with Mexico

·Annexation of Texas 1845

Mexico recalled its ambassador and severed diplomatic relations when the U.S. brought Texas into the union.

·Texas Boundary Dispute

During the Spanish-Mexican era the southeastern boundary had been the Nueces River. The Texans claimed the territory to the Rio Grande River (south of the Nueces) and Polk supported the Texas claim.

·Slidell Mission

Polk sent a special envoy John Slidell in 1845 to Mexico with instructions to buy California for $25 million. Mexico would not permit Slidell to make his offer and this snub of a U.S. diplomat exacerbated the already tense situation between the U.S. and Mexico

·"American Blood on American Soil"

In what was a deliberately provocative act Polk sent General Zachary Taylor and 4,000 men into the disputed territory between the Nueces and Rio Grande rivers. Polk prepared to ask Congress to declare war on the basis of unpaid claims that were owed to Texas (now the U.S.) by Mexico and Slidell's diplomatic rejection by the Mexican government. Before Polk could deliver his war message to Congress news came of bloodshed in the disputed area with 16 Americans being killed or wounded. Polk's war message to Congress now said, "American blood had been shed on American soil."

·"Spotty Lincoln"

A first term Whig congressman from Illinois, Abraham Lincoln, introduced resolutions wanting to know the exact spot where American blood was shed on American soil and received the nickname "Spotty" for his persistence in asking this question.

·Acquiring California

Stephen Kearny traversed the Santa Fe Trail and captured Santa Fe on his way to California. Before he arrived, John C. Fremont and William Ide, with several dozen heavily armed men forced the Mexican commandant at Sonoma to surrender.

·Bear Flag Republic

The Fremont (a topographical surveyor with the army) Ide group to legitimize their conquest decided to raise a new flag over the plaza at Sonoma. With donated muslin cloth from a *Californio* woman, the wife of one of the Ide party tore a four-inch wide strip from a red petticoat and sewed it to the muslin, making a stripe along the bottom reminiscent of the stripes on the American flag. William Todd (nephew of Abraham Lincoln's future wife Mary) then drew a star in the upper left corner (in solidarity with Texas, then also fighting a war with Mexico) and a crude rendition of a grizzly bear (the captured Mexican commandant said it looked more like a pig) next to it. The words CALIFORNIA REPUBLIC were written in black in the middle, to the right of the star. This was California's attempt to be an independent nation.

·Battle of Buena Vista

General Zachary Taylor with 5,000 men after fighting his way across Mexico from the Rio Grande defeated Santa Anna and his 20,000 man army and became a national hero.

·Battle of Mexico City

General Winfield Scott after the capture of the coastal city of Vera Cruz by the U.S. navy marched to Mexico City and captured the Mexican capital in 1847.

·Trist Mission

Accompanying Winfield Scott, well connected State Department clerk Nicolas Trist was dispatched to seek an end to the Mexican War. After paying Santa Anna a $10,000 bribe, Trist, fluent in Spanish, opened negotiations. He managed to secure an armistice following the American victories at Contreras and Churubusco in August of 1847. The Polk administration, however, impatient with the slow course of events formally recalled their representative. Trist responded with a 65 page memorandum explaining why he was not coming home because he believed he was close to a final agreement and decided to ignore his summons to Washington. His decision was supported by General Winfield Scott as well as his Mexican counterparts. The document that emerged from the negotiations was basically faithful to the original instructions provided by Polk. Mexico, however, refused to give up Baja California and insisted upon maintaining a strip of land to connect that area with the mainland. Although he was angry, Polk was relieved to find a treaty to his liking and urged its ratification by the Senate. Trist's independence was not forgiven, however, and nearly 25 years passed before he could collect his pay and expenses from the government for his efforts.

·Treaty of Guadalupe Hidalgo

This treaty provided for the Mexican Cession, 525,000 square miles of territory was ceded to the United States in exchange for $15 million dollars. The United States also agreed to take over $3.25 million in debts Mexico owed to American citizens. Articles eight and nine of the treaty granted American citizenship and property rights to those Mexican citizens who did not elect to remain Mexican citizens. This treaty affected about 100,000 thousand Mexicans, including Indians, but was subject to interpretation by the legislature and the courts which often negated the property rights features.

·Results of the Mexican War

From the United States' perspective a huge block of new territory was acquired which would eventually add a number of new states to the union. The Mexican War and the tide of expansionism it unleashed underlined the political control exercised by the South in American political affairs. The addition of new lands touched off a new and bitter debate on the slavery issue, just as many had predicted. This was accelerated with the passage of the Wilmot Proviso (1846) in the House of Representatives (no slavery in any territory in the Mexican Cession). The Americans suffered losses of nearly 13,000 dead including only about 1,700 in combat—the rest succumbed to disease. It made the two major Whig generals, Taylor and Scott national heroes and both would become Presidential candidates. The war was a proving ground for young military officers (e.g. Grant, Jackson, Lee, Meade, and Sherman) who would put their skills to work in the Civil War. From the Mexican perspective the loss of about 50 percent of their territory (Texas and the Mexican Cession) was a matter of great humiliation and provoked ill feeling against the United States that has never fully dissipated. Political instability became a characteristic of Mexican domestic affairs. Also, the Treaty of Guadalupe Hidalgo has not always been adhered to by the United States. The part of the treaty dealing with property rights has been contentious and interpreted different ways by different courts.

·Gadsden Purchase

James Gadsden, as president of the South Carolina Railroad Company, had a pet dream to knit all Southern railroads into one system and then to connect it with a Southern transcontinental railroad to the Pacific. This would make the West commercially dependent on the South instead of the North. After engineers advised Gadsden that the most direct and practical route for the Southern transcontinental railroad would be south of the United States boundary, he made plans to have the Federal Government acquire title to the necessary territory from Mexico. Because of the influence of his friend and fellow empire dreamer, Secretary of War, Jefferson Davis, Gadsden was appointed U.S. Minister to Mexico by doughface President Franklin Pierce with instructions to buy from Mexico enough territory for a railroad to the Gulf of California. In 1852, Gadsden agreed to pay Santa Anna (once again back in power) $10 million for a strip of territory south of the Gila River in what is now southwestern New Mexico and southern Arizona. Many Americans were not especially proud of the Guadalupe-Hidalgo Treaty and considered the price of the Gadsden Purchase as "conscience money" for taking so much Mexican territory as a result of the Mexican War. The Gadsden Purchase was an area of 45,535 square miles—almost as large as Pennsylvania. The treaty was originally defeated in the Senate by a vote of 27-18 (2/3rds needed for passage). The amount of territory was reduced by 9,000 square miles and the price was lowered from $15 million to $10 million to assure its final ratification in 1854.

·*Californios*

In 1834, Spanish Mission lands were seized and secularized. Mexican officials in California awarded huge grants of mission lands to favored individuals, thus great ranching empires were created, and huge cattle herds ranged over the land. These ranchers were known as *Californios*, members of great land-holding families. Just like the feudal plantations in the South, Rancho life was good for these rich owners of vast tracts of land. They lived a leisurely lifestyle dedicated to family and tradition. But most *Californios* were poor ranch hands who maintained herds of cattle on the Ranchos for the rich *Californios*. Vast numbers of Indians provided the hard labor of the ranching, working as vaqueros and servants, and toiled under serf-like conditions. After the Mexican War their status was defined as persons of Spanish or Mexican descent who were American citizens by the treaty of Guadalupe Hidalgo. The life style of the *Californios* came to the end with the discovery of gold, and even the *Californios* could not benefit from the gold because of a 1848 Foreign Miners Tax which demanded $20 dollars per person per month, an unreasonably high amount for most foreign miners.

California Gold Rush

In January of 1848 James Marshall while working with a crew building a sawmill for John Sutter on the American River found a few tiny gold nuggets. Thus, began one of the largest human migrations in history as nearly a half-million people from around the world descended upon California in search of instant wealth. Some achieved their goal and became rich. Most, however, found only enough gold to barely pay their daily expenses. In a short period of time the population explosion would overwhelm the indigenous population of native "*Californios*" and Indians. By the end of 1849, the non-native population of the California territory was some 100,000 compared with the pre-1848 figure of less than 1,000. A total of $2 billion worth of precious metal was extracted from the area during the Gold Rush, which peaked in 1852. As the 49ers flocked to California, gold mining towns sprang up all over the region, complete with shops, saloons, brothels and other businesses seeking to make their own Gold Rush fortune. Those who supplied the miners were the ones who usually got rich as prices reached astronomical heights in areas affected by the Gold Rush. The overcrowded chaos of the mining camps and towns grew ever more lawless, including rampant banditry, gambling, prostitution and violence. San Francisco, for its part, developed a bustling economy and became the central metropolis of the new frontier.

UNIT XI
MULTIPLE-CHOICE QUESTIONS

Questions 1-3 refer to the following:

1. The above visual is most likely associated with which of the following?

   (A) Lewis and Clark expedition
   (B) Santa Fe Trail
   (C) California Gold Rush
   (D) Oregon Trail

2. Those who were being transported by the Conestoga Wagons were most likely

   (A) fur traders
   (B) immigrants
   (C) pioneer families
   (D) prospectors and minors

3. This visual most directly reflects which of the following continuities in United States history?

   (A) Puritan contributions
   (B) Manifest Destiny
   (C) Religious Revivalism
   (D) Constitutionalism

Questions 4-6 refer to the following:

"... our manifest destiny to overspread the continent allotted by Providence for the free development of our yearly multiplying millions.... Anglo-Saxon emigration has begun to pour down upon it, armed with the plough and the rifle, and marking its trail with schools and colleges, courts and representative halls, mills and meeting-houses. A population will soon be in actual occupation of California,... it will... necessarily become independent. All this without the agency of our government, without responsibility of our people—in the natural flow of events.... And they will have a right to independence—to self-government—to the possession of the homes conquered from the wilderness by their own labors and dangers, sufferings and sacrifices. . . . the day is not distant when the Empires of the Atlantic and the Pacific would again flow together."

John O'Sullivan, "Annexation," 1845

4. The ideas contained in the passage by O'Sullivan can be attributed to which of the following?

   (A) Ideas of a unity of purpose as stated by Thomas Jefferson in his 1st Inaugural Address
   (B) Fundamental beliefs of liberty and self government in the Declaration of Independence
   (C) Concepts of federalism dividing authority among different branches of government in the United States Constitution
   (D) Guarantees of individual rights in the Bill of Rights

5. The sentiments expressed in the above passage were closely related to another 19th century movement called

   (A) egalitarianism
   (B) social democracy
   (C) laissez faire capitalism
   (D) romantic nationalism

6. Which late 20th and 21st century concept can be considered a continuation of the ideas expressed in the above passage?

   (A) General Welfare State
   (B) Great Society
   (C) American Exceptionalism
   (D) Cultural Diversity

Questions 7-9 refer to the following:

"Independence... has become the "port of embarkation"... [for] the Santa Fe caravans, most of the Rocky Mountain traders and trappers, as well as immigrants to Oregon.... Supplies for each man's consumption... are about fifty pounds of flour, as many more of bacon, tea, coffee and twenty of sugar, a little salt. Beans.... The buffalo...[is] for fresh meat... wagons are manufactured in Pittsburgh... are usually drawn by eight mules or oxen [and] I have seen larger vehicles... with ten or twelve..., and a cargo of goods about five thousand pounds.... The arrival of a caravan at Santa Fe changes the aspect of the place at once. Instead of the idleness and stagnation which its streets exhibited before, one now sees everywhere the bustle, noise and activity of a lively market town. As the Mexicans rarely speak English, the negotiations... are in Spanish."

Josiah Gregg, *Commerce of the Prairies*, 1845

7. The commercial success of the Santa Fe Trail gave impetus to which of the following?

   (A) Homestead Act
   (B) California gold rush
   (C) Kansas-Nebraska Act
   (D) Manifest Destiny

8. The Santa Fe Trail was a 900 mile trek across the Southwest that brought a major exchange of goods between

   (A) the U.S. and Canada
   (B) Canada and Mexico
   (C) Mexico and the U.S.
   (D) Texas and Mexico

9. Shortly after the writing of this account, Santa Fe would be incorporated into the United States as a result of the Mexican Cession from the Mexican War and the Treaty of

   (A) San Lorenzo
   (B) Guadalupe Hidalgo
   (C) Bucareli
   (D) Adams-Onis

Questions 10-12 refer to the following:

"California was a late addition to the Spanish empire, her occupation taking place some two and a half centuries after the establishment of the Spaniards at Mexico City. She was one of the northern frontier units occupied as a measure of defense against restless Indians and the greater menace of foreign encroachments. Beyond this strategic value the province was esteemed very lightly by the Spaniards, and in view of the small population, the excess of expenditure over income, and the slow progress of the missions, this attitude seems to have been fitting. California, in other words, was not a fair sample of Spanish America, but only a marginal colony."

John C. Caughey, *California*, 1940

10. According to the document above the Spanish considered California to be

(A) the cornerstone of their empire in North American
(B) a important colony in the future because of the vast undeveloped mineral resources
(C) an area rich in agricultural products that could be sent to the other colonies in the Spanish borderlands
(D) a fringe colony seen primarily as a buffer against other Europeans

11. As a result of the tenuous hold on California not only did Spain lose it to Mexico, but Mexico lost it as well due to what subsequent activity?

(A) It was the final terminus to the Oregon-California trail used by the pioneer families
(B) It succumbed first to the Bear-Flag rebellion and later to the Mexican Cession
(C) The gold rush brought in a huge number of miners making it easy to wrest the area from Mexico
(D) The Mountain Men took over the Sierra Nevada Mountains in their quest for fur separating the region from the rest of Mexico

12. The documents reference to the menace of foreign encroachments was directed primarily at what country that established a foothold in Northern California?

(A) Russia
(B) Great Britain
(C) Canada
(D) France

Questions 13-15 refer to the following:

"Eyewitness accounts of Americans in California provide a rare example of culture conflict: they express both collectively and individually a deep-seated clash of values between the Anglo-American and Latin-American culture. The clash involved elements such as the Protestant's condescension toward Catholicism, the Puritans dedication to work, now familiarly known as the "Protestant Ethic;" The republican's loathing of aristocracy; the Yankee's belief in Manifest Destiny, and the Anglo-Saxon's generalized fear of racial mixture. In few places were Yankees embraced a non-Anglo-Saxon people—in Louisiana, New Mexico, Texas, Hawaii—did they document their fears as well as California."

Leonard Pitt, *The Decline of the Californios: A Social History of the Spanish-Speaking Californians, 1846-1890*, 1966

13. Despite the cultural clash between the *Californios* and the Anglo-Saxons, California was easily taken from Mexico because of

   (A) Indian raids weakened the Mexican government
   (B) A change in leadership of the Mexican government
   (C) the long drought damaged the economy
   (D) its treatment as a marginal possession of Mexico demonstrated little loyalty to Mexico

14. The clash of values in the passage above shows the culture conflict between

   (A) Anglo-Americans and Latin Americans
   (B) Catholics and Protestants
   (C) Capitalist and Socialist
   (D) Puritans and the Protestant Ethic

15. All of the following were reasons for the clash of cultures between the Anglo-Saxons and the Latin American *Californios* EXCEPT

   (A) Anglo-Saxons disgust with aristocracy
   (B) Anglo-Saxons fear of miscegenation
   (C) Anglo-Saxons loathing of the work ethic
   (D) Anglo-Saxons superior attitude toward Catholics

NO TESTING MATERIAL ON THIS PAGE

UNIT XII

SLAVERY

The complex issue of slavery in the United States has had repercussions that reach into the 21st century. Its role in the development of the U.S. economy and society has been a pivotal one that led directly to the Civil War and Reconstruction, as well as Jim Crow segregation and eventually the Civil Rights movement. No single issue in American history has been as long lasting or as dominant as this one. The unique nature of American slavery with the slave as chattel property was different from slavery in almost all other civilizations. For the 200 years of the legal existence of slavery it dominated the social, political, and economic life in the United States.

African Slavery

·Captured in Africa
Slavery in Africa existed before the Europeans arrived as the merchants of Timbuktu were supplying slaves to the Moors in North Africa and the Muslims were leading slave traders. The Portuguese replaced the Muslims as the leading slave traders and built a series of forts along the African coast that were used to give them control over the slave trade. Few Europeans actually captured slaves as they relied on Africans themselves to capture their fellow Africans. Those doing the capturing were rewarded with guns and rum and were exempt from becoming slaves themselves.

·Supplying the Market
Most of the slaves came from the Guinea Coast of West Africa that includes the modern countries of Senegal, Sierra Leone, Liberia, Gambia, Guinea, Dahomey, Ivory Coast, Ghana, Nigeria, Congo, and Angola. Some of the major tribes who were decimated by the slave trade were the Ibo, Hausa, Fulani, Ashanti, Mandingo, and Yoruba.

·Middle Passage
The euphemism used by Europeans to describe the transporting of slaves from Africa to the Americas was the "Middle Passage." Of the 15 million slaves who were taken out of Africa approximately 3 million died

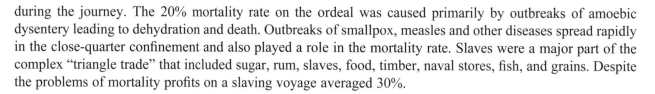

during the journey. The 20% mortality rate on the ordeal was caused primarily by outbreaks of amoebic dysentery leading to dehydration and death. Outbreaks of smallpox, measles and other diseases spread rapidly in the close-quarter confinement and also played a role in the mortality rate. Slaves were a major part of the complex "triangle trade" that included sugar, rum, slaves, food, timber, naval stores, fish, and grains. Despite the problems of mortality profits on a slaving voyage averaged 30%.

·Life on the Slave Ship
Men were shackled together right wrist and ankle to left wrist and ankle and were kept below deck most of the time. Their quarters, often called "kennels," were 16" wide, 29" high and 6' long (smaller than a coffin). They slept naked on rough wood. If the weather was clear and the captain benevolent slaves would be brought on deck at 8:00 and a meal was served at 9:00. If slaves were from the windward coast (Sierra Leone and Liberia) it consisted of boiled rice, millet, or corn meal. If they were from the "bight of Biafra" it was stewed yams. If they were from the Congo or Angola it was manioc or plantains. After the morning meal slaves were forced to jump up and down in their shackles in what was called "dancing the slaves"—a very painful forced exercise. Female slaves were never shackled and were free to have run of the ship as they were available to be sexually abused by members of the crew. To serve on a slave ship was the worst job in the merchant marine and the stench of them could be smelled five miles away.

·Training (Seasoning) the Slaves
Ninety percent of the slaves arrived in Caribbean islands where they were sold to middlemen at either set prices (the healthiest and strongest) or auctioned off. These middlemen would begin a process of breaking the spirit of the Africans (called seasoning) and making them into slaves. This could take up to two years and resulted in a 30% mortality rate. The slaves would then be shipped in a two- way trade for food and timber to Charleston, South Carolina where they would be re-distributed throughout the South.

·Shipment of Slaves
It is estimated that 12 million Africans were shipped to North and South America in the 300-year period from the 16th to the 19th centuries. Of these, approximately 645,000 were brought to the United States. The largest group of Africans were shipped to Brazil, which developed its own unique system of slavery that lasted until 1888. According to the 1860 census the slave population in the United States had grown to four million.

Colonial Legal Development of Slavery

·Jamestown
The first group of Africans to come to the English mainland colonies arrived on a Dutch ship (they had been originally taken off of a Portuguese slave ship by the Dutch) in 1619. They were traded by the Dutch Captain Jope for food. They became indentured servants, joining a small group of white indentured servants already in the colony. They voted, testified in court, and one of the group later held a white servant by indenture.

·Virginia Court (1640)
Three runaway indentured servants were captured and the Dutchmen and the Scot were given an additional year of servitude. The African, John Punch was given life servitude. He may have been the first legal slave.

·Bear Arms
By the 1640s laws were on the books in Virginia that specified that black indentured servants, unlike whites, were not allowed to bear arms.

·Prejudice
A 1662 Virginia law said, "any Christian (white) who shall commit fornication with a Negro shall pay double the usual fine."

·Miscegenation
By 1691 laws had been passed in both Maryland and Virginia that forbid miscegenation in those colonies. In time 40 states would adopt anti-miscegenation and these laws were not overturned until 1967 when the Supreme Court outlawed them in the case of *Loving vs. Virginia.*

Colonial Slavery

·Decline of Indentured Servitude
The number of people willing to become indentured servants declined in the 17th century and a new labor force was needed to pick up the slack. The African slave trade had long been controlled by the Portuguese and the Dutch, but with England becoming the dominant naval power after the War of Devolution with the Netherlands, this begin to change. Liverpool merchants financed an increasingly large slave trade from Africa to the Caribbean where 90% of the slaves were taken. Only 6% came directly to the North American colonies. The shift from indentured servants to chattel slavery of Africans was prompted by a growing lower class of former servants who had worked through the terms of their indentures and thus became competitors of their former masters. There was a constant need for more laborers. The first English colony to legalize slavery was Massachusetts.

·Barbados Slave Code
Adopted in 1661 it was the English code set up to provide a legal basis for slavery on the Caribbean island of Barbados. This code was adopted by South Carolina in 1696 and it formed the basic laws for slavery in the British North American colonies. It required that slave owners dress their slaves. However, it also denied slaves even basic rights guaranteed under English "Common Law" such as the right to life. It allowed the slaves' owners to do entirely as they wished to their slaves, including mutilating them and burning them alive, without fear of reprisal.

·Slave Laws
A 1705 Virginia law said that "All servants imported and brought into the Country [...] who were not Christians in their native Country [...] shall be accounted and be slaves. All Negro, mulatto, and Indian slaves within this dominion [...] shall be held to be real estate." Also, if a slave resisted his master and was killed the master would not be held liable. This law started the process of making slaves chattel or movable property.

American Revolution and Slavery

·Continental Congress
In 1774 the Continental Congress did agree to a temporary termination of the importation of Africans into the colonies, but, in reality, this was a tactical blow against the British slave trade and not an attack against slavery itself.

·Declaration of Independence
In an early draft of the Declaration of Independence, the British king was attacked for his involvement in the slave trade, and he was charged with going against human nature by violating the sacred rights of life and liberty. However, this section was expunged as Southern delegates feared that this condemnation of the monarch reflected on them as well.

·The Revolutionary War

At the time of the American Revolution, fewer than 10% of the half million slaves in the thirteen colonies resided in the North. Most of these northern slaves worked in agriculture. Lord Dunmore, the British governor of Virginia, offered to grant freedom to any slave who ran away from his master and joined the British army. Earlier that year, in spite of the fact that both slaves and free men had served at Lexington and Concord, the colonists had shown an increasing reluctance to have any blacks serving in the Army. However, the eager response of many slaves to Lord Dunmore's invitation gradually forced the colonists to reconsider. Slaves and freedmen were eventually recruited and in most cases slaves were granted their freedom at the end of the war. During the Revolution the armed services were largely integrated with only a few segregated units. Five thousand blacks served in the Continental Army with the vast majority coming from the North. Approximately 20,000 slaves were with the British at the end of the war and they were taken to Canada or the Caribbean and some became the founders of the British colony of Sierra Leone in West Africa.

·Vermont

In 1777 Vermont, at that time it was an independent nation even independent from the other colonies, became the first part of what would become the United States to abolish slavery.

·Ending Slavery in the North

Spurred on by the Quakers who were the first abolitionists, the Pennsylvania legislature passed a law in 1780 that provided for the gradual abolition of slavery. The preamble to the legislation argued that America had gone to war for its own freedom, it should share that blessing with those who were being subjected to a similar state of bondage. Three years later the Massachusetts Supreme Court decided that slavery was contrary to that state's constitution and that it violated the natural rights of man. Connecticut, Rhode Island, New Jersey, and New York all passed laws providing for gradual emancipation and by the ending of the slave trade in 1808, all the northern states had abolished slavery except for Delaware.

·Slavery in the South

Originally slavery developed as a solution to the labor supply needed to cultivate tobacco, rice, indigo, sugar cane and eventually cotton. It became much more than a labor supply as it became an integral part of the social system of the South. Called euphemistically the "peculiar institution" it became increasingly important economically after Ely Whitney's invention of the cotton gin in 1793. By the 1850's "cotton had become king" and the South defined itself by slavery.

·Manumission Attempts

Following the American Revolution some slave owners in Virginia did free their slaves but by 1800 laws were passed to make it more difficult to free a slave.

·Slave Ownership Patterns

Despite their numbers, slaves typically comprised a minority of the local population. Only in antebellum South Carolina and Mississippi did slaves outnumber free persons. Most Southerners owned no slaves and most slaves lived in small groups rather than on large plantations. Less than one-quarter of white Southerners held slaves, with half of these holding fewer than five. Less than 1 percent of those owning slaves (the plantation class) had more than one hundred slaves.

•Slave Laws

Some laws barred slaves from owning musical instruments or bearing firearms. All states refused to allow slaves to make contracts or testify in court against whites. About half the Southern states prohibited masters from teaching slaves to read and write although some of these states permitted slaves to learn rudimentary mathematics. Masters could use slaves for some tasks and responsibilities, but they typically could not order slaves to compel payment, beat white men, or sample cotton. Nor could slaves officially hire themselves out to others, although masters, slaves, hirers, and public officials often ignored such prohibitions. Owners faced fines and sometimes damages if their slaves stole from others or caused injuries. Courts also permitted slaves small diversions, such as Christmas parties and quilting bees, despite statutes that barred slave assemblies.

Southern Defense of Slave System

1. **Charles Pinckney**—He defended slavery as an economic system and argued that the Missouri Compromise violated the intent of the founding fathers. If the value of slaves were lost he believed the economy of the South would be ruined.

2. **John Taylor**—Along with John Randolph of Roanoke, he is the architect of the state's rights theory that held there should be no government interference in slavery, education, religion or anything that was not mentioned in the Constitution. He was opposed to the centralized government and especially the decisions of John Marshall. He was a Physiocrat in his economic philosophy and believed that agriculture was the only productive element in society. He adhered to strict Jeffersonian principles even after Jefferson had abandoned them and was a member of the "Old Republicans."

3. **John C. Calhoun**—Originally a nationalist, he became the chief southern spokesman for states rights. Calhoun believed in the law of self-preservation where man pursues his own interest and not the welfare of others. The tendency toward conflict amongst individuals called for a controlling force. He believed the majority moved by self-interest would aggrandize itself at the expense of the minority. His solution was "Concurrent Majority" as each interest (North and South) would have a voice or veto in making laws affecting that interest. If the issue could not be resolved then nullification by that interest and/or secession would logically follow.

4. **Biblical Defense**—The South used the biblical defense pointing out that slavery was sanctified in the Bible and there was not one word against it. Abraham had 318 slaves and Paul told a runaway slave to return to his master.

5. **Mud-Sill Theory**—All great civilizations must be built on a foundation that was beneath them. Greece and Rome were built on slavery according to this theory. It was argued that if America wanted to be great it must have slavery.

6. **George Fitzhugh**—In his book *Sociology of the South*, Fitzhugh argued that by their very nature Negroes were destined to be slaves. He depicted slaves as infantile and childlike who were improvident and society must prevent them from becoming a burden; hence, they needed to become slaves. Fitzhugh saw slavery as protecting the inferior Negro from being exterminated by the superior whites.

Slave Insurrections

1. **Gabriel Prosser**—He was a slave who designed a scheme for a slave revolt to slay all the whites and take control of Richmond, Virginia. He recruited supporters and organized them into military units. Authorities never discovered how many slaves were involved, but there could have been several thousand, many armed with swords and pikes made from farm tools by slave blacksmiths. On the day of the attack in 1800, the plot was disclosed by two slaves, who did not want their masters killed. Some slaves, in order to save their own lives, testified against the ringleaders. About 35 of the slaves were executed including Prosser. This attempted revolt led to laws being passed making it more difficult to free a slave.

2. **Denmark Vesey**—On July 2, 1822 former slave Denmark Vesey was executed after being tried as the leader of a conspiracy to violently rebel against slave owners and other whites in Charleston, South Carolina. Vesey was a well-respected carpenter, minister, and former household slave who

had won $1,500 in a lottery, which he used to buy his freedom and set up a carpentry shop. In 1822, he was accused of being behind a secret plot to rebel against whites, a plot that involved 9,000 slaves and had been in preparation for more than two years. Their plan was to murder as many whites as they could, then set sail for Africa or Haiti. In the wake of rumors of the plot, Charleston authorities charged 131 people with conspiracy, convicted 67 and executed at least 35.

3. **Nat Turner**—Slave Baptist preacher Nat Turner believed that God had called on him to lead his people out of slavery. A solar eclipse in 1831 was God's sign to Nat Turner that the time had come to strike the blow for freedom and Turner and seven fellow slaves murdered their master and his family while they slept. They then set out on a campaign that terrorized the countryside and killed 55 white people, picking up slave recruits as they traveled from plantation to plantation. Turner and his followers moved through Southampton County toward the county seat of Jerusalem, where they planned to capture the armory. For 48 hours, Turner and his undisciplined followers rampaged and killed until they were killed, captured, or dispersed in a confrontation with armed citizens and the state militia outside Jerusalem. Turner managed to escape and hide out for six weeks before he was captured. He and sixteen of his followers were hung. Nat Turner's rebellion set off a reign of terror for all blacks in the area as state and federal troops swept through killing as many as 200 blacks. To avoid future uprisings, new slave codes were enacted outlawing the education of slaves and putting strict controls on their movements. After this rebellion a policy of not questioning the slave system was adopted in the South because it was felt that any discussion might encourage similar slave revolts.

• Amistad Case

In 1839, 53 slaves led by Joseph Cinque, killed Ramon Ferrer, and took possession of his ship the *Amistad* as it was attempting to move them from Havana, Cuba to Port a Prince, Haiti. Cinque ordered the navigator to take them back to Africa but after 63 days at sea the ship was seized by a U.S. ship, half a mile from the shore of Long Island. The ship was towed into New London, Connecticut and the Africans were imprisoned. The Spanish government insisted that the mutineers be returned to Cuba. President Martin Van Buren was sympathetic to these demands but insisted that the men would be first tried for murder. Abolitionists took up the African's case and argued that while slavery was legal in Cuba, importation of slaves from Africa was not. The judge agreed and ruled that the Africans had been kidnapped and had the right to use violence to escape from captivity. The United States government appealed this decision and the case went before the Supreme Court. Former President John Quincy Adams at 73, defended the *Amistad* mutineers and his emotional eight-hour speech won the argument and the Africans were released. Lewis Tappan and the anti-slavery movement helped fund the return of the 35 surviving Africans to Sierra Leone where they formed a Christian anti-slavery mission in that British colony.

• Anthony Burns Case

A great deal of political heat against the Fugitive Slave Act reached a crisis level in 1854 with the capture in Boston of escaped Virginia slave Anthony Burns. Taken from a clothing store where he worked, Burns' arrest quickly became both a *cause celebre* for Northern antislavery forces as well as an opportunity for "doughface" President Franklin Pierce's administration to prove that it would enforce the controversial Fugitive Slave Law. Abolitionists organized large rallies and marched on the courthouse where Burns was being held. The city of Boston even offered to buy Burns' freedom, but this offer was refused by the Federal government. Within a few days, the administration had Federal marshals put Burns on a ship going back to Virginia and the incident seemed to be over. However, the political fallout from the "Burns Affair" continued, as nine Northern states passed stronger Personal Liberty Laws designed to prevent—or at least make it very difficult—to capture future runaways. Burns became the last fugitive returned to the South from any New England state, thus rendering the Fugitive Slave Act a dead letter.

Politics of Slavery

·British Example

The British led the way in the elimination of slavery. The Slave Trade Act was passed by Parliament in 1807 making the slave trade illegal throughout the British Empire. Led by William Wilberforce, a strong campaign for the abolition of slavery in the British Empire resulted in the Slavery Abolition Act of 1833. The British were also active in suppressing the slave trade of all nations. Between 1808 and 1860 the British West Africa Squadron seized approximately 1,600 slave ships and freed 150,000 Africans who were aboard and could have become slaves.

·Virginia Emancipation Failure

Only once, after Nat Turner's insurrection, did a southern state openly debate the possibility of ending slavery. In 1832 emancipation was narrowly defeated by 7 votes by the delegates at a Virginia constitutional convention. After this vote and Nat Turner's rebellion, the South became a closed society and there was no further discussion of emancipation.

UNIT XII
MULTIPLE-CHOICE QUESTIONS

Question 1-2 refer to the following:

"This [Underground] 'railroad' developed its own language. The 'trains' were the large farm wagons that could conceal and carry a number of fugitives. The 'tracks' were the back-country roads which were used to escape the slave catchers. The 'stations' were the homes where the slaves were fed and cared for as they moved from station to station. The 'conductors' were the fearless men and women of both races who led the slaves toward freedom and the 'passengers' or 'parcels' were the slaves who dared to break for liberty. Passengers paid no fare and conductors received no pay.... The most daring and successful conductor was Harriet Tubman, a former slave. She made 19 trips into the South to bring 300 relatives, friends, and strangers to freedom. Wanted dead or alive in the South she was never captured and never lost a passenger."

William Loren Katz, *Eyewitness: The Negro in American History*, 1967

1. The Underground Railroad was a key component of which movement?

   (A) Abolitionist
   (B) Temperance
   (C) Anti-immigrant
   (D) Civil rights

2. Which legislation after the Mexican War made it much more difficult for the Underground Railroad to function?

   (A) Wilmot Proviso
   (B) Compromise of 1850
   (C) Kansas-Nebraska Act
   (D) Ostend Manifesto

Questions 3-5 refer to the following:

"[Slave Codes] Slaves were not considered men. They had no right of petition. They were 'devisable like any other chattel.' They could own nothing; they could make no contracts: they could hold no property, nor traffic in property: they could not hire out: they could not legally marry or constitute families: they could not control their children: they could not appeal from their master: they could be punished at will: they could not testify in court: they could be imprisoned by their owners, and the criminal offense of assault and battery could not be committed on a person of a slave:... A slave could not sue his master: had no right of redemption: no right to education or religion:... Children followed the condition of the slave mother. A slave could have no access to the judiciary. A slave might be condemned to death for striking any white person."

W. E. B DuBois, *Black Reconstruction in America*, 1935

3. According to the Slave Codes described in the above passage the law regarded the black slave as

   (A) valuable labor
   (B) men before God
   (C) movable property
   (D) protected by the judiciary

4. The slave codes were legally overturned by the

   (A) Gettysburg Address
   (B) 13th & 14th Amendments
   (C) Emancipation Proclamation
   (D) 1st Reconstruction Act

5. Unlike most other historic slavery systems, slaves in the antebellum southern states were not considered to

   (A) be human beings
   (B) be contract workers
   (C) be clothed and fed by their owners
   (D) be governed by slave codes

Questions 6-8 refer to the following:

"That some desperate wretches should be willing to steal and enslave men by violence and murder for gain, is rather lamentable than strange. But that many civilized, nay, Christianized people should approve, and be concerned in the savage practice, is surprising; and still persist, though it has been so often proved contrary to the light of nature, to every principle of Justice and Humanity.... Our Traders in MEN (*an unnatural commodity!*) must know the wickedness of the SLAVE-TRADE, if they attend to reasoning, or the dictates of their own hearts.... Most shocking of all is alledging the sacred scriptures to favour this wicked practice.... *The Slave-Traders should be called Devils, rather than Christians*; a*nd that it is a heinous crime to buy them....*" The past treatment of Africans must naturally fill them with abhorrence of Christians; lead them to think our religion would make them more inhuman savages, if they embraced it..."

Thomas Paine, "African Slavery in America," April 14, 1775

6. The passage above is primarily directed against which aspect of slavery?

   (A) Inhumane treatment of the Africans during the Middle Passage
   (B) Making the Africans into slaves on West Indies Islands
   (C) Defending slavery by using the scriptures by those calling themselves Christians
   (D) The failure to include the abolition of slavery in the Declaration of Independence

7. The above excerpt could be considered an

   (A) attempt to organize an anti-slavery movement among Christians
   (B) inspiration for Thomas Jefferson's failed effort to include the issue of slavery in the Declaration of Independence
   (C) idea that would be favored by southerners of the gentlemen class
   (D) early effort by commercial interests to replace slavery with an indentured servant system

8. Paine's objections in 1775 would ultimately be partially successful with the passage of the

   (A) Slave Trade Act of 1808
   (B) Tallmadge Amendment
   (C) Missouri Compromise
   (D) Wilmot Proviso

Questions 9-10 refer to the following:

"When a new hand... is sent for the first time into the field, he is whipped up smartly and made for the day to pick as fast as he possibly can. At night it is weighed, so that his capability in cotton picking is known. He must bring in the same weight each night following. If it falls short, it is considered evidence that he has been laggard, and a greater or less number of lashes is the penalty. An ordinary day's work is 200 pounds...a slave... is punished if he or she brings in less quantity than that.... The hands are required to be in the cotton field as soon as it is light in the morning, and with the exception of ten or fifteen minutes... at noon to swallow their allowance of cold bacon, they are not permitted to be a moment idle until it is too dark to see, and when the moon is full, they often times labor till the middle of the night."

Soloman Northrop, *Twelve Years a Slave*, 1853

9. The penalty for a slave not picking the amount of cotton established by the baseline is

(A) the wages are docked
(B) sent to solitary confinement
(C) given another job
(D) lashed by a whip

10. A field hand would be most likely to engage in a work slowdown or destroy tools during a

(A) hot summer day
(B) cold winter night
(C) full moon
(D) rain storm

Questions 11-12 refer to the following:

"The stench of the hold while we were on the coast was so intolerably loathsome, that it was dangerous to remain there for any time,... but now that the whole ship's cargo were confined together, it became absolutely pestilential. The closeness of the place, and the heat of the climate,... [the] ship,... was so crowded that each had scarcely room to turn himself... This produced copious perspirations, so that the air soon became unfit for respiration, from a variety of loathsome smells, and brought on a sickness among the slaves, of which many died, thus falling victims to the improvident avarice, as I may call it, of their purchasers. This wretched situation was again aggravated by the galling of the chains, now become insupportable; and the filth of the necessary tubs, into which the children often fell, and were almost suffocated. The shrieks of the women, and the groans of the dying, rendered the whole a scene of horror...."

Olaudah Equiano, *The Interesting Narrative of the Life of Olaudah Equiano, Or Gustavus Vasa*, 1789

11. The scene that Equiano is describing was given which euphemistic name by the "slavers?"

    (A) Peculiar institution
    (B) Triangle trade
    (C) Middle passage
    (D) Slavery solution

12. Equiano describes a scene where the heat, humidity, and physical closeness created a situation where it was

    (A) too difficult to breath
    (B) an epidemic of disease
    (C) worse than death itself
    (D) preparing them for the life of a slave

Questions 13-15 refer to the following:

Act XII, 2:170

WHEREAS some doubts have arisen whether children got by any Englishman upon a negro woman should be slave or [free,] Be it therefore enacted and declared by this present grand assembly, that all children borne in this country shall be held bond or free only according to the condition of the mother, And that if any christian shall commit [fornication] with a negro man or woman, he or she so offending shall pay double the [fines] imposed by the former act.

Virginia Slave Code, 1662 (spelling corrected)

13. This slave code adopted in Virginia was an attempt to end the common practice of

    (A) midnight integration
    (B) segregation
    (C) biracial marriages
    (D) black and white socialization

14. The code in the above passage discriminates against those who commit fornication (sex outside of marriage) by

    (A) making it illegal with slaves but legal with whites
    (B) demanding jail time for those who commit it with a negro man or woman
    (C) making them pay double the usual fine if it is with a negro man or woman
    (D) deporting them back to the country they came from

15. Virginia's slave code of 1662 firmly established that

    (A) Christians were exempt from the provisions of the law
    (B) fornication was an illegal act
    (C) Englishman were free to do what they wanted with slaves
    (D) children would take the status of free or slave from their mother

UNIT XIII

EVENTS LEADING TO CIVIL WAR

From the end of the Mexican War in 1848 until the 1861 start of the Civil War, the issue of slavery in the territories dominated the U.S. political scene. The events that took place would ultimately lead to the conflagration of the Civil War. Some historians have called this generation of political leaders a "blundering one" because they blundered into the Civil War. The evidence suggests that a number of compromises were tried but that the moral issue of slavery may have been too great to compromise away.

Political Events

·Gag Resolutions

In 1836 southern Congressmen and their "doughface" allies passed a so-called "gag rule" that provided that the House of Representatives automatically table any petitions against slavery. John Quincy Adams, former President representing Plymouth in Congress, tirelessly fought the rule for eight years until he finally obtained its repeal.

·Status of New Territory

After its acquisition, Polk failed to get Congress to organize the new territories acquired in the Mexican War. The issues of California, New Mexico, and Utah were unresolved and threatened to destroy the union. It is one thing to acquire an empire and quite another to decide what to do with it once it is acquired.

·Wilmot Proviso

In 1846, freshman Pennsylvania Congressman David Wilmot introduced an amendment to the bill stipulating that none of the territory acquired in the Mexican War should be open to slavery. The amended bill twice passed the House but was rejected by the Senate. The Wilmot Proviso created great bitterness between the North and South and helped crystallize the conflict over the extension of slavery. It would lead to the Compromise of 1850.

Election of 1848

The Democratic Party was split into two factions, the Calhoun pro-slavery wing, and the Van Buren "free soil" wing. Compromise candidate Lewis Cass, who had held office under Jefferson, was nominated. He was the first doughface (a northern Democrat with pro-South views) to be nominated for President and was the first to introduce the concept of popular sovereignty to resolve sectional differences over slavery. The Barnburners (anti-slavery Democrats who were willing to burn down the barn to get rid of the rats) left the party and formed a new third party (Free Soil) with conscience Whigs that nominated former President Martin Van Buren. The Whigs sacrificed their own principles as well as their leaders Clay and Webster, and nominated Zachary Taylor, a military hero. In a close election Taylor won the Electoral College 163-127. Van Buren and the Free Soilers out-polled Cass in New York which gave the election to Taylor.

31st Congress

The Democrats controlled the Senate 35-25 but the House was divided with 112 Democrats, 109 Whigs, and 12 Free Soilers. It took 3 weeks and 63 ballots for the House to elect a Speaker and there was talk of disunion. The coalition of Whigs and Free Soilers kept the Democrats from exercising control.

Nashville Convention

Early in 1850 while Congress was debating Clay's Omnibus Bill on the Compromise of 1850, delegates from nine slaveholding states met at Nashville, Tennessee, to consider a course of action on the compromise measures being debated in Congress. Radical Southerners, who urged secession if slavery was restricted in any of the new territories, were overruled by the moderates. Consequently, the Nashville delegates, while they denounced the Omnibus Bill and reaffirmed the constitutionality of slavery, agreed to a "concession" where the geographic dividing line designated by the Missouri Compromise of 1820 would be extended to the Pacific Coast.

Compromise of 1850

Henry Clay introduced an Omnibus Bill to deal with the issues of day that was opposed by Taylor and had no chance of passing. It lumped together all of the outstanding issues in one bill. Stephen Douglas, 36-year old Northern Democrat resurrected Clay's bill and had it passed piece by piece as separate legislation. Its features included the following: California was admitted as a free state; territories of New Mexico and Utah were to be organized on the basis of popular sovereignty (voters would decide whether to have slavery or not); the slave trade, but not slavery, was abolished in the District of Columbia; a strong fugitive slave law was enacted that replaced the weak 1794 law; the Texas boundary was cut down by almost half and the Texas debt was assumed by the federal government. Passage of the Compromise was achieved by a combination of votes from Northern Democrats and conscience Whigs (who accepted it despite detesting the Fugitive Slave Law), while the bills were opposed by Free Soilers, Abolitionists, and Secessionist. Many representatives refused to vote on the different bills and were absent during the voting. Despite being castigated by New England, Daniel Webster supported the compromise in the famous 7th of March Speech, as did Clay. Calhoun led the opposition as the three powerful Senators debated the leading issues of the day for the last time—all would be dead within two years. The bills supporters received a break when President Taylor, who opposed both the Missouri Compromise and popular sovereignty, died in office and was replaced by Millard Fillmore who signed the bills.

Lopez Filibustering Expeditions

A veteran of many conflicts and wars Narcisco Lopez obtained American aid and planned a filibustering expedition to Cuba (1848) that was thwarted by Zachary Taylor. Not deterred, two years later, a new expedition against Cuba was unsuccessful. In 1851 a third expedition did gain a foothold on the island, but ended in complete defeat and the capture and execution of 50 southerners who had participated along with

López. 162 other supporters (half Americans) were sent to Spain and were released after Congress voted $25,000 to rebuild the Spanish consulate that had been sacked in New Orleans. Northerners saw this as a pro-slaveholding plot and it further convinced them that the South would stop at nothing to expand slave territory.

·*Uncle Tom's Cabin*
Publication of this book by Harriet Beecher Stowe, which was intended to show the brutality and injustice of slavery in 1852, was inspired by passage of the Fugitive Slave Law. This sentimental novel sold more than a million copies in less than a year and made household names of its characters Little Eva, Uncle Tom, and Simon Legree. Later, when Lincoln met Stowe he allegedly said, "So you're the little woman who wrote the book that made this great war!"

Doughface Presidencies—Pierce and Buchanan

·"Young America"
Name given to a movement of aggressive nationalism, manifest destiny, an active foreign policy, support for the European Revolutions of 1848, and southern expansionism. The concept would be associated with politicians such as Stephen Douglas and Franklin Pierce.

·"Doughface" Presidents
The term is loosely used to describe the presidencies of Franklin Pierce and James Buchanan, two presidents from northern states (New Hampshire and Pennsylvania) that had decidedly pro-southern views. The term was first used by John Randolph of Virginia during the Missouri Compromise debates. He considered northerners who voted with the South as "weak men, timid men, half-baked men" who were pliable and moldable by those who were strong. Many doughface political leaders had been ones who had been born and raised in the South but moved to the North as adults and established political careers.

·Election of 1852
After 49 ballots dark horse candidate Franklin Pierce, a New Hampshire Democrat, was nominated after supporters of Cass, Douglas, and Buchanan could not get the necessary 2/3rds of the delegates to vote for their candidates. Passing over Fillmore, who had proved to be effective after Taylor's death, and Webster who thought he deserved the nomination, the Whigs chose Winfield Scott, another military hero. The Democrats won 242-14 in the Electoral College and the Whigs would never nominate another Presidential candidate. The party was disappearing because of its failure to deal with the issues surrounding slavery.

·Pierce Presidency
Both a doughface and a supporter of "Young America," Pierce pursued a program of foreign economic and territorial expansion that was particularly favorable to the South. Southerners dominated this New Englander's cabinet.

·Perry and Japan
In 1853, Commodore Matthew Perry of the United States Navy, commanding a squadron of two steamers and two sailing vessels, sailed into Yokohama harbor aboard the frigate *Susquehanna*. He forced Japan to enter into an agreement with the U.S. government and demanded a treaty permitting trade and the opening of Japanese ports to U.S. merchant ships. It was clear that Perry could impose his demands by force, as Japan had no navy with which to defend itself. The treaty of Kanagawa opened up ports and made provisions for shipwrecked U.S. sailors to be taken care of in Japan.

·Kansas-Nebraska Act

With his interest in organizing the territory west of Illinois so that a transcontinental railroad could be constructed with its eastern terminus in Illinois, Stephen Douglas introduced the Kansas-Nebraska Act to Congress. After three months of debate it passed in 1854 and it allowed people in the territories of Kansas and Nebraska to decide for themselves whether or not to allow slavery within their borders. This was Lewis Cass' concept of popular sovereignty, that was now taken over by Douglas. The Act served to repeal the Missouri Compromise of 1820, which prohibited slavery in lands acquired as a part of the Louisiana Purchase north of latitude 36° 30′. The Kansas-Nebraska Act infuriated many in the North who considered the Missouri Compromise to be a long-standing binding agreement. In the pro-slavery South the act was usually supported. Douglas' motivation for introducing such a contentious bill included his courting of Southern support for his presidential ambitions; his belief in the principles of self-determination and self government; his northern railroad interests (he owned land that could be used for a railroad), which were contrary to Pierce's interest in a southern route; and, his belief that nature would preclude slavery from going into that geographic area regardless of popular sovereignty.

·Kansas Repercussions

After the Kansas-Nebraska Act passed, pro-slavery and anti-slavery supporters rushed to settle in Kansas to affect the outcome of the first election held there after the law went into effect. Charles Sumner, Salmon Chase and others published "An Appeal to Independent Democrats" opposing the Act. This would give rise to the formation of the Anti-Nebraska (later re-named Republican) Party. The Massachusetts' Emigrant Aid Society (later renamed as the New England Emigrant Aid Society) promoted the settlement of antislavery groups in Kansas with the objective of making it a free state. It brought 2,000 settlers into free towns such as Lawrence. Pro-slavery advocates in Missouri organized secret societies to promote slavery in Kansas. The Kansas Territory would become a battleground between the two opposing sides.

·Know-Nothing Party

This new political party's origin was a secret society in New York, the Order of the Star Spangled Banner. The Know-Nothing party (its official name was the American Party) was a xenophobic, anti-Catholic, political organization that emerged in the U.S. between 1852 and 1856. Nativism had been growing since the mid-1840s in response to massive immigration from Ireland and Germany. Many immigrants had become part of urban Democratic political machines, much to the resentment of non-Democratic old-stock Americans. Named the American Party, it became known as the "Know-Nothing party" because members answered "I know nothing" when asked the details about their exclusive, native-Protestant, in some ways secret, organization. Advocating exclusion of Catholics and foreigners from public office and seeking to increase the naturalization period from 5 to 21 years, the Know-Nothings won national prominence chiefly because the two major parties—Whigs and Democrats—were breaking apart over the slavery issue. It became a haven for stranded Whigs who did not want to join the new Republican Party. The party reached its peak in 1854–55, but it soon became factionalized over the slavery issue.

·Republican Party

By 1855, a new party emerged in the North that united Anti-Kansas-Nebraska men in its opposition to the extension of slavery into the territories. Anti-slavery Whigs such as William Seward, Thurlow Weed, and later Abraham Lincoln were dominant in its formation. Elements of the Know-Nothings together with the Free Soil party abolitionists and anti-Nebraska (Independent) Democrats also brought members into the new party. It was originally idealistic and won the support of both business and workingmen with its high tariff policies, and western farmers and settlers with its advocacy of a Homestead Act. After 1858 its appeal became more economic, although in time its stand against the extension of slavery into the territories would dominate all other issues.

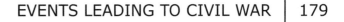
·Ostend Manifesto

This 1854 declaration issued from Ostend, Belgium, by the U.S. ministers to England, France, and Spain, stated that the U.S. would be justified in seizing Cuba if Spain did not sell it to the U.S. The incident that gave rise to this document was the seizure of the U.S. merchant ship *Black Warrior* by Spanish officials in Havana over an error in the ship's manifest. Supported by Pierce, the secret document became public and Northerners saw it as part of a plot by supporters of slavery to expand that institution. The newly formed Republicans used it to recruit more supporters.

·Walker's Filibustering Expeditions

Further evidence of a slaveholding plot to northerners were the activities of William Walker. Taking the expansionist concept of Manifest Destiny to heart and backed by isthmian canal interests (Accessory Transit Co.), Walker hired mercenary soldiers of fortune and between 1853 and 1860 made several attempts to take over territories in Mexico and Central America. He first invaded Baja, California and declared it an independent republic; he then proclaimed the annexation of the nearby Mexican state of Sonora and dubbed it the Republic of Sonora, naming himself president in 1853. Forced out by Mexico in 1854, he surrendered to United States forces and was tried for violating neutrality laws, but was acquitted by a sympathetic jury. Next, taking advantage of an existing civil war, he invaded Nicaragua where he set up a puppet government and named himself president in 1856 and issued a decree establishing slavery. Pierce's reception of Walker's emissary gave virtual recognition to his government. Forced out by a coalition of forces from neighboring Central American countries organized by Cornelius Vanderbilt (Accessory Transit Co.) in 1857, Walker returned to the U.S. and was again acquitted of violating the law. He tried another invasion of Nicaragua a few months later, but was arrested again and sent back to the U.S. In 1860, he was arrested by the British in Honduras and turned over to Honduran authorities who tried, convicted, and executed him.

·Election of 1856

The American Party nominated former president Millard Fillmore and adopted a nativist platform. A rump Whig Party still existed and endorsed the Know-Nothings nominee. Pierce and Douglas were rejected as nominees because of their involvement in the Kansas issue and the Democrats nominated James Buchanan, who had been out of the country as Minister to England, but was palatable to the South because of his involvement in the Ostend Manifesto. The newly formed Republican Party nominated military explorer John C. Fremont, who ran on the slogan of "free-soil, free men, Fremont." Buchanan carried the Electoral College vote 174-114-8 over Fremont and Fillmore. By carrying 11 free states the Republican Party now replaced the Whigs and became the nation's 2nd political party. They would elect the Speaker of the House of Representatives in 1858 and a president in 1860.

·"Bleeding Kansas"

Horace Greeley's New York Tribune first coined this term as it referred to the mini-civil war that existed in Kansas from 1855-1858. The opening of the Kansas and Nebraska territories in 1854 under the principle of popular sovereignty created rival governments—one backed by proslavery Missourians, and the other by antislavery groups. Hostilities between armed bands took place. Over a thousand Missourians crossed the border and menaced Lawrence, a free-state stronghold and looted the town. Along Pottawatomie creek John Brown orchestrated the murder of five men associated with the pro-slavery Law and Order Party, but were not themselves slave owners. The pro-slavery Lecompton Constitution was formulated and ratified after an election in which voters were given a choice only between limited or unlimited slavery; free state men refused to vote which rendered its pro-slavery results tainted. Republicans as well as a number of northern Democrats deemed it a fraud imposed by Missouri "border ruffians" who crossed into Kansas and voted although they did not live in Kansas. President James Buchanan urged Congress to admit Kansas as a slave state under the Lecompton Constitution, but Stephen A. Douglas and his followers broke with the pro-slavery Democrats, and the bill did not pass the House. At a subsequent election in 1858, despite being bribed with federal land if they passed it, Kansas voters decisively rejected the Lecompton Constitution. In 1861 Kansas would be admitted to the union as a free state.

Sumner-Brooks (1856)

Congressman Preston Brooks beat Senator Charles Sumner with his walking cane in the Senate chamber because of a speech Sumner had made three days earlier called "The Crime Against Kansas" criticizing Pierce and Southerners who sympathized with the pro-slavery violence in Kansas. In particular, Sumner lambasted Brooks' uncle, Senator Andrew Pierce Butler for supporting the "harlot" slavery. At first intending to challenge Sumner to a duel, Brooks was told that dueling was for gentlemen of equal social standing, and Sumner occupied a lower social status than Brooks, comparable to a drunkard due to the coarse language he had used during his speech. Caning was considered an appropriate chastisement. In the Senate chamber Brooks hit Sumner repeatedly until his cane broke as Sumner was trapped by his desk and was unable to get up or avoid the blows. South Carolinians sent Brooks dozens of brand new canes to replace the broken one. The *Richmond Enquirer* said, "We consider the act good in conception, better in execution, and best of all in consequences. These vulgar abolitionists in the Senate must be lashed into submission." Brooks survived an expulsion vote in the House but resigned his seat. His constituents saw him as a hero and returned him to Congress. Sumner was unable to return to duty for more than three years while he recovered, spending time in sanitariums in Europe while his constituents reelected him. He would get his revenge during Reconstruction.

Dred Scott v. Sanford (1857)

The issue of slavery in the territories was decided by the Supreme Court 6-3 in a case that became the only one since John Marshall's *Marbury v. Madison* decision to declare an act of Congress unconstitutional. Dred Scott was born a slave and had been taken by his master into the free state of Illinois and the free territory of Wisconsin. Upon his master's death, Scott sued for his freedom on the grounds that since slavery was outlawed in free territory, he had become a free man and "once free always free." This argument was rejected by a Missouri court, but Scott and his white supporters appealed to federal court, where the primary issue was whether a slave had standing—that is, the legal right—to sue or not. If Scott had standing then the Court had jurisdiction, and the justices could go on to decide the merits of his claim. But if, as a slave, Scott did not have standing, then the Court could dismiss the suit for lack of jurisdiction. The Court ruled that Scott, as a slave, could not exercise the prerogative of a free citizen to sue in federal court because he had no standing. They could have stopped at this point and should have; however, Chief Justice Roger Taney and the other southern sympathizers on the Court hoped that a definitive ruling would settle the issue of slavery in the territories once and for all. They ruled that the Missouri Compromise of 1820 was unconstitutional since Congress could not forbid citizens from taking their property—i.e. slaves—into any territory owned by the United States. A slave, Taney ruled, was chattel property, nothing more, and could never be a citizen. No Negroes, not even free Negroes, could ever become a citizen of the U.S. Not only was the Missouri Compromise unconstitutional; but, both the Compromise of 1850 and the Kansas-Nebraska Act were unconstitutional in that slaves could not be excluded from any territory by a vote of the people. This ruling made it impossible to outlaw slavery in any part of the U.S. infuriating the North and and turning former political moderates into abolitionists.

"Doughface" Buchanan

His support of admitting Kansas as a slave state under the tainted Lecompton Constitution and his earlier involvement in the Ostend Manifesto proved to Northerners that he was another doughface Democrat President just as Pierce had been.

·*Impending Crisis of the South (1857)*

Self published book by North Carolinian Hinton Helper attempted to prove by statistics from the 1850 census that slavery had degraded and impoverished most whites in the South. The book was banned in the South as being insurrectionary but became a best seller in the North and was avidly endorsed by many Republicans.

·**Panic of 1857**

Occurring during the height of the Kansas controversy and sparked by the failure of New York banks, this economic downturn was caused by inflation, overextension of credit, overexpansion of the railroads, speculation in western lands, and European wars. It hit the Northeast and Midwest especially hard while the South seemed to escape unharmed. It further convinced the South of the superiority of its cotton economy and culture. The Republican Party benefited by getting two campaign issues: higher tariffs (the tariff of 1857 was the lowest since 1812) and free homesteads as campaign issues in the election of 1858. Manufactures were convinced that the economic crisis was caused by low tariffs.

·**Lincoln-Douglas Debates**

Former Whig Congressman now turned Republican Abraham Lincoln challenged the "Little Giant" Stephen Douglas for the Illinois Senate seat in 1858. In a series of 7 debates held at different locations in Illinois the two candidates discussed the issues of the day. Douglas attacked Lincoln for his "a house divided against itself cannot stand" speech and Lincoln challenged Douglas to explain away the contradictions in his support of popular sovereignty and the Supreme Court's Dred Scot decision. In what became known as the Freeport Doctrine, Douglas explained that slavery could not exist without local laws to protect it regardless of what the Supreme Court had said. Although Lincoln won a slight popular vote plurality, Douglas was elected by the state legislature because of the inequities of gerrymandering gave the Democrats control although they received fewer votes than the Republicans. By barely losing to the better known incumbent Douglas, Lincoln established himself as a force in the Republican Party.

·**John Brown's Raid**

By 1859, Brown became convinced that slavery could only be removed by violence. Funded by Northeastern abolitionists, Brown planned to capture the U.S. government's arsenal at Harper's Ferry, Virginia to launch a slave revolt. Harper's Ferry was a "state of the art" facility for weapons production and research, with a very large stock of arms. Brown assumed that if he captured the arsenal, local abolitionist sympathizers and slaves would join him and a general rebellion against slavery would spread throughout Virginia from his base in the Blue Ridge Mountains. He set out with a racially mixed group of twenty-one men and captured the arsenal. Militia men in Virginia responded and had Brown and his force surrounded when Robert E. Lee and U.S. Marines arrived. They stormed the arsenal and Brown was captured. Ten of his men were killed, including two of his sons, five escaped, and were never caught. As he stood trial and faced the gallows and was executed Brown became a martyr to the abolitionist cause. In the South it was further proof to them that the abolitionist and "Black Republicans" were out to destroy the Southern slave system.

·**Election of 1860**

The Democrats divided into two parties when the Southern Democrats could not get a plank in the platform repudiating popular sovereignty and calling for protection of slavery in the territories. Delegates from 8 Southern states withdrew and nominated Vice-President John Breckenridge of Kentucky for President and Joseph Lane, a slaveholder who had moved to the free state of Oregon, as Vice-President. The remaining Northern Democrats nominated Douglas for President and Hershel Johnson of Georgia for Vice-President. The remnants of the American and Whig parties established the Constitutional Union Party and nominated John Bell of Tennessee for President and Edward Everett of Massachusetts for Vice-President. The confident Republicans who had taken control of the House in 1858, bypassed front runner William Seward (who was considered too radical after his "Irrepressible Conflict" speech) to nominate Lincoln for President and Hannibal Hamlin of Maine for Vice-President. The election was an electoral runaway for Lincoln 180 (18 free states), over Breckenridge 72 (11 slave states), Bell 39 (3 border slave states), and Douglas 11 (Missouri and 3 votes in New Jersey). Even if the vote for the other three candidates had been combined Lincoln would have won the Electoral College with 169 votes despite only winning 39.8% of the popular vote.

Secession

· South Carolina Secedes

By unanimous vote the South Carolina legislature called for a state convention to consider secession as soon as the results of Lincoln's election reached them. On December 20, 1860, without a dissenting vote, they passed the secession ordinance. Their grounds for leaving the union were the North's long attacks on slavery, accession to power of a sectional Republican party, and the election of a president "whose opinions and purposes are hostile to slavery." In fact, Lincoln was only opposed to keeping slavery out of the territories, not out of the states where it existed.

· Crittenden Compromise

Kentucky Senator John Crittenden introduced six constitutional amendments and four resolutions that would have re-established the 36 degrees, 30 minute, Missouri Compromise line as a demarcation point to recognize slavery south of that line. Other aspects of the compromise dealt with the return of fugitive slaves and slavery in the District of Colombia. However, Lincoln would not support it and without his support it received no support in Congress.

· "Fire Eaters"

Nickname given to the most prominent secessionists including, William Lowndes Yancey of Alabama, Edmund Ruffin of Virginia, and Robert Barnwell Rhett, Sr., of South Carolina. They had earned this label for their long and uncompromising devotion to the cause of Southern independence. Outside the inner circle of Southern political power at the national level, and hence free of the need to fashion a middle position to hold together a bisectional party coalition, the "fire-eaters" had consistently taken a hard line on Southern rights. They pushed sectional issues to their logical extreme and applauded the breakup of the national Democratic Party in 1860. Aided immeasurably by the fears provoked by John Brown's raid, they popularized the right of secession among the Southern masses. They had learned their lesson when South Carolina stood alone in the nullification crisis of 1832 and they were motivated to move quickly while resentment against Lincoln and the Republicans was the prevailing mood. "Resistance or submission" was their rallying cry and it soon resonated throughout the lower South.

· Lower South Secedes

Unlike South Carolina where the vote was unanimous, the lower South's vote for secession shows some divisions, but not much.

State	Date	Vote in Favor
South Carolina	Dec. 20, 1860	169-0
Mississippi	Jan. 9, 1861	85-15
Florida	Jan. 10, 1861	62-7
Alabama	Jan. 11, 1861	61-39
Georgia	Jan. 19, 1861	208-89
Louisiana	Jan. 26, 1861	113-17
Texas	Feb. 1, 1861	166-8

·Confederacy Formed

On February 4, 1861 southern leaders met in Montgomery Alabama, wrote a constitution and formed a provisional government. It differed slightly from the U.S. Constitution in that it stressed the sovereign and independent character of each state. The President would serve one 6 year term and he would have the power of a line item veto. Slavery was protected but "the importation of negroes of the African race from any foreign country was forbidden." This was put in to reassure British and French public opinion that the foreign slave trade would not be revived. Jefferson Davis of Mississippi was elected provisional President and Alexander Stephens of Georgia Vice-president.

·Tyler Peace Convention

Headed by former President John Tyler this convention followed the secession of the lower South and fourteen free states and seven slave states were represented. Many of the 131 delegates (which included six former cabinet members, nineteen ex-governors, fourteen former senators, fifty former representatives, twelve state supreme court justices, and one former president") were senior statesmen so the meeting was frequently referred to derisively as the "Old Gentleman's Convention." Proposals that were adopted were similar to the Crittendon plan and even these barely passed by a vote of 9-8 (voting by states).

·Unionist Moderates and the Upper South

February elections in the Upper South had resulted in Unionist victories. The legislatures of five states— Arkansas, Virginia, Missouri, Tennessee, and North Carolina—had issued calls for conventions and the secessionists suffered a sharp setback in all the elections. Moderates controlled Virginia by a 3-1 margin. Tennessee and North Carolina voted against holding conventions and Arkansas and Missouri elected Unionist majorities. By the end of February secession apparently had burnt itself out in the upper South. It was defeated either by a popular vote or, as in the case of the slave states of Kentucky, Delaware, and Missouri, by the inability of the secessionists to pressure the legislatures or governors to issue a call for conventions. A final factor accounting for the Unionist victories in the upper South was the Peace Convention called by the Virginia legislature and headed by former President John Tyler. Boycotted by some of the Northern states and all of the states that had already seceded, the convention, ended in failure. For a short time it had strengthened the hand of the Unionists in the upper South.

·Seizure of Forts

Buchanan refused to hand over the forts in Charlestown harbor after South Carolina troops seized the arsenal. Southern forces seized all other forts throughout the lower south, except Fort Sumter in South Carolina and Fort Pickens in Pensacola, Florida.

·Lincoln's Inaugural

It was conciliatory in tone but did warn the South that "…no state …can lawfully get out of the Union; that resolves to that effect were legally void; and acts of violence…against the authority of the United States are insurrectionary…."

·Fort Sumter

Before Lincoln's re-supply ships could reach the fort the Confederates fired on it for 33 hours until it caught on fire and Robert Anderson's garrison was forced to surrender. There was no loss of life on either side, except for a Confederate horse. The Civil War started on April 12, 1861.

·Lincoln's Call for Troops

His call for 75,000 volunteers for three-month terms was oversubscribed as more volunteered than were asked.

·Secession of the Upper South

It was this call for troops, and not just the armed clash at Fort Sumter, that specifically triggered secession in the upper South. The Unionist majorities suddenly dissolved once the choice shifted from supporting the Union or the Confederacy to fighting for or against fellow Southerners. The Virginia convention, which had remained in session after rejecting immediate secession on April 4, passed a secession ordinance and its decision was overwhelmingly ratified by a popular referendum. An Arkansas convention voted to go out on May 6. The Tennessee legislature, in a move later ratified by a popular referendum, approved secession on May 6. North Carolina left the union on May 20 to complete the 11 states of the Confederacy.

·Slave Border States and Regions

Both Unionist and Confederate sentiment existed in the four border slave states and western Virginia, which seceded from Virginia to became a union state.

1. **Delaware**—Although technically not in the South, slave state Delaware was divided between the pro-Union industrial area around Wilmington and the secessionist Kent and Sussex counties. There was no real attempt to leave the union, although secessionists did raid the state arsenal for arms.
2. **Maryland**—This was a hotbed of secession on the Coastal Plain (the Eastern Shore and Southern Maryland). This feeling was aggravated by the Northern troops passing through the state on their way to Washington. The first real bloodshed of the Civil War occurred in Baltimore on April 19, 1861, when the 6th Massachusetts Regiment fired on an armed mob blocking their path from one railroad station to another. The legislature met in Frederick and considered secession but never voted on it. 46,000 Marylanders enlisted in the Union army, and about 25,000 joined the Confederate army.
3. **Kentucky**—A pro-Union legislature was able to block a sovereignty convention called by the pro-secession Governor. An unofficial convention met in Russellville with representatives from 65 counties and passed an article of secession. The battlefield ultimately decided the issue when Buell defeated Bragg in 1862 to keep Kentucky safely in the Union camp. Other early Union battle victories also secured Kentucky for the Union cause.
4. **Missouri**—The Governor was pro-secession and called out the State Guard without waiting for a secession resolution. With southwestern Missouri under Confederate control, a rump legislature met in Neosho and passed a secession resolution. But when New Madrid fell in April of 1862, after a two-month siege, the Union controlled most of the Mississippi River. Overall there were over 1,000 battles and skirmishes in Missouri, as pro-Union and pro-Confederate bands fought a guerilla campaign. 100,000 Missourians fought for the Union and 30,000 for the Confederacy.
5. **West Virginia**—Military victories by McClellen and Rosecrans allowed the Union to occupy the northwestern part of the state of Virginia. In the summer of 1861 a convention met in Wheeling

and approved the creation of a new state. Over the next year, West Virginians wrangled over a constitution for the state, the principal sticking point being the abolition of slavery. Eventually, Congress passed a statehood bill enacting gradual abolition, and a statehood referendum passed in 1863. Union control of West Virginia was not assured. The Confederates captured Harpers Ferry in 1862 and held it until the end of the war. About 32,000 West Virginians fought on the Union side, and about 18,000 on the Confederate side. The Confederates made frequent raids from Virginia, with the intent of disrupting supply lines and the B & O Railroad.

6. **Eastern Tennessee**—Although a part of the Confederacy the hill country of eastern Tennessee was a hot bed of Unionist sentiment. The name Volunteers refers to the large number of soldiers from that state who joined the Union Army during the Civil War. Much of the fighting in the west during the war would take place in Tennessee.

UNIT XIII
MULTIPLE-CHOICE QUESTIONS

Questions 1-3 refer to the political cartoon:

SOUTHERN CHIVALRY — ARGUMENT versus CLUB'S.

1. The political cartoon above is depicting which historic event of the 1850s

   (A) the animosity that developed between Lincoln and Douglas in their debates
   (B) the debate between John C. Calhoun and Daniel Webster over the nature of the union
   (C) Brook's caning of Charles Sumner who only defends himself with a pen
   (D) secessionist Yancy's attack on Seward for delivering his "higher law" speech

2. The basic interpretation in the above cartoon is that

   (A) a southern gentlemen has every right to exercise the code of the south which called for dueling one's equals but chastising an inferior
   (B) the sword is mightier than the pen
   (C) sectional differences were made worse by southern violence
   (D) southern chivalry demanded that defending yourself with a club was the proper response after being attacked by arguments

3. What subsequent event shows that what is depicted in the cartoon met with the approval of southerners?

   (A) Sumner leaving the Senate to spend time in a European hospital
   (B) After resigning from the House Brooks was reflected by his constitnents
   (C) Dueling is outlawed by Congress
   (D) The failure to prosecute anyone for violence in the Senate

186

Questions 4-6 refer to the following:

"The undersigned have met in conference, first in Ostend. Belgium.... We have arrived at the conclusion, ... that an immediate and earnest effort ought to be made by the government of the United States to purchase Cuba from Spain.... But if Spain, dead to the voice of her own interest, and actuated by stubborn pride and a false sense of honor, should refuse to sell Cuba...what ought to be the course of the American government under such circumstances? Self-preservation is the first law of nature.... After we have offered Spain a price for Cuba far beyond its present value, and this shall have been refused, it will then be time to consider the question, does Cuba, in the possession of Spain, seriously endanger our internal peace and the existence of our cherished Union? Should the question be answered in the affirmative, then, by every law, human and divine, we shall be justified in wresting it from Spain if we possess the power...."

James Buchanan, John Y. Mason, and Pierre Soule, "Ostend Manifesto," October 18, 1854

4. When it became public the above document was supported by

   (A) western railroad builders
   (B) southern expansionist
   (C) anti-immigrant nativists
   (D) the Monroe Doctrine

5. Northerners were enraged at the Ostend Manifesto primarily because they saw it as

   (A) furthering the goals of Manifest Destiny
   (B) waging war for economic gain
   (C) an attempt to extend slavery
   (D) a violation of the Constitution

6. The outrage over the publication of the Ostend Manifesto enabled which newly formed political party to gain support and take over the House of Representatives?

   (A) Democrat
   (B) Whig
   (C) American (Know Nothing)
   (D) Republican

Questions 7-9 refer to the following:

".... Can a negro, whose ancestors were imported into this country, and sold as slaves, become a member of the political community... become entitled to all the rights, and privileges, and immunities, guarantied by that instrument [Constitution] to the citizen? ..."people of the United States" and "citizens" are synonymous terms, ...The question ... is, whether the class of persons described in the plea.... are constituent members of this sovereignty? We think they are not.... and can therefore claim none of the rights and privileges [of] citizens of the United States.... they were at that time considered as a subordinate and inferior class of beings, who had been subjugated by the dominant race, and, whether emancipated or not, yet remained subject to their authority, and had no rights or privileges but such as those who held the power and the Government might choose to grant them. .... [Dred Scott] could not be a citizen of the State of Missouri, within the meaning of the Constitution of the United States, and, consequently, was not entitled to sue in its courts.... The right of property in a slave is... affirmed in the Constitution. "

Roger Taney, *Dred Scott v. Sanford*, 1857

7. This Supreme Court decision overturned what previous political agreement that had stood for almost forty years?

   (A) 3/5ths clause of the Constitution
   (B) Treaty of Guadalupe Hidalgo
   (C) Annexation of Texas
   (D) Missouri Compromise

8. The ideas contained in this decision would be ultimately overturned by all of the following constitutional amendments EXCEPT

   (A) 12th Amendment
   (B) 13th Amendment
   (C) 14th Amendment
   (D) 15th Amendment

9. This decision of the Supreme Court overturned which two congressional actions that had tried to avert sectional difficulties in the 1850s

   (A) Ostend Manifesto and Talmadge Amendment
   (B) Wilmot Proviso and Gag Resolutions
   (C) Compromise of 1850 and Kansas-Nebraska Act
   (D) Crittendon Proposal and Filibustering Expeditions

Questions 10-12 refer to the following:

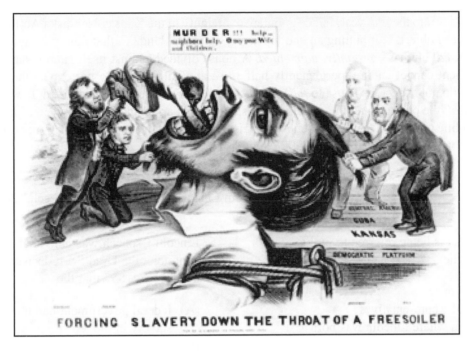

FORCING SLAVERY DOWN THE THROAT OF A FREESOILER

10. The cartoon shows the effects of what 1854 law that is forcing slavery down the throat of the freesoiler?

(A) Kansas-Nebraska Act
(B) Tallmadge Amendment
(C) Wilmot Proviso
(D) Missouri Compromise

11. The politicians doing the forcing, Franklin Pierce, Stephen Douglas, Lewis Cass, and James Buchanan, all either Presidents or presidential candidates are supporters of what political position on slavery in the territories?

(A) Ostend Manifesto
(B) Wilmot Proviso
(C) Homesteading
(D) Popular Sovereignty

12. The idea of the expansion of slavery as seen in the Democratic platform saw all the following as places for this expansion EXCEPT

(A) Cuba
(B) Kansas
(C) Nicaragua
(D) Hawaii

Questions 13-15 refer to the following:

"We are now far into the *fifth* year, [since popular sovereignty in the Kansas-Nebraska Act] was initiated, with the *avowed* object,... of putting an end to slavery agitation. Under... that policy, ... agitation has not only, *not ceased*, but has *constantly augmented*. A house divided against itself cannot stand. "I believe this government cannot endure, permanently half *slave* and half *free*. I do not expect the Union to be *dissolved*—I do not expect the house to *fall*—but I *do* expect it will cease to be divided. It will become *all* one thing or *all* the other. Either the *opponents* of slavery, will arrest the further spread of it, and place it where the public mind shall rest in the belief that it is in the course of ultimate extinction; or its *advocates* will push it forward, till it shall become alike lawful in *all* the States, *old* as well as *new*—*North* as well as *South*."

Abraham Lincoln, "House Divided Speech," June 16, 1858

13. The house that is being referred to in this metaphor is the

    (A) White House
    (B) House of Representatives
    (C) log cabin where Lincoln was born
    (D) United States

14. Which of the following fulfilled Lincoln's prophecy in this speech?

    (A) Emancipation Proclamation
    (B) Homestead Act
    (C) 13th Amendment
    (D) Civil Rights Act

15. Lincoln's speech was delivered in part to contradict the Dred Scott decision which had declared in 1857 that the

    (A) federal government had no power to regulate slavery in the territories
    (B) decision of *Marbury vs. Madison* giving the Court the power of judicial review was annulled
    (C) the issue of slavery was purely a state right's issue and the national institutions would take no stand on it
    (D) slave Dred Scott should be shipped back to Africa to end the controversy over his legal status

UNIT XIV

CIVIL WAR & RECONSTRUCTION

The four long years of the Civil War (also called the War Between the States by historical revisionist and southern apologists) was the most tumultuous period in American history. After 11 southern states seceded from the Union to form their own separate nation, battles to bring them back cost the death of 640,000 to 700,000 men, more than all the casualties in all the other wars combined. In the end it was the industrial and manpower advantage of the North along with the will to continue despite setbacks that decided once and for all the nature of the federal union.

Civil War

· Anaconda Plan
The Union strategy included starving the South into submission by a blockade, capturing the Confederate capital at Richmond, Virginia, and seizing control of the Mississippi River to divide the Confederacy. Lincoln insisted that the war was being fought to preserve the union.

· 1st Battle of Bull Run (1861)
Political demands sent General Irvin McDowell with 30,000 Union troops to Manassas Junction in Virginia where their apparent victory was turned around when Thomas Jackson arrived with Confederate reinforcements that earned him the nickname "Stonewall." Casualties were light, but many of the buggies and picnic baskets that were abandoned by Washington society that had come to view the battle from nearby hilltops hampered the Union retreat. The Confederate victory led to over-confidence in the South which thought the war would be a brief one. Lincoln replaced McDowell with George McClellan who drilled his troops incessantly but was reluctant to move his troops into battle.

· Trent Affair (1861)
The beginning of an international diplomatic crisis for President Lincoln took place when two Confederate officials sailing on the British ship *Trent* toward England were seized by the U.S. Navy. England, the leading

191

world naval power, demanded their release, and threatened war if this was not done. Lincoln eventually gave in and ordered their release saying "one war at a time."

·Grant in the West

Ulysses S. Grant captured forts Henry and Donaldson in Tennessee and then fought a major bloody battle in April of 1862 at Shiloh creek near Corinth, Mississippi with 13,000 casualties out of the 60,000 Union troops while the Confederates suffered 11,000 casualties out of the 40,000 troops engaged. The Confederates withdrew but the casualty rate convinced both sides that it would be a long and bloody conflict. Because of the carnage and the Confederates surprising Grant's forces, Lincoln was pressured to relieve Grant but resisted saying "I can't spare this man; he fights."

·New Orleans Captured

The largest southern city was taken by Admiral Farragut in April of 1862. This would take Louisiana out of the war. Later in the war, he was warned of a mine-field at Mobile Alabama, Farragut uttered the famous phrase "Damn the torpedoes, full speed ahead!"

·*Merrimac* and *Monitor* (1862)

The Confederate ironclad 'Merrimac' (CSS Virginia) sank two wooden Union ships and then battled the Union Ironclad 'Monitor' to a draw in Chesapeake Bay. Naval warfare was thus changed forever making wooden warships obsolete.

·Peninsula Campaign (1962)

McClellan's Army of the Potomac finally advanced from Washington down the Potomac River and Chesapeake Bay to the peninsula south of the Confederate capital at Richmond. President Lincoln temporarily relieved the slow moving McClellan as general-in-chief and took direct command of the Union Armies. The Battle of Seven Pines ensued as Joseph E. Johnston's army attacked McClellan's troops in front of Richmond and nearly defeated them as Johnston was badly wounded. Robert E. Lee assumed command, replacing the wounded Johnston and renamed his force the Army of Northern Virginia. Lee attacked McClellan near Richmond, resulting in very heavy losses for both armies in the "Seven Days Battles" and McClellan withdrew back toward Washington. Although outmanned the Confederates stopped the Union attack on their capital.

·2nd Battle of Bull Run (1862)

After four months as his own general-in-chief, Lincoln turned the task over to Henry Halleck who chose John Pope to head the Union Army. The Union army's 75,000 force was defeated by 55,000 Confederates under Stonewall Jackson and James Longstreet, at the second battle of Bull Run in northern Virginia. Once again the Union Army retreated to Washington and the president relieved Pope and again placed McClellan in charge.

·Antietam (1862)

As Lee attempted to take the war to Union territory, Lincoln finally achieved a victory in Maryland as McClellan and the numerically superior Union forces (they also had Lee's battle plans) defeated the Confederates. By nightfall 26,000 men were dead, wounded, or missing. Lee withdrew in good order to Virginia as McClellan failed to pursue the Confederates following the Union victory.

·Emancipation Proclamation

After the Union victory at Antietam, Lincoln issued the Emancipation Proclamation on January 1, 1863 that declared free all slaves residing in territory in rebellion against the federal government. This Emancipation Proclamation actually freed few slaves. It did not apply to slaves in the border states fighting on the Union side nor did it affect slaves in southern areas already under Union control. The states in rebellion did not act on Lincoln's order but the proclamation did show Americans and the world that the Civil War was now being fought for something greater than the preservation of the Union, it was being fought to end slavery. This strengthened the moral cause of the Union especially among the working classes in England. Lincoln had been reluctant to come to this position but had been pushed into it by the Radicals in his own political party. He initially viewed the war only in terms of preserving the Union. As pressure for abolition mounted in Congress and the country. Lincoln became more sympathetic to this idea as a purpose for fighting the war.

· Another Change in Generals

Upset with McClellan for not following up his victory at Antietam—even telling him, "If you don't want to use the army, I should like to borrow it for a while—" Lincoln replaced him with Ambrose Burnside as the new Commander of the Army of the Potomac.

· Fredericksburg (1862)

The Army of the Potomac under Burnside suffered a costly defeat to Lee with a loss of 12,653 men after 14 frontal assaults failed to dislodge a well- entrenched Confederate position. Confederate losses were 5,309 and Lee remarked during the battle, "It is well that war is so terrible—we should grow too fond of it." Lincoln replaced Burnside with Joe Hooker after this battle.

· Chancellorsville (1863)

Under Hooker, the largest Union Army ever assembled was decisively defeated by Lee's much smaller force at the Battle of Chancellorsville in Virginia. The victory was a result of Lee's own daring tactics. It was a Pyrric victory for the Confederacy as Stonewall Jackson was mortally wounded by his own soldiers in an act of "friendly fire." Union losses were 17,000 killed, wounded, and missing out of 130,000 and the Confederates lost 13,000 out of 60,000. This would be the high water mark of the Confederacy with Lee defeating an army twice his size. Lincoln replaced the retreating Hooker with George Meade, the fifth General to lead the Army of the Potomac in a year.

· Copperheads

The term refers to a person from the North who sympathized with the South during the Civil War. Although the Democratic Party had broken apart in 1860 during the secession crisis, Democrats in the North were generally more conciliatory toward the South than were Republicans. They called themselves Peace Democrats; their opponents called them Copperheads because some wore copper pennies as identifying badges. A majority of Peace Democrats supported war to save the Union, but a strong and active minority asserted that the Republicans had provoked the South into secession; that the Republicans were waging the war in order to establish their own domination, suppress civil and states rights, impose "racial equality"; and that military means had failed and would never restore the Union. Peace Democrats were numerous in the Midwest, a region that had traditionally distrusted the Northeast, where the Republican party was strongest, and that had economic and cultural ties with the South. The Lincoln administration's arbitrary treatment of dissenters caused great bitterness there. Above all, anti-abolitionist Midwesterners feared that emancipation would result in a great migration of blacks into their states. As was true of the Democratic party as a whole, the influence of Peace Democrats varied with the fortunes of war. When things were going badly for the Union on the battlefield, larger numbers of people were willing to entertain the notion of making peace with the Confederacy. When things were going well, Peace Democrats could easily be dismissed as defeatists. But no matter how the war progressed, Peace Democrats constantly had to defend themselves against charges of disloyalty. The most prominent Copperhead leader was Clement L. Vallandigham of Ohio, who headed the secret antiwar organization known as the Sons of Liberty. At the Democratic convention of 1864, where the influence of Peace Democrats reached its high point, Vallandigham persuaded the party to adopt a platform branding the war a failure. Some extreme Copperheads plotted armed uprisings. However, the Democratic presidential candidate, George B. McClellan, repudiated the Vallandigham platform. Victories by William T. Sherman and Phillip H. Sheridan assured Lincoln's reelection, and the plots failed. With the conclusion of the war in 1865, the Peace Democrats were thoroughly discredited. Most Northerners believed, not without reason, that Peace Democrats prolonged the war by encouraging the South to continue fighting in the hope that the North would abandon the struggle.

·Gettysburg (1863)
In an attempt to strengthen the peace effort in the North or possibly gain diplomatic recognition from Europe, Lee pursued the Union army into Northern soil. The tide of war turned against the South as the Confederates were defeated at the three-day Battle of Gettysburg in Pennsylvania with Union casualties at 23,000 and Confederates at 28,000. After the battle, when the battlefield was dedicated as a cemetery, Lincoln made a few preliminary remarks before the primary speaker Edward Everett delivered a two-hour oration. This two-minute speech became known as the "Gettysburg Address."

·Vicksburg
On the day after Gettysburg, July 4, 1863 the last Confederate stronghold on the Mississippi River surrendered to Grant and the Army of the West after a six-week siege. With the Union now in control of the Mississippi, the Confederacy was effectively split in two. After the twin defeats at the two "burgs" in two days, there was little chance of a southern victory but the Confederacy would fight on defensively for almost two more years.

·Quantrill's Raid
At Lawrence, Kansas, pro-Confederate William C. Quantrill and 450 proslavery followers raided the town and killed 182 civilians.

·New York Draft Riots
Anti-draft riots in New York City included arson and the murder of blacks by poor immigrant whites, primarily Irish. At least 120 persons were killed including children who were living in an orphanage that was burned and there were $2 million in damages. Union soldiers returning from Gettysburg restored order.

·Chickamauga (1863)
A decisive Confederate victory by Braxton Bragg's Army of Tennessee at Chickamauga left William Rosecrans' Union Army of the Cumberland trapped in Chattanooga, Tennessee under Confederate siege.

·Chattanooga (1863)
Grant's army ended the siege of Chattanooga as Union forces defeated the siege army of Braxton Bragg. The way was now open for the invasion of the Lower South.

·Change in Command
After the Union defeat at Chickamauga, Lincoln appointed Grant to head all the armies in the West. After Chattanooga, Lincoln appointed Grant to command all of the armies of the United States and to personally lead the Army of the Potomac. William T. Sherman succeeded Grant as commander in the West. In May of 1864, a massive, coordinated campaign of all the Union Armies commenced. In Virginia, Grant with an army of 120,000 advanced toward Richmond to engage Lee's Army of Northern Virginia, now numbering 64,000. This started a war of attrition that would last for nearly a year. In the west, Sherman, with 100,000 men advanced toward Atlanta as it engaged Joseph E. Johnston's 60,000 man Army of Tennessee.

·Cold Harbor (1964)
Grant started his Wilderness campaign with a costly mistake that resulted in 7,000 Union casualties in twenty minutes during an offensive against fortified Confederates at Cold Harbor in Virginia.

·Petersburg (1864-1865)

Located just 20 miles below Richmond was Petersburg. After failing to take the city Grant laid siege to it for 9 months after suffering 8,000 casualties in another failed frontal assault.

·Atlanta (1864)

Johnson's skillful defensive tactics slowed Sherman's march through Georgia. Jefferson Davis, frustrated with Johnson's tactics, replaced him with the rash John Hood who attacked and suffered defeats with heavy losses that allowed Sherman to take Atlanta. "Atlanta is ours, and fairly won," Sherman telegraphed Lincoln. The victory greatly helped secure Lincoln's bid for re-election.

·Shenandoah

A decisive Union victory by the cavalry troops of Philip H. Sheridan in the Shenandoah Valley in Virginia over Jubal Early's troops led to that area being laid to waste just as Georgia was under Sherman and his "march to the sea."

·Election of 1864

Abraham Lincoln was re-elected president, defeating Democrat George B. McClellan. Lincoln carried all but three states with 55 percent of the popular vote and won the Electoral College 212-21.

·Sherman's "March to the Sea" (1864)

With no army to oppose him, as Hood had decimated Joseph Johnston's 60,000 man Army of Tennessee, Sherman marched from Atlanta to Savannah destroying factories, cotton gins, warehouses, bridges, railroads, and public buildings. The path was 300 miles in length and 60 miles wide. It put into practice Sherman's belief in "total war"—destroying the enemies resources, which would destroy his will to fight.

·Freedmen

Sherman found his army surrounded by tens of thousands of former slaves. These refugees followed the army and a temporary military order was issued in January 1865 that allocated thousands of acres of land on abandoned islands along the Atlantic coast into 40-acre plots for the Freedmen. Lincoln's administration was committed to getting laws passed by Congress to make titles to the land permanent. With Lincoln's death, Andrew Johnson pardoned the former rebels and restored their property. The freedmen were often evicted or agreed to work the land under the former slave owners for wages. An opportunity to give the Freedmen economic viability was lost.

·Nashville (1964)

With only a rump army of 22,000 left, Hood decided to threaten Sherman's supply lines—although Sherman's 60,000 man army was living mostly off the land in Tennessee. In a two-day battle, Hood's army was destroyed by John Schofield and John Thomas. In four months Hood had lost Johnston's formidable army of 60,000.

·Sherman's Drive Through the Carolinas (1865)

More destructive than his "march to the sea," Shermans forces burned several towns including Columbia, the state capital. Charleston fell as he advanced into North Carolina but his progress was slowed by Johnston who had been re-instated by Lee and put together an army from the remnants of Hood's decimated forces along with other recruits from the Carolinas.

·Petersburg and Richmond (1865)

The last offensive for Lee's Army of Northern Virginia was an attack on the center of Grant's forces at Petersburg. Four hours later the attack failed and Grant's forces advanced and broke through Lee's lines as

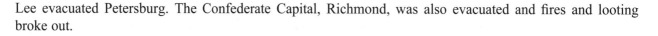

Lee evacuated Petersburg. The Confederate Capital, Richmond, was also evacuated and fires and looting broke out.

·Appomattox Court House

With less than 30,000 men, few rations, and his army surrounded, Lee surrendered to Grant on April 9, 1865. His men were paroled to return home, officers were allowed to keep their side arms, and all soldiers were allowed to retain their private horses and mules.

·Lincoln Assassinated

As the Stars and Stripes were ceremoniously raised over Fort Sumter on April 14, Lincoln and his wife Mary went see the play, "Our American Cousin" at Ford's Theater. At 10:13 p.m., during the third act of the play, John Wilkes Booth shot the president in the head. Lincoln never regained consciousness. Booth escaped but was hunted down and killed in a tobacco barn in Virginia two weeks later. Booth's co-conspirators were caught, tried, and four were executed, while three were sentenced to life in prison (later they were pardoned by Andrew Johnson) and one was acquitted.

·Surrender of Johnston at Durham

Against Jefferson Davis' wishes, Joseph Johnston surrendered his 25,000 man force to Sherman on April 26, 1865 at Durham Station, North Carolina.

·Andersonville

This Confederate prison in Georgia accounted for the deaths of 13,000 out of its 32,000 Union prisoners because of bad rations, unsanitary conditions, and inadequate medical services. The military commander Henry Wirtz was found guilty by a military commission and hanged on November 10, 1865.

Reconstruction

·Freedmen's Bureau

Even before the war ended Congress established (March 3, 1865) this federal agency to care for the freedmen. The agency provided food and medical supplies for needy blacks and some whites; hospitals were constructed in many areas of the South; more than 1,000 public schools were built throughout the South, as well as black colleges; programs were established to monitor labor agreements between freedmen and their employers; the Bureau ran a system of courts aimed at ending the exploitation of the workers; lands of Confederate officials were seized and distributed to freedmen but this program was later ended and the lands were restored to their original owners. Overall, it was a multi-purpose welfare agency.

·Lincoln's Plan

He always maintained that the states had never left the Union and while the war was in progress he appointed military governors for Louisiana, Tennessee, and North Carolina. Favoring rapid restoration to the union his plan included amnesty with some exceptions to Southerners taking a loyalty oath; recognition of state governments when 10% of the electorate of 1860 had taken a loyalty oath; and, acceptance of the 13th amendment (it had passed Congress and was in the process of being ratified by the states) outlawing slavery. Arkansas and Louisiana complied with these provisions; yet Congress refused to seat their representatives.

·Wade-Davis Bill

This was a Congressional plan for Reconstruction that provided for military governors to rule the Southern states. The majority of the citizens would be required to take the loyalty oath. Lincoln pocket-vetoed the bill. This action showed the split that was taking place between the President and Congress over the form of Reconstruction.

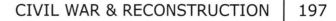

·Johnson's Plan
Upon taking over for Lincoln, Andrew Johnson tried to carry out Lincoln's ideas with some modifications. His plan included amnesty for those who signed the loyalty oaths, provisional governments to be named for each state, state constitutional conventions that would have to repeal the ordinances of secession, adoption of the 13th Amendment, and repudiation of the Confederate war debt. As Congress was not in session he was free to act and did so by recognizing the loyal governments of Arkansas, Louisiana, Tennessee, and Virginia that had been set up by Lincoln. The political moderates who were in control of Congress were willing to go along with these ideas however events would undermine their position and lead to the Radical Republicans gaining control.

·Reconstruction Proclamation
Provisional governments were organized in the seven remaining states and by December of 1865, every state had fulfilled Johnson's requirements for readmission except Texas (it would conform in April of 1866). In his first annual message to Congress, Johnson announced that the Union had been restored and the delegates from the ex-Confederate states had been chosen and were awaiting admission.

·Radical Republicans
The Radicals, a faction of the regular Republican Party and led by Thaddeus Stevens, Charles Sumner, Benjamin Wade, and Benjamin Butler tended to view the Civil War as a crusade against the institution of slavery and supported immediate emancipation. They advocated enlistment of black soldiers and they led the fight for ratification of the 13th Amendment. During the war, the Radicals were critical that Lincoln had thwarted the emancipation efforts of two of his military commanders, John C. Frémont and David Hunter. Lincoln had (initially) opposed the use of black soldiers in the Union Army. Radicals felt Lincoln's Reconstruction Plan was too lenient. In the postwar period the Radicals were advocates of a "hard peace" that would punish the South for causing the conflict. Stevens believed the states were "conquered provinces" and Sumner said they had committed "state suicide." Either interpretation meant that Congress alone, not the President, could restore them to the Union.

·Joint Committee of 15
Controlled by the Radicals this group of six Senators and nine Congressmen refused to accept Johnson's actions and devised a Congressional plan of Reconstruction.

·Events in the South
A series of events in the South weakened the position of the Moderates in Congress. Southern conventions seemed to be putting ex-Confederates in control; some states failed to revoke the ordinances of secession; both South Carolina and Mississippi refused to adopt the 13th Amendment; there was general opposition to the repudiation of the Confederate war debt; there were race riots in New Orleans and Memphis; and, the states seemed to be trying to implement aspects of the slave system by the adoption of Black Codes.

·Black Codes
These vagrancy and apprenticeship laws attempted to bind the freedmen to the land and had different degrees of harshness and leniency depending on the state. These laws were adopted in 1865-1866 by state governments in the South and were designed to regulate the lives of the former slaves. Common elements that appeared in many of the codes included: defining race by blood and the presence of any amount of black blood made one black; Freedmen who were not employed faced vagrancy charges; whites had to be present when Freedmen assembled; Freedmen were assumed to be agricultural workers and their duties and hours were tightly regulated; there were some stipulations against teaching the Freedmen to read or write; public facilities were to be segregated; and, violations of these laws could result in whipping or branding.

· Johnson's Vetoes

Both Moderates and Radicals supported a bill to extend the life of the Freedman's Bureau, which Johnson vetoed on the constitutional grounds that it was the continuance of war powers in peace time. His veto was sustained but the Moderates were disillusioned. Giving citizenship to blacks and granting them the same civil rights as other Americans (except Native Americans) was the intent of the Civil Rights Act passed by Moderates. It was also vetoed by Johnson as an unwarranted invasion of state's rights. It was the beginning of the end for Johnson politically as it was passed over his veto.

· 14th Amendment

Formulated by the "Joint Committee of 15" but also supported by most political moderates, it passed Congress and was submitted to the states for ratification. It protected rights against state infringements, defined citizenship, prohibited states from interfering with privileges and immunities, required due process and equal protection of the laws, punished states for denying the right to vote, disqualified ex-Confederate officials from holding office, and, repudiated the Confederate debt. The ratification of this amendment to the Constitution was made a condition of restoration to the Union for Southern states. Tennessee ratified it, and was restored to the Union in July, 1866. It was the only state that did not go through Military Reconstruction.

· Congressional Elections of 1866

Johnson's attempt to elect moderate Republican and Democrats (he was a Democrat) failed as his swing around the circuit backfired and the Republicans, dominated by the Radicals, captured 2/3rds control of both the House and the Senate.

· 1st Reconstruction Act

This law (Sherman Act or Military Reconstruction Act) passed in March 1867 over President Johnson's veto and it was strengthened by three supplemental acts passed later. It provided for the organization of loyal governments in all the former Confederate states except Tennessee, which, having ratified the 14th Amendment, was regarded as already reconstructed. The ten remaining states were divided into five military districts, each headed by a Major General in the U.S. Army. The military commander was responsible for seeing that each state under his command wrote a new constitution that provided for voting rights for all adult males, regardless of race. Only when the state had ratified its new constitution and the 14th Amendment would the process of political reorganization be complete. Congress reserved the right to review each case and end military rule and seat representatives.

· Military Reconstruction

Despite doubts about the constitutionality of the 1st Reconstruction Act, Johnson implemented it by appointing the commanders, each with 20,000 troops to supplant the governments previously set up by Johnson. Black voters were a majority in Alabama, Florida, Louisiana, Mississippi, and South Carolina.

· Scalawags

Southerners who cooperated with the union military commanders were derisively called Scalawags by ex-Confederates. Many of these were former Whigs or hill country farmers who joined with Carpetbaggers and Freedmen to support Republican Party policies. The term was used from the 1840s to denote a worthless farm animal and later a worthless person. This group constituted nearly 20% of the white electorate after the Civil War and many held government positions in the South and advocated moderate reforms.

· Carpetbaggers

Northerners who came to the South during Reconstruction were called Carpetbaggers. This epithet was used during the Reconstruction period (1865–77) to describe a Northerner in the South seeking private gain. The word referred to an unwelcome outsider arriving with nothing more than his belongings packed in a satchel or carpetbag. Some carpetbaggers were opportunists involved in corrupt financial schemes, but others were idealists who helped rebuild the economy in the South, helped the Freedmen, and participated in educational and social reform.

·Ku Klux Klan

Founded in Pulaski, Tennessee in 1866, this group aimed to destroy the Radical's political power in the South as well as establish white supremacy and intimidate the Freedmen. Confederate General Nathan Bedford Forest was its first Grand Wizard and the Klan, along with other secret societies like the Knights of the White Camellia, spread throughout the South.

·Congress Controls the President

A series of the laws were passed to give Congress control over the executive branch. The Army Appropriations Act limited the president's powers as Commander and Chief. Laws were passed that gave Congress control of the Electoral College. The Tenure of Office Act was passed to stop the president from controlling his Cabinet by making it illegal to remove a Cabinet official without congressional approval before a Presidential term had expired. Also, laws were passed that limited the Supreme Court's appellate jurisdiction.

·Omnibus Act

In 1868 Arkansas, Alabama, Florida, Georgia, Louisiana, North Carolina, and South Carolina all complied with the Reconstruction Acts and were re-admitted to the Union.

·15th Amendment

This suffrage amendment forbid any state from depriving a citizen of his vote because of race, color, or previous condition of servitude. Inspired as much by the Republicans goal of keeping political control in both the North and the South, as it was by idealism, it was easily ratified as the Republicans controlled the state governments.

·Texas, Mississippi, and Virginia

Readmission had been held up in these states by their refusal to approve the disenfranchising clauses of the new constitutions. They were restored to the union following ratification of the 15th Amendment in 1870.

·Impeachment of Johnson (1868)

In his last year in office Johnson was impeached by the House of Representatives by a vote of 126-47 for violating the Tenure of Office Act. He fired his Secretary of War Edwin Stanton who was working with the Radicals. There were 11 Articles of Impeachment but most were centered around his violation of the Tenure of Office Act which Johnson thought was unconstitutional. The Senate failed to remove him from office by 1 vote as 7 Republicans joined 12 Democrats to counter the 35 Republicans who voted for removal.

·Election of 1868

War hero U. S. Grant was nominated by the Republicans on a platform that endorsed Radical Reconstruction, condemned Johnson and the Democrats, advocated payment of the national debt in gold, and waffled on the issues of the tariff and black suffrage. The Democrats nominated Horatio Seymour, attacked Radical Reconstruction, and supported the Ohio Idea of paying off the national debt with greenbacks. Grant won the electoral vote 214-80 but the popular vote was much closer. His popular vote victory can be attributed to the votes of the Freedmen.

·Amnesty Act

In 1872, Congress passed a general Amnesty Act restoring full political rights to all but about 500 ex-Confederates.

· Brazil Migration

Some Southerners came to Brazil at the urging of Emperor Dom Pedro II, who longed to see them bring their cotton-planting expertise to his land. By the late 1860s, several thousand Southerners were going to Brazil from the ports of New Orleans, Galveston, Charleston, and Baltimore. They did not bring slaves with them although Brazil would not fully outlaw slavery until 1888.

· Civil Rights Act of 1875

Introduced by Charles Sumner and Benjamin Butler in 1870 it did not become law until 1875. This last attempt to help the freedmen promised that all persons, regardless of race, color, or previous condition, was entitled to full and equal employment and accommodations in "inns, public conveyances on land or water, theaters, and other places of public amusement." In 1883, the Supreme Court declared the act unconstitutional and asserted that Congress did not have the power to regulate the conduct of individuals. In 1964, a Civil Rights Act was passed that achieved the goals set forth by the 1875 law.

UNIT XIV
MULTIPLE-CHOICE QUESTIONS

Questions 1-3 refer to the following:

1. This depiction of African-American life focuses on which quality in the central scene?

   (A) Idealized, harmonious home scene romanticizing family life and the benefits of emancipation
   (B) Struggles of keeping a family together in the slave south
   (C) Irony of the peculiar institution being neither peculiar nor an institution
   (D) Terrors of slave life including auctions, hunting fugitives, and floggings

2. The word Emancipation is highlighted behind the *Statue of Freedom* and it is framed as a sunburst that supports the view that

   (A) the war should have been avoided because it did not gain freedom for the African Americans
   (B) it was an irrepressible conflict that had to be fought
   (C) economic and social issues would keep the races separate
   (D) the family and churches were the foundations of black life during Reconstrction

3. This visual from *Harper's Weekly* represents

   (A) the results of passage of the 13th, 14th and 15th Amendments to the Constitution
   (B) a strong argument for the colonizing the freedmen back to Africa
   (C) the black family benefiting from emancipation and three scenes showing the horrors of slave life
   (D) the entire history of slave life from the time when the slaves were taken out of Africa in what was called the "middle passage, to their "seasoning" process of being made slaves in the West Indies to their final settlement as chattel property in the South

201

Questions 4-6 refer to the following:

"Thus the contest was joined on the central issue which was to dominate all American history for the next dozen years, the disposition of the Territories. Two sets of extremists had arisen: Northerners who demanded no new slave territories under any circumstances, and Southerners who demanded free entry for slavery into all territories, the penalty for denial to be secession. For the time being, moderates who hoped to find a way of compromise and to repress the underlying issue of slavery itself—its toleration or non-toleration by a great free Christian state—were overwhelmingly in the majority. But history showed that in crises of this sort the two sets of extremists were almost certain to grow in power, swallowing up more and more members of the conciliatory center."

Allan Nevins, *Ordeal of the Union: Fruits of Manifest Destiny 1847-1852*, 1947

4. The two sets of extremists that the excerpt could be referring to are represented by which two paired individuals?

(A) Abraham Lincoln and Stephen Douglas
(B) John Brown and Robert Brownwell Rhett
(C) Henry Clay and Daniel Webster
(D) Mary Chestnut and Clara Barton

6. The interpretation of the causes of the Civil War that Nevins would likely support is

(A) irrepressible conflict
(B) blundering generation
(C) moral crusade
(D) geographic determinism

5. Those who demanded free entry for slavery into all the territories, and if not accommodated advocated secession were given the nick-name of

(A) Barnburners
(B) Locofocos
(C) Fire-Eaters
(D) Doughfaces

Questions 7-9 refer to the following:

"... beneath all the propaganda there was the fact of Negro slavery. Without the 'peculiar institution' there could have been no proslavery or antislavery agitators, no division on the issue ... of extension of slave territory. The northern attack on slavery was a logical product of nineteenth-century liberal capitalism. The southern defense of slavery—by planters deeply concerned about both their profits and their capital investment, was just as understandable. Enmeshed with slavery were other economic differences which contributed to sectional hate.... Between North and South there did exist a profound and irrepressible clash of material interests. ..., the question of 'inevitability' is not within the historian's province, for it is something that can never be solved by research. It should be left to the philosopher."

Kenneth Stamp, *And the War Came*, 1950

7. In the passage above the two factors that are combined as the cause of the Civil War are

(A) economic differences and slavery
(B) geographic differences and culture
(C) blundering politicians and agitators
(D) manifest destiny and expansionism

8. A conclusion that can be derived from the Stamp interpretation is that

(A) there was something inevitable about the Civil War
(B) the propaganda on both sides inflamed passions beyond the realm of reason
(C) research cannot solve all questions some have to be left to philosophers
(D) a difference of material interests had little to do with the cause of the war

9. Which of the following historians interpetations would Stamp be most likely to agree with?

(A) James G. Randall's view that a blundering generation brought about a needless war
(B) Arthur Schlesinger, Jr's view that the moral question of slavery precipitated the conflict
(C) Charles Beards belief that the roots of the controversy were differences in climate, soil, industries, labor systems and divergent social forces
(D) Rollin G. Osterweis' belief that romanticism and cultural nationalism permeated the South in the ante-belluum era making it a distinct society from the North

Questions 10-12 refer to the following:

"It may be seriously doubted whether war rises from fundamental motives of culture or economics.... Let us take all the factors—the Sumter maneuver, the election of Lincoln, abolitionism, slavery in Kansas, cultural and economic differences... could any of these... be said to have caused the war, if one omits... elements of emotional unreason and overbold leadership. If one word or phrase were selected to account for the war, that word would not be slavery, or states-rights, or diverse civilizations. It would have to be... fanaticism (on both sides) or misunderstanding, or perhaps politics.... The notion that you must have war when you have cultural variation, or economic competition, or sectional differences, is an unhistorical misconception which is stupid in historians to promote."

James G. Randall, "The Blundering Generation," 1940

10. Which of the following book titles about the causes of the Civil War would be supported by Randall's thesis?

   (A) *The Irrepressible Conflict of Irreconcilable Differences*
   (B) *An Economic Struggle Between Northern Business and Southern Planters*
   (C) *The Moral Issue Over Slavery Caused the Civil War*
   (D) *Excessive Zeal by the Irresponsible and Incompetent*

11. Because they modified an earlier interpretation that the Civil War was inevitable, historians like Randall called themselves which term regarding their interpretation?

   (A) Traditionalist
   (B) Revisionist
   (C) Culturalist
   (D) Economic Determinist

12. The interpretation in the above passage contains all of the assertions about what caused the Civil War EXCEPT

   (A) elements of emotional unreason and rash leadership
   (B) fanaticism on both sides
   (C) fundamental motives of culture and economics
   (D) a blundering generation of incompetent politicians

Questions 13-15 refer to the following:

"All persons born or naturalized in the United States, and subject to the jurisdiction thereof, are citizens of the United States and of the state wherein they reside. No state shall make or enforce any law which shall abridge the privileges or immunities of citizens of the United States; nor shall any state deprive any person of life, liberty, or property, without due process of law; nor deny to any person within its jurisdiction the equal protection of the laws."

Section 1, 14th Amendment to the Constitution

13. The 14th Amendment accomplished which primary task?

(A) Carried out the ideas of the Articles of Confederation
(B) Extended the Bill of Rights
(C) Allowed the Freedmen to vote
(D) Defined citizenship

14. The phrase "life, liberty, and property" was adopted from which earlier political thinker who's ideas strongly influenced the writing of the Declaration of Independence and Lincoln's support for emancipation?

(A) John Locke
(B) John Calvin
(C) John Winthrop
(D) John C. Calhoun

15. The main purpose of the 14th Amendment was to give freedmen rights but was interpreted by the Supreme Court to give rights to

(A) native Americans living on reservations
(B) corporations by declaring them to be a person
(C) immigrants waiting to be processed for residency
(D) homeless people living in public shelters

NO TESTING MATERIAL ON THIS PAGE

UNIT XV

POLITICS OF THE GILDED AGE

From 1868 to 1900 politicians and politics fell to an all time low (up to that time). Led by a group of non-descript politicians who served as president, the country was consumed by the new money culture and political corruption was the order of the day. The spoils system and an all powerful Congress were not kept in check by the weak presidents that can be called the "forgetables"—Grant, Hayes, Garfield, Arthur, Cleveland, B. Harrison, and McKinley. The term "Gilded Age" was first coined by Mark Twain and Charles Dudley Warner in their 1873 book, *The Gilded Age: A Tale of Today* (1873). It pointed out the ironic difference between a "gilded" and a Golden Age. The emphasis was on the many great fortunes and inequalities of wealth that were created during this period and the standard of living and way of life this wealth supported. The politics of the Gilded Age were another matter as the "forgettable" Presidents between the Civil War and Progressivism along with the wholesale corruption that existed, made this time period a tarnished one in American history. Twain summed it up this way. "What is the chief end of man?—to get rich. In what way? Dishonestly if we can; honestly if we must."

Grantism

·Grant Scandals

This term became a metaphor for the greed, corruption, and incompetence that characterized the two-term Presidency of Ulysses S, Grant from 1868 to 1876. He headed a Republican Party that had once stood for free-soil and freemen but now stood for freebooters. Historian Henry Adams once said about Grant, "the progress of evolution from President Washington to President Grant alone is evidence enough to upset Darwin. An organism as simple as Grant had no right to exist, he should have been extinct for ages." Grant's appointed cronies to his unofficial but influential "kitchen cabinet" did him no good. Also, he extensively practiced nepotism among his relatives, friends, wife's family, and neighbors for jobs. His two administrations were marked by unprecedented political and economic scandals but Grant himself did not personally engage in corrupt activities.

1. **Gold Ring**—The first scandal to taint the Grant administration was Black Friday, a gold-speculation financial crisis in September 1869, set up by Wall Street manipulators Jay Gould and James Fisk who tried to corner the gold market and tricked Grant into preventing his treasury secretary from stopping the fraud. Several of Grant's aides were suspected of inside dealings, but the president himself had been totally fooled by the Gould-Fisk scheme.

2. *Credit Mobilier*—Congressman Oakes Ames, Thomas Durant, and other influential stockholders of the Union Pacific Railroad organized the *Crédit Mobilier* construction company. Acting for both the Union Pacific and for their newly created construction company, they made contracts with themselves. Oakes Ames, as head of the *Crédit Mobilier*, in 1867 assigned contracts to seven trustees to build the remaining road that brought profits variously estimated at from $7 million to $23 million. This process depleted generous congressional grants to the Union Pacific and left it under a heavy debt by the time of its completion in 1869. The scandal became political when Ames, to forestall investigation or interference by Congress, sold or assigned shares of the *Crédit Mobilier* stock to members of Congress at par, although the shares were worth twice as much at that time. He wrote to an associate, that he had placed the stock "where it will produce the most good to us." These letters were later published in the *New York Sun* in the midst of the presidential election campaign of 1872. A subsequent investigation by Congress badly hurt the political reputations of Grant's Vice President Schuyler Colfax, Representative James Brooks, and Ames. Congress censured Ames and Brooks, but there were no prosecutions.

3. **Whisky Ring**—In 1875 over $3 million in taxes was stolen from the federal government with the aid of high government officials. Orville E. Babcock, the private secretary to the President, was indicted as a member of the ring but escaped conviction because of a presidential pardon despite Grant's earlier statement, "Let no guilty man escape."

4. **Belknap Scandal**—An investigation found that Secretary of War William W. Belknap had taken bribes in exchange for the sale of Native American trading posts. Grant accepted the resignation of Belknap but when Congress impeached Belknap for his actions, he escaped conviction since he was no longer a government official.

5. **Sanborn Incident**—In 1874, William A. Richardson, Grant's Secretary of the Treasury, hired a private citizen, John Sanborn, to collect back taxes. Richardson agreed Sanborn could keep half of what he collected and of the $213,000 Sanborn kept, $156,000 was "kicked back" to his "assistant" Richardson.

·Tweed Ring

William Marcy Tweed and a small group of men, by their control of Tammany Hall and the Democratic Party, controlled New York City's finances. They dispensed jobs and contracts in return for political support and bribes. They drained up to $200 million from city's resources as they submitted billings for city work that was never performed; they concocted phony legal agreements and a variety of kickback schemes to line their pockets. Popular support for the Ring, especially among immigrant groups, was maintained with charity and gifts to the voters. Tweed's fall came when The *New York Times* through investigative journalism, told the public of the Ring's corrupt practices. Thomas Nast, the most prominent political cartoonist of his era, made Tweed and his cronies his subjects, which were understandable to immigrants—many who could not read English but could understand the cartoons. Good government groups ("goo-goos") sponsored reform political candidates who unseated corrupt Tweed Ring officeholders. Finally, Samuel J. Tilden, a noted attorney and later governor and presidential candidate, won a conviction of Tweed for forgery and larceny. After serving one year of a 12 -year prison term he was released but was quickly rearrested on another corruption charge.

He fled to Cuba and eventually Spain where Spanish officials were able to identify and capture Tweed with the aid of a Nast cartoon. He was extradited back to the United States in 1876 to die later in a New York City jail.

Politics

·Ohio Plan

This idea formulated by George Pendleton called for the redemption of the government's war bonds in paper money rather than gold, thereby establishing "greenbacks" as permanent legal tender. It was stopped by conservative financial groups who supported deflation in the economy to help creditors not debtors.

·Crime of 73

In a move to contract the money supply, the 1873 Congress discontinued the minting of silver dollars in the Coinage Act. This action was called the "Crime of 73" by silver advocates as it contributed to deflation. Gold rose in value compared to silver from 15-1 to 40-1. Those favoring inflation to combat the depression began campaigns to persuade Congress to resume coinage of silver dollars and to repeal the act providing for the redemption (Specie Payment Resumption Act) of Civil War greenbacks into gold.

·Stalwarts and Half-Breeds

Political battles in the Republican Party were between two factions, the Stalwarts, headed by Roscoe Conkling of New York, were the party regulars who favored Grant for President and were advocates of the spoils system, and the Half-Breeds who were followers of James G. Blaine of Maine and were supporters of mild civil service reform.

·"Waving the Bloody Shirt"

This phrase refers to the Republican demagogic practice of politicians referencing the blood of martyrs or heroes to inspire support or avoid criticism. After the Civil War it gained popularity with an incident in which Benjamin Franklin Butler of Massachusetts, when making a speech on the floor of the U.S. House of Representatives, held up a shirt allegedly stained with the blood of a carpetbagger who had been whipped by the Ku Klux Klan.

·Burlingame Treaty

This 1868 treaty amended the Treaty of Tientsin and established formal friendly relations between China and the U.S. with China getting "most favored nation status." It recognized China's right of eminent domain over its territory and gave China the right to appoint consuls at ports in the United States. In an extraordinary statement it said that "citizens of the United States in China of every religious persuasion and Chinese subjects in the United States shall enjoy entire liberty of conscience and shall be exempt from all disability or persecution on account of their religious faith or worship in either country." Chinese immigration to the United States was encouraged. This treaty was reversed in 1882 by passage of the Chinese Exclusion Act.

·Election of 1876

After running two lackluster candidates against Grant and losing, the Democrats nominated New York's crusading Governor Samuel Tilden in 1876 to run against Rutherford B. Hayes, a compromise Republican from Ohio who got the nomination when the supporters of James G. Blaine and Grant became deadlocked. The Republican platform called for the continued control of the South, civil service reform, and investigation of the effects of Oriental immigration. The Democrats called for the end of Reconstruction in the South, restriction of Oriental immigration and an end to land grants for railroads. Tilden easily won the popular vote and was one electoral vote from victory when the returns in three states, South Carolina, Florida and Louisiana, were disputed. To resolve the conflict Congress appointed a congressional committee consisting of 8 Republicans and 7 Democrats and the committee decided to award all the disputed votes to Hayes giving him the election 185-184 in the Electoral College. As part of what became the Compromise of 1877 the Republicans were allowed to keep the Presidency and in return, promised to end Reconstruction, which they did with the removal of the remaining federal troops. Federal help for the former slaves was abandoned as political expediency won out over idealism.

·Hayes' Presidency

Called "granny" or "his fradulency," he tried to run a good government but failed. His wife, a teetotaler, made sure the White House was liquor free—quite a change from the hard-drinking Grant and all this did was earn him the nickname "granny." Hayes alienated the Stalwarts in his own party by appointing honest and capable men to his cabinet like Carl Schurz, Secretary of the Interior. Some notable accomplishments of the Hayes administration included: signing a bill to allow woman lawyers to argue before the Supreme Court; the Desert Land Act encouraged and promoted economic development of the arid public lands of the West as it offered 640 acres of land to anyone who would pay a $1.25 an acre and promise to irrigate the land; at the request of Argentina he arbitrated the War of the Triple Alliance between Argentina, Brazil and Uruguay against Paraguay and the Argentines hoped that Hayes would give the Chaco region to them; however, he decided in favor of the Paraguayans. He was a hard-money advocate in financial matters and the Bland-Allison Silver Purchase Act was passed over his veto. In labor disputes he took the side of business and sent in U.S. troops to quell labor unrest in the railroads. He vetoed the Chinese Exclusion Bill because it violated the Burlingame Treaty. Seven times he vetoed attempts by the Democratic controlled Congress to nullify the Force Acts, which had been passed to give the President the right to use troops in Federal elections.

·Election of 1880

The Republican convention was divided between the Stalwart faction who wanted to bring back Grant and the Half-Breeds who favored their leader, James G. Blaine. A dark horse candidate James A. Garfield of Ohio, who had ties to the Half-Breeds, was a compromise choice on the 36th ballot and Chester A. Arthur, a Stalwart and close ally of Roscoe Conkling, was chosen for vice president to balance the ticket. The Democrats gave their nomination to Winfield Scott Hancock, a Civil War general with no known political views. In a close election where only 10,000 votes separated the two candidates, Garfield would win in the electoral college 214-155 with third party candidate James Weaver of the Greenback-Labor Party getting more than 300,000 votes.

·Garfield's Term

The 4 months he was in office were marked by a political battle with Conkling and the Stalwarts when he appointed Blaine as Secretary of State and William Robertson, a political opponent of Conkling, as collector of customs at the port of New York. Conkling resigned his Senate seat in protest, as did the other Senator Tom Platt who became known as "me too" Platt. Both Senators expected the legislature to reelect them. When the legislature did not reappoint them this brought about the retirement of Conkling from public office and the decline of the Stalwarts.

·Assassination of Garfield

Charles J. Guiteau, who had been a persistent but unsuccessful applicant for an appointment in the Garfield administration, first as minister to Austria, and then as consul-general to Paris, fired two shots into Garfield at a railroad station as Garfield was on his way to a college reunion. Guiteau, a deeply disturbed man described himself as a lawyer, a politician, and a theologian, and is reported to have said, on being taken into custody: "All right, I did it, and will go to jail for it. I am a Stalwart, and Arthur will be President." A letter was found on him that stated the death of the President was a "sad necessity" that would "unite the Republican party and save the Republic." After the doctors worked on Garfield he died although at first the wounds were thought to be superficial. Guiteau was tried, convicted, and executed, despite his attempts to use an insanity defense.

·Arthur's Presidency

After the Hayes administration, Arthur brought style and drinking back to the White House and proved to be more than just a Stalwart "spoilsmen" by having a successful one-term administration. As a result of the assassination, the Pendleton Act was passed and signed by Arthur, which classified certain jobs, removed them from the patronage ranks, and set up a Civil Service Commission to administer a system based on merit rather than political connections. As the classified list was expanded over the years, it provided the American people with a competent, but sometimes arrogant, permanent government bureaucracy. In 1883, fewer than 15,000 jobs were classified; by the time McKinley became president in 1897, 86,000, almost half of all federal employees, were in classified positions. Acting independently of party dogma, Arthur also tried to lower tariff rates so the government would not be embarrassed by an annual surplus of revenue. He also successfully prosecuted the culprits of the Post-Office fraud that had occurred in Hayes' administration. His most successful action was holding off numerous "pork barrel" raids on the Treasury by the greedy Congress; they would have more success under the next Republican President, Benjamin Harrison.

·Workingmen's Party

In 1877, a workingman's association was established in San Francisco under the leadership of Dennis Kearney, an Irish immigrant and an anti-Chinese zealot. It was formed in response to the high unemployment and in sympathy with the nation-wide railroad strike of that year. Members passed resolutions supporting the striking railroad workers, calling for an end to government subsidies of railroad companies and to military intervention against strikers. The organization insisted on an eight-hour day, a confiscatory tax on wealth, as well as other radical demands. The Workingmen's Party had enough influence to have a new state constitution written and adopted in 1879 that included many anti-Chinese laws.

·Chinese Exclusion Act (1882)

This law was finally signed by Arthur, after Hayes had vetoed it. It was an example of what became known as the "yellow peril"—xenophobia against foreigners, especially Asians. The Chinese had arrived in 1848 with the gold rush. They came primarily as single men hoping to make enough money to bring their families. The Foreign Miners tax made it difficult for them to work the gold fields so they worked other jobs like cooking and laundry. Many found work building the transcontinental railroads. Often Chinese middlemen financed their ship's fare and this contracting system was so cruel it was called "pig selling." Secret societies called tongs with sinister reputations were formed among the most alienated of the Chinese. This Chinese Exclusion Act provided a 10-year moratorium on Chinese labor immigration. For the first time, Federal law forbid entry of an ethnic working group on the premise that it endangered the good order of certain localities. It also discriminated against resident Chinese by making them ineligible for naturalization.

·American Protective Association

The APA was an anti-Catholic organization (similar to the Know Nothings) founded in 1887 by Attorney Henry F. Bowers in Clinton, Iowa. Scots-Irish Protestants, Germans, and Scandinavian Lutherans were attracted to it. The APA's goals included restricting Catholic immigration, making the ability to speak English a prerequisite to American citizenship, removing Catholic teachers from public schools and banning Catholics from holding public offices. At its height in 1896, it claimed 2,500,000 members and had 20 sympathizers in Congress, but these figures were very suspect. It died out in the late 1890s.

·Immigration Restriction League

Founded in 1894 by a group of Boston lawyers, professors, and philanthropists who were upset by the large number of immigrants entering America each year. The league advocated a literacy test that passed Congress but was vetoed by Cleveland. Their goal was to keep out "new" immigrants from southern and eastern Europe.

League members considered immigrants to be inferior human beings, likely to become criminals or public charges.

·Election of 1884

After Arthur failed to get the nomination it was finally the time for Blaine, the "Plumed Knight" of the Republican Party who was known for his oratory, personal magnetism, and political acumen. The Democratic nomination was given to Grover Cleveland, the former mayor of Buffalo and the current governor of New York who ran as a "clean government" candidate. The campaign was bitter and focused on negative aspects of the candidates' character. Cleveland, years earlier in Buffalo, had fathered an illegitimate child. He had taken full financial responsibility for his offspring and publicly acknowledged that he had made a mistake. Republican opponents, however, kept the matter in the public mind by chanting, "Ma, Ma, where's my Pa? Blaine, on the other hand, was a good family man, but had apparently engaged in questionable investment schemes while on the public payroll. Much of the campaign furor revolved around the difference between private and public misdeeds. Democratic partisans used the refrain, "Blaine, Blaine, James G. Blaine, the continental liar from the state of Maine!" especially when evidence of his wrong doing surfaced in the Mulligan Letters (letters that showed his culpability in influence peddling while in Congress). A clueless Protestant minister and Blaine supporter publicly described the Democrats as the party of "rum, Romanisim, and rebellion." Blaine's failure to disavow these remarks, he was present when they were said, offended the large Irish Catholic vote in New York and he lost that state by a thousand votes, thereby losing the election. Cleveland won the popular vote by a narrow 20,000 vote margin and 219-182 in the Electoral College.

·Mugwumps

Also called the independents or Liberal Republicans this reform wing of the Party, advocates of clean government, were led by Carl Schurz who deserted Blaine for the conservative Democrat Grover Cleveland. This defection by the mugwumps illustrated the lack of real issues between the two parties; it was the man and not the party that counted. Mugwumps were often portrayed as "fence-sitters," with part of their body on the side of the Democrats and the other on the side of the Republicans. The term mugwump could have been a combination of "mug" and "wump", which meant respectively the face (mug) and the backside (*rump*) on either side or the fence. Others claim the term was of Indian origin and meant Chief.

·Cleveland's 1st Term

The only Democrat elected between 1860 and 1912, Grover Cleveland was the only President to serve two non-consecutive terms. Winning with mugwump support, they overestimated his commitment to their cause and he disappointed them by replacing hundreds of Republicans who held unclassified government jobs and replacing them with Democrats. He did insist on honesty and efficiency and carefully scrutinized all the appointments. In his fist term the civil service list of classified jobs was almost doubled from 14,000 to 27,000. He had a negative view of both man and government and vigorously pursued a policy barring special favors to any economic group. When he vetoed a bill to appropriate $10,000 to distribute seed grain among drought-stricken farmers in Texas, he wrote, "Federal aid in such cases encourages the expectation of paternal care on the part of the Government and weakens the sturdiness of our national character . . . . " He also vetoed many private pension bills to Civil War veterans whose claims were fraudulent. When Congress, pressured by the Grand Army of the Republic, passed a bill granting pensions for disabilities not caused by military service, Cleveland vetoed it. He angered the railroads by ordering an investigation of western lands they held by Government grant and forced them to return 81,000,000 acres. He also signed the Interstate Commerce Act, the first law that attempted Federal regulation of the railroads. It proved to be ineffective because there were no provisions for enforcement. He also proposed a law to settle labor disputes by arbitration but Congress and the conservative press refused to accept it. Two years into his term, the 47 year old bachelor married 21-year-old Frances Folsom, his ward, in a White House ceremony. In 1887, he called on Congress to reduce high protective tariffs that set off a political firestorm. Told that he had given Republicans an effective issue for the campaign of 1888, he commented, "What is the use of being elected or re-elected unless you stand for something?"

·Election of 1888
In a field of seven serious candidates, Benjamin Harrison was nominated by the Republicans on the eighth ballot, and unlike the campaign of Blaine against Cleveland, he ran a relatively polite campaign. Cleveland was re-nominated and both candidates limited their appearances and focused primarily on the tariff issue. The Republicans also pledged generous pensions to Civil War veterans. Harrison won the Electoral College 233-168, although he lost the popular vote by 100,000 votes.

·Harrison's Administration
Harrison was a protectionist who favored high tariffs. This was exemplified by his nurturing of the McKinley Tariff of 1890, which imposed highest import duties in history to protect American corporations and raise prices. Harrison lobbied successfully for the passage of the Sherman Silver Purchase Act of 1890, which required that silver be used in federal coinage, a concession to the western silver interests. On the other hand, Harrison advocated the conservation of forest reserves, and he embarked on an adventurous foreign policy that included U.S. expansion in the Pacific and the building of a canal across Central America. The Sherman Antitrust Act was passed, but was used more against labor unions than business trusts, as the terms trust, combination, and restraint were never defined. Czar Thomas Reed ran the Republican House as Speaker and oil, sugar, steel, silver, and copper Senators controlled the Senate.

·Election of 1892
Despite some support for political rivals Blaine and William McKinley, Harrison was re-nominated on the first ballot. The Democrats turned again to Grover Cleveland, victor in 1884 and loser in 1888. The nominee, like his opponent, did not lead a unified party. Southern and Western elements agitated for support for silver programs, but did not prevail. The primary plank in the Democratic platform called for the enactment of a tariff for revenue only—an attack on the McKinley tariff. A third party, the Populists (or People's) Party, nominated General James B. Weaver on a platform that called for free and unlimited coinage of silver and government ownership of the railroads. In the largest margin of victory in 20 years Cleveland would win 277-145 with Weaver winning 22 electoral votes.

·Cleveland's 2nd Term
The Panic of 1893 (now renamed Depression) dominated Cleveland's 2nd term. In the last days of the Harrison administration the failure of the Reading Railroad signaled the beginning of a business downturn that resulted in the failure of hundreds of banks and businesses. The stock market plunged and European investors pulled their funds from the United States. The depression soon had impact on the Europeans as well making it world wide. The ongoing agricultural depression in the West and South worsened, and as businesses failed, four million were left unemployed. Both the Sherman Silver Purchase Act of 1890, and the protectionist McKinley Tariff of 1890 were blamed for the panic which was precipitated by the gold drain on the Treasury. Cleveland believed, like most people of both major parties, that the business cycle was a natural occurrence and should not be tampered with by politicians, so he took little action. One result of the depression was a surge in business consolidations as the stronger ones gobbled up the weaker ones.

·Coxey's Army
Jacob Coxey, American businessman, reformer and later politician proposed that Congress should enact a large increase in the amount of legal tender currency in circulation (fiat money) that could be spent on public works, thereby providing jobs for the unemployed. To bring his plan to the attention of Congress and the public, Coxey enlisted the support of Californian Carl Browne, a man with a missionary zeal and unconventional

religious ideas and decided to send Washington a "living petition"—a vast army of the unemployed masses. Coxey and Browne formed an organization called the Commonweal of Christ, and left Ohio in 1894, leading an "army" of 100 followers. They hoped to attract a further 100,000 in route and to arrive in the capital for a massive May Day demonstration. Coxey arrived leading an army of 500, and he and the other leaders were arrested and the army was disbanded. Coxey's army had inspired the formation of other larger "industrial" armies in Los Angeles and San Francisco on the Pacific Coast. 1,200 members of these armies, overcoming the resistance of the railroad companies, federal marshals, the U.S. Army, and judicial injunctions, made it through to Washington. Coxey failed to get his legislation but succeeded in publicizing the plight of the unemployed and encouraged them to organize.

·Election of 1896

With the depression almost guaranteeing a Republican victory, political boss Mark Hanna engineered the nomination of his friend, William McKinley. Silver Republican delegates walked out of the convention and refused to accept the party's dedication to high tariffs and the gold standard. The Democrats convened in Chicago to select their candidate but were a divided party. Cleveland and his followers, the so-called Gold Democrats, were in the minority and the platform actually took two positions—supporting and being against "free silver." In the end this did not matter as William Jennings Bryan, a 36 year- old two-term Congressman from Nebraska, electrified the convention with his "Cross of Gold" speech that led to his nomination and the victory for the free silver advocates. In this speech, he compared the supporters of the gold standard as crucifiers of Christ and silver advocates as being true Christians. The Populist Party, forsaking most of their principles, also nominated Bryan. During the campaign, Bryan crisscrossed the country making personal appearances. McKinley stayed home and ran a front porch campaign where thousands of people came to his home and heard him speak. Bryan was depicted as a "radical socialist," while McKinley was called a "tool of business." Mark Hanna raised $3 million from business for McKinley as compared to $600,000 raised for Bryan. The electoral vote for McKinley's victory was 271-176.

·McKinley's Presidency

Although schooled in domestic issues, the new president would deal primarily with foreign policy (see Unit XIX) during his four and a half years in office. With the ending of the Depression in 1897 and the return of prosperity, economic issues ceased to be significant. McKinley would become embroiled in foreign policy.

·Election of 1900

Basically a replay of 1896 with the most significant issue being Theodore Roosevelt, Governor of New York, who was removed from that state's politics at the urging of "boss" Tom Platt by being made McKinley's Vice-Presidential nominee. At the Democratic convention, Bryan was nominated again and the major issue at the convention was whether to maintain Democratic support for the silver plank, although most Democrats thought that with the return of prosperity it was no longer necessary. Bryan campaigned rigorously and McKinley, once again, waged a front porch campaign by not venturing from the White House. The issues of currency and silver was no longer paramount and instead the campaign issues were whether the United States should give independence to the territories received in its war with Spain. Bryan called for their immediate independence, while Roosevelt, who did most of the campaigning for the Republicans, claimed that the United States had a duty to civilize the lands first. McKinley won by a larger margin than in 1896, 292-155 electoral votes. The Republicans remained in control of Congress.

· **McKinley's Assassination**

A few months after taking office for his second term, while attending a reception at the Pan-American Exposition in Buffalo, McKinley was assassinated by a poor son of Polish immigrants, anarchist Leon Czolgosz. After being tried and convicted Czolgosz's last words before his execution were "I killed the President because he was the enemy of the good people—the good working people. I am not sorry for my crime." The Republican establishment faced what they feared, Theodore Roosevelt was President.

UNIT XV
MULTIPLE-CHOICE QUESTIONS

Questions 1-3 refer to the following:

"THAT'S WHAT'S THE MATTER."

Boss Tweed. "As long as I count the Votes, what are you going to do about it? say?"

1. Thomas Nast's political cartoon against Boss William Marcy Tweed was a forerunner of which journalistic movement that exposed the abuses and corruption of both the politics and industrialists of the Gilded Age?

   (A) Anti-Masonic
   (B) Mugwuumps
   (C) Social Darwinism
   (D) Muckrakers

2. The Nast cartoons played a significant role in the downfall of Boss Tweed by

   (A) organizing women's groups against political practices
   (B) gaining support from illiterate immigrants who could not read but could understand pictures
   (C) appealing to big business corporations to curtail his power
   (D) winning approval from Good Government groups

3. Eventually political bosses like Tweed would be overthrown by the reform movement of

   (A) Populism
   (B) Pragmatism
   (C) Progressivism
   (D) Pugilism

216

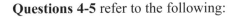

Questions 4-5 refer to the following:

"The United States surely was, in many ways, the Land of Progress. But to that image we should counterpose another—America as the Land of Flight. Millions of persons did not know where they wanted to get to; they only knew that they wanted to escape from their origins. Names were abandoned in favor of more 'American' ones.... The craving to 'get ahead' was manifest in geographical mobility and in lust for wealth as the tool of social mobility. Men who prospered changed their religions: Episcopalianism was the creed of the wealthy. City dwellers scorned their ancestors still on the farm. Second generation Americans felt contempt and shame for the outlandish ways of their parents. The United States became a country of men in flight... without traditions to guide them or visions to serve as beacons, with no havens for rest and no end but the grave, with no goal but wealth, and of wealth there is never enough."

Ray Ginger, *Age of Excess: the United State from 1877 to 1914*, 1965

4. The thesis expressed in the above passage indicates which aspect of what has been called the American character?

(A) Traditionalism
(B) Democratic institutions
(C) Upward mobility
(D) Exceptionalism

5. The conclusion reached in the passage describes which aspect of the American character?

(A) In order to be wealthy you had to be an Episcopalian
(B) Being in the Land of Progress satisfied most Americans
(C) Clearly defined goals and objectives characterized Americans
(D) Without traditions and visions having money was not satisfying

Questions 6-7 refer to the following:

"My party's in power in the city, and it's goin' to undertake a lot of public improvements. Well, I'm tipped off, say, that they're going to lay out a new park at a certain place. I see my opportunity and I take it. I go to that place and I buy up all the land I can in the neighborhood. Then the board of this or that makes its plan public, and there is a rush to get my land, which nobody cared particular for before. Ain't it perfectly honest to charge a good price and make a profit on my investment and foresight? Of course, it is. Well, that's honest graft. Or supposin' it's a new bridge they're goin' to build. I get tipped off and I buy as much property as I can that has to be taken for approaches. I sell at my own price later on and drop some more money in the bank. Wouldn't you?... It's honest graft, and I'm lookin' for it every day in the year."

William Riordan, *Plunkitt of Tammany Hall: A Series of Very Plain Talks on Very Practical Politics, Delivered by Ex-Senator George Washington Plunkitt, The Tammany Philosopher from His Rostrum— the New York County Court House Bootblack Stand*, 1905

6. The type of activity that Plunkitt openly called "honest graft" was challenged by which reform movement in the early 20th century?

(A) Populism
(B) Socialism
(C) Progressivism
(D) New Deal

7. Plunkitt's "honest graft" is illegal today and is called

(A) influence peddling or insider trading
(B) booking a bet
(C) an executive perquisite
(D) competitive bidding on contracts

To Answer Questions 8-11 refer to this chart:

Source of Imports				
Year	% from Europe	% from S. America	% from N. America	% from Asia
1865	47	36	10	5
1900	52	15	11	16
1913	49	20	12	15

8. The decline in the % of imports from South America between 1865-1900 could be attributed to

   (A) political instability in South American countries
   (B) climate change affecting weather and crop yield
   (C) U.S. boycott of South American agricultural products
   (D) an increase in trade agreements with continental Europe

9. Which of the following is the most likely reason imports from Asia slightly declined from 1900 to 1913 after more than tripling from 1865 to 1900?

   (A) The U.S. placed high tariffs on goods coming in from the leading countries of Asia
   (B) Trade barriers like quotas generally suppressed all imports from 1900 to 1913
   (C) A revolution and civil war that started in China in 1911 disrupted the economy of Asia's largest country
   (D) As Asia geared up for war the export economy took secondary importance leading to a drop in the production of trade goods

10. Generally the trend line was either steady or up regarding imports to the U.S. with the notable exception of

   (A) North America from 1865 to 1913
   (B) Asia from 1900 to 1913
   (C) Europe from 1865 to 1913
   (D) South America from 1865 to 1900

11. All of the following are true statements regarding imports into the United States EXCEPT

   (A) the imports from South America made a dramatic drop from 1865 to 1900 of more than 50% but rebounded by gaining 25% from 1900 to 1913
   (B) the largest increase in imports came from Asia between 1865 and 1900
   (C) imports from Asia did not exceed the imports from any other region until 1913
   (D) more than 100% drop in imports occurred from 1865 to 1900 from North America

Questions 12-13 refer to the following:

Frank Beard, 1884, *Judge Magazine*

12. "Another voice for Cleveland" is a reference to his earlier indiscretion which he never denied of

    (A) being caught in a gambling scandal and not paying off his debts
    (B) hiring an illegal immigrant as his maid and not paying Social Security
    (C) fathering a child out of wedlock and paying child support
    (D) running for political office and favoring plural marriage

13. What slogan did the Republicans use in the 1884 election that went along with the cartoon?

    (A) Grover! Grover! he's our man, if he can't do it no one can
    (B) Blaine! Blaine! James G. Blaine, the continental liar from the state of Maine
    (C) Cleveland, a, hop, step, and a jump from the Presidency or the Penitentiary
    (D) Ma! Ma! Where's my Pa!

For Questions 14-15 refer to the cartoon below:

C. Gordon Moffat "Uncle Sam Walks the Plank," 1899, *The Verdict*

14. According to the political cartoon which of the following is likely to make Uncle Sam walk the plank?

   (A) Labor unions
   (B) Anarchist
   (C) Populist
   (D) Business monopolies

15. Which of the following movements that the "Good Government" groups were a part of, directly reflect a subsequent historical continuity in United States history?

   (A) Socialism
   (B) Trade unionism
   (C) Progressivism
   (D) Social Darwinism

UNIT XVI

INDUSTRIALIZATION, LABOR, IMMIGRATION, URBANIZATION

From the end of the Civil War until the turn of the century and beyond, a transformation of the nation took place. Rapid and intense industrialization coupled with the growth of labor, a massive number of immigrants, and the urbanization of society ushered in a new era in American history that was a break from the agrarian past. To challenge the power of the new industrialists national labor unions were formed. The coming of immigrants from southern and eastern Europe would change the urban landscape and the composition of the cities' population. These social and economic changes would usher in a new era for the United States.

Reasons for Rapid Industrialization

The U.S. was able to rapidly industrialize after the Civil War for a number of reasons that created favorable conditions for this transformation. The U.S. would change from an agricultural nation to and industrial one during the period from 1865 to 1900.

·Agricultural Base
In order to industrialize a country needs an agricultural base that will let it release workers from farming so that they can go and work in the factories. No longer was the U.S. a subsistence agricultural country as dramatic increases in farm productivity produced a surplus so it was not necessary to have whole families working on farms. From this point on the problem would become too much farm product, not scarcity.

·Natural Resources
A country cannot industrialize unless it has the basic raw materials that industrialization calls for and the U.S. was fortunate enough to have large quantities of iron-ore and coal, the two essential components to make the single most important product in industrialization—steel. The U.S. also had vast quantities of other important raw materials like oil and copper.

223

·Labor Supply

Although relatively small in number the labor supply that did exist in the U.S. was highly skilled as the development of an artisan (often called mechanics) class was part of the American tradition. The need for unskilled labor was provided by massive waves of immigrants, first the Irish, Germans, and Chinese and later the people of the Mediterranean and Eastern Europe including Italians, Poles, Russians, Serbs, Czechs, Slovaks, Ukrainians, Magyars, Greeks, and Jews from all countries. The freedmen also contributed to the labor supply.

·Government

In order for industrialization to take place, especially under capitalism, the government must encourage it or at least not be actively opposed to it. Although the elections were close, the pro-business Republican Party usually controlled the government in the post-Civil War 19th century and it was very favorable to business. Business taxes were low or non-existent, high tariffs protected business from competition and, especially in the case of the railroads, subsidies were given to encourage the expansion of industry.

·Entrepreneurial Class

A country needs risk takers in order to provide the business acumen and innovation needed to industrialize. No country has ever had as many of these individuals as the United States. Many individuals would come from Europe or from "old stock" America, to risk everything for success. This would be done in order to realize what became known as the "American dream."

·Technological Inventions

This aspect of industrialization was more important in the U.S. than other nations because of the relatively small size of the labor force. The addiction to machines and the tradition of the "Yankee tinker" were characteristics of Americans and inventions were numerous—Bessemer-Kelly in steel processing, Bell with the telephone, Westinghouse the air brake, and Edison, nearly everything including the light bulb and motion picture camera.

·Infrastructure

Much of the social overhead, so important to industrialization, had been provided by the federal and state governments during the road building, canal, and early railroad stages of the antebellum period. This transportation system was in place and would be augmented by the building of the major transcontinental railroads.

·Capital Accumulation

Fortunately, much of this important element in industrialization was available from the success of earlier commercial economic enterprises. When more money was needed much of it was borrowed from England and other European countries, which provided the funds necessary for these economic ventures.

Philosophical Beliefs

·Social Darwinism

Philosophers and sociologists like Herbert Spencer and William Graham Sumner applied Charles Darwin's theory of evolution in the biological world to the social world. They argued that if men were left completely free to do as they pleased, evolution would take place and they would eventually evolve and become perfect. Those who could not evolve would perish according to the concept of "survival of the fittest." Any type of government or public charity would be bad for society, as it would slow down this "weeding out" process. At a banquet honoring Spencer, Henry Ward Beecher stated that he expected to meet Spencer again in heaven as the final proof of "survival of the fittest." It was implied if not actually stated that the "fit" should be left free to overcome the "unfit" if progress was to be achieved. The accumulation of wealth and success proved "fitness;" disease, poverty, or failure proved "unfitness." Men were born unequal and any attempt to equalize them by government laws would be an artificial interference that was contrary to the laws of nature. These ideas became perverted into racism as it was believed some races were superior—the Anglo-Saxon, Teutonic people—while others were inferior and could be eliminated just like the "unfit." Business used this philosophy to justify all its actions as it gave scientific sanction to not only business competition but also to monopolies who were providing a public service by eliminating the "unfit." The courts consistently struck down laws that attempted to help the non-privileged by saying government interference would violate natural laws. All areas of academia including history and the social sciences were affected by Social Darwinism. A college professor could be dismissed for arguing against these theories or for advocating low tariffs.

·Robber Barons or Captains of Industry

A fierce historical debate exists between those who argue that these great industrialists were Robber Barons (the term derives from the medieval German lords who illegally charged exorbitant tolls against ships traversing the Rhine river) or Captains of Industry. Some feel that the powerful industrialists of the "Gilded Age" should be referred to as "robber barons." This view accentuates the negative. It portrays men like Cornelius Vanderbilt, John D. Rockefeller, Andrew Carnegie and J.P. Morgan as cruel and ruthless businessmen who would stop at nothing to achieve great wealth. These "robber barons" were accused of exploiting workers and forcing horrible working conditions and unfair labor practices upon labor. Another view of the industrialist is that of being a "captain of industry." The term "captain of industry" viewed these men as ingenious and industrious leaders who transformed the American economy with their business skills. They are praised for their skills as well as for their later philanthropy once they had achieved great wealth.

·Gospel of Wealth

In an essay titled *Wealth* in 1889, Andrew Carnegie argued that the accumulation of wealth was beneficial to society and the government should take no action to impede it. Carnegie believed the rich were trustees of their money, holding it until proper public uses could be discovered for philanthropic and charitable purposes. It was the duty of the man of wealth to set an example of modest living, as he was a trustee and agent for his poorer brethren. He believed his superior wisdom, experience, and ability should be used to benefit the poor better than they would or could do for themselves. Unlike many of his contemporaries, Carnegie practiced what he preached and spent his last years giving away much of his vast fortune. One of his many charitable ventures was the funding of more than 2,800 public libraries. Carnegie wrote, "The man who dies rich dies disgraced."

Industrialists

1. **Andrew Carnegie**—Andrew Carnegie's family immigrated to America when he was a young boy. Determined to escape the poverty of his native Scotland, Carnegie, started work at an early age as a bobbin boy in a cotton mill and later became a telegraph clerk and operator. He went on to become the richest man in the world. With savings and profits from investments, one investment of $40,000 yielded a million dollars in dividends. He left the railroads and devoted all his energies to the ironworks, later steel, business. His life was a classic example of the Horatio Alger theme of rags to riches coming true. Carnegie became a powerful businessman and a leading force in the American steel industry by crushing his competitors and exploiting his workers. Once amassing his fortune he would give away millions to libraries, concert halls, other public enterprises, and the cause of world peace.

2. **John D. Rockefeller**—A leading industrialist with an image not quite as positive as Carnegies, Rockefeller rose from the rustic origins of his snake oil salesman father, and pious mother, to become the world's richest man by creating America's most powerful and feared monopoly,

Standard Oil. Branded "the Octopus" by muckrakers, the trust refined and marketed nearly 90% of the oil produced in America. Critics, led by Ida Tarbell's muckraking expose, charged that his empire was built on unscrupulous tactics including grand-scale collusion with the railroads, predatory pricing, industrial espionage, and wholesale bribery of political officials. Rockefeller spent more than thirty years dodging investigations until Theodore Roosevelt's trustbusters embarked on a crusade to show how Standard Oil was a bad trust. In 1911, the Supreme Court of the United States held that Standard Oil, which by then still held a 64% market share, engaged in illegal monopoly practices and ordered it to be broken up into 34 new companies. As his wealth grew, so did his giving, and adhering to Carnegie's "Gospel of Wealth" philosophy he gave to educational and public health causes, as well as to basic science and the arts. The Rockefeller Foundation remains a major funding source today.

3. **J. P. Morgan**—He became head of one of the most powerful banking corporations in the world that would finance the formation of the United States Steel Corporation, which became world's first billion-dollar corporation. When the government got into financial trouble President Cleveland appealed to the "House of Morgan" to bail them out with the issuance of bonds in the treasury crisis of 1895. At one point it was estimated that the House of Morgan controlled financial assets that were equal to the value of all the property in the twenty-two states west of the Mississippi River.

The New South

The term "New South" is used to contrast the industrial South that emerged after the era of Reconstruction to the Old South—a slavery-based plantation system of the antebellum period. The original term was used to describe the growing economy modeled after the industrial revolution in the North. The antebellum South had been rural and traditional and after the war it remained rural and impoverished still relying on cotton. Slavery was gone, but the blacks were still there and they had a role in the New South. Henry W. Grady made this term popular in his articles and speeches as editor of the *Atlanta Constitution* while proclaiming that industrialization would bring prosperity to the region. It was not until the mid 20th century that this change took place as Grady's visionary idea was more a promise than a reality.

Immigration

·Old Immigrants

Until 1890, the vast majority of immigrants came from Western and Northern Europe and, with the exception of the Irish and the Chinese, easily assimilated into American society. These WASPS (White, Anglo-Saxon, Protestants), came as families with resources and were often able to settle in towns and on farms. The Germans settled throughout the Midwest and the Scandinavians were in Minnesota and the Dakotas. Most of these immigrants brought skills with them and they became artisans, shopkeepers, and successful farmers who fit right into the melting pot theory of immigration.

·New Immigrants

Starting in the late 1880s and reaching a flood in the period between 1890 and WWI, immigrants from Southern and Eastern Europe came to America to supply the unskilled labor needed for industrialization. These immigrants were different than the primarily Protestant "Old Immigrants" as these "New Immigrants" brought their Catholic, Orthodox, and Jewish religions with them. Many were single males, like the earlier Chinese, looking for any type of work they could get. Most were forced by economic necessity to stay in the cities because that is where the unskilled laboring jobs were located. They did not have the means to travel further into the interior or to move to rural areas. They talked and looked different than most of the immigrants that had preceded them and were forced to live in the squalor of the crowded, urban, slums. From the colonial times until about 1890, 15 million immigrants had come to the U.S. In a much shorter time period from 1890 until 1920 another 15 million entered the country.

· Theories of Americanization

The idea of the "Melting Pot" or the "new man" theory of Americanization was originally stated by the French visitor to the U.S. Jean de Crevecoeur. His writing celebrated Americans for their lack of pretentiousness and their social mobility. He spelled out the acceptance of religious diversity in a melting pot as being created from a variety of ethnic and cultural backgrounds. His essential question, "what is an American, this new man?" contained its own answer. This idea of merging all groups into one homogeneous mass would be the basis of immigration policy until 1920. When the "New Immigrants" begin to arrive—this also sometimes applied to the earlier Irish—Americans saw them possessing attributes that would be undesirable in a melting pot. The idea of assimilation emerged where the immigrants would divorce themselves from their traditional cultures and merge into the existing dominant culture. Eventually a third approach became popular which stressed that it was undesirable for immigrants to lose all their old culture, because the richness of various cultures would keep an international flavor to America in what became known as the "salad bowl" or "stewpot" metaphor. Sometimes different metaphors apply to different generations as the immigration historian Marcus Hanson has shown with the idea of Hanson's Law: "what the son wishes to forget the grandson wishes to remember."

Settlement Houses

· Hull House

One of the first and most important of the settlement houses was Hull House founded by Jane Addams in 1889 in Chicago. Its main purpose was to provide social and educational opportunities for working class people in the neighborhood, many of whom were recent immigrants. There were classes in literature, history, and art; domestic activities such as sewing; free concerts and free lectures on current issues; and clubs both for children and adults. Later, it branched out and offered services to lessen some of the effects of poverty. There was a public dispensary to provide nutritious food for the sick, a daycare center, public baths, and a homeless shelter. Hull House gradually became political as it advocated legislative reforms at the municipal, state and federal levels, addressing issues of child labor, suffrage, and immigration policy.

· Henry Street

Another prominent settlement house in New York was Henry Street headed by Lillian Wald, an American social worker and pioneer in public health nursing. In 1893, she organized a visiting nurse service, which became the nucleus of the noted Henry Street settlement house in New York City. She took care of the sick residents of the Lower East Side; this attracted the attention of Jacob Schiff, a philanthropist who secretly provided her the means to help more effectively the "poor Russian Jews" whose care she made her life's mission. The U.S. Children's Bureau (founded in 1912) was suggested by her, as were other public health services and social reforms.

Labor Unions

· National Railway Union

From his own local union William Sylvis organized a National Iron Molders Union in Philadelphia in 1859 and by 1867 Sylvis had been elected to five terms as president and had built the most powerful labor union in the nation. Just as he had seen the need for his own union to be organized on a national basis, he also thought there should be a national organization of all workers and in 1866, he helped to form the first national labor union: the National Labor Union as he was elected president but he died shortly after it was formed.

·Knights of Labor

Founded in 1869 by Uriah Stephens as the Noble Order of the Knights of Labor, it included both skilled and unskilled workers, and it proposed a system of workers' cooperatives to replace capitalism. To protect its members from employers' reprisals, Stephens favored secrecy and ritual in its meetings, but this became increasingly controversial, as did Stephens's total opposition to strikes. Terence V. Powderly replaced Stephens in 1879 and the union favored open arbitration with management and discouraged strikes. National membership reached 700,000 in 1886 but strikes by militant groups and the Haymarket Riot caused an antiunion reaction that rapidly reduced the organization's influence. A splinter group left to form the AFL.

·American Federation of Labor

In the 1880s, Samuel Gompers, head of the Cigar Makers Union was also instrumental in establishing the Federation of Organized Trades and Labor Unions, which he served as vice president from 1881 to 1886. When it re-organized in 1886 as the American Federation of Labor, Gompers was elected its first president, a position he held for nearly 40 years. As a local and national labor leader, Gompers sought to build the labor movement into a force powerful enough to transform the economic, social and political status of America's workers. He advocated craft or trade unionism, which restricted union membership to wage earners and grouped workers into locals based on their trade or craft identification. This approach contrasted with the effort of many in the Knights of Labor to organize general, community-based organizations open to wage earners. It also contrasted sharply with the "one big union" philosophy of the Industrial Workers of the World. Gompers believed in a pure-and-simple unionism (often called bread and butter unionism) that focused on economic rather than political reform as the best way of securing workers' rights and benefits. Gompers's faith in legislative reform was dashed in the 1880s after the New York Supreme Court overturned two laws regulating production of cigars that he had helped pass. Gompers saw that what the state gave, it could also take away. But what workers secured through their own economic power of negotiation in the marketplace, no one could take away. When political action was necessary, as Gompers increasingly came to believe in his later years, he urged labor to follow a course of "political nonpartisanship." He argued that the best way to increase labor's clout was to have an independent political agenda and seek the endorsement of existing political parties for the agenda.

·IWW (Industrial Workers of the World)

Called the "Wobblies," this radical group grew out of the Western Federation of Miners and favored the anarcho-syndicalist philosophy of direct action, which could result in violence. They emphasized rank-and-file organization, as opposed to empowering leaders who would bargain with employers on behalf of workers. They were one of the few unions to welcome all workers including women, foreigners, black workers and immigrants (like Mexican miners and Asian workers). After Bill Haywood became formal head of the I.W.W he led textile strikes in Massachusetts and New Jersey and helped recruit the over three million mine, mill, and factory workers that at one time or another were Wobblies.

·Molly Maguires

This was a secret organization of Irish-Americans centered in the anthracite mining districts of Pennsylvania who often got their membership from the Ancient Order of Hibernians, an Irish-American fraternal society. Its name came from a woman who led an anti-landlord organization in Ireland during the 1840s. From 1865 to 1875, the Molly Maguires dominated the mining industry of Pennsylvania. Since the police and the forces for law and order were entirely controlled by the mine owners, the Molly Maguires often resorted to violence to intimidate the police. They reached the height of their power in 1875 when they managed to organize a union in a region otherwise unorganized and to call for a strike. The Reading RR, which had extensive mining interests, hired the Pinkerton agency to infiltrate the union, and the power of the Molly Maguires was finally broken by the spying activities of James McParlan, a Pinkerton detective. Ten of the Molly Maguires were hanged.

·Haymarket Riot

In 1886, Chicago workers struck for shorter hours. An active group of radicals and anarchists became involved in the campaign and two days later a shooting and one death occurred at the McCormick Reaper plant when police tangled with the strikers. At Haymarket Square, a protest meeting was called to denounce the events of the preceding day and speakers exhorted the crowd from a wagon, which was used for a makeshift stage. Toward the end of this meeting, while police were dispersing the crowd, a bomb exploded and 8 policeman were killed. The following day, police began a roundup of radicals, agitators and labor leaders, seizing records and closing socialist and labor press offices. Eight men were finally brought to trial for conspiracy. Despite the fact that the bomb thrower was never identified, and none of these eight could be connected with the crime, Judge Joseph E. Gary imposed the death sentence on seven of them and the eighth was given fifteen years in prison. The court held that the "inflammatory speeches and publications" of these eight incited the actions of the mob. The Illinois and U.S. Supreme Courts upheld the verdict. On November 11, 1887 four men, Albert Parsons, August Spies, Adolph Fischer, and George Engel were hanged. One committed suicide in prison awaiting the death sentence. The sentences of two others were commuted from death to imprisonment for life and in 1893; Governor John P. Altgeld pardoned the three who were in prison.

·Homestead Strike

In 1892, workers belonging to the Amalgamated Association of Iron and Steel Workers struck the Carnegie Steel Company at Homestead, Pennsylvania. to protest a proposed wage cut. Just before the strike Andrew Carnegie who sometimes expressed pro-worker sentiments had left the country leaving Henry Frick in charge. Frick, determined to break the union, hired 300 Pinkerton detectives to protect the plant and act as strikebreakers. After an armed battle between the workers and the detectives in which several men were killed or wounded, the governor called out the state militia. The plant opened, nonunion workers stayed on the job, and the strike, which was officially called off on Nov. 20, was broken. The failure of the Homestead strike led to a weakening of union membership in the steel industry.

·Pullman Strike (1894)

In the 1880s George Pullman built the town of Pullman near Lake Calumet to manufacture his railway sleeping cars. All buildings in the town were company owned and rented to workers who also shopped at the company store and bought their water and gas from the Pullman Company. The company cut wages 25%, but failed to reduce the rent in the company owned housing. The workers struck and the three workers who presented the demands were laid off. By late June, sympathetic to the cause of the workers, the American Railway Union headed by Eugene Debs agreed to boycott trains carrying Pullman cars nationwide. The General Managers Association which had been formed to combat the workers appealed to President Cleveland for Federal troops on the grounds that the mail was being interfered with and Cleveland responded, "…that if it took every soldier in the U.S. Army to deliver one postcard, that card would be delivered." The strike was broken by the troops which brought forth violence and looting in Chicago. With the arrest of the leaders, the strike collapsed. Debs and 700 members of the American Rail Union were arrested and Debs spent 6 months in jail reading radical literature and eventually became a socialist.

·Mother Jones

A seamstress by trade, at 37, life changed for Mary Harris Jones when her husband and their four small children died in a yellow fever epidemic. After the epidemic had run its course, she returned to Chicago where, once again, she began to work as a dress-maker. Four years later, in 1871, she lost everything she owned in the great Chicago fire. That event also changed her life drastically, and she discovered a new path to follow. She became involved in the labor movement and began to attend meetings of the newly formed Knights of

Labor. When there was a strike, Jones organized and helped the workers. At other times, she held educational meetings. She lived with the workers, in tent colonies or in shantytowns. In lieu of a family, she would adopt America's laborers, and they would call her "Mother." In 1877, she helped in the Pittsburgh railway strike; during the 1880s she organized workers; in 1898 she helped found the Social Democratic Party; and in 1905 she was present at the founding of the Industrial Workers of the World." She was denounced in the U.S. Senate as the grandmother of all agitators. Mother Jones was proud of that title and said she hoped to live to be the great grandmother of agitators.

African Americans

·Sharecropping

When Thaddeus Stevens' idea of "40 acres and a mule" to give the freedmen economic viability was not adopted, most of the newly freed slaves were relegated to sharecropping for their livelihood. The freedman offered his labor for the right to use the land and received supplies and a share of the crop (usually half) for what he grew. This tied him to the land owned by the whites and gave him little incentive to be productive. Most freedmen could not escape this system until the job opportunities in the North as a result of WWI would bring about their migration for economic reasons.

·Jim Crow

Name taken from a minstrel show character that described the segregation system that developed in the South after Reconstruction. The system became more prominent after the failure of the Populist movement to unite poor whites and blacks in the South. Originally the laws were intended to keep African Americans from participating in the political process; but they soon became social legislation to segregate blacks from all contact with white society including separate railroad cars, drinking fountains, washrooms, public swimming pools, park benches, lunch counters, and all other public facilities. Segregation and disfranchisement laws were often supported, moreover, by lynching southern blacks. From 1889 to 1930, over 3,700 men and women were lynched; most of whom were southern blacks. In the 1890s, southern states began to systematically and completely disenfranchise black males by imposing voter registration restrictions, such as literacy tests, poll taxes, grandfather clauses, and the white primary where only whites could vote in the Democratic Party primary contests which was tantamount to election in the solid Democratic South. Another law establishing the Jim Crow system included banning miscegenation, or interracial marriages. School segregation laws also appeared on the books in nearly every southern state beginning with Tennessee and Arkansas in 1866. Virginia erected in 1869 a constitutional ban against blacks and whites attending the same schools, followed by Tennessee in 1870, Alabama and North Carolina in 1875, Texas in 1876, Georgia in 1877, Florida in 1885, Arkansas in 1873 and Mississippi in 1878.

·First Mississippi Plan

This plan was devised by the white Democratic Party in 1875 to overthrow the Republican Party by organized violence, suppression of the black vote and the disruption of elections. White paramilitary organizations were created that, unlike the Ku Klux Klan, operated openly with the members being well known locally. In Mississippi, the most notorious group were the Red Shirts who were well armed. They would persuade 10% to 15 % of white voters still calling themselves Republicans to switch to the Democratic Party. Beside the attacks, a combined fear of social, political and economic ostracism convinced carpetbaggers to switch parties or flee the state and others to re-register as Democrats. The Mississippi Plan used intimidation of the black populace who had so recently been granted their voting rights, to stop them from exercising the franchise. Planters, landlords and merchants used economic coercion against black sharecroppers with some success. The Red Shirt's violence included whippings and murders. White paramilitary groups, also called "rifle clubs," frequently provoked riots at Republican rallies, shooting down dozens of blacks in the ensuing conflicts. The violence went unchecked and the plan worked as the Republican victory by 30,000 votes in 1874 was reversed to a Democratic majority of 30,000 in 1875. The success of the white Democrats in Mississippi influenced the growth of Red Shirts in North Carolina and South Carolina as well. They were particularly prominent in suppressing black votes in majority black counties in South Carolina, and were estimated to have committed 150 murders in the weeks leading up to the 1876 election.

Second Mississippi Plan

Unlike the First Mississippi Plan of 1875-76 which used open force and violence to control the black vote, the Second Mississippi plan of 1890 was a legal mechanism devised by the legislature to circumvent the 14th and 15th amendments in ways that would not bring Federal intervention in state elections. A new constitutional convention was called due to pressure from white members of the Farmers' Alliance, the state Grange, and white, racist Democrats. The Constitution eliminated blacks from exercising suffrage by stipulating that voters had to have lived in the state for at least six years before registering to vote; pay a poll tax; pass a literacy test or be able to understand any part of the state constitution when it was read to them; and be free of any criminal convictions from a list of petty crimes. The poll tax provision disenfranchised most blacks in the state, as well as many poor whites, while the "understanding clause" opened the door to fraud and unequal treatment of blacks by white registrars. The black vote and the Republican Party practically disappeared in the South.

Supreme Court and Civil Rights

The Jim Crow segregation laws gained legal status from a series of Supreme Court rulings. In 1883, it ruled the Civil Rights Act of 1875 unconstitutional. The Court reviewed complaints involving acts of discrimination on a railroad and in public sites, including a theater in San Francisco and the Grand Opera House in New York. In declaring the law unconstitutional, Chief Justice Bradley held that the Fourteenth Amendment did not protect black people from discrimination by private businesses and individuals but only from discrimination by states. He said it was time for blacks to assume "the rank of a mere citizen" and stop being the "special favorite of the laws." Justice Harlan dissented, arguing that hotels and amusement parks and public conveyances were public services that operated under state permission and thus were subject to public laws. It was not long after the Court's decision striking down the Civil Rights Act of 1875 that southern states began enacting sweeping segregation legislation. In 1890, a Louisiana law required that blacks ride in separate railroad cars. To test the laws constitutionality, a light-skinned African American, Homer Plessy, boarded a train, where he was arrested for sitting in a car reserved for whites. A local judge ruled against Plessy and in 1896 the U. S. Supreme Court upheld the lower court's ruling in *Plessy v. Ferguson*. The Court asserted that Plessy's rights were not denied him because the separate accommodations provided to blacks were equal to those provided whites. It also ruled that "separate but equal" accommodations did not stamp the "colored race with a badge of inferiority." Again, Justice Harlan, a former slave owner, protested in a ringing minority opinion when he said, "Our Constitution is color-blind, and neither knows nor tolerates classes among citizens." This decision sanctifying segregation would last for 58 years.

Booker T. Washington and the Atlanta Compromise

Born a slave, Booker T. Washington believed that education would raise his people to equality in this country. He became a teacher who founded the Tuskegee Normal and Industrial Institute in Alabama. As head of the Institute, he traveled the country unceasingly to raise funds from blacks and whites and became a well-known speaker. His "Atlanta Compromise" speech explained his major thesis that blacks could secure their constitutional rights through their own economic and moral advancement rather than through legal and political changes. Although his conciliatory stand angered some blacks who feared it would encourage the foes of equal rights, whites approved of his views and he became the chief spokesmen for African Americans for his generation.

·W.E.B. Du Bois and the Niagara Movement

The Niagara Movement renounced Booker T. Washington's accommodation policies set forth in his famed "Atlanta Compromise" speech. The Niagara Movement's manifesto was, in the words of Du Bois, "We want full manhood suffrage and we want it now." White liberals joined with the nucleus of Niagara "militants" and with Du Bois, and founded the National Association for the Advancement of Colored People (NAACP) in 1909.

·NAACP

The oldest civil rights group was formed in 1909, partly in response to the continuing horrific practice of lynching and the 1908 race riot in Springfield Illinois. Appalled at the violence that was committed against blacks, a group of white liberals that included Mary White Ovington, Oswald Garrison Villard, Jane Addams, Florence Kelley John Dewey, William Dean Howells, Lillian Wald, Charles Darrow, Lincoln Steffens, Ray Stannard Baker and African Americans including W. E. B. Du Bois, Ida B. Wells-Barnett and Mary Church Terrell formed the organization. Its goal was to secure for all people the rights guaranteed in the 13th, 14th, and 15th Amendments to the United States Constitution. The NAACP's principal objective was to ensure the political, educational, social and economic equality of minority group citizens of the United States and eliminate race prejudice.

Urban Life

·Streetcars (Trolleys)

Although horse drawn streetcars had existed for years, in 1888, Frank Sprague installed a complete system of electric streetcars in Richmond, Virginia, This was the first large scale and successful use of electricity to run a city's entire system of streetcars. Most cities now turned to electric-powered streetcars and this would transform the former "walking cities" into streetcar or trolley cities, which would change where people lived and worked creating distance between the two and bringing about the advent of the commuter. Streetcars were responsible for expanding the city outward and marked the beginning of "urban sprawl."

·Dumbbell Tenement

James Ware created the "dumbbell" tenement (so called because of its shape) that was designed to pack a maximum number of people into a minimum amount of space while still complying with sanitary standards. The dumbbell tenement had four apartments to a floor. At the very outer edges were parlors, then living rooms and bedrooms behind them. The building grew narrower as it moved inwards, threaded through the center by a public hall with two public bathrooms for the apartments. Between each tenement was a shallow airshaft, 50 feet long and about 10 feet wide. Although these were supposed to provide ventilation, they tended instead to be dumping grounds for garbage. Thus, the breathing conditions inside the tenements were worse than they would have been without an air -shaft. Each dumbbell tenement was six stories tall and designed to house three hundred people in eighty-four rooms. Immigrant muckraker Jacob Riis wrote *How the Other Half Lives* that exposed the terrible conditions of tenement housing. As immigrant families increased their income, they fled the dumbbell tenements of the inner city for better housing, yet there were always more to take their place. Thousands had been built by the turn of the century and would dominate inner city housing until WWI.

·Department Stores

Department stores first appeared in the mid 19th century, usually evolving from dry goods establishments. The rise of the department store was an urban phenomenon. As cities grew, larger numbers of customers dictated a broadening of items for sale. Roads and rapid transit such as trains, subways and streetcars, converged on downtown areas, concentrating populations and encouraging retailers to locate there. John Wanamaker in Philadelphia and New York expanded his stores with aggressive promotions and advertising that earned him the titles of "Merchant Prince" and "The Father of Modern Advertising." Marshall Field in Chicago built the largest department store in the world. These two pioneers along with others created massive retail behemoths with low fixed prices, pleasant clerks, and fashionable merchandise that transformed the shopping experience.

·Mail Order Houses

The idea of a dry goods mail-order business was first conceived in 1872 by Aaron Montgomery Ward after several years of working as a traveling salesman among rural customers. He found that rural customers wanted "city" goods but were often forced to pay high prices by small town retail stores who offered no guarantee of quality or much variety in order to get them. By eliminating middlemen Ward could cut costs and make a wide variety of goods available to rural customers. They could purchase goods by mail and pick them up at the nearest train station. To advertise his goods Ward created a catalog, which became known as the "Wish Book" and was favored in homes across America. In 1896, Ward faced serious competition in the mail order business when Richard W. Sears introduced his first general catalog. By 1900 Ward's had total sales of $8.7 million, compared to $10 million for Sears, Roebuck & Company, and the two companies were to struggle for dominance in this market for much of the 20th century.

·Chain Stores

The idea of two or more retail stores being run by the same company, with the same name, and selling the same kinds of merchandise started in 1859. George Gilman and George Hartford founded the Great Atlantic & Pacific Tea Company (better known as A & P) grocery stores in New York City. The idea caught on and was copied by many other establishments. Eventually, all kinds of stores moved to the chain store model, selling groceries, clothing, shoes, prescription drugs, books, jewelry, furniture, hardware, and music. By the end of the twentieth century, chain stores were selling about one third of all merchandise in America.

·Dime Stores

These stores were also known as five-and-ten-cent stores or variety stores started in the late nineteenth century and developed into a major part of U.S. retailing until their demise in the 1970s. The dime store format influenced some of the first chain stores and became an important outlet for American mass-manufactured merchandise that was created during the industrialization era. Frank Woolworth was the father of the dime store and learned the concept while running a five-cent booth in the store in Watertown, New York. In 1879, Woolworth opened his first store in Utica, New York but that store failed. His next store in Lancaster, Pennsylvania succeeded and by 1899 he owned fifty-four stores. Woolworth eliminated the wholesaler and entered into a buying arrangement with other store operators across the country. After a merger with these other chains in 1911, the F. W. Woolworth Company became the dominant variety store chain in the United States. The five-and-ten-cent stores copied the department store concept of a variety of merchandise. The dime stores lowered prices for house wares and other products, so European immigrants and rural Americans, who had moved to the cities, could afford to buy the products. The stores' major merchandise classifications included toys, notions (sewing supplies), china, glassware, stationery, shoes, and Christmas ornaments. Candy and toiletries also became big sellers. The U.S. manufacturing industry provided low-price merchandise, and the major variety store chains also sent buyers to scout Europe for distinctive and cheap goods. The stores also featured lunch counters that became popular, making Woolworth's the largest seller of restaurant food in the world.

UNIT XVI
MULTIPLE-CHOICE QUESTIONS

Questions 1-4 refer to the following:

"Francis Bowen declared that laissez faire means 'things regulate themselves'...which means, of course, that God regulates them by his general laws.... Whether the economists described the laws of economics in supernaturalistic or naturalistic terms they were agreed that the one great disturbing force...was the legislation of the state.... Belief that self-interest is a universal motive of human action...[was the] basis for the *laissez –faire* convictions of the political economists.... It was but natural for those economists who tended to identify the laws of nature with the laws of God to attribute to the design of the Lord the benefits deriving from the pursuit of self-interest.... Free competition was a third basis on which economists rested their trust in laissez faire.... A fourth factor that led the political economists to champion the idea of the negative state was their conviction that government is, at best, an inefficient agency."

Sidney Fine, *Laissez Faire and the General Welfare-State: A Study of Conflict in American Thought 1865-1901*, 1964

1. Late 19th century economist tended to accept the tenant that

   (A) the laws of nature and the laws of God operated together
   (B) the laws of nature were superior to the laws of God
   (C) human action was based on a concern for your fellow man
   (D) the pursuit of self- interest had a detrimental effect on God's laws

2. The ideas expressed in the above secondary source would be most in accord with which of the following movements in United States History?

   (A) Progressivism
   (B) New Deal
   (C) 60s Counterculture
   (D) 80s Neo-Conservatives

3. All of the economists who supported laissez faire agreed that

   (A) government was a necessary evil to keep men from harm
   (B) government was inefficient and a disturbing force when it passed laws
   (C) government should operate with the laws of God to create a just society
   (D) as long as men were left free to pursue their economic goals government could be tolerated

4. Which of the following late 19th ideas or movements was an extension of the ideas expressed in the selection from Fine's book?

   (A) Social Gospel
   (B) Settlement House
   (C) Social Darwinism
   (D) Socialism

Questions 5-7 refer to the following:

"Of one thing we may be certain at the outset. The durability of *Origins of the New South* is not a result of its ennobling and uplifting message. It is the story of the decay and decline of the aristocracy, the suffering and betrayal of the poor whites, and the rise and transformation of a middle class. It is not a happy story. The Redeemers are revealed to be as venal as the carpetbaggers. The declining aristocracy are ineffectual and money hungry, and in the last analysis they subordinated the values of their political and social heritage in order to maintain control over the black population. The poor whites suffered from strange malignancies of racism and conspiracy-mindedness, and the rising middle class was timid and self-interested even in its reform movement. The most sympathetic characters in the whole sordid affair are simply those who are too powerless to be blamed for their actions."

Sheldon Hackney, "*Origins of the New South* in Retrospect," 1972

5. Hackney's interpretation of C. Vann Woodward's book *Origins of the New South*, is that Woodward is basically negative about every group in the South EXCEPT

(A) Redeemers
(B) Carpetbaggers
(C) Poor whites
(D) Blacks

6. According to Hackney, in *Origins of the New South*, the rising middle class reformers

(A) subordinated the values of their political and social heritage to maintain control over the blacks
(B) were just as venal [corrupt] as the carpetbaggers
(C) suffered from strange malignancies of racism and conspiracy
(D) were timid and self interested even as reformers

7. The document above is an interpretation (Hackney's), of the interpretation (Woodward's), in *Origins of the New South* that is

(A) ennobling and uplifting message
(B) a story of decay, decline, suffering, betrayal
(C) durable as the ultimate happy story
(D) mostly sympathetic to the powerful Redeemers and aristocracy

Questions 8-10 refer to the following:

"As the tensions of the time steadily mounted, and the demands of laissez-faire right-wing conservatives grew more insistent upon judicial intervention,... The pressures of the 1890's, however, weakened the position of the moderates.... [as] conservative fears approached near panic, a major sector of the moderates broke from the center position... coalesced with the right wing in the burgeoning neo-Federalism, and sealed the triumph of the new judicialism...neo-Federalism of the 1890's opened the door to what was to prove in succeeding decades a full proliferation of judicial obstructionism. The Supreme Court of the United States became, instead of an instrument of constitutional democracy, an impediment to constitutional democracy. Exaggerating its powers beyond proportion in the period 1890-1937, confusing its proper role in the American scheme of government, the Court for a long while seriously weakened its real value."

Arnold M. Paul, *Conservative Crisis and the Rule of Law:*
Attitudes of Bar and Bench, 1887-1895, 1960

8. The judicialism of neo-Federalism that the passage refers to is a reference to the Supreme Court decisions of the early 19th century of

(A) Thomas Jefferson
(B) John Marshall
(C) Roger Taney
(D) Henry Clay

9. One reason why the Supreme Court intervened in the 1890s to start the process of judicial obstructionism was because it

(A) wanted to obstruct the political ideology of the dominant political party
(B) endorsed the ideas of imperialism that begin to assert itself in terms of U.S. foreign policy
(C) feared that the new immigrants from southern and eastern Europe were taking over
(D) wanted to blunt the impulses of reform movements like Populism and Progressivism

10. The era of judicial, neo-Federalism ultimately ended in 1933 when which program became the prevailing political philosophy that brought about a change in the Supreme Court?

(A) Great Society
(B) Return to Normalcy
(C) New Deal
(D) Reform Democracy

Question 11-13 refer to the following:

Chinese Occupations in California, 1868

Merchants and traders	2,000
Engaged in manufacturing for themselves	200
In other occupations	1,000
Washhouses	1,800
Laborers in factories and in other capacities in cities and towns	3,500
Mechanics	1,000
House servants	3,000
Laborers on the Pacific railroad	10,000
Miners	13,084
Farm laborers	2,000
Fishermen	200

Shih-shan H. Tsai, *China and the Overseas Chinese in the United States 1868-1911*, 1983

11. Compared to their 19th century occupations of railroad laborers or miners Chinese workers in the 21st century U.S. have

    (A) monopolized the ship building industry
    (B) an unemployment rate that is higher than the national average
    (C) shifted towards math and science oriented professions that require a higher education
    (D) became mostly farm laborers in the San Jouquin Valley in California

12. Fourteen years after these occupation statistics about the Chinese immigrants were compiled

    (A) China forbid the export of skilled labor to the U.S.
    (B) the number of Chinese working in California more than doubled to 80,000
    (C) the Coolie Labor Law was passed that established a set number of Chinese who could immigrate to the U.S. each year
    (D) Chinese Exclusion Act halted immigration and prohibited the Chinese from becoming U.S. citizens

13. Restrictions against Chinese immigration were finally lifted when China became an ally of the U.S. in which 20th century war?

    (A) WWI (Great War)
    (B) WWII
    (C) Korean War
    (D) Vietnam War

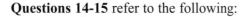

Questions 14-15 refer to the following:

"In a 1938 essay, "The Problem of the Third Generation Immigrant," [Marcus] Hansen first presented Hansen's Law: 'What the son wishes to forget the grandson wishes to remember.' This law predicts that ethnicity is preserved among immigrants, weakens among their children, and returns with the grandchildren. Children of immigrants tend to reject the foreign ways of their parents, including their religion, and want to join the American mainstream, but the next generation wants to retain the values of their ancestors."

Jane Lang, Neenah Historical Society, nd

14. A fundamental reason why Hansen's law operates is because

   (A) the children of first generation immigrants have the dual responsibility of maintaining both cultures in their identity
   (B) grandchildren are secure in their Americanism while the children of immigrants are not
   (C) Immigration laws tend to favor the acculturation process of rewarding immigrant groups who have become Americanized
   (D) the process of assimilation is evenly distributed among all generations of immigrant groups

15. Which modern day concept tends to support the position of the grandson over the son according to the principle established by "Hansen's Law"?

   (A) Assimilation
   (B) Melting Pot theory
   (C) Americanization
   (D) Cultural Diversity

UNIT XVII

THE FRONTIER WEST

From the Civil War to the end of the 19th century the American West played a prominent role in U.S. history. The idea of a "frontier" was a place that was on the edge between the known and the unknown, the settled and the wild, and has a prominent place in American history. The frontier was a place where you are on your own, where the rules have not been made. Sometimes it is a particular geographic territory, such as the North American continent west of the Missouri River. Sometimes it is more a state of mind that a particular geographic location. The final subduing and settling of the West involved miners, cowboys, pioneers and a 30 year war against the Plains Indians.

Settling the West

·Homestead Act

Making good on their campaign pledge, the Republicans passed this law in 1862 that turned over vast amounts of the public domain to private citizens. 270 million acres, or 10% of the area of the United States was claimed and settled under this act. A homesteader had only to be the head of a household and at least 21 years of age to claim a 160-acre parcel of land. Settlers from all walks of life including newly arrived immigrants, farmers without land of their own from the East, single women, and former slaves came to get this "free land." Each homesteader had to live on the land, build a home, make improvements on it and farm it for 5 years before claiming it as their land. A total filing fee of $18 was the only money required.

·Transcontinental Railroads

In 1862, after years of hostile debate, Congress passed the Pacific Railway Act which authorized the building of the transcontinental railroad with the Union Pacific Railroad building west from Omaha, Nebraska and the Central Pacific Railroad building east from Sacramento, California. The Act granted subsidies for building that amounted $16,000 on the plains, $32,000 in the Great Basin and $48,000 through the mountainous terrain for each mile of track laid. In addition, the Pacific Railway Act gave the Transcontinental Railroads' alternate sections of public land on each side of the track for each mile of track built. In the end the various

239

transcontinental railroad companies acquired 33 million acres of free land. The Irish supplied the labor for the Union Pacific while the Chinese built the Central Pacific and the two lines met at Promontory Point, Utah in 1869. The Central Pacific was organized by California's "Big Four"—Collis Huntington, Leland Stanford, Charles Crocker, and Mark Hopkins. Another one of the transcontinental railroads was the Atchison, Topeka, and the Santa Fe, which went from Kansas City to the West Coast. The only one of the railroads to not be built with subsidies and free land was James J. Hill's Great Northern which went from St. Paul Minnesota to Seattle Washington. In order to create traffic Hill promoted farm settlements along the entire route. A Southern route going through the Gadsden Purchase land went from New Orleans to Los Angeles and became consolidated as the Southern Pacific. The impact of the train on the virgin land of the West cannot be over stated; the time to get from the East to the West was shortened from five months to one week. Another innovation the RR brought was the standardization of time zones in 1883 to stop the contradictory and confusing schedules.

·Long Drive and the Cattle Trails

With the advent of the railroad in the West, the herds of wild longhorn cattle in the Southwest could now be brought to market by the combination of the "long drive" and the livestock transportation on the railroad. The Chisholm Trail went from San Antonio, Texas to Abilene, Kansas where the cattle were transshipped to the East Coast. Other cattle trails included the Goodnight-Loving from Texas to Ogallala, Nebraska, and the Western Trail from Texas to Cheyenne, Wyoming. Cowboys, black, white, and Mexican vaqueros drove herds in size from 1,000 to 10,000 over the sparsely populated, unfenced plains. Once the railroads brought more settlers who began to fence off the plains, the cattle drive was doomed. The great blizzard of 1886-1887 along with over-grazing brought it to an end after a successful 20 year run. It exists today in the folklore of America.

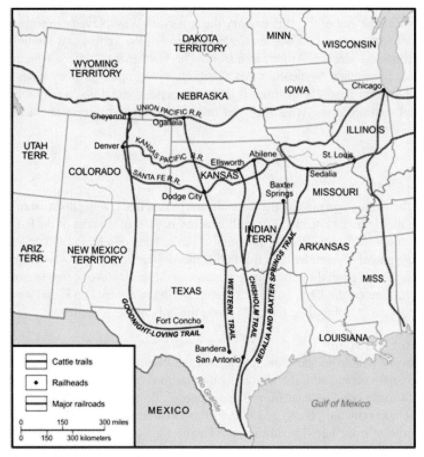

CATTLE TRAILS

·Mining

The Colorado Gold Rush was the boom in the prospecting and mining of gold that began in 1859 (when the land was still in the Kansas Territory) and lasted throughout the early 1860s. It is still considered to be the largest gold rush in American history and it followed approximately a decade after the California Gold Rush. It brought a dramatic influx of emigrants into the region of the Rocky Mountains, exemplified by the phrase "Pikes Peak or Bust." The prospectors provided the first major white population in the area, leading to the creation of many early towns in the region, including Denver and Boulder. Another mining venture was the Colorado silver boom that started in 1879, with the discovery of a lode at Leadville, that brought in over $82 million dollars worth of silver during the silver boom. The boom was largely the consequence of large-scale purchases of silver by the United States Government authorized by Congress in 1878. Other gold and silver rushes occurred in Nevada with the discovery of the Comstock Lode in 1859, as well as "rushes" in Montana, Idaho, and South Dakota, which would lead to the displacement of the Native American Indians. Throughout much of the Old West during this time, there was little local law enforcement and the military had only concentrated presence in the area at specific locations, primarily forts. The enterprising miners relied on vigilante justice including "lynch law." Brooklyn born writer Bret Harte captured the social life of these towns in his short stories like "The Luck of Roaring Camp" and "The Outcasts of Poker Flat."

·Pioneers

In the early days of the Wild West, a great deal of the land was in the public domain, open both to livestock raising as open range and to homesteading. Buffalo hunters, railroad workers, drifters, and eventually pioneers all used this land. With the invention of barbed wire by Joseph Glidden in 1874, which solved the problem for pioneers of fencing off their land, this helped to end the cattle range and impeded the "long drive." Life on the frontier was harsh and the first homesteaders to settle on the Great Plains—in what are now the states of Kansas, Nebraska, and the Dakotas—found good land there, but almost no trees suitable for building log cabins as they'd done on other frontiers. American ingenuity solved the problem by using the materials that were available to build the sod house or dugout. Life on this frontier has been captured by Laura Ingalls in, "*Little House on the Prairie*," Willa Cather's "*O' Pioneers*, and *Giants in the Earth* by Ole Edvart Rolvaag.

·Buffalo Soldiers

In 1866, Congress established two cavalry and four infantry regiments (later consolidated to two) whose enlisted composition was to be made up of African-Americans. The majority of the new recruits had served in all black units during the Civil War. The mounted regiments were the 9th and 10th Cavalries, soon nicknamed Buffalo Soldiers by the Cheyenne and Comanche. Until the early 1890's they constituted 20 percent of all cavalry forces on the American frontier.

Indian Wars

·Causes

Expansion into the plains and mountains by miners, ranchers and pioneer settlers led to increasing conflicts with the indigenous population of the West. A series of wars between 1862 and 1890 resulted in the removal of most tribes to reservations controlled by the federal government.

·Little Crow & Dakota War (1862)

When the government reneged on a treaty and provisions and the annuity money that were promised arrived late or not at all, the Dakota Sioux of Minnesota, under Little Crow's leadership went to war capturing or killing nearly 1,000 whites. With the arrival of veteran Civil War troops the rebellion was put down, Little Crow was killed, and 40 of his followers were tried and hung. The Sioux lands were confiscated and the Dakota Sioux were relocated to the Great Plains.

·1st Sioux War (1862)

As the government attempted to build a mining road from Bozeman, Montana to Fort Laramie, Wyoming through the best Sioux hunting grounds, the buffalo fled and war was waged. When an 82 man military force led by W. J. Fetterman were all killed in a short-lived Indian victory, the government abandoned the Bozeman trail in return for the Sioux accepting a permanent reservation in the Dakota territory.

·Sand Creek Massacre (1864)

A former Protestant minister J. M. Chivington massacred 300 peaceful Cheyenne Indians at Sand Creek Colorado, men, women, and even children as he justified this action when he said, "nits make lice."

·Apache War

The war started in 1861 and the Apaches held their own for a long time under the leadership of their greatest chief Cochise. The conflict eventually ended with the capture of Geronimo in 1886, and the remnants of his tribe were forced on to reservations in the Southwest.

·2nd Sioux War (1875)

With the discovery of gold in the Black Hills of Dakota in 1875, the Sioux had their lands invaded by gold seekers despite the treaty guarantees. Once again at war, the Sioux had one notable victory when the tactics of Sitting Bull, a medicine man, and Crazy Horse's leadership inspired a combined force of Sioux and Cheyenne that annihilated George Custer and 264 army troops at the Little Bighorn river in Montana. Despite this victory the Sioux would surrender in 1877 and once again return to a smaller reservation.

·Chief Joseph and the Nez Perce

In 1877, the Nez Pierce were told to give up their land and ordered to a reservation but refused to go. Instead, Chief Joseph tried to lead 800 of his people to Canada fighting the U.S. Army along their 1,100 mile journey as they crossed Idaho and Montana but were trapped just forty miles from Canada. After a five-day fight, the remaining 431 remaining Nez Perce were beaten. As they were sent to reservations in Oklahoma, Chief Joseph said, "Hear me, my chiefs. I am tired. My heart is sick and sad. From where the sun now stands, I will fight no more forever."

·Ghost Dance

By the 1880's the U.S. government had managed to confine almost all of the Indians on reservations, usually on land so poor that the white man could conceive of no use for it themselves. The rations and supplies that had been guaranteed by the treaties were of poor quality if they arrived at all. Graft and corruption were rampant in the Indian Bureau and by 1890 conditions were so bad on the reservations with starvation conditions existing that the situation was ripe for a major movement. This movement originated with a Paiute Indian named Wovoka, who announced that he was the messiah come to earth to prepare the Indians for their salvation. Representatives from tribes all over the nation came to Nevada to meet with Wovoka and learn to dance the Ghost Dance and to sing Ghost Dance songs. As they participated some of the Indians would fall into a trance and many feared that it might end in violence. The Bureau of Indian Affairs banned the Ghost Dance and white settlers were fearful of what might happen. Ghost Dance prophecy said that the buffalo and antelope would return, and deceased ancestors would rise to once again roam the earth now free of violence, starvation, and disease. The natural world would be restored, and the land once again would be free and open to the Indian peoples, without the borders and boundaries of the white man.

·Massacre at Wounded Knee (1890)

After Sitting Bull was killed on his reservations in an incident involving U.S. soldiers who went to put down the Ghost Dance (ironically, Sitting Bull did not believe in the Ghost Dance) tensions were high between the military and the Indians. Big Foot feared for the safety of his band and led them to Pine Ridge Reservation.

When he saw the 7th Cavalry approaching he surrendered to the military. The military took Big Foot and his band to Wounded Knee where they disarmed the Indians. As the soldiers were searching for other weapons a shot rang out which resulted in the soldiers opening fire with their rifles and especially Hotchkiss guns (an early machine gun) killing somewhere between 250-350 Sioux with the loss of 25 soldiers lives. Only 4 Sioux men and 47 women and children survived the massacre.

Results of Indian Wars

·Dawes Severalty Act (1887)

Government officials and reformers alike began to promote allotment in severalty—the division of Indian lands into individually owned parcels—and the sale of leftover lands as a solution to the "Indian problem." This law tried to impose private property ownership on Native Americans by dividing their reservations into individual farms and making each Indian into a yeoman farmer. It supported the federal policy of assimilating Indians into the American mainstream and worked in conjunction with government-sponsored education programs and Christian missionary work. The President could decide which reservations would undergo allotment in severalty. The original legislation specified varying amounts based on a person's age and family status, but it was amended in 1891 to provide at least eighty acres to each person. The federal government could purchase so-called "surplus" land—anything remaining after the allotments were made—but the allotments themselves were to be held in trust for twenty-five years. At the end of the trust period, Indians would receive full ownership rights to their lands. Subsequent amendments got rid of the trust period and allowed Indians to lease or sell their lands. Between the sale of "surplus" land and the sale of allotments, many tribes lost most of their reservations. Some tribes successfully resisted allotment, while others escaped it because their land was of little interest to non-Indians. This program of destroying the reservations would be in effect until it was repealed in the 1930s.

·A Century of Dishonor

After attending a translated lecture by Chief Standing Bear about the federal government's forcible removal of the Ponca Indians from their Nebraska reservation to Indian Territory, Helen Hunt Jackson became a leading figure in taking up the cause of the Indians. Emotionally moved by what she heard, Jackson became a relentless crusader for the remaining tribes. In addition to exposing the government's mistreatment of Native Americans in her writings, she circulated petitions on their behalf, raised money for lawsuits, wrote letters to newspaper editors, and attempted to arouse public opinion on behalf of the Indians' deteriorating condition. Her book, *A Century of Dishonor* published in 1881, was an impassioned documented plea on behalf of the Indians that caused a national sensation by exposing broken treaties, dishonest deals, unfulfilled promises, and the federal government's corrupt mismanagement of its Indian wards. Her later popular novel *Ramona* is still performed as a "passion play" about the plight of the California Indians.

·Oklahoma Land Rush

On March 2, 1889 Congress passed the Indian Appropriations Bill, proclaiming that unassigned lands were part of the public domain. This was the first step toward the famous Oklahoma Land Rush. In April of 1889, people who gathered on the Arkansas and Texas borders of Oklahoma could seek a parcel of unclaimed land and file for ownership with the federal government. Most of these people were from Kansas and Missouri, but people from all over the country were part of the pack. At noon, the "Boomers" burst westward in droves on the Sante Fe Railroad, in covered wagons, and on horseback. They frantically raced to secure the best parcels of land before anyone else could. As the fastest riders on horseback went ahead they found spread across the horizon covered wagons and even men on foot who had already occupied the prime places. As many as 90% these settlers had jumped the gun, earning themselves the name "Sooners." Those who entered the territory legally would challenge these premature claims in court, but the government's officials claimed that all squatters had been chased out prior to the land rush, which was untrue, as only a few had been chased out. The best land went to the "Sooners" or cheaters, while those who obeyed the rules, the "Boomers," got the worst land.

Literature of the Frontier West

·Mark Twain

His western experience began as a feature writer for the Virginia City *Territorial Enterprise*. It was as this paper's reporter at the Nevada constitutional convention that Clemens began to sign his work "Mark Twain." After two years of doing daily reports on the goings on of a Nevada mining town he went to San Francisco where he wrote for newspapers and periodicals. With the publication of "The Celebrated Jumping Frog of Calaveras County," Twain's self deprecating style first emerged. Another work, *Roughing It*, with Charles Dudley Warren (1872), was a autobiographical account of his years in the West told in his humorous style of travel writing. It places a self-confident observer within a setting which he both misinterprets, and ironically understands only too well. This element of self-conscious irony, remembered from his western experience, would become the hallmark of his best works.

·Bret Hart

It is rather unusual for someone from Brooklyn in New York City to capture the spirit and character of the American west as Bret Hart did in his memorable heart-rending tales of frontier California. The short stories *The Luck of Roaring Camp* and the *Outcasts of Poker Flat* are the best examples of this genre. These works earned him acclaim during the 1860's as the "new prophet of American letters" and Eastern magazines courted him for submissions.

·Laura Ingalls (Wilder)

Born in Wisconsin, her restless father settled on land not yet open for homesteading in what was then Indian Territory near Independence, Kansas—an experience that formed the basis of her Little House Series and her most famous novel *Little House on the Prairie*. These books are written in third person, with Laura Ingalls acting as the central character and protagonist, and are classified as historical fiction rather than as autobiography. Several of the later books are almost purely autobiographical. Her daughter, author, and political theorist Rose Wilder Lane, assisted her mother with the editing of the works.

·Ole Rolvaag

O. E. Rolvaag's *Giants in the Earth* narrates the story of a Norwegian immigrant family's struggles on the American plains from 1873 to 1881. It chronicles the story of Norwegian pioneers making the long trek from a fishing village in Norway to the Dakota Territory. Although the westward migration meant opportunity, the settlers must deal with the isolation and the boredom of prairie life; primitive housing; long, freezing winters, and plagues of insects in the summer. These conditions are hard enough for people of robust nature, eager for a new life, but for people of delicate sensibility life on the prairie becomes unbearable. *Giants in the Earth* deals with the themes of immigration, fear and loneliness, myth, and religion.. The novel details the triumphs, hardships, and ultimate tragedies of South Dakota farmers as they try to wrest a livelihood from a land that, while fertile, often proves actively hostile to human habitation. It is a realistic portrayal of the immigrant experience.

·Dime Novels & the West

During the golden days of the Wild West (1850s-1880s) the "Dime Novels" glamorized the lives of outlaws, cowboys, ranchers, and lawmen. The tales grew larger and grander and flooded the market with their descriptions of the West. Readers considered these fanciful tales as fact. Some myths of the Old West legends were born out of these "Dime Novels" that created adventure stories that were told from generation to generation. While these were being written and the West was being settled, the public's desire for entertainment and heroes in

this last frontier made "Dime Novels" a success from the outset. In June of 1860, *Malaeska: the Indian Wife of the White Hunter* was published and it is considered to be the first "Dime Novel". It told the story of an Indian who married a white settler and the tragedy that ensued. Within a few months of its release it had sold over 50,000 copies. The "Buffalo Bill" stories came along in 1872, and created a persona for the public that many people still associate with the west today.

·Myths and Tall Tales

The Frontier West was a treasure trove of myths, tall tales, and legends. Most of these featured individuals who demonstrated American superlatives. A good example of this is Pecos Bill a cowboy hero with superhuman abilities. He is the embodiment of superlatives that contribute to the concept of "American Exceptionalism:" he is the strongest, meanest, and greatest of the cowboys and his attributes include the invention of calf roping, the practice of cattle branding, and the creation of the six-shooter. Not only could he ride any horse but he also rode a panther and a tornado according to legends. Another example of the mythic figure of the Tall Tale is Paul Bunyan. A larger-than-life folk hero who embodied frontier vitality he is a symbol of might, the willingness to work hard, and the resolve to overcome all obstacles. Paul and his boon companion Babe the Blue Ox, whom he dug Lake Michigan for so Babe would have a place to drink, have been a part of the American culture ever since the beginning of the 20th century.

·"Turner Thesis"

Influenced by the census report of 1890, historian Frederick Jackson Turner wrote "The Significance of the Frontier in American History," which said, "the existence of an area of free land, its continuous recession, and the advance of American settlement westward"—was the central story of American history. The process of westward expansion had transformed a desolate and savage land into modem civilization. It had also continually renewed American ideas of democracy and individualism and had, therefore, shaped not just the West; but, the nation as a whole. Turner's concern was that there was no longer an unbroken frontier line, which could mean the end of Americanization and possibly democracy. "The frontier," he claimed, "is the line of most rapid Americanization," the presence and predominance of numerous cultural traits—"that coarseness and strength combined with acuteness and acquisitiveness; that practical inventive turn of mind, quick to find expedients; that masterful grasp of material things... that restless, nervous energy; that dominant individualism." All these traits could all be attributed to the influence of the frontier. If the frontier was gone a different America could emerge. Concomitant to his basic thesis was the idea that "free" or cheap land existed as a "safety valve" for people to escape to from the East. Modern scholars have attacked his views and feel he ignored the presence of the numerous Native Americans whose subjugation was required by the nation's westward march, as well as he assumed that the bulk of newly acquired lands were actually democratically distributed to yeomen pioneers rather than speculators. Despite this, the "Turner Thesis" lives on, as do its critics.

UNIT XVII
MULTIPLE-CHOICE QUESTIONS

Questions 1-4 refer to the following:

"any person... who has never borne arms against the United States Government... shall,... be entitled to enter one quarter section or a less quantity of unappropriated public lands,... at the time the application is made, be subject to preemption at one dollar and twenty-five cents, or less, or eighty acres or less of such unappropriated lands, at two dollars and fifty cents per acre... that the person having filed such affidavit shall have actually changed his or her residence, or abandoned the said land for more than six months at any time, then and in that event the land so entered shall revert to the government. Sec. 6. *And be it further enacted*, That no individual shall be permitted to acquire title to more than one quarter section under the provisions of this act;..."

Homestead Act, May 20, 1862

1. The availability of land like that provided in the Homestead Act gave rise to

   (A) the Turner thesis that free or cheap land existed as a "safety valve" for people to escape from the East to the democracy of the West
   (B) hordes of immigrants from Southern and Eastern Europe who bypassed the East to settle on the frontier
   (C) a great migration of blacks leaving the South and the sharecropping system to farm in the West
   (D) a number of workers leaving industrial and manufacturing jobs for more money that could be made in agriculture

2. One of the unintended consequences of the Homestead Act was the

   (A) depopulation of the major urban centers of the East
   (B) overcrowding of the western states with pioneer homesteaders
   (C) displacement of the Indians from their ancestral lands
   (D) opening up of the West to settlement created an immediate demographic change of population disbursement

246

3. Much of the land that was sold by the government

   (A) was soon abandoned by the homesteaders because they failed to make improvements on it
   (B) embodied the Republican Party's philosophy of free soil, free labor, and free men
   (C) had to be subsidized with government expenditures for irrigation systems and fertilizer
   (D) was contaminated by toxins in the soil that had to be removed before they were farmed

4. The Homestead Act was based on principles established by Thomas Jefferson which advocated

   (A) a diversified market economy with extensive trading among the various regions
   (B) a specialized economy taking advantage of the law of comparative advantage
   (C) a neo-mercantilist philosophy of exporting more than you imported
   (D) an agrarian economy of yeoman farmers tilling their own land

Questions 5-10 refer to the document below:

"An act to provide for the allotment of lands in severalty to Indians on the various reservations...

... where any tribe or band of Indians has been, or shall hereafter be, located upon any reservation created for their use,... the President of the United States be... authorized, whenever in his opinion any reservation or any part thereof of such Indians is advantageous for agricultural and grazing purposes .... to allot the lands in said reservations in severalty to any Indian located thereon in quantities as follows:

To each head of a family, one-quarter of a section;

To each single person over eighteen years of age, one-eighth of a section;

To each orphan child under eighteen years of age, one-eighth of a section; and,

To each other single person under eighteen ... one-sixteenth of a section; . . .

SEC. 5.... [Secretary of Interior] shall . . . declare that the United States does and will hold the land thus allotted, for the period of twenty-five years, in trust for the sole use and benefit of the Indian to whom such allotment shall have been made, . . . and that at the expiration of said period the United States will convey the same by patent to said Indian, or his heirs ... free of all charge or encumbrance whatsoever: . . .

SEC. 6. ... said allottees, ... shall have the benefit of and be subject to the laws, both civil and criminal, of the State or Territory . . . . And every Indian born within the territorial limits of the United States to whom allotments shall have been made ... and has adopted the habits of civilized life, is hereby declared to be a citizen of the United States...

Dawes Severalty Act, 1887

5. The Dawes Severalty Act took land away from which of the following?

   (A) Western Farmers
   (B) Tribal Nations
   (C) Individual Indians
   (D) United States Government

6. One purpose of the Dawes Act was to make Indians into which historic individuals that Jefferson exalted as being the backbone of American society

   (A) tax paying citizens
   (B) members of tribes
   (C) yeoman farmers
   (D) businessmen

7. What did Indians that had received the allotment have to do in order to be declared citizens of the United States?

   (A) Swear to support the Constitution
   (B) Renounce their allegiance to tribal laws
   (C) Register to vote as U.S. citizens
   (D) Adopt the habits of civilized life

8. Under the allotment system the amount of land a head of household would receive was

   (A) 160 acres
   (B) 80 acres for each child in the family
   (C) 1 square mile
   (D) 40 acres

9. The condition of the land that the President could make available for allotment had to be

   (A) the best land available for farming
   (B) land located close to a water source for irrigation
   (C) advantageous for agricultural and grazing
   (D) in parcels that were a minimum of 160 acres

10. Which theory usually associated with immigration did the Dawes Act support?

   (A) Melting pot
   (B) Assimilation
   (C) Stew pot
   (D) Salad bowl

Questions 11-12 refer to the following:

"Be it enacted by the Council and House of Representatives of the Territory of Wyoming: Sect 1. That every woman of the age of twenty-one years, residing in this territory, may, at every election to beholden under the laws thereof, cast her vote. And her rights to the elective franchise and to hold office shall be the same under the election laws of the territory, as those of electors. Sect 2. This act shall take effect and be in force from and after its passage. Approved, December 10, 1869"

House of Representatives, Wyoming Territory, "An Act to Grant to the Women of Wyoming Territory the Right of Suffrage and to Hold Office," 1869

11. Wyoming became the first area of the United States to carry out what had been proposed in the

(A) Kentucky and Virginia Resolutions
(B) Wilmot Proviso
(C) Declaration of Sentiments
(D) Emancipation Proclamation

12. Which of the following is the primary reason why Wyoming voted to allow women to vote before any other state or territory in 1869?

(A) Strong religious tradition established by Protestant families
(B) Homestead Act guaranteed it
(C) Influence of the dominant cattle culture on public policy
(D) With 6,000 adult males and 1,000 females men hoped women would be more likely to come if they had the right to vote.

Questions 13-15 refer to the following:

"The fate of the brave and gallant Custer has deeply touched the public heart... a monument is proposed... But a truer monument, more enduring than brass or marble, would be an Indian policy intelligent, moral, and efficient... we make solemn treaties with them as if they were civilized and powerful nations... the infamy of violating treaties... is undeniable, and we are guilty of both the folly and the infamy. We make treaties... and [have] swindlers and knaves execute them... so long as we undertake to support the Indians as paupers... we shall have the most costly and bloody Indian wars... [We need] the adoption of a system which should be neither puerile nor disgraceful, and which would tend to spare us the constant repetition... [of] the slaughter of Custer and his brave men."

Editorial, *Harper's Weekly*, August 5, 1876

13. In the immediate aftermath of what has been called "Custer's last stand"

    (A) U.S. troops flooded the West crushing the Indian populations
    (B) a new Indian policy was adlopted to treat the Indians as sovereign nations
    (C) laws were executed to stop the killing of the buffalo
    (D) a new "Trail of Tears" removed the plains Indians to Canada

14. The idea of supporting the Indians mentioned in the document is a continuity of which earlier policy?

    (A) Andrew Jackson's removal policy
    (B) Treating the Indians as Jeffersonian farmers
    (C) Adhering to the philosophy of veneration of primitive cultures
    (D) Binding treaties supported by toth the Indians and Anglo settlers

15. Which of the following contributed the most to the Indians losing their foothold on the Great Plains

    (A) Adoption of the Ghost Dance which weakened the will of the Indians to oppose the incursions by the Whites
    (B) The tactics of the "Buffalo Soldiers" in capturing the Indians and putting them on reservations
    (C) Their inability to grow crops because of severe drought conditions
    (D) The extermination of the buffalo and the invention of barbed wire

UNIT XVIII

CULTURE & SOCIETY

Accompanying the changes to America that industrialism brought were significant changes in culture and society. New styles of architecture, literature, and art as well as the development of new forms of popular culture characterized the era. The influence of the industrial revolution was not just a business and economics change but it resulted in many other more esthetic changes as well. The end of the 19th century brought forth aspects of culture and society that seem modern compared to earlier time periods.

Architecture:

· Richardsonian Style
A style of architecture named for Henry Hobson Richardson was a revival style based on Romanesque precedents of the 11th century. This style is characterized by massive stone walls, dramatic semicircular arches, and a new dynamism of interior space with the best example being the Marshall Field Building in Chicago.

· Skyscraper
George Fuller worked on solving the problems of the "load bearing capacities" of tall buildings and invented the skyscraper when he built the Tacoma Building in 1889—the first structure ever built where the outside walls did not carry the weight of the building. Using Bessemer steel beams, Fuller created steel cages that supported all the weight. His Flatiron Building, designed by Daniel Burnham, was one of New York City's first skyscrapers. The term "skyscraper" was first used during the 1880s, shortly after the first 10 to 20 story buildings were built. These building were made possible by combining several innovations—steel structure, elevators, central heating, electrical plumbing pumps and the telephone. These structures came to dominate American skylines at the turn of the century. The world's tallest building when it opened in 1913 was architect Cass Gilbert's 793-foot Woolworth Building, a leading example of tall building design.

· "Form Follows Function"

Louis Sullivan became the first modern architect by abandoning historic styles and creating original forms and details. Older architectural styles were designed for buildings that were wide, but Sullivan was able to create aesthetic unity in buildings that were tall. Often using masonry walls with terra cotta designs he intertwined vines and leaves with geometric shapes. The exterior of a new office building should reflect its interior structure and functions. Hence, the term "form follows function" described this feature. Ornamentation, when it was used, should be derived from nature, according to Sullivan, as he rejecting the ubiquitous arches of classical architecture. Other architects imitated Sullivan's style and his later work formed the foundation for the ideas of his student, Frank Lloyd Wright, the creator of "modernism" in architecture.

· Buildings

The latter part of the 19th century was a time of new technologies in construction. The revolutionary modular construction featured large spans in the structural skeleton that could be mass-produced and used on buildings like exhibition halls and railway stations. The use of cast iron as building material and the invention of twisted-wire cable extended main spans of bridges in Europe and the United States.

· Brooklyn Bridge

Designed by John Roebling, who died from tetanus after an injury when he started to build the bridge, this structure was completed by his son Washington Roebling after 13 years of construction in 1883. Stretching 5,989 feet (1,825 meters) over the East River, it connected the New York city boroughs of Manhattan and Brooklyn. It was the longest suspension bridge in the world, the first steel-wire suspension bridge, and its twin towers were the highest structures in New York except for the steeple on Trinity Cathedral. It is considered both an engineering and architectural marvel and was celebrated by Hart Crane in his epic poem, "*The Bridg*e," featuring the celebrated line, "Oh! harp and altar."

Social Ideas:

· "Acres of Diamonds"

This was the name for a popular speech/sermon given by the minister Russell Conwell that stressed the rewards of work, education, and praised the rich as being righteous. He felt it was a grand ambition for men to make money so the rich could use it to benefit their fellow man. Conwell chastised those who were poor telling them that they had a duty to be rich and the best people were among the richest people. Through this lecture, Conwell debunked the idea that it was noble to be poor. He illustrated that it is people's duty to honestly earn riches, because people can do more good with riches than without. In his view, God was responsible for directing wealth to those who could use it for beneficial purposes. In an era when many Americans would pack public halls to hear speeches given by the greatest citizens of their day, Russell Conwell read his world-famous lecture 6,000 times, and used the income he earned delivering it to establish a small seminary to train Baptist ministers that became Temple University.

· Horatio Alger

He is the writer of over 130 dime novels of children's literature that may have ultimately sold over 200 million copies. These stories were used to show how the social and economic mobility in America enabled young poor youth to rise to the top through both "pluck and luck." Many of his works have been described as rags to riches stories, showing how underclass boys might be able to achieve the American dream of wealth and success through virtues of hard work, faith, thrift, clean living, tenacity, courage, determination, and concern for others. His novels often traced the rise of street urchins to positions of wealth and prominence. The popular stories repeated the same theme *ad nauseum*, became bestsellers, and fit perfectly with the philosophy of Social Darwinism.

·Chautauqua

This was a self- improvement movement founded in 1874 by Lewis Miller in western New York on Lake Chautauqua. The program first focused on training Sunday School teachers but quickly expanded from that to offer correspondence degrees. It also offered a summer camp for families that promised "education and uplift" that was so popular that in less than a decade independent Chautauquas, often called assemblies, sprang up across the country. As with the early Lyceum movement, the goal of the Chautauqua assemblies was to offer informational and inspirational stimulation to rural and small-town America. In 1878, the New York Chautauqua initiated the first book club in the U.S. eventually sponsoring more than 10,000 local reading circles in towns all across the land. At the turn of the century, traveling Chautauqua's were first introduced, and in their heyday there were 21 such troupes operating on 93 circuits, reaching a phenomenal 35 million people a year.

The Arts

·Currier and Ives

This name was used by a New York printmaking firm from 1857 until 1907 and it depicted a certain style of lithographs. Nathaniel Currier was a printmaker and businessman and James Ives started as the firm's bookkeeper in 1852, and five years later became Currier's partner. Neither man was an artist, so all the Currier & Ives prints published by the partners, were drawn and lithographed by others. The Currier & Ives firm was in the business of producing lithographed prints to be sold to the general public for framing and display. Calling themselves "Printmakers to the People," they provided a pictorial history of the 19th centuries growth from an agricultural society to an industrialized one. The firm produced a variety of images, including pictures of newsworthy events and prints depicting every subject relating to American life: sports, games, home life, religion, children, hunting, fishing, entertainment, trains, ships, cities, and other genre pieces.

·Realism in Painting

The second half of the 19th century has been called the positivist age. It was an age of faith that all knowledge derived from science could solve human problems. In the visual arts this spirit is shown by the widespread rejection of the imagination of Romantic subjectivism in favor of Realism—the accurate objective description of the ordinary, observable world. This change was especially seen in painting. Realism's goal was not to imitate past artistic achievements but the truthful and accurate depiction that nature and contemporary life offered to the artist. The artificiality of both Classicism and Romanticism in art was unanimously rejected by the realist.

·Thomas Eakins

Eakins was an artist who worked from life choosing as his subject the people of his hometown of Philadelphia. He painted several hundred portraits and produced a number of large paintings that brought the portrait out of the drawing room and into the offices, streets, parks, rivers, arenas, and amphitheaters of his city. These active outdoor venues allowed him to paint the subjects that most inspired him in a realistic way.

·Winslow Homer

Winslow Homer was a self-taught American landscape painter and printmaker known for his maritime subjects. Homer gained acclaim as a genre painter in the late 1870s and early 1880s. At this time he painted mostly rural or idyllic scenes of farm life, children playing, and young adults courting. After moving to an English coastal village, he recaptured his boyhood interest in the sea, and painted the local fishing folk. Many of these paintings took as their subject young women mending nets or looking out to sea. Returning to the U.S. he painted the seascapes that strongly influenced succeeding generations of American painters for their direct interpretation of man's stoic relationship to neutral and sometimes harsh wilderness. In the winter, Homer ventured to warmer locations in Florida, Cuba, and the Bahamas and while on these fishing vacations he experimented freely with the water-color medium. Paintings like "Crack the Whip" are studies in Americana that he specialized in at various times in his career.

· James McNeil Whistler

Known best for his *Arrangement in Grey and Black, No. 1: Portrait of the Artist's Mother* (1871) usually called "Whistler's Mother," he was a painter of realism who was accepted by the French artistic community, as an American-born, British-based artist. He was a leading proponent of the "art for art's sake" school and his art was subtle and delicate while his public persona was combative. Late in his career he turned to Oriental influences in his works.

· Ashcan School

These painters also used urban life as inspiration for their works. Members of the "Ashcan School," a group of painters who gained notoriety at the turn of the century depicting squalid slums and modern loneliness were painters like John Sloan and George Bellows who created images of prizefighting and prostitution. These painters, along with the writers of the time, used the reality of their surroundings to open the eyes of many Americans, forcing them to confront a new, urban world.

· Photography

The new-found fascination with the camera as a means of capturing the realities of a single instant, unchanged by sentimentality, led to photography becoming an art form. Alfred Stieglitz (1864-1946) is called the father of modern photography because he became the driving force in the fight to have photography recognized as an art form. *Camera Work* was one of the greatest accomplishments in his mission to bring the level of photographic art in the United States up to the level of work being produced in England and Europe.

Literature

· Realism

By the late 19th century, America's growing cities yielded a new type of artistic expression—realism. In writing and painting artists left the idyllic imagery of Romanticism behind, and began depicting the realities of their new urban surroundings or rural areas that had been evacuated by movements to the city. Using plot and character development, a writer stated his or her philosophy about how much control mankind had over its own destiny. For example, romantic writers such as Ralph Waldo Emerson celebrated the ability of human will to triumph over adversity. On the other hand, Mark Twain, William Dean Howells and Henry James, influenced by the works of European writers, believed realism was grounded in the faithful reporting of all facets of everyday American life. These American realists believed that humanity's freedom of choice was limited by the power of outside forces. They drew upon the grim realities of everyday life, showing the breakdown of traditional values and the growing plight of the new urban poor. American realists built their plots and characters around people's ordinary, everyday lives. Additionally, their works contained regional dialects and dialogue that connected well with the public. As a result, readers were attracted to the realists because they saw their own struggles in print. The modern scientific revolution advocated that truth and knowledge be based on empirical data. Reinforcing that notion, the industrial revolution proclaimed that a better civil society could be built upon machinery and factory labor. It changed America. People left rural homes for opportunities in urban cities. With the development of new machinery and equipment, the U.S. economy became more focused on factory production; Americans did not have to chiefly rely on farming and agriculture to support their families. At the same time, immigrants from all over the world crowded into tenements to take advantage of new urban opportunities. In the end, the sweeping economic, social, and political changes that took place in post-war life allowed American Realism to prevail as a literary form.

·Henry James (1843-1916)

Henry James was a noted American-born essayist, critic, and author in the realism movement who wrote *Daisy Miller* (1879), *The Ambassadors* (1903), *The Turn of the Screw* (1898), and *The Portrait of a Lady* (1881). His works were often serialized in the *Atlantic Monthly* and featured narrative romances with highly developed characters with a setting of social commentary on politics, class, and status, as well as explorations of the themes of personal freedom, feminism, and morality. He was known for his comparisons of the Old World with the New. In his short stories and novels he employed techniques of interior monologue and point of view to expand the readers' understanding of character perception and insight.

·William Dean Howells (1837-1920)

Although he wrote over a hundred books in various genres, including novels, poems, literary criticism, plays, memoirs, and travel narratives, Howells is best known for his realistic fiction, including *A Modern Instance* (1881), on the then-new topic of the social consequences of divorce; *The Rise of Silas Lapham* (1885), his best-known work and one of the first novels to study the American businessman; and *A Hazard of New Fortunes* (1890), an exploration of cosmopolitan life in New York City.

·Mark Twain [pseudonym of Samuel Langhorne Clemens] (1835-1910)

Twain was an American humorist, lecturer, essayist, and author of realism who first came to note when he wrote *The Innocents Abroad* in 1869. This travel literature chronicled Twain's pleasure cruise on board a chartered vessel through Europe and the Holy Land with a group of religious pilgrims in 1867. It was the best selling of Twain's works during his lifetime. *The Adventures of Tom Sawyer* (1876) followed and it was met with lukewarm enthusiasm but its characters would become beloved and inspiring in numerous adaptations to the stage, television, and film. The 2nd novel in his Tom Sawyer adventure series, *Huckleberry Finn* (1885), was met with outright controversy in Twain's time but is now considered one of the great American novels. With a backdrop of colorful depictions of Southern society and places along the way, Huck Finn and Jim, Miss Watson's slave, decide to flee on the Mississippi river to the free states. Their journey has become a metaphor of idealistic freedom from oppression, broken family life, racial discrimination, and social injustice. Ernest Hemingway wrote "All modern American literature comes from one book by Mark Twain called *Huckleberry Finn*." Twain also collaborated on the *Gilded Age* (1873) with Charles Dudley Warner and wrote *A Tramp Abroad* (1880), a non-fiction satirical look at his trip through Germany, Italy, and the Alps as a sequel to *Innocents Abroad*. This was followed by *The Prince and the Pauper* (1882) and the time traveler novel, *A Connecticut Yankee in King Arthur's Court* (1889).

·Jack London

He became a leading spokesman for socialism and a popular writer of fiction. Born illegitimate in San Francisco in 1876 and because his mother was ill, he was raised by an ex-slave, Virginia Prentiss who would remain a major maternal figure while he grew up. His working class family moved around the Bay Area before settling in Oakland. He worked at various hard labor jobs, gathered oysters on San Francisco Bay, served on a fish patrol to capture poachers, sailed the Pacific on a sealing ship, joined Kelly's Army of unemployed working men, and hoboed around the country. He became acquainted with socialism and was known as the "Boy Socialist of Oakland" for his street corner oratory. He would run unsuccessfully several times on the socialist ticket for mayor. He chose to become a writer instead of living life as a factory worker and spent the winter of 1897 in the Yukon that provided him with the background material for his stories. He produced more than fifty stories, novels, and political essays. Although *The Call of the Wild* (1903) brought him lasting fame, many of his short stories became classics. His critique of capitalism and poverty in *The People of the Abyss* (1903), and discussion of alcoholism in *John Barleycorn* (1913) have left a lasting legacy. London's long voyage (1907-09) across the Pacific in a small boat provided material for books and stories about Polynesian and Melanesian cultures. He was instrumental in breaking the taboo over leprosy and popularizing Hawaii as a tourist spot. A well known public figure, he used his pulpit to support socialism, women's suffrage, and prohibition. His novel *The Sea Wolf* became the basis for the first full-length American movie.

Regionalism

The writing during this period was also very regional. The industrial revolution called for standardization, mass production of goods and streamlined channels of distribution. America was leaping into a new modern age and people feared that local folkways and traditions would be soon forgotten. Responding to these sentiments, realistic writers set their stories in specific American regions, rushing to capture the "local color" before it was lost.

Naturalism

For many of these artists daily life included the ugly side of the city—corruption, poverty, and an increasing divide between the social classes. Urbanization also brought with it a variety of new stories to tell or new themes to express. At another extreme were naturalists Stephen Crane and Frank Norris who supported the ideas of Emile Zola and the determinist movement. Naturalists argued that individuals have no choice because a person's life was dictated by a combination of heredity and the environment. Naturalism was a literary movement of the late nineteenth century that was an extension of realism—a reaction against the restrictions inherent in the realistic emphasis on the ordinary. Naturalists insisted that the extraordinary is real, too. In place of the middle-class realities and refinements of William Dean Howells, the naturalists wrote about the fringes of society—the criminal, the fallen, the down-and-out, in the form of sordid realism. Naturalism came largely from scientific determinism. Darwinism was especially important to the movement, as the naturalists perceived a person's fate as the product of blind external or biological forces. But in the typical naturalistic novel, chance played a part as well.

Women

"Cult of True Womanhood"

In the last half of the nineteenth century, Victorian ideals still held sway in American society, at least among members of the middle and upper classes. Strict, hierarchical Victorian thought promoted a so-called "cult of true Womanhood," which preached the four cardinal virtues of piety, purity, submission and domesticity. Much of this was believed more than practiced but the belief in the myth made it just as important as if it was reality.

Victoria Woodhull

She was a woman ahead of her time as she ran for President in 1872. She advocated many reforms that have been adopted today: the 8-hour work day, graduated income tax, social welfare programs, and profit-sharing. Born Victoria California Claflin in Homer, Ohio to a poor family, she was only 15 when she was married for the first time to Canning Woodhull. A complex woman she offered her hospitality to prostitutes and royalty alike. Although she was opposed to the organized Christian religion, she lived its principles by feeding the hungry, caring for the sick, and visiting the prisons. She believed that living those principles was more important to saving souls than preaching the Gospel of Christ. Her newspaper was the first to print the Communist Manifesto in English; and yet, she was also the first female stockbroker on Wall Street. After being nominated for the U.S. Presidency by the Equal Rights Party, her opponents, instead of debating her on the issues, attacked her personally. They called her everything from a witch to a prostitute and accused her of having affairs with married men. She used her personal funds as publisher of a New York journal, "Woodhull & Claflin's Weekly" and the stock brokerage firm, "Woodhull, Claflin & Company" to fund her campaign. This almost put her into bankruptcy. When she died at the age of 89 in 1927 she was a rich widow of a British banker.

·Charlotte Perkins Gilman

An original thinker on women's issues, where others saw the right to vote as a panacea, Gilman realized that political equality would not mean much unless women achieved economic equality as well. Considered a prophet before her time her first book was *In This our World* (1893), a collection of satiric poems with feminist themes. She became famous with her lectures on women's issues, ethics, labor, human rights, and social reform. Gilman's best-known work is *Women and Economics* (1898), in which she attacked the prevailing division of social roles. According to Gilman, male aggressiveness and maternal roles of women are artificial and not necessary for survival any more. "There is no female mind. The brain is not an organ of sex." She argued that only economic independence could bring true freedom for women and make them equal partners to their husbands. In her book *Concerning Children* she was an early advocate of professional child-care.

·Isadora Duncan

She is known as the founder of "modern dance," with her "New System" of interpretive dance, blending together poetry, music and the rhythms of nature. She did not believe in the formality of conventional ballet and gave birth to a more free form of dance, dancing barefoot and in simple Greek apparel. She was recognized for her passionate dancing and she ultimately proved to be the most famous dancer of her time. Her father was a poet and her mother was a pianist and music teacher and she was inspired artistically by them. Isadora did not believe in marriage but did have love affairs with a stage designer, with a millionaire, and had a child by each. She later married a Russian poet, but was soon divorced. She died tragically in 1927 when her scarf became entangled in spoke wheels of a Bugatti sports car.

Popular Culture

·Circus

The circus was a primary form of entertainment and information for the nineteenth century population, especially outside cities and larger metropolitan areas. By the beginning of the twentieth century there were more than 100 circuses traveling around the country, performing for as many as 12,000 spectators at each show. P. T. Barnum, later partnered with James Bailey, and the Ringling Brothers led the way with their product being called "The Greatest Show on Earth."

·Baseball

Invented by Abner Doubleday, Baseball became known as "America's pastime." The first truly professional team was the Cincinnati Red Stockings, formed in 1869 and financed by a group of Ohio investors. Baseball's popularity throughout the country convinced manager Harry Wright that people who happily paid "seventy-five cents to one dollar" to see theatrical performances would pay to see a baseball game, more popular by far than theatricals. He wanted to assure that patrons got their money's worth, so he drilled the team, insisted they be businesslike on the field, dressed them in knickers to increase their running speed, and nagged them on diet, drink, tobacco and clean living. The National League of Professional Baseball Players was formed out of the old National Association, that had lost support because of the Panic of 1873, and the fact that fans complained of drunkenness at games and players were accused of staging games just for gamblers. The new league tightened the rules for players, including forbidding players to drink, barred gambling, and played no games on Sunday. No beer was served at ball-parks. More importantly, power was vested in the owners, not the players. In 1882, owners of teams from other big cities formed the rival American Base Ball Association, called the "Beer Ball League" by supporters of the National League. Games cost only a quarter, teams played on Sunday, and ballparks sold alcoholic beverages. This league attracted bigger, more boisterous crowds, mostly immigrants and working class men whose only day off was Sunday. Middle-class, native-born fans remained loyal to the National League. Starting around 1880, twelve barnstorming teams were formed to bring the game to small towns. The first series advertised as " the world's championship" was played in 1886 between the Chicago White Stockings and the St. Louis Browns with the Browns winning 4 games to 2.

·Croquet

Brought over from England, this game became a popular pastime especially in the 1890s in America. Women's dresses when playing allowed them to expose their ankles—this was risque and could excite the men. Given the nature of Victorian courting codes, it is not surprising that young people, particularly women, relished the game, which gave them the opportunity to socialize out of earshot of chaperons. With the introduction of lawn tennis and the onset of World War I, the interest in croquet nearly died out.

·Bicycling

The diamond-frame safety bicycle gave women unprecedented mobility, contributing to their emancipation in Western nations. In the 1890's the cycling craze led to new fashions, including the revival of Amelia Bloomer's Turkish trousers or *bloomers*, which helped liberate women from corsets and other restrictive clothing. The popular song "Bicycle Built for Two" or "Daisy Belle" with the lyric, "But you'll look sweet, upon the seat, of a bicycle built for two" ushered in a new era in popular music. Some social scientist believed that bicycles enlarged the gene pool for workers, by enabling them to reach the next town. They also changed social patterns of behavior by increasing the courting radius. In urban areas, bicycles helped reduce crowding in inner-city tenements by allowing workers to commute from distant dwellings. Bicycles also reduced dependence on horses, and allowed people to travel distances, as they were more energy efficient and faster than walking.

·Gibson Girl

In the late 19th and early 20th century at the end of the Victorian era, illustrators for popular magazines influenced society and the pen-and-ink drawings of Charles Dana Gibson created the feminine ideal—the Gibson girl. Tall, slender, spirited, independent, yet feminine, she wore a classic "shirtwaist" dress, often with a plumed hat. "Her flowing skirt was hiked up in back with just a hint of a bustle." She was poised, patrician, and well bred, in a word, "classy." The "spark" in her eyes exemplified the American spirit of resourcefulness, adventurousness, and liberation from European traditions. She would be replaced in the 20th century by less refined women as the American ideal.

Music and Shows

·Popular Music

Popular music in the American 1890's continued traditions as well as offering innovations. The town band provided entertainment in nearly every community as it played waltzes and two-steps for local dances and concerts. The most legendary bandleader of the era was John Philip Sousa, director of the U.S. Marine Corps Band from 1880-1892. Between 1879 and 1915 he wrote 140 military marches, such as "Stars and Stripes Forever," the "Washington Post," and "Semper Fidelis." The piano became the central entertainment center of the home in the 1890s, a symbol of culture and prestige where women and girls played the instrument for the enjoyment of other family members, friends, or suitors. Religious and ethnic themes, current fads, as well as courtship were the subjects of popular songs. Parlor music was sentimental, written in waltz time, with lyrics telling tales ending in death or a lover's departure. Popular music was beginning to emerge as an industry in the 1890's as pianists demanded sheet music. One of the first hits in the popular music was "After the Ball," written in 1892 by Charles K. Harris. It was the first song to sell a million copies of sheet music. Other popular songs included "The Band Played On," "On the Banks of the Wabash," and "Daisy Belle."

·Minstrel Show

One of the most popular forms of entertainment in the nineteenth century was a traveling variety show called a minstrel show. Minstrel troupes such as Ed Christy and his Christy minstrels, featured songs and dances (usually presented by white performers in blackface), and short skits and jokes by recurring characters—one of whom was Jim Crow. By the 1890s there was less emphasis on the imitation of plantation life and more

emphasis on current song hits. Minstrel shows in the nineties also featured "coon songs"—songs whose lyrics stereotyped and ridiculed African American culture. Both black and white composers wrote such songs. By the end of the century, minstrel shows in the North generally gave way to vaudeville, the variety show that quickly became the nation's favorite form of entertainment.

· Ragtime

Blacks frequently used syncopation and rhythmic accents in their performances. The first rags were written for piano, although the style could be used on many instruments and eventually led to the development of jazz. Rags were played not just in parlors, but in saloons, gambling halls, and juke joints. Scott Joplin's "Maple Leaf Rag," published in 1899 became a best seller. Joplin was a black pianist and performer who tried to move ragtime from the saloon to the concert hall.

· Vaudeville

It was a theatrical genre of variety entertainment in the United States and Canada from the early 1880s until the early 1930s. Vaudeville developed from the concert saloon, minstrel shows, side-shows at circuses, dime museums and burlesque. During its heyday vaudeville was America's most popular form of entertainment. People flocked to their local "Palace" to see the top stars of the day doing their acts. Acrobats, animal acts, dancers, singers and old-time comedians provided popular entertainment for the masses. The vaudeville actors roamed the country with a smile and a suitcase and brought joy and excitement to the communities that they visited. The focal point of vaudeville was the Palace Theater in the heart of New York's theater district, at Broadway and 47th Street. It was every performers ambition to "play the Palace in New York," it meant they had arrived.

UNIT XVIII
MULTIPLE-CHOICE QUESTIONS

Questions 1-3 refer to the following:

"The great vogue of the bicycle...enlarged both the area of nearby travel and the vogue of out-of-door exercise.... Along with the use of the bicycle, open–air sports were coming everywhere into vogue; women for the first time participated in more strenuous activities than the orthodox croquet and archery of older decades. The nineties saw the sudden rise of the 'Gibson girl' as a recognized feminine type; also the entry of women into the field of practical employment.... In the middle nineties the art of after dinner speaking reached its prime... when chairs had been pushed back, napkins tossed besides the coffee cups and cigars lighted up to introduce the real business of the evening, the assemblage awaited the exchange of epigram and persiflage from well known wits at the speakers' table reflected one of the bright spots in New York life."

A.D. Noyes, *The Market Place*, 1938

1. The "Gibson Girl," so prominent in the 1890s was followed by which female icon of the 1920s"

   (A) damsel in distress
   (B) girl next door
   (C) flapper
   (D) pin up

2. The verbal exchange of epigram and persiflage by the after dinner speakers is a reference to the highly sought after skill possesed by the speakers of

   (A) irony and paradox
   (B) metaphor and symbol
   (C) intellect and emotion
   (D) wit and banter

3. Popular song of the 1890s also titled "On a Bicycle Built for Two" that celebrated a new craze is

   (A) Daisy Belle
   (B) After the Ball
   (C) The Band Played On
   (D) Sidewalks of New York

262

Questions 4-6 refer to the following:

"If Paul Bunyan possesses only a slight and insubstantial basis in folk tradition, he has achieved a considerable impact on American thought.... the legend bursts from print into a variety of art forms and pageants, sculpture, ballet, musical suite, lyric opera, folk drama, radio play, oil painting, lithography, wood carving, and even a glass mosaic mural celebrate the giant lumberjack and his blue ox [Babe].... Actually the nation's newspapers, rather than the lumberjacks of the northwoods have nourished Old Paul in the hearts of his countrymen.... He is the pseudo folk hero of twentieth- century mass culture... pressed into service by writers, journalists, and promoters to exemplify 'the American spirit.' Twentieth- century America, ripe and self-confident and saving the world for democracy, thirsted for a New World Thor, or Hercules... to symbolize her might. And so Paul Bunyan..."

Richard Dorson, *American Folklore*, 1959

4. American hero's that represent the spirit of the Paul Bunyon superlatives in the 21st century come primarily from

(A) narrative history
(B) comic books and movies
(C) rock and roll music
(D) epic poetry

5. As a figure of folklore Dorson sees Paul Bunyan as being

(A) a substantial figure in the folk tradition with a long history in American folklore
(B) of the oral tradition of folklore passed down from generation to generation
(C) created by publicists of the 20th century to satisfy the mass culture
(D) the quintessential icon of historic folklore going back to colonial times

6. His popularity soared along with American confidence as a result of

(A) ending unlimited immigration by establishing quotas by passage of the Immigration Act of 1924
(B) the U.S. acquiring an empire as a result of the Spanish American War
(C) opening up Oklahoma land for settlement by boomers and sooners
(D) U.S. participation in World War I

Questions 7-9 refer to the following:

"Retreat to the wilderness was a middle class response to urban pressures.... Sigrud Olson... professional guide...catering to vacation executives, [said] 'I have seen them come from the cities..., worried and sick at heart... change under the stimulus of wilderness living... into happy, carefree, joyous men....' Wild nature was a nuisance to the man on the land unless he profited by it. But those who dealt in symbols and myths found the wilderness a major force in shaping the American character.... But the taste for the primitive was a sophisticated appetite. Overindulged it led to spiritual indigestion... any protracted, genuine association with nature means a reversion to a state of brutal savagery... the average American knew pure solitude and virgin wilderness intimately in volumes of wilderness adventure [writers].... Arm-chair adventures into primeval solitude were far less arduous than those of reality."

Peter J. Schmitt, *Back to Nature: The Arcadian Myth in Urban America*, 1969

7. According to the passage above those who valued the wilderness

   (A) knew it more by reading about it than actually experiencing it
   (B) usually satisfied their wilderness yearnings by trips to Yosemite and Yellowstone
   (C) was primarily indulged in by the upper class elites
   (D) were willing to support the cause by staying away from nature in order to preserve it

8. The patron saint of the agrarianism of the "Arcadian Myth" was which historic political figure?

   (A) Benjamin Franklin
   (B) George Washington
   (C) Alexander Hamilton
   (D) Thomas Jefferson

9. The "back to nature" movement in the late 19th century inspired an important aspect of which reform movement?

   (A) Populism
   (B) Progressivism
   (C) New Deal
   (D) Great Society

Questions 10-12 refer to the following:

"Between 1850 and 1900 Americans bought one hundred million copies of William Holmes McGuffey's school readers.... As an apostle of religion, morality, and education, McGuffey wanted to bolster Midwestern civilization against the dangers inherent in new frontiers.... McGuffey worried so much about frontier dangers that he overlooked the revolutionary changes in transportation, manufacturing, and management... taking place.... Moreover, children learned that village and country life surpassed that in cities. As a rule, McGuffey simply ignored urban ways and used them as examples of corruption... McGuffey's emphasis on rural and village life pleased an agrarian age. His readers thus gained strength... [from] a... culture, uncomplicated by urban and industrial problems. This very strength, however, became a source of weakness as village and farm gave way to city and factory. McGuffey ideals retreated slowly."

Lewis Atherton, *Main Street on the Middle Border*, 1954

10. From the above passage the ideas in *McGuffey's Readers* could be considered

   (A) Liberal
   (B) Moderate
   (C) Revolutionary
   (D) Conservative

11. An education based on *McGuffey's Readers* dominated for half a century until is was supplanted by the educational ideas of

   (A) Progressives
   (B) Democrats
   (C) Republicans
   (D) Socialists

12. An education based on *McGuffey's Readers* would tend to ignore having an understanding of which of the following?

   (A) Village hamlet culture
   (B) Jeffersonianism
   (C) Immigration
   (D) Mississippi Valley geography

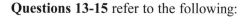

Questions 13-15 refer to the following:

"Be it enacted… That whoever…shall sell…or shall offer to sell, or to lend, or to give away, or in any manner to exhibit, or shall otherwise publish… or shall have in his possession…an obscene book, pamphlet, paper, writing, advertisement, circular, print, picture, drawing or other representation, figure, or image on or of paper or other material, or any cast instrument, or other article of an immoral nature, or any drug or medicine, or any article whatever, for the prevention of conception… On conviction thereof in any court of the United States…he shall be imprisoned at hard labor in the penitentiary for not less than six months nor more than five years for each offense, or fined not less than one hundred dollars nor more than two thousand dollars, with costs of court."

Comstock Law, 1873

13. The law in the passage above as it was enforced was primarily used to stop what practice that is now legal

    (A) sex magazines
    (B) nude paintings
    (C) book publications
    (D) birth control

14. The sweep of the Comstock Law was so broad and during the height of its power

    (A) newspapers were considered contraband and could be seized by government officials
    (B) some anatomy books could not be mailed to medical students
    (C) the post office refused to deliver publications that violated the 1st Amendment
    (D) information about venereal disease could not be sent through the mail

15. The dismantling of the Comstock laws took a long time and the decision in 1965 in *Griswold v. Connecticut* enhanced the process by applying which standard to relations between adults?

    (A) "Full faith and credit"
    (B) "Inherent powers of the Constitution"
    (C) "Life, liberty, & property clause"
    (D) "Right to privacy"

UNIT XIX

IMPERIALISM

From the time of Washington's "Farewell Address" through most of the 19th century the U.S. adopted an isolationist foreign policy. This would change in the time period around the turn of the century. From an isolationist past the country embarked on foreign policy adventures to become an imperialistic power that would transform the nation. This move toward an internationalist foreign policy lead the U.S. to join the western European nations in fighting the Great War (later renamed WWI).

19th Century Foreign Policy

· France in Mexico

When the American Civil War ended in 1865, the United States began supplying the republicans with arms in order to overthrow the French established monarchy of Maximilian and Carlotta. The U.S. Congress had unanimously passed a resolution opposing the establishment of the Mexican monarchy in 1864. With the Civil War over the U.S. demanded that France withdraw their forces from Mexico and the U.S. officially protested to Austria the presence of Austrian volunteers in Mexico. Napoleon III withdrew his French troops that would lead to the defeat of the monarchy by the republican forces of Benito Juarez and the execution of the Austrian King Maximillan. *Cinco de Mayo*—or the fifth of May—commemorates the Mexican army's victory over France at the Battle of Puebla.

· Santa Domingo

From 1868 to 1873 with the pro-U.S. annexation government in power in Santa Domingo (Dominican Republic), overtures were made to the United States about annexation. Grant sent his secretary, General O. E. Babcock to the Dominican Republic to negotiate a treaty by which the republic would become part of the United States. Although ratified by the Dominican Senate, this treaty was opposed in the United States Senate, under the leadership of Charles Sumner, and was finally rejected. In 1871, three commissioners were appointed by Grant to gather more information about annexation. Although their report was favorable to annexation, no action was taken.

267

·Hawaii

Originally a trading post in the 18th century, New England missionaries arrived in 1820 and settled in to Christianize the indigenous population. To aid in converting a society with an oral tradition to Christianity, the missionaries developed an alphabet for the Hawaiian language, began translating the Bible, and started printing other important information for many Hawaiians to read. In less than 20 years, the missionaries had established a school system that reflected Western culture and the Protestant religion. Under the Hawaiian holistic view of the world that incorporated all things from the ocean to the sea, no one owned the land. An 1848 law instituted a new system of private property ownership and divided up the land. Within decades, title to thousands of acres of land had fallen into the hands of non-Hawaiians. Even the Crown lands, owned by the King and his successors, were often sold or leased to foreigners in payment of debts or in exchange for foreign goods and supplies. The descendants of the missionaries became the sugar planters and after 1875 Hawaiian sugar came into the U.S. duty free. The U.S. government leased Pearl Harbor from the Hawaiian crown in 1887 to build a naval base. When Queen Liliuokalani came to the throne in 1891 with her slogan of "Hawaii for the Hawaiians," the sugar planters led by Samuel Dole, along with the help of the U.S. Minister John Stevens and U.S. Marines, overthrew the monarchy, imprisoned the Queen, confiscated the Crown lands, and made them part of the public domain. The new government controlled by the sugar interests asked to be annexed to the U.S. President Cleveland refused but it would happen under McKinley in 1897.

·Alaska

Russia lacked the financial resources to support major settlements or a military presence along the Pacific coast of North America and permanent Russian settlers in Alaska never numbered more than 400. Defeat in the Crimean War further reduced Russian interest in this region and Russia offered to sell Alaska to the United States in 1859 but the U.S. Civil War delayed the sale. After the war, Secretary of State William Seward agreed to purchase Alaska for $7.2 million. The Senate approved the treaty, President Andrew Johnson signed it and Alaska became part of the U.S. in 1867. Skeptics dubbed the purchase of Alaska "Seward's Folly," but the Secretary of State was vindicated when a major gold deposit was discovered in the Yukon in 1896 and Alaska became the gateway to the Klondike gold fields.

·Pago Pago

By 1872, the U.S. Navy Department was interested in a coaling station in the Pacific to supply the new steam-powered ships. It believed Pago Pago on the island of Tutuila in the Samoan Islands was available. A German company based in the Samoan Islands at Apia were opposed to the U.S. interest, as were some New Zealanders, but they were unable to get their governments to move to make the islands a protectorate. The United States won the friendship of the Samoan chieftain in the Pago Pago area, and in 1878, a treaty was signed. Pago Pago became a naval station for the U.S. Navy—beginning what would become American Samoa.

·Pan-American Conference

The brainchild of Secretary of State James G. Blaine, the first Pan-American Conference was held in Washington, D.C. in 1889. The conference was a meeting between the United States and various countries in Latin America and its goal was to improve economic and political relations between the participants. Many South and Central American nations did not trust the United States and thought the customs union plan proposed by the U.S. was unilaterally favorable to the Americans. In addition, the U.S. delegates had trouble negotiating the customs union for free trade due to the embarrassing fact that the Republican-controlled Congress was simultaneously working on legislation to raise tariffs. The final agreement failed to establish the customs union as the delegates settled for a clause that encouraged reciprocity (trade) agreements. This would result in some lowering of tariffs. The issue of arbitration was also not resolved because the Latin American countries viewed the U.S. proposals as a violation of sovereignty. The conference did set up the Pan-American Union to hold additional meetings in the future.

·Samoa Partition

The Berlin Conference of 1889 was called because of conflicting claims in the islands between the U.S. and Germany. Great Britain supported the German claims in return for Germany supporting the British imperialistic claims elsewhere. This resulted in a tripartite protectorate of the islands by the United States, Germany, and Great Britain. Popular disapproval in the United States of "foreign alliances" led to the dissolution of this agreement and its partition in 1899. Tutuila and some small islands were placed under American control and the rest went to Germany.

·Pribilof Islands

During the 1880s, Americans hunted seals on the Pribilof Islands, which the U.S. had acquired from Russia in 1867. As the price of seal skin increased Canadians began conducting sealing in the open waters beyond the three mile limit. In 1886, U.S. government revenue cutters, claiming to protect "American property," began seizing Canadian sealing vessels. After bellicose statements by both the U.S. Congress and the British, an international tribunal was convened that upheld the Canadians right to hunt seals in international waters, but imposed some restrictions. In 1911, an international conference banned pelagic seal hunting in the Bering Sea but provided compensation to Canada.

·Venezuelan Boundary Dispute

The Venezuelan boundary dispute officially began in 1841 when the Venezuelan government protested alleged British encroachment on Venezuelan territory. In 1876, Venezuela protested, broke diplomatic relations with Great Britain, and appealed to the United States for assistance citing the Monroe Doctrine as justification for U.S. involvement. The U.S. did nothing but for the next 19 years Venezuela repeatedly petitioned the U.S. for help, asking it to either support arbitration or intervene with force. In 1895, invoking the Monroe Doctrine, newly appointed U.S. Secretary of State Richard Olney sent a strong note to British Prime Minister and Foreign Secretary Lord Salisbury, demanding that the British submit the boundary dispute to arbitration. Salisbury's response was that the Monroe Doctrine had no validity as international law. The United States found that response unacceptable, and in 1895, President Grover Cleveland asked Congress for authorization to appoint a boundary commission, proposing that the commission's findings be enforced "by every means." Congress passed the measure unanimously and talk of war with Great Britain began to circulate in the jingoist U.S. press. Faced with pressure from the Boer situation in South Africa, Britain agreed to submit the issue to arbitration. Venezuela agreed, certain that the commission would decide in its favor. However, when the commission supported a line that the British had offered the Venezuelans in 1835, the Venezuelans quietly ratified the commission's finding. The Anglo-Venezuelan boundary dispute asserted for the first time a more outward-looking American foreign policy, particularly in the Western Hemisphere. Internationally the incident marked the United States as a world power and gave notice that under the Monroe Doctrine it would assert its power in the Western Hemisphere.

·Open Door Policy

By the late 19th century, Japan and the European powers had carved much of China into separate spheres of influence, where they each had economic dominance in their sphere. The U.S., coming late to imperialism, held no sphere of influence in China. In 1899, U. S. Secretary of State John Hay proposed an "Open Door" policy in China in which all nations would have equal trading and development rights throughout all of China. Such a policy would put all the imperialist powers on equal footing in China and would limit the advantages of having a sphere of influence. Russia, Japan, Germany, France, and Great Britain had worked hard to establish their dominance in China and were unlikely to give these up willingly. The various powers gave evasive and conflicting responses to Hay's announcement; but Hay interpreted their response as acceptance of the Open Door policy that was "final and definitive."

· Boxer Revolt

Beginning in 1898, groups of peasants in northern China began to band together into a secret society known as the Righteous and Harmonious Fists, called the "Boxers" by westerners because the society practiced boxing and callisthenic rituals which they believed would make them impervious to bullets. At first, the Boxers wanted to destroy the Ch'ing (Manchu) dynasty that had ruled China for over 250 years. When the Empress Dowager secretly backed the Boxers, they turned solely to ridding China of foreigners. By late 1899, bands of Boxers were massacring Christian missionaries and Chinese Christians. In June 1900, the Boxers surrounded the foreign legations in Peking and began a two-month siege. The siege was broken when the Boxers finally fell to an international force, the Eight-Nation Alliance, eventually numbering 54,000 troops of which 3,400 were U.S. forces. The Boxer Protocol set an indemnity of $332 million on China of which the U.S. was to receive $24.5 million. After accepting $4 million to settle private claims the U.S. used the unpaid balance to educate Chinese students in the U.S. Many of them would be involved in overthrowing the Ch'ing (Manchu) dynasty in 1911 and eventually establishing a republic in China.

Cuba and the Spanish American War—

· Cuba

A war of independence from Spanish rule had began in 1895, in part because of the economic hardship that was caused by the McKinley tariff and its high duties on Cuban sugar. The guerrilla warfare was succeeding until Spain's General Weyler adopted the policy of Reconcentration—to separate the guerillas from their civilian support base. Thousands of civilian Cubans were herded into over-crowded, disease-ridden camps where prisoners also suffered from malnutrition. In the U.S. press, Weyler was called a "butcher" and the "yellow journalism" of William Randolph Hearst and Joseph Pulitzer fed the war fever. The sugarcane fields, many owned by U.S. companies, were being burned. Congress passed a resolution recognizing Cuban belligerency, but President Cleveland stated he would not mobilize the army even if Congress declared war. Due partly to U.S. pressure Spain removed Weyler and granted Cuba autonomy in domestic affairs. The new government proclaimed by the rebels rejected Spain's offer, opting instead for full independence. In 1898, the United States sent to Havana harbor the battleship *Maine*, with words of friendship expressed to Spain through diplomatic channels, and Spain sent a naval ship to New York in exchange. The *Maine* blew up, killing 266 and Spain proposed a joint investigation of the incident that the U.S. refused. A U.S. inquiry concluded that a mine placed under the ship destroyed the *Maine*. Today it is known to have been an internal explosion, just as the Spanish investigation showed. "Remember the *Maine*" became a slogan of the jingoes who wanted war. Relations with Spain deteriorated further with the publication of a private letter stolen from the Havana mail and published in Hearst's newspaper. It was from Spanish minister to the U.S. Dupuy de Lome who called the President "weak and a bidder for the admiration of the crowd…and a would- be politician." The "yellow press" was outraged and Du Lome resigned, but the damage had been done. McKinley detested war, he had hoped that political pressure and negotiations would resolve the conflict in Cuba, but he gave into the passion that swept the nation. He requested authority from Congress to intervene in Cuba, and it passed by a vote of 311 to 6 in the House and 42 to 35 in the Senate. An ultimatum was sent to Spain to either leave Cuba or face war. When Spain refused to leave Cuba the Spanish-American War began.

· Teller Amendment

This last part of the war resolution said that the U.S. had no intention of exercising control or sovereignty over Cuba and the people of Cuba would adopt their own government after peace had been restored.

·Spanish American War
In what Secretary of State, John Hay called "The Splendid Little War," the U.S. victory created a nation with global interests and in one brief clash of arms the U.S. acquired Guam, Puerto Rico, and the Philippine Islands from Spain while Cuba was granted independence. In the battle of Manila Bay, the six-ship Asiatic squadron of Commodore George Dewey, destroyed with heavy casualties a larger but outgunned and antiquated Spanish fleet. The U.S. flotilla emerged unscathed, with only eight wounded. Guam, one of the Mariana Islands in the western Pacific, surrendered to Captain Henry Glass on the *Charleston* as the Spanish commander on the island had not heard of the outbreak of the war, and his garrison had no ammunition to defend itself. In one noted land battle, Theodore Roosevelt made a name for himself as a member of Leonard Wood's Rough Riders, a volunteer group, who participated in the Battle of San Juan Hill. In the Battle of Santiago Bay the American navy defeated the Spanish battle fleet and it marked the end of centuries long Spanish power in the western hemisphere. Eighteen hundred Spaniards died in the battle, in contrast to one American death and one American wounded sailor. All of the Spanish ships were beached, either burning or sinking. Two weeks later the Spanish forces defending Santiago surrendered and the war ended.

·Treaty of Paris of 1898
Commissioners from the United States and Spain met in Paris to produce a treaty that would bring an end to the war after six months of hostilities. Although the Conference discussed Cuba and debt questions, the major conflict concerned the situation in the Philippines. Spanish commissioners argued that Manila had surrendered after the armistice and therefore the Philippines could not be demanded as a war conquest. Eventually they yielded because they had no other choice, and the U.S. ultimately paid Spain $20 million for possession of the Philippines. Andrew Carnegie offered to pay the $20 million to the U.S. government so the Philippines could get their independence. Independence was 48 years away. The islands of Puerto Rico and Guam were also placed under American control, and Spain relinquished its claim to Cuba.

·Platt Amendment
The United States occupied Cuba for five years after 1898. In 1901, Secretary of War Elihu Root drafted a set of articles (later known as the Platt Amendment) as guidelines for future United States-Cuban relations. Despite considerable Cuban resistance, they became a part of the 1902 Cuban Constitution. Passed as a rider to the Army Appropriations Act, the amendment gave to the U.S. the naval base at Guantánamo Bay; forbid Cuba from transferring its land to any power other than the U.S.; mandated that Cuba would contract no foreign debt without guarantees that the interest could be paid from normal revenues; gave the U.S. the right to intervene in Cuban affairs when the U.S. deemed it necessary; and, prohibited Cuba from negotiating treaties with any other country than the United States.

·Results of the War
The United States humbled a European country and acquired an empire, which was contrary to the long established U.S. foreign policy set forth in Washington's Farewell Address and the Monroe Doctrine. Total battle deaths were 379 while total deaths numbered 5,462, mainly from yellow fever, embalmed (contaminated) beef and other non-battle causes.

Arguments for Imperialism

·*Our Country*
One of the more influential promoters of the superiority of the Anglo-Saxon culture as a justification for imperialism was Josiah Strong, a Congregational clergyman and social reformer. Strong's 1885 work, *Our Country*, asserted "...every race which has deeply impressed itself on the human family has been the representative of some great idea—one or more—which has given direction to the nation's life and form to its civilization." The Anglo-Saxon is the representative of two great ideas, according to Strong—civil

liberty and pure spiritual Christianity. Strong was certain that the United States, by its landmass and growing population, would become the center of Anglo-Saxonism and prove its evolutionary advancement in the Social Darwinistic world. In the struggle for survival, the Anglo-Saxons, with a "genius for colonization," would civilize and Christianize the world.

· Albert Beveridge's "March of the Flag"

This speech, first delivered in Indianapolis in 1898 by Senate candidate, Albert Beveridge of Indiana, justified territorial expansion as essential to the nation. His remarks suggested a special destiny for America, a destiny built upon superior racial qualities and a responsibility to give to others its economic, political and social institutions. Beveridge said, "…It is a glorious history our God has bestowed upon His chosen people; a history heroic with faith in our mission and our future… Shall the American people continue their march toward the commercial supremacy of the world? Shall free institutions broaden their blessed reign as the children of liberty wax in strength, until the empire of our principles is established over the hearts of all mankind?" Over the next three months, approximately 300,000 copies of this speech were published in pamphlet form. Beveridge gave the speech again and again to audiences and his view that America had a special destiny to fulfill helped to convince Americans that it had a responsibility to take control of the Philippines, Puerto Rico and Cuba. The economic arguments of his speech were used to justify a strong U.S. presence in China.

· Missionary Influence

Information that the U.S. government received regarding foreign countries often came from Protestant missionaries "laboring for the Lord" in what they saw as the virgin lands of other countries. Once the churches were involved, the U.S. government would tend to follow. The missionaries view of native people, usually strongly influenced by their religion, was often accepted as fact by U.S. government officials.

· Mahan's Thesis

In 1890 U.S. Navy officer Alfred Thayer Mahan published an historical study of English, French, and Dutch sea power in the seventeenth and eighteenth centuries called *The Influence of Sea Power Upon History*. He concluded that a countries "greatness" was due to its Navy and its control of the seas. This scholarly work contained geopolitical implications that naval forces should be used as instruments of national policy. In 130 subsequent articles and eighteen additional books, Mahan elaborated on the theme of command of the seas as a prerequisite to great power status. His ideas led to the belief that the U.S. must construct modern warships, occupy key positions along the main water routes of the world, acquire coaling and provisioning stations, and keep its enemies out of its defensive perimeter. Influential politicians including Henry Cabot Lodge, Theodore Roosevelt, and John Tracy accepted his arguments and were instrumental in getting them adopted as policy.

· Economic Arguments

Implied in the arguments of both Beveridge and Mahan were economic arguments for imperialism. Many felt that the promotion of markets abroad could solve the problem of industrial overproduction in the U.S. and American businessmen were convinced they could outsell their foreign rival anywhere in the world if they could only gain access to the markets. Much of the interest in the U.S. gaining a foothold in China was based on the idea of selling goods to the Chinese.

· Psychological Reasons

After decades of domestic unrest including the Panics of 1873 and 1893 (renamed a depression), the American people were ready for something that could unite them rather than divide them and make them feel proud. If foreign adventures were introduced people tended to forget the ills at home. The stirring deeds of European empire builders like Cecil Rhodes, Richard Burton, and Pierre de Brazza excited Americans who had a desire for adventure of their own, as they had become bored with domestic crises. The idea of exporting American institutions like democracy to "backward peoples" had a certain altruistic appeal.

Foreign Policy of the Progressive Presidents

· Theodore Roosevelt

Practiced a type of diplomacy often called "Big Stick" or "Gunboat Diplomacy" that asserted U.S. power by both diplomatic and military means. It was used to describe the assertion of U.S. dominance as a moral imperative. The term originated from an African proverb, "Speak softly and carry a big stick; you will go far." Roosevelt first used it when he asked Congress for money to increase U.S. naval preparedness to support his diplomatic objectives. The press used the phrase to describe Roosevelt's Latin America policy as well as his domestic policy of regulating monopolies.

· Hay-Pauncefote Treaty

Came about because of Roosevelt's desire to build a canal across the Central American isthmus that was being stopped by the Clayton-Bulwer Treaty of 1850 that specified that neither the U.S. nor Great Britain could build a trans-ocean canal without the consent of the other country. In this treaty the British renounced all joint rights to any canal, giving the U.S. sole rights to construct, control, and maintain a canal with the stipulation that the canal would be neutral and that the U.S. was forbidden to fortify it.

· Walker Commission

Originally a Nicaraguan route had been favored by the Walker Commission, which had studied the issue and determined the price the New Panama Canal Co., (successor to the bankrupt French De Lesseps Company) was asking for its holdings and franchises, $109 million, was considered exorbitant. When the company lowered its price to $40 million, the commission reversed itself and recommended the Panama route.

· Spooner Amendment

Passed as an amendment to the Hepburn Act which recommended the Nicaraguan route, it negated that decision and recommended the purchase of the property rights of the New Panama Canal Company for $40 million. It also stated that Columbia (owner of Panama) grant to the U.S. perpetual control over the waterway; established the Isthmian Canal Commission; and, authorized the President to purchase the Nicaraguan route if negotiations for the Panama route failed. Intense lobbying by the New Panama Canal Company's William Cromwell and Philippe Bunau-Varilla convinced Senators to switch to the Panama route after receiving postage stamps showing an active volcano in Nicaragua.

· Hay-Herran Convention

In return for a payment of 10 million and an annual fee of $250,000, the U.S. would receive a 99- year lease (with a renewal option) over a canal zone 6 miles wide. After a great deal of debate it was ratified by the U.S. Senate, but rejected by the Colombian Senate who wanted $25 million, since they were not going to get any part of the $40 million going to the New Panama Canal Company, whose charter would expire in 1904. This refusal of Colombia to sell the land at what they considered to be a low price gave the U.S. an excuse to help take the land by force.

· Panama Revolution

Panama wanted to sell the land to the U.S. to build the canal, but when Colombia refused, a revolution was planned in New York by Philippe Bunau-Varilla, a French citizen with the tacit approval of the U.S. Roosevelt sent a gunboat, the *Nashville* to protect "American lives in Panama." This meant that no country was going to land on the isthmus, not even its rightful owner Columbia (invasion by land was impossible because of the impenetrable Panamanian jungle). Panama declared its independence from Colombia, and the United States immediately recognized this declaration. The revolution resulted in two deaths, a donkey and a "Chinaman." Colombia would have re-conquered the area, endangering American interests, but U.S. military presence kept

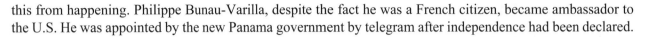

this from happening. Philippe Bunau-Varilla, despite the fact he was a French citizen, became ambassador to the U.S. He was appointed by the new Panama government by telegram after independence had been declared.

·Hay-Bunau-Varilla Treaty

The terms of the treaty were: the United States was to receive rights to a canal zone and would extend five miles on either side of the route; and, Panama was to receive a payment of $10 million; Panama was to receive annual rental payments of $250,000. Also, the U.S. guaranteed the independence of Panama and the neutrality terms of the Hay-Pauncefote Treaty would be honored.

·Building the Canal

The U.S. succeeded in building the canal where the French De Lesseps Company (builders of the Suez Canal) had failed. Having to overcome yellow fever, malaria, and massive landslides, the U.S. used the technology of a lock system and created two lakes to deal with the issue of too much water and equalizing the difference in water level of the two oceans. The U.S. success under the chief engineers John Stevens and later George Goethals was the largest and most difficult engineering project ever undertaken. Success was also due to the efforts of Dr. Walter Reed who eradicated Yellow Fever by exterminating the mosquitos that caused it.

·Insular Cases

These are several U.S. Supreme Court cases decided early in the 20th century on how to govern the new territories acquired by the U.S. as a result of the Spanish-American War. The U.S. Constitution was silent on this subject and the cases were the court's response to a major issue in the United States presidential election of 1900 that attempted to answer the question posed by the American Anti-Imperialist League, "Does the Constitution follow the flag?" Essentially, the Supreme Court said that full constitutional rights did not automatically extend to all areas under American control and that inhabitants of unincorporated territories such as Puerto Rico, "even if they are U.S. citizens," may have no constitutional rights. The Court in these cases established the doctrine of territorial incorporation. Under this doctrine, the Constitution only applied fully to incorporated territories such as Alaska and Hawaii; it only applied partially in the new unincorporated territories of Puerto Rico, Guam and the Philippines.

·Alaskan-Canadian Boundary Dispute

The discovery of gold in the Canadian Klondike in 1896 brought to a head the long-standing disagreement between the United States and Canada over the Alaska-Canada boundary. The treaty of 1867, by which the United States had bought Alaska from Russia, established the boundary of southeast Alaska (the Panhandle) as 30 miles (48 kilometers) from the coast. The entrance to the Klondike was through an inlet called the Lynn Canal. The Canadians claimed that the boundary ran across inlets from headland to headland. This would have placed the Lynn Canal within Canada. The United States held that the line followed all the windings of the coast. The problem was referred to a joint arbitration commission of three Americans, two Canadians, and one Britain. While the commissioner met Roosevelt brandished the "big stick" intimating that if the U.S. did not receive satisfaction it would employ military force in the disputed area. The commission meeting in London in 1903 upheld the U.S. claim by a vote of four to two.

·Venezuelan Debt Crisis

Long living beyond its means, Venezuela defaulted on its $22 million European debt. The European holders of the debt, Great Britain, Italy, and Germany responded by erecting a blockade along the Venezuelan coast and firing upon coastal fortifications to try to force the *caudillo*, Cipriano Castro, to pay the debt. Roosevelt stood by at first but became suspicious of Germany when they began to bomb the Venezuelan ports. Castro asked the U.S. to arbitrate and the Europeans accepted limited arbitration that was settled by the Hague tribunal in 1904.

·Roosevelt Corollary to Monroe Doctrine

Partially as a result of the situation in Venezuela, Roosevelt, in his address to Congress in 1904 claimed that the United States had the right to not only oppose European intervention in the Western Hemisphere but to intervene itself in the domestic affairs of its neighbors if those neighbors proved unable to protect U.S. investments. Roosevelt issued his corollary stating: "Chronic wrongdoing, or an impotence which results in a general loosening of the ties of civilized society [however], may in America, as elsewhere, ultimately require intervention by some civilized nation, and in the Western Hemisphere the adherence of the United States to the Monroe Doctrine may force the United States, however reluctantly, in flagrant cases of such wrongdoing or impotence, to the exercise of an international police power.... While [our Southern neighbors] obey the primary laws of civilized society they may rest assured that they will be treated by us in a spirit of cordial and helpful sympathy.... It is a mere truism to say that every nation, whether in America or anywhere else, which desires to maintain its freedom, its independence, must ultimately realize that the right of such independence can not be separated from the responsibility of making good use of it."

·Dominican-Republic

The first application of the Roosevelt Corollary occurred in the Dominican Republic when the U.S. government became the financial agent to oversee the repayment of that country's debt from customs duties. The U.S. government assumed responsibility for all Dominican debt as well as for the collection of customs duties and the allocation of those revenues to the Dominican government and to the repayment of its domestic and foreign debt.

·Portsmouth Peace Conference

Called by Roosevelt to end the Russo-Japanese War in 1905 it would establish the balance of power in the Pacific for the next century. The war and the treaty signaled the emergence of Japan as a world power as its dominant rights in Korea were recognized, and it consolidated its territorial and economic position in Manchuria. Because of the role played by Roosevelt, the U.S. became a significant force in world diplomacy and Roosevelt was awarded the Nobel Peace Prize for his back channel efforts before and during the peace negotiations, even though he never came to Portsmouth. The treaty contained language ratifying the secret Taft-Katsura agreement, whereby the U.S. agreed not to interfere in Korea as long as Japan did not interfere with U.S. interest in the Philippines. This international affair settled immediate difficulties in the Far East and created four decades of peace between the two nations.

·Algeciras Conference

In 1880, the major European nations and the United States decided at the Madrid Conference to preserve the territorial integrity of Morocco and to maintain equal trade opportunities for all. In 1904, France sought to gain Spanish and British support against the opposition of Germany, to take control of Morocco. France concluded a secret treaty with Spain to partition Morocco, and secretly agreed with Great Britain (the Entente Cordiale) not to oppose British aims in Egypt in exchange for a free hand in Morocco. In 1905, France asked the Sultan of Morocco for a protectorate, but this was thwarted when Emperor William II visited Tangier and declared support for Morocco's political integrity. Germany insisted on a conference and Roosevelt persuaded France and Great Britain to attend. An agreement was reached where Germany accepted the principles of the earlier Madrid Conference; German investments were protected; but French and Spanish interests were given marked recognition by the decision to allow France to patrol the border with Algeria, and to allow France and Spain to police Morocco. The Algeciras convention was ratified by the U.S. Senate with a caveat that it was not to be construed as a departure from the traditional U.S. policy of noninvolvement in European affairs.

·San Francisco School Crisis

In the aftermath of the 1906 earthquake and fire, the San Francisco School Board attempted to segregate Japanese, Chinese, and Korean children into separate "Oriental" schools. Japan vigorously objected and claimed this violated an 1894 treaty. Roosevelt brought the school board to Washington and persuaded San Francisco to desegregate its schools, and in return, in 1907 he negotiated a "gentlemen s agreement" with Japan to keep out agricultural laborers. In order to indicate that the U.S. had not been intimidated by Japan, Roosevelt sent the U.S. fleet on a world cruise, including a stop in Japan, to demonstrate the might of the U.S. Navy, now 2nd in the world after the British.

·Root-Takahira Agreement

It went further than the earlier Taft-Katsura Memorandum by maintaining the existing status quo in the Pacific, respect each others territorial possessions, upheld the Open Door policy, and supported by peaceful means the independence of China. By accepting the existing status quo the U.S. recognized Japan's imperialist presence in Manchuria and Korea.

·Taft's Dollar Diplomacy

From 1909 to 1913, President William Howard Taft and Secretary of State Philander C. Knox followed a foreign policy characterized as "dollar diplomacy." Knox, a corporate lawyer who had founded the giant conglomerate U.S. Steel, believed that the goal of diplomacy was to create stability and order abroad that would best promote American business and commercial interests. Knox felt that not only was the goal of diplomacy to improve financial opportunities, but also to use private capital to further U.S. interests overseas. Taft shared this view and used it to justify U.S. interventions in the Caribbean and Central America, especially in measures undertaken to safeguard American financial interests in the region. In China, Knox secured the entry of a House of Morgan banking conglomerate into a European-financed consortium financing the construction of a railway from Huguang to Canton. In spite of successes, "dollar diplomacy" failed to counteract economic instability and the tide of revolution in places like Mexico, the Dominican Republic, Nicaragua, and China.

·Nicaraguan Intervention

The adoption of the Knox-Castrillo Convention of 1911, gave the U.S. the right to intervene in Nicaragua by refunding the national debt under U.S. protection of the customs house. This loss of sovereignty by Nicaragua resulted in a revolt that was put down by US Marines who would remain in the country until 1933.

·Canadian Reciprocity

Because of negative provisions of the Payne-Aldrich tariff of 1909, the Taft administration signed a reciprocity agreement with Canada that reduced or eliminated duties on most Canadian agricultural commodities, with the U.S. receiving the same treatment for its products. A firestorm occurred in Canada when Taft and others made comments that this was a prelude to the U.S. annexation of Canada. The Canadian government fell and the new government ended the reciprocity agreement.

·Lodge Corollary

When a Japanese syndicate began negotiations for purchase of a site in Baja California, a Senate resolution introduced by Henry Cabot Lodge viewed with "grave concern" the possession of strategically important areas "by any corporation…which has a relation to another Government," that is not American. This extended the Monroe Doctrine to non-European nations as well as to foreign companies.

·Wilson's Diplomacy

In theory, the foreign policy of Woodrow Wilson differed decidedly from that of Roosevelt and Taft, substituting morality for "big stick" and "dollar." Wilson tried to re-make U.S. foreign policy by adhering to idealistic principles but reality often forced him to take other measures. Unlike his Republican predecessors,

McKinley, Theodore Roosevelt, and Taft, who had viewed the United States as an emerging power that needed to extend its influence throughout the world in order to serve national interests, Wilson was opposed to this imperialistic policy. He brought to the White House a new way of looking at America's relations with the outside world. Even though he too believed that the United States was the most politically enlightened nation under God, he felt that all peoples throughout the world had the right to self-determination—that the people in every country should have the right to choose their own governments. Wilson, along with his Secretary of State Bryan, felt that it was America's duty to protect democracy and free peoples in other countries. It was not so easy to adhere to these principles when the U.S. became involved in the Mexican Revolution.

·Mexican Revolution
U.S. backed dictator Porfirio Diaz was forced to flee to France after numerous uprisings in 1910 ended his 34-year reign. His elected successor, liberal, Francisco Madero, was murdered by Victoriano Huerta who took power in 1913. It was difficult for the United States to remain apart from this conflict because Americans had invested heavily in Mexico and 40,000 U.S. citizens lived there. If Wilson had followed conventional policy and the urgings of American business interests in Mexico, he would have recognized Huerta (as most European governments did), who promised to respect and protect all foreign investments and concessions. Favoring the liberal Madero government, Wilson refused to recognize Huerta's government saying he was going to "teach Mexico to elect good men." Wilson not only refused to recognize Huerta, but he also tried to force him to step down from office and hold free elections. When Huerta refused to cooperate, and after an incident at Tampico involving the U.S. Navy, Wilson received authorization from Congress to prevent Huerta from receiving arms from Germany and ordered the U.S. Navy to bombard the port of Vera Cruz. War seemed certain between the U.S. and Mexico but the ABC (Argentina, Brazil, and Chile) countries offered to mediate the dispute. Wilson continued to support Huerta's opponents, Venustiano Carranza (Madero's successor) and Pancho Villa. Carranza and his army occupied Mexico City and emerged victorious by the summer of 1915 and Wilson granted him *de facto* recognition. Villa, hoping to provoke a war between the U.S. and Mexico, executed 17 U.S. citizens at Santa Isabel and raided Columbus, New Mexico, burning the town and killing 17 inhabitants. Wilson sent a punitive expedition under General John J. Pershing into Mexico in pursuit of Villa; but the wily guerrilla eluded Pershing, and, the deeper the U.S. forces penetrated into Mexican territory, the more agitated the Carranza government became. There were two serious skirmishes between regular Mexican and U.S. troops in the spring, and full-scale war was averted only when Wilson withdrew Pershing's column a few months later. Relations between the two governments were greatly improved when Wilson extended *de jure* recognition to Carranza's regime in April, 1917. Thereafter, Wilson adamantly rejected all further foreign and American suggestions for intervention in Mexico. During this conflict almost all of the revolutionaries felt a growing sense of nationalism and called for a reduction in the prominent role played by foreigners, namely the U.S. in Mexico's economy.

·Bryan's Cooling Off Treaties
After becoming Secretary of State, William Jennings Bryan negotiated more than 30 treaties with nations getting them to submit to arbitration of all international disputes to a permanent investigating commission. According to these agreements countries could not resort to armed conflict until the commission had submitted its report. In this scholarly study he included remarks on the geopolitical implications of naval forces used as instruments of national policy.

UNIT XIX
MULTIPLE-CHOICE QUESTIONS

Questions 1-3 refer to the following:

"... the Americans may reasonably look forward to a time when they will have produced a civilization grander than any the world has known. Among the most striking features of the Anglo-Saxon is his money-making power... We have seen . . . that, although England is by far the richest nation of Europe, we have already outstripped her in the race after wealth.... [A] characteristic of the Anglo-Saxon is what may be called an instinct or genius for colonizing. His unequaled energy, his indomitable perseverance, and his personal independence, made him a pioneer. He excels all others in pushing his way into new countries. It was those in whom this tendency was strongest that came to America, and this inherited tendency has been further developed by the westward sweep of successive generations across the continent. So noticeable has this characteristic become that English visitors remark it. Charles Dickens once said that the typical American would hesitate to enter heaven unless assured that he could go farther west."

Josiah Strong, "Anglo-Saxon Predominance," 1891

1. Which earlier movement in America offers some proof to what is being asserted in the passage?

   (A) Jacksonian democracy
   (B) Market revolution
   (C) Great Awakening
   (D) Manifest Destiny

2. The arguments used by Strong reflect a philosophy of racial superiority called

   (A) Social Darwinism
   (B) Socialism
   (C) Transcendentalism
   (D) Gospel of Wealth

3. Strong's racial argument in favor of Anglo-Saxon superiority and his "genius for colonizing" statement was an attempt to justify which imperialistic action that was taking place in the early 1890s?

   (A) Alaska
   (B) Cuba
   (C) Hawaii
   (D) Samoa

Questions 4-6 refer to the following:

"What Will He Do," Minneapolis Tribune 1898

4. The political cartoon above takes the position that

(A) imperialism and the assumption of colonies is dangerous to the U.S.
(B) the President must quickly act to protect American democracy
(C) returning the Philippines to Spain would be like throwing them off a cliff to certain death
(D) world public opinion demands that the Philippines captured after the official end to hostilities should remain Spanish colonies

5. The Minneapolis Tribune cartoon best reflects which viewpoint?

(A) The U.S. should avoid returning the Philippines to the corrupt chaos of Spanish rule and they should be given their immediate independence
(B) As legitimate "spoils of war" possession of the Philippines had been earned by American forces and they should be retained as a colony
(C) Owning colonies invite attacks by other nations so to avoid future wars the U.S. should not retain ownership of them
(D) Care for Filipinos as they are in the words of Rudyard Kipling in the "White Man's Burden" "half devil and half child" and ill prepared for self-government

6. The superiority of America over the stereotype of the uncivilized Filipino was a part of the U.S. philosophy of

(A) Exceptionalism
(B) Social Darwinism
(C) Cultural Diversity
(D) Social Gospel

Questions 7-9 refer to the following:

"Anglo-American and Canadian-American tensions... persisted in the 1865-1895 period. Union leaders remained irate over Britain's favoritism toward the South during the Civil War, especially the outfitting of Confederate vessels in British ports... Seward filed damage claims against the British, even proposing at one point that Britain cede to America British Columbia or the Bahama [s] Islands in lieu of a cash settlement. The secretary was also annoyed that British officials would not permit American soldiers to pursue destitute Sioux Indians into Canadian territory. Canadians and Americans squabbled over Fenian raids, tariffs, boundaries, fishing rights in the North Atlantic and seal hunting. The neighbors to the north bristled upon hearing renewed and arrogant prediction that the United States would one day absorb Canada."

Thomas Patterson, J. Garry Clifford, Kenneth J. Hagan,
American Foreign Policy: A History to 1914, 1988

7. Conflicts between the U.S. and the British were used by American politicians to gain favor with the electorate by the practice taking a hard stand against the British called

   (A) "stirring the witches brew"
   (B) "tied to her apron strings"
   (C) "the devil's advocate"
   (D) "twisting the lion's tail"

8. The idea of America acquiring British Columbia and/or the Bahamian Islands from the British was a continuation of which earlier U.S. movement or policy?

   (A) Manifest destiny
   (B) Colonialism
   (C) Populism
   (D) Gospel of wealth

9. For the most part relations between Canada and the U.S. have been amicable although the passage above mentions five areas of conflict between the countries. Despite these differences the one thing that Canada objected to the most was

   (A) unlimited immigration from the U.S. into Canada
   (B) over-fishing in the Pacific by the U.S. ships based in Alaska
   (C) annexation of Canada into the U.S.
   (D) U.S. domination of cargo ships on the Great Lakes

Questions 10-12 refer to the following:

"Organized groups like the Asiatic Exclusion League, backed by labor unions and otherwise "progressive forces," advocated the segregation of all Asian children in San Francisco schools. With newspapers conducting inflammatory anti-Japanese campaigns... there were boycotts waged against Japanese-owned restaurants and frequent attacks on Japanese individuals in the city. On October 11, 1906, the San Francisco Board of Education ordered all Japanese and Korean school children to join the Chinese, who were already segregated. This action caused an uproar in Japan and led to the unprecedented involvement of a U.S. president—Theodore Roosevelt—in local San Francisco politics. Roosevelt considered the anti-Asian California legislators and politicians, "idiots" and was genuinely concerned that San Francisco's inept handling of its Japanese school children might bring Japan (which had just defeated the Russians) and the U.S. to the brink of war."

Frederik L. Schodt, *The Four Immigrants Manga*, 1999

10. The reasons for the segregation of Asians in the San Francisco schools was part of a movement or attitude called the

    (A) red menace
    (B) green movement
    (C) yellow peril
    (D) purple power

11. Historically, a tradition of xenophobia had been established exemplified by the ideas of which earlier mid 19th century political group?

    (A) Knights of Labor
    (B) Know Nothings
    (C) Mugwumps
    (D) Abolitionists

12. The Japanese-San Francisco school board crisis was eventually solved by which of the following

    (A) Gentlemen's Agreement
    (B) Kyoto Protocol
    (C) San Francisco-Tokyo Pledge
    (D) Open Door Policy

Questions 13-15 refer to the following:

"To the Americans and the British...Western supremacy meant Anglo-American supremacy.... Right thinking men believed that 'assimilation'—everyone agreed that imperialism was an ugly word—was an economic opportunity, a moral duty, [and] God's will.... President McKinley, the kindest of men, believed there was more to expansion than that—it was the least we could do for less fortunate people. On the question of annexing the Philippines, he had prayed to God for guidance, and it came to him in the night: 'there was nothing left to do but to take them all and to educate the Filipinos and uplift and Christianize them and by God's grace to do the very best we could by them as our fellowmen for whom Christ also died.' So it was with a sense of moral obligation... that McKinley undertook his [duties]... as leader of a new America."

Walter Lord, *The Good Years: From 1900 to the First World War*, 1960

13. The superiority expressed in the passage above was based on which philosophy of the late 19th and early 20th century?

    (A) Cross Cultural
    (B) Pragmatism
    (C) Existential Relativism
    (D) Social Darwinism

14. Which of the following opinions is the LEAST accurate and does NOT reflect Filipino life in 1900?

    (A) Anglo-American supremacy
    (B) Assimilation was an economic opportunity, a moral duty, and God's will
    (C) Duty to Christianize the Filipinos
    (D) The Filipinos were less fortunate people

15. The sentiments expressed by President McKinley regarding what to do about the Philippines came primarily from which historical frame of reference?

    (A) Social
    (B) Religious
    (C) Intellectual
    (D) Economic

UNIT XX
REFORM & PROGRESSIVISM

Along with economic growth industrialism in the last half of the 19th century brought many abuses. After the Civil War a number of reform movements emerged that were different from the reform movements of the ante-bellum period. By the early 20th century these movements would culminate with reforms enacted during what became known as the Progressive Era—a reform movement and time period that would ameliorate some of the worst abuses of industrialism.

Farmer's Discontent

·Grange (1867)

Oliver Kelly founded this national, secret, farm organization, the Patrons of Husbandry, to protect farmers from capitalist monopoly. Many members held the more conservative view that the organization should serve the educational and social needs of the farming community, and not be a proponent of protection against capitalists and middlemen. Others took a more militant position and wanted to do something about the rising price of getting their produce to market, the high cost of credit, and the tariff issue. The organization was involved with state railroad legislation by getting a number of laws passed called the Granger laws. In the case of *Munn v. Illinois* the court ruled that states could regulate commerce within a state to safeguard the greater public interest. The scope of this decision was later narrowed in the 1886 case of *Wabash v. Illinois* where the Supreme Court ruled that only Congress could pass legislation regulating interstate commerce and as a result the Interstate Commerce Act was passed creating the Interstate Commerce Commission. Kelley and others envisioned the organization as a secret society, with passwords, secret signals, and other covert means of identification. Membership was open to farmers and their families and the Grange admitted women into its ranks. It was a social organization that allowed farmers to meet with other farmers to talk about their common problems. It also created many cooperatives but most of those were unsuccessful. It had more success in its non-controversial advocacy of agricultural education and cheap textbooks.

283

·Greenback-Labor Party

This political party was formed in response to what agrarians and debtors called the "Crime of 1873"—the demonetization of silver enacted by the Coinage Act of 1873 that would lead to a deflationary trend of about 1.7% a year increase in the general Consumer Price Index (CPI) from 1875 to 1896. Basic to their political beliefs was inflating the currency by issuing Greenbacks (paper money). Other issues included in the Greenback-Labor Party platform were a graduated income tax, a limited work week, laws to protect labor, and the exclusion of Chinese immigrants. Their candidate James B. Weaver polled a million votes in the election of 1876.

·Farmers' Alliances

Three regional alliances were formed—Northern, Southern, and Colored—that were in general agreement on issues but could not get together in any form of affiliation. Their proposals were the typical agrarian ones: issuance of Greenbacks, free and unlimited coinage of silver; government ownership of communication and transportation, graduated income tax, a sub-treasury plan to loan farmers money with their crops as collateral, and restrictions on immigrants owning land.

Urban Movements

·*Wealth Against Commonwealth*

An anti-monopoly movement formed around Henry Demarest Lloyd's book that argued, "Nature is rich; but everywhere man, the heir of nature, is poor" as it exposed the monopolistic evils of the Standard Oil Company in what became the first work of investigative journalism or muckraking.

·Single Tax

In his best selling 1879 book, *Progress and Poverty*, Henry George argued that economic problems stemmed from the unavailability of land for those who needed access to it. The injustices of rent robbed the working-man of his wages and wild speculation in land led to poverty. His simple solution was a single tax on land, to absorb all rents, with no taxes on wages or interest. A single tax would eventually lead to the ownership of land as common property, rather than as individual property. George believed that the single tax would raise wages, increase earnings of capital, abolish poverty, give employment, and relieve other economic ills through a massive redistribution of wealth. He saw it as the perfect panacea for the economic problems in the U.S. Henry George clubs were formed to disseminate his views.

·Nationalist Clubs

Edward Bellamy's best selling utopian novel, *Looking Backward*, anticipated a future America (the year 2000) of nationalized industry, equal distribution of wealth, and the destruction of class divisions. This vision countered the problems Bellamy saw in contemporary society. In this utopian world, loyalty to the solidarity of the state holds society together. Bellamy called this philosophy, Nationalism. In 1888, the first of the Bellamy Nationalist Clubs was formed and the movement soon spread across the country attracting such notable personalities as William Dean Howells and Edward Everett Hale. The main purpose of the clubs was to create and promote the practical realization of Bellamy's utopian vision. Members became involved with other reform political groups and the Nationalists were represented at the 1892 Populist Party convention.

·Kellogism

Edward Kellogg was the founder of a plan to bring about social equality by making credit available free of interest. The movement also wanted to inflate the currency by issuing Greenbacks in which paper money would be backed by bullion. Kellogism also advocated flexible currency, low interest on land, and only government owned banks.

·Coin's Financial School (1893)

William H. Harvey, an advocate of free coinage of silver, published a pamphlet *Coin's Financial School*, which stated the money issue in simple everyday terms. He argued that farmers were the targets of American and British financial interests and he believed that reliance on gold alone tended to tighten the money supply and lower prices. The unlimited coinage of silver would expand the money supply and raise farm prices. It would help the debtor by making more money available to pay off his debts. This booklet, containing many cartoons, sold a million copies and helped prepare the way for the Populist campaign.

Populists

·Omaha Convention

What emerged in Omaha in 1892 was a conglomeration of many unhappy groups into the People's or Populist Party. The Omaha Platform set out the basic tenets of the Populist movement that included inflation of the currency through bimetallism, along with an appeal to labor unions that included a shorter work week, immigration restriction, getting rid of Pinkertons in strikes, and legislation supporting secondary boycotts. The movement emerged out of the cooperative crusade organized by the Farmer's Alliance in the 1880s and was combined with other urban reform movements. The Preamble to the Populist Platform was written by Minnesota lawyer, farmer, politician, and novelist Ignatius Donnelly. The radical nature of the movement can be shown by his rhetoric that said, "The fruits of the toil of millions are boldly stolen to build up colossal fortunes for a few." For a short while the Populist did what Mary Lease had urged by "raising less corn and more hell." The delegates embraced the platform with great enthusiasm. Many of the specific proposals urged by the Omaha Platform—the graduated income tax, the secret ballot, the direct election of Senators, the eight-hour day—won enactment in the Progressive and New Deal eras of the next century.

·Populist Candidates and Elections

The Populist made a positive showing in the 1892 elections as their candidate for President James Weaver (stepping in for the early favorite Leonidas Polk, who had died) polled more than 1 million votes, 8.5 % of the total, and carried six mountain and plains states with 22 electoral votes. By fusing with the Democrats in certain states, the party elected five senators, ten members of the U.S. House of Representatives, three governors, and nearly 1,500 state legislators, nearly all in the Northwest. It could also claim the support of numerous Republicans and Democrats in Congress who had been elected by appealing to Populist sentiment. After the Depression of 1893, the Populist turned more toward the silver issue and away from their other broader goals. The election of 1896 seemed to be ideal for them to extend their support and maybe gain control of certain states. However, they abandoned their principles by becoming enamored with the silver issue, and the Democratic candidate William Jennings Bryan, whom they endorsed, although they did run their own candidate for Vice-President, Tom Watson. Bryan's defeat was a disaster for them as they began to disintegrate after the 1896 election.

Progressivism

·Middle Class and the Progressives

One of the reasons Progressivism succeeded where Populism had failed was the support it received from the middle-class. Most progressives were educated, affluent, middle-class men and women, who began their reforming activities by trying to improve their own communities. Many progressives were lawyers, businessmen, and publishers who felt trapped between the burgeoning power of the corporation above, and the increasingly violent clamoring of working class labor below. In many ways, they were protecting their own class's unique interests, for how could an independent middle class flourish when faced with the specter of either despotic corporate control from above or anarchy and socialism from below? These men hoped for a return of old-fashioned Jeffersonian individualism that they felt was endangered by corporate interests, labor unions, and urban political machines. They also wanted to achieve structural and political efficiency in business and government in what later became known as "Taylorism." Frederick Taylor developed this system of applying science to engineering to improve labor productivity and economic efficiency.

·Muckrakers

This name given to American journalists, novelists, and critics who attempted to expose the negative impact of industrialism including the abuses of business and corruption in politics. The term derived from the word muckraker used by President Theodore Roosevelt in a speech in 1906, in which he agreed with many of the charges of the muckrakers but he compared them to a character from John Bunyan's *Pilgrim's Progress* who could look no way but downward with a muckrake in his hands and was interested only in raking the filth. With the advent of the national mass-circulation magazines such as *McClure's*, *Everybody's*, and *Collier's* the muckrakers were provided with funds for their investigations and with a large enough audience to arouse nationwide concern. It was the revelations of the muckrakers that would lead to the Progressive political reform movement. All aspects of American life interested the muckrakers as they exposed injustice and corruption in business and government. The most famous muckrakers and their major works were Lincoln Steffens, *The Shame of the Cities* that exposed corruption at the municipal level; Ida Tarbell, *The History of the Standard Oil Company* exposed monopolistic practices; David Graham Phillips, *Treason in the Senate* about how individual Trusts controlled Senators; Upton Sinclair, *The Jungle* about the horrendous conditions in the meat packing industry, and Jacob Riis,' *How the Other Half Lives* about the misery of those who lived in the tenements in the slums.

·Municipal Progressives

This movement started in the cities with the primary goal being to overthrow "boss rule." Good government groups (called Goo Goos) wanted to end the unholy alliance between the boss and immigrant groups, abolish franchise politics, rid cities of tenements and slums, and clean up the areas of vice known as "red light districts" often in Five Points areas. Leading examples of municipal reformers who succeeded were Tom Johnson in Cleveland, Sam "Golden Rule" Jones in Toledo, and Hazen Pingree in Detroit. These Progressive mayors attacked corruption in municipal government and formed nonpartisan leagues to defeat the entrenched bosses and their political machines. Both the Council-Manager and Commission forms of city government were adopted to take politics, graft, and cronyism out of local governments and replace them with professionalism.

·Wisconsin Plan

Reformers turned to state politics, where Governor Robert La Follette made Wisconsin a model of progressive reform. He won from the legislature an anti-lobbying law directed at large corporations, a state banking control measure, and a direct primary law. Taxes on corporations were raised, a railroad commission was created to set rates, and a conservation commission was set up. Wisconsin became the model that other progressive governors like Hiram Johnson in California and Woodrow Wilson of New Jersey followed.

·State Level Progressivism

In state after state, Progressives advocated a wide range of political, economic, and social reforms. They adopted the Australian (secret) ballot, direct primaries, the initiative, the referendum, and the recall, non-partisan elections, and civil service reform. They struck at the excessive power of corporate wealth by regulating railroads and utilities, restricting lobbying, limiting monopolies, and making corporations pay taxes. To correct the worst features of industrialization, Progressives advocated worker's compensation, child labor laws, minimum wage and maximum hours legislation (especially for women workers), and widows' pensions.

Progressive Presidents

·Theodore Roosevelt's 1st Term

After taking over for McKinley, Roosevelt earned a reputation for trust-busting, which was somewhat a misnomer because he was more interested in regulating the monopolies than breaking them up. Gaining fame for breaking up the Northern Securities Company, a railroad holding company, he tried to get Congress to pass legislation abolishing abuses without destroying combinations. He also won widespread approval for forcing arbitration upon a reluctant management during the Anthracite coal strike of 1902 by threatening to send in solders to run the mines. His policies, much more even handed between business and labor than earlier administrations, implemented his concept of the square deal, "We must see that each is given a square deal, because he is entitled to no more and should receive no less." He also took tentative steps toward addressing the concerns of farmers and other small shippers who believed the railroads were treating them unfairly. His early Progressivism was more pragmatism than doctrinaire reform. As President he stands out because he was so different from the "forgettable" Presidents of the late 19th century.

·Election of 1904

With many minor party candidates in the field, the Democrats abandoned Bryan and nominated the "gold bug" judge Alton Parker. By acclamation the Republicans nominated Roosevelt who defeated the conservative Democrat 336-140 in the Electoral College and pledged on election night that "under no circumstances will I be a candidate or accept another nomination."

·Theodore Roosevelt's 2nd Term

Now President in his own right, Roosevelt became the nation's first environmental President by setting aside 190 million acres for national forests, coal and water reserves, and wildlife refuges. An important step in the conservation movement was the creation of the Inland Waterways Commission to study ways to relieve transportation congestion. This would lead to the White House Conservation Conference which would study the problems of natural resources in general. Gifford Pinchot was appointed head of the National Conservation Commission, which systematically studied the availability and use of mineral, water, forest, and soil resources. Along with conservation, Roosevelt partially accomplished his goal of railroad regulation when the Hepburn Act gave the Interstate Commerce Commission the power to set maximum railroad rates. After reading Upton Sinclair's pro-socialist muckraking novel, *The Jungle*, he got Congress to pass the Pure Food and Drug Act in 1906 and the Meat Inspection Act. The Panic of 1907 resulted in the drop in stock prices and business failures; this marred an otherwise successful Presidency.

·Election of 1908

With Theodore Roosevelt retiring to hunt animals in Africa, his anointed successor was William Howard Taft his Secretary of War. For the third time the Democrats nominated Bryan who was defeated 321-162 in the Electoral College.

·William Howard's Taft's Presidency

Taft's disposition was suited to judicious administration rather than the presidential activism and stewardship of Roosevelt. Although he came to the White House promising to continue Roosevelt's agenda, he was more comfortable executing the existing law rather than demanding new legislation from Congress. He was a true trust-buster as his Attorney General George Wickersham filed 90 anti-trust cases compared to 44 under Roosevelt. Other Progressive measures passed during Taft's term were the Mann-Elkins Act, that placed telephone, telegraph, cable and wireless companies under ICC jurisdiction and the Mann Act or White Slave Traffic Act that prohibited interstate transportation of women for immoral purposes. The first of the Progressive Amendments to the Constitution, the 16th—allowing the income tax—was passed during Taft's administration and submitted to the states for ratification.

·Paine-Aldrich Tariff

Despite his positive Progressive accomplishments Taft begin to split with the Progressive elements in his party. The Republican platform of 1908 pledged revision of the tariff downward, and to this end President Taft called (1909) Congress into special session. The House promptly passed a tariff bill, which called for some reduced rates. The Senate substituted a bill by Nelson W. Aldrich, which made fewer downward revisions and increased numerous rates. It was the first change in tariff laws since the Dingley Act of 1897. Progressives denounced it and urged Taft to veto it. He not only signed the Payne-Aldrich high tariff, he defended it by calling it "the best bill the Republican Party ever passed." It lowered 650 tariff schedules, raised 220, and left 1,150 unchanged. Although the Payne-Aldrich Tariff Act was less aggressively protectionist than the McKinley Tariff Act (1890), it was protectionist.

·Pinchot-Ballinger Controversy

To further alienate the Progressives in his party, Taft failed to support the insurgents' attempt to curtail the power of the dictatorial Speaker of the House of Representatives, Joseph Cannon. The final break with the Progressives came when Taft supported his Secretary of the Interior Richard Ballinger against Gifford Pinchot, who accused Ballinger of harming the conservation cause and aiding the corporations, by allowing public water power sites in Wyoming and Montana to be transferred to private interest. By siding with Ballinger against Pinchot, Taft further alienated Roosevelt, who first became upset with Taft over the breaking up of the Steel Trust, a trust approved by Roosevelt when he was President.

·Republican Nomination for Election in 1912

This was the first year for Republican primaries with Roosevelt winning 9 out of 12 states (8 by landslide margins). Taft won only the state of Massachusetts (by a small margin) and he even lost his home state of Ohio to Roosevelt. Progressive Senator Robert La Follette of Wisconsin won two states. After the primaries were over La Follette had 36 delegates, Taft 48 delegates, and Roosevelt 278 delegates. However, 36 states did not hold primaries and these delegates were controlled by the "Old Guard" conservatives of the Republican Party. Many of the state delegates chosen in state convention were contested, but as Taft controlled the Republican National Committee, which had the power to make decisions on the contested delegates, they awarded 235 of the contested delegates to Taft and only 19 to Roosevelt. This assured Taft's nomination.

·Bull Moose Party

The Roosevelt and La Follette supporters, who condemned the Taft nomination as fraudulent, formed a Progressive Party out of the earlier Progressive League that had failed to capture control of the Republican Party. La Follette, their original choice for President, stepped aside so Roosevelt could be nominated by acclamation along with Governor Hiram Johnson of California as his running mate. The Progressive platform called for the direct election of U.S. Senators, the initiative, referendum, and recall, women's suffrage, reduction of the tariff, and other social reforms.

·New Nationalism

Drawing much of his inspiration from Herbert Croly's *The Promise of American Life* (1909), Roosevelt formulated a program called the "New Nationalism," that he unveiled at a speech at Osawatomie Kansas. He argued that the federal government had a positive interventionist role to play in the advancement of progressive democracy and that the New Nationalism "maintains that every man holds his property subject to the general right of the community to regulate its use to whatever degree of public welfare may require it." Trusts should not be dismantled but should be controlled and regulated in the public interest. Roosevelt also proposed a comprehensive program of labor and social legislation. The New Nationalism was a realistic attempt to come to terms with the modern corporate age. It was the most progressive program proposed by the three presidential candidates.

·Election of 1912

The Democrats nominated Virginia born Woodrow Wilson, a former Princeton Professor of history, recently elected governor of New Jersey, after the early leader Champ Clark could not secure the 2/3rds votes needed for nomination and Bryan switched his support to Wilson. Wilson's New Freedom program insisted that government should be used only for the negative purposes of sweeping away privilege and restoring unfettered competition. He called for the dismantling of trusts and monopolies and returning the country to a type of Jeffersonian democracy. Roosevelt denounced this as anachronistic, arguing that large corporations had become indispensable in the modern age. Wilson denounced the New Nationalism as elitist and detected in it the seeds of despotism. Wilson won the Electoral College 435 to 88 for Roosevelt and 8 for Taft. He carried 42% of the popular vote with Roosevelt getting 28% and Taft 23%. Third Party candidates led by the Socialist Eugene Debs took 7% of the vote.

·Wilsonian Progressivism

Upon taking office Wilson signed the Underwood Tariff, the first reduction in tariff rates since before the Civil War. The bill also included an income tax, permitted by the new 16th Amendment. Wilson supported the Federal Reserve Act of 1913, which created a centralized banking system to act as a lender of last resort to forestall bank crises and to permit a more elastic currency. The availability of money could be readily expanded or contracted to suit the nation's needs. To curb the monopolistic practices of trusts, Wilson pushed through Congress the Federal Trade Commission Act of 1914 that established a commission with authority to prevent business practices that could lead to a monopoly. He also supported the Clayton Antitrust Act of 1914, a law intended to bolster the poorly enforced Sherman Act by banning interlocking directorates where a few people controlled an industry by serving simultaneously as directors of related corporations. It also exempted labor unions from the category of illegal combinations and gave workers the right to strike. Under Wilson's direction, Congress passed a series of labor laws designed to ban child labor, shorten workdays, and, in the Workmen's Compensation Act, provide injury protection for federal employees. Wilson also supported reforms benefiting farmers, such as low-interest loan programs.

·17th Amendment

One of the main goals of Progressivism was achieved with the passage of the 17th Amendment, the direct election of U.S. Senators by the people, not the state legislatures. The Senatorial selection system set up by the "founding fathers" became an inconsistent mess. Consecutive state legislatures sent different Senators to Congress, forcing the Senate to work out who was the qualified candidate. The selection system was corrupted by bribery and influence peddling. In several states, the selection of Senators was left up to the people in referendums, where the legislature approved the people's choice and sent their choice to the Senate. First proposed by the Populists in their Omaha Platform, the direct election was also part of the "Wisconsin Idea" championed by Republican progressive Robert La Follette and Nebraska Republican reformer George Norris. In the early 1900s, Oregon pioneered direct election and experimented with different measures over several years until it succeeded in 1907. Soon after, Nebraska followed suit and laid the foundation for other states to adopt measures for direct election. Articles written by early 20th-century muckrakers, especially David Graham Phillips, *Treason in the Senate*, also provided arguments for getting rid of the tainted system where certain powerful trusts would often control the Senators.

·18th Amendment

America officially went dry on January 16, 1920. This was the day the Volstead Act enforcing the 18th Amendment went into effect. The Act defined the terms "beer, wine, or other intoxicating malt or liquors" to mean any beverage with greater than 0.5% alcohol by volume. The Amendment itself had been ratified a year earlier by 36 of the 48 states but did not define what constituted an alcoholic beverage. It was now unlawful to manufacture, transport or sell alcohol anywhere in the United States. The advocates of Prohibition had waged a 70-year campaign to ban alcohol and had high hopes for what was to be called a "noble experiment." The organization of the Women's Christian Temperance Union in 1874 marked the formal entrance of women into the temperance movement and gave great impetus to its cause. The WCTU was headed by Frances E. Willard, who was equally committed to the principle of equality of the sexes. Temperance was to bridge the gap, she believed, between men and women, "Drink and tobacco are the great separatists [sic] between men and women. Once they used these things together, but woman's evolution has carried her beyond them; man will climb to the same level . . . but meanwhile ... the fact that he permits himself fleshly indulgence that he would deprecate in her, makes their planes different, giving her an instinct of revulsion." Supporters of prohibition anticipated that alcohol's banishment would lead to the eradication of poverty and vice while simultaneously ennobling the common man to achieve his highest goals.

Women's Suffrage

·Early Efforts

An organized movement on behalf of women's suffrage, led by women but open to men, first emerged in the United States in 1848 with the Seneca Falls Convention's controversial resolution, insisted on by Lucretia Mott and Elizabeth Cady Stanton, favoring women's right to vote. Stanton and Susan B. Anthony refused to support the 15th Amendment because it did not enfranchise women. They formed the National Woman's Suffrage Association (NWSA) in 1869. Conservative women, led by Lucy Stone and Julia Ward Howe, supported the 15th Amendment and campaigned for the passage of state laws to enfranchise women. They established the rival American Woman's Suffrage Association (AWSA) in 1869.

·Wyoming

Suffrage success began in 1869 when the Wyoming Territory approved full and equal suffrage for its roughly one thousand women. In 1890, Wyoming became the first state with women's suffrage and by 1900, Utah, Colorado, and Idaho joined Wyoming in allowing women to vote.

·*Minor v Happersett*

This 1874 Supreme Court case determined that Missouri had been within its constitutional rights in denying a woman, Virginia Minor, the right to vote. Victoria Woodhull had urged women to try to vote, arguing that the 14th Amendment forbade the states to limit citizens' rights. This idea was adopted by NWSA and Susan B. Anthony organized seventy suffragists nationwide—among them, Minor—to vote in the 1872 elections. When denied the right to vote she sued the registrar, arguing that her rights of citizenship had been unlawfully abridged. When the case reached the Supreme Court, however, the justices declared that voting was not among the privileges guaranteed to all citizens and was therefore not protected by the Fourteenth Amendment. This decision convinced NWSA that woman's suffrage could be won only by a new constitutional amendment.

·Constitutional Amendment

In 1878, a constitutional amendment was proposed that provided "The right of citizens to vote shall not be abridged by the United States or by any State on account of sex." This same amendment would be introduced in every session of Congress for the next 41 years.

·A United Movement

The differing approaches—whether to seek a federal amendment or to work for state amendments—kept the women-suffrage movement divided until 1890, when the two societies, NWSA and AWSA were united as the National American Woman Suffrage Association.

·New Zealand
It became the first country to allow women to vote in 1893, which gave encouragement to the women's suffrage movement in the United States.

·Progressive Party
In 1912, Theodore Roosevelt's Progressive (Bull Moose) Party became the first national political party to have a plank supporting women's suffrage.

·Carrie Chapman Catt
From 1890 to 1900 she organized the National American Woman Suffrage Association and became its president in 1900. She led the campaign to win suffrage through an amendment to the U.S. Constitution with her "Winning Plan" program that united all of the state leaders to concentrate on a national rather than state by state effort to win the right to vote. After the ratification of the Nineteenth Amendment (1920), she organized the League of Women Voters for the political education of women.

·Alice Paul
More militant than Catt, she broke with the NAWSA in 1914 and co-founded the Congressional Union. In 1916, she founded the National Woman's Party. She led pickets at the White House and Congress and despite America's entry into World War I refused to abandon these tactics. She and her colleagues were arrested and imprisoned; they engaged in hunger strikes and endured forced feedings at the hands of authorities. Ultimately her tactics, as well as persuasion from Carrie Chapman Catt, induced President Woodrow Wilson to make the suffrage amendment a priority, a stand he had previously refused to take. Along with Catt, Paul was a pivotal force in the passage and ratification in 1920 of the 19th Amendment.

·Passage and Ratification of 19th Amendment
After President Woodrow Wilson announced his support of the amendment, the next day the House of Representatives narrowly passed the amendment but the Senate refused to even debate it. With the Senate finally voted it failed by two votes. The National Woman's Party urged citizens to vote against anti-suffrage senators up for election in the fall of 1918. This tactic succeeded and after the 1918 election, most members of Congress were pro-suffrage. In 1919, the House of Representatives passed the amendment by a vote of 304 to 89, and 2 weeks later the Senate passed it 56 to 25. After a long arduous state-by-state fight over ratification it was finally ratified by the 36th state, Tennessee on August 18, 1920.

Supreme Court Decisions

·*US v. E. C. Knight Co.* (1895)
In its first judicial interpretation of the Sherman Antitrust Act the court in an 8-1 decision determined that a defendant with a near monopoly on sugar refining was not engaged in commerce but manufacturing which was not a part of commerce and could not be regulated. This decision made the Sherman Act ineffective until a later court would overturn it.

·Insular Cases (1901)
These cases involving people living in the islands that were now under U.S. control established the principle that the Constitution did not necessarily follow the flag. The people of an annexed territory did not have all the privileges of U.S. citizenship but that Congress could extend these privileges if it wanted to.

Northern Securities Co, v. US (1904)

It revived the moribund Sherman Antitrust Act when it upheld the government 5-4 in its suit that broke up a railroad holding company. It held that the stock transactions constituted an illegal combination in restraint of interstate commerce and came within the scope of the Sherman Act.

Lochner v. New York (1905)

Lochner was convicted under a New York law prohibiting bakery employees from working more than 10 hours per day. By a 5-4 margin, the Supreme Court overturned his conviction by rejecting the argument that the law was necessary to protect the health of bakers, calling it an unreasonable, unnecessary and arbitrary interference with the right and liberty of the individuals, both employer and employee alike, to exercise the 14th Amendment right to contract.

Danbury Hatters Case (1908)

Officially the case of *Loewe v. Lawler* was a unanimous decision in which the court decided that a secondary boycott by a labor union was a conspiracy in restraint of trade within the meaning of the Sherman Anti-Trust Act; thus, it applied that law to labor unions for the first time.

Muller v. Oregon (1908)

Oregon enacted a law that limited women to ten hours of work in factories and laundries a day. Business owners attacked it on the grounds that, like the New York law in the *Lochner* case, it bore no relation to the women's health or safety. Louis Brandeis seized upon the opening in the *Lochner* case, namely, that if he could show how the Oregon law related to worker health and safety, then the Court would have to sustain it. His highly unusual brief become known as a "Brandeis Brief" and it changed jurisprudence by making it more open to the everyday facts of life. It called upon justices to take into account the effect of their decisions on the real world and on the lives of real people. He covered the traditional legal precedents in just two pages, and then filled over 100 pages with historical, sociological, economic and physiological statistical data on the effects of long working hours on the health of women. The court not only acknowledged the brief, a highly unusual step, but conceded that women were, in fact, different from men, and needed this type of protection.

UNIT XX
MULTIPLE-CHOICE QUESTIONS

Questions 1-4 refer to the following:

"... You come to us and tell us that the great cities are in favor of the gold standard; we reply that the great cities rest upon our broad and fertile prairies. Burn down your cities and leave our farms, and your cities will spring up again as if by magic; but destroy our farms and the grass will grow in the streets of every city in the country.... If they dare to come out in the open field and defend the gold standard as a good thing, we will fight them to the uttermost. Having behind us the producing masses of this nation and the world, supported by the commercial interests, the laboring interests and the toilers everywhere, we will answer their demand for a gold standard by saying to them: You shall not press down upon the brow of labor this crown of thorns, you shall not crucify mankind upon a cross of gold."

William Jennings Bryan, "Cross of Gold Speech," 1896

1. The speech above is usually associated with which political philosophy or movement?

   (A) Conservatism
   (B) Liberalism
   (C) Populism
   (D) Progressivism

2. The speech compares the gold standard to

   (A) a train wreck
   (B) Jesus' suffering and death
   (C) natural disaster
   (D) the Declaration of Independence

3. When Bryan makes his allusion to the importance of farms compared to cities this idea most directly reflects which of the following continuities in United States history?

   (A) Jacksonianism
   (B) Federalist
   (C) Social Darwinism
   (D) Jeffersonianism

4. Bryan concludes his speech with a metaphor taken from

   (A) religion
   (B) sports
   (C) politics
   (D) cards

293

Questions 5-7 refer to the following:

"On the land question the Populist demands distinctly foreshadowed conservation. 'The land,' according to the Omaha declaration, 'including all the natural resources of wealth, is the heritage of all the people and should not be monopolized for speculative purposes....' This one time dangerous Populist doctrine has now won all but universal acceptance. It would thus appear that much of the Populist program has found favor in the eyes of later generations. Populist plans for altering the machinery of government with but few exceptions have been carried into effect.... William Allen White wrote recently, 'They abolished the established order completely and ushered in a new order.' Thanks to this triumph of Populist principles, one may almost say that in so far as political devices can insure it, the people now rule."

John D. Hicks, "The Persistence of Populism," 1931

5. Which of the following government agencies in the late 20th and early 21st century represent a continuation of the ideas described in the passage above?

   (A) Department of Housing and Urban Development (HUD)
   (B) Social Security Administration
   (C) Environmental Protection Agency (EPA)
   (D) Civil Rights Division of the Justice Department

6. Hick's assertion that "the people now rule" is best supported by which of the following?

   (A) 19th Amendment to the Constitution
   (B) Supreme Court decision in Brown v. The Board of Education of Topeka, Kansas
   (C) The Roosevelt Corollary to the Monroe Doctrine
   (D) Simpson-Mazzoli Act of 1986 on Immigration Reform

7. The passage above asserts that the Populist movement proved to be a success because it

   (A) elected its candidate William Jennings Bryan for President in 1896
   (B) established a permanent political party
   (C) immediately overturned the power structure in the United States
   (D) was favored by later generations

Questions 8-10 refer to the following quotation:

"I contend that the period from approximately 1900 until the United States' intervention in the war, labeled the "progressive era" by virtually all historians, was really an era of conservatism. Moreover, the triumph of conservatism...was a result not of any impersonal, mechanistic necessity but of the conscious needs and decisions of specific men and institutions.... In brief, conservative solutions to the emerging problems of an industrial society were almost universally applied.... It is business control over politics... rather than political regulation of the economy that is the significant phenomenon of the Progressive Era."

Gabriel Kolko, *The Triumph of Conservatism:*
A Reinterpretation of American History, 1900-1916, 1963.

8. The ideas expressed in the passage above support which of the following interpretations?

    (A) Political reform cured the evils of the industrial era
    (B) Conservative business interest gained control over progressivism
    (C) Progressivism resulted in the political regulation of the economy
    (D) The United States entry into World War I brought an end to progressivism

9. The interpretation in the above passage is contrary to the generally accepted view of historians that Progressivism

    (A) as a successful reform movement that curbed the power of the business class
    (B) instituted permanent changes in the economic structure of the nation
    (C) carried out the republican democracy found in the Preamble to the Constitution
    (D) is the embodiment of 19th century classical liberalism

10. Which of the following movements in 1950s to the 1980s could be considered similar to the ideas expressed in the passage?

    (A) The Civil Rights movement of the 1950s and 1960s
    (B) The Counter Culture movement of the 1960s and 1970s
    (C) The Beats critique of the conformist society of the 1950s
    (D) The Neo-Conservative movement of the 1980s

Questions 11-13 refer to the following:

"With the advent of Progressivism, the strategy of consensus bore fruit. The suffragists had already defined the vote for women as a means of humanizing government, and in a period of generalized commitment to "reform," they were able to identify their own cause with the larger effort to extend democracy and eliminate social injustice. Progressivism...represented an effort to clean up the most obvious causes of corruption, disease, and poverty... suffragists argued convincingly that extension of the franchise to females would help in the task of improving society... the society at large defined the goals of Progressivism,... the suffragists succeeded in making the vote for women a prominent item on the agenda of reform."

William Henry Chafe, *The American Woman: Her Changing Social, Economic, and Political Roles, 1920-1970*, 1972

11. Which of the following activities from the late 19th century closely resembles the agenda of reform that is alluded to in the passage?

(A) Regulation of large corporations
(B) Efforts to restrict immigration
(C) Gospel of Wealth
(D) Settlement houses

12. Which of the following movements supported by the suffragetts as well as the progressives represented an effort to clean up disease and poverty in the cities?

(A) Adoption of the referendum, initiative, and recall
(B) Getting rid of vice, gambling, and prostitution by eradicating red-light districts
(C) Support for monetary reform by passage of the Federal Reserve Act
(D) Adoption of the 17th Amendment to extend democracy to the United States Senate

13. Suffragettes hitched their wagon to Progressivism by arguing that society could be improved by

(A) following the ideas of the Social Gospelers
(B) enacting legislation that would establish family planning centers
(C) granting the right to vote to women
(D) eliminating social injustice by adopting a program of aid to children of unmarried mothers

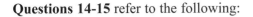
Questions 14-15 refer to the following:

Edward Windsor, "The Finishing Touch" *Harper's Weekly*, 1912

14. This cartoon refers to the election of 1912 in which the bull, or in this case the bull moose symbol is being skewered by the professor. Who are the two presidential opponents represented by the bull moose and the professor?

    (A) Grover Cleveland and William Howard Taft
    (B) Theodore Roosevelt and Woodrow Wilson
    (C) William Jennings Bryan and William McKinley
    (D) Benjamin Harrison and James Garfield

15. The lances from the picadors already piercing the hide of the Bull Moose are labeled "Investigations, Campaign Contributions, Political Deals, Tariff Questions" and the finishing touch is the sword. What is all of this trying to represent?

    (A) The Democrats putting to death the Progressive Party
    (B) Republicans accused of campaign violations
    (C) The control the Progressive Party will have over Congress
    (D) Historical situation where the political parties are seen as being in a bull ring

UNIT XXI

WORLD WAR I & 1920'S FOREIGN POLICY

Despite the historic tradition of the U.S. staying out of the affairs of Europe, a number of factors would lead the U.S. into World War I. From its involvement in this conflict the U.S. would emerge as the leading country in the world. The war and the peace treaty that followed would forever change the course of U.S. history. Instead of just being concerned with domestic matters, foreign policy would dominate the American political agenda through much of the 20th century.

U.S. Response to Hostilities in Europe

·Neutrality Proclamation
With the outbreak of the Great War (later renamed WWI), Wilson issued a Proclamation of Neutrality and urged Americans to be "impartial in thought as well as in action."

·Declaration of London
Bryan asked the belligerents to accept this 1909 agreement that had never been ratified and the Central Powers complied. France and Russia made their acceptance conditional upon the British acceptance and the British gave conditional acceptance with exceptions for its contraband provisions. The Declaration of London comprised 71 articles dealing with many controversial points, including blockades, contraband, and prizes. In general it was a restatement of the existing law, but with a high regard for the rights of neutrals. Although the U.S. Senate ratified the Declaration, unanimous ratification by the signatories did not follow, and the code never went officially into effect. After the U.S. backed off on getting support for the Declaration, based on the influence of Colonel House, Wilson diplomatic adviser and an Anglophile, Great Britain increased its contraband list and revived the doctrine of continuous voyage which enabled them to seize goods once considered fair trade for neutrals.

·Loans to Belligerents

The U.S. government announced that these loans were inconsistent with the true spirit of neutrality, but Robert Lansing, another Anglophile and later Secretary of State, negated this statement by saying short-term credits were acceptable. Wilson would reluctantly agree with the Lansing policy, paving the way for massive loans to the Allied belligerents.

·German Submarines

By declaring the waters around Great Britain a war zone Germany announced that ships would be destroyed on sight without provisions for the safety of passengers and crew. The traditional policy of firing a shot across the bow and boarding a ship was untenable for submarines for if they surfaced they could easily be rammed and sunk by merchant ships. Germany warned U.S. citizens not to travel on belligerent ships, but the U.S. reply was that this would be "an indefensible violation of neutral rights" if someone was killed on one of these ships

·Sinking of the *Lusitania*

In 1915, the Lusitania left port in New York for Liverpool to make her 202nd trip across the Atlantic. On board were 1,959 people, including 159 Americans. Fourteen miles off the coast of Ireland a torpedo hit the starboard (right) side of the *Lusitania* and almost immediately, another explosion rocked the ship. At the time, the Allies thought the Germans had launched two torpedoes to sink the *Lusitania*. However, the Germans said their U-boat only fired one torpedo. Many believe the second explosion was caused by the ignition of ammunition hidden in the cargo hold—the ship was carrying thousands of cases of ammunition and some small arms. It was the damage from the second explosion that made the ship sink within 18 minutes. Though there had been enough lifeboats for all passengers, the severe listing of the ship while it sank prevented most from being launched. Of the 1,198 passengers and crew that died, 128 were U.S. civilians. Although the public was opposed to intervention and Wilson ran for re-election in 1916 on the slogan "he kept us out of war," the sinking of the *Lusitania* heightened tensions between the U.S. and Germany and helped to tilt American public opinion in favor of joining the war on the side of the Allies.

·Wilson's Notes to Germany

After the sinking of the *Lusitania* Wilson sent three diplomatic notes to Germany, each harsher than the previous one, protesting the German action of sinking unarmed ships. Bryan resigned as Secretary of State because he refused to sign the second note, as it might involve the U.S. in war. New Secretary of State Robert Lansing had no trouble signing the notes and the third one was an ultimatum that warned the Germans that a repetition of the acts would be regarded as being "deliberately unfriendly."

·*Arabic* Pledge

After the British steamer *Arabic* was sunk with the loss of two American lives, the German Ambassador on his own authority pledged, "Liners will not be sunk by our submarines without warning and without safety of the lives of non-combatants…" Germany offered an apology and an indemnity for the loss of American lives.

·*Sussex* Pledge

A French passenger ship was sunk with several Americans injured and the anti-German, Anglophile, Secretary of State Robert Lansing urged Wilson to sever diplomatic relations with Germany as this violated the *Arabic* pledge. Instead Wilson issued an ultimatum threatening to break relations unless Germany abandoned its present methods of submarine warfare. Germany agreed to Wilson's demands but made a counter proposal that the U.S. compel the Allies to respect the rules of international law.

·Virgin Islands Purchased
Fearful that Germany would take these Caribbean islands from Denmark and use them as a naval base, the U.S. bought them from Denmark in 1917 for $25 million.

·Unrestricted Submarine Warfare
With the failure of the German peace initiatives and Russia pulling out of the war, the Germans informed the U.S. that they would resume submarine attacks against all neutral and belligerent ships in the war zone.

·Diplomatic Break with Germany
After the *USS Housatonic* was sunk, Wilson severed diplomatic relations with Germany in March 1917.

·Zimmerman Note
Newspapers published an intercepted telegram (received from British intelligence) from German, Foreign Minister, Arthur Zimmermann to his ambassador in Mexico. He proposed a German-Mexican alliance and promised "Mexico is to re-conquer the lost territory in New Mexico, Texas, and Arizona." U.S. public opinion was enraged.

·Arming of Merchant Ships
Wilson asked Congress for the authority to arm these U.S. ships but 12 Senators led by isolationist Robert La Follette filibustered the bill until the end of the session. Wilson, upon the advice of Lansing, ordered the merchant ships armed without the specific approval of Congress.

U.S. Enters WWI

·Declaration of War
After getting unanimous advice from his cabinet for war, Wilson requested that Congress declare war on Germany on April 6, 1917. It was approved in the House 373-50, and in the Senate 82-6. Most opposition came from German American districts in the isolationist Midwest. Because of their animosity toward Great Britain there was also some Irish opposition to the war as well.

·American Expeditionary Force (AEF)
It took nearly a year for the U.S. Army to be trained and transported to Europe. The British and French wanted to send U.S. troops to reinforce their troops already on the battle lines. However, General John Pershing, AEF commander, refused to break up American units and insisted on a separate U.S. army with its own sector on the front. The German spring offensive of 1918 was stopped by the Allies with the U.S. now playing a major role at Chateau-Thierry, Belleau Wood, the 2nd Battle of the Marne, and Cantigny. The U.S. offensive in the Meuse–Argonne involved 1.2 million troops and resulted in 120,000 U.S. casualties. Total battle deaths for the U.S. in WWI were more than 117,000.

·Committee of Public Information
The most important wartime agency was the Committee of Public Information headed by newspaperman George Creel. He established a successful system of voluntary censorship by the press and his massive propaganda campaign effectively created support for the Allied cause and depicted the Germans as vicious beasts and barbaric Huns.

·War Industries Board
Some order came to the procurement of supplies and materials for the war effort with the appointment of Bernard Baruch; he became one of the first $1 a year man, to head this agency. For the most part planning was haphazard as *laissez faire* was still the dominant philosophy. Lessons from this debacle would be learned and WWII would be totally directed by the government.

·Espionage Act

In an attempt to stifle dissent this law was passed in 1917, which made it a crime for a person to convey information with the intent to interfere with the operation or success of the armed forces of the United States or to promote the success of its enemies. Many of those punished with up to $10,000 fines or 20 years in jail, were socialist or radicals including many newspapers. German-American newspapers, pacifist publications and Irish nationalist publications were also banned.

·Sedition Act

This 1918 law was an amendment to the Espionage Act of 1917 and made it a crime to utter, print, write or publish any disloyal, profane, scurrilous, or abusive language about the United States' form of government, flag, or armed forces during war. It was an attempt by the United States government to limit "freedom of speech" and prominent individuals like Eugene Debs, Victor Berger, and Bill Haywood were sentenced to jail.

·*Schenk v. United States*

Charles Schenk, Secretary for the Socialist Party, had been convicted for distributing 15,000 leaflets critical of the war effort and especially the draft to men of draft age. The leaflet urged readers to "Assert your rights--Do not submit to intimidation." Writing for the Court in *Schenk*, Justice Oliver Wendell Holmes asked whether "the words create a clear and present danger that they will bring about substantive evils Congress has a right to prevent?" Holmes's test seemed to demand little more than that the government show that the words in the leaflet had a bad effect. No proof was demanded that the words actually persuaded anyone to evade the draft, or even that they were highly likely to have that effect. Schenk's conviction was upheld, which was a major attack on the 1st Amendment and the establishment of the "clear and present danger" rule.

·*Debs v United States*

This case involved a speech, "Socialism is the Answer," given by Socialist Eugene Debs in 1918 before 1, 200 persons in Ohio. Debs was prosecuted for remarks such as: "I might not be able to say all that I think, but you need to know that you are fit for something better than slavery and common fodder." The Supreme Court again using its "clear-and-present-danger test," ruled that if a speech had a bad tendency, the speech was illegal. They voted to uphold Deb's ten-year sentence.

Peace Conferance

·14 Points

Presented to Congress these became the Allies war objectives as determined by Wilson:
1. open covenants (treaties) openly arrived at;
2. freedom of the seas in peace and war;
3. removal of economic barriers to free trade;
4. reduction in national armaments;
5. adjustment of colonial claims with people having equitable claims with the government;
6. evacuation of Russian territory and Russian right of independence;
7. evacuation and restoration of Belgium;
8. evacuation of French territory and restoration of Alsace-Lorraine to France from Germany;
9. readjustment of Italian frontiers along nationality lines;
10. autonomy for people of Austria-Hungary;
11. evacuation of Serbia, Montenegro, & Rumania & free access to the sea for Serbia;
12. Turkish part of Ottoman Empire given sovereignty but other parts of Ottoman Empire given autonomy and the Dardanelles were opened to all nations;
13. independent Poland was established with access to the sea through German territory;

14. general association of nations established for guaranteeing political independence and territorial integrity for all states (League of Nations);

·Armistice
Germany surrendered on November 11, 1918 ending the war.

·Peace Treaties
Wilson was treated as a hero when he arrived in Paris to personally head the U.S. delegation. The Paris Peace Conference opened in January of 1919, and meetings were held at various locations in and around Paris for over a year. Leaders of 32 states, representing about 75% of the world's population, attended but negotiations were dominated by the five major powers responsible for defeating the Central Powers: the United States, Britain, France, Italy and Japan. Besides Wilson, the dominant figures were Georges Clemenceau (France) David Lloyd George (Britain), and Vittorio Orlando (Italy). Wilson was forced to compromise with the allied leaders on issues that were not a part of his 14 Points in order to get them to agree to Point 14, his association of nations. Eventually five treaties emerged from the Conference and were named after the Paris suburbs of **Versailles** (Germany), **St. Germain** (Austria), **Trianon** (Hungary), **Neuilly** (Bulgaria) and **Serves** (Turkey).

·Versailles
The main terms of the Versailles Treaty were: (1) the surrender of all German colonies as League of Nations mandates; (2) the return of Alsace-Lorraine to France; (3) cession of Eupen-Malmedy to Belgium, Memel to Lithuania, the Hultschin district to Czechoslovakia; (4) Poznania, parts of East Prussia and Upper Silesia went to Poland; (5) Danzig became a free city; (6) plebiscites were to be held in northern Schleswig to settle the Danish-German frontier; (7) occupation and special status for the Saar under French control; (8) demilitarization and a fifteen-year occupation of the Rhineland; (9) German reparations of £6, 600 million; (10) a ban on the union of Germany and Austria; (11) an acceptance of Germany's guilt in causing the war; (12) provision for the trial of the former Kaiser and other war leaders; (13) limitation of Germany's army to 100,000 men with no conscription, no tanks, no heavy artillery, no poison-gas supplies, no aircraft and no airships; (14) the limitation of the German Navy to vessels under 100,000 tons, with no submarines. Germany signed the Versailles Treaty under protest and they were especially incensed at the "war guilt" clause and the unspecified reparations.

·League of Nations
Despite Wilson's efforts to establish and promote the League of Nations, for which he was awarded the Nobel Peace Prize in 1919, the United States neither ratified the charter nor joined the League due to opposition from isolationists and Republicans in the U.S. Senate. The isolationists, often called the "irreconcilables," were led by Senator William E. Borah of Idaho. The Republicans were led by Henry Cabot Lodge and were willing to join the league but only under certain conditions that were contained in Lodge's 14 Reservations. The peace treaty genuinely troubled Lodge, chairman of the Senate Foreign Relations Committee, taking particular exception to Article X of the League Covenant, which he and others felt required all League members to come to the aid of any member state under attack. Wilson was unwilling to compromise to get the League passed although he had often compromised with the other allied leaders at the Paris Peace Conference; furthermore, he suffered a stroke which physically limited his effectiveness in getting the League of Nations and peace treaties passed by Congress. The Lodge resolution failed on a 39-55 vote. The Senate then considered a resolution to approve the treaty without reservations of any kind, which failed on a 38-53 vote. The isolationist group voted against the treaty and the league on both votes, which doomed it. After 55 days of debate, the Senate had rejected the Treaty of Versailles and Wilson's League of Nations.

Foreign Policy and Events to 1932

·Influenza Pandemic (1918-1919)
Erroneously called the Spanish Flu, it accounted for 30 to 50 million deaths world-wide. Half of the U.S soldiers killed in WWI succumbed to the flu and there were nearly 700,000 deaths in the U.S.

·Columbia Treaty, 1921
As a result of this treaty the U.S. paid Columbia $25 million for the loss of Panama. A similar treaty had been rejected by the Senate in 1914 because of Theodore Roosevelt's influence when he denounced it as blackmail. This was a tacit admission that the U.S. had been wrong in participating in taking Panama from Columbia—it was conscience money.

·Washington Naval Armaments Conference of 1922
As a result of this conference in Washington D.C. 9 treaties were drafted and signed by the leading naval nations. A 10 -year naval building holiday was agreed to and the tonnage of capital ships (battleships and heavy cruisers) would be based on a ratio of 5 (Great Britain), 5 (U.S.), 3 (Japan), 1.67 France, and 1.67 (Italy). Other features were agreements to respect each nation's rights in the Pacific Ocean and an endorsement of the Open Door principal by guaranteeing China's independence and territorial integrity.

·World War Foreign Debt Commission
Wilson had previously rejected a British proposal, endorsed by France, to cancel the debts owed to them (German Reparations and other loans to allies) if the U.S. would cancel the British debt of $4 billion. Based on their capacity to pay, the debtor nations accepted obligations of over $11.5 billion which would be payable over a 62 year period with an average interest rate of 2.135%. In the Balfour Note, the British agreed to not ask for more from its debtors than they owed the U.S. but the U.S. remained adamant about re-payment. As President Calvin Coolidge said, "They hired the money, didn't they?" In 1925, the U.S. agreed to a drastic reduction in principal by canceling 60% of France's debt, 80% of Italy's and reducing the interest rate. Ultimately agreements were reached with 17 nations. The U.S. insistence on partial debt payments contributed to anti-U.S. sentiment in Europe and resulted in increasing isolationism in America. Only Finland made all of their payments.

·Dawes Plan (1924)
After Germany stopped payment of its reparations and France and Belgium occupied the Ruhr, runaway inflation and unemployment crippled the German economy. The U.S.'s desire to collect its war debts from the Allies was predicated on the German's paying their reparations. The U.S. proposal laid out a more manageable schedule for German reparations payments, linked to a complex system of new taxes in Germany, stabilization of the German currency on the gold standard, placing the *Reichsbank* under Allied supervision, and, most important, massive American loans. The loans made possible German payments to the Allies, who in turn, repaid their debts to the United States. The plan went into effect in September and did enable Germany to resume paying reparations for a while.

·League of Nations
Although the U.S. did not join the League it sent five permanent representatives to Geneva to monitor League activities and by 1931, 212 U.S. persons had been appointed to participate in more than 40 League conferences.

·Withdrawal from Latin America
1. **Nicaragua**—U.S. Marines who had been in Nicaragua since 1912 were removed for a short time in 1925, but were brought back to fight against the revolutionary forces of Augusta Sandino. The American trained National Guard led by Anastasio Somoza took power and the Somoza family

would rule until 1979 when they would be overthrown by a new group of leftist revolutionaries called Sandinistas.

2. **Dominican Republic**—After occupying the Dominican Republic for eight years, because of government mismanagement and failure to pay its debts, the U.S. withdrew its Marines in 1924 after a constitutional president was chosen and took office.

3. **Honduras**—U.S. intervened but quickly withdrew its forces after helping to settle an election dispute in 1925.

· World Court
A U.S. attempt to join the World Court, supported by most politicians as well as Harding, Coolidge, and Hoover, was stopped by the Senate's insistence that the World Court accept a U.S. reservation related to advisory opinions.

· Kellogg-Briand Pact
Also known as the Pact of Paris this 1927-1928 agreement called for the renunciation of war as an instrument of national policy. Eventually 62 nations would sign the agreement that was rendered rather ineffective by the fact that there were no enforcement provisions and countries got around it by no longer declaring war.

· Young Plan (1929)
Revised the Dawes Plan by scaling down the amount of reparations Germany owed to $8 billion payable over 58 1/2 years at 5.25% interest. It provided for further reduction if the U.S. would reduce the amount of war debts owed to it by the Allies, which the U.S. refused to do.

· London Naval Conference, 1930
Great Britain, U.S. and Japan scrapped a few battleships and the U.S. failed to get its proposal for the abolition of all offensive armaments adopted. After Germany withdrew from the League of Nations the conference broke up.

· Hoover Debt Moratorium, 1931
In light of the world-wide depression Hoover proposed a one year moratorium on both inter-allied war debts and German Reparations. France's delay in accepting the proposal led to the closure of all German banks.

· Japanese Invasion of Manchuria, 1931-32
Starting with the incident at Mukden, Japan took over Manchuria and created a puppet state called Manchukuo under the Chinese heir to the Ching (Manchu) dynasty, Henry Pu Yi.

· Stimson Doctrine, 1932
Secretary of State Henry Stimson announced that the U.S. would not recognize any agreement which impaired the sovereignty of China over its territory. Japanese forces expelled the Chinese forces from Shanghai but withdrew when the League of Nations adopted the non-recognition principle of the Stimson Doctrine. Japan stayed in control of Manchukuo.

UNIT XXI
MULTIPLE-CHOICE QUESTIONS

Questions 1-3 refer to the following:

1. This propaganda poster depicts which World War I opponent of the U.S. as a brutish ape?

   (A) Russia
   (B) Germany
   (C) China
   (D) Congo

2. The beast is in the act of disrobing if not ravaging which personification of America?

   (A) "It girl" Clara Bow
   (B) America's sweetheart Mary Pickford
   (C) Sex siren Theda Bara
   (D) Columbia/Lady Liberty

3. This poster would not be sponsored today by the U.S. government about an enemy of the U.S. primarily because of

   (A) political correctness
   (B) standards of decency
   (C) censorship of violence
   (D) animal rights groups

306

Questions 4-6 refer to the following:

"...frustrations felt by progressives during the First World War and the subsequent disclosure by historians and journalist of the shoddy motives that had apparently been at the base of American intervention. Some were pacifist who felt vindicated by the failure of the Versailles Treaty. Others had supported the war and apparently felt guilty about the results of their action. Still others examined the quickly opened diplomatic documents of Russia and the Central Powers and discovered evidence that Germany, the chief object of hatred during the war, was probably less guilty... than her ally Austria or... America's allies Russia and France. The moral and religious fervor which the war had been conducted contrasted painfully with the story of sordid imperialistic intrigue, diplomatic conniving, deceitful secret treaties, peace initiatives squashed by America's allies, undemocratic methods used by leaders even as they mouthed Wilson pieties..."

Robert M. Crunden, *From Self to Society*, 1919-1941, 1972

4. The results of WWI caused which reform minded group to become frustrated with America in the 1930s

   (A) Progressives
   (B) Instrumentalist
   (C) Pragmatist
   (D) Darwinians

5. Those journalists and historians who became critical of the U.S. involvement in World War I are called

   (A) peaceniks
   (B) traditionalists
   (C) revisionists
   (D) extremist

6. A group of young people who succumbed to the disillusionment created by WWI and the end of Progressive reform by becoming expatriates and moving to Europe, especially the left bank of Paris, were called

   (A) a selfish generation
   (B) lost generation
   (C) baby boomers
   (D) silent generation

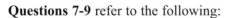

Questions 7-9 refer to the following:

"Arms merchants have long carried on a profitable business arming the potential enemies of their own country. In England today in Bedford Paale there is a cannon captured by the British from the Germans during the World War. It bears a British trademark, for it was sold to Germany by a British firm before the war.... Arms makers engineer "war scares." They excite governments and peoples to fear their neighbors and rivals, so that they may sell more armaments. But the arms merchant does not see himself as a villain,... he is simply a businessman who sells is wares under prevailing business practices. The uses to which his products are put and the results... are apparently no concern of his, no more than they are, for instance, of an automobile salesman.... One British arms manufacturer... compared his enterprise to that of a house-furnishing company which went so far as to encourage matrimony to stimulate more purchases of house furnishings."

C. Engelbrecht and F.C. Hanighen, *Merchants of Death*, 1934

7. The interpretation in the above passage basically was reiterated in the

(A) Nye Committee Report
(B) Stimson Doctrine
(C) quarantine the agressor speech
(D) Lend-Lease Act

8. The "merchants of death" in the above passage have similarities to which of the following?

(A) Those whom FDR called "this generation of Americans have a rendezvous with destiny"
(B) Eisenhower's warning that "we must guard against the acquisition of unwarranted influence, whether sought or unsought, by the military-industrial complex"
(C) Truman's observation that, "We shall never be able to remove suspicion and fear as potential causes of war until communication is permitted to flow, free and open, across international boundaries"
(D) Lyndon Johnson's belief that "The guns and the bombs, the rockets and the warships, are all symbols of human failure.

9. The belief that the arms manufacturers led the U.S. into the Great War contributed to which legislation during the 1930s that made it impossible for the U.S. to give help to those threatened by aggressor nations?

(A) Smott-Hawley
(B) Volstead Act
(C) Securities and Exchange Legislation
(D) Neutrality Acts

Questions 10-11 refer to the following:

10. In the political cartoon above what is the temptation?

    (A) Germany is being tempted to invade Mexico
    (B) Arizona, New Mexico, and Texas are tempted to form a regional trading cartel
    (C) Mexico is being tempted to side with Germany in WWI
    (D) Immigrants from Mexico are being tempted to cross the border to the U.S.

11. What is Mexico being promised if they side with the Central Powers in WWI?

    (A) Return of territories taken from them by the U.S. in the 19th century
    (B) Most favored nation status in trade relations with Germany
    (C) Their pick of British, French, and Dutch territories in the Caribbean
    (D) Unlimited munitions to arm themselves from Germany and its allies

Questions 12-15 refer to the following:

"The traditionalists frowned, complained, and sighed about the "Americanization" of Europe. America, like its films, was all brilliant energy and no substance. The nation was a gross contradiction in terms, they said. Against the mindless patriotism of Americans should be set a physical disunity of the country; against the architectural grandeur of New York, that city's incredible filth; against the prudery and puritanism of America, her criminality and indecent sexuality; against the humanism of her ideals; her racism and lynchings, against the piety of her religion, the burlesque of her Bible-thumping evangelists. The adjectives and similes that the British and French had reserved for Germans were now redirected at Americans."

Modris Eksteins, *Rites of Spring: The Great War and The Birth of the Modern Age*, 2000

12. According to the passage above the impact that America had on Europe because of the close proximity they had with each other in World War I was

   (A) a negative one according to the Europeans
   (B) an appreciative Europe for what the U.S. had done to help them in the war
   (C) the adoption of French and British culture because of the exposure to those countries
   (D) almost non-existent, neither good nor bad

13. Much of the passage above demonstrates

   (A) European admiration for Americans
   (B) An objective assessment of the American character
   (C) contradictions that are a part of the United States
   (D) fear and loathing the British and French had for the Germans

14. The rather negative view of Americans by Europeans was written after the United States had

   (A) sacrificed men and money in helping western Europe in WWI
   (B) demanded territorial concessions at the Treaty of Versailles
   (C) forced American culture and language on the Europeans
   (D) withdrawn its forces from Europe leaving it open to invasion by the communists

15. The ideas expressed about America in the excerpt would be most opposed by advocates of

   (A) "return to normalcy"
   (B) American Exceptionalism
   (C) the Great Society
   (D) the Counterculture

UNIT XXII

THE ROARING TWENTIES

The decade after WWI which lasted from 1919 to 1932 was a turbulent one that was characterized by political reaction against the Progressivism that had preceded the Great War. This decade was also marked by significant social changes and upheavals that made it a schizophrenic time period—part liberal, part conservative, part radical, part reactionary. One historian has noted that it was as much a "nervous generation" as it was a "roaring one." In either case, it was a memorable decade and once again domestic policies would dominate.

Politics—Domestic Policy (Wilson and Harding)

·Volstead Act
Implementation legislation for the 18th Amendment passed by the Republican Congress in 1919 over Wilson's veto put into force the 18th Amendment by defining intoxicating liquids as anything that exceeded 1/2 of 1% alcohol.

·Background to Red Scare and Palmer Raids
The year 1919 saw a great deal of social conflict—a wave of strikes, the passage of both Prohibition and Women's Suffrage, and the Chicago race riot. A series of bombings by suspected anarchists began in the summer 1919. On June 2, bombs went off in eight cities, including Washington DC, where Attorney General A Mitchell Palmer's home was partially destroyed.

·Red Scare
The climate of repression established during World War I with the Espionage and Sedition Acts, continued after the war ended with an attack on all radicals who were thought to be Bolsheviks or "reds."

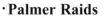

·Palmer Raids

The climactic phase of this anti communist crusade occurred during the "Palmer Raids" of 1918-1921. A. Mitchell Palmer, Wilson's Attorney General, believed communism was "eating its way into the homes of the American workman." Palmer's men began a series of raids against radicals and leftists. Without warrants, they destroyed union offices and the headquarters' of Communist and Socialist organizations, as well as other radical groups. They concentrated whenever possible on aliens rather than citizens, because aliens had fewer rights. In one raid they seized 249 resident aliens including the feminist anarchist and writer Emma Goldman who was singled out for opposing the draft and promoting birth control. They illegally put them on a ship bound for Finland and the Soviet Union. The events of 1919-1920, in which no evidence of a Bolshevik conspiracy were found, was the first of a series of "Red Scares" in American history in which the government would clamp down on real or imagined domestic revolutionaries.

·ACLU Formed

The postwar Red Scare, the Palmer raids, new laws on criminal syndicalism, the use of red flags, the need to repeal the Espionage Act and to secure amnesty for wartime dissidents, led to the formation of the American Civil Liberties Union in 1920.

·Presidential Election of 1920

Political bosses of the Republican Party nominated a likable, lightweight, Ohio Senator Warren G. Harding who defeated the Democratic candidate Governor James Cox of Ohio and won the 1920 Presidential election with the largest popular vote in history. Eugene Debs running as the Socialist candidate from prison (convicted of violating the Espionage Act) received almost a million votes.

·"Return to Normalcy"

This "catch-phrase" made up by Harding described his political philosophy and program which meant going back to a time period before Progressivism and the Great War when business was dominate and society was less complex.

·Andrew Mellon

Industrialist who became Secretary of the Treasury and his pro-business economic policies dominated the 1920s. His influence was so great over economic policy in the 1920s that it was said that three Presidents (Harding, Coolidge, & Hoover) served under him.

·Esch-Cummins Transportation Act

It provided for the return of the railroads to private control following their takeover by the government during WWI.

·Immigrant Act of 1921

Closing the door to immigration this law established a quota system by limiting immigrants to 3% of their nationals that were in the U.S. in 1910.

·Fordney-McCumber Tariff Act of 1922

With support from farmers and businessmen, the Republican Congress passed the Emergency Tariff Act raising duties on agriculture products, wool and sugar in 1921 as a stop gap measure. Later in 1922, Congress passed the Fordney-McCumber Act that contained the highest rates in U.S. history and completely repudiated the low tariff policy that Wilson had established with the Underwood tariff.

·Harding's Death, August 2, 1923

After 2 1/2 years in office Harding died and was universally honored and mourned throughout the nation. The scandals that would symbolize his administration were still in just the rumor stage but would come to light after Coolidge became President.

·Calvin Coolidge

He succeeded to the Presidency on the death of Harding. He was a former Governor of Massachusetts, who first came to prominence in the Boston police strike of 1919 when he asserted that no one was permitted to "strike against the public safety." Devoted to laissez faire economics he believed the "chief business of the American people is business." As President he supported Mellon's tax reduction plan, U.S. adherence to a World Court, and prohibition enforcement. He opposed cancellation of the allied debts and payment of the veterans bonus. He would easily win election in his own right in 1924 but declined to run again in 1928.

Harding Scandals—

·Daugherty and Ohio Gang

A group of politicians led by Harry Daugherty, a long-time political operative who was the principal manager of Harding's ascendancy and became Attorney General, this group betrayed their public trust through a number of scandals. Daugherty was forced to resign because of irregularities in the Justice Department, payments received from violators of the prohibition statues, and failure to prosecute graft in the Veterans Bureau.

·Teapot Dome/Elk Hills

Secretary of Interior Albert Fall (a member of the Ohio Gang), after receiving kickbacks, leased Teapot Dome Oil Reserves (Wyoming) to Harry Sinclair and Elk Hills Reserves (California) to E. L. Doheny. Fall was sentenced to 1 year in prison for bribery and the oil leases were cancelled in 1927. The name Teapot Dome became a metaphor for all of the Harding scandals.

·Charles Forbes

Another member of the Ohio Gang who as head of the Veterans Bureau was indicted for fraud, conspiracy, and bribery and served two years in prison and was fined $10,000.

·Thomas Miller

Custodian of Alien Property who was sent to prison in 1927 for conspiring to defraud the government by selling valuable German patents seized in the war for far below market price.

Politics—Domestic Policy—(Coolidge)

·Soldiers Bonus Act

Original a bill to give Veterans a bonus was vetoed by Harding in 1922. The 1924 bill was vetoed by Coolidge but passed over his veto by Congress. Payment was to be in the form of a 20-year endowment but would become a major issue in 1931-32 when Veterans demanded immediate cash payments.

·Ku Klu Klan

A revived KKK that started in Stone Mountain Georgia in 1915 reached its peak strength in the early 1920s with over 5 million members. This new KKK broadened its lists of hated groups beyond African Americans to include Catholics, Jews, most immigrants especially ones from Southern and Eastern Europe as well as certain tendencies in modern thought including internationalism, pacifism, Darwinism, birth control, and the repeal of prohibition. Exposès of Klan activities included the conviction of Grand Dragon David Stephenson of second degree murder in Indiana that would lead to a falling off of Klan membership in the latter 1920s to about 9,000 in 1930.

·Immigration Act of 1924

Changed the quota of the 1921 law to 2% of nationals instead of 3% and changed the year to establish the quota to 1890 in order to discriminate against Southern and Eastern Europeans who had primarily entered the U.S. after that date. Japanese were to be totally excluded which abrogated the Gentlemen's Agreement of 1906. No restrictions were placed on countries in the Western Hemisphere including Mexico.

·McNary-Haugen

This farm relief bill proposed that the federal government boost agricultural prices by buying up surpluses at a fair price level, disposing of them on foreign markets at a loss, and recovering that loss through a fee assessed against agricultural producers. This bill passed Congress a number of times in the 1920s but failed to override Coolidge and Hoover's Presidential vetoes.

·Presidential Election of 1924

Coolidge and his running mate Charles Dawes were nominated on a platform that supported reduced taxes, lower government expenditures, the Fordney–McCumber tariff, armament limitations, and the U.S. adherence to a World Court. The Democrats nominated conservative businessman John Davis on the 103rd ballot and their platform favored a competitive tariff, disarmament, the League of Nations, and it denounced the Ku Klux Klan and the "Harding Scandals." A new Progressive Party was formed that nominated Robert La Follette and its platform called for the government ownership of railroads and water power resources, abolition of the use of the injunction in labor disputes, collective bargaining for farmers and labor, child labor laws, limitations on the Supreme Court's power of judicial review, and controls over agriculture commodity trading. Coolidge won easily but not by as big a margin as Harding in 1920. La Follette made a creditable showing with 4.8 million votes to Coolidge's 15.7 million and Davis' 8.4 million.

·Bruce Barton

Advertising executive of Batten, Barton, Dunstine, and Osborne who came from a religious background and published *The Man Nobody Knows: A Discovery of the Real Jesus* in 1925. His retelling of the life of Jesus depicted him as the world's first business executive and super-salesman who trained 12 field men to spread a message throughout the world. The book was a nonfiction bestseller in the United States for two years.

·Scopes Trial

In response to Tennessee passing the Butler Act against teaching in public school, "any theory that denies the story of divine creation of man as taught in the Bible," high school coach and substitute teacher John Scopes in Dayton, Tennessee was charged with violating the law by teaching evolution. Defended by Clarence Darrow and prosecuted by William Jennings Bryan among others, Scopes was convicted and fined $100 (later overturned by an appellate court on a technicality) by the judge. This widely publicized 1925 trial (called the Monkey Trial by writer H. L. Mencken) tended to discredit fundamentalist religion and gave a boost to the acceptance of the theory of evolution and the ideas of the modernists in religion.

·Trial of Billy Mitchell

Colonel Mitchell, an advocate of air power, was subject to court martial for insisting that the military was incompetent by not preparing capital ships for being attacked and sunk by air planes. He was convicted for this military heresy, resigned from the service, and died in 1936. The military admitted its error in 1942 when he was posthumously restored to the service with the rank of Major General.

·Sacco-Vanzetti Case

Sacco and Vanzetti, two anarchist Italian immigrants were accused of killing a paymaster and his guard in Braintree, Massachusetts in 1920. During the trial, the prosecution emphasized the men's radical political beliefs and they were also accused of unpatriotic behavior by fleeing to Mexico during WWI. After a seven

week trial they were found guilty of first degree murder and sentenced to death. Felix Frankfurter, later a Supreme Court Justice, characterized Judge Thayer's instructions to the jury as "a farrago (hodge podge) of misquotations, misrepresentations, suppressions and mutilations. ... The opinion is literally honeycombed with demonstrable errors, and infused by a spirit alien to judicial utterance." The men were executed in 1927 despite the efforts of Jane Addams, John Dos Passos and many other prominent individuals to get them a new trial. In 1977, 50 years after their deaths, Massachusetts Governor Michael Dukakis issued a proclamation declaring that Nicola Sacco and Bartolomeo Vanzetti had not received a fair trial. Modern evidence suggests that Sacco may have been guilty but that Vanzetti was not.

·Revenue Act of 1926

Mellon's fiscal program supported by Coolidge reduced personal income and inheritance taxes and ended public access to income tax returns by repealing the publicity clause.

Social and Cultural

·Flappers

According to some accounts the name derived from the sound that un-buckled galoshes made which the newly liberated women wore as a fashion statement. The flapper became a metaphor of the Jazz Age. With short hair and skirt, compressed silhouette, turned-down hose and powdered knees—the flapper, compared to the gentile Gibson girl of an earlier generation, was a rebel. The new, energetic dances of the Jazz Age, required women to be able to move freely, something "old ironsides" (corsets) didn't allow. Replacing the pantaloons and corsets were underwear called "step-ins." No longer confined to the home, the flapper offended the older generation because she defied conventions of acceptable feminine behavior by smoking in public, drinking, dancing the Charleston and other sensuous dances, and engaging in an openly sexual manner often while riding in the newly popular automobiles . Unfortunately for their parents, flappers didn't just use cars to ride in, the back seat became a location for the new popular sexual activity—necking and petting.

·Prohibition

A good example of the "law of unintended consequences," the 18th Amendment radically changed the U.S. in ways that its supporters never envisioned. It was undertaken to reduce crime and corruption, solve social problems, eliminate prisons and poorhouses, and improve health and hygiene in America. Instead, it provided a steady income for organized crime, made a large number of Americans lawbreakers, and it led some drinkers to switch to opium, marijuana, patent medicines, cocaine, and other dangerous substances that they would not have been likely to encounter except for the absence of alcohol.

·Lost Generation

Gertrude Stein used this term to describe the expatriates who became disillusioned with America after WWI and fled to Paris to live on the left bank of the Seine River. Seeking a bohemian lifestyle and rejecting the values of American materialism, these intellectuals, poets, artists and writers, once full of youthful idealism sought the meaning of life, drank excessively, had love affairs and created some of the best American literature. The most well known of these "ex-pats" were F. Scott Fitzgerald, Ernest Hemingway and John Dos Passos. The "Lost Generation" defines a sense of moral loss or aimlessness apparent in literary figures during the 1920s. World War I seemed to have destroyed the idea that if you acted virtuously, good things would happen. Many good, young men went to war and died, or returned home either physically or mentally wounded and their faith in the moral guideposts that had earlier given them hope, were no longer valid—they were in effect, "lost."

·Fads and Crazes

The frivolity of the 1920s is shown by a number of examples of fads and crazes that account for much of the zany interpretation of the era.

1. **Flagpole Sitting**—Started by Alvin "Shipwreck" Kelly, who ultimately would set the record of 49 days in front of 20,000 admirers, this fad lasted from 1924 to 1929 and involved hundreds of participants and thousands of spectators.
2. **X-Word Puzzles**—Originally called word-cross, the name evolved into "cross-word," and were first published in the *New York World*. In 1924, a fledgling publishing house Simon & Schuster put out a collection of the *World's* puzzles in book form that launched the craze.
3. **Dance Marathons**—The craze begin in 1923 when Alma Cummings broke the existing British record by dancing for 57 hours and wearing out six partners in the process. It was soon taken over by promoters who realized that good money could be made from commercializing and standardizing the contests. These would last into the 1930's as contestants would try to win money and prizes to combat the effects of the Great Depression.
4. **Mahjong**—American mahjong, which was mainly played by women after being imported from China in the 1920s, grew into a craze. Part of fad for the tile-playing women was to decorate rooms in Chinese style and dress Chinese.
5. **Freudianism**—The ideas of the Austrian psychiatrist neurologist Sigmund Freud became popular during the 1920s and ushered in an age of "pop psychology" that remains today. People were fascinated with his theories of unconscious influences of sex and the operations of id, ego, and superego on behavior.

·Model T

Henry Ford's invention called the Tin Lizzie or the Flivver came of age in the 1920s as the price was continually reduced until it reached $260 in 1925. It changed America as the new emerging middle class were able to purchase a car, often on the newly created installment plan. By 1925 more than 50% of the families in the North owned cars and automobiles passed cotton to become the #1 U.S. export by 1929.

·Films and Radio

Both of these reached a height of popularity in the 1920s that brought about the standardization and nationalization of the culture. Movie theatres, the people's palaces, featured such performers as Mary Pickford, ironically "America's Sweetheart," although born in Canada, Rudolf Valentino, "The Great Lover," Theda Bara, "The Vamp," Clara Bow, "The It Girl," and the best paid and most popular silent film star, Charlie Chaplin. From 1923 to 1930, 60% of American families purchased radios; and, politics, sports, and cultural programs became available to everyone.

·Literature and the Arts

The 1920s featured an outpouring of literature and other artistic fields that still resonate today with their focus on many themes that had been ignored by earlier generations.

1. **Sherwood Anderson**—His *Winesburg Ohio* showed the crippling effects of small town life on the people. In style and his psychological insights, with the characters dominating the plot, this plain style prose group of short stories or tales has became a "patron saint" of modern literature.
2. **Sinclair Lewis**—His influential works included *Main Street* and *Babbit* with themes of a women's attempt to break with small town provincialism and the conformity and the materialism of the emerging middle class that became known as "Babbitry." In *Elmer Gantry* he showed the hypocrisy of religious fundamentalism with the title character based on the popular real life evangelist Billy Sunday.

3. **Ernest Hemingway**—*The Sun Also Rises* told of the experiences of the expatriates in Europe and his *Farewell to Arms* expressed disillusionment with the war.

4. **F. Scott Fitzgerald**—*This Side of Paradise* and *The Great Gatsby* chronicled the new emerging culture and especially its focus on youth.

5. **William Faulkner**—In a number of works including *The Sound and the Fury* and *Absolum Absolum*, Faulkner laid bare the restricted culture of the South and its stultifying impact on its people.

6. **Edna St. Vincent Millay**—An American poet and playwright and the first woman to receive the Pulitzer Prize for Poetry in 1923. As a long time resident of Greenwich Village she was also known for her unconventional, bohemian lifestyle as well as her many love affairs. Her best-known poem is "First Fig" from *A Few Figs from Thistles* (1920):

    My candle burns at both ends;
    It will not last the night;
    But ah, my foes, and oh, my friends--
    It gives a lovely light!

7. **T. S. Eliot, e. e. cummings, Ezra Pound, and Edward Arlington Robinson**—Their poetry presented themes of alienation in modern life and was often presented in new experimental forms that dissected society during the Jazz Age.

·Jazz

The syncopated rhythm of the music that would give its name to the age had roots in a number of types of music and it was originally formulated in New Orleans. Creative forces included songwriter George Gershwin, bandleaders King Oliver, Duke Ellington, and Paul Whiteman, and performers Bessie Smith, Jack Teagarden, Jelly-Roll Morton, Bix Beiderbecke, Louis Armstrong and Al Jolson.

·Modernism and Art-Deco

These were two forms of architecture that characterized the 1920s. Frank Lloyd Wright's prairie houses ushered in Modernism, which featured abstract styles and simplified geometric forms. New materials and structural technologies allowed architects to create structures that had previously been impossible. The catch-phrase "form follows function" indicated that this style had an absence of the ornamentation of the Richardsonian style that preceded it. Art Deco, a decorative and architectural style of the period 1925–1940 was characterized by geometric and streamlined designs, bold colors, and the use of plastic and glass. The Miami Beach version featured pastels with nautical motifs.

·Artists

Paintings of artists like Georgia O'Keeffe and Edward Hopper expanded the subject matter and the techniques of art. With paintings like "Black Hollyhocks and Blue Larkspur" O'Keefe featured flowers so prominent that they would be noticed as she painted the natural landscape simple in form with vivid and dramatic color. Hooper, the best-known American realist of the inter-war period, once said: "the man's the work. Something doesn't come out of nothing." His works of lonely roads and vacant rooms were modern in their bleakness and simplicity, but were also full of nostalgia for the Puritan virtues of the American past.

Personalities

·Charles Lindbergh

This adventurer and explorer became the greatest American hero in history by his 33 hour, non-stop, flight across the Atlantic to Le Bourget Field near Paris in 1927. At the age of 25, he had performed the greatest piloting feat in the history of aviation. Crowds of people cheered as the "Spirit of St. Louis" landed. "Lucky

Lindy" or the "Lone Eagle" was given the greatest of all the ticker tape parades when he returned to New York City. He was decorated with countless awards and received both the Congressional Medal of Honor and the Distinguished Flying Cross. His quiet unassuming nature made him an ideal hero.

·Margaret Sanger

In working with poor women as a nurse on the "lower east side" in New York, Sanger was aware of the effects of unplanned and unwelcome pregnancies on women. Her own mother's health had suffered as she bore eleven children. Sanger believed in the importance of health care to women's lives and their health could be improved by the availability of birth control, a term she's credited with inventing. She attempted to overturn the Comstock Act of 1873 that was used to stop the distribution of birth control devices and information.

·Billy Sunday

A former professional baseball player, Billy Sunday became a "fire-and-brimstone" fundamentalist minister. After a night of drinking he attended a church service and became "born again." His evangelistic sermons were directed against political liberalism, evolution, alcohol, and other aspects of modern America. His energy and vitality won many converts and he accumulated a small fortune through contributions at his sermons.

·Jimmy Walker

Became mayor of New York City in 1926 with the help of Governor Al Smith and the Tammany Hall political machine. Initially the city was prosperous under his regime with many public works projects along with the proliferation of speakeasies during the Prohibition era. His extra marital affairs with "chorus girls" were widely known and even after he left his wife for a showgirl it did not hurt his popularity. Despite a threatened strike by the transit workers he managed to maintain the 5-cent subway fare, adding to his popularity. He won re-election in 1929, defeating Republican Fiorello La Guardia and Socialist Norman Thomas. The stock market crash ended his popularity—his flamboyant style was not suited for the Great Depression. Increasing social unrest led to investigations into corruption within his administration, and he was eventually forced to testify before an investigative committee. After being pressured by Governor Franklin Roosevelt, Walker resigned in 1932 and left for Europe until the danger of criminal prosecution passed.

·Gertrude Ederle

New York born Trudy became the first woman to swim the English Channel in 1926 at the age of 19. Her time of 14 hours 39 minutes for the 35-mile distance broke the previous record by more than 2 hours and stood as the women's record for 35 years. Returning to New York, her ticker tape parade was the largest until Lindbergh's a year later. From 1921 to 1925, she set 29 United States and world records for swimming races ranging from the 50-yard to the half-mile. In the 1924 Summer Olympic Games in Paris, she won one gold and two bronze medals.

·Aimee Semple McPherson

Also known as Sister Aimee, she was a Canadian-born evangelist and media celebrity in the 1920s and 1930s. She was a pioneer in the use of modern media, especially radio, and attracted a huge following. By 1920, McPherson was permanently established in Los Angeles and her revivals were often standing room only. One of these was held in a boxing ring, with the meeting before and after the match. In 1923 she and her followers dedicated the Angelus Temple and called her new breed of Christian church the Foursquare Gospel, a complete gospel for body, soul, spirit, and eternity. McPherson developed a large group of devoted followers in her 5000 seat church. McPherson thrived on publicity and sensationalism and her most famous stunt occurred in 1926, when McPherson, believed to have drowned in the Pacific Ocean, "miraculously" reappeared in the Mexican desert. Many doubted her tale of kidnapping and mistreatment, claiming she had been in hiding with one of her male followers. A resulting court battle attracted national attention. She was involved with well-publicized vendettas with other religious groups and died after overdosing on sleeping pills in 1944.

African Americans

·Race Riots

Major race riots occurred in 1919 in Chicago, 1921 in Tulsa, and 1921 in Washington D. C. in which hundreds of blacks were killed by rampaging whites.

·Great Migration

By 1920, the African-American population had nearly doubled in the major cities of the North: Chicago, St. Louis, New York City, Philadelphia, Indianapolis, Washington DC, Cleveland, Detroit, Pittsburgh, and Boston were the major cities of black migration from the South. The core area of many of these cities became dominated by the African American community often forming black ghettos in the inner-city area. African-Americans who stayed in the South were mainly employed as farmers, tenant farmers, or sharecroppers. Those who moved to the North were able to secure higher paying manufacturing jobs.

·Marcus Garvey

Jamaica born and schooled in England, he founded the UNIA (Universal Negro Improvement Association) that stood for black pride as he championed the 'back to Africa' movement of the 1920s. Garvey formed the Black Star Lines with $10,000,000 invested by his supporters and he purchased two steamships to take African Americans to Africa. With the failure of the enterprise Garvey was arrested and charged with fraud and in 1925 was sentenced to five years imprisonment. He had served half of his sentence when President Coolidge commuted the rest of his prison term and had him deported to Jamaica. He spent his remaining years traveling and lecturing around the world and died in London in 1940. His ideas of black pride would be revived in the 1960s.

·A. Philip Randolph

A leading civil rights advocate who formed and led the Brotherhood of Sleeping Car Porters in 1925, the largest labor union representing black workers. Later he would play a prominent role in influencing presidents in ending segregation.

·Harlem Renaissance

After the American Civil War, liberated African-Americans searched for a safe place to explore their new identities as free men and women. They found it in the Harlem district of New York City. The Harlem Renaissance was a flowering of African-American social thought that was expressed through music (Louis Armstrong, Fats Waller and Billie Holiday), literature (Langston Hughes, Zora Neale Hurston, and W.E.B. DuBois), theater (Paul Robeson) and dance (Josephine Baker). The *New Negro Movement* as it was called was not a school, nor did the writers associated with it share a common purpose; nevertheless, they had a common bond as they dealt with black life from a black perspective. The legacy of the Harlem Renaissance opened doors and deeply influenced the generations of African American writers that followed.

UNIT XXII
MULTIPLE-CHOICE QUESTIONS

Questions 1-4 refer to the following:

"[President Warren G.] Harding capitalized on an immense feeling of nostalgia for the years before the war, for the days when life was simpler. In a speech,... in Boston, Harding caught the spirit of the country in urging a return to 'not heroism, but healing, not nostroms, but normalcy,' thereby coining a word and defining a mood. The country, bemused by Wilsonian rhetoric, wanted to return to a reality that was concrete.... The election of 1920, declared the Republican vice-presidential candidate Calvin Coolidge... was 'the end of a period which has seemed to substitute words for things.' Harding had no qualification for being President except that he looked like one—which is, given the mythological role of the President in American culture, not an unimportant consideration."

William E. Leuchtenburg, *The Perils of Prosperity*, 1914-1932, 1958

1. Harding found a receptive audience for his "return to normalcy" philosophy as

   (A) immigration was populating the U.S. with the reactionary peasant class of Europe
   (B) people were tired from causes like the reform movements and War War I
   (C) the traditional attitude in the U.S was a deeply conservative one
   (D) the modern world could not keep up with the dramatic changes in society

2. The politics of the Harding era was a vivid contrast to which political reform movement that came before it?

   (A) Progressivism
   (B) Populism
   (C) Social Darwinism
   (D) Industrialism

3. By his wish to return to what he perceived to be the normal condition in the U.S. Harding is advocating which description of change on the political spectrum?

   (A) Liberalism
   (B) Conservatism
   (C) Moderation
   (D) Radicalism

4. Leuchtenburg describes Harding as having what single qualification for being president that was not an unimportant one?

   (A) Experience
   (B) Background
   (C) Political philosophy
   (D) He looked like one

320

Questions 5-6 refer to the following:

5. The battle in the 1920 over religion was between religious modernists and religious

   (A) Catholics
   (B) Orthodox
   (C) Reformers
   (D) Fundamentalists

6. The civil trial in 1925 that divided the nation between the two religious factions and their respective stand on evolution is called the

   (A) Darwin Trial
   (B) Genesis Trial
   (C) Scopes Monkey Trial
   (D) *Brown vs. Board of Education of Topeka, Kansas*

Questions 7-9 refer to the following:

"As an ex-flapper I'd like to say a word in her behalf. I who have tasted the fruits of flappery and found them good—even nourishing... A flapper lives on encouragement... a flapper is proud of her nerve... she is shameless, selfish, and honest... she considers these attributes virtues. She takes a man's point of view as her mother never could.... She can take a man—the man of the hour—at his face value with no foolish promises that will need... breaking.... [There are] different types of flappers. There is the prep-school type—still a little crude.... She has not the finish of the college flapper who has learned to be soulful, virtuous on occasions, and, under extreme circumstances, even highbrow... if she wants you badly enough she will come out in the open and work for you with the same fresh and vigorous air that you would work to win her...."

George E. Mowry (ed.), *The Twenties: Fords, Flappers, & Fanatics*, 1963

7. This description by a self-professed flapper shows that compared to earlier women arch-types she is a

   (A) debutante
   (B) classy lady
   (C) progeny of Republican motherhood
   (D) rebel

8. The flapper replaced which woman who had been the feminine ideal for most of society before her time?

   (A) Pin-up
   (B) "Girl next door"
   (C) Gipson Girl
   (D) Femme fatale

9. One significant way that the flapper differed from traditional women's types is that she

   (A) adopted the habits and behaviors associated more with men
   (B) was free to pursue religious and domestic interests within organized groups and the focus of her life did not have to be stretched beyond her own front porch
   (C) demonstrated the Victorian ideals of piety, purity, submissiveness, and domesticity
   (D) became a paragon of the virtues of the cult of domesticity

Questions 10-12 refer to the following:

"Surely part of the reason why young women seemed so much more interested in their private affairs and the pursuit of pleasure after 1920 was precisely because the adventure had gone out of what had been for a generation or more almost traditional activities. As long as going to college, joining a woman's club, working for the vote or participating in the social justice movement called for a certain boldness, and at least a mild taste for adventure, the best and bravest young women were moved to service. When these activities became tame and routine, they ceased to be outlets for spirited youth. Adventure was... in struggling against not social problems but social conventions. Drinking, smoking, dancing, sexual novelties, daring literature, and avante-garde society now filled the vacuum created by the collapse of social feminism."

William L. O'Neill, *Everyone Was Brave: A History of Feminism in America*, 1969

10. From the passage above the author seems to be saying that once women solved serious social problems and women's issues, the sense of adventure was passed and they turned to

    (A) challenging generally accepted standards, norms, criteria, and customs
    (B) working for the greater good on mankind in the anti-war or peace movement
    (C) extending women's rights throughout the world
    (D) liberating their sisters in countries that oppressed women

11. It can be inferred that O'Neill believes the social feminist greatest accomplishment that led to their undoing was the

    (A) ending of assigned marriages
    (B) ratification of the 19th Amendment
    (C) invention of the birth control pill
    (D) passage of women's right to work laws

12. From the militant suffragettes before the war young women had morphed into which social type in the 1920s interested in drinking, smoking, dancing, and sex?

    (A) Gibson Girl
    (B) Vargas Girl
    (C) Flapper
    (D) Feminist

Questions 13-15 refer to the following:

"I learned that not everything in America was what it seemed to be. I discovered, for instance, that a spare tire could be filled with substances other than air, that one must not look too deeply into certain binoculars, and that the Teddy Bears that suddenly acquired tremendous popularity among the ladies very often had hollow metal stomachs. 'But,' it might be asked, 'where do all these people get the liquor?' Very simple. Prohibition has created a new, a universally respected, a well-beloved, and a very profitable occupation, that of the bootlegger who takes care of the importation of the forbidden liquor… The filthy saloons, the gin mills which formerly flourished on every corner and in which the laborer once drank off half his wages, have disappeared ... a great deal of poison and methyl alcohol has taken the place of the good old pure whiskey… as a consequence of the law, the taste for alcohol has spread ever more widely among the youth.... My observations have convinced me that many fewer would drink were it not illegal."

Count Felix von Luckner, "I learned that not everything in America was what it seemed to be, *Seeteufel erobert Amerika*," 1928

13. What was the main thing that the German visitor learned about America?

   (A) Things were different then they appeared
   (B) If drinking was legal more people would do it
   (C) Prohibition has created the despised occupation of the bootlegger
   (D) Because of the law fewer young people are drinking

14. According to the German visitor all of the following were changes that prohibition brought about EXCEPT

   (A) a newly respected and beloved occupation of the bootlegger has emerged
   (B) filthy saloons and gin mills have disappeared
   (C) good old pure whiskey has replaced methyl alcohol
   (D) people drank openly without attempting to hide what they were doing

15. Which of the following illustrates the validity of the law of unintended consequences (outcomes that are not the ones intended by a purposeful action) as it applies to prohibition?

   (A) It was a popular law
   (B) Among youth drinking became more widespread
   (C) Prohibition has been successful by stopping the importation of foreign liquor
   (D) Spare tires, binoculars, and Teddy Bears were used to conceal illegal alcohol

UNIT XXIII

CRASH OF 1929 & THE 1930'S

In the economic and social history of the United States no single event had as great an impact as the stock market crash of 1929 and the Great Depression of the 1930s. Many in this generation developed a depression mentality that would last through World War II and the rest of their lives. They would always be concerned about economic security and would practice frugality that has been lost by recent generations of Americans.

1920s Background

·Stock Market

As the Dow Jones Industrial Average (the historic indicator of stock prices) soared, many investors pushed prices upward by buying up shares (ownership in corporations) without regard to their value. Because of the apparent booming economy, stock ownership was considered a safe investment by most economists. To speculate even further, investors often purchased stock on margin—the borrowing of stock for the purpose of gaining even more leverage. For every dollar invested, a margin user would borrow 9 dollars worth of stock. Because of this leverage, if a stock went up 1%, the investor would make 10%! This also worked the other way around, exaggerating even minor losses into a huge loss. If a stock dropped too much, margin holders could lose all of their money. From 1921 to 1929, the Dow Jones went from 60 to 381. Millionaires were created instantly based on stock speculation. Soon stock market trading became America's favorite pastime as investors jockeyed to make a quick killing. Investors mortgaged their homes, and foolishly invested their life savings in hot stocks such as Ford and RCA. To the average investor, stocks were a sure thing. Few people actually studied the fundamentals of the companies they invested in. Thousands of fraudulent companies were formed to hoodwink gullible investors. Most investors never even thought a crash was possible. To them, the stock market "always went up."

·Economic Problems of 1920s

On the surface the economy seemed to be booming during the latter 1920s because of the speculative fervor of the stock market. But underneath this financial facade there were serious flaws in the economy. The stock market crash of 1929 signaled the start of the Great Depression but was not responsible for causing it. Fundamental flaws in the economy begin to surface in the late 1920s but these were hidden because of the surge in stock market prices. Agricultural prices were depressed, durable goods purchases had slacked off, the high tariff policy restricted oversees markets, the strong building boom of the early 1920s had tapered off, coal and textiles industries were depressed and the new technology was laying off workers. Businesses were not investing but putting their excess profits (in part, because of the low tax policy of Andrew Mellon) into the stock market. Consumers were doing the same, and when they did purchase items they were buying them without money by using installment purchases. The most important factor leading to the Great Depression was that there was a mal-distribution of income as too few people controlled most of the wealth, which led to under-consumption by the consumer sector of the economy.

·Mellon Plan

It has been said that during the 1920s three presidents (Harding, Coolidge, and Hoover) served under Secretary of the Treasury, Andrew Mellon. His policies undid the progressive taxes of World War I on the wealthy as he dropped income tax rates from 77% to 25%, dropped the estate tax from 40% to 20%, repealed the excess profits tax, and repealed the gift tax. By concentrating money at the top this fueled the speculative bubble that resulted in a stock market crash and the Great Depression.

Crash and the Great Depression

·Election of 1928

After Coolidge's surprise announcement that he would not run for President in 1928, the logical heir apparent was self-made millionaire engineer, Herbert Hoover, who served as Secretary of Commerce under Harding and Coolidge. The Democrats choose the charismatic governor of New York, Al Smith as their candidate. Smith was the first Catholic ever nominated by a major party and would lose 5 southern states because he favored repeal of the 18th Amendment and because of his religion. Hoover won in a landslide with 444 electoral votes to 87. It would take 32 more years before another Catholic was nominated for President.

·Stock Market Crash of 1929

Throughout the 1920s wild speculation in the stock market had driven prices up to unfathomable heights that had no correlation to the actual value of the companies receiving the investment. From 1921 to 1929, the Dow Jones went from 60 to 400 and stock market trading became America's favorite pastime. Investors mortgaged their homes, and foolishly invested their life savings in hot stocks, often buying on margin with only a 10% down payment. The investor Joseph Kennedy (father of Jack, Bobby, and Ted) sold all of his stock after a shoeshine boy gave him stock advice. This saved the Kennedy family fortune.

·Early Warnings

On March 25, 1929, the stock market suffered a mini-crash. It was a prelude of what was to come. By the spring of 1929, there were additional signs that the economy might be headed for a serious setback. Steel production went down; house construction slowed, and car sales waned. At this time, there were also a few reputable people warning of an impending major crash; however, as month after month went by without one, those that advised caution were labeled as pessimists and ignored. Both the mini-crash and the "nay-sayers" were nearly forgotten when the market surged ahead during the summer of 1929. The continual increase of stocks seemed inevitable. When economist Irving Fisher stated, "Stock prices have reached what looks like a permanently high plateau," he was stating what many speculators wanted to believe. On September 3, 1929, the stock market reached its peak with the Dow Jones Industrial Average closing at 381.17. Two days later, the market started dropping. At first, there was no massive drop. Stock prices fluctuated throughout September and into October until the massive drop on Black Thursday.

·Black Thursday–October 24, 1929

On the morning of Thursday, October 24, 1929, stock prices plummeted. Vast numbers of people were selling their stocks. Margin calls were sent out. People who had leveraged their stocks by borrowing now had to come up with money or they would lose their stocks. People across the country watched the ticker as the numbers it spit out spelled their doom. The ticker was so overwhelmed that it quickly fell behind. A crowd gathered outside of the New York Stock Exchange on Wall Street, stunned at the downturn. False rumors circulated of people committing suicide by jumping out of the windows of office buildings. To the great relief of many, the panic subsided in the afternoon. When a group of bankers pooled their money and invested a large sum back into the stock market, their willingness to invest their own money in the stock market convinced others to stop selling. The morning had been shocking, but the recovery was amazing. By the end of the day, many people were again buying stocks at what they thought were bargain prices. On "Black Thursday," 12.9 million shares were sold—double the previous record.

·Black Tuesday–October 29, 1929

Four days later on Tuesday the stock market fell again, for good. This time there was no rebound. Although the market had closed on an upswing on Black Thursday, the low numbers of the ticker that day had shocked many speculators. Hoping to get out of the stock market before they lost everything (as they thought they had on Thursday morning), they decided to sell. This time, as the stock prices plummeted, no one came in to save it. Just as the sniffles are symptoms of a cold the stock market crash was a symptom of the depression. Not the cause, just a symptom.

Great Depression and Hoover's Response

·Hoover's Relief Policy

It is ironic that the man credited with teaching America to economize during WWI, and feeding Europe in the aftermath of the war, would fail miserably in providing relief to Americans in the Great Depression. His philosophy based on the "bootstrap theory" of rugged individualism stressed that the economy would right itself as long as there was minimal interference in it by the government, especially the national government. He was opposed to direct federal relief for the unemployed and believed any help for them should come from private agencies or local government. He also tended to blame the depression on factors outside of the U.S. and did not see any fundamental flaws in the American economic system.

·Smoot Hawley Tariff

In June of 1930, Congress exacerbated the effects of the depression by raising tariffs to the highest in history. The original intention behind the legislation was to increase the protection for domestic farmers against foreign agricultural imports as Hoover had pledged to do in his campaign. But once the tariff schedule revision process got started, it proved impossible to stop as calls for increased protection flooded in from the industrial sector and every special interest group. Soon a bill meant to provide relief for farmers became a means to raise tariffs in all sectors of the economy. European countries retaliated and the result was that international trade came to a standstill.

·Wickersham Commission

Appointed by Hoover to study Prohibition it concluded that effective enforcement was hindered by the lucrative returns of the bootlegging industry, public antipathy or hostility to the 18th Amendment, and that enforcement should be by the federal government, not the states. The commission favored the revision of the 18th Amendment to allow for the sale of light beer and wine. Hoover did not favor any changes and called Prohibition "a great social and economic experiment, noble in motive and far-reaching in purpose." He did not call it a "noble experiment" but that phrase has been credited to him.

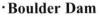

·Boulder Dam

Authorized under Coolidge and begun under Hoover (to be completed under Roosevelt in 1936 and renamed Hoover Dam) this massive public works project dammed the Colorado River to provide irrigation, flood control and electric power. It was a harbinger of public works projects in the future during the New Deal.

·Norris-LaGuardia Act

This was a controversial pro-labor union law that outlawed "yellow dog contracts" and restricted the Supreme Court's ability to issue injunctions to restrain strikes, boycotts, and picketing.

·Reconstruction Finance Corporation

This was Hoover's federal program to loan money to banks, insurance companies, large corporations, and railroads with the hope that this would check deflation and create employment and purchasing power by the consumers. The RFC was capitalized at $500 million and authorized to borrow up to $2 billion. Hoover believed giving money to the large institutions would trickle down and help those below. As some put it, feeding the horses to feed the sparrows.

·Unemployment & GDP (Gross Domestic Production)

From essentially full employment in 1929 when the unemployment rate was 3.2 percent the country moved into massive unemployment in 1933 when the unemployment rate reached 25 percent. By 1940 the unemployment rate was still at 15%. The GDP declined from $791 billion in 1929 to $577 billion in 1933.

·Bonus Army (1932)

A thousand veterans marched on Washington D. C. (later joined by 17,000 more) to demand early payment of their WWI bonuses. The House authorized the payment but the Senate defeated it and the government provided funds for the veterans to return to their homes. Most did but 2,000 refused to disband and after the police failed to remove them Hoover called out army under Douglas MacArthur. His forces routed them and destroyed their shanty town camps with infantry, cavalry, and tanks in what became known as the Battle of Anacostia Flats—the army waging war on the WWI veterans.

·Soup Kitchens

During the Great Depression "soup kitchens" provided the only meals some unemployed Americans received. These were often private charities sponsored by churches, service groups, and even individuals. The notorious gangster Al Capone sponsored the first one in Chicago. In time most municipalities supported them. Soup kitchens served mostly soup and bread. Soup was economical because water could be added to serve more people if necessary. The long lines of people waiting to get soup were usually called "bread lines." When President Hoover made his infamous remark that "prosperity was just around the corner" the radio comedians Amos and Andy retorted that you couldn't see around the corner because the bread lines were too long.

·Brother, Can You Spare a Dime

In "Brother, Can You Spare a Dime," E. Y. Harburg created an "Everyman" narrator for his song; a person who has built railroads, skyscrapers, and tilled the fields. This person has contributed to the vast bounty of the land (through his plow) and kept faith with the promise of the land by bearing guns for it in time of war. There is irony the lines where he described the half-million "boots" that went slogging through hell "Full of that Yankee Doodle-de-dum" in WWI that helped to build a dream of "peace and glory ahead." How can he now be standing in a breadline? The tune contributed to the overall theme by sounding like a funeral dirge.

·Tramps & Hobos

Traditionally a tramp or hobo was a long-term homeless person who traveled from place to place as an itinerant vagrant, traditionally walking, riding the rails or hiking all year round. Vast armies of tramps were created by the joblessness of the Great Depression. While some tramps did odd jobs from time to time, they were mostly unemployed and homeless, living off the land and eating in soup kitchens. Many unemployed heard about work hundreds of miles away, or even half a continent away, and the only way they could get there was by illegally hopping on freight trains. More than two million men and perhaps 8,000 women became hoboes. According to one account at least 6,500 hoboes were killed in one year either in accidents or by railroad "bulls," brutal guards hired by the railroads to make sure the trains carried only paying customers.

·Hoovervilles & Hoover Blankets

In what became a form of "gallows humor," Hooverville was the popular name for shanty towns built by homeless people during the Great Depression. They were named after President Herbert Hoover indicating the disdain people felt for him because he let the nation plunge into the Great Depression. The term was allegedly created by the publicity chief of the Democratic National Committee, Charles Michelson, and the name stuck. These settlements were often formed on empty land close to soup kitchens and consisted of jerry-rigged shacks and tents featuring scraps of lumber, cardboard, tar -paper and sometimes tin. City dumps, construction sites, and trash bins provided materials for constructing shelters. Gutted old cars made acceptable homes, as did stacks of fruit boxes and worn tires. If a shelter was built well enough, a resident could sell it. There was always turnover, since people continually came and went in the shantytowns. Public officials did not officially recognize these Hoovervilles and occasionally removed the occupants for technically trespassing on private lands, but they were frequently tolerated out of necessity. Other variations of the Hooverville were: Hoover blankets, newspapers wrapped around you to keep warm; Hoover flags, pockets turned inside out with nothing in them; and Hoover hogs, wild jackrabbits caught and killed for food. Even today tent cities are often called Hoovervilles.

·Apple Sellers

In what became a common sight during the Great Depression were people selling apples on street corners for 5 cents each. In 1930, the International Apple Shippers Association was faced with an oversupply of fruit and came up with a unique solution to clear out their warehouses and give the unemployed a way to make a little money. They sold apples on credit to the unemployed. Apple vendors could be found standing over a fruit crate on the corner of every major American city. By the end of November there were 6,000 people selling apples in New York. The trend spread, and soon there were pitchmen of all persuasions standing alongside the apple sellers, hawking everything from patent medicines, to pencils, to neckties. Many cities soon passed ordinances, however, banning street vendors as a nuisance to the public. The selling of apples became a metaphor for the despair people felt during the Great Depression.

·Dust Bowl

The Dust Bowl of the 1930s lasted about a decade and was centered in the western half of Kansas, eastern Colorado, New Mexico and the Texas and Oklahoma panhandles. Its primary area of impact was on the southern Great Plains. The agricultural devastation helped to lengthen the Depression and the effects were felt worldwide. The movement of people on the Plains was also profound. Poor agricultural practices and years of sustained drought caused the Dust Bowl. Plains grasslands had been deeply plowed and planted for wheat. During the years when there was adequate rainfall, the land produced bountiful crops. But as the droughts of the early 1930s deepened, the farmers kept plowing and planting and nothing would grow. The ground cover that held the soil in place was gone. The Plains winds whipped across the fields raising clouds of dust to the sky which could darken it for days, and even the most well sealed homes could have a thick layer of dust on furniture. In some places the dust would drift like snow, covering farms. As John Steinbeck wrote in his 1939 novel *The Grapes of Wrath*: "And then the dispossessed were drawn west- from Kansas, Oklahoma, Texas, New Mexico; from Nevada and Arkansas, families, tribes, dusted out, tractored out. Car-loads, caravans, homeless and hungry; twenty thousand and fifty thousand and a hundred thousand and two hundred thousand.

They streamed over the mountains, hungry and restless—restless as ants, scurrying to find work to do...." This great migration found many ending up in the San Joaquin Valley in central California or the Willamette Valley in Oregon.

Social Life of the 1930s

·Radio

Radio reached its zenith of popularity in this decade and by 1939 about 80 percent of the population owned radio sets. Comedians such as Jack Benny, Fred Allen, George Burns and Gracie Allen, Amos and Andy, and Fibber McGee and Molly were popular. The "soap opera," so-named because they were sponsored by companies selling soap, dominated the daytime airwaves just as they would television two decades later. The heroics of the Lone Ranger, the Green Hornet, the Shadow, and Jack Armstrong, All-American Boy, thrilled listeners and sold countless boxes of cereal and soap. News broadcast by commentators like Edward R. Murrow kept the public aware of the impending crisis in Europe. Franklin Roosevelt used this media in his "fireside chats" to influence public opinion. One of the most dramatic moments in radio history occurred on May 6, 1937, when the German airship Hindenburg burst into flames as it was about to land in New Jersey. The horror of the incident was dramatically conveyed live by reporter Herb Morrison. On October 30, 1938, twenty-three-year-old Orson Welles broadcast on his Mercury Theater the H.G. Wells' story "War of the Worlds." Despite the disclaimer at the beginning and end of the program, the tale of a Martian invasion of earth panicked many listeners who mistook the play for an actual newscast of an event.

·Music of the 1930s

Three songs that depicted the time of the Great Depression were "Brother, Can You Spare a Dime," by Yip Harburg, "Life is Just a Bowl of Cherries," by Lew Brown, and "We're in the Money," by Al Dubin. Later in the decade Woody Guthrie wrote "This Land is Your Land" to try to uplift the spirits of everyone. George Gershwin's American folk opera "Porgy and Bess" was first performed in 1936. In 1938, Kate Smith sang Irving Berlin's "God Bless America" and made the song her own.

·Films of the 1930s

In 1930, the Motion Picture Production Code, administered by Joseph I. Breen (and former Postmaster General Will Hays) set film guidelines regarding sex, violence, religion, and crime (not yet strictly enforced until the Production Code Administration of 1934). For more than 30 years this code would heavily censure what could be shown in films. Olympic swimming champion Johnny Weissmuller made his screen debut as the vine-swinging man of the jungle in "Tarzan, the Ape Man." Curly-haired, dimpled, child star Shirley Temple became the most popular film personality of the 1930s. 1939 became the greatest year in film history which included releases of "The Wizard of Oz," "Gone with the Wind," "Mr. Smith Goes to Washington," "Wuthering Heights," "Stagecoach," "Gunga Din," "Love Affair," and "Goodbye Mr. Chips."

·Dance Marathons

During the height of the Great Depression, young people across America gathered to participate in Dance Marathons. These endurance contests offered the unemployed hopes of temporary fame, some money, and the opportunity to dance their cares away. Prizes ranged from $1,000 to $5,000, but many contestants participated solely for the promise of food and shelter. Serious competitors danced for days, even weeks at a time and the record stands at 5,148 hours and 28.5 minutes. The contestants were usually allowed a few minutes of rest for every hour of dancing. Success came to those who had the ability to keep their partner moving at all times. Police and health officials attempted time and time again to shut down these contests for health reasons but usually failed. For the unemployed, these tests of stamina and displays of fatigue provided an escape from the dreariness and hopelessness of the Great Depression.

·Regionalism in Art

The 1930s saw the beginning of the American regionalist style with Grant Wood's, "American Gothic" being the best known. Artists that adopted this style included, Thomas Hart Benton, Georgia O'Keeffe with her southwestern themes, and Edward Hopper with his realistic scenes from city life.

·Architecture

Many of the nation's most memorable skyscrapers (the Empire State Building, the Chrysler Building, and Rockefeller Center) were completed in the early 1930's. In 1937 the Frank Lloyd Wright masterpiece of home design "Falling Water" was built. Art-Deco continued to be popular with its new name Streamline Moderne. The style emphasized curving forms, long horizontal lines, and nautical elements (such as railings and porthole windows) and reached its height in the late 1930s.

·Leisure Activities and Games

President Roosevelt helped make stamp collecting a popular hobby. Parlor games and board games became the rage, and in 1935 Parker Brothers introduced the game of Monopoly and 20,000 sets were sold in one week. Gambling increased as people sought any means to add to their income. Between 1930 and 1939 horse racing became legal in 15 more states bringing the total to 21. Interest in spectator sports such as baseball grew. Stars like Babe Ruth, Lou Gehrig and Joe DiMaggio drew fans into the stadium, and those who could not attend the games gathered around their radios to listen to the play-by-play. The 1932 Winter Olympics, held at Lake Placid, New York, renewed interest in winter sports. Jesse Owens, an African American athlete won four gold medals in track-and-field at the 1936 Olympics in Berlin to demolish Adolph Hitler's Aryan superiority message.

·Literature

Many of the writers from the Lost Generation of the 1920s continued to be productive after returning to America in the 1930s. Hemingway, Fitzgerald, and Dos Passos were still writing. Thornton Wilder's, *Our Town* with its bare stage that stripped the play of everything that was not essential to give it a profound, strange, otherworldly significance, was a surprise hit. Some of the novels of this period explored what was happening in the country during the Great Depression. John Steinbeck's *The Grapes of Wrath* chronicled the life of a displaced Oklahoma family who had lost its farm to the drought of the Dust Bowl. James T. Farrell wrote a trilogy of novels about an Irish-American named *Studs Lonigan* and his attempt to rise above his poor beginnings. Richard Wright took on the issue of racial prejudice and the plight of blacks in *Native Son*. Erskine Caldwell's novel, *Tobacco Road* described the life of poor whites in the rural South. There were notable works in other forms of literature as poet Carl Sandburg published his poem "The People, Yes;" Ogden Nash wrote light verse for the New Yorker magazine, Dr. Seuss delighted children with his rhyming books for youngsters learning to read, and the public speaking instructor, Dale Carnegie, wrote a book whose title *How to Win Friends and Influence People* became a part of the language.

·Big Bands and Swing

The Big Band Era is generally regarded as having occurred between the years 1935 and 1945. The popularity of jazz eclipsed all other forms of music. The appearance of Benny Goodman and his big band at the Palomar in Los Angeles in August of 1935 is often referred to as the official start of the "swing era." A Big Band is a large musical ensemble that plays various forms of jazz music. The term is synonymous with the bands of the "swing era," that were popular through the 1930s and 1940s. Music for big band is highly 'arranged', in contrast to the improvisational nature of most jazz combos. In New York, a new dance known as the Lindy Hop (named after Charles Lindbergh's famous trans-Atlantic flight) was catching on in ballrooms like the Savoy where some of its most significant adaptations occurred. A new generation was searching for their own identity, searching for excitement for something to call their own. Jazz music through its evolution into swing and these new and energetic dances offered the whole package. Although the swing phenomenum spread slowly and in small pockets at first, national publicity through radio and publications assisted in propelling this form of jazz to the pinnacle of its popularity. Leading band leaders of the Big Band and Swing Era included: Duke Ellington, Count Basie, Bob Crosby, Benny Goodman, Tommy Dorsey, Woody Hermann and a host of others. They were often accompanied by star singers like Frank Sinatra, Helen O'Connell, Bob Eberly, Ella Fitzgerald, Dick Haymes, and Helen Forrest.

UNIT XXIII
MULTIPLE-CHOICE QUESTIONS

Questions 1-3 refer to the following:

"The American experiment in self-government was now facing what was, excepting the Civil War, its greatest test.... And through [out] the world the free way of life was in retreat.... Thirty-three days before... while Franklin Roosevelt celebrated his fifty-first birthday... one hundred thousand massed Storm Troopers and National Socialist marched through the darkened streets of Berlin... waving swastika banners... Many had deserted freedom, many more had lost their nerve. But Roosevelt, armored in some inner faith, remained calm and inscrutable, confident that American improvisation could meet the future on its own terms.... He was calm and unafraid... the collapse of the older order meant catharsis, rather than catastrophe... [the] crisis could change from calamity to challenge. The only thing America had to fear was fear itself."

Arthur Schlesinger Jr., *The Crisis of the Old Order*, 1957

1. The passage above is written as Franklin Roosevelt

   (A) was ready to take the oath of office as President
   (B) contemplated signing the Atlantic Charter
   (C) prepared to meet with British Prime Minister Winston Churchill
   (D) finishes his first term as President of the United States

2. The phrase "many had deserted freedom" was a reference to

   (A) the capitulation of China to the war-lords
   (B) Fascist and totalitarian governments taking over countries in Europe
   (C) the economic crisis that loomed on the horizon as people turned to panaceas
   (D) religious uniformity imposed on everyone who was not Christian

3. The "greatest test" that Schlesinger was alluding to was

   (A) the issue of the decline in morals and values afflicting America
   (B) how to rid the world of the threat of the spread of communism
   (C) solving the economic problems of the Great Depression
   (D) helping the people of Asia and Africa achieve their independence from their colonial rulers

333

Question 4-5 refer to the following:

"Revolution ... is not for the United States. Revolution requires temper, and America is without temper. He turns on the radio and listens to the mouthings of Amos 'n' Andy. He can smile at a jest while his children fed in public schools at the expense, often, of inadequately paid school-teachers.... He can even grow enthusiastic over bootleg whiskey. He can argue that the depression hits the rich and poor alike.... As simple as a Russian peasant, in his intellectual process, he insists on an easy, simplified, quick scheme... for reconstruction. Utterly uneducated, he is ready to jump to irrational conclusions.... He believes today that political magic will save him.... As long as every American believes that he has as many chances as John D. Rockefeller to become a millionaire... he will not become a revolutionist."

George Sokolsky, "Will Revolution Come," 1932

4. From the context of the passage above it is clear that the author feels

   (A) America is ripe for revolution
   (B) the lower classes will rise up and overthrow the upper classes
   (C) the Great Depression has made the typical American so angry that he is ready to do something about it
   (D) a revolution is not possible when the typical American has such a favorable opinion of the rich

5. Which group in an earlier time period had an attitude that was similar to what Sokolsky is describing?

   (A) Sons of Liberty
   (B) African slaves
   (C) Indentured servants
   (D) Poor whites in the South

Questions 6-8 refer to the following:

"They used to tell me I was building a dream
And so I followed the mob
When there was earth to plow or guns to bear
I was always there right on the job

They used to tell me I was building a dream
With peace and glory ahead
Why should I be standing in line
Just waiting for bread

Once I built a railroad, I made it run
Made it race against time
Once I built a railroad, now it's done
Brother, can you spare a dime

Once I built a tower up to the sun
Brick and rivet and lime
Once I built a tower, now it's done
Brother, can you spare a dime?

Once in khaki suits, gee we looked swell
Full of that Yankee-Doodly-dum
Half a million boots went slogging through Hell
And I was the kid with the drum

Say, don't you remember, they called me "Al"
It was "Al" all the time
Why don't you remember, I'm your pal
Say buddy, can you spare a dime"

E.Y. Yip Harburg, "Brother, Can You Spare A Dime," 1931

6. The lyrics to this song describe conditions during the

    (A) Civil War
    (B) Trail of Tears
    (C) Great Depression
    (D) Cold War

7. Once in khaki suits, gee we looked swell
Full of that Yankee-Doodly-dum
Half a million boots went slogging through Hell
And I was the kid with the drum

    The preceding lyrics from the song are a reference to:
    (A) Spanish American War
    (B) World War I (Great War)
    (C) World War II
    (D) Korean War

8. The conditions described in the song closely resemble which economic time period in the U.S.

    (A) 1920-1925
    (B) 1942-1947
    (C) 1983-1988
    (D) 2007-2012

Questions 9-10 refer to the following:

"...the evictions in Philadelphia are frequently accompanied not only by the ghastly placing of a family's furniture on the street, but the actual sale of the family's household goods by the constable. These families are, in common Philadelphia parlance, 'sold out.'... a family of 10 had just moved in with a family of 6 in a 3-room apartment... it is an almost everyday occurrence in our midst. Neighbors do take people in. They sleep on chairs, they sleep on the floor... There is scarcely a day that calls do not come in to all of our offices to find somehow a bed or a chair. The demand for boxes on which people can sit or stretch themselves is hardly to be believed....

Dorothy Kahn, "U.S. Congress, Senate, Subcommittee on Unemployment Relief," 1931

9. Besides the time period of the Great Depression and 1930s, another era when homelessness became an issue is

    (A) during the American Revolution
    (B) in the 21st century
    (C) the 1950s
    (D) when the Civil War was taking place

10. Who is taking on the responsibility of finding shelter for the poor and the homeless in Philadelphia according to this document?

    (A) Local poor houses
    (B) State government
    (C) Religious centers
    (D) Neighbors

Questions 11-12 refer to the following:

11. The above photograph is a depiction of which 1930s event

    (A) dropping of the atomic bomb
    (B) prairie fires in the Midwest
    (C) dust bowl
    (D) anarchist fire-bombing

12. The tragic event pictured in the photograph is also described in which novel that told the story of these victims?

    (A) Margaret Mitchell's, *Gone With the Wind*
    (B) T. S. Eliot's, *The Wasteland*
    (C) Pearl S. Buck's, *The Good Earth*
    (D) John Steinbeck's, *The Grapes of Wrath*

Questions 13-15 refer to the following:

"Of all American presidents, Herbert Hoover was the most single mindedly committed to a system of beliefs. His pragmatism was well hidden, and what there was of it emerged only after great prodding from events... his... principles of individualism... prevented his sanctioning federal relief to the unemployed, [and] dictated the tone and content of his veto of the bill to create a government corporation to operate Muscle Shoals. The government... should not compete with private enterprise.... enterprises should be 'administered by the people... responsible to their own communities. Directing them solely for the benefit of their communities not for the purpose of social theories or national politics. Any other course deprives them of liberty.'"

Carl N. Degler, "The Ordeal of Herbert Hoover," 1963

13. The description of Herbert Hoover in the passage above infers that he was a (an)

(A) pragmatist
(B) progressive
(C) populist
(D) ideologue

14. The government corporation that was created under FDR at Muscle Shoals was the

(A) WPA
(B) TVA
(C) NRA
(D) CCC

15. As President, Herbert Hoover was known for his inability to deal with which problem because of his ideology?

(A) Rise of fascism in Europe
(B) Cold War
(C) Great Depression
(D) Populism

UNIT XXIV
FDR & THE NEW DEAL

The Great Depression would dominate the lives of Americans in the 1930s and lead to a transformation of American society. The relationship between the people and the government was forever changed with the adoption of the policies and programs of Franklin Delano Roosevelt called the New Deal. These programs and policies were an attempt to lessen the effects of the Great Depression and to put in place reforms that would act as automatic stabilizers against the down periods of the business cycle.

The New Deal

·Election of 1932

Franklin Delano Roosevelt, governor of New York, and distant cousin of Theodore Roosevelt, was nominated by the Democrats to face Hoover. He pledged a "new deal" (metaphor taken from cards that described the President's program) for the American people in his acceptance speech. Republicans stuck with Hoover who was overwhelmed in the Electoral College 472-59. FDR won 57% of the popular vote to Hoover's 40% and various socialist parties polled 3%.

·FDR's Philosophy

One of the reasons for the seeming inconsistency of the New Deal was that FDR did not have a specific, well-formulated, political philosophy. He governed as a pragmatist and was willing to try different approaches to any problem. If one did not work he would try another. His primary goals in taking office were to get people back to work; raise the value of agricultural products; have strict supervision of banking and investment; and put in safeguards against the return of the system that allowed the Great Depression to happen.

·Three R's

FDR would use broad executive authority to achieve the three "R's" of the New Deal—relief, recovery, and reform.

· "Brain Trust"

This was the name for a group of unofficial advisors to FDR, often from Ivy League academia, who helped him formulate his policies that became known as the New Deal. Rexford Tugwell, Raymond Moley, and Adolph Berle were prominent members of the "brain trust."

· "Lame Duck" Amendment

The 20th Amendment to the Constitution which shortened the time between an election (November) and Congress and the President taking office from March to January 3 (Congress) and January 20 (President) was passed by Congress and ratified by the states.

· Assassination Attempt

FDR was uninjured as assassin Giuseppe Zangara fired 6 shots at the presidential party and killed Mayor Anton Cermak of Chicago as well as wounding several others in Miami Beach.

· Inaugural Address

Filled with memorable phrases "the only thing we have to fear is fear itself," being a "good neighbor" in foreign policy, and "evil of the old order," it sought to inspire Americans to overcome the adversity they faced. What FDR said was not that different than what Hoover had said, but the way he said it with confidence made a difference.

"100 Days"

· 73rd Congress

"100 Days" is the name given to the special session of the 73rd Congress that passed the bulk of the New Deal legislation in just over three months. The Democratic controlled Congress was almost entirely compliant and gave the President everything he wanted.

· Bank Holiday

By calling it a Bank Holiday, FDR was trying to relieve fear and give it a positive spin when he ordered all the banks closed. This stopped people from withdrawing all of their money and ended the panic. He then signed the Emergency Banking Act that closed all of the insolvent lending institutions and allowed the Treasury Department to only reopen the solvent ones. While many lost their life savings because their banks never reopened, the panic was eased. The President was also given broad power over transactions in credit, currency, and gold and silver (could not be hoarded or exported).

· Fireside Chats

FDR was a master communicator with the American people and one of the successful techniques he used was the "fireside chat." He gave 30 of these evening radio talks to the American public straight from the White House and the addresses gave people a sense of hope and security during the difficult times of the Great Depression.

· Economy Act

In a move designed to balance the budget, government salaries were cut by 15%, veteran's pensions were reduced, and the government was re-organized. Pulling money out of the economy ran counters to what he was trying to do with his other programs that were putting money into the economy. This inconsistency did not faze FDR although it did little to help the economy.

· Beer-Wine Revenue Act

While the 18th Amendment (Prohibition) was in the process of being repealed, the Volstead Act was amended to allow the sale of 3.2% (alcoholic content) beer. It levied a tax of $5 on every barrel of wine or beer produced.

·Civilian Conservation Corps (CCC)

A program designed to tackle the problem of unemployed young men between 18 and 25 years old it is often considered the most successful of all the New Deal alphabet agencies. CCC camps were set up all over the United States with the majority of the projects in the West. The organization was based on the training program of the armed forces with officers in charge of the men. The pay was $30 dollars a month with $22 dollars of it being sent home to dependents. The men planted trees to stop soil erosion, built public parks, drained swamps to fight disease, restocked rivers with fish, worked on flood control projects and a range of other work that helped to conserve the environment. Between 1933 and 1941 over 3,000,000 men served in the CCC as it trained primarily unemployed urban youth to work in a healthy environment. Labor unions had some reservations about implementing a program with $1 a day wages but it was so successful that it basically escaped criticism.

·Federal Emergency Relief Act (FERA)

Harry Hopkins, FDR's closest advisor was chosen to head this agency that authorized $500 million in immediate grants to states for relief projects. Half of the money was given outright and the other half was distributed on a matching fund basis as states and local agencies devised the projects the money was to be spent on.

·Agricultural Adjustment Act (AAA)

It provided immediate relief to farmers by setting prices for agricultural products and paying subsidies to farmers for curtailing production of certain crops that were in surplus. It tried to eliminate the crop surplus by granting subsidies for non-production and to provide parity price supports for farm products based on their prices between 1909 and 1914. The Thomas Amendment to this bill gave the President the authority to inflate the currency by devaluing the gold content of the dollar; adopting free coinage of silver at a ratio of gold to be determined by the President; and, issue up to $3 billion in paper currency.

·Unemployment

14 million people—one quarter of the nation's work force were out of work. Apple selling on street corners symbolized the plight of the unemployed.

·Tennessee Valley Authority (TVA)

In what proved to be the most socialistic of the New Deal agencies, a public corporation was established to construct dams and power plants along the Tennessee River Valley. Electricity was produced for residents, many of whom lacked it previously, fertilizer was sold, and the agency was authorized to sell aluminum and munitions to the government. This program would revitalize a large rural area in the South affecting the states of Tennessee, Alabama, North Carolina, Georgia, Kentucky, Mississippi, and Virginia.

·Federal Securities Act (FSA)

Congress passed the Federal Securities Act in 1934. Before securities could be offered for sale they had to be accompanied by full and true information listing their assets and liabilities. The absence of information or misleading information could result in prosecution. A Federal Trade Commission was set up to supervise the stock market (replaced by the Security and Exchange Commission headed by Joseph Kennedy in 1934) and the margin requirement was changed to make it more difficult to speculate. The commission had five members and enforced the publication of stock prospectuses and the regulation of exchange practices.

·Glass Steagall Banking Act

Legislation that prohibited commercial banks from owning, underwriting, or dealing in corporate stock and corporate bonds. This separated investment banks from commercial banks to keep bankers from speculating in the stock market.

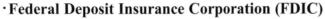

·Federal Deposit Insurance Corporation (FDIC)

Established to make sure people would never lose their life savings again if there was a run on the banks and bank closures resulted. Deposit insurance coverage initially was set at $2,500 and then raised in midyear to $5,000.

·Home Owners Refinancing Act (HOLC)

Capitalized at $200 million it allowed homeowners to exchange their mortgages for bonds with better terms to keep them from being foreclosed on. It would go out of business in June 1936 after providing loans for one million mortgages.

·National Industrial Recovery Act (NRA)

It passed on the last day of the "100 Days" Congress with a goal of stimulating competition to revive business and reduce unemployment. Based on the principle of industrial self-regulation, fair competition codes were adopted—supervised by the government—to benefit both producers and consumers by establishing fair trade. These codes were exempt from anti-trust laws and compliance was to be voluntary; those who cooperated received the blue eagle "seal of approval" and displayed the motto "we do our part."

·Section 7A

A part of the NIRA, it established the right of labor unions to collectively bargain with employers and established the National Labor Board to enforce this right.

·Public Works Administration

Established as part of the NIRA, it was authorized to supervise the construction of roads, public buildings and other projects while providing employment. Secretary of the Interior Harold Ickes, a Republican, was chosen to head the agency that was authorized to spend $3.3 million on its projects. It would ultimately spend $4.5 million on 34,000 projects that were carefully scrutinized by Ickes before they were funded.

Other Alphabet Agencies

·Civil Works Administration (CWA)

Partly because the PWA was too slow to act, this emergency relief program was created for the purpose of putting 4 million jobless to work on federal, state, and local projects and Harry Hopkins was put in charge. It was heavily criticized for spending most of its $933 million on salaries and wages for "make work" projects that were called "boondoggles."

·Farm Mortgage Refinancing Act (FMRC)

It authorized $2 billion to further the refinancing of farm debt bonds with more favorable terms.

·Gold Reserve Act of 1934

The United States nationalized gold and prohibited private gold ownership except under license. The President was empowered to devalue the gold dollar by up to 40%, a power that was exercised for the first time one day after the Act went into effect. The Federal Reserve took title to all the gold that had been collected. This act also changed the value/price of gold from $20.67 per ounce to $35 per ounce, which meant that all of the silver certificates the people had recently received for their gold now were worth 40% less.

·Securities and Exchange Commission (SEC)

This agency of the U.S. government created by the Securities Exchange Act of 1934 was charged with protecting the interest of the public and investors in connection with the public issuance and sale of securities (stocks and bonds). It would regulate the stock exchanges and Joseph Kennedy was appointed as its first chief administrator.

· **Railway Retirement (Pension) Act**

A 1934 law that provided a comprehensive retirement system for railway employees based on employer and employee contributions. This act was subsequently declared unconstitutional but it would be a forerunner of Social Security.

· **Federal Housing Administration (FHA)**

Established by the National Housing Act to insure loans for construction, renovation or repairs of houses. It would result in a permanent program to guarantee lower interest rate loans for buyers. It reduced the interest rate from 6% to 4% for those who qualified for the program.

· **Indian Reorganization Act (Wheeler-Howard), 1934**

In response to the Great Depression, John Collier (1884-1968), Commissioner of Indian Affairs in the Franklin D. Roosevelt administration, developed plans for reservation-centered relief programs and official support of tribal governments. Collier believed tribes could restore their identities and cultures through local organizations. This was accomplished through the passage of the Wheeler-Howard Act, also known as the Indian Reorganization Act, that reversed the U.S. policy favoring Indian assimilation (Dawes Act) and became the basis for United States policy that recognized the right of self-determination for Native Americans. The law curtailed the land allotment system, permitted tribes to establish formal governments with limited powers, and allowed the formation of corporations to manage tribal resources. Funds were authorized for educational assistance and to assist tribes in repurchasing tribal lands that had been lost under the Dawes Act.

Demagogues Opposed to FDR

· **American Liberty League**

A right wing organization formed in 1934 by conservative Democrats such as Al Smith (the 1928 Democratic nominee for President), members of the du Pont family, and many industrialists who believed the Roosevelt administration was leading the U.S. toward socialism, bankruptcy, and dictatorship. The League spent between half a million and $1.5 million dollars in promotional campaigns; its funding came mostly from the DuPont family who were deeply involved in a para-military plot to overthrow the government in 1934. Popular Marine General Smedley Butler came forward to the U.S. Congress in 1934 to report that a proposed coup had been plotted by wealthy industrialists to overthrow the government of President Franklin D. Roosevelt. Though the investigating congressional committee corroborated most of the specifics of his testimony, no further action was taken.

· **Huey Long**

Governor and later Senator of Louisiana (he held both jobs at once for a while), Long was a radical populist known as the "Messiah of the Rednecks," who, as governor, sponsored many reforms that endeared him to the rural poor. He ruled the state like a dictator by ending municipal government and so controlling the legislature that it once passed 44 bills in 22 minutes. An ardent enemy of corporate interests, he championed the "little man" against the rich and privileged; he was colorful, charismatic, controversial, and gave himself the nickname "Kingfish" because, he said, "I'm a small fish here in Washington. But I'm the Kingfish to the folks down in Louisiana." Huey Long was the determined enemy of Wall Street, bankers and big business whom he thought controlled FDR. His goal was for government to confiscate the wealth of the nation's rich and privileged. He called his program "Share Our Wealth" and it called upon the federal government to guarantee every family in the nation an annual income of $5,000, so they could have the necessities of life, including a home, a job, a radio, and an automobile. He also proposed limiting private fortunes to $5 million, legacies to $5 million, and annual incomes to $1 million. Everyone over age 60 would receive an old-age pension. His slogan was "Every Man A King" and he was a real threat to FDR's New Deal. The threat ended when Long was assassinated by Dr. Carl Weiss, in Baton Rouge in 1935.

·Father Coughlin

Starting in 1926 and lasting until 1941, Father Coughlin broadcasted weekly sermons over the radio. By the early 1930s the content of his broadcasts had shifted from theology to economics and politics. He began as an early Roosevelt supporter, coining a famous expression, that the nation's choice was between "Roosevelt or Ruin." Later in the 1930s he turned against FDR over his agricultural policy and the U.S. joining the World Court. He became one of the president's harshest critics. His popular following raised huge amounts of contributions, as he was getting 80,000 letters a week, for his "Shrine of the Little Flower." His money solutions endeared him to Mid-western farmers as he wanted to nationalize the banks and have an inflationary monetary system. His broadcast had strains of anti-Semitism and the Catholic Church had trouble controlling him.

·Francis Townsend

Was a 66-year-old retired physician who developed a plan in which the government would impose a 2% sales tax to provide seniors a monthly income of $200 provided that they spent the money in the same month. He argued that turning the nation's elderly population into robust consumers would solve the underlying problem of weak demand. "Townsend Clubs" sprang up across the country as his message of care for the elderly meshed with people's desire for a panacea for hard times. In 1934, he set up the Old-Age Revolving Pensions organization, headed by Robert Clement who ran a PR campaign that gained followers across the nation. FDR's adoption of Social Security pre-empted Townsend by providing old age insurance but there is no question that Townsend pushed FDR in the direction of Social Security.

Second New Deal

·Origins

In the face of these pressures from left and right, President Roosevelt backed a new set of economic and social measures. Prominent among these were measures to fight poverty, to counter unemployment with work, and to provide a social safety net. Whereas, the First New Deal had concentrated its energies on relief and recovery programs, the Second New Deal had a decidedly reform element to it.

·Works Progress Administration (WPA)

The ideas of the British economist John Maynard Keynes were finally imbedded into the New Deal through this program. Harry Hopkins was chosen to lead the WPA, a massive agency created in 1935 by a $5 billion public works bill. It expanded the New Deal programs to put the unemployed to work on public works projects that primarily (90%) employed unskilled blue-collar workers in construction projects across the nation. It also employed some white-collar artists, musicians, photographers and writers on smaller-scale projects. More than 3/4ths of both the employment and expenditures went to public facilities such as highways, streets, public buildings, schools, airports, utilities, bridges (including the Golden Gate), sewers, parks, libraries, bookbinding, sidewalks, and recreational fields. The WPA built 650,000 miles of roads, 78,000 bridges, 125,000 buildings, and 875 miles of airport runways. Only 7% percent of the budget was allocated to arts projects that presented 225,000 concerts to audiences totaling 150 million, and produced almost 475,000 works of art. It became the most widely criticized of the New Deal agencies for the huge amount of money spent, over $11 billion in all, and the fact that "make work" boondoggle projects were sometimes funded to get money into the hands of the unemployed. The 7% spent on art projects were widely criticized as a waste of money by conservatives.

·Rural Electrification Administration (REA)

Morris Cooke led the Rural Electrification Administration to build electrical systems in rural areas, and make loans to farmers to adopt labor saving electrical appliances. The percentage of electrified farms in the nation increased from 10% in 1935 to 40% in 1941.

·National Youth Administration (NYA)

This program was designed to help youth in urban settings just as the CCC helped youth with rural areas.

·Wagner Act or National Labor Relations Act of 1935

Officially the Wagner-Connery Labor Relations Act it is sometimes called the "*Magna Carta*" of labor unions. This 1935 law was designed to satisfy the complaints of labor organizations against provisions of the Recovery Act of 1933 as it affected them, and also to remedy their disappointment at losing the advantages of collective bargaining by the invalidation of the NRA and section 7A by the Supreme Court. The act declared it the policy of the U.S. to encourage collective bargaining and to protect employees' freedom of self-organization their employment as to their employment through representatives of their own choosing. A New National Labor Relations Board was created to enforce the provisions of this law.

·Social Security

In part due to the pressure from Long and Townsend, the Social Security Act was passed by Congress in 1935 to provide unemployment insurance and establish old age pensions. This would be done through a tax levied on employers and a retirement system based on contributions from both employers and employees. By this act, responsibility for unemployment was returned to the states as a joint federal-state program, financed by an "offset" tax that allowed states to collect 90% of the tax themselves and run their own programs. This type of system had been in place in other countries since Otto Von Bismarck had introduced them into Germany in the 1880s.

·Revenue Act of 1935 (Wealth Tax Act)

This so-called "soak the rich" scheme attempted to achieve a wider distribution of wealth by changing the federal tax structure, increasing estate and gift taxes, and making sure corporations paid at least 13% of their income in taxes regardless of their profits. These new taxes were highly progressive and took up to 75% of the incomes over one million and increased the surtax rate on individual incomes that were above $50,000. FDR was considered a trader to his class (the rich) by these actions and he was vigorously opposed by most wealthy people in the election of 1936.

Politics, Individuals, and the Court

·*Schecter Poultry Corp. v. United States*

In this so-called "sick chicken" case the Supreme Court ruled unanimously that the NIRA Act of 1933 was unconstitutional on the grounds that the NIRA codes gave power to the Executive that belonged with Congress. A major setback to the New Deal, it is the first of many Supreme Court decisions that would go against FDR and lead to his court-packing proposal of 1937.

·*U.S. v. Butler*

Supreme Court ruled 6-3 that the Agricultural Adjustment Act was unconstitutional on the grounds that the act did not levy a tax but tried to control production, exceeding government responsibilities.

·Election of 1936

The Republicans, not saddled with Hoover, were confident as they nominated Governor Alf Landon (the Kansas Coolidge) for president. Their platform condemned the New Deal and charged that regulated monopoly had replaced free enterprise. The Democrats re-nominated both FDR and Vice-President John Nance Garner and FDR prophetically predicted in his acceptance speech, "To some generations much is given. Of other generations much is expected. This generation of Americans has a "rendezvous with destiny." The saying as Maine goes so goes the nation was changed to as Maine goes so goes Vermont. FDR won the Electoral

College 523-8 taking every state but Maine and Vermont. The Democrats increased their overwhelming majorities in Congress to 76-16 in the Senate and 331-89 in the House.

·Court Packing

After his landslide victory, FDR lambasted the justices of the Supreme Court for eviscerating his programs. "We have been relegated to the horse-and-buggy definition of interstate commerce," he complained about the "Nine Old Men"—six justices were age 70 or older, and the youngest was 61. Re-elected to a second term by an even larger majority than in 1932, and given an even larger Democratic majority in Congress, Roosevelt, had been the only 20th-century president not to have appointed a Supreme Court justice in four years. He came up with a solution to "the court problem." He called for all federal judges to retire by age 70. If they failed to do so, the president could appoint another judge to serve in tandem with each one older than 70. Roosevelt could have appointed six more Supreme Court justices increasing the size of the court to 15 members. Opposition immediately surfaced even from his friends and a committee of Congress issued a scathing report that called FDR's plan "a needless, futile and utterly dangerous abandonment of constitutional principle … without precedent or justification." The Senate voted 70-20 to send his judicial-reform measure back to committee, where all the controversial language was stripped from it. FDR's "court-packing scheme" robbed him of much of the political capital he had won in two landslide elections. But to some extent, the president lost the battle but won his war with the Supreme Court. First, the court's philosophy began to change even as Congress debated the merits of judicial reform. Owen J. Roberts, the youngest jurist, began to vote Roosevelt's way in close decisions, giving FDR 5-4 wins rather than losses by the same margin. Then before long, the "Nine Old Men" began to retire of their own volition, enabling the president to appoint a "Roosevelt Court." Prominent, liberal, judicial minds like Felix Frankfurter, Hugo Black, and William O. Douglas began to replace the "old guard" bringing about a fundamental change in the Supreme Court.

·Eleanor Roosevelt

Married to her fifth cousin once removed, Franklin Roosevelt, Eleanor Roosevelt shattered the ceremonial mold in which the role of the "First Lady" had traditionally been fashioned. She became her husband's "eyes and ears," traveling around the country and gathering the grass-roots knowledge he needed to understand the people he was leading. She gave a voice to people who did not have access to power and was the first "First Lady" to speak in front of a national convention, write a syndicated column, earn money as a lecturer, be a radio commentator and hold regular press conferences. Her talents for public speaking, organizing, and articulating social problems made her the conscience of the New Deal. She was involved in a variety of reform organizations, dedicated to the abolition of child labor, the establishment of a minimum wage, the passage of legislation to protect workers and the underclass, and civil rights for African Americans.

·Francis Perkins

As Secretary of Labor for the 12 years of Franklin D. Roosevelt's presidency, and the first woman to hold a Cabinet post, she brought to her office a deep commitment to improving the lives of workers. Serving as the first Labor Secretary after passage of the Wagner Act her role influenced the political agenda of the administration by moving it closer to the values of economic justice and security for all.

UNIT XXIV
MULTIPLE-CHOICE QUESTIONS

Questions 1-4 refer to the following:

"Perhaps the most striking alteration in American thought which the depression fostered concerned the role of government in the economy. Buffeted and bewildered by the economic debacle, the American people in the course of the 1930's abandoned, once and for all, the doctrine of laissez faire. This beau ideal of the nineteenth century economists had become, ever since the days of Jackson, an increasingly cherished shibboleth of Americans. But now it was almost casually discarded. It is true that the rejection of laissez faire had a long history; certainly the Populists worked to undermine it. But with the depression the nation at large accepted the government as a permanent influence in the economy...."

Carl Degler, *Out of Our Past*, 1959

1. By discarding *laissez faire* the United States was abandoning which philosophy that had dominated the country since the post-bellum 19th century?

   (A) Agrarianism of Thomas Jefferson
   (B) States' rights sectionalism
   (C) Social Darwinism
   (D) Social Gospel

2. Besides the Populist another group not mentioned that worked to undermine some aspects of *laissez faire* at the turn of the century were the

   (A) Federalist
   (B) Neoconservatives
   (C) Plutocrats
   (D) Progressives

3. The economic debacle that "buffeted and bewildered" Americans in the 1930s was the

   (A) coming of World War II
   (B) Great Depression
   (C) growth of Labor Unions
   (D) Gospel of Wealth

4. The program that led to the dismantling of the "beau ideal" of 19th century economists is called the

   (A) New Deal
   (B) Great Society
   (C) Fair Deal
   (D) New Frontier

347

To Answer Questions 5-7 refer to the chart below:

Economics

	Unemployment	GNP	Consumer Prices	Manufacturing	Investment	Stocks
1929	3.2	104.4[a]	73.3[b]	58[b]	16.2[c]	260.2[d]
1930	8.7	95.1	71.4	48	10.3	210.3
1931	15.9	89.5	65.0	39	5.5	136.6
1932	23.6	76.4	58.4	30	.9	69.3
1933	24.9	74.2	55.3	36	1.4	89.6
1934	21.7	80.8	57.2	39	2.9	98.4
1935	20.1	91.4	58.7	46	6.3	106.0
1936	16.9	100.9	59.3	55	8.4	154.7
1937	14.3	109.1	61.4	60	11.9	154.1
1938	19.0	103.2	60.3	46	6.7	114.9
1939	17.2	111.0	59.4	57	9.3	120.6
1940	14.6	121.0	59.9	66	13.2	110.2
1941	9.9	138.7	62.9	88	18.1	98.2

[a] $ Billions in 1929 Prices
[b] 1947-49 = 100 bse
[c] Gross Private Domestic Investment ($ Billions)
[d] Average Prices of Stocks (1941-43 = 100)

5. This chart leaves out what important economic indicator that comprises half of the "misery index" in modern economic analysis?

(A) Labor productivity
(B) Salary and wages
(C) Inflation Rate
(D) Return on Capital

6. Using the chart an economic observation that could be supported by the data is

(A) improvement in the economy lasted until 1938 when a sharp downturn occurred that was especially severe with the rise of unemployment and the fall in manufacturing
(B) stocks and investments moved steadily upward equaling the pre-depression highs by 1940
(C) the consumer price index showed a steady drop in prices for each year in the 1930s
(D) unemployment finally reached its pre-depression lows in 1941

7. All of the following economic indicators had a greater value in 1941 than they did in 1929 EXCEPT

(A) GNP
(B) Investments
(C) Manufacturing
(D) Stocks

Questions 8-9 refer to the following:

A SHORT WEIGHT ARTIST

SOCIAL SECURITY ACT

OLD AGE INSURANCE

CONGRESS

Special

Townsend Weekly, May 25, 1940

8. The cartoon above is trying to suggest that

   (A) the Social Security Act passed by Congress is not adequate to the needs of the elderly

   (B) applauds Franklin Delano Roosevelt for his New Deal program

   (C) argues that government bureaucracy denies qualified old people from getting what they need

   (D) speculates that the approaching cost for military preparedness requires cut-backs in the aid given to the elderly poor

9. The idea for the Old Age Insurance part of the Social Security Act came from which of the following?

   (A) Huey Long's, Share the Wealth Plan

   (B) Father Coughlin's National Union for Social Justice

   (C) Liberty League's Program

   (D) Dr. Francis Townsend's Plan for Old Age Pensions

Questions 10-12 refer to the following:

"In the field of racial equality, where there was no crisis as in economics... there was no "new deal..." the permanent caste structure remained unaltered by the kind of innovations that at least threatened the traditional edifice in economics. The white South was left, as it had been since the Compromise of 1877, to deal with Negroes as it chose—by murder, by beatings, by ruthless exclusion from political and economic life; the Fourteenth Amendment waited as fruitlessly for executive enforcement as it had in all earlier administrations since Grant.... The warm belief in equal rights held by Eleanor Roosevelt, as well as FDR himself... could have led to important accomplishments but the clear goal of ending segregation, as with comparable objectives in economics, was never established."

Howard Zinn, "Middle-Class America Refurbished," 1966

10. The passage above points to a fundamental difference between the New Deal and which other reform movement over the issue of civil rights?

(A) Populism
(B) Progressivism
(C) Great Society
(D) New Federalism

11. Zinn laments the fact that the 14th Amendment was not used to end segregation and this would not occur until which Supreme Court case unanimously overthrew the "separate but equal doctrine"?

(A) *Brown vs. the Board of Education of Topeka, Kansas*
(B) *Plessy vs Ferguson*
(C) *Regents of the University of California v. Bakke*
(D) *Griswold v. Connecticut*

12. Where the New Deal innovations threatened the elaborate social structure and foundation of the economy the edifice that remained untouched was the

(A) social system
(B) caste structure
(C) hegemony of the business class
(D) government bureaucracy

Questions 13-15 refer to the following:

13. The political cartoon above is directed against FDR's

    (A) alphabet agencies passed by Congress in 100 Days
    (B) court packing plan for the Supreme Court
    (C) mindless actions against the institutions of government
    (D) attempts to change the architectural structure of buildings

14. The cartoonist is critical of FDR for trying to

    (A) demonstrate his physical strength
    (B) act like a biblical figure
    (C) tear down the twin pillars of democracy
    (D) appeal to the masses for support for his program

15. The two New Deal agencies that the court had declared unconstitutional in the Schechter and Butler cases that especially enraged FDR were the

    (A) NRA & AAA
    (B) TVA & REA
    (C) Social Security & FDIC
    (D) WPA & CCC

UNIT XXV
EVENTS LEADING TO WWII

After the ordeal of the Great Depression, the generation that Tom Brokaw would name the "Greatest Generation" would find themselves facing a world war. The events leading up to what would be called World War II comprise the foreign policy of the 1930s and the war itself would last until 1945. A generation of Americans would know nothing but depression and war for more than 15 years. Their fortitude and ability to endure earned them the title the "Greatest Generation."

Latin American Diplomacy

·Good Neighbor Policy
FDR continued Hoover's policy of having better relations with Latin America and even gave it a name in his first inaugural when he said, "In the field of world policy I would dedicate this nation to the policy of the good neighbor." No longer would "big stick" or "gunboat diplomacy" be the order of the day in the relations between the U.S. and Latin America.

·Montevideo Conference
Secretary of State Cordell Hull supported the declaration that said, "No state has the right to intervene in the internal or external affairs of another" that was unanimously adopted at the conference. This was a complete repudiation of the Roosevelt Corollary to the Monroe Doctrine.

·London Economic Conference
FDR refused to support currency stabilization of the gold-block nations (France, Belgium, Switzerland, Italy, and the Netherlands) and limited U.S. participation to a discussion of bilateral tariff treaties. This FDR announcement effectively scuttled the conference and signified the U.S. drift toward isolationism in foreign affairs.

·Modification of the Platt Amendment
During the midst of a revolution and civil war, Cuban conservatives led by U.S. backed dictator Fulgencio Batista negotiated a treaty that removed previous limitations on Cuban sovereignty. Furthermore, Sumner Welles negotiated the Jones-Costigan Sugar Control Act that reduced and stabilized duties on Cuban sugar.

·Buenos Aires Conference
Attended by FDR, who declared in his opening remarks that this hemisphere was "wholly prepared to consult together for our mutual safety and our mutual good" if threatened by non-American states.

·Declaration of Lima
It reaffirmed the sovereignty of the American states and expressed the determination to resist "all foreign intervention." It also provided for consultation between the nations if the "peace, security, or territorial integrity" of any country was threatened.

·Mexico and the Expropriation Settlement
Under Lazaro Cardenas, Mexico had nationalized the properties of British and U.S. oil companies. Secretary of State Hull insisted on fair compensation for the expropriation, which would amount to $450 billion according to the oil companies. Ultimately two U.S. oil companies would get approximately $34 billion for their claims but the issue would be settled.

Diplomacy with Europe

·Recognition of the USSR
Following the fall of the Alexander Kerensky government to the Bolsheviks in 1917 the U.S. refused to recognize the government of the USSR. FDR changed this in 1933 by granting recognition based on the Soviets pledge to refrain from interfering in the domestic affairs of the U.S. and granting religious freedom to U.S. citizens in Russia. Neither of these stipulations were honored by the Soviet Union but *de jure* recognition remained.

·Johnson Debt Default Act
It kept the U.S. from making loans to countries who were in default (WWI debt) which meant only Finland could receive loans as they were the only one not in default.

·Nye Investigation
Senator Gerald Nye of North Dakota headed a Senate Committee Investigating the U.S. involvement in the Great War and concluded that the "Merchants of Death," consisting of American bankers and arms merchants were responsible for it in their quest to make money. This committee strengthened isolationism, led to the U.S. abandonment of its traditional policy in support of neutral rights, and led to the various neutrality acts of the 1930s.

·Neutrality Acts
1. **Neutrality Act of 1935**—After Italy invaded Ethiopia the President was authorized to prohibit arms shipments to nations at war. Also, U.S. citizens traveling on belligerent vessels did so at their own risk. FDR signed it but complained it would "drag us into war instead of keeping us out."
2. **Neutrality Act of 1936**—Extended the Act of 1935 and forbid the extension of loans or credits to belligerents.

3. **Neutrality Acts of 1937**—In response to the Spanish Civil War between the Fascist Falange and the Popular Front government of the Republic, Congress passed a joint resolution forbidding the export of munitions to either side in Spain. This worked against the Republic as the *Falange* could get all the arms they needed from fellow Fascist states Germany and Italy. Another feature of the resolution was that other products had to be paid for on delivery.

·Reciprocal Trade Agreements

Under leadership of FDR and Cordell Hull, Congress passed the Reciprocal Trade Agreements Act that gave the President the authority to lower tariff rates by 50% without Congressional approval. Hull worked out reciprocity agreements with 21 nations by 1939.

·Quarantine of Aggressor Speech

In a speech at the isolationist "hot bed" of Chicago, FDR urged that the only means of preserving peace was to have the international community quarantine the aggressors. Public opinion turned against FDR, as isolationism still dominated the U.S.

·Ludlow Amendment

This Resolution by Representative Louis Ludlow of Indiana was introduced into Congress a number of times. It proposed a constitutional amendment that would have prohibited a congressional declaration of war unless it was confirmed by a nationwide referendum. The only exception was if the U.S. or its territorial possessions were invaded. FDR used his influence to have the resolution returned to committee by a close vote of 209-188. Republicans and Democrats from western states supported the resolution.

Dictators in Europe and International Events

·Germany Violated the Versailles Treaty

After rising to power legally the National Socialists under Adolph Hitler proceeded to violate the Treaty of Versailles by adopting compulsory military service in 1935 and marching troops into the supposed demilitarized Rhineland in 1936.

·Nuremberg Laws (1936-1939)

Laws adopted by the Nazi's after gaining power in Germany that denied citizenship to the Jews. The Law for the Protection of German Blood and German Honor prohibited marriages and extra-marital intercourse between Jews and Germans and also the employment of German females under 45 years old in Jewish households. The Reich Citizenship Law stripped Jews of their German citizenship and introduced a new distinction between "Reich citizens (Germans)" and "nationals." By 1936, Jews were prohibited from participation in parliamentary elections and signs reading "Jews Not Welcome" appeared in many German cities (these signs were taken down in the late summer in preparation for the 1936 Olympic Games in Berlin). In the first half of 1938, numerous laws were passed restricting Jewish economic activity and occupational opportunities. A law was passed (effective January 1, 1939) requiring all Jews to carry identification cards.

·Spanish Civil War (1936-1939)

On the outbreak of the Spanish Civil War, FDR declared that the United States government would remain neutral in the conflict. The U.S. also took measures to restrict its citizens from selling arms to the Nationalists or the Republicans. However, some Americans did take part in the fighting to stop the Fascist (Nationalist) from taking over Spain. The Abraham Lincoln Battalion was established by Americans fighting for the Republic. It was a part of the International Brigade consisting of nationals of other countries fighting the Fascist. An estimated 3,000 men fought in the battalion and these included over 1,000 industrial workers (miners, steel workers, longshoremen) and 500 students or teachers. About 30% were Jewish and 70% were between 21 and

28 years of age. The majority were members of the American Communist Party; whereas, others came from the Socialist Party of America and the Socialist Labor Party. The Abraham Lincoln Battalion suffered heavy casualties at Jarama and by the end of the Spanish Civil War, there were only 150 American soldiers left in that battalion. Over the course of the war over one-third of the volunteers from the United States had been killed. In the end it was to no avail as the help that Francisco Franco and the *Falange* received from Germany and Italy enabled him to defeat the Republic and establish Fascism in Spain that would last from 1939 to 1976.

·Appeasement

This term describes the policy of giving into the demands of the Fascist dictators in order to stave off war in Europe. British Prime Minister Neville Chamberlain was its chief architect and French Prime Minister Eduard Daladier its chief supporter. It fit in well with the U.S. policy of isolationism. Chamberlain genuinely believed that Germany had been badly treated by the Allies after it was defeated in the Great War. He therefore thought that the German government had genuine grievances and that these needed to be addressed. He also thought that by agreeing to some of the demands being made by Adolf Hitler of Germany and Benito Mussolini of Italy, he could avoid a European war.

·Italy's Invasion of Ethiopia (1935)

There was little international protest to Benito Mussolini when he sent large numbers of troops to Eritrea and Italian Somaliland, two colonies of Italy that bordered Ethiopia on the North and Southeast, in anticipation of invading Halle Selassie's kingdom. In a war that lasted seven months, Ethiopia was outmatched by Italy in armaments—a situation exacerbated by the fact that a League of Nations arms embargo was not enforced against Italy. Gaining revenge for their defeat at Adua (Adowa) in the First Italy-Abyssinian War of 1896, Italy's victory was the first direct military act of aggression by a European fascist state.

·*Kristallnacht*

A pogrom that came to be called *Kristallnacht* (the Night of Broken Glass) occurred in Germany on the nights of November 9 and 10, 1938. Gangs of Nazi youth roamed through Jewish neighborhoods breaking windows of Jewish businesses and homes, burning synagogues, and looting. In all 101 synagogues and almost 7,500 Jewish businesses were destroyed. 26,000 Jews were arrested and sent to concentration camps. Jews were physically attacked and beaten and 91 died. The official German position on these events, which were clearly orchestrated by Minister of Propaganda Joseph Goebbels, was that they were spontaneous outbursts.

·*Anschluss*

In defiance of the Treaty of Versailles, Germany annexed Austria in 1938 while the western powers who were supposed to guarantee Austrian independence did nothing. Many pro-NAZI Austrians welcomed the unification with Germany (Anschluss).

·Munich Pact (1938)

Hitler's demand for the Sudetenland part of Czechoslovakia was agreed to by Chamberlain and Daladier at the Munich Conference in 1938. The Munich Agreement was popular with most people in Britain because it appeared to have prevented a war with Nazi Germany—"peace in our time" was how Chamberlain described it. However, some politicians, including Winston Churchill and Anthony Eden, attacked the agreement. These critics pointed out that not only had the British government behaved dishonorably, but it had lost the support of the Czech Army, one of the best in Europe. When Eduard Benes, Czechoslovakia's head of state, protested this decision, Neville Chamberlain told him that Britain would be unwilling to go to war over the issue of the Sudetenland. The German Army marched into the Sudetenland in October of 1938 and was welcomed by the cheering Germans in that region. As this area contained nearly all the Czechoslovakian's mountain fortifications, it was no longer able to defend itself against further aggression. By March 1939, the whole of Czechoslovakia was under the control of Germany and Hitler's promise of no more territorial acquisitions after the Sudetenland was proven to be a lie. The Czech Army was disbanded and the Germans took control of the country's highly developed arms industry. Hungary and Poland participated in the dismemberment as each took large sections of Czechoslovakia.

·Italy and Albania

As Germany annexed Austria and moved against Czechoslovakia, Italy saw itself becoming a second-rate member of the Axis. After Hitler invaded Czechoslovakia without notifying Mussolini in advance, the Italian dictator decided, in early 1939, to proceed with his own annexation of the neighboring Balkan state of Albania. Despite some stubborn resistance, especially at Durrës, the Italians took over the country and King Zog and his family went to London and established an Albanian government in exile. This would be the first of many governments established in exile in London.

·Germany-USSR Non Aggression Pact

In 1939, Hitler was preparing for war and was planning against the possibility of a two front war. Since fighting a two front war in the Great War had split Germany's forces, and weakened them, this played a large role in Germany losing. Hitler was determined not to repeat the same mistake. German Foreign Minister Joachim von Ribbentrop contacted the USSR to arrange a deal. Ribbentrop met with the Soviet Foreign Minister Vyacheslav Molotov in Moscow and together they arranged two pacts—an economic agreement and a Nazi-Soviet Non-Aggression Pact. The economic agreement committed the Soviet Union to provide food products and raw materials to Germany in exchange for finished products such as machinery. Publicly, this agreement stated that the two countries would not attack each other. If there were ever a problem between the two countries it was to be handled amicably. A secret protocol held an agreement between the Nazis and Soviets that greatly affected Eastern Europe. For the Soviets for agreeing to not join a possible future war against Germany, Germany gave the Soviets the Baltic States (Estonia, Latvia, and Lithuania). Poland was also to be divided between the two countries along the Vistula, and San Rivers. These new territories gave the Soviet Union the buffer (in land) that it wanted to feel safe from an invasion from the West. It also provided Hitler with some assurance that his eastern flank would not be attacked if he launched a war against France.

·Fate of the *St. Louis* (1939)

After *Kristallnacht*, (see page 360) many Jews within Germany decided that it was time to leave. It was difficult to get out of Germany but a group boarded the passenger ship *St. Louis*, which was to take Jewish refugees from Germany to Cuba. Once the refugees arrived in Cuba they would await their quota number to be able to enter the United States. After arriving in Havana harbor the Cuban cabinet met and decided the passengers aboard the *St. Louis* would not be allowed to land, not even 250 to allow room for return passengers. The ship cruised around Cuba and then headed north as negotiations continued on what to do with the refugees. The ship followed the Florida coastline in the hope that the United States would accept the refugees. There were talks of allowing the ship to land at the Isle of Pines or even the Dominican Republic. None of this worked out and the ship was ordered to return to Germany. Several countries took some of the refugees after it returned to Hamburg—181 to Holland, 224 to France, 228 to Great Britain, and 214 to Belgium. Having crossed the Atlantic Ocean twice, the passengers' original hopes of freedom in Cuba and the U.S. turned into a tragedy as they returned to Germany. Rejected by the world, many of the passengers would be put into concentration camps and were executed in the Holocaust.

East Asia

·Mukden Incident

After a skirmish with Chinese soldiers, Japan occupied Manchuria and set up the puppet government of Manchuko under the last heir to the Ching (Manchu) dynasty, Henry Pu Yi in 1931. Since offensive war had been outlawed by the Kellogg-Briand Pact, aggression by one nation against another was called an "incident."

·Tydings-McDuffie Act

Also known as the Philippines Independence Act, it was approved in 1934 and provided for the independence of the Philippines by 1946. During the transitional intervening time period the U.S. would keep military forces in the Philippines and the President was granted power to call into service all military forces of the Philippines. U.S. naval bases would be maintained until 1947. Also, as a part of this act was the reclassification of all Filipinos as aliens for the purpose of immigration to the United States with a quota of fifty immigrants per year.

·Japan Invades China

The Second Sino-Japanese War (1937–1945) was a major war between the Republic of China and the Empire of Japan, both before and during World War II. The Japanese invasion was a strategic move made by the Imperial Japanese Army as part of their large-scale plan to control Asia as a part of their "New Order in East Asia" plan, also called the Co-Prosperity Sphere. The early battles were commonly known as "incidents" supposedly provoked by China, in order to downplay Japan's illegality in these invasions. The 1931 invasion of Manchuria by Japan was referred to as the "Mukden Incident." The last of these was the "Marco Polo Bridge Incident of 1937," marking the official beginning of full- scale war between the two countries. Shanghai was taken after a bitter battle and the European community so prominent there had to abandon the city. From 1937 to 1941, China fought alone against Japan. After the attack on Pearl Harbor, the Second Sino-Japanese War merged into the greater conflict of World War II..

·Rape of Nanjing

After having lost the Battle of Shanghai, Chiang Kai-shek knew the fall of Nanjing (Nanking) was simply a matter of time. Chiang and many of his advisors flew to Chongqing (Chungking), which would become China's capital for the next seven years. After two days of Japanese attack, under heavy artillery fire and aerial bombardment, the army retreated and that turned into a rout. Chaos ensued as soldiers stripped the clothes off of civilians in an attempt to blend in and others were shot in the back as they attempted to flee. The Japanese entered the walled capital city of Nanjing, free of any military resistance. For six weeks following the fall of Nanjing, Japanese troops engaged in rape, murder, theft, and arson. An American missionary, John Magee, was able provide film documentation and first-hand photos of the massacre. The International Military Tribunal for the Far East later stated that 20,000 to 80,000 women were raped. Rapes were often performed in public, sometimes in front of spouses or family members. A large number of the rapes were systematized where soldiers would search door-to-door for young girls. After being taken captive and gang raped the women were then killed, often by mutilation. Most estimates of the Nanking Massacre range from 200,000 to 400,000 killed. Besides the civilian killings, the Japanese army did not take prisoners of war and captured and surrendered Chinese soldiers were executed after combat.

·Panay Incident

On December 12, 1937 Japanese planes bombed a U.S. gunboat on the Yangtze River in China. The ship sank as 2 sailors were killed and 30 wounded. Japan and the United States were not at war at the time. The Japanese claimed that they did not see the United States flags painted on the deck of the gunboat, apologized, and paid an indemnity. Nevertheless, the attack and reports of the "Nanjing Massacre" caused U.S. opinion to turn sharply against the Japanese.

World War II in Europe

·Germany invaded Poland (1939)

World War II official began when Germany invaded Poland on September 1, 1939. At the beginning of the attack, Great Britain and France sent Hitler an ultimatum—withdraw German forces from Poland or Great Britain and France would go to war against Germany. On September 3, with Germany's forces penetrating deeper into Poland, Great Britain and France both declared war on Germany. Utilizing a new type of warfare, Poland would fall within a month. The term *"blitzkrieg"* ("lightning war") was coined by newspapermen to convey the rapid and mechanized air and land attack on Poland.

· U.S. Neutrality
FDR responded to the outbreak of war in a fireside chat when he said the U.S. would remain a neutral nation but he could not ask every American to be "neutral in thought."

· Occupation of the Baltic States
After the occupation and partition of Poland, the Soviet Union started pressuring Finland, Estonia, Latvia, and Lithuania to accept territorial changes and Soviet bases on their soil. Eventually all the states except Finland signed pacts of "defense and mutual assistance," which permitted the Soviet Union to station troops on their land. In June of 1941 these three countries would be incorporated into the USSR where they would remain until the USSR broke apart in the early 1990s. The takeover of the Baltic states had been agreed to by Germany and the USSR in a secret part of the von Ribbentrop-Molotov Agreement.

· Russo-Finnish War
After World War II broke out the USSR, still angry from the loss of Finland as a colony as a result of WWI, took advantage of its nonaggression pact with Germany to make several far-reaching demands on Finland. These demands included the demilitarization of the Mannerheim Line (the Finnish fortification line across the Karelian Isthmus), a 30-year lease on Hanko as a naval base, and the cession of several islands in the Gulf of Finland. In return, Russia offered extensive but valueless districts along the eastern border of Finland. Finland balked and the USSR, denouncing the Russo-Finnish nonaggression pact of 1932, attacked Finland on November 30, 1939. The Russians first concentrated their efforts on the eastern border of Finland, but the Finns, superior in winter warfare and ably commanded by Field Marshall Karl Mannerheim, repulsed the attacks. World sympathy was with Finland, especially in the U.S. because the Finns were the only people to pay their WWI war debt to the U.S. Sweden and Norway sent volunteers and supplies, and some supplies came from France and Great Britain. Finally, however, small Finland was no match for the USSR. Air bombardments and frontal attacks on the Karelian Isthmus brought about a peace treaty March 12, 1940. Finland ceded part of the Karelian Isthmus, Vyborg (Viipuri), and several border territories to the USSR.

· *"Sitzkrieg"* or Phony War
For 6 months after the fall of Poland both sides sat behind their defensive lines (*Maginot* in France and *Siegfried* in Germany) and dropped leaflets instead of bombs to convince the other side to get out of the war.

· Denmark and Norway
The inactivity ended when Germany marched into Denmark on April 9, 1940, occupying it without a fight. The primary reason for Germany invading Norway was Germany's dependence on Swedish iron ore shipped from the Norwegian port of Narvik. By securing access to Norwegian ports, Germany could obtain the iron ore supply it needed for war production in spite of the British naval blockade. The Danes hid or helped to escape their 7,500 Jews to keep them from being shipped to the concentration camp Theresienstadt. The French and the British came to the defense of Norway, which was the first actual fighting on land between the Axis and Allies. The battle for Narvik went back and forth and by May 28th, the Allies had succeeded in recapturing it from German forces; but the German invasion of France and the Low Countries led to the general Allied retreat from Norway as it soon surrendered to the Germans and the occupation began.

· Vidkun Quisling
The first of the collaborators who would work with the Nazi occupiers was a Norwegian fascist politician and officer Vidkun Quisling. After the Allies withdrew he staged a coup and held the office of Minister President

in occupied Norway from February 1942 to the end of World War II. The King and the elected Social Democratic cabinet of Johan Nygaardsvold went into exile in London. Quisling's name became synonymous with traitor and a strong resistance movement that required 400,000 German troops to control existed in Norway. Norway, during the occupation opposed this "puppet government" and Quisling was executed by a firing squad after the war.

·Low Countries and France
In less than a month Belgium, the Netherlands, and Luxembourg were for would be overrun and France, with a larger army than Germany, would fall in 12 days. The Maginot line proved useless once the Germans went around it by going through Belgium and getting behind it. Italy invaded southern France after the Germans had effectively disabled the French military.

·Dunkirk
In what the British call a "miracle," 338,226 British and French troops, surrounded by the German army on the coast of France, were evacuated from the French coast to Great Britain by 861 vessels, mostly privately owned, that came from England.

·Occupied and Vichy France
The armistice with Germany divided France into occupied and unoccupied zones. The Germans would directly control three-fifths of the country, an area that included northern and western France and the entire Atlantic coast. The remaining southern part of the country would be administered by the French government at Vichy, under 83 year old Henri Petain. Other provisions of the armistice included the surrender of all Jews living in France to the Germans. Over the next four years Henri-Philippe Petain led the right-wing government of Vichy France. The famous revolutionary principles of "Liberty, Equality, Fraternity" were replaced by "Work, Family, Fatherland." Prominent figures in the collaborationist Vichy government included Pierre Laval and Jean-Francois Darlan. Vichy retained control of the French colonies. An exiled Free French government would be established in London under Charles De Gaulle. The French underground or resistance, the *maquis*, attempted to hamper the German war effort and were a force in Brittany and the French Alps.

·Battle of Britain
Germany attempted to bomb the British into submission in preparation for a cross-channel invasion. From July to October in 1940, the German Luftwaffe bombed on a daily basis British shipyards, airfields, factories, land transportation, and especially the cities including London, that was called the "blitz." After losing approximately 2,000 planes, the invasion of Britain would be abandoned as the Germans prepared for the invasion of the USSR. 915 British fighter planes were lost by the Royal Air Force, of which Prime Minister Winston Churchill said, "Never in the field of human conflict was so much owed by so many to so few."

·Axis in the Balkans
Hitler primarily used diplomacy to conquer Romania by first obtaining an oil and arms pact and later forcing Romania to settle its land claims with other Balkan nations. After the abdication of the King it became a satellite state, similar to Slovakia after the Czech and Moravian parts of Czechoslovakia had been annexed to Germany. Germany in November of 1940 brought Hungary, Romania, and Slovakia into the Axis (a Tripartite Pact that Germany, Italy, and Japan had concluded in September of 1940). Italy tried, but failed, to conquer Greece.

·Naval War in the Mediterranean
With naval victories over Italy at Taranto and Cape Matapan, the British navy effectively bottled up the Italian fleet keeping it in port for the duration of the war. Mussolini's pledge of the Mediterranean being *Mare Nostra*,

our sea, was a hollow promise. Even daily bombings of Malta failed to bring that island nation under Italian control.

· Yugoslavia and Greece

In preparation for the invasion of the USSR, Germany overran Yugoslavia after first trying to take it through diplomacy. Greece, which the Italians had failed to conquer, was easily defeated by the Germans with the last island Crete taken by paratroopers as the British still controlled the sea. Approximately 35,000 British soldiers defending Greece became prisoners of war.

· Battle of the North Atlantic

This 6 year naval battle pitted Nazi Germany's U-boats against convoys from North America to the United Kingdom, protected mainly by the British and Canadian navies and air forces, which were later aided by United States ships. In all German losses would include 783 submarines with the Allies losing 175 military ships and 3500 merchant ships.

· Germany Invades Russia

The nature of the war changed on June 22, 1941 as German, Finish, and Romanian troops established a 2000 mile front with the invasion of the USSR from the Arctic to the Ukraine. The Axis forces quickly approached Leningrad (put under siege) and the outskirts of Moscow, where the Russian winter set in to stop their advance.

U.S. Policies and Actions

· "Cash and Carry"

By repealing the arms embargo, a new Neutrality Act was passed in 1939. Congress authorized the export of arms and munitions to belligerents on a "cash and carry" basis. In other words they had to be paid for in hard currency, no credit allowed, and had to be hauled away in their own ships. This was a major departure from the earlier isolationist neutrality acts.

· Destroyers for Bases

In order to help the British defend themselves against a cross channel invasion, the U.S. sent 50 obsolete destroyers to Great Britain. In return the U.S. received the right to use bases on the British possession of Bermuda, Antigua, British Guiana, Jamaica, St. Lucia, Newfoundland, and Trinidad.

· U.S. and Preparedness

FDR's 1940 budget called for the production of 50,000 planes and $2 billion in expenditures for national defense. Surplus or outdated arms, munitions, and aircraft were shipped to Great Britain.

· Smith Act (Alien Registration Act)

A 1940 law that was designed to check subversive activities required fingerprinting of all resident aliens, and made it against the law to advocate the overthrow of the government of the U.S. by force or violence, or to become a member of any group dedicated to teaching that doctrine.

· Committee to Defend America by Aiding the Allies (1940)

Its first chairman was the prominent Republican editor from Kansas, William Allen White. This group gave political cover to FDR as he moved the country away from isolationism.

· America First Committee (1940)

To counter the interventionist "White Committee," Robert E. Wood formed an isolationist group to oppose the U.S. getting involved in the war. Supported by groups ranging from extreme reactionaries to leftist-pacifists, these isolationists used Charles Lindbergh as a popular spokesman.

·Election of 1940

The Republicans nominated a former Democrat Wendell Willkie, who agreed with FDR on almost all of the issues. The Democrats broke Washington's two term precedent by drafting Roosevelt after he told them he had no desire for a third term. FDR won the Electoral College 449-82 but the popular vote was much closer than in 1936.

·Act of Havana

Delegates at the Pan American Conference, meeting in Havana in 1940, established trusteeships over European colonies in the Western Hemisphere, whose colonial rulers had been overrun by the Germans. This policy applied to Dutch and French colonies in the Caribbean, South America, and off the Canadian coast. The American states sought to prevent Fascist infiltration into the Western Hemisphere via these colonies.

·Selective Service (1941)

The first peacetime U.S. draft of compulsory military service was adopted. This law provided for registration of all men between 21-35 and resulted in registering over 16 million men for military service.

·"Four Freedoms" (1941)

In his annual report to Congress FDR enunciated the "Four Freedoms:" freedom of speech and expression, freedom of worship, freedom from want, and freedom from fear.

·Lend-Lease Act (1941)

Because the British had exhausted their credits for war supplies this law enabled any country, whose defense the president had deemed vital to the interest of the U.S., to receive war supplies by sale, transfer, exchange, or lease. The initial amount was $7 billion but $50 billion would eventually be authorized by Congress.

·Greenland (1941)

A U.S.-Denmark agreement pledged the United States to defend Greenland for its defense was considered essential to the security of the Western Hemisphere. The U.S. would construct, maintain, and operate defense installations on the island for the duration of the war.

·Iceland (1941)

At the invitation of the Icelandic government the U.S. landed forces in Iceland to prevent its occupation by Germany.

·Atlantic Charter (1941)

This document was signed on the warship *Prince of Wales* in Argentia Bay, Newfoundland by FDR and Winston Churchill. The Atlantic Charter was a proclamation of the goals of the United States and Great Britain for World War II. It denounced territorial gains as a result of the war, proclaimed self-determination for all nations, recognized freedom of the seas, freedom from fear of aggression, and disarmament of aggressor nations. This charter was used as the basis for some of the fundamental principles of the United Nations, and it was signed by the 26 nations at war with the Axis.

Japan and the Pacific

·Indochina

Japan was able to negotiate the occupation of French Indochina (Vietnam, Laos, Cambodia) through the Matsuoka-Henry-Pact. It permitted the Japanese to station troops in French Indochina. When the Vichy-French hesitated at ratifying the pact the Japanese occupied Langson and bombarded Haiphong, in order to intimidate both the French administration and the Thai government. The French administration was merely tolerated by the Japanese and following the Japanese attack on Pearl Harbor, the Japanese coerced the Vichy-

French administration to sign another agreement, which virtually ceded the administration of Indochina to the Japanese, in all but name.

·U.S. Trade Restrictions on Japan

In July of 1940, the United States placed an embargo on the export of scrap metal and petroleum without a special license, and of all aviation gasoline to Japan, while continuing to permit trade in other commodities. In response to the Japanese move on Indochina, Japanese assets in the United States were frozen, and similar action was taken by Great Britain and the Netherlands.

·Japan's Ultimatum to the U.S.

A new cabinet was formed in Japan and General Hideki Tojo, Minister of War in the Konoye cabinet, retained that position and also became Prime Minister and Minister of Home Affairs. The Imperial Conference decided on a final attempt to reach an agreement with the United States but if a settlement favorable to Japan was not achieved by December 1, 1941, war would commence. The Japanese ambassador in Washington, Kichisaburo Nomura, and a special envoy, Saburo Kurusu, were instructed to present Japan's last proposal for a temporary settlement. Under its terms both countries would agree to: no new armed expansion in Southeast Asia or the South Pacific; Japan would withdraw its troops from southern Indochina on the conclusion of the agreement and from northern Indochina when the war with China ended; the United States would give Japan a free hand to bring the war against China to a successful conclusion; and it would lift the embargo on strategic exports to Japan, release Japanese assets in the United States, agree to supply petroleum as generously as in the period 1936-1940; and, join with Japan to ensure access by both countries to the resources of the Netherlands East Indies. This proposal was an ultimatum.

·U.S. Answer

It suggested that Japan evacuate both China and Indochina immediately and recognize Chiang Kai-shek's regime as the only government of China. A favorable trade treaty would be negotiated between Japan and the United States, and Japanese assets would be unfrozen. In addition, the two governments would enter into a multilateral nonaggression pact for the Far East.

UNIT XXV
MULTIPLE-CHOICE QUESTIONS

Questions 1-3 refer to the following:

"In response to Japanese activities in the Far East, 1931-1933, the Hoover administration adopted a policy of refusing to recognize political or territorial changes made in violation of American treaty rights... At the time of Japan's Twenty One Demands upon China, in 1915, Secretary of State William Jennings Bryan had announced a similar nonrecognition policy. But the Hoover administration elaborated the formula by associating it with the Kellogg-Briand or Paris Pact of 1928, whose signatories (including Japan) renounced war as an instrument of national policy, and with the Nine Power Treaty of 1922, which bound the nine powers (including Japan) to respect the Open Door in China and Chinese territorial... integrity. Non-recognition—as a corollary of these treaties came to be known variously as the Stimson, the Hoover-Stimson or the Hoover doctrine."

Richard N. Current, "The Stimson Doctrine and The Hoover Doctrine," 1954

1. Which incident in the Far East in 1931 led to the issuing of the Stimson Doctrine?

   (A) Rape of Nanking by Japanese soldiers that resulted in mass murder and rape for six weeks as they conquered the Chinese city
   (B) Occupation of Shanghai by Japan and the expulsion of the European colonial concessions
   (C) Dispute near the Chinese city of Mukden that led to the Japanese conquest of Manchuria
   (D) The Boxer Rebellion with its objective of overturning the Manchus and eliminating foreigners from China

2. The historic U.S. recognition policy that was the basis of the Stimson doctrine had first been debated during the

   (A) Jacksonian era and its policy toward Native Americans
   (B) discussion over issuing the Monroe Doctrine to curtail Spanish intervention in the Latin American revolutions
   (C) issuing of the Open Door Note to protect the territorial hegemony of China
   (D) 1790s as Jeffersonians and Federalists argued bitterly over a proper response to the French Revolution

3. The influence of the Stimson Doctrine caused which action that alienated Japan from the world community?

   (A) An international boycott of Japanese trade goods
   (B) League of Nations ordering Japan to leave Manchuria
   (C) An expeditionary force formed by the European colonial powers to protect their interests in the Far East
   (D) The U.S. launching a preemptive air strike against Japan to enforce the provisions of the Open Door policy

Questions 4-6 refer to the following document:

"The President of the United States... and the Prime Minister, Mr. Churchill, representing His Majesty's Government... to make known certain common... policies of their respective countries on which they base their hopes for a better future for the world. **First**, their countries seek no aggrandizement, territorial or other; **Second**, they desire to see no territorial changes that do not accord with the freely expressed wishes of the peoples concerned; **Third**, they respect the right of all peoples to choose the form of government under which they will live;... **Fourth**,... access, on equal terms, to the trade and to the raw materials of the world which are needed for their economic prosperity; **Fifth**, they desire to bring about the fullest collaboration between all nations in the economic field...; **Sixth**, after the final destruction of the Nazi tyranny, they hope to see established a peace which will afford to all nations the means of dwelling in safety within their own boundaries... [and} may live out their lives in freedom from fear and want; **Seventh**, such a peace should enable all men to traverse the high seas and oceans without hindrance; **Eighth**, they believe that all of the nations of the world,... must come to the abandonment of the use of force. Since no future peace can be maintained if land, sea or air armaments continue... disarmament of such nations is essential. They will ... encourage... peace-loving peoples [to end] the crushing burden of armaments."

Atlantic Charter, [Churchill's edited copy] 1941

4. The Atlantic Charter was similar to which earlier document in U.S. history?

    (A) Emancipation Proclamation
    (B) Monroe Doctrine
    (C) 14 Points
    (D) Declaration of Independence

5. The Atlantic Charter was the basis of which subsequent international organization?

    (A) United Nations
    (B) North Atlantic Treaty Organization
    (C) League of Nations
    (D) North American Free Trade Agreement

6. The eight points of the Atlantic Charter established which of the following?

    (A) The foundations of what became the General Agreement of Trade and Tariffs
    (B) The justification for the outbreak of the Cold War
    (C) The cornerstone of the Anglo-American bilateral alliance
    (D) The war aims of the allied nations in World War II

Questions 7-8 refer to the following:

"The Committee finds that: Loans to belligerents [go] against neutrality, for when only one group of belligerents can purchase and transport commodities the loans act in favor of the belligerent.... Loans extended to the Allies in 1915-1916, led to a very considerable war boom and inflation.... The foreign policy of the United States from 1914 to 1917 was, in fact, affected by our growing trade with the Allies as well as by natural sympathies. The neutral rights we claimed were simply not enforced against our largest customers.... It is not desirable for the Nation that any foreign belligerent or any bankers representing them be allowed to get into a position as they did in 1915, when sudden stoppage of sterling... can influence an administration into a reversal of our neutrality policy...."

Senator Gerald Nye, "Conclusions of the Nye Committee on War Profits," June 6, 1936

7. The conclusions that the Nye committee came up with supported which interpretation on the reason why the U.S. became involved in WWI

(A) defending neutral's rights
(B) make the world safe for democracy
(C) "merchants of death" influenced the decision
(D) German unrestricted submarine warfare

8. The sentiments of the Nye committee reinforced which view of foreign policy that had had dominated the 1930s?

(A) Interventionism
(B) Internationalism
(C) Expansionism
(D) Isolationism

Questions 9-11 refer to the following:

".... It seems to be unfortunately true that the epidemic of world lawlessness is spreading. ... And mark this well! When an epidemic of physical disease starts to spread, the community approves and joins in a quarantine of the patients in order to protect the health of the community against the spread of the disease.... War is a contagion, whether it be declared or undeclared. It can engulf states and peoples remote from the original scene of hostilities. Yes, we are determined to keep out of war... Most important of all, the will for peace on the part of peace-loving nations must express itself to the end that nations that may be tempted to violate their agreements and the rights of others will desist from such a cause. America hates war. America hopes for peace. Therefore, America actively engages in the search for peace."

Franklin D. Roosevelt, "Quarantine Speech," 1937

9. This speech by Franklin Roosevelt in Chicago in 1937 unleashed criticism from what subsequent political group?

(A) Committee to Defend the Allies
(B) Keep American Strong Committee
(C) America First Committee
(D) Internationalist Brigade

10. The epidemic that Roosevelt is referring of world lawlessness would ultimately result in which war being waged?

(A) World War I
(B) World War II
(C) Korean War
(D) Vietnam War

11. The terminology used in this speech by Roosevelt was later adopted by John F. Kennedy when he used the word quarantine in response to the

(A) Bay of Pigs
(B) Berlin Airlift
(C) Gunboats in the Bay of Tonkin
(D) Cuban Missile Crisis

Questions 12-13 refer to the following:

".... But the crisis of 1938, culminating at Munich, could hardly be ignored. Munich, as we discovered in retrospect, was the great divide of American opinion on the war, after it, isolationism slowly receded.... Most Americans then found that there supposed unconcern with the affairs of Europe was predicated on the assumption that no unfriendly power could dominate that continent. When Nazi Germany threatened to secure such mastery, most Americans abandoned their neutrality.... Business opinion divided sharply. While part of it remained stubbornly loyal to isolationism, a growing minority, finally to become a majority, discovered that America could not, and ought not, to remain aloof."

Roland N. Stromberg, "American Business and the Approach of War, 1935-41," 1953

12. Which incident does the passage above see as a watershed event in transforming American public opinion away from neutrality?

(A) Signing of the Molotov-Ribbentrop or German-Soviet Non-aggression Pact
(B) Italian invasion of Abyssinia from its African colony of Eritrea
(C) Nationalist *Falange* under Francisco Franco with the aid of Nazi Germany and Fascist Italy overthrowing the Spanish Republic or Loyalist
(D) Agreement between Britain, France, Germany, and Italy in which the Sudetenland region of Czechoslovakia was ceded to Germany

13. Isolationism begin to recede in the late 1930s when which laws were modified to enable the U.S. to give support to Great Britain and the other Allies?

(A) Stimson Doctrine
(B) Nine Power Treaty
(C) Neutrality Acts
(D) Atlantic Charter

Questions 14-15 refer to the following:

... this government (U.S.) has acquired the right to lease naval and air bases in Newfoundland, and in the islands of Bermuda, Bahamas, Jamaica, St. Lucia, Trinidad, Antigua, and in British Guiana,... The right to bases in Newfoundland and Bermuda are gifts—generously given and gladly received. The other bases mentioned have been acquired in exchange for fifty of our over-age destroyers. This is not inconsistent in any sense with our status of peace. Still less is it a threat against any nation. It is an epochal and far-reaching act of preparation for continental defense in the face of grave danger. Preparation for defense is an inalienable prerogative of a sovereign state. Under present circumstances this exercise of sovereign right is essential... [for] our peace and safety."

Franklin D. Roosevelt, "Destroyers for Bases Agreement with Great Britain," 1940

14. Why were the bases in Newfoundland and Bermuda gifts instead of a trading exchange like the other islands?

(A) No destroyers were received in return for the gifts
(B) They were considered independent countries
(C) White populations dominate Newfoundland and Bermuda and on the other islands blacks or racial mixtures were majorities
(D) Newfoundland was controlled by Canada and Bermuda was a part of the U.S. sphere of influence

15. What ultimately proved to be the most important part of the destroyers for bases deal was the

(A) firepower it gave the British navy to blockade German ports
(B) it was the start of the wartime Anglo-American partnership
(C) U.S. received greater advantages than the British which made the U.S. feel obligated to defend the British
(D) fact that some of the destroyers were sent to the USSR to shore up their defenses against a German invasion

UNIT XXVI
WORLD WAR II

Once in a while a war can be categorized as a good war and World War II fits that description. Despite the debate between the internationalists and the isolationists leading up to the war, after Pearl Harbor the war was universally supported by the American people. Unlike other wars there was no anti-war sentiment, draft riots, or speakers and writers against the war. There was no need for wartime legislation against dissenters. A united country faced the Axis powers.

Early Battles & Strategy

· Attack on Pearl Harbor

The specific Japanese attack on Pearl Harbor on December 7, 1941 came as a surprise to the commanders there and to officials in Washington, who had expected an attack to occur in Southeast Asia. The attack lasted a total of two hours and twenty minutes and included strikes at Wheeler Field in the middle of the island, Oahu, the naval air station at Kaneohe, Ford Island and Ewa Field. Twenty-nine Japanese aircraft were shot down. The attack killed 2,403 Americans and wounded 1,178 others. Fourteen ships, including eight battleships, were put out of service and the battleship *Arizona* was a total loss. Seventy-seven aircraft of all types were destroyed. Three U.S. aircraft carriers, the *Saratoga*, *Lexington* and *Enterprise*, had been out to sea and aircraft carriers, not battleships would prove to be the decisive naval weapon in WWII. President Roosevelt described the attack at Pearl Harbor as a "dastardly deed" and a day that would "live in infamy." On December 8, 1941 Congress declared that a state of war had been thrust on the United States by Japan. In accordance with the Tripartite Pact and in response to Japanese requests, Germany and Italy declared war on the United States on December 11. Congress reciprocated the same day.

· Attack on Philippines, Singapore, Malay, Hong Kong, and Guam

On December 8, 1941, the Japanese bombed and strafed Clark Field in the Philippines for a little more than an hour then left, leaving the base in total ruin. Most of the U.S. aircraft had been destroyed on the ground. On the same morning that the Japanese attacked Pearl Harbor and the Philippines, they moved against the British at Hong Kong, against Southeast Asia's only independent country, Thailand, and against the British on the Malay Peninsula. Saigon in Indochina was the staging area for these assaults. Two days later Japanese troops invaded Guam and landed at various points in the Philippines, including Luzon and Mindanao. On December 15, their forces invaded the British controlled area of northern Borneo, an area that was important because of its oil.

·Get Germany First

Despite the anger that was felt against the Japanese for their "sneak attack" on Pearl Harbor, the government strategy was that Hitler and Germany were the greater threat and that most of the war effort would be directed against them. A strong revenge factor against Japan was resisted by both the U.S. government and military, as the war in Europe took up most of the U.S. resources. As the focus of the war effort turned to Europe, the Pacific theatre was in a holding pattern.

U.S. and the War in Europe

·North Africa

In what was called " Operation Torch," the U.S. joined the British in removing German and Italian troops from North Africa. In October 1942, the British launched a counteroffensive westward in Egypt, around 100 miles west of Alexandria. At El Alamein, the German drive led by Erwin Rommel toward the Suez Canal was stopped. In November, U.S. and British forces landed at Casablanca and Algiers in French controlled North Africa. Stalin was unhappy about this invasion because he wanted a landing somewhere in France that would take pressure off of the Soviet forces fighting the Germans alone. Roosevelt had promised that this landing in Europe would happen that year. Hitler was relieved because he had feared a landing closer to home. The success of the Americans and British in North Africa included a deal with Admiral Darlan who was on the side of the pro-German government at Vichy. Charles de Gaulle, leader of the "Free French," was outraged and felt that the allies had betrayed him. Hitler responded to the Allied invasion by moving troops into what had been the unoccupied area of France that included the Mediterranean coastline. The regime at Vichy accepted this move and declared it would defend itself against the Allies in its North African territory. Some French forces fought with determination against the Allies. With Darlan's defection some went over to the side of the Allies, while others continued to resist the invasion. Green U.S. forces suffered a humiliating defeat to the Germans at Kasserine Pass and this further convinced the British that the U.S. would play a subservient role in the fighting. This proved to be a wrong assumption. By mid-1943 all of North Africa was controlled by the Allies and 250,000 Axis troops had been captured at Tunis. After "Torch" the U.S. was the dominant military force for the Allies.

·Sicily Conquered

From Tunis, the Anglo-American invasion of Sicily called Operation Husky was launched. The island was conquered in just over a month and the Italian defeat led to the resignation of Mussolini and the appointment of Pietro Badoglio as the Italian leader who dissolved the Fascist Party.

·Italy Invaded

After Southern Italy was invaded by both British and American forces, Italy accepted the Allied terms of unconditional surrender. When the Italians surrendered, including the Italian fleet, the Germans took over most of Italy. It would take 6 months of heavy fighting to inch up the Italian peninsula and liberate Rome.

·USSR & Germany

After the disastrous German defeat at Stalingrad, the Russians began a 13 month advance that would relieve the siege of Leningrad, re-take all of the Ukraine and the western republics, and enter Poland.

·D-Day at Normandy

A true second front in Europe was finally accomplished with the invasion of Normandy in northern France in Operation Overlord. In June of 1944, 4,000 war ships and 11,000 planes protected 176,000 troops assaulting the coast from 4,000 invasion craft in a 60-mile front.

·Liberation of France, Belgium, and Luxembourg

Within 3 months after the Normandy landings the allied army of more than 2 million men liberated most of Western Europe and entered Germany.

·Battle of the Bulge

In mid-December in 1944, three German armies advanced into the semi-mountainous, heavily forested Ardennes region of eastern Belgium and northern Luxembourg. Their goal was to reach the sea, trap four allied armies, and force a negotiated peace on the Western front. Over a million men, 500,000 Germans, 600,000 Americans, and 55,000 British fought for three days with 100,000 German casualties, killed, wounded or captured and 81,000 American casualties, including 23,554 captured or missing and 8,000 killed. Even though the German offensive achieved total surprise, the determined American stand at Bastogne where the American commander answered "nuts" when asked to surrender, this stand thwarted the ambitious German goal. What the Germans accomplished was to create a "bulge" in the American line, which was quickly reversed with the arrival of reinforcements. It proved to be the last gasp of the German army; yet, fighting would continue for another 5 months.

·VE Day

As Russian and American troops met on the Elbe River, Russian troops entered Berlin to find that Hitler had committed suicide and unconditional surrender was achieved on May 8th, 1945.

U.S. Home Front in WWII

·Rosie the Riveter

During World War II, an unprecedented number of American women responded to government encouragement to enter the high-paying world of the heavy war-production industry. Women who had worked at pink-collar jobs, or in lower-paying women's industrial jobs, flocked to war production work as an opportunity to learn new skills and make higher wages. Called "Rosie the Riveter" after a popular song, they symbolized the total commitment of the U.S. to the war effort. Between 1941 and 1945, 6.5 million women entered the work force, a 57% increase from the pre-war years.

·Rationing

A complex system of rationing was developed starting in May of 1942. The U.S. Office of Price Administration (OPA) froze prices on most everyday goods, starting with sugar and coffee. War Ration Books were issued to each American family dictating how much of any product could be bought. Rationed foods included meats, butter, fats and oils, and cheese, and later such varied items as canned, bottled and frozen fruits and vegetables, beans, peas, and processed foods such as soups, baby foods, baked beans, and catsup. The first nonfood item rationed was rubber, which led to gasoline rationing of three gallons a week for most people. The national maximum "Victory Speed" was 35 miles an hour. During World War II, a person was allowed 48 coupons per year for clothes. With pants taking 6 coupons, dresses 5 and shirts or blouses 4, it did not take much clothing to use up the coupons, and rationed shoes were the most difficult item of all to deal with, especially with growing boys and girls. Most Americans agreed to rationing without complaint as it was all part of the total war effort. Children's toys were made of wood as metal, rubber, and plastic had gone to war.

·Victory Gardens

Because commercially canned goods were rationed, the Victory Garden became an indispensable source of food for the home front. The Victory Garden was a household activity during the war where crops were planted on any piece of land that was vacant. Vacant lots in urban areas flourished when planted with vegetables, although this cut into the areas used for sandlot baseball by young people. At its peak, it is estimated that nearly 20,000,000 Victory Gardens were supplying about 40 % of all vegetables produced in the U.S.

·Recycling and Conservation

The federal government encouraged Americans to conserve and recycle materials such as metal, paper, and rubber, which factories could then use for wartime production. Lots of everyday household trash had value: kitchen fats, old metal shovels, even empty metal lipstick tubes.

·Fashion

War conservation even influenced American fashion. In 1942, the War Production Board began dictating styles for civilian apparel that would conserve cloth and metal for the war effort. For example, menswear rid itself of vests, elbow patches on jackets, and cuffs on pants. Women's clothing also relied on fewer materials and skirts became shorter and narrower. Patriotic women begin wearing two-piece bathing suits to conserve on cloth, which created the biggest public stir since Amelia Bloomer's Turkish trousers in the 19th century.

·Zoot Suit Riots (or sailor riots)

The Zoot Suit Riots occurred in the context of national and global racial conflicts during the World War II era. From June 3rd to June 7th in 1943, sailors (later joined by soldiers) invaded East Los Angeles, marched down the streets, broke into bars and theaters, and attacked Mexican Pachuchos wearing clothing called zoot suits —wide-legged, "pegged," pleated, pants, a long coat with wide lapels, and wide, padded shoulders, and often a felt hat with a feather. None of the sailors or soldiers who were committing the violent acts were arrested by the Police or the Sheriff's office, in fact, the servicemen were portrayed in the local press as heroes stemming the tide of the "Mexican Crime Wave." The police practice was to accompany the caravans of soldiers and sailors in police cars, watch the beatings, and jail the victims. Finally, at midnight on June 7th, because the Navy believed it had an actual mutiny on hand, the military authorities did what the city of Los Angeles would not do, they moved to stop the rioting of their personnel. Los Angeles was declared off limits for all military personnel and this ended the attacks on the Hispanic population. In the aftermath, the city council voted to ban Zoot Suits.

·War Bonds

At first they were called Defense Bonds and they were U.S. Government issued bonds to finance the war effort. The name was changed to War Bonds after the Japanese attack on Pearl Harbor. The bonds were set to yield a 2.9% return after a ten- year maturity. The War Bonds the government wanted people to buy were the Series E bonds. Secretary of the Treasury Henry Morgenthau sold the first Series E bond to President Franklin D. Roosevelt. The bonds were zero-coupon bonds that sold at 75 percent of their face value in denominations of $10, $25, $50, and up to $100,000.

·Japanese Relocation (Concentration) Camps

After the beginning of World War II, Franklin D. Roosevelt signed Executive Order 9066 that rounded-up 120,000 Americans of Japanese heritage and assigned them to 10 internment camps—officially called "relocation centers"—in California, Idaho, Utah, Arizona, Wyoming, Colorado, and Arkansas. FDR's executive order was fueled by anti-Japanese sentiment among farmers who competed against Japanese labor, politicians who sided with anti-Japanese constituencies, and the general public whose anger was heightened by the Japanese attack of Pearl Harbor. More than 2/3rd of the Japanese who were interned in the spring of 1942 were citizens of the United States. In Canada, similar evacuation orders were established. The U.S.

internment camps were overcrowded and provided poor living conditions although families were usually kept together. The irony of internment was that the Japanese on Hawaii, a much more significant part of the population, were not put into camps. Two important legal cases were brought against the United States concerning the internment. The landmark cases were *Hirabayashi v. United States* (1943), and *Korematsu v. United States* (1944). The defendants argued that their 14th and 5th amendment rights had been violated by the U.S. government because of their ancestry. In both cases, the Supreme Court ruled in favor of the government. In 1968, the government began reparations to Japanese Americans for property they had lost. In 1988, Congress passed legislation that awarded formal payments of $20,000 each to the surviving internees.

·Election of 1944

FDR was nominated for a 4th term along with a little known Senator from Missouri, Harry Truman for Vice-President. The Republicans nominated Governor Thomas Dewey of New York. The Democrats won 432-99 in the Electoral College and continued to control the Congress. Four months into his 4th term Roosevelt died of a cerebral hemorrhage and Truman took over to finish out the war.

War in the Pacific

·Japan's Ascendancy

In the six months after Pearl Harbor Japan took over Hong Kong, Guam, Wake Island, the Philippines, Attu and Kiska in the Aleutians Islands, Netherlands East Indies and the Mariana, Caroline, and Solomon island groups. These were almost uncontested—due to the official policy of getting Germany first (called ABC-1) except in the Philippines where more than 11,000 U.S. troops were forced to surrender on Corregidor and many died as they were marched through the Bataan peninsula to prisoner of war camps. The British suffered the largest defeat to Japan when 70,000 of their troops were captured when Singapore fell.

·Doolittle's Raid

On April 18, 1942 nine days after Japan overran the Bataan Peninsula in the Philippines, Colonel James Doolittle led sixteen B-25 bombers off of the carrier *Hornet*. They traveled 600 miles and surprised Tokyo, bombing that city, doing little damage, but helping American morale. The planes landed or crashed in China after running out of fuel and one plane landed in the Soviet Union where its crew was interned.

·Coral Sea (1942)

The reason that the Battle of the Coral Sea came about was because the Japanese were intent on capturing Port Moresby, New Guinea. If Japan managed to take Port Moresby they would have a full control over the Coral Sea and they could cut Australia out of the war. The Battle of the Coral Sea was the first time that two fleets clashed, and that neither fleet saw each other. The battle was all between airplanes. The battle was technically a draw but Japan was damaged enough that they could not continue their move on Port Moresby so it is seen as a U.S. victory

·Guadalcanal (1942-1943)

The attack on the Japanese-occupied island of Guadalcanal in the Solomon Islands by the Allied navies and 16,000 United States troops, was the first offensive by U.S. land forces in the Pacific Campaign. After a 6-month battle U.S. soldiers finally secured Guadalcanal, it was the first step in a long string of invasions that would eventually lead to the surrender of Japan. The capture of the island was the first breach of the perimeter that Japan had established during the first six months of the Pacific War and the first defeat for the Japanese Imperial Army.

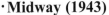

·Midway (1943)
Fought near the Central Pacific island of Midway, it is considered the decisive naval battle of the war in the Pacific. Before this battle the Japanese were on the offensive, capturing territory throughout Asia and the Pacific. By their attack, the Japanese had planned to capture Midway to use as an advance base, as well as to entrap and destroy the U.S. Pacific Fleet. Because of communication, intelligence successes, and some luck, the U.S. Pacific Fleet surprised the Japanese forces, sinking four Japanese carriers that had attacked Pearl Harbor only six months before, while losing one carrier. After Midway, the Americans took the offensive in the Pacific.

·Island Hopping
This idea was to capture certain key islands, one after another, until Japan came within range of American bombers. Some islands would be left alone to wither on the vine because taking every island took up too many resources. The plan eventually succeeded, but only after a long and difficult struggle. Japanese soldiers believed in fighting to the death, which made it difficult to capture the key islands. Hard fought victories at Tarawa, Kwajalein, Saipan, Guam, and Iwo Jima paved the way for the U.S. taking the Philippines and Okinawa.

·Philippines-Leyte Gulf (October ,1944)
This naval battle brought about the annihilation of the Japanese fleet, as they lost 2 battleships, 4 carriers, 9 cruisers and 9 destroyers. This battle paved the way for the U.S. retaking all of the archipelago of the Philippines.

·Okinawa
On April 1, 1945, a combined Army-Navy-Marine force landed on Okinawa for what turned out to be the last major battle of WWII. The conflict raged for 83 days with 12,500 Americans (the largest single total number of deaths in one battle in U.S. history) being killed. Nearly 100,000 Japanese were killed and more than 200,000 Okinawans were killed. Kamikaze suicide fighters sank 34 U.S. ships and damaged 361. The carnage of this battle was a contributing factor in convincing the U.S. to use the atomic bombs on Japan at Hiroshima and Nagasaki.

·Hiroshima
On August 6th, 1945 a single atomic bomb, that had been developed and tested as a part of the secret Manhattan project in Alamogordo, New Mexico, was dropped on this Japanese city killing an estimated 80,000 people and heavily damaging 80% of the city. In the following months, an estimated 60,000 more people died from injuries or radiation poisoning. The earlier "fire-bombing" of Tokyo resulted in more than 100,000 deaths; but it did not have the same emotional impact of the atomic bomb at Hiroshima.

·Nagasaki
A second atomic bomb was dropped on Nagasaki on August 9th killing 39,000 with 70,000 dying of bomb related causes later.

·VJ Day
On August 14th or 15th (depending on the side of the international dateline), marked the end of the Burma Campaign, the Second Sino-Japanese War, and the Pacific War as well as other military conflicts in Asia. Japan's emperor Hirohito was allowed to keep his throne contrary to the Potsdam principle of unconditional surrender.

Conferences and the Holocaust

·Casablanca

Held in French Morocco in January of 1943, FDR and Churchill established "unconditional surrender," agreed in principle on a second front (Churchill wanted it in the Balkans and Italy and FDR favored France), and made Dwight D. Eisenhower Supreme Commander in North Africa.

·Cairo Declaration

This was made at a conference held in Egypt with Chiang Kai Shek, FDR, and Churchill. They declared that the war was being fought to restrain and punish the aggression of Japan and that the Allies had no thoughts of territorial expansion. Japan would be stripped of all the islands in the Pacific that it had seized or occupied since 1914, and all the territories Japan had taken from China, such as Manchuria, Formosa, and the Pescadores, would be restored to the Republic of China. Japan would also be expelled from all other territories it had taken and Korea would become free and independent.

·Teheran

The 1st meeting of the "Big Three" (FDR, Stalin, and Churchill) occurred in November of 1943, in Iran. Stalin reaffirmed the USSR's commitment to enter the war against Japan and coordination of the Russian offensive with the allied invasion of France in a second front was discussed.

·Moscow Conference

Churchill and Stalin divided up the Balkans into spheres of influence with the USSR getting Rumania, Bulgaria, and Hungary, the two countries sharing Yugoslavia, and Great Britain getting Greece. FDR did not take part in this agreement and indicated he would not be bound by it.

·Yalta

The 2nd meeting of the "Big Three" in February of 1945 in the Crimea in Russia. USSR agreed to enter the war in the Pacific within three months after Germany's surrender. The format for an international organization, the United Nations, was established, procedures for the dismemberment of Germany were discussed and a 4th zone of occupation would be given to the French. FDR accepted the USSR's control of Outer Mongolia, Kurile Islands, half of Sakhalin Island and Port Arthur (Darien). FDR and Stalin agreed that 50% of the German reparations would go to the USSR. The Polish government was to be broadened by including non-communists in exile in London and free elections were promised. Major war criminals would be punished.

·Potsdam

A third meeting of a new "Big Three" that included the holdover Stalin, Truman, and Clement Atlee (replacing Churchill) met in July of 1945 in Germany. There were disagreements on many major issues although the de-militarization and de-nazification of Germany was agreed to, along with the development of democratic institutions and the destruction of the war capacity of Germany. Specific reparations were agreed to and the German navy would be divided up amongst the three major Allied powers. The USSR would receive German Koenigsberg (Kaliningrad), and Poland's boundaries would be re-adjusted, losing territory in the east to the USSR, and gaining territory in the west from Germany. A council of Foreign Ministers would draft peace settlements for the Balkans.

·"Final Solution"

In what is today called the Holocaust and Hitler euphemistically called his "Final Solution," up to 12 million humans—6 million of them Jews—were systematically killed in an act of genocide the world had never seen before or since. Although concentration camps existed throughout Germany and the areas it controlled, some camps were specifically earmarked for exterminations (usually in Poland) such as Auschwitz, Sobibor and

Treblenka. Executions also took place at work camps in Germany such as Dachau and Bergen-Belsen. In addition to Jews, those being killed were Slavs, especially Poles, Serbs, Ukrainians, Russians, communists, homosexuals, Romany (gypsies), the mentally ill, the physically disabled, intelligentsia, Jehovah's Witnesses, trade unionists, and psychiatric patients. The method of extermination was typically poison gas, usually in "gas chambers," although many prisoners were killed in mass shootings, by starvation or by sadistic actions of the SS guards who ran the camps. It was carried out without mercy for children or babies and often victims were made to suffer before finally being killed. The Nazis carried out cruel and deadly medical experiments on prisoners. The Allies, especially the U.S., despite some individual acts of heroism have been strongly criticized for not issuing visas to Jews who attempted to leave areas under German control before and during the war and the failure of the military to either bomb the camps or the railroads servicing the camps. As the Soviet armed forces advanced into Poland in 1944, the camps were closed and partly or completely dismantled to conceal what had taken place.

UNIT XXVI
MULTIPLE-CHOICE QUESTIONS

Questions 1-4 refer to the following:

"Yesterday, December 7, 1941—a date which will live in infamy—the United States of America was suddenly and deliberately attacked by naval and air forces of the Empire of Japan.... bombing... the American island of Oahu.... The United States was at peace with that nation,... it [is] obvious that the attack was deliberately planned many days or even weeks ago. During the intervening time the Japanese Government has deliberately sought to deceive the United States by false statements and expressions of hope for continued peace.... Yesterday the Japanese Government also launched an attack against Malaya. Last night Japanese forces attacked Hong Kong,... Guam... the Philippine Islands..., Wake Island. And this morning the Japanese attacked Midway Island.... I ask that the Congress declare that since the unprovoked and dastardly attack by Japan on Sunday, December 7, 1941, a state of war has existed between the United States and the Japanese Empire."

Franklin Roosevelt, "Day of Infamy," December 8, 1941

1. The main Japanese attack took place in which territorial possession of the United States?

   (A) Puerto Rico
   (B) American Samoa
   (C) Tahiti
   (D) Hawaii

2. This action by Japan would end which powerful group's strong influence on American foreign policy?

   (A) Interventionist
   (B) Internationalists
   (C) Isolationists
   (D) Exceptionalists

3. As a result of the Japanese "sneak" attack on Pearl Harbor and other Pacific possessions

   (A) the U.S. would be involved in its own war with Japan separate from the war going on in Europe
   (B) all the wars going on in Europe, Asia, and the Pacific Islands would be combined into one war—World War II
   (C) United States territorial possessions in East Asia and the Pacific Islands would be permanently lost to U.S. control
   (D) the way would be open for the Union of Soviet Socialist Republics to spread their influence into Asia

4. The attack on Pearl Harbor was a surprise only because of its location as the U.S. expected an attack because

   (A) it had broken the Japanese code and knew an attack was forthcoming
   (B) the U.S. was historically aware that Japan had launched "sneak" attacks in the past to start wars
   (C) the rival imperial ambitions of Japan and U.S. meant a war was inevitable
   (D) economic conditions in Japan gave it no choice but to expand geographically

379

Questions 5-6 refer to the following:

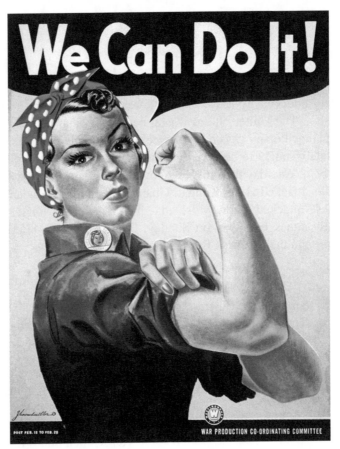

5. The poster above represents the role of women

   (A) in their quest to get equal voting rights as suffragettes
   (B) as workers in the household
   (C) taking over for men in industrial and manufacturing jobs
   (D) in joining the WACS and WAVES

6. Along with the poster above what popular novelty song sang the praises of women who took the traditional manufacturing and industrial jobs of men and contributed greatly to the American cause?

   (A) "Over There"
   (B) "I Am Woman"
   (C) "It's a Long Way to Tipperary"
   (D) "Rosie the Riveter"

Questions 7-9 refer to the following:

"The mass production industries never like the idea of employing women.... [But] experience is proving to the plant manager that a woman can do almost all of the jobs he thought were exclusively masculine. But he does run into limitations on heavy lifting... and here he begins to... fit the job to the worker instead of the worker to the job, The fact that... a woman can lift only a little more than half as much as a man is cancelled if a woman is given a mechanical hoist to lift the work up to her. Once the work is in place she will do the job as well as a man—better if it is routine, monotonous, repetitive, painstaking, and intricate, as most production jobs are.... The differences between men and women are not only physical they are psychological and social as well."

A. G. Mezerak, "The Factory Manager Learns the Facts of Life," 1943

7. One conclusion that can be drawn from the passage above is that

   (A) women can do the heavy lifting as well as a man
   (B) only men can do most mass production jobs
   (C) women can do most production jobs better than men
   (D) there is essentially no difference between men and women and doing a job

8. The reason that women moved into the mass production industries by 1943 is that

   (A) affirmative action policies required employers to hire them
   (B) women had better skills for mass production jobs than did men
   (C) men were unwilling to work at industrial jobs that paid so little
   (D) there was a labor shortage of men who had gone to war

9. Managers were able to solve the issue of women not being able to lift as much weight as men by

   (A) having weight lifting rooms available for women to improve their upper body strength
   (B) fitting the job to the worker by using mechanical devices
   (C) using alternative production materials that were much lighter in weight
   (D) employing only large and strong women who had the strength to lift heavy objects

Questions 10-12 refer to the following:

Some of the Rationed Goods in the U.S. During World War II

Rationed Items	Rationing Duration
Tires	January 1942 to December 1945
Cars	February 1942 to October 1945
Bicycles	July 1942 to September 1945
Gasoline	May 1942 to August 1945
Fuel Oil & Kerosene	October 1942 to August 1945
Solid Fuels	September 1943 to August 1945
Stoves	December 1942 to August 1945
Rubber Footwear	October 1942 to September 1945
Shoes	February 1943 to October 1945
Sugar	May 1942 to 1947
Coffee	November 1942 to July 1943
Processed Foods	March 1943 to August 1945
Meats, canned fish	March 1943 to November 1945
Cheese, canned milk, fats	March 1943 to November 1945
Typewriters	March 1942 to April 1944

10. In addition to rationing during WWII products were also saved for the war effort by

    (A) having women work in defense plants
    (B) conservation
    (C) contributing to charities
    (D) technology

11. The reason that tires were the first item rationed is because

    (A) tires were needed for the production of tanks in the war effort
    (B) replacement tires for vehicles would take a long time to make
    (C) Japan had overrun Malaya and the East Indies where 99% of the rubber came from
    (D) most of the tires in the U.S. were for passenger cars that would not be made in 1942 and 1943

12. When petroleum products became in short supply in 1973 because of an Arab oil embargo as a consequence of the Yom Kippur war, a form of rationing was adopted that called for

    (A) buying gas on odd or even days based on the last number of your license plate
    (B) mandatory curtailment of the number of miles driven
    (C) changing the non-gasoline uses of petroleum to other products that were in plentiful supply
    (D) not purchasing any petroleum products from countries that were participating in the embargo

Questions 13-15 refer to the following:

13. Rationing was justified on the basis that

    (A) finite resources should be preserved to protect the ecology
    (B) people were living "green" to protect the environment
    (C) consumer goods should be limited to help the war effort
    (D) the economy was still suffering from the effects of the Great Depression

14. Rationing was based on which of the following principles

    (A) might makes right
    (B) he who has the gold makes the rules
    (C) crony capitalism
    (D) shared sacrifice

15. Items that were subject to rationing included all of the following EXCEPT

    (A) sugar
    (B) shoes
    (C) rubber
    (D) wood

NO TESTING MATERIAL ON THIS PAGE

UNIT XXVII
TRUMAN 1940S & THE COLD WAR

The time period between the end of WWII and the Eisenhower 1950s was a transitional one in American History. After more than a decade of FDR being president, Harry Truman, who became the president in April, 1945 was faced with ending WWII and leading America in the new postwar world. What became known as the Cold War would dominate his administration and the development of the policy of containment as a strategy to fight this war would be his major contribution to winning this 40+ year struggle.

Aftermath of WWII

· Demobilization

Tremendous pressure was put on Truman to "bring the boys home." The armed forces were quickly reduced from 11 million to 2 million and at the time of the Korean conflict they would be down to 1 million.

· Inflation

With pent-up demand at an all time high from the 15 years of depression and rationing in WWII, and purchasing power from war-time savings bursting, prices soared immediately following the war. In 1946 alone inflation was running at 32% where it had only been 34% during the entire four years of WWII. Truman wanted rationing and price controls continued until shortages and inflation could be stopped, but the Republican controlled Congress elected in 1946 would not go along. Eventually a compromise Anti-Inflation Act would be passed, and the Office of Economic Stabilization was formed to replace the war-related boards that were abolished.

· Employment Act of 1946

This law made the federal government responsible for creating and maintaining full employment. It established the President's Council of Economic Advisers to furnish the expertise that was supposedly needed to anticipate and avoid future recessions. The Act provided that full employment was to be maintained by "compensatory spending"—that is, the government was to make up for "inadequate" private sector spending if a recession occurred. The law did not specifically endorse deficit spending and an unbalanced budget, but this Keynesian approach was inherent in the law. This anti-recessionary program was put into effect when the President's economic advisers foresaw a decline in the business sector.

·Legislative Reorganization

In order to become more streamlined, at least in theory, the Legislative Reorganization Act cut the number of standing committees in the House from 48 to 19 and from 33 to 15 in the Senate. Little was accomplished, as the elimination of standing committees led to the proliferation of subcommittees in Congress.

·Mine Workers Strike

One of the few unions to strike in WWII, the United Mine Workers' 1943 strike brought about the government seizure of the mines. Strikes in 1945–47, although successful, cost both John L. Lewis, president of the union $10,000 in fines and the union $3.5 million that was later reduced to $700,000 when the miners returned to work. The fines were for violating an injunction barring the union from striking. To make matters worse for labor, Truman used the National Guard to seize the mines.

International Organizations

·Nuremberg Trials

In 1945, the Allied Control Council issued Control Law No. 10, establishing the basis for "the prosecution of war criminals and similar offenders." Each of the occupying authorities were authorized, in its occupation zone, to try persons suspected of committing war crimes. Twelve trials, involving over a hundred defendants and several different courts, took place in Nuremberg from 1945 to 1949. The first and most famous of these trials was the Trial of the Major War Criminals Before the International Military Tribunal (IMT), which tried 24 of the most important captured leaders of Nazi Germany. The defendants themselves often took the stand, trying to put their actions in as positive of a light as possible. Many of the defendants claimed to know nothing of the existence of concentration camps or midnight killings. Other defendants used their testimony to emphasize that they were merely following orders. A few of the defendants, namely Albert Speer and Hans Frank, confessed their mistakes and offered apologies for their actions. The Nazi leaders were convicted of committing "crimes against humanity" and were executed. There has been some criticism of the verdicts reached as they seemed to contradict existing international law that had up to that time upheld the absolute sovereignty of the nation state. What has become the "Nuremburg principle" says that there is a higher law, the law of mankind or humanity, than the laws of the nation state, and it is a criminal act if this law is violated.

·United Nations

The name was coined by U.S. President Franklin D. Roosevelt, who first used it in the "Declaration by United Nations" in January 1942, when representatives of 26 nations pledged to fight against the Axis Powers. In 1945, representatives of 50 countries met in San Francisco at the United Nations Conference on International Organization to draw up the United Nations Charter. Those delegates deliberated on the basis of proposals worked out by the representatives of China, the Soviet Union, the United Kingdom and the United States at Dumbarton Oaks in the United States. The charter was signed in 1945 by the representatives of 50 countries. Poland, which was not represented at the Conference, signed it later and became one of the original 51 members. The United Nations officially came into existence in October of 1945 when the charter was ratified by China, France, the Soviet Union, the United Kingdom, the United States and a majority of other signatories.

·International Monetary Fund (IMF)

It came about in 1944 during the United Nations Monetary and Financial Conference. Representatives of 45 governments met in Bretton Woods, New Hampshire with the delegates to the conference agreeing on a framework for international economic cooperation. The IMF was formally organized in 1945, when the first 29 countries signed its Articles of Agreement. Its goal was to stabilize exchange rates and assist the reconstruction of the world's international payment system in the aftermath of the war. Countries contributed to a pool that could be borrowed from, on a temporary basis, by countries with payment imbalances.

·World Bank

Also created at the Bretton Woods Conference in 1944 was the World Bank, an international financial institution that provides leveraged loans to developing countries for capital programs. Its stated goal is reducing poverty. The World Bank is made up of International Bank for Reconstruction and Development (IBRD), and the International Development Association (IDA).

Domestic Issues and Policies

·G.I. Bill of Rights

Officially called the Serviceman's Readjustment Act, it was designed to provide opportunities to returning war veterans of World War II. The bill, signed by FDR in 1944, provided federal aid to help veterans adjust to civilian life in the areas of hospitalization, purchases of homes and businesses, and especially in education. The act provided tuition, subsistence, books, supplies, equipment, and counseling services for veterans to continue their education in vocational school or college. The Federal Government would subsidize tuition, fees, books, and educational materials for veterans and contribute to living expenses incurred while attending college or other approved institutions. Moreover, veterans were free to attend the educational institution of their choice and colleges were free to admit those veterans who met their admissions requirements. Approximately eight million veterans received educational benefits in the seven years after the act was passed. Servicemen were also given unemployment compensation of $20 a week for up to one year. Vets could buy homes with no money down as a part of the Veterans' Administration loan program, and they could buy small businesses or farms with loans from the government. The impact of the bill was tremendous, the generation that had suffered in the Great Depression and WWII were able to receive an education, start businesses, and buy homes with government help.

·Housing Shortage

Few houses had been built during the Great Depression and WWII and 3 million married couples were sharing a dwelling unit with another family. Government loans to veterans by the G.I. bill was one solution to this problem.

·Levittown

During his service in Hawaii, Lieutenant William Levitt realized that the urgent need for post-war housing and the availability of cheap farmland provided a golden opportunity for his family to capitalize on some Long Island property, 25 miles east of Manhattan they had taken an option on. They would divide the former potato field of Hempstead into small lots and build simple, inexpensive mass-produced (just like Henry Ford had done for automobiles) homes for veterans and their families. These returning servicemen were entitled to low-interest, insured "GI Loans," which would make the new Levitt homes easily affordable and, therefore, highly attractive. The new development ultimately consisted of 17,400 homes and 82,000 people. The Levitt's perfected the art of mass-producing houses by dividing the construction process into 27 different steps from start to finish. The company or its subsidiaries produced lumber, mixed and poured concrete, and even sold appliances. They built as much of the house that they could off-site in carpentry and other shops. The assembly-line production techniques could produce up to 30 of the four-bedroom Cape Cod houses—all the homes in the first Levittown were the same—each day. Levittown would be the catalyst that would lead to the development of suburbia, all across the nation but especially in the west where land was available near the cities.

·Taft-Hartley Act

Called a "slave labor" act by organized labor it modified provisions in the earlier pro labor Wagner and Norris- LaGuardia Acts to put restraints on labor unions. The act established control of labor disputes on a new basis by enlarging the National Labor Relations Board and providing that the union or the employer must, before terminating a collective-bargaining agreement, serve notice on the other party and employ a government mediation service. The government was empowered to obtain an 80-day injunction against any strike that it deemed a peril to national health or safety. The act also prohibited jurisdictional strikes (dispute between two unions over which should act as the bargaining agent for the employees) and secondary boycotts (boycott against an already organized company doing business with another company that a union was trying to organize); and declared that it did not extend protection to workers on wildcat strikes; outlawed the closed shop; and permitted the union shop only on a vote of a majority of the employees. In a section that was later ruled unconstitutional it attempted to forbid labor unions from contributing to political campaigns. It was passed over Truman's veto.

·Hoover Commission

In the spirit of bi-partisanship former President Herbert Hoover headed a commission that reorganized the executive branch of government. Many of its recommendations were adopted in its final report and it succeeded in streamlining the federal government.

·Integration of the Armed Forces (1948)

By executive order, based on the report of a Presidential committee, Truman wiped out segregation and discrimination in the armed forces.

·FEPC (Federal Employment Practices Committee) Formed

In 1948 Truman sent a message to Congress that recommended a permanent civil rights commission, a Congressional committee on civil rights, a federal anti-lynching law, laws against discrimination, laws protecting the right to vote, and the formation of the FEPC. By executive order Truman banned discrimination in the hiring of federal employees.

·Alger Hiss Case

Former communist Whittaker Chambers, a senior editor of Time magazine, appeared before the House Un-American Activities Committee (HUAC) and identified Alger Hiss, former state department official and several other officials of having been members of a Communist cell whose purpose had been to infiltrate the U.S. government. At one point HUAC was ready to drop their investigation but persisted primarily because of the prodding of a young Congressman from California, Richard Nixon. Hiss was indicted on two counts of perjury (the statue of limitations on espionage had expired). One charged him with lying that he had passed classified State Department documents and the other with lying that he had ever known Whittaker Chambers. Throughout the trial that followed he vigorously maintained his innocence and it ended in a hung jury, 8-4 voting for conviction. A second trial found him guilty and this verdict was upheld by an appeals court. This trial would give impetus to the "Mc Carthyism" that would follow.

·Election of 1948

Republicans, confident of victory, once again nominated Governor Thomas Dewey of New York for President. The Democrats re-nominated Truman and their adoption of a strong civil rights plank resulted in Southern delegates walking out and forming their own political party called the Dixiecrats, who nominated South Carolina Governor Strom Thurmond for President. Another group, the liberals, upset with Truman over his tough stance on the USSR, left the Democratic Party and formed a new Progressive Party that nominated former cabinet member and Vice-President Henry Wallace for President. In an unexpected political upset,

Truman defeated Dewey 303-189 in the Electoral College with Thurmond taking 39 electoral votes. The Democrats recaptured control of Congress with a majority of 12 in the Senate and 93 in the House.

·Communists on Trial

Eleven top leaders of the U.S. Communist Party were put on trial and convicted of violating the Smith Act. The Supreme Court in the case of *Dennis v. US* upheld the convictions.

·"Hollywood 10"

The House Un-American Activities Committee (HUAC) began an investigation into the Hollywood Motion Picture Industry. HUAC interviewed 41 people who were working in Hollywood who became known as "friendly witnesses." During their interviews they named nineteen people who they accused of holding left-wing views. One of those named, Bertolt Brecht, a playwright, gave evidence and then left for East Germany. Ten others: Herbert Biberman, Lester Cole, Albert Maltz, Adrian Scott, Samuel Ornitz,, Dalton Trumbo, Edward Dmytryk, Ring Lardner Jr., John Howard Lawson and Alvah Bessie refused to answer any questions. HUAC found them guilty of contempt of Congress and the courts agreed. Each was sentenced to 6-12 months in prison. If people refused to name names when called up to appear before the HUAC, they were added to a blacklist that had been drawn up by the Hollywood film studios. Over 320 people were placed on this list that stopped them from working in the entertainment industry.

·Fair Deal

After his reelection, Truman proposed his own extension of the New Deal that would provide economic security, conservation, and housing and went far beyond FDR's initiatives in civil rights, national health insurance, federal aid to education, and agriculture subsides. After battling with Congress he failed to get national health insurance but did get an increase in the minimum wage. Most of his other proposals were not enacted.

·Point Four

In the 4th section of his Inaugural Address Truman called for a program of technical assistance to the underdeveloped areas of the world to be funded by $45 million in foreign aid from the U.S.

·McCarthyism

In 1950, Joseph McCarthy, junior senator from Wisconsin, made a speech in Wheeling, West Virginia and claimed to have a list of 205 (later reduced to 57) people in the State Department known to be members of the American Communist Party. For the next two years, McCarthy's committee investigated various government departments and questioned a large number of people about their political past. Some lost their jobs after they admitted they had been members of the Communist Party. McCarthy made it clear to the witnesses that the only way of showing that they had abandoned their left-wing views was by naming other members of the Party. This witch-hunt and anti-communist hysteria became known as "McCarthyism." Some left-wing artists and intellectuals were unwilling to live in this type of society and went to live and work in Europe. At first, McCarthy mainly targeted Democrats associated with the New Deal policies of the 1930s. Truman and members of his Democratic administration such as George Marshall and Dean Acheson, were accused of being soft on communism. Many whom McCarthy accused were denied reelection and most people refused to speak out against McCarthy, especially politicians because they feared that they would be accused of being soft on communism. His power and influence became so great that he targeted anti-American books in libraries. His researchers looked into the Overseas Library Program and discovered 30,000 books by "communists, pro-communists, former communists and anti anti-communists." After the publication of this list, these books were removed from the library shelves. Public libraries removed Robin Hood because of its theme of robbing from the rich to give to the poor. Ultimately McCarthy would over-reach when he accused the U.S. Army of having been infiltrated by the communists. In televised hearings, McCarthy's "bullying tactics" were exposed by Army council Joseph Welch which would eventually lead to his downfall.

· McCarran Act

Officially the Internal Security Act, it was passed over Truman's veto and provided for the registration of Communist and Communist front organizations and during national emergencies the internment of communists.

· 22nd Amendment

This amendment restricted the President's to two terms or 10 years total if they had succeeded into the office. As a sitting president Truman was exempt from its provisions but he chose not to run in 1952.

· McCarran-Walter Immigration Act

This act codified existing law while making some modifications in it. The quota system was retained but racial restrictions were abolished. The policy of restricting the numbers of immigrants from certain countries was continued. A preference system that selected which ethnic groups were desirable immigrants was adopted. The law defined three types of immigrants: relatives of U.S. citizens who were exempt from quotas (would be admitted without question); regular immigrants whose numbers were not supposed to exceed 270,000 per year; and refugees. The Act allowed the government to deport immigrants or naturalized citizens suspected of being engaged in subversive activities and also barred suspected subversives from entering the country.

Foreign Policy

· United Nations

Trygve Lie of Norway was elected the first Secretary General of the United Nations as it played a role in many of the foreign policy decisions of the post-war era.

· Philippines Independence (1946)

In accordance with the Tydings-McDuffie Act approved in 1934, the U.S. gave the Philippines their independence after the removal of the Japanese. The Philippines becoming independent would start a move for independence that would result in most of the colonized areas of the world becoming independent nation states in the next 30 years.

· Iranian Crisis

At the outbreak of World War II, Iran declared its neutrality but the country was soon invaded by both Britain and the Soviet Union. The occupation of Iran proved of vital importance to the Allied cause and brought Iran closer to the Western powers. Soviet pressure on Iran continued as British and American troops evacuated in keeping with their treaty agreement. Soviet troops remained in the country. There were two reasons why the USSR finally left Iran: first, Stalin was persuaded to withdraw his troops when Iran agreed to give the Soviets an oil concession; second, he withdrew as a result of United States, British, and UN pressure. In either case, this conflict over Iran marked the beginning of the Cold War between the USSR and the U.S. that would last for more than 40 years.

· Iron Curtain Speech

At Westminster College in Fulton, Missouri in 1946, Winston Churchill delivered his "Iron Curtain" speech to a crowd of more than 4,000 people. The speech was actually titled, "The Sinews of Peace," but contained the memorable line, "From Stettin in the Baltic to Trieste in the Adriatic an "iron curtain" has descended across the Continent. Behind that line lie all the capitals of the ancient states of Central and Eastern Europe. Warsaw,

Berlin, Prague, Vienna, Budapest, Belgrade, Bucharest and Sofia…." This metaphor by Churchill would indicate the dividing line in Europe between the countries that would wage the Cold War for the next 45 years.

·Containment

George F. Kennan, a career Foreign Service Officer and student of history, formulated the policy of "containment," in what was known as the "long telegram" to the state department. It became the basis of United States strategy for fighting the Cold War (1947-1989) with the Soviet Union. Kennan's ideas, were adopted by the Truman administration. They first came to public attention in 1947 in the form of a journal article in *Foreign Affairs*, written under the pseudonym "X." Kennan wrote, "The main element of any United States policy toward the Soviet Union, must be that of a long-term, patient but firm and vigilant containment of Russian expansive tendencies." To that end, he called for countering "Soviet pressure against the free institutions of the Western world" through the "adroit and vigilant application of counter-force at a series of constantly shifting geographical and political points, corresponding to the shifts and maneuvers of Soviet policy." This policy, Kennan predicted, would "promote tendencies which must eventually find their outlet in either the break-up or the gradual mellowing of Soviet power." Both the left and the right heavily criticized Kennan's policy. He suffered both condemnation and a number of policy defeats in the early 1950s. Despite these criticisms, containment remained the basic strategy of the United States throughout the Cold War. On the one hand, the United States did not withdraw into isolationism; it did not move to "roll back" Soviet power, as John Foster Dulles and others on the right had advocated. Each succeeding administration after Truman's, until the collapse of communism in 1989-1991, adopted a variation of Kennan's containment policy and made it their own. In the end, the USSR did exactly what Kennan had predicted they would do 40 years earlier—the strain was too great and it collapsed.

·Truman Doctrine: Greece and Turkey

The Soviets did not return their armies to a peacetime status after 1945. They and their allies challenged the West in Greece, Turkey, and Iran. Britain was too weak to play its former role in that region and announced to the U.S. that it was withdrawing from the eastern Mediterranean and Middle East. The U.S. filled the gap left by the withdrawal of both the British and French. Truman responded to Soviet pressure by announcing that the United States would support any country threatened by communist aggression. Soon after the proclamation of the Truman Doctrine in 1947, the United States sent economic and military aid to Greece and Turkey, to stop the spread of communism in those countries. With the help of U.S. aid the communist led rebellion was stopped in Greece. In Turkey, to counter the move of the USSR, the warship *Missouri* was sent to the straits and Truman announced that the U.S. would aid the UN with military power to protect the nations in the Near East from "coercion or penetration." The USSR's demand for revision of the Montreux Convention (it provided for exclusive Turkish administration of the "straits") to allow for joint Russian and Turkish administration, was adamantly opposed by the U.S.

·"Baruch Plan"

Bernard Baruch proposed the establishment of an international atomic development authority similar to the one proposed by the earlier Acheson-Lilienthal report. This organization would control all activities dangerous to world security and possess the power to license and inspect all other nuclear projects. Once in effect, no more bombs should be built and existing bombs would be destroyed. It was idealistically thought that abolishing atomic weapons could lay the groundwork for reducing and subsequently eliminating all weapons, thus outlawing war altogether. The "Plan," in Baruch's words was "the last, best hope of earth," and deviated from the optimistic tone of the Acheson- Lilienthal plan, which had intentionally remained silent on enforcement, and set specific penalties for violations such as illegally owning atomic bombs. The Soviet Union, not a nuclear power yet, insisted upon retaining its United Nations veto and argued that the abolition of atomic weapons should precede the establishment of an international authority. The Baruch plan, although approved by the General Assembly, was never put into effect because of the opposition from the USSR.

Rosenberg Case

Ethel and Julius Rosenberg were executed for espionage in Sing Sing Prison in 1953. They had been convicted of giving American atomic secrets to the USSR during World War II. The government charged that in 1944 and 1945 the Rosenbergs had persuaded Ethel's brother, David Greenglass—an employee at the Los Alamos atomic bomb project—to provide them and a third person, Harry Gold, with top-secret data on nuclear weapons. Although the government was convinced of their guilt, many people were not, and the debate over their guilt or innocence did not stop with their deaths. Many claimed that the political climate of McCarthyism made a fair trial impossible. Leftists in the United States and abroad organized a campaign to save the Rosenbergs and received the support of many liberals and religious leaders. Subsequent declassified government documents have, however, indicated that Julius Rosenberg did spy for the Soviets but that the government's case against Ethel Rosenberg was quite weak. They were the only Americans executed for espionage during the Cold War.

Marshall Plan (1948)

Officially titled the European Recovery Program, the idea named for Secretary of State George Marshall was for the U.S. to give Europe $11 billion so they could rebuild their economies and this would help stop the potential spread of communism as part of the policy of containment. The money offered required the European nations to get together and draw up a rational plan on how they would use the aid. For the first time, they would have to act as a single economic unit and cooperate with each other. Marshall also offered aid to the Soviet Union and its allies in Eastern Europe, but Stalin denounced the program as a trick and refused to participate. The Marshall Plan, benefited the American economy as well. The money would be used to buy goods from the United States, and they had to be shipped across the Atlantic on American merchant vessels. The plan worked and by 1953 the United States had pumped in $13 billion, and Europe was economically viable again. Also, communism did not spread in western Europe.

Coup in Czechoslovakia

While the debate over the Marshall Plan was going on in Congress—it was still in doubt whether it would pass or not—a coup in Czechoslovakia established communism in that country. When the Red army liberated Prague in 1945 the government that was formed was a National Front coalition in which three socialist parties—Czechoslovak Social Democrats or KSČ (communists) and Czechoslovak National Socialist Party predominated as the Slovak Popular Party was banned for collaborating with the Nazis. Other conservative, democratic parties, such as the Republican Party of Farmers and Peasants, were prevented from resuming activities in the postwar period. The dominant National Socialist Party of Eduard Benes allowed the communist KSC to gain control over such key ministries as information, internal trade, finance, and interior (including the police apparatus). Through these ministries, the communists were able to suppress noncommunist opposition, place party members in positions of power, and create a solid infrastructure for the takeover. A cabinet crisis precipitated the February, 1948 coup. National Socialist ministers, backed by all noncommunist parties, demanded a halt to the communists' blatant use of the Ministry of Interior's police and security forces to suppress non-communists. The twelve non-communist ministers resigned, in part, to induce Beneš to call for early elections where it was expected the communists would lose support. Beneš refused to call for elections and would not accept their resignations. The communist-controlled Ministry of Interior deployed police regiments and began to take over sensitive areas with their "action committees." These committees also purged all governmental and political party organs of "unreliable elements." On February 25, Beneš, perhaps fearing Soviet intervention, capitulated by accepting the resignations of the dissident ministers and received a new cabinet that completed the communists takeover. He died three months later after the communist coup.

·OAS

As a sign of inter-American cooperation the Organization of American States was established in 1948 with the adoption of the Charter of Bogota. This regional association would work for general cooperation and the promotion of peace between the countries of Latin America and the U.S.

·Israel Created by the UN

Following World War II, Great Britain, still controlled Palestine from its left over WWI mandate from the League of Nations. It continued its policy of limiting Jewish immigration to Palestine as it had done before the war. The Zionist (movement for the establishment of a Jewish homeland) conducted an underground war against the British, as well as applying pressure on the British government through the United States to relent and let more European survivors from the holocaust into Palestine. In 1947, the British rammed the Jewish illegal immigrant ship *Exodus* on the high seas. They towed it to Haifa where it was the subject of extensive publicity, generating public sympathy for the Zionist cause. The passengers eventually disembarked in Hamburg, Germany. The incident set the world and particularly U.S. opinion against the British, and caused the British to intern illegal immigrants thereafter in Cyprus, rather than attempt to return them to Europe. In 1947, the General Assembly of the United Nations voted to partition Palestine (both the U.S. and USSR voting in favor) by a vote of 33-13 with 10 abstentions into Jewish and Arab states as the British gave up their mandate. The state of Israel was established on May 15, 1948 after which the Arab states declared war on the new country.

·Berlin Airlift

In response to the U.S., French, and British adoption of a single currency, Stalin cut off all rail lines, canals and roads that entered West Berlin through the Russian sector of East Germany with the hope of getting the West to abandon the city. This cut off supplies of food and fuel meant the only way for the Allies to supply their sectors in Berlin was to fly in supplies. The massive effort to supply the 2 million West Berliners with food and fuel for heating, called Operation Vittles, begin in June, 1948, and lasted until September, 1949, although the Russians lifted the blockade in May of that year. After 11 months it became clear that the Allies would stand firm and the Russians gave in. The Allies remained in their sectors in Berlin. During the around-the-clock airlift some 277,000 flights were made, many at 3-minute intervals by U.S. and British planes. By spring of 1949, an average of 8,000 tons was being flown in daily. More than 2 million tons of goods—coal accounted for about 2/3rds—were ultimately delivered.

·NATO

Based in part on a resolution of former isolationist Senator Arthur Vandenberg that called for a U.S. association with regional and other collective arrangements affecting national security, the North Atlantic Treaty Organization was formed in 1949. NATO was set up largely to discourage an attack by the Soviet Union on the non-communist nations of Western Europe. The original members of NATO included the U.S., Canada, Belgium, Denmark, France, West Germany, Greece, Iceland, Italy, Luxembourg, the Netherlands, Norway, Portugal, Spain, Turkey, and the United Kingdom. NATO was established not only to discourage communist aggression but also to keep the peace among former enemies in Western Europe. In World War II, for example, Italy and Germany had fought most of the other countries that later became NATO members. In forming NATO, each member country agreed to treat an attack on any other member as an attack on itself. Militarily, the United States was the alliance's most powerful member, in part, because of its large supply of nuclear weapons. The NATO countries believed that the Soviet Union would not attack Western Europe if Soviet leaders thought such an attack would trigger war with the United States. NATO's policy is known as deterrence because it is designed to deter an attack. Dwight Eisenhower became the first NATO commander.

·Communists take China: Nationalists to Formosa

When the Japanese surrendered ending WWII, the Nationalists and the Communists resumed their Civil War as they scrambled to seize territory that had been occupied by the Japanese. Despite substantial amounts of military aid from the U.S. to help Chiang Kai Shek's Nationalist, corruption and disillusionment with his government led to Communist gains. Beginning in the latter half of 1947, the Communists began winning important victories in Hunan, Hupeh, and Manchuria and as the Communist armies grew, they inflicted heavier and heavier losses on Nationalist forces. In the last year of the Civil War, the Communists inflicted over a million and a half causalities on the Nationalist Army and it disintegrated in mid-1949. On October 1, 1949, before all of China had been conquered, Mao Tse Tung declared the establishment of the People's Republic of China. Four days later the Nationalist government fled to Chungking and then across the sea to Formosa (Portugal's name for Taiwan). China would consist of two governments: the mainland Communist government and the Taiwanese Nationalist government. With the U.S. fleet protecting the Nationalists the Communist under Mao Tse Tung were not able to bring about the complete unification of China.

·Korean Police Action

After WWII, Korea was taken from Japan and divided into two separate nations. South Korean President Syngman Rhee and North Korean General Secretary Kim Il-Sung were each intent on reuniting the peninsula under their own system of government. When United States Secretary of State Dean Acheson told the National Press Club that America's Pacific defense perimeter was made up of the Aleutians, Ryukyus, Japan, and the Philippines, this omission of Korea inadvertently sent a message to North Korea and the USSR that the U.S. might not defend South Korea. This led to North Korea invading South Korea in 1950 and forcing the U.S. and Korean forces to the far southern tip of the island around Pusan. Fortunately for the U.S., the USSR was boycotting the Security Council because Communist China was not in the UN; the Security Council condemned the North Korean action by a 9-0 resolution and called upon its member nations to come to the aid of South Korea. The U.S. and 15 other nations formed a "UN force" to pursue this action. President Truman characterized these hostilities as not being a "war," but a "police action." U.S. commander Douglas Mac Arthur made an amphibious landing at Inchon behind the North Korean lines that led to the U.S. breaking out of Pusan and rolling the North Korean troops all the way back to the Chinese border. At this point China sent in hundreds of thousands of volunteers that pushed the UN forces back toward the original line of demarcation between the two countries. When MacArthur publicly disagreed with Truman about the war by wanting to extend the "limited war" to bombing targets in China, Truman fired MacArthur. Both sides consolidated their positions and war became a stalemate that would ultimately result in a armistice that would establish the border between the two countries at the 38th parallel, almost the same location that had existed before the war.

UNIT XXVII
MULTIPLE-CHOICE QUESTIONS

Questions 1-4 refer to the following:

"The very existence of the Greek state is today threatened by the terrorist activities of several thousand armed men, led by Communists,... The British Government, which has been helping Greece, can give no further financial or economic aid... The British government has informed us that,... it can no longer extend financial or economic aid to Turkey. As in the case of Greece, if Turkey is to have the assistance it needs, the United States must supply it. I believe that it must be the policy of the United States to support free peoples who are resisting attempted subjugation by armed minorities or by outside pressures.... I believe that our help should be primarily through economic and financial aid.... I therefore ask the Congress to provide authority for assistance to Greece and Turkey in the amount of $400,000,000... I ask the Congress to authorize...American civilian and military personnel to Greece and Turkey..."

Harry S. Truman, "The Truman Doctrine," March 1947

1. In a speech before Congress, President Harry Truman took the unprecedented peace-time step of

   (A) signing a formal military alliance with Greece and Turkey
   (B) combating communist aggression by sending combat ground troops to fight the enemy
   (C) forming an alliance with Great Britain to assist Greece and Turkey's fight against aggression
   (D) supporting free people who were being subjugated by armed groups

2. The action taken in Greece and Turkey indicated what shift in public opinion in U.S. foreign policy?

   (A) A desire to reaffirm the Neutrality Acts of the 1930s
   (B) A growing acceptance in Congress for U.S. engagement in the world
   (C) The movement to bring the boys home now that the war was over
   (D) Bipartisonship in foreign policy led by Republican leaders like Senator Robert Taft

3. After being battered in WWII, which country would no longer be the traditional financial and economic supporter of Greece and Turkey

   (A) Germany
   (B) Soviet Union
   (C) Great Britain
   (D) United States

4. The Truman Doctrine was the first specific example of the implementation of which policy that would govern U.S. foreign policy for the next 40 years?

   (A) Containment
   (B) Isolationism
   (C) Neoconservatism
   (D) Colonization

395

Questions 5-6 refer to the following:

"Before he could build Levittown, Mr. Levitt had to get the approval of the Town of Hempstead... because ... they were different from most housing.... They had no basements. Why? 'It was for cost and speed,' Mr. Levitt said, ' we were in a hurry. It takes time to build cellars, and we wanted to build 150 houses a week.' 'Today the cellar is a rarity—all over the world... but in 1947 a house was expected to have a basement. We filed plans and the Hempstead Town building inspector turned them down.... [on] general principles, so we applied for an amendment to the building code.... Thanks to newspaper articles, it seemed that all the veterans in Nassau County came to the hearing... the Town Supervisor, wanted to table the matter, but the veterans refused to go home and the town board was forced to vote, and they passed it."

Irvin Molotsky, "Levittown 30 Years Later," October 2, 1977

5. The reason that Levittown was built in potato fields on Long Island was to

(A) create an instant slum of identical houses away from the city center
(B) provide cheap homes for returning WWII veterans who could buy them on the G.I. bill
(C) institute a commuter culture with people living far away from their work
(D) keep the returning soldiers separated from the rest of society

6. Levittown had a major demographic impact on the United States by creating which innovation for housing?

(A) Tenements
(B) Slums
(C) Row houses
D) Suburbia

Questions **7-8** refer to the following:

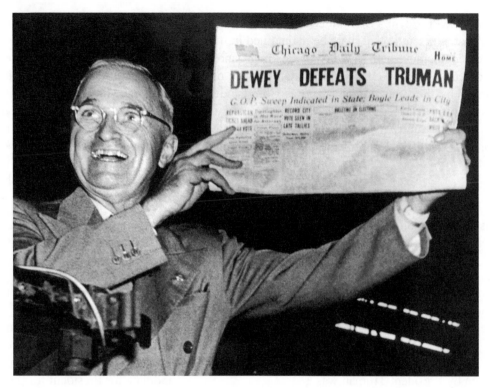

Chicago Tribune, November 3, 1948

7. The irony of this photograph of Harry Truman holding up the Chicago Tribune headline is

   (A) neither candidate was able to secure a majority in the Electoral College
   (B) Truman defeated Dewey not the other way around
   (C) Strom Thurmond the Dixiecrat candidate received 39 electoral votes
   (D) four major candidates in the race each polled more than a million votes

8. Which institution was damaged the most by the unexpected results of this 1948 election?

   (A) National Republican Party
   (B) Electoral College
   (C) Supreme Court
   (D) Polling organizations

Questions 9-12 refer to the following:

"Establishing the President's Committee on Equality of Treatment and Opportunity In the Armed Forces. "WHEREAS it is essential that there be maintained in the armed forces of the United States the highest standards of democracy, with equality of treatment and opportunity for all of those who serve in our country's defense. NOW, THEREFORE, by the virtue of the authority vested in me as President of the United States, by the Constitution..., and as Commander in Chief of the armed services, it is hereby ordered as follows: It is hereby declared to be the policy of the President that there shall be equality of treatment and opportunity for all persons in the armed forces without regard to race, color, religion, or national origin. This policy shall be put into effect as rapidly as possible...."

Harry S. Truman, "Executive Order 9981," July 26, 1948

9. In the passage above, this Executive Order ended what governmental practice in the armed forces?

(A) Integration
(B) Separatism
(C) Segmentation
(D) Segregation

10. This decision by President Truman was a forerunner of the 1954 Supreme Court decision of *Brown vs. the Board of Education of Topeka, Kansas* that declared what practice as being unconstitutional?

(A) Busing in schools
(B) Relying on the property tax for school funding
(C) Segregating children in public schools
(D) Failing students and holding them back from graduation

11. This action as well as the Civil Rights position of President Truman had what immediate political repercussion in the 1948 presidential election?

(A) The Republicans abandoning their position on equal rights for minorities
(B) A splintering in the Democratic party creating a 3rd party the Dixiecrats
(C) Black voters supporting a Democratic candidate for President for the first time
(D) The unpopularity of this decision assured Truman's defeat

12. The issuing of this executive order started a process that over the next 20 years would end

(A) Jim Crow
(B) adverse condemnation proceedings
(C) right to work laws
(D) sharecropping system

Questions 13-15 refer to the following:

"Conservatism in its crisis of despair turns to fascism: so progressivism in its crisis of despair turns to Communism. Each in a sober mood has a great contribution to make to free society: the conservative in his emphasis on law and liberty, the progressive in his emphasis on mass welfare. But neither is capable of saving free society. Both, faced by problems they cannot understand and fear to meet, tend to compound their own failure by delivering free society to its totalitarian foe. To avoid this fate, we must understand as clearly as possible the reasons for the appeal of totalitarianism."

Arthur Schlesinger Jr. *The Vital Center: The Politics of Freedom*, 1949

13. The passage above is especially critical of extreme conservatism and extreme liberalism for

   (A) giving a free society over to totalitarianism
   (B) their emphasis on law, liberty, and mass welfare
   (C) taking a sober approach in their contribution to a free society
   (D) having a movement to turn to in the crisis of despair

14. The dominant political ideology of the 1920s, 1950s, and 1980s that would be critical of Schlesinger for his view of

   (A) fascism
   (B) progressivism
   (C) conservatism
   (D) communism

15. A possible reason why Schlesinger calls his book *The Vital Center* is because he favors

   (A) progressivism
   (B) conservatism
   (C) totalitarianism
   (D) a middle ground

NO TESTING MATERIAL ON THIS PAGE

UNIT XXVIII
EISENHOWER 50S & THE COLD WAR

The desire of a generation who had gone through the Great Depression and WWII for conformity and security was thwarted by the growing conflict with the communist world. There was a conservative tinge to this Eisenhower decade (looked on with nostalgia by modern day neo-cons) with the focus on materialism, conformity, and security. Underneath that placid surface was a great deal of unease and strife that is often ignored by the "Happy Days" interpretation. The postwar Civil Rights movement that would come to fruition in the 1960s started in this decade.

Politics and Domestic Events

· Election of 1952
After 20 years of Democratic rule the nation was ready for a change. After a spirited convention (the first one on TV) the Republican political moderate, Dwight D. Eisenhower gained the nomination from the conservative Robert Taft. Eisenhower overwhelmingly defeated the drafted Democratic candidate Illinois Governor Adlai Stevenson 442-89. During the campaign the power of television was demonstrated for the first time when Richard Nixon, Eisenhower's Vice-Presidential nominee, used it to blunt criticism that he had received secret money from an illegal "slush fund" and in the speech he only admitted to receiving a dog that his daughter named Checkers and he refused to give the family dog back. This "Checkers" speech saved Nixon's political career.

· Moderate Republicanism
A member of the internationalist wing of the party, the genial Eisenhower saw himself as a conservative on money issues and more liberal on issues dealing with human beings. Despite his rhetoric to stop the "creeping socialism" of the New Deal, his administration reflecting the philosophy of "dynamic conservatism" expanded Social Security and unemployment benefits, established the Department of Health Education and Welfare, and increased federal aid to education. He genuinely tried to balance the budget but only three of the eight he submitted to Congress were balanced.

·Eisenhower Economics

He initially reduced federal spending by 10% and eliminated 200,000 government jobs. However, when his initial passivity failed to halt the recession of 1953-54; he resorted to both fiscal policy (increasing government spending) and monetary policy to stimulate the economy.

·Suburbia

The move to the suburbs continued from the late 1940s and by the end of the decade more than 1/3rd of the total population lived in the suburbs. Veteran's Administration (VA) and FHA loans continued to give people access to low interest mortgages to buy cheap suburban housing built on the Levittown model. Suburbia became more than just a place to live but it also brought in a lifestyle change. The backyard instead of the porch or step became the focal point of outdoor living and the automobile became a mainstay of family life.

·End of McCarthyism

After McCarthy began investigating communist infiltration into the military, Eisenhower finally turned on him for his "book burning" (McCarthy's influence led to the removal of 30,000 books in the Overseas Library Program. The end of McCarthy would come with the Congressional hearings on alleged subversives in the Army when the Army's counsel Joseph Welch skewered him with these words as the hearings were on national television, "Little did I dream you could be so reckless and cruel as to do an injury to that lad…. Have you no sense of decency." Welch's decency resonated and McCarthy's bullying did not come across well on the new media. The Senate would finally censure McCarthy in 1954 for "conduct unbecoming a member" and he would die three years later in 1957 with little influence and no respect.

·Dixon-Yates Scandal

Eisenhower's desire to dismantle the "creeping socialism" of the TVA failed. In 1954, he had the Atomic Energy Commission award a major power plant contract in the Tennessee Valley area to the private firm Dixon-Yates. A later congressional inquiry found improprieties in the way the contract was awarded and the administration had to sue to block the contract it had awarded. The TVA continued as a government enterprise as it does today.

·St. Lawrence Seaway

The U.S. contributed $134 billion to Canada's $338 billion in this project that linked the Great Lakes to the Atlanta Ocean through the St. Lawrence river in Canada. Eisenhower supported this almost New Deal type of project to the chagrin of many conservatives in his own party.

·Federal Highway Act of 1956

Based on his experience with the German autobahn after WWII, Eisenhower supported the largest public works project in the nation's history as $32 billion dollars would be spent building the nations 41,000 mile Interstate Highway system. This system would tie together the nations highways and render older highways like the fabled Route 66 obsolete. In time, it became the largest highway system in the world and the largest public works project in history. Americans could now travel non-stop from the Atlantic to the Pacific and from the Gulf of Mexico to Canada. About 1/3rd of the total number of miles driven in the U.S. are on the Interstate Highway system.

·Communist Control Act

This 1954 law deprived the Communist party of its rights and immunities and subjected Communists to penalties under the Internal Security Act.

·Social Security Act Amendments

Under Eisenhower, benefits were raised, more workers were added to its coverage, disability insurance was provided, and the minimum age for women to collect was lowered to 62.

·1956 Elections

Eisenhower won easily against Stevenson but he was more popular than his party as Democratic majorities in Congress were established that would last until 1994. The electoral vote was 457-73 with Stevenson only winning seven Southern states. The apparent domination of Congress by the Democrats was somewhat of an illusion as conservative southern Democrats often sided with conservative Republicans to form a majority.

·Termination Policy

To promote Native Americans to assimilate into mainstream American society the Relocation Act of 1956 urged them to move to urban areas. Termination had started in 1953 when most federal funding to the tribes and the reservation system was ended. By 1958, protests by Native Americans led Eisenhower to reverse termination.

·Sherman Adams Scandal

Eisenhower's chief of staff was forced to resign when it was disclosed that businessman Bernard Goldfine had given him a vicuna coat and an oriental rug in return for Adams' intervention with the FTC and the SEC to give Goldfine preferential treatment.

·National Defense Education Act (NDEA)

$295 million in federal money was loaned to college students at 3% interest with the stipulation that 50% of the loan could be forgiven if the student taught in public schools for five years. An additional $280 million was given to state schools for facilities in science or modern foreign languages.

·Landrum-Griffin Act

A 1959 law that attempted to crack down on union corruption by banning ex-convicts from holding union offices, required frequent elections of officers, and regulated the investments of union funds. Union power and membership, that had reached its height in 1957, steadily declined after that date and by the 21st century became less than half of what it had been.

·Alaska and Hawaii

In January of 1959 Alaska was added as the 49th state and in August of that same year Hawaii became the 50th state.

Foreign Policy

·Brinker Amendment (1953)

After extended debate, this bill limited the scope of international treaties and imposed controls over the power of the President to negotiate treaties and executive amendments. It failed to pass by one vote in the Senate, 60-31.

·Korean Armistice

After two years of negotiations an armistice was finally reached three weeks after Eisenhower went to Korea as he promised he would do during the 1952 Presidential campaign. South Korea gained 1,500 more miles of territory than it had before the war and the line separating the two Koreas was established just north of the 38th parallel.

·Mutual Defense Agreement with Spain

This provided Spain with U.S. military and economic aid while the U.S. would be allowed to build air and naval installations in Spain. As Spain was not a part of NATO the U.S. was now committed to Spain's defense.

·Atoms for Peace

Eisenhower proposed that nuclear countries turn over some of their stockpiles of uranium and fissionable materials to the International Atomic Energy Agency for peaceful purposes. The USSR rejected the proposal but Eisenhower was able to achieve some of it by working with the UN.

·Dulles' Foreign Policy

Secretary of State John Foster Dulles initiated a new foreign policy based on rolling back communism through the twin threats of brinkmanship and massive retaliation. In calling for the liberation of all nations that had fallen under Soviet control since 1945, he believed the U.S. should go to the brink of war and the other side would back down because of the threat of nuclear massive retaliation by the U.S. Despite this rhetoric and condemnation of Truman's containment, Eisenhower tended to rely on diplomacy and covert action to achieve his ends and generally continued Truman's policy. The deficiencies of Dulles' policy were apparent when the U.S. failed to intervene in the Hungarian revolt even after the Hungarians pleaded for help.

·SEATO Pact

It was to be an Asian version of NATO as the U.S., UK, France, New Zealand, Pakistan, the Philippines and Thailand formed the Southeast Asian Treaty Organization (SEATO) in 1954. The pact pledged joint action against aggression upon any member nation, but unlike NATO, there was no unified military command. In an addendum the U.S. said it applied only to Communist aggression.

·Covert Actions and the CIA

A new tactic emerged under Eisenhower to overthrow governments that were deemed to be leftist or unfavorable to the U.S. by using the CIA.

1. **Iran**—When Mohammad Mossadegh, the elected leader in Iran, nationalized British owned oil fields Eisenhower cut off aid to Iran and authorized the CIA to organize a coup against the Iranian leader. It succeeded and the young, pro-U.S. Shah Reza Pahlavi became the leader of Iran.
2. **Guatemala**—In 1954, when President Jacobo Arbenz took over uncultivated sections of Guatemala's largest plantations, including those of the American owned United Fruit Company, and distributed the land to the rural poor, the CIA led forces bombed the capital and installed a new pro-U.S. government that reversed the land reform program.

·Formosa Resolution (1995)

In response to threats on Taiwan by Chinese Foreign Minister Chou en-Lai and the shelling of Nationalist held islands Quemoy and Matsu, Congress passed the Formosa Resolution authorizing the president to use armed force "as he deems necessary to defend Formosa and the Pescadores (an island group)." This was followed by the U.S.–Nationalist Chinese Mutual Security Pact ratified by the Senate by a 65-6 vote.

·Austrian Peace Treaty (1955)

An agreement between the four occupying powers (U.S., USSR, United Kingdom, and France) restored Austria's sovereignty and declared it's military to be neutral in perpetuity. This showed that the Western powers and the USSR could work together to achieve a common objective.

·Baghdad Pact

To block USSR pressure in the Middle East this agreement between the UK, Turkey, Pakistan, Iran, and Iraq, was promoted by the U.S. Ironically, the U.S. declined to formally join as it would have alienated U.S.

relations with Egypt. The U.S. sent observers to Pact meetings, participated in defense and anti-subversion committees, and formally joined the military committee in 1957. After Iraq withdrew from the Pact, its name was officially changed to the Central Treaty Organization (CENTO).

·Hungarian Uprising (1956)

In response to Dulles' call for countries to overthrow communism, Hungary deposed their communist leaders, took to the streets to demand democracy, and their moderate leaders withdrew Hungary from the Warsaw Pact. Khrushchev used Soviet tanks to crush the revolt as the Hungarians pleaded for help from the West. Eisenhower was unwilling to risk nuclear war with the Soviets and refused to help. U.S. immigration laws were loosened to allow 40,000 Hungarian refugees to flee to the U.S. Most of these came via neutral Austria.

·Suez Crisis (1956)

After the U.S. government cancelled its offer of financial help to Egypt to build the Aswan Dam because the Soviet Union was also giving assistance, President Gamal Abdel Nasser seized the Suez Canal and nationalized it. When he refused to let Israeli ships pass through the canal, Israel invaded Egypt. France and England followed by invading Egypt claiming they were protecting the canal. The USSR and the U.S. working together brought about the withdrawal of the Israeli, French, and British forces and averted a nuclear confrontation in the process. A UN emergency force was installed to act as a buffer between Egypt and Israel and Israel was forced to give up the territory it had captured militarily.

·Sputnik

The launching of a 184 pound space satellite by the USSR in 1957 called Sputnik I, and Sputnik II which contained the dog "Laika," panicked the U.S. as the public feared that the Soviets' ability to launch satellites also translated into the capability to launch ballistic missiles that could carry nuclear weapons from Europe to the U.S. The Sputnik launch marked the start of the space age and the U.S.-USSR space race and would lead directly to the creation of National Aeronautics and Space Administration (NASA) and changes in education to emphasize math and science as well as the introduction of Advanced Placement programs into American high schools.

·Eisenhower Doctrine (1957)

After the Suez crisis, Eisenhower asked and received from Congress, the authority to extend economic and military aid to any Middle East nation "requesting assistance against armed aggression from any country controlled by international communism."

·Lebanon

The Eisenhower Doctrine was applied when U.S. Marines landed in Lebanon in 1958 at the request of the Lebanese government to restore order and bolster the pro-Western and Maronite Christian Lebanese government of President Camille Chamoun against internal opposition and threats from Syria and the United Arab Republic.

·Spirit of Camp David

Nikita Khrushchev's visit to the U.S. in 1959 generated good will and a thawing of the Cold War as he and Eisenhower established amicable relations and made plans for a full summit of world leaders in Paris to be held the following year. The trip was marred by Walt Disney's refusal to allow Khrushchev to visit Disneyland under the "thin" excuse of security reasons which made the Premier furious.

·Cuban Revolution

After four years in the jungle, Fidel Castro overthrew the U.S. backed Fulgencio Batista regime in Cuba in 1959. His nationalism, anti-American rhetoric and broad based social and economic revolution, led him to seize two U.S. and British owned oil refineries. Eisenhower cut the quota on Cuban sugar, which led to the nationalization of all big foreign and Cuban businesses. Eisenhower broke diplomatic relations with Cuba and an embargo was placed on most exports to Cuba that still exists today. Castro turned to the USSR for support and turned his country into a communist nation.

· U-2 Incident
American pilot Francis Gary Powers was shot down and captured while flying over the Soviet Union. NASA released a CIA cover story that said it was a weather research plane but Power's confession to the Soviets that he was spying forced Eisenhower to admit he had authorized the flights. This unprecedented admission of espionage activities by a head of state caused a great deal of ill will for the U.S. in the new emerging "Third World" of former colonies who were recently independent. It gave Khrushchev the opportunity to scuttle the Paris Summit, as well as the planned trip by Eisenhower to the USSR. After being sentenced to 10 years in prison, Powers was exchanged for Soviet master spy Rudolf Abel in 1962.

· Farewell Address
In leaving office Eisenhower warned the nation against the growing power of the military-industrial complex as defense spending had more than tripled in the decade.

Social and Cultural

· TV
Just as the automobile had revolutionized American society in the 1920s, the television had the same impact on the 1950s. By the end of the 1950, 46 million households owned at least one television set. Popular programs like the "Texico Star Theatre" (Milton Berle) and "I Love Lucy" (Lucille Ball and Desi Arnez) reached millions of viewers and advertisers were spending more than $1.5 billion to convince viewers to buy their products. Society changed dramatically as social life now revolved around the "tube." The traditional family meal was changed with Swanson's invention of the TV dinner, in part, child-rearing would become a function of the TV, and national sporting events would eventual revolve around TV coverage. High quality live shows like "Playhouse 90," and news documentaries like Edward R. Murrow's "See it Now," indicated that this innovative medium could enhance American life. However, the race for profits, the power of advertising, and the tendency to appeal to the lowest common denominator, soon led it to be called a "vast wasteland" by the head of the FCC Newton Minow.

· *Film Noir*
French term meaning black film used to describe the dark and downbeat look and themes of American crime and detective films of the 1940s and 1950s. These included such classics as *The Maltese Falcon*, *Murder My Sweet*, *Double Indemnity*, *The Woman in the Window*, and *Laura*. These films reflected the tensions and insecurities of the time period, and were the opposite of the optimism of Hollywood's musicals and comedies. Fear, mistrust, bleakness, loss of innocence, and despair are all a part of this genre, reflecting the chill of the Cold War period when the threat of nuclear annihilation was ever-present. The criminal, violent, misogynistic, hard-boiled, or greedy perspectives of anti-heroes in *film noir* were a metaphoric symptom of society's evils. These films with their strong undercurrent of moral conflict, purposelessness and sense of injustice were rarely happy or had optimistic endings. A *film noir* story frequently developed around a cynical, hard-hearted, disillusioned male character who encountered a beautiful, amoral, seductive *femme fatale* who would use her feminine wiles and sexuality to manipulate him into becoming the fall guy for a crime—usually murder. After a betrayal or double-cross, she was frequently destroyed as well, often at the cost of the hero's life. The primary moods of classic *film noir* were melancholy, alienation, bleakness, disillusionment, disenchantment, pessimism, ambiguity, moral corruption, evil, guilt, desperation and paranoia. The titles of many *film noir*

classics often reflected the nature or tone of the style and content itself: *Dark Passage. The Naked City, Fear in the Night, Out of the Past, Kiss me Deadly*, and *Touch of Evil.*

·Folk Music

Folk songs have a long history in the U.S. and they range in subject matter from war, work, civil rights, and economic hardship to nonsense, satire and love songs. Over the years they rarely enjoyed commercial success. There is a message in folk music that is usually sung in the ballad style. Folk music becomes prevalent during times of trouble, hardships, or turmoil. The earliest folk songs came from the slave fields as spirituals such as "Down by the Riverside, "We Shall Overcome," and "Follow the Drinking Gourd." The early 20th Century brought folk music back into America as workers struggled and struck for child labor laws and better working conditions. Joe Hill was an early folk songwriter and union agitator and his songs adapted the tunes of Baptist hymns. In the 1930s, folk music enjoyed a resurgence as the stock market crashed and workers everywhere were displaced and scrambled for jobs. A series of droughts and dust storms encouraged farmers out of the Dust Bowl region and toward promises in California and Oregon. Woody Guthrie, one of those workers who headed to California, wrote hundreds of folk songs including his classic—"This Land is Your Land." In the 1950s and 1960s, folk music emerged again with themes of Civil Rights and the War in Vietnam. American folksingers gathered in coffee houses and at hootenannies and continued the legacies of Woody Guthrie, Pete Seeger, and The Weavers. Out of this came the protest songs of Bob Dylan, Joni Mitchell, Joan Baez, Judy Collins, Peter, Paul, and Mary and a host of others. This 1960s folk revival offered political commentary as well as the powerful promise for change.

·Youth Rebellion

The rebellion was evident in many forms ranging from college panty raids in the early 50s to genuine juvenile delinquency of gangs in New York and other urban centers as shown in "West Side Story." Biker gangs as depicted in the popular film starring Marlon Brando, "The Wild One;" and the general alienation of youth symbolized by actor James Dean in "Rebel Without a Cause" created a stereotype. The media played up this youth rebellion by focusing on the superficial and the sensational. The Broadway musical West Side Story portrayed alienated youth in its story along with an updated Romeo and Juliet theme. All of these would start a tendency for youth to rebel in each subsequent generation. A form of youth rebellion that started in the 1950s would come to fruition in the turbulent 60s.

·Beatnik Culture

The "beat"(nik was added by detractors after Sputnik in 1957) movement in the United States in the 1950s rejected middle-class American values, customs, and tastes, especially ones of conformity and security in favor of radical politics, mystical religions, and exotic jazz, art, and literature. This bohemian movement had its own symbols (coffee houses, black clothing, berets, folk music, and poetry readings) that separated it from conventional America. The anti-middle class message of the beats, against materialism and the competitive corporate world, was spread by poet Allen Ginsberg's *Howl* and the novelist Jack Kerouac's *On the Road*. In substance this culture had an affinity to the earlier "Lost Generation" of expatriates of the 1920s.

·Rock and Roll

A new type of music emerged that combined elements of rhythm and blues, blues, boogie woogie, jazz, folk, gospel, and country and western. Its name came from Cleveland disc jockey Allen Freed who saw white teenagers dancing to, and buying rhythm and blues records, that had been traditionally written and recorded for blacks. Black R & B performers like Fats Domino and Joe Turner continued to be popular but Rock and Roll took on white roots with the popularity of Bill Haley and the Comets,' "Rock Around the Clock," featured in the film about teen rebellion, "The Blackboard Jungle." Rock and Roll continued to grow in popularity because of the influence of Elvis Presley, a white singer who sang black, and the popularity of the T.V. show,

Dick Clark's "American Bandstand." Other prominent figures in the rise of Rock and Roll included Little Richard, Chuck Berry, and Buddy Holly.

·Literature

A number of writers became critical of the culture of the post-WWII era.

1. ***Catcher in the Rye***—J. D. Salinger's protagonist Holden Caulfield lashed out against the hypocrisy and phoniness of the world around him.
2. ***Invisible Man***—Ralph Ellison's story of an African American man who searched for his place in a society that is both indifferent and hostile to him.
3. ***The Lonely Crowd***—David Reisman's sociological treatise about how society had transformed the individual from being inner-directed with fixed and certain goals to other-directed or conforming to the will of the masses.
4. ***The Man in the Grey Flannel Suit***—Sloane Wilson novel, made into a successful film, captured the dissatisfaction that the corporate world had brought to the individual who longs for a more vital and authentic existence.
5. ***From Here to Eternity***—James Jones anti-war WWII story that was made into a popular film.
6. ***A Raisin in the Sun***—Borrowing the title from Langston's Hughes poem about how a dream deferred dries up like a "raisin in the sun," Lorraine Hansberry's accurate portrayal of the life and dreams of an African American family ushered in a new consciousness about the black experience.

UNIT XXVIII
MULTIPLE-CHOICE QUESTIONS

Questions 1-5 refer to the following:

"By the summer of 1955 Eisenhower's in-between concept of the President's role, his conservative-liberal domestic policies, his mixed attitudes in foreign affairs, his warm but unaggressive personality, were sweeping him to a political potency unapproached since the heyday of Franklin Roosevelt. The right wing of the Republican Party lay at his feet, powerless, if not shattered... Senator Mc Carthy was now duly censored by the Senate... by a vote of 67-22.... Why were there so few calls for 'real liberalism.' Adlai Stevenson would soon answer:... 'I agree that it is a time for catching our breath; I agree that moderation is the spirit of the times.' Moderation, middle of the road—the phrases were filling the country..." A UCLA coed summarized the findings..., 'What, in general did she want out of living?' 'Why, a good sensible life'.... 'But,... not too darned sensible.'"

Eric F. Goldman, *The Crucial Decade and After: America, 1945-1960*, 1956

1. The passage above mentions that the right-wing of the Republican Party lay at Eisenhower's feet. What did Eisenhower do to mollify the right wing of his party?

   (A) Connect all the major highways by building the interstate highway system
   (B) Participate in a joint venture with Canada in building the St. Lawrence Seaway
   (C) "Under God" was added to the Pledge of Allegiance and "In God We Trust" was put on all money
   (D) Broadening social security coverage and increasing the monthly amounts as well as other reforms in the system

2. By saying she did not want her life to be "too darned sensible" the UCLA coed was

   (A) trying to moderate her statement of a good sensible life
   (B) making a sensible life the ultimate goal of life
   (C) taking a position that could not be defended about life
   (D) living life to the fullest by burning the candle at both ends

3. According to the passage above the Eisenhower era was characterized by

   (A) conservatism
   (B) classical liberalism
   (C) radicalism
   (D) moderation

4. The most important political issue during the crucial decade of 1945 to 1955 was

   (A) the Great Depression
   (B) Cold War
   (C) Civil Rights
   (D) Counter Culture

5. Senator McCarthy was censored by the U.S. Senate for

   (A) acting contrary to senatorial traditions by using tactics that debased the Senate into a forum for hate and character assassination
   (B) accepting bribes and kickbacks for doing favors for special constituents
   (C) sexual behavior and indiscretions
   (D) steering government contracts for millions of dollars into corporate monopolies from his home state of Wisconsin

409

Questions 6-8 refer to the following:

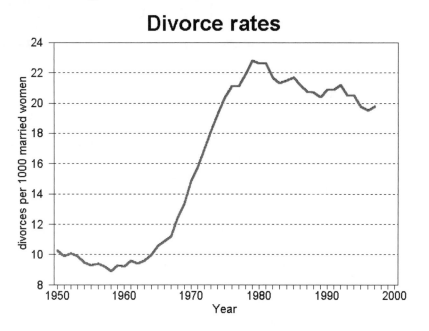

Divorce rates

6. A valid conclusion that can be derived from the chart is that the generation who led the way in the number of divorces were the

   (A) G.I. or "Greatest Generation"
   (B) Baby Boomers
   (C) Generation X
   (D) Millenials

7. Which of the following is a likely reason for the decline in divorces during the 1950s?

   (A) The continuation of an economic downturn made divorce too expensive for most couples
   (B) Divorces had been common and prevalent in the war years and this was a normal correction
   (C) Societal pressure of the woman as wife and mother created a stigma for women who divorced and did not keep their home and family together
   (D) The Catholic Church made it more difficult for women to get annulments of marriages that ended in divorces that would allow them to remarry

8. The dramatic increases in divorces starting in 1962 and reaching its peak in 1980 can be attributed in part to all of the following EXCEPT

   (A) the publication of Betty Friedan's book, *The Feminine Mystique*, defining "the problem that has no name," and launching the feminist movement that showed how dissatisfied many women were with their role as a suburban housewife and mother
   (B) a launching of the counter-culture with its disavowal of the middle class values of the dominant culture
   (C) the wide dissemination of modern means of birth control including the "pill"
   (D) the establishment of the marriage penalty in the tax code which made being married less desirable on an economic basis

For Questions 9-12 refer to the following chart:

...Domestic Intercity Freight Traffic by Type of Transportation: 1939 to 1957 (selected years)

Year	Total Traffic Volume	Railroads Vol.	%	Motor Vehicles Vol.	%	Inland Waterways Vol.	%	Oil Pipelines Vol.	%	Airways Vol.	%
1957	1,352,131	626	46	261	19	232	17	233	17	6	.04
1951	1,178,075	655	56	188	16	182	15	152	13	4	.03
1945	1,027,115	691	67	67	7	142	14	126	12	.09	.009
1939	543,534	339	62	53	10	96	18	55	10	.01	.002

9. From the table above which of the following statements are true regarding the domestic intercity freight traffic by type of transportation from selected years from 1939 to 1957?

(A) The only mode of transportation whose % went up every year over the four selected years was the oil pipelines
(B) Over two-thirds of freight traffic was being transported by railroads by the end of WWII
(C) The type of transportation that was the steadiest with the least amount of change was oil pipelines
(D) Total traffic volume was so low in 1939 because of WWII

10. Which type of transportation showed the greatest decline from 1939 to 1957?

(A) Railroads
(B) Motor Vehicles
(C) Inland Waterways
(D) Oil Pipelines

11. Which of the following statements is accurate regarding intercity freight traffic from 1939 to 1957?

(A) During the entire period Railroad freight traffic was more than 50% of the total traffic
(B) The mode of transportation that almost tripled between 1939 and 1957 was motor vehicles
(C) Inland waterways increased its share of freight traffic from 1939 to 1957
(D) Both inland waterways and motor vehicles decreased their % of freight traffic carried during WWII

12. In modern times a compenent of freight traffic that was almost non existent the years 1939-1957 is

(A) trucks
(B) ships
(C) planes
(D) buses

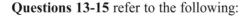

Questions 13-15 refer to the following:

"... we have been compelled to create a permanent armaments industry of vast proportions.... We annually spend on military security more than the net income of all United States corporations. This conjunction of an immense military establishment and a large arms industry is new in the American experience. The total influence—economic, political, even spiritual—is felt in every city, every State house, every office of the Federal government. We recognize the imperative need for this development. Yet we must not fail to comprehend its grave implications. Our toil, resources and livelihood are all involved; so is the very structure of our society. In the councils of government, we must guard against the acquisition of unwarranted influence, whether sought or unsought, by the military industrial complex. The potential for the disastrous rise of misplaced power exists and will persist...."

Dwight D. Eisenhower, "Farewell Address," 1961

13. The primary reason why the U.S. felt "compelled to create a permanent armaments industry of vast proportions" was the

(A) need to stop the aggression of the fascist countries Germany, Italy, and Japan
(B) fear of international communism
(C) imperialistic solutions to solve the problems of the world
(D) protection of the countries of the United Nations by U.S. forces

14. The phrase Eisenhower used to describe what the U.S. needed to guard against was the influence of the

(A) banks and financial services industry on the economy
(B) policies of creeping socialism in our government
(C) military-industrial complex
(D) international community on foreign policy

15. Eisenhower's concern in 1961 is borne out by which fact about U.S. defense spending in the 21st century?

(A) 40% of the world's total is spent by the U.S., more than the next 15 countries combined
(B) The amounts are justified by the many wars the U.S. is/and has been fighting throughout the world
(C) In the post Cold War era it is a smaller percentage of GDP than at any time in the 20th and 21st centuries
(D) Most of the spending is directed against a threat posed to U.S. security by our adversaries Russia and China

UNIT XXIX
CIVIL RIGHTS MOVEMENTS
OF THE 50s, 60s, 70s

The Civil Rights movement that started during the Truman presidency continued during the Eisenhower 50s and reached fruition during the turbulent 60s. In less than two decades the Jim Crow segregation system that had existed since the end of Reconstruction was overturned. It took a combination of legal challenges, peaceful means of protest, and economic boycotts to end legal segregation.

Eisenhower Years

· *Brown vs. Board of Education of Topeka*

This 1954 case overturned the 1896 case of *Plessy v. Ferguson* that had established the doctrine of "separate but equal" segregation in public facilities. Linda Brown was an eight-year old black girl who had to cross Topeka, Kansas to attend grade school, while her white friends were able to attend classes at a public school just a few blocks away. The Topeka School system was segregated on the basis of race, and under the separate but equal doctrine, this arrangement was acceptable and legal. The lead attorney for the NAACP that represented the plaintiffs was Thurgood Marshall who later became the first African American on the Supreme Court. The Supreme Court's unanimous ruling written by Chief Justice Earl Warren in ringing words declared, "We conclude that, in the field of public education, the doctrine of 'separate but equal' has no place. Separate educational facilities are inherently unequal. Therefore, we hold that the plaintiffs and others similarly situated for whom the actions have been brought are, by reason of the segregation complained of, deprived of the equal protection of the laws guaranteed by the Fourteenth Amendment." The *Brown* decision initiated educational and social reform throughout the United States and was a catalyst in launching the modern Civil Rights movement.

· **Southern Manifesto**

Opposition to the Brown decision was intense as 101 southern members of Congress signed this document. It denounced the Brown decision as "a clear abuse of judicial power....which is destroying the amicable

413

relations between the white and Negro races." A number of southern members of Congress refused to sign it including Senate Majority Leader Lyndon Johnson of Texas.

·White Citizens Councils

These were formed in response to the Brown decision and they favored continued segregation of the races. They were successful for a time in blocking integration by using legal maneuvers as well as the economic pressure of mortgage foreclosures, job dismissals, and the withdrawal of credit. In some instances they forced the closure of the public schools. They were aided by the Supreme Court which used the term "all deliberate speed" in its ruling in the Brown decision. This enabled school districts to drag their feet and one year after the ruling there was not a single black student attending schools with whites in eight southern states.

·Montgomery Bus Boycott (1955-1956)

This event started when Rosa Parks refused to give up her seat on a bus to a white man in violation of state and local laws. Parks was arrested and fined $10 for not moving to the back of the bus. Under the leadership of Rev. Dr. Martin Luther King, Jr. a boycott was launched lasting more than a year that resulted in the bus company losing 65% of its normal income. Montgomery city officials struck a blow to the boycott when they announced that any cab driver charging less than the 45-cent minimum fare would be prosecuted. Since the boycott began, the black cab services had been charging blacks only 10-cents to ride, the same price as the bus fare, but this service would now be illegal. To further stop the boycott the Montgomery municipal government indicted 89 blacks under an old law prohibiting boycotts. King was the first defendant to be tried and as press from around the nation looked on, he was ordered to pay a $500 fine plus $500 in court costs or spend 386 days in the state penitentiary. Other tactics were used to stop the boycott such as bombing King's house. Finally, on November 13, 1956, the U.S. Supreme Court upheld an earlier federal court's ruling, declaring segregation on buses unconstitutional. The Montgomery Bus Boycott was officially over and the buses were integrated.

·Little Rock 9

Inspired by the Brown decision, nine black students attempted to integrate Little Rock High School in 1957. Governor Orville Faubus ordered the Arkansas National Guard to monitor the school. When the group of students arrived at Central High on September 3, they were kept from entering the school by the National Guardsmen. On September 20, an injunction against Governor Faubus was issued and three days later the group of nine students returned to Central High School. Although the students were not physically injured, several black reporters were as a mob of 1,000 townspeople prevented the students from remaining at school. Finally, after a great deal of pressure and many diplomatic efforts, President Eisenhower intervened militarily ordering 1,000 paratroopers of the 101st Airborne to Little Rock as well as nationalizing the Arkansas National Guard. These troops would guarantee that the school would be integrated and that the "Little Rock 9" would be protected as they attended classes. This was the first instance since Reconstruction where federal troops were used to protect the civil rights of black citizens in the South.

·Civil Rights Act of 1957

Eisenhower never publicly gave support to the Civil Rights movement believing that you could not force people to change their beliefs and such changes had to come from the heart, not as the result of legislation from Washington. However, he did push through during his presidency the 1957 Civil Rights Act that aimed to ensure that all African Americans could exercise their right to vote. Southern Democrats in the Senate watered down the bill with the provision that any person found guilty of obstructing someone's right to register, faced the prospect of punishment by jury trial in the South. This meant the accused had to face an all-white jury as only whites could be jury members. Political support and public confidence for the Act were eroded when Eisenhower publicly admitted that he did not understand parts of it.

·Civil Rights Act of 1960

As a reaction to a violent outbreak of bombings against churches and schools in the South, the 1960 Civil Rights Act introduced penalties that were to be levied against anybody who obstructed someone's attempt to register to vote or someone's attempt to actually vote. A Civil Rights Commission was also created but both the 1957 and 1960 laws only increased black voting by 3%. Politicians from the South were furious over what they saw as Federal interference in state's affairs.

·Greensboro Sit-In (1960)

This student protest began on February 1, 1960, when four North Carolina A&T freshmen sat down at the downtown Woolworth lunch counter and tried to order something to eat and drink. They were told that people of their race had to stand up at another counter to eat. The young men stayed until the store closed and students returned to sit-in the next day. This peaceful protest continued for nearly six months, and similar protests sprang up across the South. In July 1960, three local stores changed their policies to allow integrated lunch counters that served people regardless of race or color and allowed anyone to sit down when there was an empty seat.

·Freedom Rides

The first Freedom Rides took place in the late 1940s and were unsuccessful. The Freedom Riders of the early 1960s, organized by the Congress of Racial Equality (CORE) headed by James Farmer, rode through the South seeking integration of the bus, rail, and airport terminals. After training in non-violent techniques, black and white volunteers sat next to each other as they traveled through the South in 1961. There were no incidents in the upper South but when they reached the lower South these thirteen volunteers were attacked in Georgia, Alabama and Mississippi. One bus was destroyed and the riders on another bus were attacked by men armed with clubs, bricks, iron pipes and knives. The Attorney General, Robert Kennedy, sent John Seigenthaler to accompany the Freedom Riders and he was beaten as well by the mob. In Birmingham, the passengers were greeted by members of the Ku Klux Klan who committed further acts of violence. At Montgomery, the state capital, a white mob beat the riders with chains and ax handles. The Ku Klux Klan hoped that this violent treatment would stop other young people from taking part in Freedom Rides. However, over the next six months more than a thousand people took part in Freedom Rides. With the local authorities unwilling to protect these citizens, President John F. Kennedy sent Byron White and 500 federal marshals from the North to do the job.

Kennedy Years

·Meredith at Old Miss (1962)

A 29 year- old Air Force veteran, African American James Meredith tried to enroll in a class at the University of Mississippi and met violent opposition including that of the governor Ross Barnett. Kennedy ordered federal marshals and federal troops to Mississippi as well as federalizing the National Guard to assure Meredith's admittance. He would ultimately get his degree at the cost of $4 million in government expenditures for his protection.

·Voter Education Project

Supported by Kennedy, Martin Luther King attempted to register disenfranchised African American voters in the South.

·University of Alabama Integration

Governor George Wallace backed down from his refusal to allow the integration of the University of Alabama when Kennedy federalized the National Guard in that state.

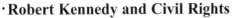

·Robert Kennedy and Civil Rights
By enforcing provisions of the 1957 and 1960 Civil Rights Laws, the Attorney General who was the President's brother brought more than 50 suits in 4 states to secure the right to vote for African Americans.

·Executive Order
Issued by President Kennedy in 1962, it prohibited racial or religious discrimination in housing built or purchased with federal aid.

·March on Birmingham
In 1963, Martin Luther King attempted to desegregate Birmingham, Alabama. Despite the Southern Christian Leadership Conferences non-violent approach, scenes of water cannons and police dogs used by the police on demonstrators caused an international outcry that led to federal intervention by the Kennedy administration. "Jim Crow" signs in Birmingham came down and public places were more open to blacks. The Birmingham campaign in shutting down the city became a model of direct action protest. By attracting media attention to the adverse treatment of blacks, Birmingham brought national attention to the issue of segregation. Although desegregation occurred slowly in Birmingham, the campaign was a major factor in the national push towards the Civil Rights Act of 1964.

·March on Washington D. C. (1963)
A. Phillip Randolph, who had first proposed the idea of a march on Washington in 1944 to pressure FDR to have the defense industry hire African Americans, addressed the crowd of an estimated 200,000 by demanding passage of meaningful civil rights legislation; an immediate end to all school segregation; protection for all civil rights protestors against police brutality; a major public works program for all unemployed; a federal law prohibiting racial discrimination in the workplace; a $2 minimum wage; and self government for the District of Columbia.

·"I Have a Dream Speech"
Martin Luther King delivered the most famous speech at the Washington civil rights demonstration (March on Washington) when he declared "I have a dream that my four little children will one day live in a nation where they will not be judged by the color of their skin, but by the content of their character."

Johnson Years

·Civil Rights Act of 1964
"All persons shall be entitled to the full and equal enjoyment of the goods, services, facilities, privileges, advantages, and accommodations of any place of public accommodation, as defined in this section, without discrimination or segregation on the ground of race, color, religion, or national origin."
1. Public accommodations included any inn, hotel, motel, or other establishment which provides lodging to transient guests, other than boarding houses of five rooms or less in which the proprietor lives;
2. any restaurant, cafeteria, lunchroom, lunch counter, soda fountain, or other facility principally engaged in selling food for consumption on the premises, including, but not limited to, any such facility located on the premises of any retail establishment; or any gasoline station;
3. any motion picture house, theater, concert hall, sports arena, stadium or other place of exhibition or entertainment.

·Affirmative Action
When Congress approved Title VII of the Civil Rights Act of 1964 it was intended to ban job discrimination. It had affirmed a color-blind system that hiring was to be done without regard to race, religion, sex, or national

origin. Nixon's modification of Johnson's affirmative action program transformed the system from one that was designed to protect individuals to one that would protect designated groups. After 1970, many American institutions were required to set aside what in effect were quotas. This dramatic and rapid transformation took place as a result of Nixon's executive decision and court interpretations. Critics of the system called it reverse discrimination and much of it was upheld in a series of divided court decisions.

·Voting Rights Act of 1965
This law empowered the federal government to oversee voter registration and elections in counties that had used tests to determine voter eligibility or where registration or turnout had been less than 50% in the 1964 presidential election. It also banned discriminatory literacy tests and expanded voting rights for non-English speaking Americans. In a 5-4 decision the law was significantly weakened by the Supreme Court in 2013.

Protests and Black Power

·Watts Riot of 1965
The Watts riot began when white police officers stopped an intoxicated black driver in South Central Los Angeles. He resisted arrest and was forcibly subdued while rumors spread that the police had attacked a pregnant black woman. The incident snowballed into a five-day conflagration, with blacks destroying a thousand businesses as they cried "burn, baby burn" and thirty-four people died, more than 1,000 were hospitalized and nearly 4,000 were arrested. This was the first episode in a series of "long hot summers" in the '60s, when blacks went on to riot and loot in one city after another. African Americans believed that a history of police brutality and the poverty that existed in the black ghettos contributed to the rioting. In Detroit in 1965, there were 43 deaths, more than 7,200 arrests, and about 2,500 stores trashed. In the past urban riots had been whites on blacks. This marked a change as some blacks would destroy and burn up their own neighborhoods as an example of the protests of the 1960s.

·Selma to Montgomery
On Sunday March 7, 1965, about 525 people began a fifty-four mile march from Selma, Alabama to the state capitol in Montgomery. They were demonstrating for African American voting rights and to commemorate the deaths of freedom-riders. On the outskirts of Selma, after they crossed the Edmund Pettus Bridge, the marchers, in plain sight of photographers and journalists, were brutally assaulted by heavily armed state troopers and deputies in an event that became known as Bloody Sunday. After seeing the event on television Civil Rights leaders descended on Selma and Martin Luther King Jr. led a 5 day 54 mile march from Selma to Montgomery Alabama under protection of a federalized National Guard. As 25,000 protestors stood before the state house in Alabama the Voting Rights Act of 1965 passed Congress.

·Black Power
Rejecting the non-violent, integrationist, legalistic and coalition building approach of traditional civil rights groups like the NAACP, the Black Power movement advocated black control of organizations (SNCC was reorganized so only blacks could serve as leaders), self-determination, and a new racial consciousness and racial pride among blacks in the United States. The Black Power movement encouraged the improvement of African American communities, rather than the fight for complete integration and featured slogans such as "Black is Beautiful." The movement also featured a return to African roots with hairstyles such as the natural "Afro" instead of the Conk (straitening of the hair by processing it with lye).

·SNCC
The Student Nonviolent Coordinating Committee (SNCC) was a political organization formed in 1960 by black college students dedicated to overturning segregation in the South and giving young blacks a stronger voice in the civil rights movement. In 1966, a faction of SNCC committed to black separatism and headed by

Stokely Carmichael took over the organization from John Lewis, who favored integration. SNCC then began to eject its white members. Carmichael soon issued a call for Black Power with its insistence on racial dignity and black self-reliance and the use of violence as a legitimate means of self-defense. Carmichael and his successor as chairman of SNCC, H. "Rap" Brown, became national symbols of black radicalism.

·CORE

Originally organized in 1942 by an interracial group of students in Chicago, the Congress of Racial Equality had some success in integrating facilities in the North in the 1940s and 1950s. It organized the Freedom Rides in 1961, and in 1964 CORE participated in the Mississippi Freedom Summer project where three CORE activists, James Chaney, Andrew Goodman and Michael Schwerner were killed while trying to register blacks to vote. In 1966, under mounting pressure, the original founder James Farmer stepped down as National Director and was replaced by the more militant Floyd McKissick. McKissick endorsed the term "Black Power" and was a much more acceptable leader to the increasingly radicalized black community.

·Martin Luther King Jr.

Starting with his leadership in the Montgomery bus boycott, King became a leading spokesman for integration with his emphasis on using the civil disobedience of Henry David Thoreau and the non-violent protest of Mahatma Gandhi. The Southern Christian Leadership Conference (SCLC) was established in 1957 to coordinate the action of local protest groups throughout the South. Under King's leadership, the organization utilized the power and independence of black churches as the strength of its activities. After the success of the march on Washington, King's "I Have a Dream" speech, and the Selma March, King and the SCLC were often criticized for being too moderate and overly dependent on the support of white liberals by the growing Black Power movement. It was during this period that SCLC began to shift its attention toward economic inequality. Seeing poverty as the root of inner-city violence, SCLC planned the Poor People's Campaign to push for federal legislation that would guarantee employment, income, and housing for economically disadvantaged blacks. King's assassination by James Earl Ray in 1968 set off a wave of riots in 125 cities in 29 states.

·Malcolm X

Originally named Malcolm Little and later called El-Hajj Malik El-Shabazz, Malcolm X became a Black Muslim while serving a prison term. His charisma led to him quickly becoming very prominent in the movement with a following equaling that of its leader, Elijah Muhammad. In 1963, Malcolm X was suspended by Elijah Muhammad because of a speech where Malcolm X suggested that President Kennedy's assassination was a matter of the "chickens coming home to roost." He formed a rival organization of his own, the Muslim Mosque, Inc., and after a pilgrimage to Mecca, converted to orthodox Islam with his new belief that there could be brotherhood between blacks and whites. In his Organization of Afro-American Unity, formed after he returned from Mecca, his tone was still that of militant black nationalism but no longer favoring separation. The popularity of his autobiography added to his influence, but he was assassinated in 1965 by Black Muslims who were never prosecuted for the crime.

·Black Panthers

In 1966 in Oakland, California Huey Newton and Bobby Seale founded the Black Panther Party for Self-Defense. The Black Panthers were a militant organization that fought to establish revolutionary socialism through mass organizing and community based programs. An early leader was Eldridge Cleaver who gained prominence for his book *Soul on Ice* explaining the black experience and character written while he was in prison. The Black Panther Party took the position that black people in America and the Vietnamese people were waging a common struggle, as comrades-in-arms, against a common enemy the U.S. government. In 1967, a small group of Black Panther Party members, led by Bobby Seale, marched into the California legislature fully armed as a protest against a pending gun control bill (which became the Mulford Act) aimed at the Black Panther Party. In 1967, Huey Newton was shot, arrested and charged with the murder of a white police officer after a gun battle on the streets of Oakland. Young whites, angry and disillusioned with America over the Vietnam War, raised their voices with young, urban blacks, with the cry—"Free Huey!" After three mistrials, Newton was cleared in 1971 and he fled to Cuba in 1974 to avoid drug and murder charges. The Black Panthers began to develop a series of social programs to provide services to black poor people promoting a model for an alternative, more humane society. These programs, the most popular being the Free Breakfast for Children Program, were referred to as "survival programs," and were operated by Party members under the slogan "survival pending revolution." With many of its members under indictment, in jail, in exile, or no longer alive, the Black Panthers fell apart in the late 1970s.

Women's Movement

·*The Feminine Mystique*

This book written by Betty Friedan in 1963 sparked a national debate about women's roles as it defined women's unhappiness as ''the problem that has no name.'' Friedan blamed the idealized image of femininity that she called the "feminine mystique" as the problem. According to Friedan, women had been encouraged to confine themselves to the narrow roles of housewife and mother, forsaking education and career aspirations in the process. Because of the "mystique" women had been denied the opportunity to develop their own identities, which could ultimately lead to problems for women and their families. Friedan saw the "feminine mystique" as a failed social experiment that World War II and the Cold War helped to create.

·Title VII

This section of the Civil Rights Act of 1964 (ironically included at the insistence of southern politicians who were trying to scuttle the bill) prohibited discrimination in employment on the basis of sex as well as race. This would lead to expanded economic opportunities for women.

·NOW

The National Organization of Women began at a 1966 conference on the status of women in order to form a civil rights organization for women. Founded by Betty Friedan, Pauli Murray, and Shirley Chisholm, it's goals were: passage of a constitutional amendment guaranteeing equal rights for all; enforcement of Title VII of the Civil Rights Act; maternity leave benefits; child care; equal and unsegregated education; equal job training opportunities; and abortion rights. Friedan became NOW's first President.

·National Women's Political Caucus

Founded by Gloria Steinem and a member of Congress Bella Abzug, it worked to put women in political office and supported candidates who were sympathetic to women's issues.

·Ms. Magazine

First published in 1972, it took up issues that had not been covered in traditional women's magazines. Called Ms. by its founder Gloria Steinem it helped popularize that title for women to replace Miss or Mrs., when a women's marital status was considered irrelevant or unknown.

·Women in Education

Women's Studies courses became prevalent in college and former all male schools went co-educational. From 37% of the college graduates in 1960 women constitute 59% of college graduates today. Under Title IX of the Educational Amendment Act of 1972, women's athletics were to receive equality with men's athletics. The growth of women's sports teams in high school and college is directly attributable to this law.

·Radical Feminists

Grassroots organizations that favored more dramatic protests such as ridiculing the 1968 Miss America contest in Atlantic City by crowning a sheep as the winner and, allegedly (never proven), burning their bras and other female accoutrements in protest of their feminine enslavement. Consciousness-raising sessions were held for women to talk openly about their situation and bond with other women.

·Equal Rights Amendment

"Men and women shall have equal rights throughout the United States and every place subject to its jurisdiction." This amendment was introduced in every session of Congress from 1924 until it passed in reworded form in 1972. The Equal Rights Amendment passed the U.S. Senate and then the House of Representatives, and the proposed 27th Amendment to the Constitution was sent to the states for ratification. Congress placed a seven-year deadline on the ratification process. Like the 19th Amendment before it, the ERA barreled out of Congress, getting 22 of the necessary 38 state ratifications in the first year. But the pace slowed as opposition began to organize—only eight ratifications in 1973, three in 1974, one in 1975, and none in 1976. Arguments by ERA opponents such as Phyllis Schlafly, right-wing leader of the Eagle Forum, claimed that the ERA would deny woman's right to be supported by her husband, privacy rights would be overturned, women would be sent into combat, and abortion rights and homosexual marriages would be upheld. States'-rights advocates said the ERA was a federal power grab, and business interests such as the insurance industry opposed a measure they believed would cost them money. Opposition to the ERA was often led by fundamentalist Christian religious groups. In 1977, Indiana became the 35th and last state to ratify the ERA. Other states postponed consideration, defeated ratification bills or passed rescission bills. As the 1979 deadline approached ERA advocates appealed to Congress for an indefinite extension of the time limit and Congress granted an extension until June 30, 1982. The political tide turned more conservative and in 1980 the Republican Party removed ERA support from its platform and Ronald Reagan was elected president. ERA did not succeed in getting three more state ratifications before the deadline passed.

·Anti-Feminism

Women opposed to the women's movement especially the radical feminist began to emerge and Phyllis Schlafly led a campaign against passage the equal rights amendment that eventually succeeded and kept that amendment from becoming law. With these attacks the word feminism became a pejorative one to many individuals and the first wave of the movement seemed to stall out.

Hispanic Movement

·Hispanic

This term refers to those who had come from Spanish speaking lands in the Western Hemisphere. Recently the preferred term has been changed to Latino.

·Grape Boycott

Led by Cesar Chavez, founder of the United Farm Workers Union, this national boycott of table grapes lasted from 1965 to 1970. It led to the signing of contracts that gave farm workers significant benefits and made Chavez a national hero to Hispanics.

·Chicanos

An ethnic label connoting pride that was adopted by many Mexican Americans. In the late 1960s, Mexican-American youth, inspired by the farm workers' strike in California, the African American freedom struggle, and the youth revolts of the time, began using the label 'Chicano' to describe their cultural heritage and assert their energy and emerging militancy. In appropriating a word that previously had a negative connotation, Mexican-American youth turned 'Chicano' into a politically charged term used for self-identification that was a cultural as well as a political movement. This militancy led to the formation of the Brown Berets that was patterned after the Black Panther Party who wore Black Berets.

·Braceros

The program of bringing temporary agricultural workers from Mexico into the U.S. that started in WWII was ended in 1965 primarily because Mexican Americans complained about the poor working conditions. Cesar Chavez and Dolores Huerta led the movement to end this guest worker program. Another reason for its demise was the increase in immigration, both legal and illegal, from Latin American countries in the 1960s.

·Civil Rights and Hispanics

Originally classified as white, Hispanics did not receive the same protections as other minorities until a federal court in 1970 ruled Mexican Americans constituted a "identifiable ethnic minority with a pattern of discrimination."

·Bilingual Education Act

Passed in 1968 it provided money for schools to develop programs where students would be taught in both Spanish and English. The Supreme Court ruled the law constitutional in 1974 when it said schools had to meet the needs of children with limited knowledge of English. There was never agreement on just how the act would be implemented in the classroom. Parents and community activist typically favored enrichment models based on multilingual, multicultural curricula, while educators largely endorsed programs of compensatory education that would assimilate children to traditional English-speaking classrooms. Enrichment models treated the non-English language as an asset to be preserved, while compensatory models treated it as a barrier to be overcome in learning English. Throughout the Act's history, controversy over the role of native-language instruction and English immersion persisted. The original Act and its many revisions were nullified by the No Child Left Behind Act under George W. Bush.

·La Raza Unida

This was an attempt to organize the diverse Hispanic community into a national political party. It had some success in electing officials in south Texas.

·MEChA

Formed in 1969, the *Movimiento Estudiantil Chicano de Aztlán* was formed to promote an awareness of Chicano history by education and political action. Members of MEChA said the organization's main purpose was to educate Chicano youth into seeing the value of education, and to provide college preparatory outreach to high school students. It also favored the *reconquesta* of the Southwest into a Spanish dominated culture. Popular on college campuses, it called for civil rights for Mexican illegal immigrants and demanded Spanish language and cultural education.

·Brown Power

As a movement of racial pride, it was an intense attachment to "Mexican culture"—the whole complex of family, feelings, food, music, history and social mannerisms that are accepted as "Mexican." It was also a protest against poor education, jobs, and economic misery in the Southwestern barrios as well as a consciousness of the Indian past and the historic land issue question with the dominant Anglo culture.

Native Americans

·Native Americans

A new name adopted by Indians in the United States (Indians in Canada have adopted the name First Nations) that is often used in place of Indians. The term became the political correct way of describing the indigenous people in North America. The term Indian given to the indigenous people by Europeans fell into disrepute but has been revived in recent years because of the popularity of gaming (formerly called gambling) at "Indian Casinos."

·Early Accomplishments

After the abandonment of Eisenhower's termination policy in 1963, various tribes negotiated with museums and universities for a return of sacred objects that had been taken away and they filed numerous lawsuits to regain their historic lands.

·AIM (1968)

American Indian Movement organized in Minneapolis-St. Paul by a group of Indian ex-cons including Clyde Bellecourt, Dennis Banks and George Mitchell. They put pressure, through sit-ins and other methods, on the "War on Poverty" bureaucracy to ensure greater Indian representation in decision-making, and they helped Indians organize themselves for self-protection against the police and the judicial system.

·Alcatraz (1969-1971)

In accordance with U.S. law that said abandoned federal property would revert to the Indians, the abandoned federal prison in San Francisco Bay was taken over by AIM and occupied for 19 months. The federal government initially insisted that the Indian people leave the island, placed an ineffective barricade around the island, and eventually agreed to demands by the Indian council that formal negotiations be held. The Indians led by Richard Oakes wanted the deed to the island, the establishment of an Indian university, a cultural center, and a museum. The siege ended when the government turned off the electricity and removed the water barge that had been supplying fresh water. Most people left and public support had waned as the originally group of 100 (80 UCLA students) had been replaced by other urbanites including many from the drug culture of the Haight-Asbury district. On June 10, 1971, armed federal marshals, FBI agents, and special -forces police swarmed the island and removed five women, four children, and six unarmed Indian men. The occupation was over but it had gained a great deal of publicity for the Indian movement.

·Wounded Knee (1973)

For 71 days, members of the Oglala Sioux, many who were members of AIM (American Indian Movement) held residents of Wounded Knee captive as they declared the town liberated from outside control. The U.S. Marshall's office immediately surrounded the town with a major military force. When the siege was lifted the issues of corruption of the reservation system, broken treaties, and the desire for Indians for self-determination, as well as the poverty of Indians came to the attention of the nation.

·Court Challenges

A series of court challenges resulted in some land being returned to the Indians and some tribes receiving millions of dollars in claims settlements by the federal government.

·Casinos

In recent years Indians have built a number of gambling casinos on tribal land that have become a huge source of revenue for some tribes. Quirks in federal and state law allow the tribes to build these gambling halls as they are considered sovereign nations. The Indian term for these gambling establishments is "gaming." Since the early 1980s, several tribes in Florida and California began raising revenues by operating bingo games offering larger prizes than those allowed under state law. When the states threatened to close the operations, the tribes sued in federal court—*Seminole Tribe vs. Butterworth* (1979) and *California vs. Cabazon Band* (1987) and won. The courts formally recognized Indians right to conduct gaming operations as long as the games are not criminally prohibited by the states. In 1988, Congress formally recognized, but limited the rights of Native Americans to conduct gaming operations with the passage of the Indian Gaming Regulatory Act (IGRA). The

IGRA required tribes to negotiate with states concerning games to be played and regulations of those games while it ensures that tribal governments are the sole owners and primary beneficiaries of gaming. The states as promoters of the IGRA collect significant tax revenues off of Indian gaming (i.e. gambling).

UNIT XXIX
MULTIPLE-CHOICE QUESTIONS

Questions 1-3 refer to the following:

"We conclude that, in the field of public education, the doctrine of "separate but equal" has no place. Separate educational facilities are inherently unequal. Therefore, we hold that the plaintiffs and others similarly situated for whom the actions have been brought are, by reason of the segregation complained of, deprived of the equal protection of the laws guaranteed by the Fourteenth Amendment. This disposition makes unnecessary any discussion whether such segregation also violates the Due Process Clause of the Fourteenth Amendment."

Brown v. Board of Education of Topeka, Kansas, 1954

1. The concept of "separate but equal" overturned in the Brown decision, was originally established by the Supreme Court in which earlier court decision?

    (A) Gibbons v. Ogden
    (B) Plessy v. Ferguson
    (C) Marbury v. Madison
    (D) Dred Scott v. Sanford

2. The part of the Constitution that the court used for their ruling in the Brown case was the

    (A) due process of law clause the 14th Amendment
    (B) establish justice and insure domestic tranquility clause of the preamble
    (C) equal protection of the laws clause in the 14th Amendment
    (D) freedom of speech clause of the 1st Amendment

3. What term did Chief Justice Warren use, speaking for a unanimous court, that means intrinsic or belonging by nature, to describe separate educational facilities?

    (A) Natural
    (B) Lawful
    (C) Constitutional
    (D) Inherent

Questions 4-6 refer to the following:

4. What did Rosa Park do in 1955 that inspired this political cartoon?

    (A) Spoke out against discrimination in church
    (B) Enrolled in an all-white university in the South
    (C) Refused to move to the back of the bus as required by law
    (D) Sat in at a lunch counter that was for whites only

5. Rosa Park's arrest for defying segregation laws in 1955 directly resulted in

    (A) the 13 month Montgomery bus boycott that ended segregation on public busses
    (B) integration of the public high schools in the states that had been part of the Confederacy
    (C) the Civil Rights Act of 1964 giving Americans the right to be served in facilities which are open to the public—hotels, restaurants, theaters, and retail stores
    (D) the right to vote in all federal elections

6. The actions of Rosa Park in 1955 inspired all of the following civil rights actions EXCEPT

    (A) sit-in to integrate Woolworth's lunch counter by four black college students in Greensboro North Carolina in 1960
    (B) racially mixed groups of "freedom riders" who brought attention to the movement as they rode integrated busses that were physically attacked by segregationists
    (C) the 1960 Supreme Court decision in *Boynton v. Virginia* that overturned a judgment against a black law student for trespassing by being in a restaurant in a bus terminal which was designated "whites only"
    (D) the Supreme Court striking down the "separate but equal" doctrine of *Plessy v. Ferguson* for public education and requiring the desegregation of schools

Questions 7-8 refer to the following:

"... we have not made a single gain in civil rights without determined legal and nonviolent pressure.... We know through painful experience that freedom is never voluntarily given by the oppressor. It must be demanded by the oppressed.... For years now I have heard the words (sic) 'Wait!' It rings in the ear of every Negro with a piercing familiarity. This 'Wait' has almost always meant 'Never.' We must come to see with the ... jurist of yesterday that 'justice... delayed is justice denied.' We have waited for more than three hundred and forty years for our constitutional and God-given rights. I guess it is easy for those who have never felt the stinging darts of segregation to say, 'Wait,...' Any law that degrades human personality is unjust. All segregation statues are unjust...

Martin Luther King Jr., "Letter from a Birmingham Jail," 1963

7. Gains in civil rights for black American basically meant an end to which system?

(A) Jim Crow
(B) Jim Dandy
(C) Stepin Fetchit
(D) Uncle Tom

8. In the passage above Martin Luther King Jr., is speaking out against

(A) those who use non-violent pressure to achieve their goals
(B) gradualists who want the civil rights movement to end segregation to slow down
(C) the belief that justice delayed is justice denied
(D) violent actions taken by civil rights radical advocates

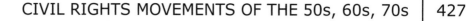

Questions 9-11 refer to the following:

"I have a dream that one day this nation will rise up and live out the true meaning of its creed: "We hold these truths to be self-evident: that all men are created equal...."

I have a dream that my four little children will one day live in a nation where they will not be judged by the color of their skin but by the content of their character....

when we allow freedom to ring,... we will be able to speed up that day when all of God's children, black men and white men, Jews and Gentiles, Protestants and Catholics, will be able to join hands and sing in the words of the old Negro spiritual, "Free at last! free at last! thank God Almighty, we are free at last!"

Martin Luther King Jr., "Speech" 1963

9. The passage above is a speech that was part of which movement?

(A) Populism
(B) Progressivism
(C) Civil Rights
(D) Counter Culture

10. Which government program to designed to help African Americans has been interpreted by some conservative critics as going against King's speech when he said, "I have a dream that my four little children will one day live in a nation where they will not be judged by the color of their skin but by the content of their character?"

(A) Voting Rights Act of 1965
(B) Philadelphia Plan/Affirmative Action
(C) Title IX
(D) Civil Rights Act of 1964

11. Martin Luther King Jr's speech refers to which of the following documents?

(A) Declaration of Independence
(B) Constitution
(C) Bill of Rights
(D) Emancipation Proclamation

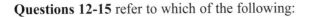

Questions 12-15 refer to which of the following:

"The problem that has no name—which is simply the fact that American women are kept from growing to their full human capacities—is taking a far greater toll on the physical and mental health of our country than any known disease.... The problem lay buried, unspoken for many years in the minds of American women. It was a strange stirring, a sense of dissatisfaction, a yearning that women suffered in the middle of the twentieth century in the United States. Each suburban housewife struggled with it alone. As she made the beds, shopped for groceries, matched slipcover material, ate peanut butter sandwiches with her children, chauffeured Cub Scouts and Brownies, lay beside her husband at night, she was afraid to ask even of herself the silent question 'Is this all'....The feminine mystique has succeeded in burying millions of American women alive."

Betty Friedan, *The Feminine Mystique*, 1963

12. The document above indicates that women in the 1950s were unhappy because

    (A) their status was being defined solely by their role as a wife and mother
    (B) the had little control over Cold War terror like their fear of "the bomb"
    (C) they wanted to return to their previous roles modeled after "Rosie the Riveter"
    (D) the suburban lifestyle offered few material comforts

13. Which of the following organizations was formed and inspired by Friedan's book?

    (A) CORE
    (B) NAACP
    (C) NOW
    (D) MECHa

14. All of the following were considered to be successes for the women's movement launched by Friedan's book EXCEPT

    (A) *Griswold v. Connecticut*
    (B) Ratification of the Equal Rights Amendment
    (C) Launching of Ms Magazine
    (D) Title IX of the Education Amendments of 1972

15. When the document uses the term feminine mystique, this mystique is the

    (A) aura of mystery that surrounds the women in the 1950s
    (B) uplifting of women to a superior status in the household
    (C) high regard that the 1950s women felt for the battles that earlier feminist had fought
    (D) suburban homemaker or housewife ideal of femininity

UNIT XXX
NEW FRONTIER &
GREAT SOCIETY–THE 60S

Following the tranquility at least on the surface of the 1950s, the 1960s ushered in a time period of social upheaval and tremendous change in America, culminating in a war that is still being fought over in American society. The Cold War heated up in America's failed 10- year attempt to stop communism in Vietnam. From Kennedy's New Frontier to Johnson's Great Society, and Nixon's New Federalism, the 60's brought forth political changes that had as great an impact on America as the New Deal did. But it was the social changes that were attempted that gave the 1960s its caché.

Kennedy's Domestic Policy

·Election of 1960

The youngest man ever elected President, 43-year-old John Kennedy defeated Eisenhower's Vice-President, Richard Nixon by 120,000 votes with more than 68 million cast. The electoral vote went for Kennedy 303-219 and did not reflect just how close the election was as Kennedy barely won Texas and Illinois which secured his victory. Many felt that Kennedy won the election by his appearance in the first of four joint television appearances, called debates, with Nixon. After this election TV would dominate all political campaigns and candidates would have to spend much of their time raising money for TV advertisements.

·Inaugural Address

In a charismatic speech Kennedy made an idealistic appeal and urged his fellow Americans to "ask not what your country can do for you—ask what you can do for your country." He followed the tradition laid down by earlier Presidents and gave his program a catchy title—"The New Frontier."

·Peace Corps

Established by Executive Order, this program would send volunteers to 3rd World countries (new emerging or developing countries in Africa and Asia that were not aligned with either the U.S. or USSR) to help their economic development. Volunteers served as teachers, engineers, public health workers, technicians and in

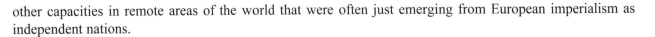

other capacities in remote areas of the world that were often just emerging from European imperialism as independent nations.

·Jawboning Business

After helping to negotiate non-inflationary wage agreements in the steel industry Kennedy became incensed when steel management announced significant price increases. After calling their increases, "a wholly unjustified and irresponsible defiance of our public interest" he met with them in the White House and got them to back down and rescind the price increases.

·Tax Cut

In order to stimulate the economy Kennedy announced his support for a general tax cut that Congress approved. Dropping the top marginal rate from 91% to 70%, Kennedy hoped it would lower the unemployment rate of 6.7%.

·Man on the Moon

Kennedy supported a multi-billion dollar program to put a man on the moon by the end of the decade (Neil Armstrong and Buzz Aldrin would do it in 1969). This was a Cold War commitment as the U.S. did not want to fall behind the USSR in space exploration.

·Minimum Wage

It was increased in stages from $1 an hour to $1.25 an hour over a three year time period.

·23rd Amendment

Passed by Congress during the Eisenhower administration it became law in 1961 and gave District of Columbia citizens 3 electoral votes in Presidential elections.

·John Birch Society

Right wing organization founded in 1958 by 12 men led by Robert Welch, Jr., for the purpose of combating communism and promoting various ultraconservative causes. The name came from John Birch, an American Baptist missionary and U.S. Army intelligence officer who was killed by Chinese communists in 1945, making him, in the society's view, the first hero of the Cold War. The "Birchers" believed that the U.S. and Soviet governments were controlled by a conspiratorial cabal of internationalists, greedy bankers, and corrupt politicians. If left unexposed, traitors inside the U.S. government would betray the country's sovereignty to the United Nations for a collectivist New World Order, managed by a "one-world" socialist government. Welch saw collectivism as the main threat to Western Civilization, and liberals as communist traitors who provided cover for the gradual process of collectivism. The movement reached its high point in the 1960s, supporting Barry Goldwater for President in 1964, and it had somewhere between 60,000 and 100,000 followers. When it turned on Eisenhower calling him a possible "conscious, dedicated agent of the Communist Conspiracy" former conservative supporters of Welch like William F. Buckley, Jr., and Russell Kirk denounced the movement. At its height the Society successfully attacked local governments, libraries, school boards, parent-teacher associations, teachers, mental health programs, the ecumenical movement, and it led the impeach Chief Justice Earl Warren movement."

Warren Court Decisions

·Civil Liberties

These expanded individual rights, curtailed the influence of religion in schools, established the right to privacy, and extended democracy in government. An attempt was made to "impeach Earl Warren" by those opposed to his judicial activism.

· *Mapp vs. Ohio* (1961)
Established the principle that evidence secured by state officials through unreasonable search and seizure must be excluded from a trial.

· *Engel v. Vitale* (1962)
The court ruled that a school sponsored non-denominational prayer violated the establishment of religion clause of the Constitution.

· *Abington Township v. Schempp* (1963)
Struck down mandatory daily bible readings in school.

· *Gideon v. Wainwright* (1963)
A right to an attorney in all cases potentially punishable by a jail sentence was established.

· *Miranda v. Arizona* (1964)
Statements obtained by the authorities when a suspect is in custody were ruled to be inadmissible unless the suspect was informed of his right to remain silent, anything he says may be used against him, his right to an attorney, and that if he cannot afford an attorney one will be provided for him. These so-called "Miranda" warnings would change police interrogation methods.

· *Baker vs. Carr* (1962)
Established the principle of one man, one vote by requiring Congressional districts to be roughly equal in population.

· *Reynolds v. Sims* (1964)
The court ruled that the state legislatures would be required to be reapportioned according to population.

· *New York Times v. Sullivan* (1964)
Public officials could not be awarded damages in libel suits unless the defamatory falsehoods were written with the intent of actual malice.

· *Griswold v. Connecticut* (1965)
A statute that banned giving advice on birth control was unconstitutional on the grounds that it violated the right of privacy. It struck down the Comstock laws banning contraception among married couples but let stand other aspects of the Comstock laws.

Kennedy Foreign Policy

· Flexible Response
It was adopted as a policy that would use conventional forces as well as nuclear options to replace Eisenhower's brinkmanship and massive retaliation. Kennedy strengthened the regular military and created Special Forces units like the Green Berets. He also encouraged the European countries to supply more troops for NATO that would release some U.S. conventional forces to be deployed elsewhere in the world.

· Alliance for Progress
This was Kennedy's 10-point program to help the undeveloped countries of Latin America with a $20 billion dollar U.S. commitment. It was seen as a Marshall Plan for Latin America, but it was only marginally successful.

·Bay of Pigs

Originally this was a CIA plan, approved by Eisenhower, to overthrow Castro in Cuba with an invasion force of Cuban exiles who had been trained by the CIA in Guatemala. Despite misgivings, in 1961 Kennedy approved of landing the 1500 man force based on the CIA's calculation that it would spark a popular uprising against Castro. There was no uprising and after three days, 1,200 men were captured by Castro's forces. Later they would be ransomed for $52 million in food and medical supplies. The failure of this venture made the U.S. look weak, inept, and incompetent to the rest of the world. The USSR interpreted this as a sign that they could take more aggressive action against the U.S.

·Vienna Summit

Talks held in 1961 in which Khrushchev insisted the West must recognize the sovereignty of East Germany and remove all troops from West Berlin.

·Berlin Wall

In 1961, in order to stop East Germans from escaping to West Berlin, a barbed wire barrier was put up that was then replaced by a 12 foot tall concrete wall. Streets, the railway and the S-Bahn (city railway) were severed, and stations of the U-Bahn (underground railway) were closed. The Wall included guard towers lining large concrete walls circumscribing a wide area (later known as the "death strip") containing anti-vehicle trenches and other defenses. The East German government claimed that the Wall was an "anti-fascist protective rampart" intended to stop aggression from the West. After its erection, around 5,000 people attempted to escape by circumventing the wall, with figures of the resulting death toll varying between 98 and 200. East Germans would not be allowed to travel to the West until 1989 when the Wall fell.

·Cuban Missile Crisis

After the failed Bay of Pigs invasion Castro asked the USSR for defensive weapons. The USSR gave both offensive and defensive weapons—the U.S. spotted the launching pads in its U-2 over flights of Cuba. Kennedy called for the withdrawal of the missiles and ordered a quarantine of Cuba to keep Russian ships from bringing the missiles to the sites. U.S. warships were set to intercept the Russian freighters when Khrushchev agreed to have them turn around. In return, the U.S. pledged not to invade Cuba and indicated that it would pull some missiles out of Turkey at a later date. The Cuban Missile Crisis was the closest the world ever came to nuclear war. The United States armed forces were at their highest state of readiness ever and Soviet field commanders in Cuba were prepared to use battlefield nuclear weapons to defend the island if it was invaded. Khrushchev had overreached and Kennedy's strong stand was seen as a victory for the U.S. in the Cold War. This more than negated the harm done by the failed Bay of Pigs invasion.

·Red Phones

In an attempt to lessen tensions between the U.S. and the USSR direct lines of communication were established between the White House and the Kremlin in what became known as the red phone "hot line."

·Limited Nuclear Test Ban Treaty

Kennedy originally mentioned this in his commencement speech titled "A Strategy of Peace" at American University. In September of 1963, the U.S., USSR, and Great Britain signed an agreement to not conduct nuclear weapons tests in the atmosphere, underwater, or in outer space. They were still allowed to conduct underground tests.

·Kennedy's Assassination

While riding in a motorcade in Dallas to heal a rift in the Democratic Party he was shot and killed by Lee Harvey Oswald who was captured later that day. While in custody, Oswald was shot and killed by Jack Ruby, a Dallas nightclub owner. Chief Justice Earl Warren headed a special Presidential Commission on the assassination, and in an 888-page report concluded that Oswald was the lone assassin. Over the next 30 years conspiracy theorists believed that others beside Oswald were involved in the assassination. A House of Representatives Committee on Assassinations in 1978 concluded that Oswald fired three shots at Kennedy, but another gunmen fired a fourth shot. Modern historical scholarship supports the idea that Oswald was the lone gunman. Vice-President Lyndon Johnson of Texas succeeded Kennedy as President.

Great Society

·Johnson's Ann Arbor Speech

Lyndon Johnson said, "The Great Society rests on abundance and liberty for all. It demands an end to poverty and racial injustice. The Great Society is a place where every child can find knowledge to enrich his mind and to enlarge his talents. It is a place where leisure is a welcome chance to build and reflect, not a feared cause of boredom and restlessness. It is a place where the city of man serves not only the needs of the body and the demands of commerce but the desire for beauty and the hunger for community. It is a place where man can renew contact with nature. It is a place which honors creation for its own sake and for what is adds to the understanding of the race. It is a place where men are more concerned with the quality of their goals than the quantity of their goods." This speech would launch a massive governmental program known as The Great Society.

·Great Society Program

This program included civil rights laws as well as initiatives launched between 1964 and 1967 designed to expand the social welfare system and eliminate poverty.

·Economic Opportunity Act (1964)

This created an Office of Economic Opportunity to oversee a variety of community-based antipoverty programs. It was based on the concept that the best way to deal with poverty was not simply to raise the incomes of the poor but to help them better themselves through education, job training, and community development. "Community action" would allow the poor to participate in the framing of programs that were designed to help them.

·War on Poverty

$1 billion was appropriated in 1964 and another $2 billion in the following two years. The programs created included Job Corps, whose purpose was to help disadvantaged youths develop marketable skills; Volunteers in Service to America (VISTA), a domestic version of the Peace Corps, which sent middle-class young people on "missions" into poor neighborhoods; the Model Cities program for urban redevelopment; Upward Bound, which assisted poor high school students entering college; legal services for the poor; the Food Stamp program; and Project Head Start, which offered preschool education for poor children.

·Abandonment of the Program

Despite the idealistic beginnings mounting political opposition to the community action programs as well as budgetary pressures caused by the expansion of the Vietnam War brought the War on Poverty to a premature end after 1967. It had a mixed record of success with some programs like Head Start lasting but most were terminated as the U.S. failed in its attempts to win both the war on poverty and the war in Vietnam.

·Election of 1964

Johnson ran for election in his own right and was opposed by a conservative Senator from Arizona, Barry Goldwater, who gained control of the Republican Party from the more moderate eastern establishment. The Democrats successfully depicted Goldwater as a dangerous political extremist as Johnson carried all but 6 states and won the Electoral College 486-52 while winning 61% of the popular vote. The Democrats increased their congressional majority and some pundits speculated that the Republican Party was in danger of becoming extinct like the Federalist and Whig Parties had become. Johnson saw this overwhelming victory as a mandate to achieve whatever he wanted.

·89th Congress (Great Society Program)

1. **Elementary and Secondary School Act**—The first large-scale program of federal aid to elementary and secondary schools with $1.3 billion being allocated on the basis of the number of needy children.
2. **Medicare**—It provided medical care for those over 65 through the Social Security system.
3. **Omnibus Housing Act**—Rent supplements were provided for low income families.
4. **Department of Housing and Urban Development**—New cabinet position established with African American Robert Weaver as the first head of HUD.
5. **National Foundation for the Arts and Humanities**—Federal funding for painters, actors, dancers, musicians, community theatres and others involved in the arts.
6. **Water Quality Act**—Required states to enforce water quality standards for all water within their boundaries.
7. **Clean Waters Restoration Act**—$3.5 billion for the construction of sewage treatment plants and authorized payment of up to 50% of the cost for cleaning up non-interstate waters.
8. **Immigration Reform**—Quota Act of 1924 based on national origins was rescinded and an annual limit of 290,000 immigrants was established with no more than 20,000 from any one country.
9. **Higher Education Act**—Provided the first federal scholarships to college undergraduates.
10. **Veterans Educational Benefits**—Granted to all who served for 180 days or more on active duty since 1955.
11. **Department of Transportation**—Created a new cabinet position to coordinate federal programs in air, rail, and highway transportation.

Turbulent 1960s

·Port Huron Statement (1962)

This manifesto was written in Port Huron, Michigan at a meeting of Students for a Democratic Society and many believe launched the student protest movement and counterculture of the 1960s. The "Statement" reflected the dissatisfaction and disillusionment many young people were feeling in the 1960s as students objected to the way college administrators attempted to control their personal lives; were opposed to the political environment of the Cold War; the bomb (nuclear weapons); racial bigotry; and the materialistic value system that dominated the U.S. The driving force behind the document was Tom Hayden, a University of Michigan student from a working class background whose radicalism helped to usher in a political movement called the New Left.

·Counterculture

The 1960s movement of youth who reacted against the materialism, conformity, and security based ideology of the 1950s to challenge the ethos of the prevailing system. It was a social and political reaction to what was seen as the hypocrisy of the mainstream middle class culture from which it sprang. Most of the individual elements of the value system of the counterculture stem from values of the mainstream culture, and claimed to hold, but actually did not practice according to this youth movement. Popular belief has simplistically characterized the movement as "sex, drugs, and rock and roll" and like all stereotypes there was some truth to it. But at its core it was more than just a caricature of jaded youth; it was an intellectual movement that challenged the prevailing life-style and advocated an alternative one. An example of a counterculture idea was the expression "do your own thing." On the surface it sounded selfish or narcissistic but what it meant was to do something for its own sake, something to be enjoyed, but it did not have to be done well or have utilitarian value.

· Free Speech Movement (1964)

The Free Speech Movement was a student protest that emerged when administrative officials tried to ban students from setting up information tables on the campus of the University of California, Berkeley in 1964. The issue became one of free speech and academic freedom and is seen as a starting point for the many student protest movements of the 1960s and early 1970s. Student activists, many members of the pro-Civil Rights political movement on campus called SLATE, and some of whom had traveled with the Freedom Riders and worked to register African American voters in the South over the summer, organized into a loose coalition with Mario Savio, a philosophy student, as their spokesman. The center of the protest was Sproul Hall, the campus administration building, that protesters took over in a massive sit-in that all but shut down the university. The sit-in ended when police arrested over 800 students. After a great deal of disturbance, the University officials slowly accepted the student demands and UC Berkley would become a hot bed of radicalism, student dissent, and the counterculture movement throughout the 1960s and beyond.

· Summer of Love, Flower Power, and Hippies (1967)

Refers to the cultural phenomena of the counterculture movement, (called the "hippie movement" by those who wanted to cash in on it commercially) of going to the Haight-Ashbury district of San Francisco in 1967. This was launched by a human "Be-In" that took place in Golden Gate Park as Jerry Rubin, Timothy Leary, Allen Ginsberg, and the rock group the Jefferson Airplane all participated in a celebration of counterculture values and experiences. John Phillips of "The Mamas and the Papas" wrote the lyrics for the song that promoted the upcoming Monterey Pop Festival (the first rock music festival to be held) and his lyrics became an anthem for what would then be renamed the "hippie movement:"

> If you're going to San Francisco,
> be sure to wear some flowers in your hair.
> If you come to San Francisco,
> Summertime will be a love-in there.

To many, 1967 would be the high water mark of the counterculture movement as that which followed became more commercialized and in many instances explotative. The word hippie came from hipster, a term used to describe beatniks of the 1950s who had settled into San Francisco's North Beach bohemian areas. The hippies adopted the counterculture values of the Beat Generation, created their own communities, often communal in structure, listened to psychedelic rock music, embraced the sexual revolution, and used drugs like marijuana and LSD to explore alternative states of consciousness.

· Yippies (1968)

Originally a "put-on," this so-called Youth International Party or Yippies poked fun at both the "hippie" culture and the political establishment. They ran a pig for President, threatened to put LSD in the water supply of Chicago during the Democratic nominating convention and, in general, created havoc and mayhem as they attempted "to rewrite the stuffy textbook of revolution with children's crayons rather than the pen of political analysis." Led by Abbie Hoffman, Jerry Rubin, and Paul Krassner (who coined the name), the movement received a great deal of publicity during the five-month Chicago Seven Conspiracy trial in 1969. Hoffman and Rubin were the most colorful of the seven defendants accused of criminal conspiracy and inciting a riot at the 1968 Democratic National Convention.

·1968: Year of Protest and Rage

With the assassinations of Martin Luther King Jr. and Robert Kennedy, along with the Tet Offensive in Vietnam, the riots at the Democratic Convention in Chicago, student protests shutting down Colombia University in New York and the Sorbonne in Paris among others, and Prague Spring in Czechoslovakia, this year was the most turbulent of any in the turbulent 60's and would go down in history as one of the most turbulent of all time.

·Woodstock

The name for a peaceful gathering of nearly 400,000 of the counterculture in Bethyl, New York in 1969 for a combination "happening," "be-in," music /art festival, and anti-war protest. Featuring a varied group of folk and rock artists such as Joan Baez, Blood, Sweat & Tears, Country Joe McDonald, Creedence Clearwater Revival, the Grateful Dead, Jefferson Airplane, Jimi Hendrix, Janis Joplin, Richie Havens, Santana, Joe Cocker, The Who, Sha Na Na, and John Sebastian it lasted for three days amidst the drugs, music, rain, and mud. There was no violence but there were vast amounts of mood modifying drugs. The term Woodstock became a metaphor for counterculture events of the 1960s.

Johnson's Foreign Policy

·Dominican Republic

In 1965 Johnson sent 22,000 U.S. troops to the Dominican Republic on the grounds that a band of Communist conspirators had taken over the country. In what became the Johnson Doctrine, he claimed a domestic revolution ceased to be a local concern when the object was the establishment of a communist dictatorship. Most Latin Americans and many in the U.S. were critical of this action as there was little evidence of communist involvement and the U.S. put back into power former officials in the dictatorial right-wing Rafael Trujillo regime that had been overthrown by the people.

·Building Bridges (1964-1968)

A Consular Treaty with the USSR was negotiated and ultimately signed that provided for diplomatic immunity for all officials and employees of each country and prompt notification of the detainment of a citizen of either country and access to them by their own consular authorities.

·Outer Space Treaty

Signed by 60 countries in 1967, it provided for the peaceful use of outer space banning weapons of mass destruction, testing, military bases, and claims of ownership or national sovereignty in space.

·Six Day War (1967)

By using the "hot line" the U.S. and USSR stayed out of the conflict. The USSR would re-equip the defeated Arab air forces. France would quit selling its Mirage fighter planes to Israel. The U.S. would step into the void and began selling advanced fighter planes to Israel and become their main military arms supplier. In this war, Israel would take control of the Sinai Peninsula and Gaza from Egypt, the Golan Heights from Syria, and Old Jerusalem and the land on the West Bank of the Jordan River from Jordan. It was a total Israel victory.

·Pueblo Seizure

A U.S. intelligence gathering ship with its 83-man crew was captured by North Korea in 1968. Nearly a year later the crew was released after signing a statement of the guilt for spying despite the U.S. contention that they had been in international waters when captured. This was a blow to the prestige of the U.S. at a time when the War in Vietnam was reaching its peak.

UNIT XXX
MULTIPLE-CHOICE QUESTIONS

Questions 1-4 refer to the following:

"Any new left in America must be, in large measure, a left with real intellectual skills....A new left must consist of younger people who matured in the postwar world,... The university is an obvious beginning point. A new left must include liberals and socialists, the former for their relevance, the latter for their sense of thoroughgoing reforms in the system.... A new left must start controversy across the land.... a militant left might awaken its allies, and by beginning the process towards peace, civil rights, and labor struggles... To turn these possibilities into realities will involve national efforts at university reform by an alliance of students and faculty. They must wrest control of the educational process from the administrative bureaucracy.... They must make debate and controversy, not dull pedantic cant, the common style for educational life.... As students, for a democratic society, we are committed to... vision... If we appear to seek the unattainable, it has been said, then let it be known that we do so to avoid the unimaginable."

Excerpts from the "Port Huron Statement" of the Students for a Democratic Society, 1962

1. The New left differed from the old left of the 1930s by its disavowal of

   (A) classical liberalism
   (B) utopian socialism
   (C) intellectualism
   (D) class struggle maxism

2. The Port Huran statement was written in part because students were frustrated with

   (A) the idealism of the New Frontier
   (B) the conservatives domination of the government
   (C) the pace of reform of traditional liberalism
   (D) the failure of youth to embrace rock music

3. The social movement of the 1960s that most resembles the "new left" is the

   (A) counterculture
   (B) beats
   (C) lost generation
   (D) baby boomers

4. The new left of the 1960s were different from the old left of the 1930s because many of the old left of an earlier time period had been

   (A) anarchists
   (B) communists
   (C) royalists
   (D) bohemians

437

Questions 5-8 refer to the following:

"Just a little rain falling all around,
The grass lifts its head to the heavenly sound,
Just a little rain, just a little rain,
What have they done to the rain?

Just a little boy standing in the rain
The gentle rain that falls for years.
And the grass is gon
And rain keeps falling like helpless tears,
And what have they done to the rain?

Just a little breeze out of the sky,
The leaves pat their hands as the breeze blows by,
Just a little breeze with some smoke in its eye,
What have they done to the rain?

Just a little boy standing in the rain,
The gentle rain that falls for years.
And the grass is gone,
The boy disappears,
And rain keeps falling like helpless tears,
And what have they done to the rain?"

Malvina Reynolds, "What Have They Done to the Rain," 1962

5. The type of music that is captured in this protest song popular in the 1950 & 1960s is

(A) swing
(B) folk
(C) rock
(D) disco

6. This song during the 1960s was protesting against

(A) nuclear fallout
(B) water pollution
(C) cloud seeding
(D) pesticides

7. The "they" being referred to in the song are

(A) corporate executives
(B) agri-business farmers
(C) politicians in the U.S. & USSR
(D) those who do not recycle

8. From the perspective of the 21st century this song's protest could be directed against

(A) developing countries industrialization
(B) UN failure to stop environmental damage
(C) loopholes in the Kyota Protocols
(D) acid rain

Questions 9-12 refer to the following:

"These sprays, dusts, and aerosols are now applied almost universally to farms, gardens, forests, and homes nonselective chemicals that have the power to kill every insect, the "good" and the "bad," to still the song of birds and the leaping of fish in the streams, to coat the leaves with a deadly film, and to linger on in soil all this though the intended target may be only a few weeds or insects. Can anyone believe it is possible to lay down such a barrage of poisons on the surface of the earth without making it unfit for all life? They should not be called "insecticides," but "biocides...." Since DDT was released for civilian use, a process of escalation has been going on in which ever more toxic materials must be found. This has happened because insects, in a triumphant vindication of Darwin's principle of the survival of the fittest, have evolved super races immune to the particular insecticide use...."

Rachael Carson, *Silent Spring*, 1962

9. This 1962 book inspired which movement that would have a major impact on U.S. government policy?

(A) Environmental
(B) Genetic
(C) Gerontology
(D) Biological engineering

10. The metaphorical title of the book is a reference to which environmental change

(A) rivers that no longer have enough water in them to flow
(B) song birds could no longer be heard in springtime
(C) loss of habitat for plants and animals because of pesticides
(D) failure of the snow pack to provide an adequate supply of fresh water

11. Silent Spring's impact on legislation was similar to which earlier book that brought about the Pure Food and Drug Act and Meat Inspection Act of 1906?

(A) Lincoln Steffens, *Shame of the Cities*
(B) Oscar Handlin, *The Uprooted*
(C) John Spargo, *Bitter Cry of the Children*
(D) Upton Sinclair, *The Jungle*

12. Which current U.S. environmental concern, highlighted by Al Gore's book *An Inconvenient Truth*, owes its debt to what Rachel Carson accomplished with *Silent Spring*?

(A) Auto emissions
(B) Population explosion
(C) Climate change
(D) Fossil fuels

Questions 13-15 refer to the following:

"If you're going to San Francisco
Be sure to wear some flowers in your hair
If you're going to San Francisco
You're gonna meet some gentle people there

For those who come to San Francisco
Summertime will be a love-in there
In the streets of San Francisco
Gentle people with flowers in their hair

All across the nation such a strange vibration
People in motion
There's a whole generation with a new explanation
People in motion people in motion

For those who come to San Francisco
Be sure to wear some flowers in your hair
If you come to San Francisco
Summertime will be a love-in there

If you come to San Francisco
Summertime will be a love-in there"

John Phillips, "San Francisco (Be Sure to Wear Some Flowers in Your Hair)," 1967

13. This song is considered to be emblematic of which 1960s social event or "happening"?

(A) Summer of Love
(B) Woodstock
(C) March on Washington
(D) Free Speech movement

15. Names given to those who went to San Francisco in 1967 included all of the following EXCEPT

(A) counterculture
(B) hip cats
(C) hippies
(D) flower children

14. The song written by John Phillips of the Mama's and the Papa's for Scott McKenzie was intended to advertise what 1967 event that would launch a new venue for singers to perform—the rock festival?

(A) Altamont
(B) Monterey Pop Festival
(C) Woodstock
(D) US Festival

UNIT XXXI
VIETNAM WAR

For almost 30 years the U.S. was involved in the politics of Vietnam from 1945 to 1975 during the presidencies of Truman, Eisenhower, Kennedy, Johnson, Nixon and Ford. From what started out as support for French imperialism ended up as a 10 year full scale war resulting in the loss of not only Vietnam to communism, but the death of more than 59,000 U.S. soldiers in America's longest war. As America's first losing war, it had an impact on the U.S. psychological make-up that still exists today.

Truman Years

·World War II
During WWII Japan overran Vietnam, Cambodia, & Laos (Indochina) and replaced the French, who had colonized the country in the 19th century as the rulers of Indochina.

·Ho Chi Minh (1945)
After Japan had been defeated, a power vacuum occurred in Southeast Asia as the French were still interned as the Japanese forces were removed. Into this vacuum, a native nationalist movement, the Viet Minh, took power across Vietnam in what became known as the "August Revolution." Ho Chi Minh (leader of the Viet Minh), declared the independent Democratic Republic of Vietnam and made an overture to the Americans by quoting the Declaration of Independence.

·Allies & France
The major allied victors of World War II (United Kingdom, U.S. and Soviet Union) all agreed that the area belonged to the French. Because the French did not have the forces to immediately retake Vietnam, the major powers agreed that British troops would occupy the South while Nationalist Chinese forces would take the North. After the British landed they rearmed the French forces as well as some of the Japanese forces to aid them in retaking the southern part of Vietnam.

441

·Colonial War

At the USSR's urging, Ho Chi Minh tried to negotiate with the French who were reestablishing their control in Vietnam. In 1946, the Viet Minh won elections across central and northern Vietnam but the French landed in Hanoi and they ousted the Viet Minh from the city. The Viet Minh began a guerilla war against French rule that would last from 1949 to 1954.

·U.S. and France

The Truman administration supported the French in retaking Vietnam after WWII both diplomatically and financially. The U.S. created a Military Assistance and Advisory Group to deal with French requests for aid, gave advice on strategy, and help in the training of Vietnamese soldiers. By 1954, the U.S. was paying $1 billion in support of the French military and contributing 80% of the cost of the war. Twice the U.S. considered military intervention on the side of the French, but the siege of Dien Ben Phu and the ultimate French defeat put and end to that idea.

Eisenhower Years

·Dienbenphu

After the Vietnamese Communist forces, or Viet Minh, defeated the French colonial army at the Battle of Dien Bien Phu in 1954, the colony was granted independence. The 11,721 prisoners that were captured by the Viet Minh forces of General Giap (4,436 were wounded) broke France's will to fight. It was the first time a colonized people had a major victory and captured an army of a European colonial power.

·Geneva Accords (1954)

According to the Geneva settlement, Vietnam was temporarily partitioned at the 17th parallel into a communist North and a non-communist South. Some signers of the Geneva accords hoped that elections to unify North and South Vietnam could be scheduled to take place in 1956, but the elections were never held. Neither the U.S. nor the two Vietnams had signed the election clause in the accord, and were thus not bound to honor it. Initially, it seemed that a partitioned Vietnam would become similar in nature to a partitioned Korea that had been created earlier.

·Forming Two Countries

Freedom of movement between the two areas was allowed for 300 days. Communist forces regrouped in the north and non-Communist forces in the south. During this period some 900,000 people, many of whom were Catholics or individuals fleeing the land reform program initiated by the Ho Chi Minh government, migrated south.

·North Vietnam

North Vietnam, where the Viet Minh were the strongest adopted the Communist government of Ho Chi Minh. He maintained good relations with both China and the USSR, and received a great deal of aid from both countries while skillfully protecting the independence of his country.

·South Vietnam

It was initially placed under the control of the discredited, French-backed government of Bao Dai. He would soon be forced out of power and went into exile in France.

·Ngo Dinh Diem

In 1955 after the South Vietnamese monarchy was abolished and Bao Dai removed from power, Prime Minister Ngo Dinh Diem became President of a new South Vietnamese Republic. The Republic of Vietnam government of Diem, with the support of Eisenhower, had no interest in holding elections that threatened to bring communist influences into the South. Diem was faced with a war-torn economy and serious political and military problems. His authoritarian policies—rigid press censorship, interference with elections, restriction of opposition parties, nepotism, and mass arrests—drew increasing criticism. The Eisenhower administration increased its military and economic aid to combat the communist threat and put pressure on Diem for democratic reforms. He dispatched military advisers to train a South Vietnamese army, and U.S. unleashed the Central Intelligence Agency (CIA) to conduct psychological warfare against the North.

· **National Liberation Front**

The NLF was a communist political group from the South who wanted to take over the Diem government. With support from Ho Chi Minh, the Viet Cong, the military arm of the NLF, begin to take over large areas of South Vietnam. By late 1961, the Viet Cong had won control of virtually half of South Vietnam with little local opposition.

Kennedy Years

· **Military Advisors**

From the 900 U.S. military advisors that were in Vietnam when Eisenhower left office, Kennedy increased the number to 16,000 in 1963. This increase in forces included combat troops along with advisors.

· **Counter Insurgency**

This plan was adopted in 1961 that included both military and social goals for Vietnam.

· **Diem's Failure**

Widespread opposition to the U.S. supported, corrupt, Diem regime manifested itself in the immolation of Buddhist monks that were captured on camera by television. Kennedy became critical of the Saigon government and said in a TV interview that the U.S. could only play a supporting role in Vietnam; it was their war to win or lose.

· **Strategic Hamlet**

Counter insurgency was carried out by this plan of U.S. advisors living in villages, in order to strike out against Viet Cong insurgents. All this plan accomplished was a disruption of traditional village life.

· **Diem's Assassination**

With tacit U.S. approval, a military coup led to Diem's assassination in November of 1963. A military junta replaced him. Kennedy would be assassinated less than a month later.

The Johnson Years

· **Junta Politics**

The military junta who replaced Diem had their own power struggle and air force officer Nguyen Cao Ky emerged as the new leader of the Republic of Vietnam.

· **NLF and Viet Cong Expansion**

The political revolutionaries the National Liberation Front and their guerilla military arm the Viet Cong begin to widen their control over large areas of South Vietnam especially in the countryside.

· **Planned Escalation**

During the first 6 months of 1964, the U.S. initiated a program of covert operations against North Vietnam (who were aiding the NLF and Viet Cong) including intelligence gathering for South Vietnam commando raids. Bombing North Vietnam was considered but it ran counter to Johnson campaign criticism of Goldwater who had suggested bombing to discourage North Vietnam infiltration of the South.

·Maddox and Turner Joy
Two U.S. destroyers who were gathering intelligence to direct South Vietnamese commando raids were allegedly fired on by North Vietnamese PT boats on August 4, 1964 in the Gulf of Tonkin.

·Gulf of Tonkin Resolution
Concealing the activities of the two destroyers, Johnson asked Congress for authority to take all necessary measures to repel any armed attack against the forces of the U.S. in a resolution that amounted to a "functional equivalent of a declaration of war" according to Undersecretary of State Nicolas Katzenbach. It passed the House 414-0 and the Senate 88-2. The two Senators voting against it Ernest Gruening of Alaska and Wayne Morse of Oregon were defeated when they ran for reelection because of their opposition to the resolution.

·U.S. Troop Buildup
From 23,000 in 1964, U.S. troops would increase to 184,000 in 1965, 385,000 in 1966, 485,000 in 1967 and 536,000 in 1968. With the large number of troops committed more of the fighting was done by the U.S.; this ran counter to Johnson's campaign speech that said, "We don't want our American boys to do the fighting for Asian boys." The build-up was to convince North Vietnam that they could not win a military victory. The buildup had little impact on the North as they insisted it was a civil war and the U.S. had to negotiate with the NLF.

·Mekong Delta Project
This is the name for Johnson's proposed economic plan to win the "hearts and minds" of the South Vietnamese with a TVA type of program of dams on the Mekong River.

·Search and Destroy
The U.S. military commander William Westmoreland convinced Johnson that "search and destroy" operations would bring victory to the U.S. by 1968. This tactic replaced the strategic hamlet approach and amounted to U.S. troops going on patrol to find the Viet Cong and kill them. Success was measured by the amount of kills (body count) that was difficult to estimate as the Viet Cong took their dead with them when they escaped back into the jungle. There was a tendency to inflate the number of kills to make the body count higher than it should have been. These suspect numbers led to a credibility gap; the U.S. government statements were no longer believed by the American people.

·Napalm and Agent Orange
Air strikes often amounted to defoliation of the tropical rain forest; the dropping of Napalm became a favorite tactic of the military. Napalm was a syrupy type of jellied gasoline used to ignite areas and Agent Orange was the code name for a powerful herbicide and defoliant used by the U.S. military in its herbicide warfare program.

·Operation Rolling Thunder
The code name for a sustained bombing campaign against North Vietnam with its purpose being to destroy the will of the North Vietnamese to fight, to destroy industrial bases and air defenses (SAMs), and to stop the flow of men and supplies down the Ho Chí Minh Trail that went through neutral Laos into South Vietnam. Starting in March 1965, Operation Rolling Thunder gradually escalated in intensity to force the Communists to negotiate but was weakened by the fact that the two principal areas where supplies came from, Haiphong and the Chinese border, were off limits to attack. It was stopped during the Presidential elections of 1968.

·South Vietnam Elections
Johnson's dislike of the arrogance of the military dictatorship of Nguyen Cao Ky resulted in Nguyen Van Thieu being elected President.

·Anti-War Movement
As Johnson escalated the war a significant anti-war movement developed. Protests included the burning of draft cards, teach-ins at universities, and large demonstrations including a march on the Pentagon of 55,000 protestors that were met by soldiers with fixed bayonets. Many in the counterculture adopted opposition to the Vietnam War as their new cause. Those who were opposed to the war were called doves and were considered unpatriotic by those who favored the war.

·Hawks and Hard Hats
A significant group of often working class individuals symbolized by the "hard hat" staged counter protests against the demonstrators. These so-called hawks often wanted to expand the war and they were especially critical of what they saw as the long-haired, hippie, counterculture for their lack of patriotism in supporting the war.

·Internal Dissent
The architect of the war, Secretary of Defense Robert McNamara reported to the President that neither the "pacification" program of subduing the countryside, nor the air war against the North was succeeding. He resigned from the administration, and his doubts began to erode the internal consensus that the administration had about the war. The war in Vietnam had been known as "McNamara's War" and his misgivings gave more fuel to the anti-war movement.

·Tet Offensive (1968)
After being assured by the government that there was a "light at the end of the tunnel" in the Vietnam War, the Viet Cong and North Vietnamese surprised the U.S. when they launched a major attack against South Vietnam cities during the lunar new year *Tet*, the most important holiday in Vietnam. It took months for the U.S. forces to lift the siege at Khe Sanh, recapture Hue, and force the Viet Cong out of Saigon where they had invaded the U.S. embassy. Although technically a U.S. victory, it was a turning point in the War as it raised questions about the ability of the U.S. to end the war. From this point on the anti-war movement would gain strength and the U.S. would begin the long process of extricating itself from the war.

·McCarthy's Crusade
A Democratic Senator from Minnesota who had voted for the Gulf of Tonkin Resolution, Gene McCarthy became disillusioned with the war and challenged Johnson for the Democratic nomination for President in 1968. Joined by an unofficial army of students and some members of the counterculture (who cleaned up their act by cutting their hair), these anti-war volunteers helped McCarthy gain 42% of the vote in the New Hampshire primary to Johnson's 48%. Although it was a Johnson victory it was so below expectations that it was considered a defeat. Robert Kennedy, brother of martyred President John Kennedy, announced that he would also be running for President on an anti-war platform to challenge Johnson as well as McCarthy for the nomination.

·Johnson's Announcement
With polls showing his possible defeat in the upcoming Wisconsin primary, Johnson declared in a TV address, "I shall not seek, and I will not accept, the nomination of my party for another term as President."

Nixon Years

·"Peace with Honor"

Slogan used by Nixon during his winning 1968 campaign (see Unit 32) as he promised to bring peace with honor in Vietnam, but did not specify how this was to be done.

·Vietnamization

Name for Nixon's plan to turn the fighting over to the ARVN (Army of the Republic of Vietnam) and bring U.S. troops home on a flexible timetable. To increase the size of the ARVN, a mobilization law was passed that called up into the army all men in South Vietnam between ages seventeen and forty-three. In June of 1969, Nixon announced the first of the U.S. troop withdrawals. The 540,000 U.S. troops were to be reduced by 25,000. Another 60,000 were to leave the following December.

·Nixon Doctrine

This policy proclaimed that the U.S. would honor its existing commitments but that in the future Asians and others would have to fight their own wars without the support of large bodies of American ground troops.

·Bombing Cambodia

In response to a new offensive by the Communist forces, Nixon secretly authorized the bombing of neutral Cambodia.

·My Lai

In 1968, U.S. forces massacred 350-500 civilians in a small village in South Vietnam. The commander William Calley was court-martialed and sentenced to life imprisonment (later reduced) for leading this massacre. Calley claimed he was following a direct order and many sympathized with him and saw him as a fall guy for higher ups, especially Captain Ernest Medina. This massacre left an indelible scar on the U.S. attempt to win over the "hearts and minds" of the Vietnamese people.

·Cambodian Incursion

A pro-West coup against the neutralist government resulted in Nixon ordering a joint ARVN-U.S. invasion that captured some caches of supplies but ultimately resulted in larger areas of Cambodia coming under the control of the Communist *Khymer Rouge*.

·Kent State

In 1970 in response to a student protest against the illegal bombing of Cambodia, four students (two who were not protesting but just walking to class) were killed and nine wounded when the Ohio National Guard fired on them in what a later investigation called "unwarranted and inexcusable." The National Guard claimed they were acting in self-defense and none of them were convicted for any wrong doing. More than 450 college campuses were shut down protesting the killing of the students at Kent State. American troops firing on American college students further weakened the war effort.

·Jackson State

A week after Kent State at the nearly all black college in Mississippi, two African American (innocent bystanders) students were killed and 9 were wounded by police, the highway patrol, and National Guard units.

·Repeal of the Gulf of Tonkin Resolution

In part because of the hearings held by Senator William Fullbright started in the Johnson years, and his Foreign Relations committee that was critical of the war, the Gulf of Tonkin Resolution was repealed in the Senate, in 1970 but not in the House.

·Pentagon Papers, 1971

Daniel Ellsberg, a Pentagon official, leaked to the *New York Times* a secret history of the Vietnam War. This 47-volume government study had been ordered by Secretary of Defense, Robert McNamara and it revealed a considerable degree of miscalculation, bureaucratic arrogance, and deception on the part of U.S. policymakers in the staging of the Vietnam War. The Justice Department obtained a court injunction against further publication on national security grounds, but the Supreme Court ruled that constitutional guarantees of a free press overrode other considerations and allowed further publication. Ellsberg was indicted on charges of espionage, theft, and conspiracy but in 1973 a federal judge dismissed all charges against him because of improper government conduct.

·Secret Peace Negotiations

Starting in 1969, National Security Advisor Henry Kissinger met with North Vietnam's Le Duc Tho 12 times in Paris to talk about peace. These secret talks held some hope of progress unlike the formal peace talks that had been going on since 1968.

·Bombing Hanoi and Haiphong

The U.S. increased its bombing of North Vietnam, mined Haiphong Harbor and all other ports, and blockaded the North to stop it from getting supplies in what became known as the Christmas bombing and the "madman theory." By depicting Nixon as so extreme that he might launch nuclear weapons it was hoped that this strategy would force North Vietnam to agree to peace.

·Paris Peace Accord of 1973

This agreement called for the U.S. withdrawal of all military forces within 60 days, release of all U.S. POWs, a cease-fire with 130,000 North Vietnamese troops being allowed to stay in place in the South, an end to military activities in Laos and Cambodia, military replacement aid and unlimited economic aid by the U.S. toward the Saigon regime, and formation of a National Council of National Reconciliation and Concord composed equally of members of the Saigon regime and NLF (Viet Cong). U.S. POWs were released and the last U.S. troops were withdrawn from South Vietnam.

Ford Years

·Communist Victory in Indochina

Ford asked Congress, to no avail, for more weapons for the ARVN as the North Vietnamese with their Viet Cong allies quickly over-ran South Vietnam in 1975. TV captured the evacuation of thousands of Vietnamese, who had been closely allied with the U.S., by helicopter as Saigon fell. Ford allowed the refugees into the U.S. where 300,000 of them would eventually settle—many of them in an area of Orange County, California called Little Saigon. At the same time South Vietnam was falling, the pro-Western Long Nol government fell to the Communist Khmer Rouge in Cambodia, as U.S. citizens and embassy personal were evacuated by helicopter. The fall of Indochina after U.S. involvement for 14 years brought about 6.5 million refugees from South Vietnam, 2.1 million from Cambodia, and over 1 million from Laos.

UNIT XXXI
MULTIPLE-CHOICE QUESTIONS

Questions 1-3 refer to the following:

"Lyndon Johnson had lost it all, and so had the rest of them; they had, for all their brilliance and hubris and sense of themselves, been unwilling to... learn from the past and they had been swept forward by their belief in the importance of anti-Communism (and the dangers of not paying sufficient homage to it) and by the sense of power and glory, omnipotence and omniscience of America in this century... Lyndon Johnson had known better, he had entertained no small amount of doubt.... He and the men around him wanted to be known as being strong and tough.... [The] leaders of a democracy [had not] bothered to involve the people of their country in the course they had chosen;... They had manipulated the public, the Congress, and the press from the start, told half truths.... When their predictions turned out to be hopelessly inaccurate... the faults were not theirs, the fault was with this country which was not worthy of them."

David Halberstam, *The Best and the Brightest*, 1969

1. A reason why Lyndon Johnson relied so heavily on the advice of the "so-called" "Best and Brightest" political advisors was that

   (A) his own judgment told him the experts knew the truth and should be followed
   (B) he trusted men who had not had to climb the political ladder by running for county sheriff
   (C) his insecurities about foreign policy compared to his expertise on domestic policy
   (D) he was concentrating on his renomination and reelection

2. The failure of the endeavor in Halberstam's book brought about a halt to which domestic program that Lyndon Johnson had championed?

   (A) Great Society
   (B) New Frontier
   (C) Fair Deal
   (D) New Federalism

3. Halberstam's description of men in the *Best and the Brightest* is similar to

   (A) the former Confederacy and its delusions of the "Lost Cause" after the Civil War
   (B) the fatal flaw of hubris that causes the Greek tragic hero to fall
   (C) a belief that "American exceptionalism" would prevail over adversity
   (D) the U.S. was like the biblical shining "City upon a Hill," and exempt from historical forces that have affected other countries

Questions 4-6 refer to the following:

"Saigon [is] almost luxurious. The... complex where so many of my friends work, has a golf course, Olympic-size swimming pool, etc. But with all the surface glitter and bustle of Saigon, I came away with a very gloomy feeling. The people are frantically trying to make every last cent they can from the Americans before [the soldiers] leave. My friends are somewhat depressed. It now seems they have to rewrite all their reports because the truth they are putting out is too pessimistic. The higher echelons, for their career's sake and the plans of Nixon's Vietnamization, will not allow a bad situation to exist—no matter how true it may be! I saw myself... some reports that were to go to Abrams... and how they had to be changed to get to him. What a disgrace—and still people are dying every day."

Sp/5 Thomas Pellaton, *Dear America: Letters from Vietnam*, 1985

4. The description of conditions for the U.S. military in Saigon is that it is a

(A) slum
(B) country club
(C) boring place
(D) overly religious

5. The excerpt is an example of

(A) soldiers grousing about how difficult life is in the military
(B) U.S. boasting about how well the soldiers are treated by the Vietnamese
(C) the false reporting of what was happening that contributed to the credibility gap
(D) the positive outlook about the luxurious life style that prevailed in Saigon

6. Nixon's attempt to create an impression that the U.S. was undertaking a diminshed role was through Vietnamization which was

(A) to turn the fighting and the conduct of the war over to the Vietnamese while the U.S. provided arms and supplies
(B) to win over the hearts and minds of the people by having U.S. troops stay in people's houses
(C) the Strategic Hamlet Program that represented the unifying concept for a strategy designed to pacify rural Vietnam (the Viet Cong's chosen battleground) and to develop support among the peasants for the central government.
(D) to extend the war into Laos and Cambodia by destroying safe havens in those countries

Questions 7-9 refer to the following:

"...To promote the maintenance of international peace and security in Southeast Asia.

Whereas naval units of the communist regime in Vietnam, in violation of the principles of the Charter of the United Nations and of international law, have deliberately and repeatedly attacked United States naval vessels lawfully present in international waters,...

Whereas these attacks are part of a deliberate and systematic campaign of aggression....

Whereas the United States is assisting the peoples of Southeast Asia to protect their freedom...

Resolved by the Senate and House of Representatives of the United States of America in Congress assembled, That the Congress approves and supports the determination of the President, as Commander in Chief, to take all necessary measures to repel any armed attack against the forces of the United States and to prevent further aggression....

Sec. 3. This resolution shall expire when the President shall determine that the peace and security of the area is reasonably assured..."

Text of Joint Resolution, August 7, Department of State Bulletin, 24 August 1964

7. This joint resolution of Congress in the passage above is commonly called the

   (A) Quemoy and Matsu Resolution
   (B) Gulf of Tonkin Resolution
   (C) Defense of Vietnam Resolution
   (D) Bay of Pigs Resolution

8. This resolution was used as the justification by the United States for a war that is similar to a resolution passed for which subsequent war in which no declaration of war was passed either?

   (A) World War II
   (B) Korean War
   (C) Iraq War
   (D) Grenada War

9. All of the following are true implications of this joint Congressional resolution EXCEPT

   (A) The only two Senators who voted against it, Ernest Gruening and Morse Wayne were defeated for reelection
   (B) It authorized the President to wage war without a formal declaration of war
   (C) The President later acknowledged that U.S. ships were not under attack and may have been shooting at whales or flying fish
   (D) It was later replaced by a Declaration of War by Congress

Questions 10-13 refer to the following:

"We don't smoke marijuana in Muskogee
We don't take no trips on LSD
We don't burn no draft cards down on Main Street
We like livin' right, and bein' free

I'm proud to be an Okie from Muskogee
A place where even squares can have a ball
We still wave Old Glory down at the courthouse
And white lightnin's still the biggest thrill of all

We don't make a party out of lovin'
We like holdin' hands and pitchin' woo
We don't let our hair grow long and shaggy
Like the hippies out in San Francisco do

And I'm proud to be an Okie from Muskogee
A place where even squares can have a ball
We still wave Old Glory down at the courthouse
And white lightnin's still the biggest thrill of all

Leather boots are still in style for manly footwear
Beads and Roman sandals won't be seen
Football's still the roughest thing on campus
And the kids here still respect the college dean...."

Merle Haggard and Roy Edward Burns, "Okie from Muscogee," 1967

10. This song was written to extoll the virtues of

(A) intellectuals and academicians
(B) traditional values and lifestyle
(C) liberalism and reform
(D) middle class suburbia

11. This song was directed against all of the following groups in American culture EXCEPT

(A) Hard Hats
(B) Students for a Democratic Society (SDS)
(C) Counterculture
(D) Doves

12. The song extolls the virtues of which of the following?

(A) Psychedelics
(B) Cannabis
(C) "Acid"
(D) Illegal alcohol

13. Which of the following is a positive image in the song?

(A) Burning draft cards
(B) Roman sandals
(C) College football
(D) Long hair

Questions 14-15 refer to the following:

"After Korea everyone said there would be no more Koreas. And there weren't. But there was Vietnam. Now it is a cliché to say there will be no more Vietnams. And there probably won't be—in Vietnam. But unless our military power to fight counterrevolutionary wars is reduced, and unless our attitudes change, there might very well be further military interventions.... We are allied with 42 nations and judging from past behavior, consider virtually every noncommunist country in the world to be vital to our security... Having intervened actively for thirty years, it has become almost a reflex action... No more Vietnams? It would be unwise to take any bets on it. The heady rhetoric of the 1960s has been deflated, but great power still provides an irresistible temptation."

Ronald Steel, *Pax Americana*, 1967

14. Which two American wars in the 21st century could be interpreted has fulfilling the prediction that Steel made when he stated he would not take any bets of there being no more Vietnams?

   (A) Kuwait and Iran
   (B) Iraq and Afghanistan
   (C) Grenada and Haiti
   (D) Lebanon and Tunisia

15. What does Steel say has become a reflex action of the United States?

   (A) Military intervention
   (B) Opposing communism
   (C) Aligning with countries
   (D) No more Vietnams

UNIT XXXII
NIXON TO CARTER: THE 70S

Much of what is ascribed to the 1960s actually occurred in the early 1970s. Nixon's remarkable political comeback and overwhelming reelection would end in the disgrace called "Watergate." Both Ford and Carter would be plagued by problems that they were unable to solve as President. Socially, the U.S. would eventually move away from the counterculture to a value system based on materialism—an attempt to return to some of the values of the 1950s or even the earlier 1920s.

Richard M. Nixon:

·Election of 1968

1. **Democrats**—Robert Kennedy's assassination, after he won the California primary over Gene McCarthy, paved the way for Hubert Humphrey (Johnson's Vice President) to get the Democratic nomination. He gained the nomination from the political bosses and party regulars. Humphrey won no primaries, in what became the last convention that actually nominated a President instead of the coronation of a Presidential nominee. In future years nominations would be decided by delegates chosen in state primaries, caucuses, and conventions.

2. **Republicans**—United behind the suddenly resurrected Richard Nixon, who had been out of office for eight years after losing to Kennedy in 1960 and being overwhelmingly defeated when he ran for governor of California in 1962, the Republican platform stood solidly behind the war and Nixon's secret plan to end it.

3. **American Independent**—With its pro-war position this newly formed party nominated George Wallace, former segregationist governor of Alabama for President and General Curtis Le May for Vice-President.

4. **Other Third Parties**—All of these took a handful of votes away from the major candidates and included the Socialist-Labor, Socialist Worker, Peace and Freedom, Prohibition, Communist and Free Ballot parties.

453

5. **Results**—In a close election Nixon won the popular vote by 500,000 out of more than 73 million votes cast and the electoral vote 302-191 over Humphrey and a divided Democratic Party with Wallace winning 46 electoral votes. Nixon ran ahead of his party as the Democrats maintained control of the House 243-192 and the Senate 58-42.

Foreign Policy

·Nuclear Non-Proliferation Treaty

1969 agreement that had been negotiated over the previous four years that banned the spread of nuclear weapons to non-nuclear states and was signed by the USSR, U.S., and 60 other nations not including nuclear powers France and the People's Democratic Republic of China.

·Okinawa

This island was turned over to Japan's administration and the U.S. agreed to remove its nuclear weapons from its $2 billion military base complex but the U.S. would retain the bases.

·Berlin Accord

Recognized the existence of East and West German nations and established formal diplomatic recognition between the two countries. The 4 occupying powers (U.S., USSR, Great Britain, and France) agreed to the accord.

·Detenté

In a reversal of 25 years of official American policy, Nixon would adopt the policy of better relations between the U.S. and the USSR and China.

·China Policy

A U.S. policy shift occured in 1971 submitted a resolution to the UN recommending that Beijing replace Taiwan on the Security Council while Taiwan would continue its membership in the General Assembly. The General Assembly voted 76-35 with 17 abstentions to admit Beijing to the Security Council and expel Taiwan from all UN bodies.

·"Ping Pong Diplomacy"

U.S. table tennis team visited and competed in China starting the move toward the termination of restrictions on travel, permitting foreign subsidiaries of U.S. companies to trade in non strategic goods, and the lifting of the 20 year trade embargo on Chinese goods.

·Nixon's Visit to China

To seek normalization of relations, Nixon's historic visit to China in 1972 signaled an end to the U.S. isolation of China.

·Moscow Summit

Nixon met with General Secretary Leonid Brezhnev and laid the groundwork for a treaty dealing with the USSR on weapons and the environment.

·SALT I

These talks held over a number of years in Helsinki and Vienna were finalized when an agreement was reached over ABM systems in both countries. Richard Nixon and Leonid Brezhnev signed the Anti-Ballistic Missile Treaty and the Interim Agreement Between The United States of America and The Union of Soviet Socialist Republics on Certain Measures With Respect to the Limitation of Strategic Offensive Arms. A number of statements were also agreed to.

·CIA in Chile

Nixon feared that the Socialist Salvador Allende's land reform program and nationalization of foreign industries was a major threat to the U.S. The CIA offered bribes, and engaged in propaganda but failed to defeat him when he ran for election. After his election, foreign aid was cut off from Chile and the CIA worked for three years to overthrow him. They finally succeeded in 1973 when General Augusto Pinochet seized the government and killed Allende. Trade and economic relations were quickly restored to Pinochet's government as it abolished civil liberties, ended economic reform, and killed thousands of political opponents. Congress belatedly investigated the U.S. involvement in the overthrow of Chile's elected government, but its condemnation was too late to do any good.

·War Powers Act of 1973

Passed over Nixon's veto this anti-Imperial Presidency law required the president to report to Congress within 48 hours after committing troops or substantially enlarging combat units in a foreign country. Authorization to use troops would be limited to 60 days unless Congress extended it for 30 more days. A declaration of war would lift the restriction.

·1973 Arab Oil Embargo

The 1973 attack on Israel in the Yom Kipper war and Israel's ultimate victory despite heavy initial casualties led to the Arab oil boycott because of the U.S. support for Israel. This led to long lines at the gas stations, lowered thermostats, a 55 mile per hour speed limit, and Congressional approval for the building of an Alaska pipeline. After five months the embargo was lifted but OPEC (Organization of Petroleum Exporting Countries) quadrupled its crude oil prices that led to a disruption in U.S. international trade as well as domestic inflation.

Domestic Policy

·New Federalism

Nixon wanted to reverse Johnson's Great Society and the flow of money to the Federal government. His revenue sharing amounted to returning tax money to local governments where it might be used for law enforcement and civic projects instead of liberal programs like jobs for the unemployed.

·Great Society Extension

Despite his desire to end the Great Society programs Nixon ended up expanding many liberal programs and accepted others passed by a Democratic Congress:

1. **Social Security**—He boasted benefits
2. **Job Corps**—Expanded the program
3. **Low Cost Housing**—Established a new program
4. **26th Amendment**—Lowered the voting age to 18, which resulted in most people under the age of 25 not voting in subsequent elections
5. **EPA**—Established the Environmental Protection Agency that had been inspired by the publication of Racial Carson's 1962 book, *The Silent Spring*, that focused on the harm done to the environment by commercial pesticides
6. **OSHA**—Occupational and Safety Health Administration which investigated businesses for infractions of environmental and safety regulations
7. **Urban Mass Transit**—Created a fund of $3.1billion in grants and loans to states and localities to create mass transit
8. **Water Quality Improvement Act of 1970**—Passed by Congress as a result of the Santa Barbara California oil-spill which established liability for polluters up to $14 million and authorized the federal government to clean them up

9. **Clean Air Act of 1970**—Expanded on the previous clean air and air quality acts of 1963, 1965, and 1967 by requiring cars to emit less carbon monoxide and hydrocarbons after 1975
10. **National Environmental Policy Act of 1969**—Required environmental impact statements for all major activities that had an impact on the environment
11. **Food Stamps and Medicaid**—Nixon signed bills increasing appropriations for these Great Society entitlement programs

·Anti-Great Society

Nixon cut off funds for urban renewal, job training, and education. He abolished the Office of Economic Opportunity and refused to spend funds that Congress allocated in health, housing, education, and the environment. He impounded more than $15 billion in funds that were earmarked for 100 programs. This is an example of his concept of the Imperial Presidency practiced by both Johnson and Nixon where the President could defy the law. Later the courts would rule these impoundments unconstitutional as the president was exercising a veto power that was not in the Constitution.

·Family Assistance Plan

FAP was an attempt to streamline the welfare bureaucracy and stop welfare cheating by giving poor families $1600 a year with a stipulation that the head of household sign up for job training. Both liberals and conservatives attacked it and it passed the House but died in the Senate.

·Imperial Presidency

Both Johnson and Nixon are known as the "Imperial Presidents" because of their conception of the office as that of an emperor more than "Mr. President." Presidential salaries were increased in 1969 to $200,000 with a travel allowance of $40,000 un-taxable and an official allowance of $50,000 taxable. As a symbol of the "Imperial Presidency" Nixon attempted to change the uniforms of the white house officers to have them resemble a European type of "Swiss Guard." This idea was short lived. The concept of the "Imperial Presidency" puts the President beyond constitutional limits and involves the creation of a large, complex bureaucracy shielding the President.

·Nixon Court

To replace retiring Chief Justice Earl Warren in 1969 Nixon chose a political conservative Warren Burger. He also tried, but failed, to appoint Clement Haynesworth and Harrold Carswell who were rejected by the Senate because of ethical improprieties, racial views, and deficient intellect. Three other conservatives, Harry Blackmun, Lewis Powell, and William Rehnquist were appointed to fill vacancies but the court did not always make conservative rulings especially on issues like abortion, desegregation, and the death penalty. It's most controversial decision was legalizing most abortions in the case of *Roe v. Wade* in 1973.

·Earth Day

An event suggested by Senator Gaylord Nelson that focused national attention on the harm being done to the environment. On April 22, 1970, millions of Americans participated in environmental teach-ins, anti-pollution protests, cleanup projects, walked or biked to school or work, and peacefully protested the degradation of the environment. The movement would wane with the realization of the high economic costs of cleaning up the environment but would be revived periodically over the next 40 years.

·Philadelphia Plan

In 1969, a plan was developed that required construction trade unions working on federal contracts to establish "goals and timetables" for hiring minority apprentices. The plan was then extended to all federal contracts requiring thousands of employers to establish quotas (called set-asides) for hiring minority subcontractors. Nixon went far beyond Johnson's "affirmative action" which was designed to protect individuals. The

Philadelphia Plan gave privileges to certain groups that were not available to everyone. It also had the purpose of integrating labor unions that were predominately white. Educational institutions also adopted this controversial approach and critics called it reverse discrimination. The courts have upheld most of its principles in a series of very controversial decisions.

·Watergate Break-In

On June 17, 1972, two months before Nixon's re-nomination, five burglars were arrested at the Watergate Hotel and Office Complex in Washington D. C. as they attempted to "bug" the offices of Democratic National Committee Chairman Larry O'Brien. Links were established between the burglars and E. Howard Hunt, a White House consultant, and G. Gordon Liddy, counsel to the Committee to Reelect the President (CREEP). The burglar's carried money that was traceable to the President's reelection campaign but Nixon stated that no one in his administration was involved.

·Weathermen

As SDS and other radical groups lost power they were replaced by groups such as the Weathermen— revolutionaries who were willing to use violence to bring down American institutions. Taking their name from a lyric in the Bob Dylan song, "Subterranean Homesick Blues," they lived an underground existence and committed acts of terrorism against the U.S. and especially the Vietnam War.

·Presidential Election of 1972—

1. **Reforms** in the nominating process after Humphrey's tainted victory in 1968 led to proportionate representation (quotas) of women, minorities, and young people and anti-war candidate Senator George McGovern was nominated on the first ballot after more prominent Democrats fell by the wayside. He was the first candidate to win a nomination by only winning primaries and caucuses.
2. **The Democratic platform** called for withdrawal from Vietnam, ending the draft, amnesty for war resisters, and a guaranteed income above the poverty line.
3. **Nixon and Spiro Agnew** were re-nominated and the Republican platform favored Nixon's foreign policy, welfare reform, revenue sharing, national health insurance, and opposed amnesty for war resisters and busing to achieve racial balance in schools.
4. **McGovern Vice-Presidential** choice Senator Thomas Eagleton of Missouri was forced to withdraw from the ticket two weeks after the convention when reporters discovered he had been hospitalized three times for depression and had received shock treatments. R. Sargent Shriver, former head of the Peace Corps became the new Vice-Presidential candidate after 6 others had refused McGovern's offer to run with him.
5. **A $50 million war chest** helped Nixon receive the most overwhelming electoral victory in U.S. history since Monroe's election in 1820 when he had no opponent.
6. **Results**—Nixon's 520-17 (Massachusetts and D. C.) victory in the Electoral College and 61% to 38% in the popular vote was overwhelming. The Republicans gained 13 seats in the House to still remain in the minority and lost 2 Senate seats as well as one Governorship.

·Watergate Aftermath and Cover-Up

1. **Early Cover Up**—Between the break-in and Nixon's re-nomination documents were destroyed in HR Haldeman's (White House Chief of Staff) office; Howard Hunt's safe was emptied; the FBI was pressured to limit its investigation to avoid implementing the CIA; $460,000 of CREEP campaign funds were siphoned away from the $60 million to support the burglary defendants; and the Deputy Director of CREEP Jeb McGruder committed perjury before a grand jury.
2. **Woodward and Bernstein**—Two young investigative reporters for the *Washington Post*, Bob Woodward and Carl Bernstein revealed that a White House secret fund had financed spying

and sabotaging of the stronger Democratic candidates. This included correspondence containing a letter that destroyed the candidacy of candidate Ed Muskie who was ahead of Nixon in the polls. Other aspects of this sabotage included false leaks to the press; the seizure of confidential campaign files; and Nixon's appointments secretary Dwight Chapin hireing Donald Segretti who recruited agents to perform various other "dirty tricks" on the Democrats. One source who confirmed much of the wrongdoing and was given the cover name "Deep Throat," to keep his identity secret. He was later revealed to be Mark Felt the #2 man at the FBI.

3. **Judge John Sirica**—At the trial of the Watergate 7, the judge, unhappy with the questioning by the federal prosecutors, personally interrogated defense witnesses. Five defendants pleaded guilty and two others were convicted by the jury. One defendant James McCord was given a 20 year sentence with the hope that this would pry information out of him.

4. **Irvin Committee**—A seven man Senate Select Committee was formed headed by North Carolina Senator Sam Irvin to conduct a Watergate inquiry. These televised hearing brought out much of the chicanery of the Nixon White House.

5. **Dean's Testimony**—White House Counsel John Dean testified that the President had been a party to the cover-up for 8 months and that offers of executive clemency to the burglars had been made. Without corroboration it was his word against Nixon's.

6. **Enemies List**—At the insistence of Nixon, Charles Colson, his special counsel, had put together in 1971 a list of more than 200 individuals and 18 organizations that were on a list including politicians, members of the press, academia, and Hollywood celebrities that were considered enemies. The FBI and IRS were asked to spy on them and harass them with tax audits.

7. **Plumbers**—Concerned that the press might expose his illegal campaign activities, Nixon created a secret investigative unit called the "Plumbers" to stop security leaks. In order to discredit Daniel Ellsberg, who had leaked the Pentagon Papers, they broke into his psychiatrist's office to get damming information against him but they found nothing they could use. G. Gordon Liddy came up with the plan to break into the Democratic headquarters and copy documents and wire-tap the phones. Attorney General John Mitchell approved these actions of the "Plumbers" in his new capacity as head of CREEP.

8. **Special Prosecutor**—Harvard law professor Archibald Cox was appointed to investigate all aspects of Watergate and to have complete independence from the White House.

9. **Revelations at Irvin Hearings**—Bob Haldeman, John Erlichman, Mitchell and other White House and CREEP figures were questioned. Vice Chairman Senator Howard Baker of Tennessee continually asked two questions: "What did the President know and when did he know it?" Except for Dean most witnesses exhibited "selective amnesia."

10. **White House Tapes**—White House aide Herbert Butterfield told the Senate Select Committee that Nixon had installed a tape recording system in his own office in 1971.

11. **Saturday Night Massacre**—Special Prosecutor Cox asked for the tapes but Nixon refused on the grounds that it would endanger national security. When Cox went to court to force Nixon to hand over the tapes Nixon ordered him fired. Attorney General Elliot Richardson refused to fire Cox and resigned. Deputy Attorney General William Ruckelshaus refused to fire Cox and was fired for this refusal. Finally, Solicitor General Robert Bork fired Cox.

12. **Agnew Resigns**—Pleading "no-contest" to charges of bribery (accepting kick-backs) and income tax evasion, Vice-President Spiro Agnew resigned and Nixon quickly nominated Gerald Ford (who was confirmed by Congress) to replace him as required by the 25th Amendment ratified in 1964.

13. **Nixon Finances**—Nixon had only paid $800 a year in taxes on an annual salary of more than $200,000 a year and had paid no state income taxes in California, his legal residence. Other financial scandals also weakened him.

14. *United States v. Nixon*—The Supreme Court unanimously ruled that Nixon had to release the tapes.

15. **"Smoking Gun"**—Despite the fact that 18 minutes had been erased from one of the tapes, there was convincing evidence that Nixon had ordered the CIA to halt the investigation of the case just days after the break-in. One tape clearly demonstrated that Nixon directed the cover-up.

16. **House Judiciary Committee**—Voted overwhelmingly (28-10, 27-11, 21-17 on the three counts) to impeach Nixon for obstruction of justice in covering up Watergate; violating the rights of U.S. citizens by using the FBI, CIA, and IRS to harass them if they were considered his enemy; and refusing to turn over the tapes.

17. **Nixon Resigns**—When his close supporters in Congress told him that he was going to be impeached by the full House and removed from office by the Senate he resigned on August 8, 1974.

18. **Ford's Pardon**—A month after taking office Gerald Ford, the only unelected President, pardoned Nixon for all crimes he had committed or might have committed in the White House. Many felt Nixon had escaped justice while others felt as Ford did that, "Our long national nightmare is over."

19. **Convictions**—Four Cabinet members, advisors Haldeman and Ehrlichman, along with 19 other men served prison terms ranging from 25 days to 52 months for their involvement in the illegal activities known as "Watergate."

Gerald Ford

Domestic Issues

· Rockefeller as VP

In accordance with the 25th Amendment, Ford nominated Nelson Rockefeller for Vice President who was confirmed by Congress.

· Stagflation

A new economic phenomena emerged that was not supposed to happen according to classical economic theory. An increase in unemployment, negative growth rates, and rising prices created "Stagflation," an economic condition that plagued both the Ford and James Carter presidencies. In 1974 and 1975 the recession became the worst since the Great Depression.

· WIN

Ford's approach to the economy was a program he called Whip Inflation Now (WIN) that consisted of tight monetary policy, reduced federal spending, a 5% tax surcharge, and tax and spending assistance to some industries. He vetoed a number of bills passed by Congress dealing with health, housing, and education.

· Auto Industry

After the oil embargo of 1973 most Americans did not want the "gas guzzling" cars the U.S. auto industry produced. Instead they turned to imports, primarily Japanese which went from 17% of the U.S. market to 37% from 1970 to 1980.

· Steel Industry

Unable to compete with foreign steel, the steel industries market share fell to 14% in 1980 from what had been 60% in 1946. Congress refused to go along with quotas, tariffs, and other limits on imports that the industry requested.

· Assassination Attempts

In two separate incidents in California in September of 1975 two different women failed in their attempts to assassinate Ford with handguns.

Foreign Policy

· Vietnam

In 1975, the North Vietnamese with their Viet Cong allies overran Saigon and reunited the country under communist control. Americans witnessed the end of a thirty year war as they watched U.S. helicopters evacuating Vietnamese who had supported the U.S. from the American Embassy.

· Mayaguez

The new communist government of Cambodia in 1975 seized a U.S. merchant ship with a crew of 39 aboard. They were freed as a result of military action but at the cost of 41 American soldiers.

Jimmy Carter

· Election of 1976—

1. Former Governor of Georgia Jimmy Carter won a number of early caucuses and primaries to gather enough delegates to defeat better known candidates for the Democratic nomination. He chose Senator Walter Mondale of Minnesota as his running mate.
2. Gerry Ford won the early primaries for the Republican nomination but had to withstand a challenge from Ronald Reagan, who won primaries in the South and Southwest, and barely defeated Reagan at the convention 1187 to 1070 delegates.
3. In the first campaign paid by public funds each candidate spent $21.8 million with Carter winning a close election 297-240 in the Electoral College and 50.1% to 48% in the popular vote. The Democrats kept control of Congress with a 62-38 margin in the Senate and 292-143 in the House.

Domestic Policy

· Inauguration

In order to show an abandonment of the Imperial Presidency of Johnson and Nixon, Carter's inauguration was informal and he and his wife walked down Pennsylvania Avenue to the White House after being sworn in.

· Energy Program

Carter's attempt to bring about energy conservation failed when Americans would not give up their "gas guzzling" automobiles. He tried to cut consumption by taxing it. He did succeed in getting a new cabinet department on energy.

· More Stagflation

Economic woes continued under Carter with inflation running at more than 10% and a lack of growth in the economy. He tried to curtail these problems by tax cuts and a public works program. Calling the tax system a disgrace his call for reform was ignored by the overwhelmingly Democratic Congress. Bank interest rates on borrowing reached 20% in 1980, which brought a halt to the building industry.

· Oil Crisis

As a result of the Iranian Revolution, OPEC (Organization for Petroleum Exporting Countries) pushed oil prices to more than $30 a barrel as gasoline prices tripled in the U.S. This fueled inflation and indicated the end of the era of "cheap oil."

· Three Mile Island

A breakdown in the cooling system of a nuclear power plant in 1979 resulted in fears it could overheat and release radioactivity outside the system. Changes in the law placed a moratorium on new construction or operating licenses for plants effectively ending the building of nuclear energy power plants.

Foreign Policy

· Vietnam Draft Evaders

They were granted full pardons if they had not been involved in violent acts. Deserters were not covered under the plan and it is estimated that only 15% of the draft evaders ever took advantage it.

· Human Rights

This issue became the cornerstone of Carter's foreign policy. A deeply religious Christian he applied the moral principles of his private life to his political policy. He strongly criticized governments that violated the basic rights of its citizens and his support of dissidents in the USSR led Soviet leaders to accuse him of meddling in their internal affairs.

· Panama Canal

Carter negotiated an agreement to restore the sovereignty of the Panama Canal Zone and the Canal to Panama in the year 2000. The U.S. would maintain the right to defend the neutrality of the Canal.

· Camp David Accords

In 1978, after two weeks at the Presidential retreat in Camp David, Maryland, Carter got Israeli Prime Minister Menachem Begin and Egyptian President Anwar Sadat to agree to a peace treaty between the two countries. Israel traded land for peace by giving the Sinai Peninsula (captured in the 6-Day War) back to Egypt. For their efforts both Sadat and Begin would share the Nobel Peace Price in 1978 and later Sadat would be assassinated by nationals of his own country opposed to the peace treaty. Despite this diplomatic success Carter would be overwhelmingly defeated by Ronald Reagan when he ran for reelection.

· Iran Hostage Crisis

In response to the exiled Shah of Iran's admission (1979) to the United States for medical treatment, the American embassy in Teheran, with 90 people inside, was seized by Muslim militants. Fifty two remained in captivity until the end of the crisis 444 days later. Carter applied economic pressure by halting oil imports from Iran and freezing Iranian assets in the United States. He did not blockade Iran to try to force them to give up the hostages. In April of 1980, the United States failed in an attempted rescue mission that resulted in three of eight helicopters being damaged in a sandstorm and eight Special Forces commandos being killed in the desert. With the death of the Shah in Egypt in 1980 and the invasion of Iran by Iraq, the Iranians were willing to resolve the crisis. On the day of Reagan's inauguration the hostages were freed and the U.S. released $8 billion in Iranian assets and gave Iran immunity from lawsuits arising from the incident.

· Response to USSR Invasion of Afghanistan

With the Soviet invasion of Afghanistan in 1979, Carter placed a boycott on selling grain and high tech machinery to the USSR and ordered the U.S. Olympic team not to participate in the 1980 Olympics to be held in Moscow. The SALT II Treaty, which had been carefully negotiated by Carter, would never be ratified by the Senate because of the Soviet Union's invasion of Afghanistan. The invasion would become the USSR's Vietnam. The Soviets failed attempt to impose a communist government on Afghanistan would eventually lead to the dismemberment of the USSR.

· Failure of Leadership

A naval engineer and technocrat by nature Carter failed to lead Congress or the American people. As a political outsider surrounded by fellow Georgians he never gained the respect of Congress nor did they fear him. His skills of analysis of a problem did not transfer to leadership abilities. Along with bothJohn Adams, John Quincy Adams, Martin Van Buren, Benjamin Harrison, Herbert Hoover and George Bush, he failed to win reelection.

UNIT XXXII
MULTIPLE-CHOICE QUESTIONS

Questions 1-3 refer to the following:

"... in the field of foreign policy Nixon met the test of his encounter with destiny. He understood what was at stake in the world. In the midst of unbridled emotions, he held fast to the truth that America's credibility must not be squandered, especially by its leaders. He fought for America's honor in distant jungles into which his predecessors had committed our troops, convinced that we had no right to abandon those who had depended of us and that tens of millions would curse the abdication his critics wished to impose on us. Against the rhetoric of a lifetime, he bravely affirmed the impossibility of an international order that excluded China, a quarter of the human race... he perceived that resistance to Communist aggression requires a psychological foundation that positions America as the defender of a structure of peace..."

Henry Kissinger, *Years of Upheaval*, 1982

1. Kissinger's comment "honor in distant jungles" was a reference to

   (A) Korean War
   (B) battles in the South Pacific
   (C) Vietnam War
   (D) Malay Peninsula

2. The statement "against the rhetoric of a lifetime" was a reference to Nixon

   (A) defending his family and expenditure of money in the "Checkers speech"
   (B) going to China despite a lifetime of speaking out against the Chinese communist regime
   (C) attempting to bring the Soviet Union and China together to end the cold war between Moscow and Beijing
   (D) willingness to set aside the crucial question obstructing the normalization of relations concerning the political status of Taiwan

3. The event preceding Nixon going to China that paved the way was

   (A) the exchange of table tennis (ping-pong) players between the United States and People's Republic of China (PRC) in the early 1970s
   (B) China's attendance at the peaceful 1972 Olympics in Munich, Germany
   (C) Participation by both countries in the manning of the space station
   (D) Soldiers from both countries joining a United Nations peace-keeping force in southern Sudan

Question 4-6 refer to the following:

"First, the United States will keep all of its treaty commitments.

Second, we shall provide a shield if a nuclear power threatens the freedom of a nation allied with us or of a nation whose survival we consider vital to our security. Third, in cases involving other types of aggression, we shall furnish military and economic assistance when requested in accordance with our treaty commitments. But we shall look to the nation directly threatened to assume the primary responsibility of providing the manpower for its defense."

Richard Nixon, "Nixon Doctrine," or "Guam Doctrine," 1969

4. The Nixon Doctrine was issued primarily to

(A) stop the Soviet Union from advancing into Afghanistan
(B) get the U.S. prepared from the invasion of Kuwait and Iraq
(C) appease the anti-war movement in the U.S.
(D) prepare for an exit strategy of what he called "peace with honor" in Vietnam

5. As a result of the Nixon Doctrine and the implementation of this policy in Southeast Asia

(A) there was an increase in the training of South Vietnamese troops and strong motivation to bring the American soldiers home
(B) counter-insurgency forces would be relocated to the Middle East
(C) the U.S. would increase the production of nuclear weapons
(D) a Soviet Union and U.S. partnership would be formed against the Chinese communists

6. The Nixon Doctrine resulted in turning the ground fighting over to the Vietnamese as the U.S. only involved itself in military training, providing weapons, and economic assistance in a policy and program called

(A) Nixonianism
(B) Vietnamization
(C) Counter Insurgency
(D) Americanization

Questions 7-10 refer to the following:

"One of the most surprising acts of Nixon...concerned racial discrimination in employment... the so-called Philadelphia Plan... required construction unions in Philadelphia employed on government contracts to set up "goals and timetables" for the hiring of black apprentices. In 1970, this mechanism was incorporated in government regulations governing all federal hiring and contracting,... one third of the national labor force,... the Nixon administration transformed the meaning of "affirmative action." When Congress approved Title VII...to ban job discrimination, it had affirmed a meritocratic and color-blind principle: hiring was to be done without regard to race, religion, sex, or national origin.... After 1970, however, many American institutions...were required to set aside what in effect were quotas.... This dramatic and rapid transformation... took place as a result of [Nixon's] executive decision... and court interpretations. Affirmative action of this sort never had the support of democratically elected representatives."

James T. Patterson, Grand Expectations: *The United States, 1945-1974*, 1996

7. Along with the executive branch of the government, the institution that supported the change in interpretation of affirmative action is the

(A) state governments
(B) Congress
(C) Supreme Court
(D) Republican Party

8. According to the interpretation in the passage above "affirmative action"

(A) was changed from a system based on individual ability to one based on race
(B) was transformed into a system that followed the color–blind principle
(C) would treat all apprentices the same in terms of hiring practices
(D) construction unions in Philadelphia were banned from discriminating in their hiring of workers

9. Critics of the Philadelphia Plan called it a system of

(A) set asides
(B) reverse discrimination
(C) goals and timetables
(D) meritocracy

10. In the Supreme Court decision of *Regents of the University of California v. Bakke the Supreme Court* narrowly upheld "affirmative action" created by the Philadelphia Plan by a 5-4 vote on the basis that

(A) the use of quotas was permissible as long as they did not exceed 15%
(B) the term set asides was legal but quotas were not
(C) race could be one of the factors considered in choosing a diverse student body
(D) Bakke had been discriminated against but the court did not have the authority to right the wrong

Questions 11-13 refer to the following:

"The financing of public schools is a national disgrace: First states are carved into local school districts, some of which are wealthy and some poor. Second, the major share of school financing is tied to local taxes, usually on real property, raised within each district for the support of the district's schools. It follows, as it must, that rich districts can raise large revenues by levying taxes at low rates, while poor districts must levy taxes at high rates to produce even minimal revenues. Last year, in *Serrano v. Priest*, the supreme court of California held California's version of grotesque school finance system unconstitutional, upholding a complaint of school children and taxpayer-parents that the California scheme violates both the equal protection clause of the fourteenth amendment and the analogous provisions of the California Constitution."

Kenneth L. Karst, "Responsibilities and Opportunities in the Development of Federal Constitutional Law," 1972

11. According to the above passage the reason why the financing of public schools is a national disgrace is because

(A) not enough total revenue is spent on the funding of schools
(B) rich districts can generate more money from property taxes than poor districts that have higher tax rates, which means children of the poor have less educational opportunities
(C) the right to an education is a natural right that is being denied by the way that school districts raise money for the education of school children
(D) it has failed to convene a process to build consensus on what elements constitute an adequate education environment in California

12. The Supreme Court of California used the same rationale to declare the school finance system unconstitutional as U.S. Supreme Court had used to declare segregation illegal in which decision?

(A) *Muller v. Oregon*
(B) *Plessy v. Ferguson*
(C) *Brown v. Board of Education of Topeka, Kansas*
(D) *Serrano v. Priest*

13. Along with some provisions of the California Constitution the court ruled the California system of providing school funding also violated which part of the U. S. Constitution?

(A) Right of privacy clause in the 1st Amendment
(B) Privileges and immunities clause of the 14th Amendment
(C) Supremacy clause of Article IV, Section 2
(D) Equal protection clause of the 14th Amendment

Questions 14-15 refer to the following:

".... Title IX of the Education Amendments of 1972 prohibits discrimination on the basis of sex in federally funded education programs or activities... the statute is perhaps best known for prohibiting sex discrimination in intercollegiate athletics. Indeed, the provisions regarding athletics have proved to be one of the more controversial aspects of Title IX.... Proponents of the existing regulations point to the dramatic increases in the number of female athletes in elementary and secondary school, college, and beyond as the ultimate indicator of the statute's success in breaking down barriers against women in sports. In contrast, opponents contend that the Title IX regulations unfairly impose quotas on collegiate sports and force universities to cut men's teams in order to remain in compliance. Critics further argue that the decline in certain men's sports, such as wrestling, is a direct result of Title IX's emphasis on proportionality in men's and women's college sports."

Jody Feder, Legislative Attorney, "Title IX, Sex Discrimination, and
Intercollegiate Athletics: A Legal Overview," December 2, 2008

14. Title IX was inspired by which earlier federal law that barred discrimination on the basis of race?

(A) Civil Rights Act of 1964
(B) Voting Rights Act of 1965
(C) Equal Pay Act of 1963
(D) Executive Order 11246 of 1965

15. Title IX is characterized by which of the following achievements?

(A) Absolute parity between men's and women's collegiate athletic teams
(B) The same amount of money spent on men's and women's sports
(C) An increase in participation by both men's and women's athletic teams
(D) A decrease in the amount of money spent on the revenue sports of football and basketball

UNIT XXXIII
REAGAN 80S & CLINTON 90s

Recent United States history from Ronald Reagan's election in 1980 to George W. Bush re-election in 2004 brought about a conservative political resurgence in the United States. Not since the 1920s had the political climate been as conservative. Beginning in what had been the failed Goldwater revolution of 1964, this revolution extended into the Clinton years and beyond and may still be the dominant political ideology in the U.S. Even the one Democrat elected in those 28 years from 1980 until 2008, Bill Clinton, was a political moderate and Democratic centrist in the tradition of Eisenhower's middle of the road policies. Not only did the country swing right politically, but socio-economically and culturally as well, with an increased emphasis on job, career, family, and home. Technology would transform America during the latter years of this time period, and the end of the Cold War would bring about new political threats.

Reagan's Domestic Policy

·Election of 1980

After almost capturing the Republican nomination from Gerald Ford in 1976, former actor and California governor Ronald Reagan easily won the nomination over George Bush, who became his Vice-presidential running mate. Jimmy Carter was re-nominated by the Democrats despite a fierce challenge from Senator Ted Kennedy. In what was thought to be a close election ended up a Reagan Electoral College landslide 489-49 with Carter carrying only 6 states and the District of Columbia. Republicans easily captured control of the Senate by gaining 12 seats and their 33- seat gain in the House created a more conservative body in spite of its nominal Democratic majority.

·Boll Weevils, Gypsy Moths, Blue Dogs

During the administration of Ronald Reagan, the term "boll weevils" was applied to a bloc of conservative Democrats, who consistently voted for tax cuts, increases in military spending, and deregulation favored by the Reagan administration. "Boll weevils" was sometimes used as a political epithet by the Democratic Party leaders. Most of the boll weevils either retired from politics, or like Senators Phil Gramm, Richard Shelby, and Ben Nighthorse Campbell switched parties and joined the Republicans. The term "boll weevil" is not used today and has been replaced by the term "blue dog" Democrat. A much smaller group of northeastern Republicans would vote with the Democrats on social issues and were called the "gypsy moths." With the domination of conservatives in the Republican Party political moderates like the "gypsy moths" have disappeared.

·Assassination Attempt

Shortly after taking office, Reagan was shot by John Hinkley (found not guilty by reason of insanity at his trial but he remains in prison today) but quickly recovered and his ebullient spirit during this ordeal endured him to most Americans.

·Reaganomics

Following the ideas of supply-side economist Arthur Laffer and others, Reagan believed that a cut in the marginal (highest) tax rates would bring about more tax revenue in the long run as businesses and individuals would take this additional income to invest, which would create more jobs. It would bring in more aggregate tax revenue. Another part of this supply side theory that Reagan implemented as President was the easing of government regulatory rules on business and corporations.

·Economic Recovery Act

This law provided budget and tax cuts that structurally changed government policy. Personal income taxes were cut 25% and the top marginal rate was lowered from 75% to 50%. The maximum tax on long-term capital gains (money made from investments like stocks and real estate) went from 28% to 20% (later it would be lowered to 15%) and the amount of estate and gift tax exempt from taxes was raised from $175,000 to $600,000. Along with tax cuts, budget cuts were enacted on educational, social and cultural programs that amounted to $32.5 billion. With the tax cuts, budget deficits were projected to be $100 billion a year for three years. Reagan abandoned the long sought after Republican goal of a balanced budget and the national debt soared during his Presidency—the largest percentage increase in the history of the country.

·Firing Air Traffic Controllers

Reagan fired more than 11,000 air-traffic controllers in 1981 for staging what he called an illegal strike for higher wages and fewer hours on a stress-filled job. The move was a major blow to the power of labor unions and President Clinton would rescind their lifetime ban in 1993.

·Military Build-up

In order to build-up the navy to a 600 ship level, modernize the nuclear air force by purchasing 100 B-1 bombers, and implement the Strategic Defense Initiative (called Star Wars after the popular film), the Defense budget increased from $197 billion to $279 billion in fiscal 1985 although it remained a smaller share of GDP than it had been during the Vietnam War.

·Social Security

Payroll tax increases, reduction in the growth rate of benefits (COLA), and the eventual raising of the retirement age for full benefits were enacted. For the most part Social Security was running a surplus and that surplus was used to pay for other government services to keep the debt from soaring out of control.

·"Choice" and "Right to Life"

The fallout from the Supreme Court's 1973 decision in *Roe v. Wade* that legalized abortions in the first trimester continued. The country became divided between pro-choice (women's right to an abortion) and pro-life (restrictions or prohibitions on abortion). A number of Supreme Court cases narrowed the scope of abortion rights but did not reverse the Row decision.

· Election of 1984

Reagan and Bush were re-nominated and the Republican platform opposed tax increases, the Woman's Equal Rights Amendment (it failed as only 35 of 38 states ratified it in the time allowed), and declared that prospective federal judges should be nominated only if they were opposed to abortion. Former Vice-President Walter Mondale won the Democratic nomination after a bruising battle with Senator Gary Hart and Jesse Jackson, a black civil rights activist. He nominated a woman, Representative Geraldine Ferraro of New York, as his running mate. Reagan won the greatest electoral victory since FDR's in a 515-13 landslide with Mondale only carrying his home state of Minnesota and the District of Columbia.

· Affirmative Action

In a series of cases, this controversial government program started by Johnson and Nixon was generally upheld by the courts.. These "set asides or preferences"—opponents called them quotas or reverse discrimination—for designated minorities (this could include African Americans, women, Hispanics, Native Americans, Inuits in Alaska, native Hawaiians in Hawaii, and Portuguese in Rhode Island) were held to be constitutional by a sharply divided Supreme Court. Some believe that this issue more than any other moved many former New Deal Democrats to become Reagan Democrats who often supported Republicans.

· Supreme Court

In 1981, President Reagan, who had pledged during the 1980 presidential campaign to appoint the first woman to the Supreme Court, appointed Sandra Day O'Connor as an Associate Justice of the Supreme Court, replacing the retiring Potter Stewart. She would become one of the two swing votes that would dominate the court for the next 20 years. With the retirement of Warren Burger, conservative Associate Justice William Rehnquist was appointed Chief Justice and another conservative Antonin Scalia was appointed to Rehnquist's seat. Robert Bork, another conservative was nominated by Reagan to succeed retiring Justice Lewis Powell but after being extensively questioned by the Senate he was rejected 58-42. Reagan's next nominee Douglas Ginsberg was forced to withdraw his name after allegations of drug use while a Harvard Law School professor became public. Finally, a moderate conservative Anthony Kennedy would be unanimously confirmed, and would become one of the two swing votes along with O'Connor to decide issues on the court.

· Income Tax Reform

The concept of the Progressive income tax was abandoned as 14 tax brackets were compressed into two—15% and 28%. A number of low- income wage earners were removed from the tax roles and many tax deductions and shelters that had been used by the middle class were eliminated. The corporate tax rate was cut from 46% to 34%, but corporations and some individuals were made subject to an alternative minimum tax.

· Welfare Reform

At a cost of 3.3 billion over 5 years, changes were made in the AFDC (Aid to Families with Dependent children) to force one person in a two-parent family to participate in a job search, and if the search failed to find a job, they would have to take a job in a public works program if one could be found. A number of other bureaucratic changes were also made in the system.

· Rise of the Religious Right

Conservative evangelical Christians formed a powerful group sometimes called "movement or social conservatives" who were united around the issues of overturning *Roe v. Wade*, returning mandatory prayer and bible reading to the schools, censorship of anti-family media, antifeminism, teaching creationism (now renamed intelligent design) in schools as an antidote to Darwinian science, opposition to sex education in the schools and opposition to laws for "gay" rights. A political organization, the Moral Majority was founded by the Reverend Jerry Falwell to carry out the agenda of the Christian Conservatives.

·Reagan Scandals

Attorney General Ed Meese resigned after an independent counsel rendered a critical report. Two Reagan aides, Lyn Nofziger and Michael Deaver were convicted of violating federal ethics laws for activities after they left office.

·Simpson-Mazzoli Act of 1986

Officially the Immigration Reform and Control Act (IRCA), the Simpson-Mazzoli Act imposed sanctions on employers who knowingly hired illegal aliens (this part was never enforced). It also offered legal amnesty to immigrants who could prove that they had been living continuously in the U.S. since 1982, which led to 3 million illegals or undocumented immigrants becoming citizens. The law was supposed to solve the problem of illegal immigration, but twenty years later the number of illegal aliens or undocumented immigrants as their supporters called them had soared to an estimated 12 million or more. By 2014, the issue was once again before Congress, which remained deadlocked over a solution.

·Savings and Loan Scandal

Reagan's program of deregulation for the so-called "Thrifts" or Savings and Loans resulted in a massive failure of lending institutions that would ultimately bring about a $1 trillion bail-out of these institutions by the American taxpayer. The Garn–St. Germain Depository Institutions Act of 1982 put S & L's on an equal footing with commercial banks as they could now pay higher interest rates for deposits, borrow money from the Federal Reserve, make commercial loans, and issue credit cards. Deregulation of S & L's gave them the capabilities of banks but they did not have the same regulations as banks. They now had the rights but not the responsibilities. With their new found freedom these "Thrifts" made shaky commercial real estate loans and they were usually overmatched as they tried to compete with banks. A large number of S & L defaults and bankruptcies ensued, and the S & L's that had overextended themselves were forced into insolvency proceedings themselves. The government agency FSLC that insured the S & L's went bankrupt as well. Most of the S & L's were absorbed into existing banks thus ending the S & L system.

·National Debt

The national debt hit a 47-year low just as Reagan was taking office. It climbed steadily under Reagan and George H. Bush, declined under Clinton and made a quick turn upward under George W. Bush and his successor Democrat Barack Obama. The traditional pattern of running large deficits only in times of war or economic downturns was broken during much of the 1980s. In 1982, [Reagan's 1st budget year] partly in response to a recession, large tax cuts were enacted. However, these were accompanied by substantial increases in defense spending. Although reductions were made to non-defense spending, they were not sufficient to offset the impact on the deficit. As a result, deficits averaging $206 billion were incurred between 1983 and 1992. These unprecedented peacetime deficits increased the debt held by the public from $789 billion in 1981 to $3.0 trillion in 1992. Republicans and conservative Democrats who supported a large debt argued that it was a smaller % of the GDP than it had been in earlier years so it was not a problem. In the 21st century the debt would soar beyond all recognition to $17 trillion. It started with Reagan who nearly tripled the debt.

Reagan's Foreign Policy

·Central America

Carter had ignored the left wing take over of Nicaragua by the Sandinistas but Reagan accused them of being a forward base for Cuba and the Soviet Union take over of Central America. Reagan provided military advisors and covert aid from the CIA to prop up the pro-American government of Guatemala. He also claimed that the Sandinistas were shipping weapons to revolutionary forces in El Salvador.

·Lebanon

In 1982, as part of a multinational peacekeeping force, Reagan sent 800 U.S. Marines to Lebanon to maintain a cease fire which allowed PLO fighters passage to neighboring Syria by Israel, which was then occupying southern Lebanon. Once the PLO left, Israel would withdraw from Lebanon. After the PLO left the international force including U.S. troops was withdrawn. However, after 700 refugees were massacred Reagan ordered the U.S. forces back. As Israel withdrew, the U.S. found itself in the middle of a civil war. In April 1983, Hezbollah terrorists—which received financial and logistical support from Iran and Syria—detonated a truck bomb in front of the American Embassy in Beirut killing 17 Americans including 8 CIA agents. In response to these attacks on the U.S., Reagan ordered warships to shell the camps of anti-American militias. The terrorists retaliated in 1983 and blew up the Marines' barracks at the Beirut airport killing 241 U.S. servicemen. Reagan ordered air strikes against Hezbollah's leadership. The small remaining U.S. force had little hope of influencing events in Lebanon. Against the opposition of the diplomats, the surviving Marines were withdrawn to U.S. vessels. Reagan described the withdrawal as "redeployment," but he would never again send ground troops into Lebanon or any other place in the Middle East. Two days after the withdrawal he turned to an invasion of Grenada in the Caribbean to restore U.S. prestige.

·Grenada

For years the CIA had engaged in efforts to destabilize the Caribbean island of Grenada, which had adopted a movement of social reform under leftist leaders. The major justification for the U.S. invasion was the protection of the lives of the 800 American students at the U.S.-run St. George's University School of Medicine. Another reason for the invasion was the reported Cuban military buildup on the island. Actually less than 100 of the 750 Cubans on the island were military. The Reagan administration was also concerned about an airport under construction on the southern tip of the island, near the capital of St. George's. Reagan repeatedly charged that it was to be a Soviet/Cuban air base but in fact it was to be a larger civilian airport for the tourist trade. The spark that set off the U.S. invasion was the assassination of Maurice Bishop, the Premier who had been head of the leftist reform movement, by a pro-Cuban Marxist group. After a U.S. invasion, fighting continued for several days and the total number of American troops reached some 7,000 along with 300 troops from various neighboring Caribbean islands. The invasion was the first major operation conducted by the U.S. military since the Vietnam War and 19 U.S. soldiers were killed, some by "friendly fire," and 106 were injured. Cuban and Grenadian losses were 100 dead and 350 wounded. On a per capita basis the new government of Grenada would receive more U.S. foreign aid than any other country.

·Reagan-Gorbachev Summits

Reagan met with Mikhail Gorbachev, a personable and energetic new leader of the USSR, who initiated the radical policies of *Glasnost* (openness) and *Perestroika* (restructuring), in four summits at Geneva, Reykjavik, Washington D. C., and Moscow. The two leaders signed the INF (intermediate range nuclear forces), banning all intermediate range nuclear missiles from Europe. Reagan who had entered office calling the Soviet Union an "evil empire" showed his realism in working with Gorbachev to start the end of the Cold War.

·Bombing Libya

Following a terrorist bombing at a *discotheque* in West Berlin frequented by American military personnel, in which Libya was implicated, the U.S. retaliated militarily against targets in Libya, and imposed broad unilateral economic sanctions. The attack lasted about ten minutes with 45 total U.S. aircraft involved. Several targets were hit, Qadaffi, the main target escaped, but some of his family were injured and killed. Civilian and diplomatic sites in Tripoli were struck as well, notably the French embassy, when a number of bombs missed their intended targets.

·Iran-Contra

The Iran-Contra affair was a Byzantine network of deals involving arms sales to Iran, designed to win the release of U.S. hostages being held in Lebanon, and to raise money to fund the Nicaraguan Contras trying to overthrow the Marxist government. This botched enterprise took years to unravel, and Congress televised hearings into the matter that made household names of bureaucrats Oliver North, Richard Secord, John Poindexter, Robert McFarlane, and Elliott Abrams. Much of the truth about the incident had been in documents shredded by North and his staff but the scandal exposed the U.S. government as weak and unprincipled, contributing to a growing distrust in the political process by the early 1990s. Convictions were rare in the Iran-Contra affair (North's and Poindexter's were overturned on appeal), and the few verdicts that were handed down in court amounted to little more than slaps on the wrist. On December 24, 1992, outgoing president George H. Bush pardoned former secretary of defense Caspar Weinberger and five other defendants, asserting that it was "time for the country to move on." But independent counsel Lawrence Walsh, who spent more than seven years and $40 million unraveling the scandal issued his own report and saw it differently. The Iran-Contra affair was the direct result of two major dilemmas facing the Reagan administration in the early 1980s: (1) how to fund, train, and arm an army of Nicaraguan exiles (known as Contras) to overthrow the socialist Sandinista government, especially after the U.S. Congress passed the Boland Amendment that made it illegal to do so in 1982; and, (2) how to win release of American hostages being held by Islamic radicals in Beirut. Money from the sale of arms to the Iranians was diverted to the Contras, violating the Boland Amendment and its ban on military aid to the Nicaraguan rebels. What was more surprising was that Reagan had vowed never to negotiate with terrorists, which was exactly was what he was doing with the Iranians. Much to the chagrin of the Democrats, none of this had any lasting impact on Reagan's popularity, as he continued to be the "Teflon" President—nothing stuck, no matter how sordid it was.

George Herbert Bush's Domestic Policy

·Election of 1988

The leading Democratic candidate Gary Hart self-destructed in a sex-scandal when a photograph of him with his mistress on the boat "Risky Business" was made public. Governor Michael Dukakis of Massachusetts was nominated over Senator Al Gore and Reverend Jesse Jackson. Vice-President Bush won the Republican nomination after a spirited battle with Senate Majority Leader Bob Dole. Bush overwhelmed Dukakis 426-111 in the Electoral College and 402 out of 408 House incumbents won re-election showing the power of incumbency and gerrymandering to create safe districts.

·Inaugural Address

Bush advocated a kinder, gentler nation in his inaugural when he stated that America's purpose was "to make kinder the face of the nation and gentler the face of the world."

·ADA

The Americans with Disabilities Act gave protection in employment and public accommodations to those with disabilities that were similar to the protections for women, racial, and ethnic groups in the Civil Rights Act of 1964. The law caused havoc with many small businesses as they tried to comply.

·Thomas Nominated (1991)

A firestorm erupted when Bush nominated Clarence Thomas to replace the retiring justice Thurgood Marshall on the Supreme Court. Senate hearings centered on his competence, his conservatism, and especially on sexual harassment charges leveled at him by an African American college professor, Anita Hill. He was confirmed by a close vote of 52-48 and has voted with Anthony Scalia in almost all the Supreme Court cases and has only spoken twice in oral arguments. Earlier David Souter was confirmed as a nominee to replace William Brennan, and this Republican's voting record sided with the liberals on many controversial decisions.

·Keating Scandal

Of all the S & L scandals the most notorious one involved Charles Keating because it had an impact on five U.S. Senators. Keating, head of Lincoln Savings in Irvine, California, was convicted of fraud, racketeering, and conspiracy in 1993, and spent time in prison before his convictions were overturned. Five U.S. senators were implicated in an influence-peddling scheme to assist Keating and three of them—Alan Cranston, Don Riegle, and Dennis DeConcini—had their political careers ended while two others—John Glenn and John McCain—escaped relatively unscathed.

·Watts Riots II

In 1992, riots took place in the South-Central part of Los Angeles causing $1 billion in damage and 50 deaths. African Americans were outraged when four white policemen were acquitted for the savage beating of Rodney King, a black man whose experience had been captured on videotape.

·27th Amendment

It forbid Congress from accepting mid-term pay increases.

·The Economy

Bush was plagued by a bad economy right from the start and unlike the teflon Reagan, everything stuck to Bush. Partly as a result of Reagan's economic policies the budget deficit increased the national debt by more than a trillion dollars during Bush's one term as President. Unemployment exceeded 7% officially and was much higher than that in certain regions of the country like California where it was more than 10%.

·"No New Taxes"

Contrary to the pledge he had made in the campaign of "read my lips, no new taxes," Bush agreed to $133 billion in new taxes passed by Congress to attempt to stem the tide of large budget deficits. Going back on his 1988 campaign pledge probably did more than anything to deny him reelection in 1992.

George Herbert Walker Bush's Foreign Policy

·Tiananmen Square

Beijing China was the site of a pro-democracy student demonstration in the spring of 1989, a demonstration violently crushed by the Chinese military. Scenes of the brutal crackdown were broadcast throughout the world. Students had assembled and camped in the square for two weeks and made demands for free speech and a free press as they erected a symbolic Statue of Liberty named the "Goddess of Democracy." The government responded when the army launched an assault on the unarmed civilians in the square. They stormed the area with tanks and machine guns, firing into the crowd at random. Hundreds of young students were killed and thousands wounded in the attack. Afterward all dissent was shut down in China. China experienced nearly three years of economic sanctions and scorn from the international community after the massacre, yet the Chinese government continued its hardline policies toward all civilian dissent.

·End of the Cold War

Starting in Poland with the Solidarity labor movement toppling the communist government, communism fell in Hungary, Czechoslovakia, East Germany, Romania, and Bulgaria in rapid succession in 1989.

·Berlin Wall Falls

The Wall fell as the combined result of both internal and external pressures. The evolution of the USSR played a crucial role in this process. On his first official visit to West Germany in May 1989, Mikhaïl Gorbachev, whose ambition was to save his country from decline and ruin through an innovative policy based on restructuring (*perestroïka*) and openness (*glasnost*), informed Chancellor Kohl that the Brezhnev doctrine had been abandoned—Moscow was no longer willing to use force to prevent democratic transformation of its satellite states. Hungary decided to pull down the iron curtain and opened up its border with Austria. Germans poured out of East Germany and within six months, over 220,000 East Germans had passed over to the West. After the fall of Honeker and the Communist Party, the official destruction of the Wall began on June 13th, 1990 by 300 East German border guards, and was completed by 600 sappers equipped with 13 bulldozers, 55 excavators, 65 cranes and 175 lorries in November. Six segments were kept to commemorate the wall.

·Panama Invasion

The U.S. invaded Panama in 1989 and captured dictator Manuel Noriega who had been indicted in the U.S. for drug trafficking and money laundering. The invasion involved 27,684 U.S. troops and over 300 aircraft with U.S. casualties 24 dead and 324 wounded. The Organization of American States (OAS), United Nations General Assembly, and United Nations Security Council (vetoed by the U.S.) all passed resolutions condemning the invasion. The U.S. established a new government under Guillermo Endara. The U.S. military did not anticipate the widespread looting and lawlessness that followed the invasion that ruined many Panamanian businesses.

·Gulf War/Desert Storm-Build-up

Iraq invaded Kuwait in 1990 on the pretense that Kuwait was illegally "slant-drilling" for oil across Iraq's border. Iraq also claimed that historically Kuwait was a part of Iraq. The UN immediately imposed economic sanctions on Iraq and the U.S., under UN auspices put together a coalition force of 660,000 where U.S. troops represented 74% of the coalition. Despite some reluctance, in the end many nations were persuaded to join the coalition by Iraq's belligerence towards other Arab states, along with offers of U.S. economic aid or debt forgiveness. The U.S. gave a number of reasons for getting involved in the crisis including its long standing friendship with Saudi Arabia: which was now threatened by Iraq; Iraq's history of human rights abuses under President Saddam Hussein; and the potential that Iraq might develop nuclear weapons or weapons of mass destruction in the future.

·Gulf War I

The coalition forces opened the war with thousands of bombing raids using sophisticated missiles and destroying Iraq's Air Force, it's command and communications facilities, most military targets, and its infrastructure. Iraq countered the coalition's bombing raids by launching missile attacks on coalition bases in Saudi Arabia and on Israel. Iraq hope to draw Israel into the war and draw other Arab states to its side. In 1991 the U.S.-led forces began Operation Desert Storm, the ground portion of the campaign would last four days and ended with Iraq exiting Kuwait, the Iraq army totally routed, and the coalition forces having few casualties. After Bush declared a cease-fire he did not allow the U.S. forces to proceed to Baghdad without UN authorization. At the urging of the U.S. there was a Shiite uprising in the south and a Kurdish uprising in the north. However, when no American support was forthcoming, Iraqi generals remained loyal and brutally crushed the Kurdish troops and Shiite insurgents. Millions of Kurds fled across the mountains to Kurdish areas of Turkey and Iran. The war cost the U.S. $71 billion, but $53 billion of this was paid for by other countries in the coalition. Germany and Japan, who were not part of the military coalition because of WWII treaties, made substantial financial contributions. George H. Bush's failure to remove Saadam Hussein was highly criticized and a later Gulf War would be fought. One negative result of the Gulf War was the sharp revival in Islamic extremism, which would replace the Soviet Union as the chief threat to the U.S. Another negative result of the Gulf War was the fact that many returning coalition soldiers reported illnesses following their participation, a phenomenon known as Gulf War Syndrome. Possible causes included exposure to radioactive materials, oil fires, and the fast series of anthrax vaccine given to soldiers (normally it is given over months).

·Final End to Cold War

The Warsaw Pact nations disbanded their military alliance in 1991 effectively ending the Cold War. They would each go different directions with many turning to Western Europe and the U.S. for economic revival and political influence.

·Yugoslavia Break-Up

Bush recognized the independence of Slovenia, Croatia, and Bosnia-Herzegovina as they broke away from Yugoslavia (Serbia). The U.S. ambassador was withdrawn from Yugoslavia in protest of the violence against Bosnia.

·Soviet Union Break-Up

Gorbachev resigned as the former USSR broke up into Russia and 14 other independent countries—Latvia, Estonia, Lithuania, Belarus, Moldova, Ukraine, Armenia, Azerbaijan, Georgia, Uzbekistan, Tajikistan, Kazakhstan, Turkmenistan, and Kyrgyzstan.

Clinton's Domestic Policy

·Election of 1992

George H. Bush and his Vice-president Dan Quayle were easily re-nominated despite a challenge from conservative journalist and television commentator Pat Buchanan. Governor Bill Clinton of Arkansas was nominated over a large field of candidates when other prominent Democrats declined to run because they thought G. H. Bush was unbeatable. Clinton, a member of the Democratic Leadership Council, a centrist group, chose fellow southerner and Vietnam War veteran Senator Al Gore as his running mate. The Clinton-Gore ticket, running on the issue of the economy ("It's the economy stupid" was the campaign strategy formulated by political advisor James Carville) surprised G. H. Bush and won the Electoral College easily 370-168. The campaign was marked by the third party candidacy of Texas billionaire businessman H. Ross Perot who actually led in the polls at one time, but after dropping out and then re-entering the campaign, he finished with 19% of the popular vote and no electoral votes.

·"Don't Ask, Don't Tell"

In trying to end the ban on gays in the military, Clinton faced fierce opposition and settled for what becomes known as the "don't ask, don't tell" policy of tacitly accepting gays in the military without asking their sexual orientation. This along with the fact that Clinton had not served in Vietnam and had protested the Vietnam War, would earn him the enmity of the military and weaken his Presidency right from the beginning.

·Health Care Reform Failure

Clinton appointed a task force headed by First Lady, Hillary Rodham Clinton, to come up with a comprehensive plan to provide universal health care for all Americans. This complex and complicated 1,000 page proposal, after first gaining acceptance from much of the health-care community, came under withering attack from conservatives, libertarians, and parts of the insurance industry, with and ad campaign that derided the proposal as "Hillarycare." It was a complex and confusing bureaucratic nightmare that was depicted as being against middle class values. Liberals who wanted a simple Canadian style single payer plan also opposed it. The Democratic controlled Congress began to offer different plans, which further weakened the administration's HMO based plan, and after a year of debate the plan was dead. This political defeat would contribute greatly to the Republican success in the elections of 1994, when they captured control of the House of Representatives for the first time in 40 years.

·Terrorist Attacks

A radical Muslim group bombed the World Trade Center in New York in 1993 killing 6 people in the process. In 1995, a federal office building in Oklahoma City was bombed by home grown terrorist Timothy McVey killing 168 people. These attacks by both foreign and domestic terrorists should have alerted the U.S. to the dangers in the world that still existed after the fall of communism but the U.S. was slow to wake up to these threats.

·Congressional Elections of 1994

In what became known as the Republican Revolution, dissatisfaction with Clinton's early policies as well as a Republican program called the "Contract with America," led to Republicans capturing both house of Congress. As a result of a 54-seat swing in membership (34 incumbents and 20 open seats) from Democrats to Republicans, the Republican Party gained a majority of seats in the House for the first time since 1954. The creator of the contract, Newt Gingrich, became Speaker of the House of Representatives. Control of the Senate from Democrats to Republicans was changed for the first time since 1986 as the Republicans captured 8 Senate seats from the Democrats unseating two incumbents and winning six open seats. After the election, two Democrats, Richard Shelby of Alabama and Ben Nighthorse Campbell from Colorado switched allegiance to the Republican Party further strengthening its gains.

·Unfunded Mandates

An accomplishment of the new Republican Congress was passage of the Unfunded Mandates Reform Act of 1995. It was a requirement that committees of Congress, when writing a bill that would impose new duties on states, local governments or private companies, obtain an estimate of the additional costs they would entail and make those part of their report on the legislation. Under the newly approved procedure, any mandate that would cost state or local governments more than $50 million a year, or private business $100 million, legislators would have to vote specifically that the benefit was worth the cost. This legislation was bitterly opposed by the Democrats whose 40-year grip on the House of Representatives had allowed them to pass any mandates in the past without accountability. Clinton showed his centrist tendencies as a fiscal conservative by signing the measure.

·Welfare Reform

Fulfilling a campaign promise of "ending welfare as we know it," Clinton signed into law the Personal Responsibility and Work Opportunity Act of 1996. It replaced the old welfare system AFDC (Aid to Families of Dependent Children) with a plan that limited welfare to five years and distributed welfare money to the states as block grants to be doled out as the states wanted (sometimes not even used for welfare). Liberal Democrats vehemently opposed this law and Clinton's assumption that after 5 years all the recipients would find jobs was an overly optimistic assumption.

·Government Shutdown

In a showdown between Clinton and Gingrich over the budget, the government was shut down for a few days in 1995 until, in the face of public displeasure, Gingrich backed down and a budget was adopted.

·Election of 1996

Clinton and Gore were unanimously re-nominated by the Democrats and faced the last of the WWII candidates—eight who had become President (Eisenhower, Kennedy, Johnson, Nixon, Ford, Carter [at the Naval Academy], Reagan, and G. H. Bush)—Robert Dole, former Senate Majority Leader and Vice-presidential candidate with Ford in 1976. Helped by a buoyant economy and the success of his triangulation policy of appealing to moderates, Clinton won the electoral vote 379-159 although the Republicans remained in control of Congress.

· Affirmative Action

Clinton finessed this controversial issue by pledging to "mend it, not end it." California voters had passed a law forbidding the use of preferences in government hiring and higher education admissions. Other states were gearing up to follow suit. It stayed in place but was under constant attack as many who had once thought it a noble idea turned against it.

· Economic Prosperity

During his two terms there was unprecedented economic prosperity with low unemployment, a low inflation rate, high revenues that balanced the budget (with help from money from the Social Security trust fund) for the first time in three decades. High tech, media, the internet, and new service businesses fueled an economy that continued to grow throughout the decade.

· Brady Bill

One of Clinton's legislative accomplishments was passage of the Brady bill, named for Reagan's Press Secretary who had been wounded and suffered brain damage in the assassination attempt on Reagan. This law required a 5- day waiting period for a background check before a handgun could be sold. A number of loopholes (exempting gun shows from its provisions was the major one) made the law relatively ineffective, and the Supreme Court further eviscerated it by saying it violated the 10th Amendment in *Prinz v. US*.

· Family and Medical Leave Act

Under the Family and Medical Leave Act of 1993 (FMLA), most Federal employees were entitled to a total of up to 12 workweeks of unpaid leave during any 12-month period for the birth or care for a son or daughter, or care of a spouse, children, or parents. A key factor in FMLA is that an employee who takes the leave maintains their health care benefits and is allowed to return to the job that they left when the leave is over.

· Big Tobacco

Clinton helped negotiate a deal between the various state attorney generals who were suing the tobacco companies and the companies themselves. The deal would force the cigarette makers to pay $368 billion over 25 years for anti-smoking campaigns and for health costs related to tobacco smoking; allow the FDA to regulate nicotine as a drug, but not eliminate it for 12 years; restrict advertising; and force the industry to reduce youth smoking. In return, the industry would receive immunity from future class-action lawsuits and from punitive damages for past wrongdoing. The industry's legal liability would be capped at $5 billion per year. The deal was heavily criticized by public health advocates, including former Surgeon General C. Everett Koop and former federal drug administration chief David Kessler. Senator Richard Durbin quoting John Randolph of Roanoke said, "This amendment, to paraphrase an old literary quote, shines and stinks like rotten mackerel by moonlight."

· Whitewater

A failed 1970s Arkansas real estate venture by the Whitewater Development Corp. in which Governor (later President) Bill Clinton and his wife, Hillary Rodham Clinton, were partners was investigated by Special Prosecutor Kenneth Starr after Clinton's personal attorney Vincent Foster committed suicide. Accusations of impropriety against the Clintons and others centered around improper campaign contributions, political and financial favors, and tax benefits. Although nothing conclusive concerning the Clintons' involvement in the Whitewater deal was proven, in fact they lost money on the deal, an additional investigation would surface that would lead to Clinton's impeachment.

· Clinton Sex Scandals

Allegations of sexual misconduct had plagued Clinton during his political career. Paula Corbin Jones, a former Arkansas state worker claimed that Clinton had accosted her sexually in 1991, when he was governor of Arkansas. Seeking to show a pattern of behavior on Clinton's part, Jones's lawyers questioned several women believed to have had relations with him including Monica Lewinsky, who first denied having such a relationship. Clinton denied having had an affair with Lewinsky, an unpaid intern at the White House. Starr had previously received tape recordings made by Linda R. Tripp (a former coworker of Lewinskys) of telephone conversations in which Lewinsky described her involvement with the President. Asserting that there was a "pattern of deception," Starr obtained from Attorney General Janet Reno permission to investigate. Clinton publicly denied having had a relationship with Lewinsky and charges of covering it up by saying, "I did not have sex with that woman." Meanwhile lawyers for Paula Jones released papers revealing, among other things, that Clinton, in his January deposition, had admitted to a sexual relationship in the 1980s with Arkansas entertainer Gennifer Flowers, a charge he had long denied. Judge Susan Webber Wright dismissed the Jones suit saying she had been subjected to "boorish behavior" not sexual harassment. Starr granted Lewinsky immunity from perjury charges, and Clinton agreed to testify before the grand jury. Clinton then went on television to admit the affair with Lewinsky and ask for forgiveness.

·Impeachment

Starr sent a 445-page report to the House of Representatives, recommending four grounds for impeachment: perjury, obstruction of justice, witness tampering, and abuse of authority. The report described sexual acts along with misdeeds that many people thought were unnecessary and actually prurient. After reviewing the report, the House Judiciary Committee sent Clinton 81 formal inquiries and his parsing of the language with his legalistic and defensive answers did not help his cause. Rejecting a resolution of censure pushed by the Democrats, the committee and later the entire House, voting mostly on party lines (228-206), recommended two counts of impeachment. After a trial in which testimony relating to the charges was limited, the Senate rejected both counts of impeachment. The perjury charge lost, 55–45, with 10 Republicans joining all 45 Democrats in voting against it; the obstruction charge drew a 50–50 vote.

·Aftermath

During the Starr inquiry Monica Lewinsky was granted immunity from perjury charges. While his trial was going on in the Senate, Clinton settled the Paula Jones suit and was ordered by Judge Wright to pay $90,000 to Jones' lawyers. The day before he left office, Clinton admitted to giving false testimony in the Jones case and accepted a five-year suspension of his law license and a $25,000 fine in return for the independent counsel not prosecuting him. A Maryland grand jury indicted Linda Tripp for illegally tapeing phone calls but the charges were later dropped when the evidence against her was ruled inadmissible.

·Repeal of the Glass-Steagall Act

The Gramm-Leach-Bliley Act (GLBA) of 1998 was the result of an agreement between Clinton and the Republican dominated Congress that repealed part of the Glass-Steagall Act of 1933. The Glass-Steagall Act prohibited any one institution from acting as any combination of an investment bank, a commercial bank, and an insurance company. This Act made the merger that had already occurred of Citibank, Smith Barney, Primerica, and Travelers into Citigroup legal. Many see GLBA as a major contributing factor that lead to the financial meltdown in 2007.

·Clinton Pardons

Upon leaving office Clinton further tarnished his reputation by pardoning more than 100 people on his last day in office. Several of the people he pardoned were well connected and even notorious, but not deserving. Even Clinton supporters were openly critical of these actions although charges that the pardons were obtained through bribery were unfounded.

Clinton's Foreign Policy

·NAFTA Ratified

Negotiated by Bush, Clinton gave strong support for the North American Free Trade Agreement that eliminated trade barriers between Mexico, the U.S., and Canada despite fears that jobs would go south to Mexico, and that the environment would suffer.

·Czechoslovakia

In 1992 during the "Velvet Revolution," a country created from the Austro-Hungarian Empire after WWI divided into two separate countries—the Czech Republic and the Slovak Republic.

·Haiti

A UN Security Council resolution authorized member states to use all necessary means to facilitate the departure of Haiti's military leadership and to restore Haiti's constitutionally elected government to power. The United States took the lead in forming a multinational force to carry out the UN's mandate by means of a military intervention. Clinton dispatched a negotiating team led by former President Jimmy Carter to persuade the de facto authorities to step aside and allow for the return of constitutional rule. With intervening troops already airborne, General Raoul Cedras and other top leaders agreed to accept the intervention and a 21,000 member international force entered Haiti to oversee the end of military rule and the restoration of the constitutional government. The military leaders and their families departed Haiti and President Jean Bertrand Aristide and other elected officials in exile returned to power in 1994.

·Somalia

The Battle of Mogadishu was fought between U.S. Special Forces and Somali guerrilla fighters loyal to warlord Mohamed Aidid. This resulted in 18 Delta Force Rangers being killed and two Black Hawk helicopters lost in an 18-hour battle. As a result of this all action against Aidid was stopped and American politicians were reluctant to use military intervention in 3rd World or "developing" countries. This would lead to the failure to assist in halting genocide in Rwanda in 1994. The U.S. would strictly use air power, but no ground forces, when it intervened in the Balkans later in the 1990s.

·WTO

Clinton strongly supported the creation of the World Trade Organization (1995), an international economic organization that emerged out of the last round of GATT (General Agreement on Trade and Tariffs) meetings held in Punta del Este, Uruguay. It was a permanent organization designed to liberalize trade between nations and it has now grown to 153 member nations. Conferences held in Singapore and Geneva were without incident but protestors to the organization disrupted its meeting in Seattle in 1999 objecting to the human and environmental cost of globalization. Some of the violent protestors who destroyed property in their protest were anarchists who did not have had foggiest idea of what the WTO was or purported to be.

·Landmines

The Clinton administration won ratification of the Chemical Weapons Convention (signed 1993), but it refused to join in a major international treaty banning land mines, primarily because of hundreds of thousands of land mines in Korea.

·Kosovo and Yugoslavia

Failure to achieve a negotiated settlement in Kosovo resulted in a 78-day U.S.-led NATO air war that forced Yugoslavia (Serbia and Montenegro) to cede control of the province, but not before Yugoslav forces had made refugees of millions and killed several thousand.

· Oslo Accords

The Oslo I Accord was officially called the Declaration of Principles on Interim Self-Government Arrangements and was an attempt in 1993 to set up a framework that would lead to the resolution of the ongoing Israeli–Palestinian conflict. It was the first face-to-face agreement between the government of Israel and the Palestine Liberation Organization highlighted by the famous handshake between Yitzhak Rabin and Yasser Arafat at the White House. Later, Rabin was assassinated by a Israeli at a peace rally. Clinton failed to get the Israelis and the PLO to agree to a settlement at a Camp David summit at the end of his presidency.

UNIT XXXIII
MULTIPLE-CHOICE QUESTIONS

Question 1-4 refer to the following:

"Reagan left three major adverse legacies at the end of his second term. First, the privately held federal debt increased from 22.3 percent of GDP to 38.1 percent [$1 trillion to $3 trillion] and, despite the record peacetime expansion, the federal deficit in Reagan's last budget was still 2.9 percent of GDP. Second, the failure to address the savings and loan problem early led to an additional debt of about $125 billion. Third, the administration added more trade barriers than any administration since Hoover. The share of U.S. imports subject to some form of trade restraint increased from 12 percent in 1980 to 23 percent in 1988. There was more than enough blame to go around for each of these problems. Reagan resisted tax increases, and Congress resisted cuts in domestic spending. The administration was slow to acknowledge the savings and loan problem, and Congress urged forbearance on closing the failing banks."

William A. Niskanen, *Reagonomics: An Insider's Account of the Policies and the People*, 1988

1. The passage above tends to blame Reagan along with which institution for the adverse legacies at the end of his second term?

   (A) Republican Party
   (B) Government Bureaucracy
   (C) House of Representatives and Senate
   (D) Federal Trade Commission

2. Reagan's plan of tax relief for the rich was based on the premise that it would enable them to

   (A) purchase more European properties to have second and third homes
   (B) leave a greater inheritance to their children
   (C) reap the rewards of all of the hard work that they had done to amass a fortune
   (D) spend and invest by hiring workers which would bring in more tax revenue

3. The program that became known as Reaganomics had all of the following features EXCEPT

   (A) lower marginal tax rates especially on the upper income levels
   (B) increase the progressive features of the existing income tax
   (C) stop excessive government regulations
   (D) end social spending that hampered growth

4. Reagan's economic program was based on a theory called

   (A) supply side or trickle down
   (B) Keynesianism
   (C) bottom up economics
   (D) monetarism

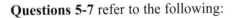

Questions 5-7 refer to the following:

"When the United States invaded Grenada and refused to allow any reporters to go along, it seemed... that the American people agreed with the government... because no one asked the American people's opinion.... When they did through polls... the public said the government should have let the press go along... just as the press had gone along and covered WWII without managing to lose the war...; the only other time in recent memory that an invading country refused to allow the world press into the country it was invading was when the Soviet Union invaded Afghanistan. The Reagan administration argued that reporters could not be trusted to be fair in their coverage. Senator Jeremiah Denton ... said, 'the... media are running the country...' If we are, we are doing a terrible job of it.... There have been many instances [where] politicians have taken power and muzzled the press. There is no instance where the press has taken power and muzzled the politicians."

Linda Ellerbee, *And So It Goes: Adventures in Television*, 1986

5. The passage is making the argument that first surfaced in colonial America in the

(A) Zenger case
(B) Albany Conference
(C) Writs of Assistance case
(D) Stamp Act Congress

6. The primary charge made against the Reagan administration was that in forbidding the press from covering the invasion

(A) they were protecting the U.S. from bad publicity
(B) the students on the Caribbean Island were given time to escape their captors
(C) they were in violation of the 1st Amendment
(D) they were carrying out the provisions of the Patriot Act

7. Which of the following comments supports the interpretation in the above passage?

(A) The public have an insatiable curiosity to know everything. Except what is worth knowing. Journalism, conscious of this, and having tradesman-like habits, supplies their demands—Oscar Wilde
(B) were it left to me to decide whether we should have a government without newspapers or newspapers without a government, I should not hesitate a moment to prefer the latter—Thomas Jefferson
(C) There are laws to protect the freedom of the press's speech, but none that are worth anything to protect the people from the press—Mark Twain
(D) One of the shrewdest ways for human predators to conquer their stronger victims is to steadily convince them with propaganda that they're still free—N.A. Scott

Questions 8-10 refer to the following:

"Although the Cold War involved much more than Soviet-American relations, that rivalry—strategic, political, ideological, and economic—lay at its core. This competition ended because Soviet strength eroded and the Soviet empire disintegrated... the Soviet Union's inability to compete economically with the United States was probably the decisive factor in its demise. The Kremlin gained rough military equivalency, but the success came at tremendous cost. Compared to the United States the Soviet Union was forced to devote a much larger share of its gross national product to defense. Diverting investment from more productive sectors and from consumer goods ultimately undermined the regime's capacity to satisfy its own people and to act as a Great Power."

David S. Painter and Melvin P. Leffler, *Origins of the Cold War*, 1994

8. The passage above attributes the demise of the Soviet Union from its inability

   (A) to improve the standard of living for ordinary Soviet citizens
   (B) to keep up with its bitter rival, the United States, militarily
   (C) to train political leaders to keep order in a continually turbulent system
   (D) to alter its ideology to adjust to changing to changes in world politics

9. The competition between the United States and the Soviet Union ended in favor of the U.S. because the USSR was ultimately not able to compete

   (A) politically
   (B) strategically
   (C) ideologically
   (D) economically

10. Because its productive capacities were stronger the United States was able to recover from its losing 10-year war in Vietnam better than the Soviet Union was able to recover from its 10-year war in which country?

   (A) Iran
   (B) Iraq
   (C) Afghanistan
   (D) Kuwait

Questions 11-13 refer to the following:

"America must ask more of our students, our teachers, and our schools.... We will bring together business and schools to establish new apprenticeships, and young people the skills they need to find productive jobs tomorrow. Lifelong learning will benefit workers throughout their careers... we will offer a plan to end welfare as we know it.... We will offer people on welfare the education, training, child-care and health care they need to get back on their feet. Then, after two years, they must get back to work.... It's time to end welfare as a way of life. We must reinvent government to make it work again. We'll push innovative education reform to improve learning, not just spend more money. We'll use the Superfund to clean up pollution, not just increase lawyers' incomes."

Bill Clinton, "Address Before a Joint Session of Congress on Administrative Goals," 1993

11. Just as it took Nixon to go to China to open up relations with that country, it took a Democrat to accomplish which of the following reforms?

    (A) Get rid of poverty in America
    (B) Pass civil rights laws
    (C) Stop environmental damage
    (D) End welfare as we know it

12. Compared to Ronal Reagon Clinton's reforms offered in this Congressional address did not focus on

    (A) tax cuts
    (B) foreign policy
    (C) debt reduction
    (D) climate change

13. The concept or idea contained in the Clinton speech that was a major part of Progressive Educator John Dewey's ideas was

    (A) the Superfund
    (B) reinventing government
    (C) lifelong learning
    (D) apprenticeships

Questions 14-15 refer to the following:

"Sometimes I wish I could just skip my senior year and go to Stanford. I've learned enough—I'm bored and I've learned all I am going to learn from high school.... We have always lived in the Tenderloin section in San Francisco... your friends are always from your people—your own nationality... I have two Vietnamese friends. It is difficult to break into any new group... My one Vietnamese friend knows a few Chinese but it is more than they are polite to her rather than they are friends. Scholastically, Galileo is not the best high school.... Most Asians do pretty well in school, and there is always some jealousy by the black and Spanish students.... If they are jealous, I can't do anything about it. I work hard, they can too. Besides, the Vietnamese are supposed to raise the math and science scores in... San Francisco schools,... we help improve the system..."

Ho Xuan Tam, *Voices from Southeast Asia: The Refugee Experience in the United States*, 1991

14. Tam's comments tend to refute which widely accepted view of the immigration experience?

(A) Salad bowl
(B) Melting pot
(C) Assimilation
(D) Cultural pluralism

15. What role do the Vietnamese students play in the San Francisco schools?

(A) They are viewed as the natural leaders in the school because of their work ethic
(B) Their enthusiasm about school is infectious and makes the other students want to learn
(C) The integrate well into to school community and provide diversity to the school landscape
(D) They are like hired guns in westerns, brought in to raise the test scores

NO TESTING MATERIAL ON THIS PAGE

UNIT XXXIV
U.S. IN 21ST CENTURY—
BOOM-BUBBLE-BUST DECADE

The 21st century ushered in the presidencies of two men who could not have been more different—although their policies ended up being similar. George W. Bush's administration attempted to return to the days of Reagan, but events would prove his undoing and he ended being a very unpopular two term president. The return of the Democrats to power under Barack Obama in 2008 was a political surprise. Not because of the Democrat's victory, but because a political neophyte was able to defeat a formidable group of candidates for the nomination including a New York Senator who was the wife of former President Clinton, as well as a war-hero, and long time Senator, John McCain to become the first African American to be elected President.

George W. Bush's Presidency

·Election of 2000
George W. Bush, son of former president George H. Bush and Governor of Texas called himself a "compassionate conservative" and easily won the Republican nomination. He chose Washington insider Dick Cheney as his running mate. Al Gore, Vice president under Bill Clinton chose a consistent critic of Clinton, Senator Joe Lieberman, the first Jewish nominee, as his running mate. Significant third-party candidates included Patrick Buchanan (Reform) and Ralph Nader (Green). Although Gore won the popular vote by more than 500,000, the electoral college votes of three states remained too close to call in the days following the election: Oregon (7), New Mexico (5), and Florida (25). With Bush having won 246 electoral votes and Gore 255, the election hung on which of the candidates would win Florida's crucial 25 electoral votes. After the mandatory machine recount in Florida revealed that Bush held the lead by only a few hundred votes, the election began its tortuous journey through various Florida county recounts and the judicial system, ultimately ending in the U.S. Supreme Court.

·Supreme Court Ruling
The court divided 5–4 in its decision to reverse the Florida Supreme Court, which had ordered manual recounts in certain counties, saying the recount was not treating all ballots equally, and was thus a violation of the

Constitution's equal protection and due process guarantees. The Supreme Court ruled that the Supreme Court of Florida would need to set up new voting standards and carry them out in a recount, but also mandated that this process and the recount take place by midnight, December 12, 2000, the official deadline for certifying Electoral College votes. Since the court made its ruling just hours before the deadline, it ensured that it was too late for a recount. In a scathing dissent, Justice John Paul Stevens said, "Although we may never know with complete certainty the identity of the winner of this year's presidential election, the identity of the loser is perfectly clear. It is the nation's confidence in the judge as an impartial guardian of the rule of law." From uncounted votes, "hanging chads," the infamous "butterfly ballot" that had many liberal seniors in West Palm Beach voting for conservative Pat Buchanan, the confusion and ineptitude in Florida tainted the election. To the credit of the nation most American people accepted the decision of the Supreme Court and George W. Bush became the 43rd President winning 271-267 in the Electoral College.

Foreign Policy

·9/11/2001

On September 11, 2001, eight months after he took office, Bush's presidency was suddenly transformed by an act of terrorism that stunned the nation. Hijackers crashed two passenger jets into New York City's World Trade Center, demolishing its twin towers and killing more than 2,700 people. Another jet crashed into the Pentagon, and a fourth, after the passengers stormed the cockpit to thwart the hijackers, crashed in a field in Pennsylvania. The nineteen Muslims who carried out the terrorists attacks had been trained to fly by private companies in the U.S. Osama bin Laden and his Al Queda terrorist network, a group responsible for the earlier bombing of the World Trade Center in 1993, were responsible for the attack. It seemed impossible that 19 terrorists could plan and carry out this act without being detected in the U.S. but evidence of the impending attack was ignored. This event would transform the United States and accomplish the goals of the terrorists to disrupt American society.

·Patriot Act

Passed in the aftermath of 9/11, this legislation was officially titled the Uniting and Strengthening America by Providing Appropriate Tools Required to Intercept and Obstruct Terrorism Act of 2001. The law reduced restrictions on law enforcement agencies' ability to conduct searches of telephone, e-mail communications, medical, financial, and other records. It also made it easier for foreign intelligence gathering in the U.S.; expanded the Secretary of the Treasury's authority to regulate financial transactions; and gave more leeway to law enforcement and immigration authorities to detain and deport immigrants suspected of terrorism-related acts. Domestic terrorism was included in the Act. Passed by wide margins in Congress, it was supported by the Republican and Democratic parties. Opponents of the law have criticized its authorization of indefinite detentions of immigrants; searches where law enforcement officers search a home or business without the owners knowledge or permission; the expansion of authority that allows the FBI to search telephone, e-mail, and financial records without a court order; and the access of law enforcement agencies to search business financial records including the use of libraries. Since its passage, many legal challenges have been brought against the act and courts have ruled that a number of provisions are unconstitutional. Attempts to sunset the act have usually failed as the act has been reauthorized repeadedly by Congress.

·Axis of Evil

In his annual State of the Union address to Congress in 2002, Bush warned of the dangers of new attacks. He singled out three countries—North Korea, Iran, and Iraq—as making up an "axis of evil" and vowed to prevent them from using "the world's most destructive weapons" against the United States.

·Invasion of Afghanistan (2002)

Shortly after 9/11, 2001 the U.S. marked the beginning of its "War on Terrorism" by invading Afghanistan in 2002, after the government refused U.S. demands to oust the Islamic Fundamentalist Taliban and find Al-Qaeda mastermind Osama bin Laden. The anti-Taliban, Afghan Northern Alliance provided the majority of forces, while the U.S. and fellow NATO members including the United Kingdom, Canada, Australia, France, New Zealand, Italy, and Germany provided support. In a two-month battle the Northern Alliance with the U.S. and it's allies support, mainly from the air, were able to overrun all the Taliban positions. The allied forces failed to capture Osama bin Laden, despite having him cornered at the battle of Tora Bora. He escaped into a safe haven in Pakistan where the U.S. could not pursue him, as Pakistan was an ally of the U.S. and also had nuclear weapons.

·Iraq War (2003)

George W. Bush accused Saddam Hussein's government of hiding chemical and biological weapons of mass destruction from United Nation's inspectors. He also said the United States had evidence that Hussein was trying to build nuclear weapons, and that the Iraqi ruler was aiding Al Qaeda, the terrorist group that had launched the September 11 attacks. He announced and promoted the "Bush Doctrine," a policy that advocated striking out at a known enemy before the enemy attacked first. Despite opposition to the war from abroad and at home, Bush, with the support of Great Britain, ordered an invasion of Iraq on March 19, 2003 (March 20 in Iraq). U.S. led forces soon seized Baghdad and drove Hussein from power. On May 1, Bush announced the end of major combat operations as he landed on an aircraft carrier underneath a sign that said, "Mission Accomplished." But zealous supporters of Hussein and other Sunnis in Iraq who resented the U.S. occupation continued to wage guerrilla warfare against American troops. The failure to find evidence of weapons of mass destruction led to increasing criticism that Bush had exaggerated the threat from Iraq and the world increasingly turned against the U.S. policy. After declaring victory, a civil war of Shite against Sunni threatened the stability of the country. Over time, ethnic cleansing occurred as Sunnis were removed by the more numerous Shiites and relegated to small areas in Iraq. Northern regions that came under the control of the Kurds remained relatively quiet.

·Interrogation Policies

Bush authorized the CIA to use waterboarding as a enhanced interrogation technique that most experts believed was torture and violated international law. Between 2002 and 2003, the CIA considered these to be legal based on a secret Justice Department opinion that argued that terror detainees were not protected by the Geneva Conventions' ban on torture. While not permitted by the U.S. Army Field Manuals which asserted "that harsh interrogation tactics elicit unreliable information," the Bush administration believed these techniques "provided critical information" to preserve American lives. Critics argued that the information was suspect as "you can get anyone to confess to anything if the torture's bad enough." In 2006, Bush signed into law the Military Commissions Act that allowed the government to prosecute unlawful enemy combatants by military commission rather than a criminal trial. The law also denied access to *habeas corpus* so those detained could be kept incarcerated for years without being charged with a crime. The law also allowed the President to determine what constituted torture. In 2009 the ACLU sued and won release of the secret memos that had authorized the Bush administration's interrogation tactics. One memo detailed specific interrogation tactics including a footnote that described waterboarding as torture as well as the form of waterboarding used by the CIA was far more intense than authorized by the Justice Department.

·Guantanamo Bay

The oldest U.S. base overseas and the only one in a Communist country is located on the southeast corner of Cuba, in Oriente Province. In December 1903, the United States leased the 45 square miles of land and water for use as a coaling station. A treaty reaffirmed the lease in 1934 granting Cuba and her trading partners free access through the bay and required that both the U.S. and Cuba must mutually consent to terminate the lease. For a time the base was used as a detention center for refugees from Haiti and Cuba who tried to come to the U.S. After 9/11 President George W. Bush opened the prison in January 2002 to hold and interrogate foreign captives suspected of links to terrorism. As of June 2008 there were 180 detainees but at its peak the camp held about 780, most of them low level fighters while only 24 were considered to be involved in plots against the U.S.

Domestic Policy

·Tax Cuts

The top item on Bush's domestic agenda was the Economic Growth and Tax Relief Reconciliation Act of 2001 that provided a $1.35 trillion tax cut over 11 years. The highest income tax rates—28, 31, and 36 percent—were cut by 3 percentage points, while the 39.6 percent rate fell by 4.6% to 35%. A new 10 percent tax bracket was carved out of the 15 percent bracket and was available immediately although the other brackets were phased in. For the most part those at both the highest and lowest brackets received the greatest benefits from the tax cuts that would total $1.65 trillion.

·Stem Cell Research

Stem cell research, intended to develop cures for auto-immune disorders such as Type 1 Diabetes, Alzheimer's, and Parkinson's diseases was opposed by Bush with the exception of research limited to stem cells derived from embryos that had already been destroyed. He opposed federal funding that would lead to the destruction of additional embryos. This restricted use of stem cells would deter their use to find a cure for many diseases until it was ended by the Obama administration.

·Executive Orders & Signing Statements

In May of 2002, Bush issued an executive order authorizing the National Security Agency to wiretap phones and read e-mails of U.S. citizens. By April 2006, Bush had issued "signing statements" for more than 750 laws stating that he had the power to override the laws if they conflicted with his interpretation of the Constitution. This extension of executive power was reminiscent of the Imperial Presidencies of Lyndon Johnson and Richard Nixon.

·Election of 2004

After an early-spirited primary season, the Democrats nominated Senator John Kerry, a Vietnam War veteran who had later opposed that war. Bush and Cheney were re-nominated. The country was evenly divided just like in 2000 and the final decision came down to winning Ohio, which Bush finally carried with 51% of the popular vote, the same margin he won on the national level. Many pundits believed his victory there was due to the high turnout of Evangelical Christians, an increasingly important group in the Republican Party. Bush was also helped by anti-gay marriage proposals on the ballot in a number of states. Bush had backed a proposal for a constitutional amendment banning gay marriage, but the Senate blocked its approval. Bush won the Electoral College 286-252 and the Republicans remained in control of Congress.

·Medicare Extension

Bush won a major legislative victory when Congress broadly revised the Medicare program to help seniors pay for prescription drugs. But Democrats argued that the plan did too little for seniors and would undermine Medicare as a whole. The plan was incredibly complex and relied on seniors having knowledge of 42 different programs to see which one was best for them. It was an unfunded mandate, a government requirement that was not being paid for, that dramatically increased the national debt.

·Social Security
Bush called for a fundamental change in the Social Security system. He proposed allowing Americans under the age of 55 to voluntarily put part of the money they would normally contribute to Social Security into their own private retirement accounts (primarily the stock market). These proposals were stalled in Congress and Bush used most of his political capital to try to keep support for the Iraq War. Bush claimed the measure was necessary to keep the system from eventually going bankrupt, but most people were skeptical of the plan and it never came to a vote.

·Pro-Business Laws
After winning his second term, Bush had legislation passed to help business. These included: a law that made it harder for consumers to file lawsuits against businesses for providing bad products or services; legislation that made it harder to file for bankruptcy, a law favored by credit card companies but opposed by consumer groups; an energy bill providing more than $14 billion in tax benefits for businesses; legislation protecting gun manufacturers and dealers from lawsuits resulting from violent crimes committed with their products; and the Central American Free Trade Agreement, lowering trade barriers between the United States and Central American countries.

·Reform of Intelligence Services
With terrorism still a constant threat, Bush signed an intelligence reform bill to help prevent future attacks. The new law brought together 15 separate intelligence agencies under one national intelligence director. It was the most significant reform to the intelligence community in fifty years. John Negroponte, a former U.S. Ambassador to the United Nations, was appointed to the new position as Director of National Intelligence.

·Hurricane Katrina
This 2005 hurricane was the costliest and one of the deadliest hurricanes in the history of the United States. Its size caused devastation over 100 miles from the center. The storm surge caused catastrophic damage along the coastlines of Louisiana, Mississippi, and Alabama. Levees, separating Lake Pontchartrain from New Orleans were breached, ultimately flooding roughly 80 percent of the city and many areas of neighboring parishes. Most of the city's levees designed and built by the United States Army Corps of Engineers broke including the 17th Street Canal levee, the Industrial Canal levee, and the London Avenue Canal floodwall. These breaches were responsible for most of the flooding. The hurricane set things in motion but it was the human error of the improperly built and maintained levees that made the devastation so severe. The evacuation and assistance procedures for local, state, and the national government were abysmal. Bush was condemned for deliberately having incompetent people at the head of FEMA (Federal Emergency Management Agency) and for visiting the site of the disaster without ever leaving his airplane. Investigations are still going on to find out why everything went so wrong. This disaster would add more than $200 billion to the national debt that had increased during Bush's Presidency from $5.6 trillion to $8.6 trillion in just over 5 years in office, the 2nd largest increase in U.S. history. The loss of life was nearly 1500 people and five years after the event more than 100,000 residents had still not returned to New Orleans to live.

·Attorney General's Dismissal
During Bush's second term, his Justice Department dismissed seven United States Attorneys for poor performance. Attorney General Alberto Gonzales would later resign over the issue, along with other senior members of the Justice Department. The House Judiciary Committee issued subpoenas for advisers Harriet Miers and Josh Bolten to testify regarding this matter, but Bush directed Miers and Bolten to not comply by invoking the right of executive privilege. Congressional investigations focused on whether the Justice Department and the White House were using their U.S. Attorney positions for political advantage. In 2008, Congress filed a federal lawsuit and a United States district court judge ruled that Bush's top advisers were

not immune from Congressional subpoenas. In 2009, Karl Rove and Harriet Miers testified before the House Judiciary Committee. Finally, a Justice Department inquiry into the firing concluded that political considerations played a part in as many as four of the dismissals.

·Immigration

In 2006, Bush tried to create a "temporary guest-worker program" allowing 12 million illegal immigrants to work in the United States. He did not support amnesty for these illegals (called undocumented by the immigrants supporters) but argued that the lack of legal status denied the protections of laws to millions of people. Bush strongly supported the Comprehensive Immigration Reform Act of 2007, written by a bipartisan group of Senators that envisioned: a legalization program for undocumented immigrants, with an eventual path to citizenship; established a guest worker program; border and work site enforcement measures; reformed the green card application process; introduced a point-based "merit" system for green cards; and eliminated the "chain migration" of the Diversity Immigrant Visa. The public debate resulted in a substantial rift within the Republican Party as the majority of conservatives opposed it because of its legalization or amnesty provisions. The bill was eventually defeated in the Senate when a cloture motion failed to end the filibuster on a 46-53 vote. The immigration issue would continue to fester in the 21st century and would also plague the Barack Obama administration. Democratic support and Republican opposition to a plan to have a "path to citizenship" for illegal or undocumented immigrants led non-whites to overwhelmingly support Democrats and enable the Democrats to keep control of the Senate in the 2012 election.

·2006 Midterm Elections

The conduct and progress in the war in Iraq was a significant national issue, along with a series of congressional scandals. Democrats gained 31 seats in the House, enough to take control, and Republicans became the minority party after 12 years of control. As a result of the Democratic victory, Nancy Pelosi became the first woman, first Italian-American, and the first Californian elected Speaker of the House. The loss of Republican control of the House and Senate were seen as a referendum on the war, and the day after the election Bush accepted Defense Secretary Donald Rumsfeld's resignation, despite having pledged the week before that Rumsfeld would serve until Bush's second term ended. The loss of 6 Senate seats gave the Democrats a 49-49 tie with the Republicans but two independents, Joseph Lieberman and Bernie Sanders, supported the Democrats in organizing the Senate.

·Bush' Second Term Accomplishments

It was highlighted by several free trade agreements, the Energy Policy Act of 2005, alongside a strong push for offshore and domestic drilling, the nomination and confirmation of conservative Supreme Court Justices John Roberts and Samuel Alito, and more troops were sent to Iraq, that was followed by a drop in violence.

·Background of Economic Collapse

The bust of the dotcom bubble in 2001 and the fear of recession led the Federal Reserve to lower the Federal funds rate 11 times—from 6.5% in May 2,000 to 1.75% in December 2001—creating a flood of money into the economy. Cheap money was used by speculative bankers to loan money to people who had no income, no job and no assets but wanted to realize their dream of acquiring a home. This situation was made worse as more home- buyers led to more appreciation in home prices. This environment of easy credit and the upward spiral of home prices made investments in higher yielding subprime mortgages (loans made to bad risk borrowers) look like a sure thing. The Federal Reserve, pouring fuel on the fire, continued slashing interest rates to further encourage speculative fevor. Later, Alan Greenspan, head of the Federal Reserve admitted that, "I really didn't get it until very late in 2005 and 2006." In June 2003, the Fed lowered interest rates to 1%, the lowest rate in 45 years. But the bankers thought that it just wasn't enough to lend the cheap money they were getting so they decided to repackage loans into collateralized debt obligations (CDOs) and pass on the debt to another "sucker" in what became a shadow banking system. A big secondary market for originating and distributing subprime loans developed. To make matters worse the Securities Exchange Commission lowered the net capital requirement for five investment banks—Goldman Sachs, Merrill Lynch Lehman Brothers, Bear Stearns and Morgan Stanley. This enabled them to leverage up to 30-times or even 40-times their initial investment. Bond ratings agencies like Moody's and Standard and Poor's turned a blind eye to these shenanigans and made the situation worse by giving top ratings to bonds that were junk.

·The Beginning of the End
Interest rates started rising when home ownership reached a saturation point at 70% of households. From June 30, 2004, onward, the Fed raised rates that reached 5.25% and remained at that level until August, 2007. Many who had bought homes with adjustable rate mortgages at ridiculously low "teaser rates" were facing the resetting of these loans bringing about higher monthly payments that they could not afford. During the last quarter of 2005 home prices started to fall which led to a 40% decline in U.S. home construction in 2006. 2007 started with bad news as one subprime lender after another filed for bankruptcy. Financial firms and hedge funds owned more than $1 trillion in securities backed by these now-failing subprime mortgages. Bear Stearns stopped redemptions in two of its hedge funds and Merrill Lynch seized $800 million in assets from two Bear Stearns hedge funds. By the summer of 2007 the financial markets could not solve the subprime crisis and the problems spread beyond the U.S. borders.

·The End
The Federal Reserve finally took the punch bowl away from the party instead of adding more alcohol to it as they had been doing by slashing the interest rates, but the party had been going on far too long. Lehman Brothers filed for bankruptcy, Indy Mac bank collapsed, Bear Stearns was acquired by JP Morgan Chase, Merrill Lynch was sold to Bank of America, and government insured lenders Fannie Mae and Freddie Mac went bankrupt and were put under the direct control of the U.S. government. The great bubble had burst. By 2008, the Federal Reserve dropped the interest rate to 1% but this was not enough to stop a widespread financial meltdown. The U.S. government then came out with National Economic Stabilization Act of 2008 that created $700 billion to purchase distressed assets, especially mortgage-backed securities. This so-called TARP (Troubled Assets Relief Program) ended up being a boondoggle for large financial institutions as they took the money but did not loan it out and paid their employees billions of dollars in bonuses.

·Bush's Response
As all of this took place Bush seemed to look on as a disinterested bystander. "Bush fatigue" had set in and the country was looking for a new leader to deal with the economic crisis and the myriad of other problems that existed. He left office with his approval ratings in the 25% range, and the U.S. was a far different country than when Bush first won the Presidency through the intervention of the Supreme Court in 2000. He became the most unsuccessful two-term president since U. S. Grant.

Barack H. Obama's Presidency
·Democrat's Primaries & Caucuses
Although Hillary Clinton was the heavy favorite over seven other male candidates for the Democratic nomination, by skillfully maneuvering his supporters in the states that had caucuses, first term Illinois Senator Barack Obama was able to win the nomination. Obama won the first primary election battle, the Iowa caucus but Senator Clinton rallied with a comeback victory in New Hampshire. The two battled evenly in the primary states. After Super Tuesday that resulted in a draw, Obama won a string of smaller caucus states—states that almost never voted for a Democrat in a general election—that provided him with a significant lead in delegate count that Clinton's late primary victories could not overcome. Many believe a mismanaged campaign caused Hillary Rodham Clinton to lose the nomination.

·Republican Primaries

The early Republican front-runner Senator John McCain stumbled in the summer of 2007 and almost dropped out of the race. The early leader in the polls was the former mayor of New York, Rudy Giuliani, who had high name recognition due to his stewardship of the city during 9/11 but he self-destructed by not participating in the early caucuses and primaries. Former Governor Mike Huckabee, a self-defined evangelical, won the Iowa caucus. Senator McCain won the New Hampshire primary, where he had placed much of his effort, and went on to win the South Carolina primary, the state that derailed his 2000 efforts against George W. Bush. The other candidates proved to be lackluster and McCain easily won the Republican nomination.

·Election of 2008

Senator Obama selected experienced Senator Joe Biden of Delaware as his running mate. At the conclusion of the Democratic convention Senator McCain announced that little known first term Alaskan Governor, Sarah Palin was his running mate. Palin generated enthusiasm with the Republican base, something that McCain had not been able to do, but her woeful lack of experience blunted the Republican charge that Obama lacked experience. A Presidential race that was thought to be close ended up a decisive victory for Obama 365-173 in the Electoral College with Obama winning all of the swing or purple states and the traditional red Republican states of Indiana, Virginia, and North Carolina. Obama's response to the economic crisis was considered to be better than McCain's response, and the Palin factor was an overall negative for the Republicans. Obama also benefited from his decision to not accept public financing of his campaign. He raised record sums of money, especially on the Internet and was able to outspend McCain nearly three to one. The enthusiasm for the 47 year old African American was successful in bringing out the youth vote and to increase the minority vote from previous elections.

·Early Actions

After his inauguration Obama issued executive orders directing the military to develop plans to withdraw troops from Iraq and ordered the closing of Guantanamo Bay as a detention camp "as soon as practicable and no later than" January, 2010." As of December of 2014 the camp remains open as Congress has failed to allocate the funds for its closure. He also loosened up restrictions on the Freedom of Information Act and reversed George W. Bush's ban on federal funding to foreign establishments that allow abortions. The first bill signed into law by Obama was the Lilly Ledbetter Fair Pay Act of 2009 that extended the statute of limitations for equal-pay lawsuits. He also signed the reauthorization of the State Children's Health Insurance Program (SCHIP) to cover an additional 4 million uninsured children. Obama reversed a Bush-era policy which had limited funding of embryonic stem cell research to only a small number of lines. Obama stated that he believed "sound science and moral values...are not inconsistent" and pledged to develop "strict guidelines" on the research.

·American Recovery and Reinvestment Act

This $787 billion economic stimulus bill was aimed at helping an economy recover from the deepening worldwide recession—many felt that it was a depression. It included increased federal spending for health care, infrastructure, education, various tax breaks and incentives, and direct assistance to individuals. In order to get it through Congress many pet "pork barrel projects" called earmarks were a part of the bill that was heavily condemned by Republicans. Others argued against it saying you do not cure too much debt by going into more debt. Some felt the amount was too small and was not targeted to stimulate the economy, as many provisions would take years to go into effect.

·TARP

The remaining $350 billion of Troubled Asset Relief Program funds were allocated by Secretary of the Treasury Tim Geithner to stem the deflation accompanying the financial crisis.

·Public-Private Investment Program for Legacy Assets

Commonly called "the bailout," Geithner introduced this law which contained provisions for buying up to $2 trillion in depreciated real estate assets. The law spiked the stock market as all of the major stock indexes soared. He was heavily criticized for bailing out the big banks and financial institutions that had caused the problem. To many Americans it seemed like crime did pay as these Wall Street bankers received huge bonuses for their misdeeds.

·GM and Chrysler

Obama intervened in the troubled automotive industry renewing loans for General Motors and Chrysler to continue operations while reorganizing. The White House set terms for both firms' bankruptcies, including the sale of Chrysler to Italian automaker Fiat and a reorganization of GM giving the government a temporary 60% ownership in the company.

·Cash for Clunkers

Obama signed into law the Car Allowance Rebate System that lasted for two months and allowed car companies to reduce inventories with up to $4000 in subsidies for car buyers. The destruction of so-many potential used cars would have an unintended consequence on future used car markets.

·Unemployment at 10.1%

This was the highest figure since 1983 and the "underemployment" rate (a more accurate figure because it included those who were not working not just those who were looking for work) went to 17.5%.

·Sonia Sotomayor

An Appeals Court judge replaced retiring Associate Justice David Souter to become the first Hispanic (Puerto Rican) to be a Supreme Court Justice.

·Health Care and Education Reconciliation Act

Obama signed a reconciliation bill that ended the process of the federal government giving subsidies to private banks to give out federally insured loans. The government would do this directly saving students the cost of middleman fees. The law also increased the Pell Grant scholarship award, and made changes to the Patient Protection Act. The two laws were combined to prevent a Republican filibuster.

·Hate Crimes Prevention Act (Shepherd-Byrd Act)

It expanded the 1969 United States federal hate-crime law to include crimes motivated by a victim's actual or perceived gender, sexual orientation, gender identity, or disability.

·Health Care Reform

For nearly a year Congress worked to pass legislation reforming health care in the United States, a key campaign promise and a top legislative goal of the Obama administration. He proposed an expansion of health insurance coverage to cover the uninsured, to cap premium increases, and to allow people to retain their coverage when they leave or change jobs. His proposal was to spend $900 billion over 10 years and included a government insurance plan, also known as the public option, to compete with private insurance. It would make it illegal for insurers to drop sick people or deny them coverage for pre-existing conditions. It also required every American to carry health coverage. The plan included medical spending cuts and taxes on insurance companies that offered the so-called "Cadillac" or expensive plans. After months of negotiations with Republicans to achieve a bi-partisan bill that failed, House Democratic leaders introduced a 1,017 page plan for overhauling the U.S. health care system. After failing to achieve the needed 60 votes to cut off the Republican filibuster in the Senate, the Democrats resorted to the reconciliation process (a parliamentary method to allow consideration of a budget bill with debate limited to twenty hours under special Senate rules) to pass the bill by majority vote in both houses. Obama signed the bill into law on March 23, 2010. The final bill without a "public option" (a government-run health insurance agency which would compete with private health insurance companies) angered many Democrats who thought the bill looked too much like earlier bills submitted by Republicans that had originated in a conservative think-tank, the Heritage Foundation. Republicans opposed the bill and called it socialism. The main goal of Republicans in the election of 2012 was to repeal what they called "Obamacare" and what became known to Democrats as the Affordable Care Act.

·Tea Party Movement

While debate went on over the Health Care Bill, Congressmen recessed for the summer and held meeting with their constituents; these meetings were often raucous and attended mostly by individuals disgruntled with the government. Urged on by conservative TV commentators on Fox news, as well as conservative dominated talk radio, these protestors were responding to the bailout, stimulus package, and the debate going on over health care reform which they did not like. As one Tea Party member said, the government should "keep their hands off of my Medicare" failing to recognize that Medicare is a government program and an example of socialized medicine that the Tea Party opposes. This socio-political movement adopted the name "Tea Party;" a reference to the Boston Tea Party of 1773—a protest by American colonists against taxes imposed on them by the British government, and against the colonists' lack of representation in the British Parliament. Tea Party protests have sought to evoke themes, images and slogans similar to those used during the pre-revolutionary period in American history. Some have called their message a Populist one with simplistic answers for complex problems. As the mid-term 2010 elections approached it was clear that they would play a role in the nomination of and election of candidates that resulted in the Republicans regaining control of the House of Representatives and a majority of the state legislatures.

·AmeriCorps Expansion

At Obama's urging, Congress passed a $5.7 billion bill that tripled the size of the AmeriCorps service program over an eight year period. It expanded the way people from middle-school to baby boomers could earn money for college through volunteer work.

·Financial Reform

Obama and the Democrats, with the support of Republicans Olympia Snowe, Susan Collins, and Scott Brown were able to break the Republican filibuster in the Senate and passed the "Restoring American Financial Stability Act of 2010." Democrats heralded it as the greatest overhaul of Wall Street since the Great Depression. Others were not so sure. The many loopholes in the legislation caused some to call it "the Accountants' and Lawyers' Welfare Act of 2010." There was little truth to the widely circulated rumor that Wall Street was popping Champagne corks after hearing the bill had passed. In any case Wall Street remained largely unchanged, if marginally more regulated by the thousands of pages of legislation. For all their errors and lack of transparency and accountability, the large financial institutions remained relatively untouched because of the "to big to fail" philosophy.

·Torture

One major way that Obama differed from the foreign policy of George W. Bush was that the use of torture was prohibited although Obama refused to support a movement to prosecute those who had committed illegal acts.

·Climate Change

Obama appointed Special Envoys for "climate change," a concept that many conservatives derisively called "global warming" and refused to accept it as either existing or being man-made. Former Vice-President Al Gore received a Nobel Prize for his book, *An Inconvenient Truth*, on this subject, and an Academy Award for his film based on the book.

·Wars in Afghanistan and Iraq

Obama tried to refocus the U.S. on the threat from al Qaeda in Afghanistan and Pakistan. In March of 2009, he announced a new strategy with the goal to disrupt, dismantle, and defeat Al Qaeda in Pakistan and Afghanistan, and to prevent their return to either country in the future. In addition to new troops, the strategy called for more resources to the civilian effort. In early 2009, Obama announced a plan to responsibly end the war in Iraq by August of 2010 when the combat mission in Iraq would end. In August of 2010, the U.S. combat brigades left Iraq but 50,000 troops remained as well as an equal number of contractors (mercenaries). The number of troops in Afghanistan increased to 98,000 while unmanned predator drone aircraft continued to seek out and destroy U.S. enemies in an undeclared war in Pakistan.

·Nuclear Weapons

In 2009 in Prague, Obama proposed measures to reduce and eventually eliminate existing nuclear arsenals, including negotiations on further nuclear reductions with Russia, ratification of the Comprehensive Test Ban Treaty, and completion of a verified Fissile Material Cutoff Treaty. He wanted to halt proliferation of nuclear weapons in additional states and prevent terrorists from acquiring nuclear weapons or materials. He also advocated the denuclearization of North Korea through the Six-Party process.

·Clean Energy

Obama talked about a path to a clean energy economy to improve energy security, reduce the use of fossil fuels, and foster a new era of American innovation. Obama proposed spending $150 billion in clean energy research and development over ten years and wanted the U.S. to be a leader in addressing global climate change. By June of 2010 Congress had made no move to act on these ideas, and the controversial proposal of "Carbon Offsets" had been shelved for the time being.

·Social Networking

A phenomena that characterized the 21st century was the growth and importance of these new forms of communication. Starting with My Space, which was soon eclipsed by Facebook, these internet sites including Twitter and U Tube provided a new form of instant communication that went far beyond the impact of the internet and E-mail that had transformed the 1990s. These forms of communication along with the "Blogosphere" became a new community and rendered much of the old print community of newspapers and magazines as obsolete.

·BP Oil Spill

In what some called Obama's Katrina, a massive oil spill by British Petroleum (BP), the 4th largest company in the world started on April 20, 2010 when a semi-submersible exploratory offshore drilling rig in the Gulf of Mexico exploded after a blowout and sank two days later, the explosion killed eleven people and caused a massive oil spill that threatened the coasts of Louisiana, Mississippi, Alabama, Texas, and Florida. The rig was owned and operated by Transocean while BP was the majority owner of the oil field. The company's original estimates were far off and later the U.S. government said that at least 5,000 barrels a day were being leaked. An associate professor of mechanical engineering at Purdue University analyzed videotape of the leak and estimated oil flow rates at between 56,000 to 84,000 barrels per day, or the equivalent to one Exxon Valdez spill about every 3 days. The cause of the explosion was unknown as BP tried, and failed, to stop the leak by a variety of methods with exotic names like Top Cap, Junk Shot and Top Hat. With profits of $61 million daily, BP was running the well without a remote control shut-off switch used in oil-producing nations like Brazil and Norway as a last resort protection against underwater spills. The use of these devices was not mandated by U.S. regulations that were frequently written by the oil companies. BP's maintenance and monitoring crews were also understaffed in order to save money. On May 11, 2010, Congress called the executives of BP, Transocean, and Halliburton to a hearing regarding the oil spill. When asked for answers regarding the events leading up to the explosion and spill, each company (owners, operators, and builders) blamed the other. Scientists who tried to monitor the amount of oil being released were stopped by BP officials, who did not want this information released until the leak was plugged. A second, smaller leak was estimated to be releasing 25,000 barrels per day. Finally, in August of 2010, most of the leak was plugged although there was still disagreement about how much oil was still being released in the Gulf of Mexico. The total size of the leak may well have been in excess of 100,000 barrels per day at the height of its flow. This was one of the largest oil spills in history, and the worst man-made disaster ever recorded.

Off-Year Congressional Elections

Obama called the 2010 election, where the Democratic Party lost 63 seats and control of the House of Representatives, "humbling" and a "shellacking." Democrats admitted that not enough Americans had felt the effects of the economic recovery. The Democrats retained control of the Senate although their margin was narrowed to 51-47 with independents Bernie Saunders and Joe Lieberman caucusing and usually voting with the Democrats.

Death of Bin Laden

After more than 10 years of hunting, the CIA determined that Osama bin Laden was living in a large compound in Abbottabad, Pakistan, a suburban area 35 miles from Islamabad. Obama rejected a plan to bomb the compound, instead he authorized a "surgical raid" to be conducted by United States Navy SEALS. On May 1, 2011, the raid succeeded resulting in the death of bin Laden and the seizure of papers and computer drives and disks from the compound. Bin Laden's body was identified through DNA testing, and buried at sea several hours later. There were celebrations around the country although some were critical of Obama for not releasing the photographs of a dead Bin Laden.

Great Correction

Despite massive amounts of currency infused into the economy by both Quantitative Easing (printing money to buy treasury bonds) I & II, the economy remained in the doldrums with unemployment still high and property values continuing to fall. The economic malaise that started in 2001 with the dot-com bust was now entering its second decade as Americans geared up for the presidential election of 2012 with a host of Republicans, many former governors, running to take on President Obama.

Ending the War in Iraq

After nearly 9 years and a trillion dollars spent, as well as the death of nearly 4,500 U.S. service members, the war was ended to little fanfare on December 17, 2011. America's second longest war, after the Afghanistan War still going on, was finally over.

Marriage Equality

By 2012 the Gay and Lesbian community were no longer content to achieve legal status via domestic partnerships but pushed hard for the right to marry. This movement gained impetus when "don't ask, don't tell" regarding restrictions on gays serving in the military was ended in September of 2011. Ten countries and seven U.S. states accepted the right to marry by same sex couples by the beginning of 2012.

Occupy Wall Street (2011)

Centered in Zucotti Park near the New York financial district, OWS was a protest movement against social and economic inequality, high unemployment, greed and corruption, the undue influence of corporations on government, and the financial services sector of the economy. A kind of Progressive equivalent of the Tea Party, "We are the 99%" was the slogan adopted by the protestors to show the growing income disparity and wealth distribution in the U.S. between the wealthiest 1% and the rest of society. The movement spread to other cities, even internationally, but waned with the onset of winter and the actions of the police in destroying many of the OWS camps.

·Presidential Election 2012

Much of 2012 revolved around the presidential campaign. Instead of millions being spent both sides campaign's approached a billion dollars with much of it spent by political action committees (PAC) who were exempt from campaign spending limitations by the Supreme Court's Citizen's United decision. Most of the money was spent in the 9 battleground states of New Hampshire, Virginia, North Carolina, Florida, Ohio, Wisconsin, Iowa, Colorado and Nevada. The other 41 states & DC were out of play being strongly in the Republican (red state) or Democrat (blue state) camp. Mitt Romney outlasted a large group of contenders to win the Republican nomination and faced off against President Obama. The Romney campaign was languishing until he scored a decisive victory over Obama in the first presidential debate. Although Obama recouped by winning the 2nd & 3rd debates, the race remained close until the end when Obama won 8 out of the 9 contested states (purple) to gain a significant victory in the Electoral College 332-206 and just under 53% of the popular vote.

UNIT XXXIV
MULTIPLE-CHOICE QUESTIONS

Questions 1-4 refer to the following:

"The terrorists kill not merely to end lives, but to disrupt and end a way of life. With every atrocity, they hope that America grows fearful, retreating from the world and forsaking our friends.... They are the heirs of all the murderous ideologies of the 20th century. By sacrificing human life to serve their radical visions—by abandoning every value except the will to power—they follow in the path of Nazism and totalitarianism. And they will follow that path all the way, to where it ends: in history's unmarked grave of discarded lies. Americans are asking: how will we fight and win this war? We will direct... every means of diplomacy, every tool of intelligence, every instrument of law enforcement, every financial influence, and every necessary weapon of war... to the defeat of the global terror network."

George W. Bush, "Address to the Nation," September 20, 2001

1. This speech was a precursor of the U.S. invasion of which two Middle East countries?

   (A) Saudi Arabia and Kuwait
   (B) Iran and Pakistan
   (C) Afghanistan and Iraq
   (D) Egypt and Syria

2. The global terror network that President Bush is referring to in this speech is primarily which terrorist group?

   (A) Red Brigades
   (B) Al Qaeda
   (C) New People's Army
   (D) Islamic Jihad

3. The terrorists have had the most success in which of the following goals or objectives?

   (A) Taking over countries in the Middle East
   (B) Overturning feudal monarchies on the Arabian Peninsula
   (C) Threatening world peace by following the path of totalitarianism
   (D) Disrupting the American way of life

4. The United States is still at war with the "global terror" network in what has been America's longest war and has increasingly relied upon what new technology that has changed the nature of warfare in the 21st Century?

   (A) The internet
   (B) Special forces
   (C) Drones
   (D) Clean nuclear weapons

Questions 5-6 refer to the following:

Sack, *Star Tribune*, 2013

5. This cartoon is a reference to former Vice-Presidential candidates Sarah Palin's remark when she was asked about her foreign policy experience and said, "They're our next door neighbors, and you can actually see Russia from land here in Alaska." Comedian and impersonator Tina Fey simplified and distorted this quote when she had Palin saying

(A) I can see Alaska from where I live
(B) I can see Russia from my house
(C) From an island in the Bering Sea you can see Russia
(D) Russia and Alaska are contiguous

6. The cartoon's reference to Siberia is both ironic and metaphorical in that

(A) Palin in a news interview admitted that she had no idea of Siberia's location
(B) being sent to an undesirable locale as punishment for falling out of favor combined with her earlier apocryphal remark about seeing Russia from her house
(C) losing her job at Fox News, having her reality TV show cancelled, not being allowed to speak at the Republican Convention
(D) Alaska was shipping vast quantities of fish to Siberia

Questions 7-9 refer to the following:

"The nuclear thing is harder to figure. The United States..., spent nearly eight *trillion* in today's dollars on nukes in the last half of the twentieth century, which represents something like a third of our total military spending in the Cold War. Just the nuke budget was more than that half century's federal spending on Medicare, education, social services, disaster relief, scientific research (non-nuclear), environmental protection, food safety inspectors, highway maintenance, cops, prosecutors, judges, and prisons combined. What do we have to show for.... that mushroom cloud of a spending spree?... a humongous nuclear weaponry complex.... [In the] 21st century we've got thousands of nuclear missiles armed, manned, and ready to go pointed at the Soviet Union. *Er*... Russia. Whatever, at the places that still have thousands of live nuclear weapons pointed at us."

Rachael Maddow, *Drift*, 2012

7. The totality of the nuclear arsenal described in the above passage was the subject of a warning in which earlier 1961 document?

 (A) The Truman Doctrine
 (B) Eisenhower's Farewell Address
 (C) Kennedy's Inaugural
 (D) Johnson's Great Society

8. The irony of the U.S. and Russia still having thousands of nuclear weapons that can be pointed at each other in a short period of time is that

 (A) each side is waiting for the other to make the first move in dismantling the weapons
 (B) both countries are keeping the weapons aimed because they are concerned about the intentions of the other country
 (C) the countries are no longer combatants as the Cold War ended more than twenty years ago
 (D) they prefer to face each other rather than the real threat to peace, radical jihadist

9. Historically the closest the U.S. and the Soviet Union came to launching nuclear weapons at each other was the

 (A) building of the Berlin Wall
 (B) Bay of Pigs invasion
 (C) Korean War
 (D) Cuban Missile Crisis

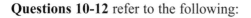

Questions 10-12 refer to the following:

"Whereas many Chinese came to the United States in the 19th and 20th centuries,... in search of the opportunity to create a better life;

Whereas the United States ratified the Burlingame Treaty on October 19, 1868, which permitted the free movement of the Chinese people to, from, and within the United States and made China a 'most favored nation'....

Whereas the House of Representatives passed legislation that adversely affected Chinese persons in the United States and limited their civil rights, including--

... 1882, the first Chinese Exclusion bill, which excluded for 20 years skilled and unskilled Chinese laborers and expressly denied Chinese persons alone the right to be naturalized as American citizens....

That the House of Representatives regrets the passage of legislation that adversely affected people of Chinese origin in the United States because of their ethnicity."

House Resolution 683, June 18, 2012

10. This recent resolution was an attempt to make amends for

   (A) discrimination against the Chinese
   (B) the hypocrisy of accepting immigrants but not giving them rights
   (C) encouragement of ethnic diversity
   (D) the inscription on the Statue of Liberty

11. The Chinese Exclusion Act was a direct violation of the sentiments expressed in the

   (A) Gettysburg Address
   (B) Bill of Rights
   (C) Constitution
   (D) Declaration of Independence

12. Four years after the Chinese Exclusion Act was passed, which monument was given to the U.S. by France that was opposed to the sentiments and laws expressed against the Chinese?

   (A) Ellis Island Memorial
   (B) USS Missouri
   (C) Statute of Liberty
   (D) Replica of the Eiffel Tower

Questions 13-15 refer to the following:

"We, the people, declare today that the most evident of truths – that all of us are created equal – is the star that guides us still; just as it guided our forebears through Seneca Falls, and Selma, and Stonewall; just as it guided all those men and women, sung and unsung, who left footprints along this great Mall, to hear a preacher say that we cannot walk alone; to hear a King proclaim that our individual freedom is inextricably bound to the freedom of every soul on Earth."

Barack Obama, "Second Inaugural Address," January 21, 2013

13. The sentiments expressed in this excerpt indicate that Barak Obama in his second term was going to have a greater focus on

    (A) foreign policy in Iraq and Afganistan
    (B) curtailing inflation to help the economy
    (C) human rights
    (D) job creation

14. The reference to Stonewall is the first time which minority group was mentioned in a Presidential inaugural speech?

    (A) Women
    (B) Hispanics
    (C) African Americans
    (D) Gays

15. In the passage above the reference to "all of us are created equal" is a reference to the

    (A) Gettysburg Address
    (B) Preamble of the Constitution
    (C) Bill of Rights
    (D) Declaration of Independence

TEST ONE

Directions: Each of the questions or incomplete statements below is followed by either four suggested answers or completions. Select the one that is best in each case and then fill in the appropriate letter in the correspoinding space on the answer sheet.

Questions 1-3 refer to the following excerpt below:

"And never have the Indians... committed any act against the Spanish Christians, until those Christians have first and many times committed countless cruel aggressions against them or against neighboring nations.... Yet into this sheepfold, into this land of meek outcasts there came some Spaniards who immediately behaved like ravening wild beasts, wolves, tigers, or lions.... More than thirty other islands in the vicinity of San Juan are for the most part and for the same reason depopulated, and the land laid waste.... We can estimate very surely and truthfully that in the forty years that have passed, with the infernal actions of the Christians, there have been unjustly slain more than twelve million men, women, and children. In truth, I believe without trying to deceive myself that the number of the slain is more like fifteen million."

Bartolome de las Casas, *Account of the Devastation of the Indies* (1552)

1. In the passage above the European's behavior is described as all of the following EXCEPT

   (A) practicing Christian charity toward the native peoples
   (B) denuding the land and killing off most of the population
   (C) acting like predatory animals toward the Indians
   (D) criminal in nature and aggressive toward the meek people they encountered

2. Bartolome de las Casas made observations that support the

   (A) idea of Christians practicing the brotherhood of man
   (B) civilizing influence Europeans had on the native people
   (C) theory that genocide was practiced on the Indians
   (D) fact that the Spanish missions supported the indigenous people

3. Which event in the 19th century most closely resembles the events described by de las Casas?

   (A) Great Awakening
   (B) Trail of Tears
   (C) Santa Fe Trail
   (D) Manifest Destiny

507

Questions 4-6 refer to the excerpt below:

"IN THE NAME OF GOD, AMEN. We,... Loyal Subjects of our dread Sovereign Lord King *James*, by the Grace of God, of *Great Britain*... Having undertaken for the Glory of God, and Advancement of the Christian Faith, and the Honour of our King and Country, a Voyage to plant the first Colony in the northern Parts of *Virginia*; Do... solemnly and mutually, in the Presence of God and one another, covenant and combine ourselves together into a civil Body Politick, for our better Ordering and Preservation, and Furtherance of the Ends aforesaid: And by Virtue hereof do enact, constitute, and frame, such just and equal Laws, Ordinances, Acts, Constitutions, and Officers, from time to time, as shall be thought most meet and convenient for the general Good of the Colony; unto which we promise all due Submission and Obedience. **IN WITNESS** whereof we have hereunto subscribed our names at *Cape-Cod* the eleventh of November, in the Reign of our Sovereign Lord King *James*, of *England*,... *Anno Domini*; 1620."

"Mayflower Compact," 1620

4. The primary purpose of the Mayflower Compact was to

(A) glorify the King of England
(B) give thanks to God and profess to being a Christian
(C) establish a political body for the colony
(D) claim the land for James I

5. The religious background of those signing the Mayflower Compact is contained in all of the following quotes from the document EXCEPT

(A) "In the name of God, Amen"
(B) "Loyal Subjects of our dread Sovereign Lord King James
(C) "by the Grace of God"
(D) "Having undertaken for the Glory of God, and Advancement of the Christian Faith...

6. The government established by the Mayflower Compact was legally a government of

(A) Plymouth, Massachusetts
(B) Great Britain
(C) England, France, Ireland, Scotland
(D) Northern Parts of Virginia

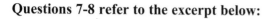

Questions 7-8 refer to the excerpt below:

"When in the Course of human events, it becomes necessary for one people to dissolve the political bands which have connected them with another, and to assume among the powers of the earth, the separate and equal station to which the Laws of Nature and of Nature's God entitle them, a decent respect to the opinions of mankind requires that they should declare the causes which impel them to the separation. We hold these truths to be self-evident, that all men are created equal, that they are endowed by their Creator with certain unalienable Rights, that among these are Life, Liberty and the pursuit of Happiness. That to secure these rights, Governments are instituted among Men, deriving their just powers from the consent of the governed..."

Thomas Jefferson, "Declaration of Independence," 1776

7. According to the passage above which of the following could be considered a statement of democracy?

(A) All men are created equal
(B) Governments get their power from the consent of the governed
(C) Laws of nature and of nature's God entitle them
(D) Life, liberty, and the pursuit of happiness

8. According to the natural rights theory propounded by John Locke and other Enlightenment thinkers which essential natural right did Jefferson leave out of the Declaration of Indepence?

(A) Freedom
(B) Equality
(C) Democracy
(D) Property

Questions 9-12 refer to the following document:

"... the American continents, by the free and independent condition which they have assumed ..., are henceforth not to be considered as subjects for future colonization by any European powers.... In the wars of the European powers in matters relating to themselves we have never taken any part,... we should consider any attempt on their part to extend their system to any portion of this hemisphere as dangerous to our peace and safety. With the existing colonies or dependencies of any European power we have not interfered and shall not interfere. But with the Governments who have declared their independence and maintain it,... any interposition for the purpose of oppressing them, or controlling... their destiny, by any European power [is]... an unfriendly disposition toward the United States.... Our policy in regard to Europe,... is, not to interfere in the internal concerns of any of its powers;... It is impossible that the allied powers should extend their political system to any portion of either continent without endangering our peace and happiness; nor can anyone believe that our southern brethren, if left to themselves, would adopt it of their own accord...."

James Monroe, "Monroe Doctrine," December 2, 1823

9. After it was issued the Monroe Doctrine was enforced in the 19th century by

   (A) established international law
   (B) the power of the British navy
   (C) frequent threatened declarations of war by the U.S.
   (D) formal alliances with the major Latin American countries

10. Which of the following is the most accurate interpretation of the significance of this document?

    (A) It warned Europe to stay out of the affairs of the Americas and the U.S. would stay out of the affairs of Europe
    (B) It paved the way for the U.S. expansion to the Pacific Coast as a fulfillment of Manifest Destiny
    (C) It encouraged Latin American countries to establish their independence from Europe
    (D) Because of this document Russia would withdraw from Northern California and the Oregon Territory issue would be settled in favor of the United States

11. The Monroe Doctrine was a continuation or continuity of advice that had been contained in which earlier document?

    (A) Declaration of Independence
    (B) Mayflower Compact
    (C) Washington's Farewell Address
    (D) Jefferson's 1st Inaugural

12. A major reason why the U.S. did not want Europe to interfere in the Western Hemisphere is because

    (A) its economic power would dominate the Western Hemisphere
    (B) the U.S. was creating a defensive alliance system among the countries of the Americas
    (C) the international community supported the U.S. efforts to suppress the slave trade
    (D) the political system of Europe was different than the U.S.

Questions 13-15 refer to the excerpt below:

Godey's Lady's Book, "The Sphere of Women," March, 1850

13. This illustration from a prominent woman's journal of the antebellum period closely aligns with which of the following concepts?

   (A) Hudson Valley School
   (B) Seneca Falls Declaration of Sentiments
   (C) Child Centered Family
   (D) Cult of Domesticity

14. The idea of women staying in the home to be the household leaders of the family, lingered until which time period when women first permanently left the home for jobs in the workforce?

   (A) 1920s & 1930s
   (B) 1940s & 1950s
   (C) 1960s & 1970s
   (D) 1980s & 1990s

15. The ideas expressed in "The Sphere of Women" followed, and to some extent, were an extension of which role of women during the Revolutionary and early National period?

   (A) Republican motherhood
   (B) Women's egalitarianism
   (C) Economic liberalism
   (D) Work, School, Church

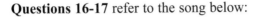

Questions 16-17 refer to the song below:

"Follow the Drinking Gourd"

"VERSE 1
When the sun comes back, and the first quail calls, Follow the drinking gourd
The old man is awaiting for to carry you to freedom If you follow the drinking gourd.

CHORUS
Follow the drinking gourd, Follow the drinking gourd,
For the old man is awaiting for to carry you to freedom If you follow the drinking gourd.

VERSE 2
The river bank will make a mighty good road The dead trees show you the way Left foot, peg foot, traveling on Follow the drinking gourd.

CHORUS
Follow the drinking gourd, Follow the drinking gourd,
For the old man is awaiting for to carry you to freedom If you follow the drinking gourd.

VERSE 3
The river ends between two hills, Follow the drinking gourd, There's another river on the other side, Follow the drinking gourd.

CHORUS
Follow the drinking gourd, Follow the drinking gourd,
For the old man is awaiting for to carry you to freedom If you follow the drinking gourd.

VERSE 4
Where the great big river meets the little river Follow the drinking gourd The old man is awaiting for to carry you to freedom If you follow the drinking gourd."

16. The basic idea behind the song is to

   (A) get your geographic and astronomy bearings
       to escape slavery
   (B) lay down your tools and to refuse to work
   (C) gather together slaves on other plantations
       for a slave uprising
   (D) save their money so eventually the slaves
       could purchase their freedom

17. The song is describing what institution that existed in the antebellum period?

   (A) African American churches
   (B) Colonization Society
   (C) Underground Railroad
   (D) Jim Crow Minstrel Show

Questions 18-21 refer to the following excerpt below:

"Four score and seven years ago our fathers brought forth on this continent a new nation, conceived in liberty, and dedicated to the proposition that all men are created equal. Now we are engaged in a great civil war, testing whether that nation, or any nation, so conceived and so dedicated, can long endure. We are met on a great battle-field of that war. We have come to dedicate a portion of that field, as a final resting place for those who here gave their lives that that nation might live. It is altogether fitting and proper that we should do this. But, in a larger sense, we can not dedicate, we can not consecrate, we can not hallow this ground. The brave men, living and dead, who struggled here, have consecrated it, far above our poor power to add or detract. The world will little note, nor long remember what we say here, but it can never forget what they did here. It is for us the living, rather, to be dedicated here to the unfinished work which they who fought here have thus far so nobly advanced. It is rather for us to be here dedicated to the great task remaining before us—that from these honored dead we take increased devotion to that cause for which they gave the last full measure of devotion—that we here highly resolve that these dead shall not have died in vain—that this nation, under God, shall have a new birth of freedom—and that government of the people, by the people, for the people, shall not perish from the earth." Abraham Lincoln, "Gettysburg Address," 1863

18. What was the "cause" that the soldiers gave their lives for according to Lincoln?

   (A) The democratic right of voting in elections
   (B) The right to bear arms
   (C) Government of, by, and for the people shall be preserved
   (D) Everyone has the free will to own and dispose of property

19. According to the document our "founding fathers" created a new nation devoted to the principle that

   (A) men were endowed with inalienable rights of life, liberty, and pursuit of happiness
   (B) the proper study of mankind is man
   (C) freedom of religion, speech, the press, assembly and petition are fundamental rights
   (D) all men are created equal

20. An action that Lincoln took to carry out the ideals expressed in the Gettysberg Address was to

   (A) adopt the Anaconda Plan
   (B) issue the Emancipation Proclomation
   (C) declare that the war was being fought to preserve the Union
   (D) appoint U.S. Grant as the commander of all the Union armies

21. What is the ironic statement that Lincoln says in the Gettysburg Address?

   (A) The speech will not be remembered
   (B) There will be a new birth of freedom
   (C) This nation is under God
   (D) Those who perished will not have died in vain

Questions 22-24 refer to the excerpt below:

"The merchant of the Black Belt is a curious institution,—part banker, part landlord, and part despot. His store... has ... everything,—clothes and shoes, coffee and sugar, pork and meal, canned and dried goods, wagons and ploughs, seed and fertilizer, ... Here, then, comes the tenant, Sam Scott, ... [who] wants him to "furnish" him,—i.e., to advance him food and clothing ... and perhaps seed and tools, until his crop is raised and sold. ... [they] go to a lawyer, and Sam executes a chattel mortgage on his mule and wagon in return for seed and... rations. As soon as... cotton leaves appear... another mortgage is given on the "crop." Every Saturday, ... Sam calls upon the merchant for his "rations;" a family of five usually gets about thirty pounds of fat side-pork and a couple of bushels of cornmeal a month.... If Sam is a hard worker and crops promise well, he is often encouraged to buy more,—sugar, extra clothes, perhaps a buggy. But he is seldom encouraged to save. When cotton rose to ten cents last fall, the shrewd merchants... sold a thousand buggies in Douglas County in one season, mostly to black men."

W.E.B. Du Bois, *The Souls of Black Folks*, 1903

22. Even if a farmer of the Black Belt is successful he remains dependent because he

   (A) lacks the skills to be a successful farmer
   (B) does not have the natural inclination to work hard
   (C) is encouraged to buy more and not to save
   (D) fails to provide his family with the basic essentials of life

23. The type of agricultural system that Du Bois is describing in the passage is called

   (A) quick-rent
   (B) headright
   (C) plantation
   (D) sharecropping

24. The fact that even if blacks did well in farming but instead of saving they spent the extra money on a buggy is an example of showing off your wealth called

   (A) discretionary spending
   (B) conspicuous consumption
   (C) wealth acquisition
   (D) *nouveau riche*

For Questions 25-26 refer to the cartoon below:

25. What action by the U.S. was an attempt to stop what was occurring as depicted in the above political cartoon?

    (A) Issuance of the Roosevelt Corollary to the Monroe Doctrine
    (B) Gentlemen's Agreement
    (C) Participation in the Boxer Rebellion
    (D) Open Door Notes of John Hay

26. The countries of Europe wielding the knives were carving up China into

    (A) condominiums
    (B) dependent states
    (C) spheres of influence
    (D) territorial possessions

Questions 27-29 refer to the cartoon below:

27. The political cartoon in the figure above expresses concern about

    (A) voting causing changes in gender roles and the disruption of the traditional family
    (B) new fashion style for women as they adopt men's clothing that reflect their changed attitude
    (C) the tranquility of the family structure in the 1920s
    (D) women getting away from their domestic duties to practice their civic duties by voting

28. The above political cartoon is a reflection of which constitutional change?

    (A) Men's joyful willingness to help in family duties now that wives had new responsibilities
    (B) Women winning suffrage with passage of the 19th amendment
    (C) Supreme Court ruling that women had the right to vote despite constitutional restrictions
    (D) Passage of the Equal Rights Amendment

29. Women's right to vote as shown in the cartoon was accomplished during a historic period of change known as

    (A) Progressivism
    (B) the New Deal
    (C) Civil Rights movement
    (D) the Great Society

Questions 30-33 refer to the definitions below:

1. **Open diplomacy**. Open covenants of peace, openly arrived at,...diplomacy shall proceed always frankly and in the public view.
2. **Freedom of the seas**. Absolute freedom of navigation upon the seas....
3. **Removal of economic barriers**. The removal, so far as possible, of all economic barriers and the establishment of an equality of trade conditions among all the nations....
4. **Reduction of armaments**. ... national armaments will be reduced to the lowest point consistent with domestic safety.
5. **Adjustment of colonial claims**. A free, open-minded, and absolutely impartial adjustment of all colonial claims,...
6. **Conquered territories in Russia**. The evacuation of all Russian territory....assure her of a sincere welcome into the society of free nations under institutions of her own choosing....
7. **Preservation of Belgian sovereignty**. Belgium,... must be evacuated and restored,
8. **Restoration of French territory**. All French territory should be freed and the invaded portions restored, and the wrong done to France by Prussia in 1871 in the matter of Alsace-Lorraine,... should be righted,...
9. **Redrawing of Italian frontiers**. A readjustment of the frontiers of Italy should be effected along clearly recognizable lines of nationality.
10. **Division of Austria-Hungary**. The peoples of Austria-Hungary,... should be accorded the freest opportunity of autonomous development.
11. **Redrawing of Balkan boundaries**. Rumania, Serbia, and Montenegro should be evacuated; occupied territories restored; Serbia accorded free and secure access to the sea;...
12. **Limitations on Turkey**. The Turkish portions of the present Ottoman Empire should be assured a secure sovereignty, but the other nationalities which are now under Turkish rule should be assured.... [of] opportunity of autonomous development, and the Dardanelles should be permanently opened....
13. **Establishment of an independent Poland**. An independent Polish state should be erected which should include the territories inhabited by indisputably Polish populations, which should be assured a free and secure access to the sea,...
14. **Association of nations**. A general association of nations must be formed under specific covenants for the purpose of affording mutual guarantees of political independence and territorial integrity to great and small states alike.

Woodrow Wilson, "Speech of 14 Points," 1918

30. This document was used to bring an end to which war?

    (A) Franco-Prussian
    (B) Great War (WWI)
    (C) WWII
    (D) Cold War

31. More than half of these points deal with which issue?

    (A) International peace
    (B) Economic opportunities
    (C) Territorial adjustments
    (D) Association of nations

32. The subsequent organization that was formed out of these 14 Points was the

    (A) North Atlantic Treaty Organization (NATO)
    (B) Association of Countries
    (C) United Nations
    (D) League of Nations

33. Special consideration was given to Serbia and Poland in the 14 Points in that they were the only countries that were guaranteed

    (A) freedom from invasion
    (B) self-determination for nationalities
    (C) sovereignty
    (D) access to the sea

Questions 34-36 refer to the excerpt below:

"...World War II caused a manpower shortage. The Mexican and U.S. governments entered into a contract [in which] Mexico would temporarily furnish farm laborers to work in the fields. The resulting *bracero* program [1942] was a war emergency measure.... The government transported Mexicans into the U.S., and guaranteed a set wage with prescribed working and living conditions.... Agricultural employers considered the continuance of the program essential for the efficient operation of their industry. They argued...that domestic workers would not do stoop labor.... A California senator even justified the... program by claiming Mexicans were more suited for stoop labor because they were built closer to the ground.... The *bracero* program stereotyped the Mexican American as a foreign field hand—not a citizen with permanent status. The man most responsible for ending the *bracero* program [1964] is Cesar Chavez."

Rudy Acuna, *A Mexican American Chronicle*, 1967

34. As a result of the ending of the *bracero* program field hands to do the stoop labor were provided primarily by

   (A) unemployed domestic workers
   (B) recent graduates of colleges who could not find jobs
   (C) field hands imported from Asia
   (D) illegal, undocumented workers from Mexico

35. After ending the *bracero* program, Cesar Chavez had success in organizing

   (A) farm workers into a union
   (B) political action committees for Mexican American
   (C) voting rights for the agricultural community
   (D) a path to citizenship for former braceros who stayed in the U.S.

36. In order to meet the labor shortage after the ending of the *bracero* program, agricultural employers turned to which group for farm labor?

   (A) Guest workers brought to the U.S. under special permits
   (B) Migrant workers often doing seasonal work in the fields
   (C) Rural workers from Eastern Europe escaping communism
   (D) Blacks leaving the south and coming west for better paying jobs

Questions 37-38 refer to the following excerpt below:

Section 1.
Equality of rights under the law shall not be denied or abridged by the United States or by any state on account of sex.

Section 2.
The Congress shall have the power to enforce, by appropriate legislation, the provisions of this article.

Section 3.
This amendment shall take effect two years after the date of ratification.

"Equal Rights Amendment," 1972

37. In giving equal rights to women this proposed amendment was similar to what earlier equal rights document?

(A) 14th Amendment
(B) Declaration of Independence
(C) Preamble to the Constitution
(D) Emancipation Proclamation

38. The ultimate fate of this "Equal Rights Amendment" was

(A) struck down by the Supreme Court for being unconstitutional
(B) enacted into law to become the 27th amendment to the Constitution
(C) withdrawn by its backers when it could not get enough support to pass in Congress
(D) failed when only 35 states ratified it and it needed 38 states

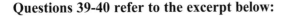

Questions 39-40 refer to the excerpt below:

"... history... teaches that simple-minded appeasement or wishful thinking about our adversaries is folly. It means the betrayal of our past, the squandering of our freedom. So, I urge you to speak out against those who would place the United States in a position of military and moral inferiority.... So, in your discussions of the nuclear freeze proposals, I urge you to beware the temptation of pride—the temptation of blithely declaring yourselves above it all and label both sides equally at fault, to ignore the facts of history and the aggressive impulses of an evil empire, to simply call the arms race a giant misunderstanding and thereby remove yourself from the struggle between right and wrong and good and evil.... the struggle now going on for the world will never be decided by bombs or rockets, by armies or military might. The real crisis we face today is a spiritual one; at root, it is a test of moral will and faith."

Ronald Reagan, "Evil Empire Speech," March 8, 1983

39. The "evil empire" that Reagan is referring to in this speech is the

    (A) Comintern
    (B) Marxist-Leninist International
    (C) Warsaw Pact
    (D) Union of Soviet Socialist Republics

40. The gist of the argument in the speech is directed against those who wanted to

    (A) stop the U.S. from expanding its nuclear arsenal
    (B) end the war in Vietnam
    (C) stop the moral and spiritual decline of religion in the United States
    (D) halt the spread of foreign ideas like socialism and progressivism

Questions 41-45 refer to the excerpt below:

"While Texas pioneers and Santa Fe traders were beginning their assault on the Mexican borderlands, another band of frontiersman—the fur traders—were blazing their trails into the heartland of the Far West. Their hour of glory was brief; the trade flourished only between the mid-1820's and early 1840's. But during those years the fur trappers played a heroic role in opening the land to more permanent setters. Theirs was the task of spying out fertile valleys that needed only man's touch to yield bountiful harvests, of spreading word of the West's riches..., of pioneering routes through mountain barriers, and of breaking down the self-sufficiency of the Indians by accustoming them to the firearms and firewater of civilization. When their day was done all the Far West was readied for the coming of the pioneer farmers?"

Ray Billington, *The Far Western Frontier, 1830-1860*, 1956

41. The ideas expressed in the passage above are part of the larger 19th century movement of

    (A) economic self-sufficiency
    (B) manifest destiny
    (C) romantic nationalism
    (D) popular sovereignty

42. Which of the following groups/events in the mid 19th century was a continuation of the process started by the fur traders?

    (A) California Gold Rush
    (B) Mormon settlement of Deseret
    (C) Oregon Trail
    (D) Irish and German Immigration

43. What government policy destroyed the livlihood of the Plains Indians to make them dependent on the government for their welfare?

    (A) Dividing the land into 640 acre sections
    (B) Providing them with armaments and alcohol whiskey
    (C) Outlawing the practice of communal living
    (D) Extermination of the buffalo

44. Because of the geographic location of where they operated the fur traders were usually referred to as

    (A) mountain men
    (B) cowboys
    (C) western pioneers
    (D) intermountain settlers

45. The fur traders task in opening the land to more settlers included all of the following EXCEPT

    (A) finding fertile valleys that only needed man's farming skills to yield bountiful harvests
    (B) spreading the word of the riches of the Far West
    (C) pioneering routes through the mountains
    (D) protecting the Indians from encroachment by white settlers

Questions 46-48 refer to the excerpt below:

"There she lies, the great Melting Pot—listen! Can't you hear the roaring and the bubbling? There gapes her mouth—the harbor where a thousand mammoth feeders come from the ends of the world to pour in their human freight. Ah, what a stirring and a seething! Celt and Latin, Slav and Teuton, Greek and Syrian,—black and yellow—Jew and Gentile—Yes, East and West, and North and South, the palm and the pine, the pole and the equator, the crescent and the cross—how the great Alchemist melts and fuses them with his purging flame! Here they shall all unite to build the Republic of Man and the Kingdom of God... what is the glory of Rome and Jerusalem where all nations and races come to worship and look back, compared with glory of America, where all races and nations come to labour and look forward."

Israel Zangwill, *The Melting-Pot*, 1909

46. The idea of the "melting pot" that Zangwill describes ran contrary to which other accepted concept regarding immigration?

 (A) Acculturation
 (B) Assimilation
 (C) Cultural diversity
 (D) Accommodation

47. The ideas expressed in the passage above are reinforced by the sentiments expressed on which other memorial or monument?

 (A) Poetic inscription on the Statue of Liberty
 (B) Tomb of the unknown soldier
 (C) Lincoln Memorial
 (D) Ellis Island Monument

48. The metaphor of the "melting pot" that Zangwill uses is part of a process that describes which characteristic?

 (A) Citizenship
 (B) Immigration
 (C) Americanization
 (D) Naturalization

Questions 49-51 refer to the photograph below:

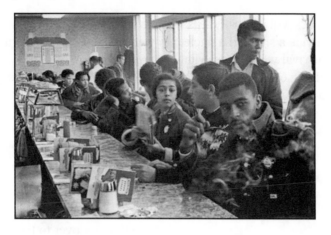

49. The specific activity that these students are engaged in is a

    (A) sit-in
    (B) hootenanny
    (C) consciousness raising
    (D) be-in

50. Which of the following was the first to engage in this activity in 1960?

    (A) Rosa Parks
    (B) UC Berkley students
    (C) Freedom Riders
    (D) North Carolina A&T freshmen

51. The purpose of this activity was to

    (A) secure voting rights for blacks
    (B) integrate lunch counters
    (C) enforce the First Amendment's right of assembly
    (D) use a school lunch program for a political statement

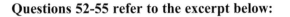

Questions 52-55 refer to the excerpt below:

• "First, the United States will keep all of its treaty commitments.
• Second, we shall provide a shield if a nuclear power threatens the freedom of a nation allied with us or of a nation whose survival we consider vital to our security.
• Third, in cases involving other types of aggression, we shall furnish military and economic assistance when requested in accordance with our treaty commitments. But we shall look to the nation directly threatened to assume the primary responsibility of providing the manpower for its defense."

Richard Nixon, "Nixon Doctrine," or "Guam Doctrine," 1969

52. The Nixon Doctrine was issued primarily to

(A) stop the Soviet Union from advancing into Afghanistan
(B) get the U.S. prepared for the invasion of Kuwait and Iraq
(C) appease the anti-war movement in the U.S.
(D) prepare for an exit strategy of what he called "peace with honor" in Vietnam

53. As a result of the Nixon Doctrine and the implementation of this policy in Southeast Asia

(A) it would increase the training of South Vietnamese troops and bring the American soldiers home
(B) counter-insurgency forces would be relocated to the Middle East
(C) the U.S. would increase the production of nuclear weapons
(D) a Soviet Union and U.S. partnership would be formed against the Chinese communists

54. The Nixon Doctrine resulted in turning the ground fighting over to the Vietnamese as the U.S. only involved itself in military training, providing weapons, and economic assistance in a policy and program called

(A) Nixonianism
(B) Vietnamization
(C) Counter Insurgency
(D) Americanization

55. The Nixon or Guam Doctrine was an extension or modification of which earlier doctrine also proclaimed by a President?

(A) Truman
(B) Hoover
(C) Roosevelt
(D) Reagan

TEST ONE

SECTION I, Part B

Time—45 minutes

4 Questions (Short Answer)

Directions: Read each question carefully and write your responses in the corresponding boxes on the free-response answer sheet.

Use complete sentences; an outline or bulleted list alone is not acceptable. You may plan your answers in this exam booklet, but only your responses in the corresponding boxes on the free-response answer sheet will be scored.

"A house divided against itself cannot stand. I believe the government cannot endure permanently half slave and half free. I do not expect the government to be dissolved; I do not expect the house to fall; but I expect it will cease to be divided. It will come all one thing or all the other. Either the opponents of slavery will arrest the further spread of it, and place it where the public mind shall rest in the belief that it is in the course of ultimate extinction, or its advocates will push it forward till it should become alike lawful in all the States, old as well as new, North as well as South."

> Abraham Lincoln, Speech at Republican State Convention Springfield, Illinois, June 17, 1858

"The framers of our government never contemplated uniformity in its internal concerns.... They well understood that the great varieties of soil, of production and of interests...required different local and domestic regulations in each locality.... In my opinion our government can endure forever, divided into free and slave States as our fathers made it—each State having the right to prohibit, abolish, or sustain slavery... This government was made upon the great basis of the sovereignty of the States, the right of each State to regulate its own domestic institutions to suit itself;..."

> Stephen Douglas, Speeches at Chicago, July 9 and Alton, October 15, 1858

1. Using the excerpts above, answer parts a, b, and c.

   (a) Briefly explain the basic interpretation of the Lincoln speech.
   (b) Briefly explain the basic interpretation of the Douglas speech.
   (c) Provide how ONE piece of evidence from the era of the Antebellum period, Civil War, and Reconstruction that is not included in the passages, and explain how it supports the interpretation in either passage.

2. Using your knowledge of United States history, answer parts a and b.

    (a) United States historians have proposed various events to mark the beginning of an American identity. Choose ONE of the events listed below, and explain why your choice best represents the beginning of an American identity. Provide at least ONE piece of evidence to support your explanation.
- Ratification of the Bill of Rights in 1791
- Washington's Farewell Address
- Revolution of 1800

    (b) Contrast your choice against ONE of the other options, demonstrating why that option is not as good as your choice.

3. Use the image above and your knowledge of United States history to answer parts a, b, and c.

    (a) Explain the point of view reflected in the image above of one of the following:
- Newly Arrived Immigrant
- Men in Top Hats
- People in Shadows

    (b) Explain how ONE element of the image expresses the point of view you identified in part a

    (c) Explain how the point of view you identified in part a helped to shape ONE specific United States government action between 1900 and 1924

4. Using your knowledge of United States history, answer parts a, b, and c.

    (a) The antebellum period was one of great economic change in the United States during what has been called a "market revolution." Analyze and explain how ONE of the following made a contribution to these fundamental changes in the American economy?
- Lowell system
- Canals
- Railroads
- Turnpikes

    (b) Provide at least one specific piece of evidence to support your point of view.

    (c) Contrast your choice against one of the other options, demonstrating why that option is not as good as your choice.

TEST ONE

SECTION II, Part B

Total Time—1 hour, 35 minutes

Question 1 (Document-Based Question)
Suggested reading period: 15 minutes
Suggested writing period: 45 minutes

Directions: Question 1 is based on the accompanying documents. The documents have been edited for the purpose of this exercise. You are advised to spend 15 minutes reading and planning and 45 minutes writing your answer.

In your response you should do the following:

- State a relevant thesis that directly addresses all parts of the questions.
- Support the thesis or a relevant argument with evidence from all, or all but one, of the documents.
- Incorporate analysis of all, or all but one, of the documents into your argument.
- Focus your analysis of each document on at least one of the following: intended audience, purpose, historical context, and/or point of view.
- Support your argument with analysis of historical examples outside the documents.
- Connect historical phenomena relevant to your argument to broader events or processes.
- Synthesize the elements above into a persuasive essay.

1. How was the relationship different between the English, Spanish, and French colonizers and the Indians they encountered during the 16th and 17th centuries?

Document 1

Source: *Missionary John Megapolensis on the Mohawks (Iroquois)*,1644 from Ebenezer Hazard, Historical Collections (Philadelphia, 1792)

The Women are obliged to prepare the Land, to mow, to plant, and do every Thing; the Men do nothing except hunting, fishing, and going to War against their Enemies: they treat their Enemies with great Cruelty in Time of War, for they first bite off the Nails of the Fingers of their Captives, and cut off some joints, and sometimes the whole of the Fingers; after that the Captives are obliged to sing and dance before them . . . and finally they roast them before a slow Fire for some Days, and eat them. . . . Though they are very cruel to their Enemies, they are very friendly to us: we are under no Apprehensions from them. . . .

They are entire Strangers to all Religion... worship and present Offerings to the Devil whom they call Otskon or *Airekuoni*. . . . They have otherwise no Religion: when we pray they laugh at us; some of them despise it entirely, and some when we tell them what we do when we pray, stand astonished.... They call us *Assyreoni*, that is, Cloth-Makers, or *Charistooni*, that is, Iron-Workers, because our People first brought Cloth and Iron among them...

Document 2

A French Jesuit missionary, 1644

To make a Christian out of a Barbarian is not the work of a day.... A great step is gained when one has learned to know those with whom he has to deal; has penetrated their thoughts; has adapted himself to their language, their customs, and their manner of living; and when necessary, has been a Barbarian with them, in order to win them over to Jesus Christ.

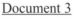

Document 3

Edward Randolph's report of King Philip's War in New England, 1675

Various are the reports and conjectures of the causes of the present Indian warre [sic]. Some impute it to an imprudent zeal in the magistrates of Boston to christianize those heathen before they were civilized and enjoining them the strict observation of their laws. . . . [T]he people, on the other side, for lucre and gain, entice and provoke the Indians to the breach thereof, especially to drunkenness, to which those people are so generally addicted that they will strip themselves to their skin to have their fill of rum and brandy. . . .

Some believe there have been vagrant and jesuitical priests, who have made it their business, for some years past, to go from Sachem to Sachem, to exasperate the Indians against the English and to bring them into a confederacy, and that they were promised supplies from France and other parts to extirpate the English nation out of the continent of America. . . .

But the government of the Massachusetts...[has] contributed much to their misfortunes, for they first taught the Indians the use of arms, and admitted them to be present at all their musters and trainings, and shewed [sic] them how to handle, mend and fix their muskets, and have been furnished with all sorts of arms by permission of the government.

Document 4

Source: Inscription Reads, "Come Over and Help Us" in this 1629 Seal of the Massachusetts Bay Colony

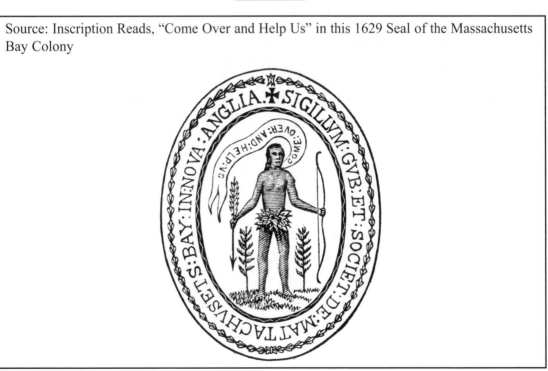

Document 5

Source: A Huron Indian to Jesuit missionary Jean de Brébeuf, 1635.

You tell us fine stories, and there is nothing in what you say that may not be true; but that is good for you who come across the seas. Do you not see that, as we inhabit a world so different from yours, there must be another heaven for us, and another road to reach it?

Document 6

Source: Bartolomé de las Casas—*A Short Account of the Destruction of the Indies*

The natives of the province of Santa Marta had a great deal of gold …. And this is the reason why, from 1498 right down to today, in 1542, the region has attracted an uninterrupted series of Spanish plunderers who have done nothing but sail there, attack, murder and rob the people, steal their gold and sail back again. Each expedition in turn—and there have been many over the years—has overrun the area, causing untold harm and a monstrous death-toll, and perpetrating countless atrocities….

The remedy for the ills that beset this territory is that Your Majesty remove from positions of authority the cruel usurpers presently in control and entrust it to someone who will love and care for it…. Those who presently govern these regions be stripped of their stewardship, so that the cruel yoke may be removed from the whole republic…. Your Majesty will also now perceive that here there are no Christians but only devils; no servants of God and the Crown but only traitors to His laws and Yours….The greatest obstacle that stands in the way of the pacification of the New World, and with it the conversion of the people to Christ, is the harshness and cruelty of the treatment meted out by "Christians" to those who surrender. This has been so harsh and so brutal that nothing is more odious nor more terrifying to the people than the name "Christian", a word for which they use in their language the term yares, which means "demons."

Document 7

Source: "A 17th Century Letter of Gabriel Diaz Vara Calderón, Bishop of Cuba, Describing the Indians and Indian Missions of Florida," Smithsonian Miscellaneous Collections, vol. 95, no. 16

"… there are 13,152 Christianized Indians to whom I administered the holy sacrament of confirmation. They are fleshy, and rarely is there a small one, but they are weak and phlegmatic as regards work, though clever and quick to learn any art they see done, and great carpenters as is evidenced in the construction of their churches which are large and painstakingly wrought....They go naked, with only the skin [of some animal] from the waist down…. The women wear only a sort of tunic that wraps them from the neck to the feet, and which they make of the pearl-colored foliage of the trees (Spanish moss), which they call guano and which costs them nothing except to gather it…. Their ordinary diet consists of porridge which they make of corn, … pumpkins, beans which they call frijoles, with game and fish from the rivers and lakes which the well-to-do ones can afford. Their only drink is water, and they do not touch wine or rum. Their greatest luxury is [a drink] which they make from a weed that grows on the seacoast, which they cook and drink hot and which they call cazina [cacina]. It becomes very bitter and is worse than beer, although it does not intoxicate them and is beneficial. They sleep on the ground, and in their houses only on a frame made of reed bars, which they call barbacoa, with a bear skin laid upon it and without any covert…. These Indians do not covet riches, nor do they esteem silver or gold, … and their only barter is the exchange of one commodity for another…. As to their religion, they are not idolaters, and they embrace with devotion the mysteries of our holy faith."

TEST ONE

Directions: Choose EITHER question 2 or question 3. You are advised to spend 35 minutes writing your answer..

In your response you should do the following.

- State a relevant thesis that directly addresses all parts of the question.
- Support your argument with evidence, using specific examples.
- Apply historical thinking skills as directed by the question.
- Synthesize the elements above into a persuasive essay.

2. Some historians have argued that the formal ending of the bracero program in 1964 marked a dramatic change in the relationship between Mexican immigrants and the United States. Support, modify, or refyte this contention using specific evidence.

3. Some historians have argued that the ratification of the 19th Amendment in 1920 marked a turning point for women in their quest for equal rights. Support, modify, or refute this contention using specific evidence.

TEST TWO

Directions: Each of the questions or incomplete statements below is followed by either four suggested answers or completions. Select the one that is best in each case and then fill in the appropriate letter in the correspoinding space on the answer sheet.

Questions 1-3 refer to the excerpt below:

"The Indians of Xicalango gave the child [Dona Marina] to the people of Tabasco and the Tabasco people gave her to Cortés... As Doña Marina proved herself such an excellent woman and good interpreter throughout the wars.... Cortés always took her with him,... she was married to a gentleman named Juan Jaramillo at the town of Orizaba. Doña Marina... was obeyed without question by the Indians throughout New Spain.... [Her relatives] were in great fear of Doña Marina, for they thought she had sent for them to put them to death, and they were weeping.... she consoled them and told them to have no fear, that when they had given her over to the men from Xicalango, they knew not what they were doing, and she forgave them... and she gave them many jewels of gold and raiment, and told them to return to their town, and said that God had been very gracious to her in freeing her from the worship of idols and making her a Christian…and in marrying her to such a gentleman as Juan Jaramillo.... That she would rather serve her husband and Cortés than anything else in the world...."

Bernal Díaz del Castillo, *The Discovery and Conquest of Mexico 1517-1521*

1. As Castillo describes it the giving of Dona Marina from the Xicalango to the Tabasco to Cortes meant that she was originally a

    (A) princess
    (B) guide
    (C) valuable economic commodity
    (D) slave

2. Some Indians and Mexicans have been critical of Dona Marina for

    (A) converting to Christianity
    (B) marrying a European Spaniard
    (C) betraying her people by acting as Cortes' interpreter
    (D) establishing control of her own empire in central Mexico

3. Which of the following later incidents or events is similar to what is described by Castillo regarding Dona Marina

    (A) Pocahontas and John Rolfe
    (B) Sacagawea and Louis & Clark
    (C) Squanto and the Separatists (Pilgrims)
    (D) Crazy Horse and George Armstrong Custer

535

Questions 4-6 refer to the excerpt below:

"It being one chief project of that old deluder, Satan, to keep men from the knowledge of the Scriptures,... It is therefore ordered that every township in this jurisdiction, after the Lord hath increased them to fifty households shall forthwith appoint one within their town to teach all such children as shall resort to him to write and read, whose wages shall be paid either by the parents or masters of such children, or by the inhabitants in general,... And it is further ordered, that when any town shall increase to the number of one hundred families or householders, they shall set up a grammar school, the master thereof being able to instruct youth so far as they may be fitted for the university, provided that if any town neglect the performance hereof above one year that every such town shall pay 5 pounds to the next school till they shall perform this order."

Old Deluder Act of 1647 passed by the General Court of Massachusetts

4. The primary purpose of education according to the passage above was to

(A) enlighten the souls of youth
(B) prepare students for a life of the mind in their older years
(C) be able to read the Bible
(D) train them to become good citizens and workers

5. According to the document above who was it that was keeping men from knowledge?

(A) Government officials
(B) The devil
(C) Ministers
(D) Parents or masters of children

6. This law started a process that would ultimately result in which of the following continuities in American history?

(A) Compulsory public education by the middle of the 20th century
(B) An emphasis on higher learning through the Land Grant system of funding colleges
(C) The parochial school movement of establishing Catholic education
(D) The "home schooling" movement in the 21st century

Questions 7-8 refer to the chart below:

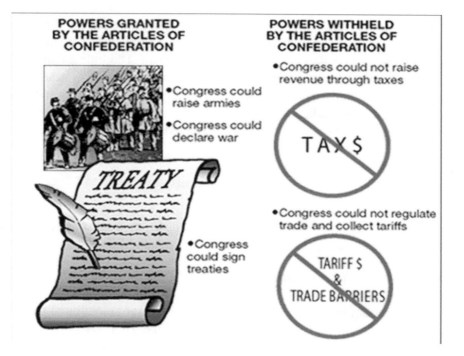

7. Which of the following interpretations does the chart above support about the Articles of Confederation?

(A) The new central government under the Articles of Confederation had unlimited powers
(B) Issues like the sale and organization of the lands in the west were the province of the state governments
(C) The government's power was over war and peace but not economic issues
(D) Each state could decide if it was going to cooperate with the Confederation government of not

8. Based on the evidence in the chart which of the following could be considered a logical continuity in United States History?

(A) A new government was needed to provide the people with fundamental rights and freedoms
(B) Issues of taxes, tariffs, and trade barriers required a stronger central government which was provided by the Constitution
(C) The Declaration of Independence was written to provide a blueprint for what a government should be that would protect people's liberty
(D) The Articles of Confederation were considered a powerful government because it could raise an army to go to war and sign a treaty to end a war

Questions 9-11 refer to the excerpt below:

"I visited... Waltham Mills... [established] before those of Lowell were set up. The establishment is for the spinning and weaving of cotton... [and] 500 persons were employed at the time of my visit. The girls earn two, and some three dollars a week, besides their board. The little children earn one dollar a week.... The managers of the various factory establishments keep the wage as nearly equal as possible, and then let the girls shift about from one to another.... The people work about seventy hours per week.... All look like well-dressed young ladies. The health is good..., it is no worse that it is elsewhere.... I saw very few shabby houses.... the place is unboundedly prosperous, through the temperance and industry of the people."

Harriet Martineau, *Society in America*, 1837

9. The conclusion in the passage above is that the prosperity of the people is due to their

    (A) great location as a trade center or *entrepot* for the exchange of goods
    (B) lack of competition from European competitors
    (C) hard work and sobriety
    (D) training and education

10. This account of the Waltham Mills by the English visitor Harriet Martineau is generally favorable about labor in the Waltham Mills but she should have been most alarmed about

    (A) the poor health of the girls
    (B) the fact that the children were dressed in rags
    (C) the shabbiness of much of the housing
    (D) a seventy hour work week

11. One of the biggest disadvantages to this system at Waltham Mills is

    (A) the isolation of the girls from their fellow female workers
    (B) upward mobility of the workers is stifled as the pay is always the same at each factory
    (C) a general culture of poverty that effects the psychological make-up of the work force
    (D) failure to instill in the girls a positive work ethic

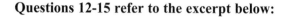

Questions 12-15 refer to the excerpt below:

"At this memorable time, Isabella [Sojourner Truth] was struck off, for the sum of one hundred dollars, to one John Nealy, of Ulster County, New York; and she has an impression that in this sale she was connected with a lot of sheep. She was now nine years of age, and .... She says, with emphasis, 'Now the war begun. ' She could only talk Dutch-and the Nealys could only talk English. Mr. Nealy could understand Dutch, but Isabel and her mistress could neither of them understand the language of the other.... She says, 'If they sent me for a frying-pan, not knowing what they meant, perhaps I carried them pot-hooks and trammels. Then, oh! how angry mistress would be with me!' ... During the winter her feet were badly frozen, for want of proper covering. They gave her a plenty to eat, and also a plenty of whippings. One Sunday morning... she found her master with a bundle of rods, prepared in the embers, and bound together with cords. When he had tied her hands together before her, he gave her the most cruel whipping she was ever tortured with. He whipped her till the flesh was deeply lacerated, and the blood streamed from her wounds-... In those hours of her extremity, she did not forget the instructions of her mother, to go to God in all her trials.... obeyed: going to him, 'and telling him all-and asking Him if He thought it was right,' and begging him to protect and shield her from her persecutors."

Olive Gilbert, "Narrative of Sojourner Truth," 1850

12. Isabella's story gives evidence that which accepted sterotype about the nature of slavery was not accurate?

  (A) Slaves were happy in their condition of servitude
  (B) Were treated better than the wage slaves in the North
  (C) Protected from physical abuse because of their economic value
  (D) Treated well because of the dictates of the Bible

13. Isabella remembered being sold along with a lot of sheep, which proves the point that slaves were

  (A) chattel property
  (B) kept together as families
  (C) better off than the poor whites
  (D) wards of the state

14. A basic misunderstanding occurred between Isabella and her new owners because

  (A) she was a Protestant and they were Catholic
  (B) she spoke Dutch and they spoke English
  (C) her owners wife was jealous of Isabella
  (D) she had been separated from her family

15. As she suffered the whippings Isabella took the advice of her mother to heart and turned to what source to get her through the ordeal?

  (A) Her family
  (B) Books
  (C) Friends
  (D) God

Questions 16-18 refer to the excerpt below:

"Now then, I say again that the opportunity to get rich, to attain unto great wealth, is here... I say that you ought to get rich, and it is our duty to get rich. How many of my pious brethren say to me, 'Do you, a Christian minister, spend your time going up and down the country advising young people to get rich, to get money?' 'Yes, of course I do.' They say, 'Isn't that awful! Why don't you preach the gospel instead of preaching about man's making money?' 'Because to make money honestly is to preach the gospel.' That is the reason. The men who get rich may be the most honest men you find in the community. 'Oh,' but says some young man here to-night, 'I have been told all my life that if a person has money he is very dishonest and dishonorable and mean and contemptible.' 'My friend, that is the reason why you have none, because you have that idea of people... ninety-eight out of one hundred of the rich men of America are honest. That is why they are rich....'"

Russell H. Conwell, *Acres of Diamonds*, 1900

16. The ideas expressed in the passage above closely resemble the ideas of which economic philosophy?

    (A) Laissez faire
    (B) Socialism
    (C) Communitarianism
    (D) Democratic liberalism

18. The ideas in Conwell's speech were similar to which ideas propounded by industrialist Andrew Carnegie?

    (A) Social Gospel
    (B) Gospel of Wealth
    (C) Reform Darwinism
    (D) Social Democracy

17. Historically speaking the ideas that Conwell states are similar to the ideas of which colonial religious group?

    (A) Quakers
    (B) Deist
    (C) Puritans
    (D) Anglicans

Questions 19-20 refer to the image below:

"The Yellow Terror in All His Glory" 1899

19. This particular cartoon depicts what international event that led to American forces being deployed in China?

(A) Asian Boundary Dispute
(B) Gentlemen's Agreement
(C) Boxer Rebellion
(D) Mejii Restoration

20. All of the following were laws directed primarily against Asians EXCEPT

(A) Page Act of 1875
(B) Chinese Exclusion Act
(C) Geary Act of 1892
(D) Burlingame Treaty Act

Questions 21-23 refer to the excerpt below:

"... it is well to bear in mind that whatever other sins the South may be called to bear, when it comes to business, pure and simple, it is in the South that the Negro is given a man's chance in the commercial world... Our greatest danger is that in the great leap from slavery to freedom we may overlook the fact that the masses of us are to live by the productions of our hands, and fail to keep in mind that we shall prosper in proportion as we learn to dignify and glorify common labour, and put brains and skill into the common occupations of life; shall prosper in proportion as we learn to draw the line between the superficial and the substantial, the ornamental gewgaws of life and the useful. No race can prosper till it learns that there is as much dignity in tilling a field as in writing a poem. It is at the bottom of life we must begin, and not at the top. Nor should we permit our grievances to overshadow our opportunities."

Booker T. Washington, "Atlanta Compromise Address," 1895

21. According to the passage above the Negro should concentrate their energies on

(A) learning manual arts and farming
(B) working to become doctors and lawyers
(C) preparing for an academic career
(D) honing their entrepreneurial skills

22. Booker T. Washington's views as expressed in the "Atlanta Compromise" were challenged by

(A) the Populist platform
(B) the Harlem Renaissance
(C) the economic impact of the Great Migration
(D) W.E.B. Du Bois and the Niagara Movement

23. The "Atlanta Compromise" as proposed by Booker T. Washington

(A) was a compromise between militant black leaders and moderates regarding social equality between the races
(B) believed vocational education, which gave blacks an opportunity for economic security, was more valuable to them than social advantages, higher education, or political office
(C) it was a deal with the Southern politicians that they would give up segregation if blacks would vote with them on political issues
(D) for a short period of time it united the poor whites with the blacks aligned against the ruling Bourbon class of southern aristocracy

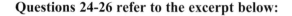

Questions 24-26 refer to the excerpt below:

"It is not true that the United States feels any land hunger or entertains any projects as regards the other nations of the Western Hemisphere save such as are for their welfare.... Any country whose people conduct themselves well can count upon our hearty friendship. If a nation... keeps order and pays its obligations, it need fear no interference from the United States. Chronic wrongdoing, or an impotence which results in a general loosening of the ties of civilized society, may in America, as elsewhere, ultimately require intervention by some civilized nation, and in the Western Hemisphere the adherence of the United States to the Monroe Doctrine may force the United States, however reluctantly, in flagrant cases of such wrongdoing or impotence, to the exercise of an international police power.... We would interfere with them only in the last resort..."

Theodore Roosevelt, "Annual Message to Congress," December 6, 1904

24. This statement by the President became known as the

(A) square deal manifesto
(B) Caribbean intervention policy
(C) Roosevelt Corollary
(D) West Indies International

25. This policy of Theodore Roosevelt's created a belief that the United States was viewed by the countries of Latin America and the Caribbean as the

(A) colossus of the north
(B) great peacemaker
(C) regional moneybags
(D) international lender

26. This Roosevelt policy of intervention was ultimately ended by the policy of Herbert Hoover and Franklin D. Roosevelt called what policy?

(A) Pan Americanism
(B) Public Spirit
(C) Co-Prosperity Plan
(D) Good Neighbor

Questions 27-29 refer to the excerpt below:

"Sec. 2 That any woman who marries a citizen of the United States after the passage of this Act, or any woman, whose husband is naturalized after the passage of this Act, shall not become a citizen of the United States by reason of such marriage or naturalization; but if eligible to citizenship, she may be naturalized upon full and complete compliance with all requirements of the naturalization laws with the following exceptions:

Sec. 3... That any woman citizen who marries an alien ineligible to citizenship shall cease to be a citizen of the United States... Sec. 5 That no woman whose husband is not eligible to citizenship shall be naturalized during the continuance of the marital status."

Cable Act or Women's Citizenship Act, Sixty-Seventh Congress, September 22, 1922

27. Aliens who were ineligible for citizenship in 1922 included

   (A) Mexicans
   (B) Latin Americans
   (C) Southern & Eastern Europeans
   (D) Asians

28. The reason behind the Cable Act's clause that took away citizenship from women who married an alien ineligible for citizenship was

   (A) fear of the "Yellow Peril" or the threat of Oriental domination through race mixing
   (B) to decrease the number of women voters now that the 19th Amendment had passed
   (C) to make sure there were enough women available for marriage to men eligible for citizenship
   (D) that non-citizens were multiplying so fast that they would soon outnumber citizens

29. The Cable Act had which restrictions on women?

   (A) Kept them from marrying or eloping without their father's consent
   (B) Took away their citizenship and they could not be naturalized if they married an illegal alien
   (C) Gave the women citizenship even if she married a foreigner
   (D) Denied women the right to vote in local, state and national elections

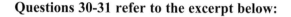

Questions 30-31 refer to the excerpt below:

"... aliens of Japanese, German, and Italian nationality living in the United States were branded as 'enemy aliens.' The leaders among them were taken into custody and interned at camps. After this initial round-up,... Germans and Italians were kept under surveillance, but Japanese immigrants and their American born children living along the Pacific Coast... were rounded up and incarcerated in so-called relocation centers... Of these, almost two thirds—64.9%—were American born.... Life in these places was not generally brutal; there were no torture chambers, firing squads, or gas ovens.... They were places of confinement with barbed wire and armed sentries... the camp personal, recruited from the local labor force, shared the contempt of the general population for 'Japs.'"

Roger Daniels, *Concentration Camps, North America: Japanese in the United States and Canada during World War II*, 1981

30. The relocation camps the Japanese were forced to live in could be considered similar to

    (A) Nazi concentration camps
    (B) Immigrant's ghettos
    (C) Indian Reservations
    (D) Settlement Houses

31. The primary reasons why the entire west coast Japanese population was put into the relocation camps and most Germans and Italians were only kept under surveillance was because

    (A) many American expatriates living in Germany and Italy would be discriminated against and put into camps in Europe
    (B) a combination of the Yellow Peril and the attack on Pearl Harbor caused near panic on the Pacific Coast
    (C) the millions of German and Italians living in the U.S. made it physically impossible to put them into relocation camps
    (D) there was still hope that differences between the U.S. and the Rome-Berlin Axis could be solved so the U.S. did not want to alienate Germany and Italy

Questions 32-35 refer to the excerpt below:

"It would be an exaggeration to say that American unassisted and alone could exercise a power of life and death over the Communist movement and bring about the early fall of Soviet power in Russia. But the United States has in its power to increase enormously the strains under which Soviet policy must operate, to force upon the Kremlin a far greater degree of moderation and circumspection than it has had to observe in recent years, and in this way to promote tendencies which must eventually find their outlet in either break-up or the gradual mellowing of Soviet power. For no mystical, Messianic movement—and particularly not that of the Kremlin—can face frustration indefinitely without eventually adjusting itself in one way or another to the logic of that state of affairs."

George F. Kennan, "The Sources of Soviet Conduct," 1947

32. The passage above served to help formulate U.S. foreign policy to address which of the following?

(A) World War I
(B) World War II
(C) Korean War
(D) Cold War

33. All of the following are examples of the U.S. successfully frustrating Soviet power EXCEPT

(A) Berlin air lift
(B) formation of NATO
(C) Vietnam War
(D) arming the mujahideen

34. What Kennan predicted in 1947 came true in the 1989/1990 symbolized by the

(A) launching of sputnik
(B) tearing down Berlin Wall
(C) adoption of the Oslo Accords
(D) shooting down the U-2

35. The adjustments the Soviet Union made in the 1980s to gradually mellow Soviet power as Kennan had predicted were

(A) *glasnost and perestroika*
(B) unification of Czechoslovakia
(C) purchasing wheat from the U.S.
(D) continuing the war with Afghanistan

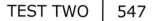

Questions 36-38 refer to the excerpt below:

"In your hands, my fellow citizens, more than mine, will rest the final success or failure of our course.... Now the trumpet summons us again—not as a call to bear arms, though arms we need—not as a call to battle, though embattled we are—but a call to bear the burden of a long twilight struggle... against the common enemies of man: tyranny, poverty, disease and war itself.... In the long history of the world, only a few generations have been granted the role of defending freedom in its hour of maximum danger. I do not shrink from this responsibility—I welcome it.... The energy, the faith, the devotion which we bring to this endeavor will light our country and all who serve it—and the glow from that fire can truly light the world. And so, my fellow Americans: ask not what your country can do for you—ask what you can do for your country. My fellow citizens of the world: ask not what America will do for you, but what together we can do for the freedom of man."

John F. Kennedy, "Inaugural Address," January 20, 1961

36. Kennedy's "Inaugural" recognizing the special role that America needs to play in addressing the various world challenges could be considered an example of which concept?

   (A) Liberalism
   (B) Conservatism
   (C) American Exceptionalism
   (D) Constitutualism

37. What program did Kennedy start to carry out the statement, "ask not what your country can do for you—ask what you can do for your country?"

   (A) Point Four
   (B) Alliance for Progress
   (C) War on Poverty
   (D) Peace Corps

38. Kennedy's statement "ask not what your country can do for you—ask what you can do for your country?" helped to usher in what characteristic that personifies the early 1960s before Vietnam war and the counterculture

   (A) New Frontier idealism
   (B) Gender equality
   (C) Imperialistic adventurism
   (D) Neo-conservativism

Questions 39-40 refer to the excerpt below:

" Article 1... Clinton swore to tell the truth, the whole truth... before a Federal grand jury of the United States. Contrary to that oath, William Jefferson Clinton willfully provided perjurious, false and misleading testimony to the grand jury concerning one or more of the following: (1) the nature and details of his relationship with a subordinate Government employee; (2) prior perjurious, false and misleading testimony he gave in a Federal civil rights action brought against him; (3) prior false and misleading statements he allowed his attorney to make to a Federal judge in that civil rights action; and (4) his corrupt efforts to influence the testimony of witnesses and to impede the discovery of evidence in that civil rights action. In doing this, William Jefferson Clinton has undermined the integrity of his office, [and] has brought disrepute on the Presidency..."

"Resolution Impeaching William Jefferson Clinton for High Crimes and Misdemeanors," 1998

39. The high crimes and misdemeanors that Clinton was impeached for revolved around which issue?

(A) Failure to protect the United States against attacks by terrorist
(B) Raised illegal campaign funds to assure his reelection in 1996
(C) Waging an illegal war without the approval of Congress
(D) His sexual misconduct with women in two separate cases

40. Besides Clinton the only other President to be impeached was

(A) Andrew Johnson
(B) Richard Nixon
(C) George W. Bush
(D) James Earl Carter

Questions 41-45 refer to the following excerpt below:

"The movement for the Constitution... was originated and carried through principally by four groups... [who] had been adversely affected under the Articles of Confederation: money, public securities, manufactures, and trade and shipping:

... the formation of the Constitution were taken by a small and active group of men immediately interested through their personal possessions in the outcome of their labors....

A large propertyless mass was, under the prevailing suffrage qualifications, excluded... from participation (through representatives) in the work of framing the Constitution.

The members of the Philadelphia Convention... derived economic advantages from, the establishment of the new system.

The Constitution was essentially an economic document based upon as recognizing the claim of property to a special and defensive position in the Constitution.

In the ratification of the Constitution, about three-fourths of the adult males failed to vote,...

The Constitution was ratified by a vote of probably not more than one-sixth of the adult males....

The leaders who supported the Constitution in the ratifying conventions represented the same economic groups as the members of the Philadelphia Convention....

... the ratification... was between substantial personality interests on the one hand and the small farming and debtor interests on the other.

The Constitution was not created by "the whole people"... [nor] "the states" as Southern nullifiers long contended; but it was... a consolidated group whose interests knew no state boundaries and were truly national in their scope."

Charles Beard, *An Economic Interpretation of the Constitution*, 1913

41. According to the historian Charles Beard's interpretation regarding the motivation of the "founding fathers" in writing the Constitution is that they were motivated primarily by their

   (A) concern for world peace and world order
   (B) altruistic attitude toward mankind
   (C) desire to change the system in the U.S. so that there would be more democracy
   (D) commercial self interest

42. Those who were excluded from the writing and the ratification of the Constitution included all of the following EXCEPT

   (A) African Americans
   (B) Women
   (C) Southern planters
   (D) propertyless white males

43. The passage in the above document indicates which of the following?

    (A) Debtors and small farmers opposed the Constitution
    (B) Personality interests had benefited from the Articles of Confederation
    (C) Members of the Philadelphia convention were not personally interested in a new government
    (D) Those who supported the Constitution were opposed to nationalism

44. The passage indicates that the Constitution

    (A) was created by the whole people
    (B) was supported by 75% of the white males
    (C) favored those who gained economic advantage from the new system
    (D) was a creation of the states that adhered to the compact theory

45. On the whole the Beard interpretation supports the view that the "founding fathers" who wrote the Constitution were opposed to

    (A) a republic
    (B) democracy
    (C) life, liberty, & the pursuit of happiness
    (D) the property class

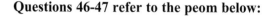

Questions 46-47 refer to the peom below:

"By the rude bridge that arched the flood,
Their flag to April's breeze unfurled,
Here once the embattled farmers stood,
And fired the shot heard round the world,
The foe long since in silence slept,
Alike the Conqueror silent sleeps,
And Time the ruined bridge has swept
Down the dark stream which seaward creeps.
On this green bank, by this soft stream,
We set today a votive stone,
That memory may their deed redeem,
When like our sires our sons are gone.
Spirit! who made those freemen dare
To die, or leave their children free,
Bid time and nature gently spare
The shaft we raise to them and Thee."

Ralph Waldo Emerson, "Concord Hymn," 1837

46. The line in the poem that is likely to be poetic license and probably not literally true is

(A) By the rude bridge that arched the flood,
(B) Their flag to April's breeze unfurled,
(C) Here once the embattled farmers stood,
(D) And fired the shot heard round the world,

47. The most powerful line in the poem and the one that reverberated and spread the idea of revolution to foreign lands is

(A) Spirit! Who made those freemen dare To die, or leave their children free,
(B) By the rude bridge that arched the flood, Their flag to April's breeze unfurled,
(C) Here once the embattled farmers stood, And fired the shot heard round the world,
(D) That memory may their deed redeem, when like our sires our sons are gone.

Questions 48-51 refer to the excerpt below:

"That if any person shall write, print, utter or publish,... any false, scandalous and malicious writing or writings against the government of the United States, or either house of the Congress of the United States, or the President of the United States, with intent to defame ... or to bring them, or either of them, into contempt or disrepute; or to excite against them,... the hatred of the good people of the United States, or to stir up sedition within the United States, or to excite any unlawful combinations therein, for opposing or resisting any law of the United States, or any act of the President of the United States, ... or to aid, encourage or abet any hostile designs of any foreign nation against United States, their people or government, then such person, being thereof convicted before any court of the United States having jurisdiction thereof, shall be punished by a fine not exceeding two thousand dollars, and by imprisonment not exceeding two years."

Sedition Act, July 14, 1798

48. The above law was directed against supporters of which political faction that was challenging the ideas and policies of the dominant Federalist Party?

(A) Whigs
(B) Progressives
(C) Jeffersonians
(D) Liberty

49. The Sedition Act as it was interpreted was directed primarily against

(A) newspapers
(B) government officials
(C) the courts
(D) state legislatures

50. To challenge this law opponents of it would likely rely upon which specific document as the basis of their challenge?

(A) Declaration of Independence
(B) Constitution
(C) Washington's Farewell Address
(D) Amendment #1 of the Bill of Rights

51. Opposition to the Sedition Act along with opposition to the Alien Act was contained in which written documents that condemned the two laws?

(A) Bill of Rights
(B) Kentucky and Virginia Resolutions
(C) Suffolk Resolves
(D) Funding and Assumption

Questions 52-53 refer to the political cartoon below:

52. In the last part of the 19th century there was little to differentiate the Democrats from the Republicans except for their positions on which issue that is alluded to in this cartoon?

 (A) Environment
 (B) Immigration
 (C) Imperialism
 (D) Tariff

53. In the first panel the lion (symbol of Great Britain) and the lamb (symbol of American industries) are together but in the second panel the lion has eaten the lamb and this represents

 (A) fear that British imperialism would crowd out American industry from oversees markets
 (B) Republicans 'belief that Democrats' tariff reform will allow the British free trade policies to devour American businesses
 (C) a belief that British policy of having twice as many capital (war) ships plus 10% as its closest rival would hamper the U.S. naval build-up
 (D) England's efforts for dismantle the Monroe Doctrine to open up Latin American trade to the commerce of their shipping industry

Questions 54-55 refer to the excerpt below:

"And provided, that the further introduction of slavery or involuntary servitude be prohibited, except for the punishment of crimes, whereof the party shall have been fully convicted; and that all children born within the said State, after the admission thereof into the Union, shall be free at the age of twenty-five years."

Tallmadge Amendment, 1820

54. The above passage applies to a bill that would admit which state into the Union?

(A) Maine
(B) Missouri
(C) Nebraska
(D) Kansas

55. The ideas expressed in the Tallmadge Amendment could be seen as a precursor to which later document?

(A) Macon's Bill #2
(B) Populist Manifesto
(C) Emancipation Proclamation
(D) Wilmot Proviso

TEST TWO

SECTION I, Part B

Time—45 minutes

4 Questions (Short Answer)

Directions: Read each question carefully and write your responses in the corresponding boxes on the free-response answer sheet.

Use complete sentences; an outline or bulleted list alone is not acceptable. You may plan your answers in this exam booklet, but only your responses in the corresponding boxes on the free-response answer sheet will be scored.

"Coming south after the war to make money and seize political power, the Northern "carpetbaggers" became the dominant figure in Southern politics for a decade. In collusion with the carpetbaggers were the "scalawags" native whites in the South who took advantage of the chance for aggrandizement...Aided by a system that gave the vote to the Negro while it disenfranchised the more substantial element among the whites,...

Elections in the South became a byword and a travesty. Ignorant blacks by the thousands cast ballots without even the names of the men whom they were voting...

As the process of carpetbag rule unfolded, honest men in the South felt increasing disgust. Conservative editors referred to the fancy state conventions as "black and tan" gatherings, "ring -streaked and speckled" conventions or as assemblies of "baboons," ragamuffins," or jailbirds."

James G. Randall, *The Civil War and Reconstruction*," 1837

"...the Southern people of both races lived as quietly and as normally during Reconstruction as in any politically disturbed period.... No attempt was made to destroy white supremacy in the social or economic sphere or to sanction interracial marriages.... One of the accepted conventions of Reconstruction scholars is that the Carpetbaggers failed because their measures were excessively radical....

A truly radical program would have called for the confiscation of land for the freedman. Land was the principal form of Southern wealth....ex-slaves could have battled for economic competence and social equality.... Radicalism of the day naively assumed that a people's salvation could be obtained through the ballot and the spelling book.... [Radicals] did not try to destroy the greatest obstacle to the Negroes' salvation, the Southern caste system..."

Francis B. Simkins, "New Viewpoints of Southern Reconstruction," 1939

1. Using the excerpts above, answer parts a, b, and c.

   (a) Briefly explain the basic interpretation in the Randall book.
   (b) Briefly explain the basic interpretation in Simkin's article.
   (c) Provide ONE piece of evidence from the era of Reconstruction that is not included in the passages, and explain how it supports the interpretation in either passage.

2. Using your knowledge of United States history, answer parts a and b.

   (a) United States historians have proposed that various groups have made a contribution to the development of the American character. Choose ONE of the groups listed below and explain what your choice has contributed to the development of the national character. Provide at least ONE piece of evidence to support your explanation.
- Puritans
- Yeoman Farmers
- Western Pioneers

   (b) Contrast your choice against ONE of the other options, demonstrating why that option is not as good as your choice.

3. Use the image above and your knowledge of United States history to answer parts a, b, c, and d.

   (a) Explain how the political cartoon describes the Senate
   (b) Explain how the political cartoon describes the Monopolists
   (c) Explain how the political cartoon describes the People
   (d) Provide at least one specific piece of evidence from 1880 to 1920 that supports the point of view in the political cartoon

4. Using your knowledge of United States history, answer parts a, b, and c.

   (a) Although the Compromise of 1850 attempted to solve sectional differences it only succeeded in delaying the Civil War for a decade. Explain how ONE of the following provisions in the compromise either helped avert the conflict or ultimately contributed to increased sectional discord:
- Texas boundary and debt
- California as a free state
- popular sovereignty in Utah and New Mexico
- slave trade in the District of Columbia
- Fugitive Slave Law

   (b) Provide at least ONE specific piece of evidence to support your point of view.

   (c) Contrast your choice against ONE of the other options, demonstrating why that option is not as good as your choice.

TEST TWO

Question 1 (Document-Based Question)
Suggested reading period: 15 minutes
Suggested writing period: 45 minutes

Directions: Question 1 is based on the accompanying documents. The documents have been edited for the purpose of this exercise. You are advised to spend 15 minutes reading and planning and 45 minutes writing your answer.

In your response you should do the following:

- State a relevant thesis that directly addresses all parts of the questions.
- Support the thesis or a relevant argument with evidence from all, or all but one, of the documents.
- Incorporate analysis of all, or all but one, of the documents into your argument.
- Focus your analysis of each document on at least one of the following: intended audience, purpose, historical context, and/or point of view.
- Support your argument with analysis of historical examples outside the documents.
- Connect historical phenomena relevant to your argument to broader events or processes.
- Synthesize the elements above into a persuasive essay.

---

1. Analyze the arguments women used in the 1848-1920 campaign to achieve the right to vote AND how were they able to combat the opposition against women's suffrage.

Document 1

Elizabeth Cady Stanton and Lucretia Mott, "Declaration of Sentiments," 1848

"We hold these truths to be self-evident: that all men and women are created equal; that they are endowed by their Creator with certain inalienable rights; that among these are life, liberty, and the pursuit of happiness; that to secure these rights governments are instituted, deriving their just powers from the consent of the governed. Whenever any form of government becomes destructive of these ends, it is the right of those who suffer from it to refuse allegiance to it, and to insist upon the institution of a new government, laying its foundation on such principles, and organizing its powers in such form, as to them shall seem most likely to effect their safety and happiness. Prudence, indeed, will dictate that governments long established should not be changed for light and transient causes; and accordingly all experience hath shown that mankind are more disposed to suffer. while evils are sufferable, than to right themselves by abolishing the forms to which they are accustomed. But when a long train of abuses and usurpations, pursuing invariably the same object, evinces a design to reduce them under absolute despotism, it is their duty to throw off such government, and to provide new guards for their future security. Such has been the patient sufferance of the women under this government, and such is now the necessity which constrains them to demand the equal station to which they are entitled. The history of mankind is a history of repeated injuries and usurpations on the part of man toward woman, having in direct object the establishment of an absolute tyranny over her. To prove this, let facts be submitted to a candid world...."

Document 2

"Dear Mrs. Stanton

Well I have been & gone & done it!!--positively voted the Republican ticket--strait this a.m. at 7 Oclock--& swore my vote in at that--was registered on Friday & 15 other women followed suit in this ward--then on Sunday others some 20 or thirty other women tried to register, but all save two were refused--all my three sisters voted--Roda De Garmo too--Amy Post was rejected & she will immediately bring action for that--similar to the Washington action--& Hon Henry R. Selden will be our Counsel--... so we are in for a fine agitation in Rochester on the question--I hope the morning's telegrams will tell of many women all over the country trying to vote.... Haven't we wedged ourselves into the work pretty fairly & fully--& now that the Repubs have taken our votes--for it is the Republican members of the Board--The Democratic paper is out against us strong & that scared the Dem's on the registry board--How I wish you were here to write up the funny things said & done--Rhoda De Garmo told them that she wouldn't swear of affirm--"but would tell the truth"-- & they accepted that When the Democrat said my vote should not go in the box--one Republican said to the other--What do you say Marsh!--I say put it in!--So do I said Jones--and "we'll fight it out on this line if it takes all winter"....If only now--all the women suffrage women would work to this end of enforcing the existing constitution--supremacy of national law over state law--what strides we might make this winter...I hope you voted too.

Affectionately, Susan B. Anthony"

Letter to Elizabeth Cady Stanton, Rochester, Nov 5th, 1872

Document 3

"It is true that many women are unmarried and not affected by any of the duties, complications, and incapacities arising out of the married state, but these are exceptions to the general rule. The paramount destiny and mission of woman are to fulfill the noble and benign offices of wife and mother. This is the law of the Creator. And the rules of civil society must be adapted to the general constitution of things, and cannot be based upon exceptional cases. "

Justice Bradley, *Bradwell v. Illinois*, 1872

Document 4

"... the Constitution, when it conferred citizenship, did not necessarily confer the right of suffrage. If uniform practice long continued can settle the construction of so important an instrument as the Constitution of the United States confessedly is, most certainly it has been done here. Our province is to decide what the law is, not to declare what it should be.

We have given this case the careful consideration its importance demands. If the law is wrong, it ought to be changed; but the power for that is not with us. The arguments addressed to us bearing upon such a view of the subject may perhaps be sufficient to induce those having the power, to make the alteration, but they ought not to be permitted to influence our judgment in determining the present rights of the parties now litigating before us. No argument as to woman's need of suffrage can be considered. We can only act upon her rights as they exist. It is not for us to look at the hardship of withholding. Our duty is at an end if we find it is within the power of a State to withhold.

Being unanimously of the opinion that the Constitution of the United States does not confer the right of suffrage upon any one, and that the constitutions and laws of the several States which commit that important trust to men alone are not necessarily void, we affirm the judgment. "

Minor v. Happerset, 1875

Document 5

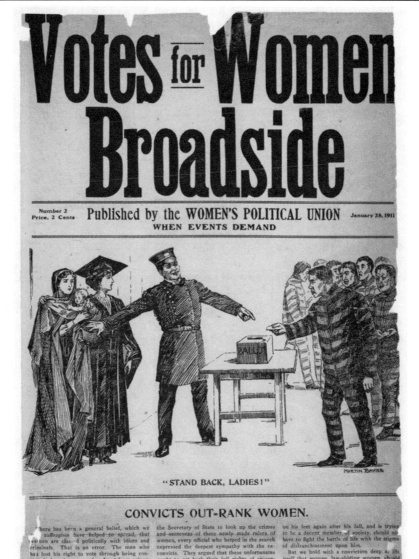

Document 6

"She's Good Enough To Be Your Baby's Mother And She's Good Enough To Vote With You

No man is greater than his mother

No man is half so good

No man is better than the wife he loves

Her love will guide him What 'ere beguile him

She's good enough to love you and adore you

She's good enough to bear your troubles for you

And if your tears were falling today Nobody else would kiss them away

She's good enough to warm your heart with kisses When your lonesome and blue

She's good enough to be your baby's mother And she's good enough to vote with you

Man plugs the world in war and sadness She must protest in vain Let's hope and pray someday we'll hear her pain

Stop all your madness, I bring you gladness

She's good enough to love you and adore you

She's good enough to bear your troubles for you

And if your tears were falling today Nobody else would kiss them away

She's good enough to warm your heart with kisses

When your lonesome and blue She's good enough to be your baby's mother

And she's good enough to vote with you

She's good enough to give you old Abe Lincoln

She good enough to give you Brandon Sherman, Robert E. Lee and Washington too

She was so true she gave them to you

She's good enough to give you Teddy Roosevelt Thomas A. Edison too.

She's good enough to give you Woodrow Wilson

And she's good enough to vote with you."

Herman Paley, 1915

Document 7

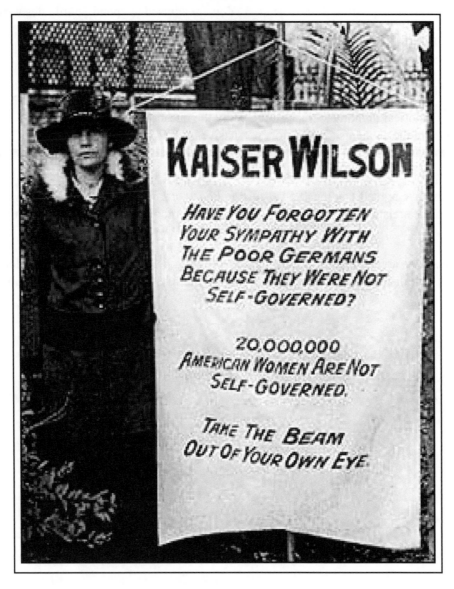

TEST TWO

Directions: Choose EITHER question 2 or question 3. You are advised to spend 35 minutes writing your answer..

In your response you should do the following.

- State a relevant thesis that directly addresses all parts of the question.
- Support your argument with evidence, using specific examples.
- Apply historical thinking skills as directed by the question.
- Synthesize the elements above into a persuasive essay.

2. Some historians have argued that the 1954 *Brown v. Board of Education of Topeka Kansas* case marked a turning point in race relations in the United States. Support, modify, or refute this contention using specific evidence.

3. Some historians have argued that the 1980s marked a turning point in both foreign and domestic policy from moderate liberalism to neo-conservatism. Support, modify, or refute this contention using specific evidence.

TEST THREE

SECTION I, Part A

Time—55 minutes

55 Questions

Directions: Each of the questions or incomplete statements below is followed by either four suggested answers or completions. Select the one that is best in each case and then fill in the appropriate letter in the correspoinding space on the answer sheet.

Questions 1-3 refer to the excerpt below:

"The Spanish scheme for colonizing the borderlands called for a central colony in New Mexico, the establishment of widely separate outposts in California, Arizona, and Texas and eventually the linking of these settlements...across the northern part of New Spain. The central colony of New Mexico was... anchored, after great effort, but more than a hundred years passed before the colonization of the three outlying provinces could be undertaken.... During their existence as Spanish outposts, they went their separate and different ways, with little intercommunication or exchange; each with its own pattern, its own special problems. The failure of Spain to consolidate its borderland outposts has had important latter day consequences. For the Spanish-speaking of the borderlands remain... separate and disparate groups, sharing a common heritage but never...functioning together."

Carey McWilliams, *North from Mexico: The Spanish Speaking People of the United States*, 1948

1. The basic interpretation of the passage above is the lands of the Spanish borderlands

   (A) enjoyed a regional government that brought the different entities together
   (B) centered around the colony of Texas with its large population and political influence
   (C) remained separate and distinct each staying within itself with little contact with the others
   (D) provided a unified barrier from encroachment by the dominant Anglo people and culture to the north

2. As different as the borderlands were they all shared a common

   (A) history
   (B) economy
   (C) geography
   (D) heritage

3. Ultimately, the fate of the Spanish borderlands was to become a part of the United States as a result of the Mexican Cession after the Mexican War EXCEPT for

   (A) Texas
   (B) New Mexico
   (C) California
   (D) Arizona

567

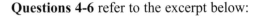

Questions 4-6 refer to the excerpt below:

"The Navigation Act of 1660 reserved the whole trade of the colonies to English ships and required that the captain and three quarters of the crew be English...colonial 'enumerated articles'—sugar, tobacco, cotton, ginger, and dies like indigo and fustic [rice, molasses, naval stores, furs and copper were added later]—could not be shipped...outside the empire. [In 1663] Parliament required...all European products destined for the colonies be brought to England before being shipped across the Atlantic...Later legislation...enforcing these laws...dealt with the posting of bonds, the registration of vessels, [and] the appointment of customs officials.... A planned economy, with England specializing in manufacturing and the colonies in the production of raw materials—this was the grand design."

John Garraty, *The American Nation: A History of the United States*, 1966

4. The Navigation Acts were directed against which commercial rival of England?

   (A) France
   (B) Spain
   (C) Italy
   (D) Netherlands

5. The Navigation Acts put into place in England an economic system that was an anathema to most businesses in colonial America called

   (A) mercantilism
   (B) commercialism
   (C) industrialism
   (D) phsiocratism

6. One of the reasons the colonials rebelled against the England is because the period of "salutary neglect" was ended by the French and Indian War. Many wanted to dismantle the economic system represented by the Navigation Acts and replace it with

   (A) a planned economy
   (B) socialism
   (C) Adam Smith's laissez faire
   (D) democracy

Questions 7-8 refer to the excerpt below:

"PERHAPS the sentiments contained in the following pages, are not YET sufficiently fashionable to procure them general favor; a long habit of not thinking a thing WRONG, gives it a superficial appearance of being RIGHT, and raises at first a formidable outcry in defence of custom. But the tumult soon subsides. Time makes more converts than reason.... Small islands not capable of protecting themselves, are the proper objects for kingdoms to take under their care; but there is something very absurd, in supposing a continent to be perpetually governed by an island. In no instance hath nature made the satellite larger than its primary planet, and as England and America, with respect to each other, reverses the common order of nature, it is evident they belong to different systems: England to Europe, America to itself."

Thomas Paine, "Common Sense," 1776

7. The passage above is arguing for

(A) fashionable arguments
(B) might makes right
(C) American Independence from England
(D) Application of Common Law

8. Paine uses examples from which of the following to make his point?

(A) Ancient Greece and Rome
(B) Religious doctrine
(C) Enlightenment thought
(D) Science and geography

Questions 9-12 refer to the excerpt below:

"Here are not aristocratical families, no courts, no kings, no bishops...no great manufacturers employing thousands, no great refinements of luxury. The rich and poor are not so far removed from each other as they are in Europe....

What then is the American, this new man? He is either a European or the descendant of a European; hence the strange mixture of blood which you will find in no other country.... He is an American,... Here individuals of all nations are melted into a new race of men, whose labors and posterity will day cause great change in the world. Americans are the western pilgrims, who are carrying along with them that great mass of arts, sciences, vigour, and industry, which begin in the east; they will finish the great circle."

Michel Guillaume Jean de Crevecoeur, *Letters from an American Farmer*, 1782

9. The passage above best describes Americans as being

(A) conservative
(B) liberal
(C) egalitarian
(D) theocratic

10. Crevecoeur's interpretation of what constitutes an American gave rise to which theory in the late 19th century describing immigration?

(A) Assimilation
(B) Melting pot
(C) Racial purity
(D) Salad bowl

11. Which of the following statement's best describes the interpretation of the American identity in the passage above?

(A) This new man, the American, derives his essential goodness from providence, destiny, and the fulfillment of idealism that comes from an advanced culture
(B) The American character is shaped primarily by the interplay of the economic forces of capitalism
(C) Republicanism brought a new way of life that was centered in the system of representative democracy that was first laid out in the Declaration of Independence
(D) It is a blend of different nationalities characterized by little social stratification and creating a new entity to carry forth the attributes of civilization

12. Which of the following concepts in the late 20th and early 21st century resembles the ideas contained in the excerpt above?

(A) American Exceptionalism
(B) Perfectibility of Man
(C) Rendezvous with Destiny
(D) We Shall Overcome

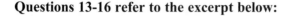

Questions 13-16 refer to the excerpt below:

"Provided, That, as an express and fundamental condition to the acquisition of any territory from the Republic of Mexico by the United States, by virtue of any treaty which may be negotiated between them, and to the use by the Executive of the moneys herein appropriated, neither slavery nor involuntary servitude shall ever exist in any part of said territory, except for crime, whereof the party shall first be duly convicted."

"Wilmot Proviso," 1846

13. The passage above was in reference to land that was acquired as a result of

(A) Mexican Cession
(B) Louisiana Purchase
(C) Northwest Ordinance
(D) Southwest Acquisition

14. The ideas expressed in the Wilmot Proviso became the centerpiece of which political party that emerged as a permanent major party in the 1850s?

(A) Whigs
(B) Democrats
(C) Republicans
(D) Federalist

15. Although the Wilmot Proviso twice passed the House of Representatives it failed to become law because it was stopped by

(A) a presidential veto
(B) the U.S. Senate
(C) the Supreme Court
(D) the major political parties

16. An alternative to the Wilmot Proviso introduced at about the same time was the concept of

(A) manifest destiny
(B) the American System
(C) territorial liberty
(D) popular sovereignty

Questions 17-18 refer to the excerpt below:

"I took my place in this narrow prison.... I laid me down in my darkened home three feet by two, and resigned myself to my fate.... I took with me a bladder filled with water... in case of too great heat; and no access to fresh air excepting three small... holes, I started on my perilous cruise. I was first carried to the express office, the box being placed on its end, so that I started with my head downwards, although the box was directed, "this side up with care...." I was carried to the depot, and from thence tumbled roughly into the baggage car, where I happened to fall "right side up." But after a while the cars stopped, and I was put aboard a steamboat, and placed on my head. In this dreadful position... my eyes were swollen out of their sockets... [After many travails] I arrived in Philadelphia... I was... carried to a house where... persons were ready... each one seized hold of some tool, opened my grave... and I swooned [fainted] away."

George Stearns, *Narrative of Henry Box Brown by Himself*, 1849

17. A conclusion that can be drawn from this account is that

   (A) it was not worth it to try to escape from slavery
   (B) slaves would take extreme measures to escape
   (C) slaves had to escape on their own without assistance
   (D) because of the ordeal involved few slaves would try to free themselves

18. Because he received some help at his final destination Henry Brown could be considered as

   (A) another success for the underground railroad
   (B) a criminal for violating the 1793 Fugitive Slave Law
   (C) the best example of the need for stronger laws against runaway slaves
   (D) a national hero for the abolitionist movement that started in Philadelphia

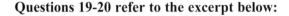
Questions 19-20 refer to the excerpt below:

"...of the... 35,000 men who went up the trail from Texas with herds during the heroic age of the cattle industry, 1866-1895, 'about one third were Negroes and Mexicans....' Negroes out-numbered Mexicans by more than two to one—slightly more than 63% whites, 25% Negroes, and slightly under 12% Mexicans.... Without the services of the... Negroes...who...helped to move herds up the cattle trails to shipping points, Indian reservations, and fattening grounds, and who, between drives, worked on the ranches of Texas and the Indian territory, the cattle industry would have been seriously handicapped... many of them were especially well-qualified top hands, rider, ropers and cooks...during the halcyon days of the cattle range, Negroes... frequently enjoyed greater opportunities for a dignified life than anywhere else in the United States. They worked, ate, slept, played and on occasion fought with their white comrades, and their ability and courage won respect, even admiration."

Kenneth W. Porter, "Negro Labor in the Western Cattle Industry, 1866-1900," 1969

19. Negroes on the cattle drive from 1866 to 1900 were treated

(A) as separate workers from the whites and the Mexicans
(B) as subservient cowboys who were only allowed to do the most menial tasks
(C) with respect, dignity, and according to the principles of equality
(D) the same as Indians who lived on reservations

20. At the same the Negro cowboy was being treated according to egalitarianism in the West, blacks in the South were living under a new emerging system called

(A) integration
(B) Jim Crow
(C) internationalism
(D) separatism

Questions 21-22 refer to the excerpt below:

"The domination of popular fiction by the so-called domestic novel during the mid nineteenth century decades reflected the recent appearance of women as a cultural, social, and economic force in American society.... These domestic novels were useful weapons in women's undeclared war against a male-oriented society. They were often anti-husband novels written in a code quickly understood by the female reader.... The aim of the domestic novel was... to teach moral lessons. It combined three powerful elements—sex, sentiment, and religion—in a potent mixture. Sex was very much there, realistically though delicately handled. The books taught that conventional sexuality was best, that deviation from it was dangerous, that immorality was punished by terrifying results. Sentimentality soaked the novel in tears.... Religion in the novels was simple... 'the religion of the heart,'... the solution to almost any problem."

Russel Nye, *The Unembarrassed Muse: The Popular Arts in America*, 1970

21. The moral lessons of domestic fiction focusing on sentimentality, sex, sentiment and religion would be challenged by Margaret Sanger and her

    (A) support for the Comstock laws
    (B) political activism for women's right to vote
    (C) innovative dance style featuring natural movement rather than rigid technique
    (D) birth control and sex education advocacy

22. Which of the following aphorisms best describes what occurred in the domestic novel?

    (A) Women's work is never done
    (B) The wages of sin are death
    (C) This above all: to thine own words be true
    (D) Nature has given women so much that the law has given them little

Questions 23-25 refer to the cartoon below:

23. In the political cartoon above the two groups that are being condemned by the cartoonist are

    (A) businessmen and labor unions
    (B) immigrants and homesteaders
    (C) Republicans and Progressives
    (D) Democrats and Populists

24. The witches are dropping negative things into the cauldron that revolve around which issue?

    (A) Monetary
    (B) Immigration
    (C) Expansionism
    (D) Cultural values

25. The cartoonist links which other movement with the Demo-Popocrats?

    (A) Communism
    (B) Socialism
    (C) Anarchism
    (D) Capitalism

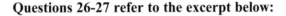

Questions 26-27 refer to the excerpt below:

"...the President of the National Association of Manufacturers in early 1932 ascribed the Depression and the growing unemployment to mass laziness. Most men... did not want to work or were 'utilizing the occasion to swell the Communist chorus.' Among the major liquidations of the Great Depression was that of business prestige and influence. From their venerated position during the twenties businessmen fell to objects of public hostility, suspicion, and ridicule,... because of their unwillingness or inability to provide or support new solutions for the pressing problems of unemployment and growing poverty. Their doctrinaire hostility to relief or reform.... fostered the public image of them as cold, indifferent, and greedy and led to their social bankruptcy."

George Mowry, *The Urban Nation: 1920-1960*, 1965

26. Which man representing the business class became a symbol of "doctrinaire hostility" to relief or reform" was

    (A) Warren Harding
    (B) Calvin Coolidge
    (C) Herbert Hoover
    (D) Franklin Roosevelt

27. The view of the President of the National Association of Manufacturers that unemployment was due to the laziness of workers is totally contradicted by which New Deal program that employed more than 5 million men who had been out of work?

    (A) Tennessee Valley Authority (TVA)
    (B) National Industrial Recovery Act (NRA)
    (C) Agricultural Adjustment Act
    (D) Works Progress Administration (WPA)

Questions 28-30 refer to the excerpt below:

"[In] this modern civilization economic royalists carved new dynasties. New kingdoms were built upon concentration of control over material things. Through new uses of corporations, banks and securities,... modern life was impressed into this royal service. There was no place among this royalty for our many thousands of small-businessmen and merchants who sought to make a worthy use of the American system of initiative and profit... It was natural... that the privileged princes of these new economic dynasties, thirsting for power, reached out for control over government itself. They created a new despotism and wrapped it in the robes of legal sanction.... And as a result the average man once more confronts the problem that faced the Minute Man.... There is a mysterious cycle in human events. To some generations much is given. Of other generations much is expected. This generation of Americans has a rendezvous with destiny...."

Franklin Delano Roosevelt, "Speech Before Democratic Convention," 1936

28. The "economic royalist" that FDR mentions is a reference to

(A) the control over the national economy demonstrated by the government bureaucracy
(B) the role of big business, financial institutions, and stock brokers in causing the Great Depression
(C) international cartels' influence on the U.S. economy
(D) entrepreneurs who provided innovative products for the consumer economy

29. To regulate the "economic royalist" and their dynasties FDR created a program of government agencies called

(A) the Great Society
(B) Populism
(C) the New Deal
(D) the New Frontier

30. The idea that this generation of Americans has a "rendezvous with destiny" was subsequently borne out by their

(A) ability to go through a number of changes in their lifetime
(B) large numbers which led them to be catered to
(C) superior use of technology to achieve success without the grind of hard work
(D) surviving the Great Depression, WWII, and creating post-war prosperity

For questions 31-33 refer to the chart below:

10 Largest Industrial Corporations (ranked in order of sales for 1957, in billions)			
Corporation	Sales in dollars	Assets in dollars	Net Profits
General Motors	11.0	7.5	.84
Standard Oil (N.J.)	7.8	8.7	.80
Ford Motor	5.8	3.3	.28
U. S. Steel	4.4	4.4	.42
General Electric	4.3	2.4	.25
Chrysler	3.6	1.5	.12
Socony Mobil Oil	3.0	3.1	.22
Gulf Oil	2.7	3.2	.35
Bethlehem Steel	2.6	2.3	.19
Swift	2.5	0.5	.14

31. A form of transportation that was almost eliminated by the preponderance of the automobile industry in the 1950s was the

    (A) bicycle
    (B) subway
    (C) railroad
    (D) streetcar

32. Which of the following is a true statement regarding information contained in the chart?

    (A) The oil companies were the only companies that had more money in their assets than in their sales
    (B) Swift had the lowest totals in all three categories of sales, assets, and net profits
    (C) Compared to sales the company with the largest profits was General Motors
    (D) General Motors and Standard Oil's net profits were greater than the net profits of the other eight companies combined

33. Which of the following gave a boost to the leading corporations?

    (A) Completion of the St. Lawrence Seaway
    (B) Heating up the Cold War
    (C) Interstate Highway Act
    (D) Statehood for Alaska and Hawaii

Questions 34-35 refer to the excerpt below:

"I am Joaquin,
lost in a world of confusion,
caught up in the whirl of a gringo society,
confused by the rules,
scorned by attitudes,
suppressed by manipulation,
and destroyed by modern society.
My fathers have lost the economic battle
and won the struggle of cultural survival.
And now!
I must choose between the paradox of victory of the spirit,
despite physical hunger,
or to exist in the grasp of American social neurosis, sterilization of the soul and a full stomach."

Rodolfo Gonzales, "I Am Joaquin," (excerpt), 1968

34. A major point made in the poem is the problems dealing with

    (A) minority rights
    (B) cultural identity
    (C) Mexican immigration
    (D) hunger in America

35. This poem became a major part of what Mexican American movement of the 1960s?

    (A) Bracero
    (B) Bario
    (C) Chicano
    (D) Hispanic

Questions 36-38 refer to the song below:

"Fighting soldiers from the sky
fearless men who jump and die
men who mean just what they say
the brave men of the Green Beret

Silver wings upon their chest
these are men Americas best
one hundred men will test today but
only three win the Green Beret

trained to live off natures land
trained in combat hand to hand
men who fight by night and day
courage take from the Green Beret

Silver wings upon their chest
these are men Americas best
one hundred men will test today
but only three win the Green Beret

Back at home a young wife waits
her Green Beret has met his fate
he has died for those oppressed
leaving her this last request

put silver wings on my sons chest
make him one of Americas best
he'll be a man they'll test one day
have him win the Green Beret"

Robin Moore and Barry Sadler, "Ballad of the Green Beret," 1966

36. This song was written to honor soldiers who served in which war?

    (A) World War II
    (B) Korean Police Action
    (C) Gulf War
    (D) Vietnam War

37. The particular head covering worn by the Green Berets was designated by which Democratic President to set them apart because of their special mission?

    (A) Harry S. Truman
    (B) Dwight D. Eisenhower
    (C) John F. Kennedy
    (D) Lyndon Baines Johnson

38. A primary reason why President Kennedy created the Special Forces of the Green Beret was his belief that the military

    (A) needed to be better trained to fight insurgencies in the 3rd world (developing countries) rather than Europe
    (B) would be able to emulate the toughness of the French Foreign Legion by emulating their headgear
    (C) should be ready to face the USSR and its communist bloc allies
    (D) had a mission to utilize advanced technology against its foes in the post-WWII world

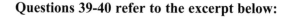

Questions 39-40 refer to the excerpt below:

"The Bush Doctrine declared America could launch first strikes to defend itself from terrorists and countries that supported terrorists in order to prevent possible attacks before they occurred. A corollary idea within the doctrine argued that promoting democratic governments—by force if necessary—was central to American security strategy. The doctrine was developed largely in response to American vulnerabilities exposed by the terrorist attacks of September 11, 2001, and provided the rationale for invading Afghanistan, where the local government provided a haven for those who launched the attack. The doctrine later provided the rationale for the invasion of Iraq (whose secular government was not aligned with Islamic terrorists) on the grounds that Iraq might have weapons of mass destruction (WMDs), which could threaten the U.S."

Anonymous, "Definition of Bush Doctrine," 2013

39. Those who formulated the Bush Doctrine were Republican strategists called the

    (A) brain trust
    (B) gang of eight
    (C) GOP Mafia
    (D) neocons

40. The U.S. justification for invading Iraq in 2003 that proved to be untrue is that Iraq

    (A) was refusing to pay its foreign debts
    (B) possessed nuclear, biological, or chemical armaments
    (C) had invaded and taken over Kuwait
    (D) was subject to an economic boycott by the United Nations

Questions 41-42 refer to the political cartoon below:

41. In the political cartoon above the caption reads, "The news reaches Bogota." What is this news?

    (A) Theodore Roosevelt sponsors "shovel ready" infrastructure projects to help the Columbian economy

    (B) The U.S. is invoking the Roosevelt Corollary to the Monroe Doctrine in Columbia because of the failure to pay its debts

    (C) Despite Columbian objections, the U.S. is building an isthmian Canal in their territory of Panama

    (D) TR offers to mediate the dispute between Colombia and Panama

42. The political cartoon above indicates the beginning of a process that will result in the

    (A) Spanish American War
    (B) Panama Canal
    (C) signing of the Gentlemen's Agreement
    (D) adoption of the Good Neighbor policy

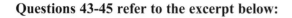

Questions 43-45 refer to the excerpt below:

"Expansionism is usually associated with crusading ideologies. In the case of Arab expansion it was Islam; in Spanish expansionism, Catholicism; in Napoleonic expansionism, revolutionary liberalism; Russian and Chinese expansionism, Marxian communism. The equivalent of these ideologies in the case of the United States was 'Manifest Destiny.' This was a mixture of republicanism, democracy, freedom of religion, Anglo-Saxonism, and a number of other ingredients. It was harnessed to the cause of continentalism in the 1840's, and, strangely enough, to insular expansionism a half century later.... Ideas are spread by propaganda, this has always been so, and, with improvement in the means of communication, has become increasingly so."

Frederick Merk, *Manifest Destiny and Mission in American History*, 1963

43. The crusading ideology of United States expansionism was

(A) providence
(B) revolutionary liberalism
(C) to control North America
(D) Anglo-Saxonism

44. The acquisition in the 1840s of Texas, Oregon and the Mexican Cession are all the products of

(A) the divine plan
(B) social mobility
(C) god's will
(D) manifest destiny

45. The term "insular expansion" a half century after the expansion of the 1840s is a reference to the

(A) acquisition of Pacific and Caribbean islands
(B) extension of the U.S. to its continental limits
(C) the reach of the progressive movement
(D) range of U.S. influence throughout the world

Questions 46-47 refer to the excerpt below:

"Keep ancient lands, your storied pomp!"
cries she With silent lips.
"Give me your tired, your poor,
Your huddled masses yearning to breathe free,
The wretched refuse of your teeming shore.
Send these, the homeless, tempest-tost to me,
I lift my lamp beside the golden door'!"

Emma Lazarus, The New Colossus, 1883

46. This poem expresses the idea of which concept in U.S. history?

(A) Know-Nothingism
(B) Xenophobia
(C) Land of opportunity
(D) Protectionism

47. The Lazarus poem is inscribed on "Liberty Enlightening the World," a statue symbolizing

(A) the concept of manifest destiny justifying territorial expansion
(B) the welcome given to foreign immigrants arriving from Europe
(C) the emancipation of Afro Americans from slavery
(D) the celebration of the capitalistic, free enterprise, economic system

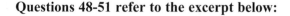
Questions 48-51 refer to the excerpt below:

"We stand for the segregation of the races and the racial integrity of each race; the constitutional right to choose one's associates; to accept private employment without governmental interference, and to earn one's living in any lawful way. We oppose the elimination of segregation, the repeal of miscegenation statutes, the control of private employment by Federal bureaucrats called for by the misnamed civil rights program. We favor home-rule, local self-government and a minimum interference with individual rights.... We oppose and condemn the action of the Democratic Convention in sponsoring a civil rights program calling for the elimination of segregation, social equality by Federal fiat, regulations of private employment practices, voting, and local law enforcement."

Platform of the States Rights Democratic Party, August 14, 1948

48. This political party split away from a major party in the election of 1948 primarily because it opposed the major party favoring

 (A) integration
 (B) ecumenicalism
 (C) cultural diversity
 (D) segregation

49. The common name given to this splinter 3rd party of 1948 is the

 (A) Populists
 (B) Progressives
 (C) Constitutional Union
 (D) Dixiecrats

50. Which of the following groups of states gave its electoral votes to the States Rights Democratic Party and their candidate Strom Thurmond in the presidential election of 1948?

 (A) Louisiana, Mississippi, Alabama, South Carolina
 (B) Maine, Vermont, Connecticut, Rhode Island
 (C) Ohio, Michigan, Indiana. Illinois
 (D) Washington, Oregon, California, Nevada

51. The formation this splinter party was caused by all of the following actions in 1948 EXCEPT

 (A) Truman's support of rights for labor unions
 (B) Issuing of Executive Order 9981 de-segregating the armed forces
 (C) The commitment to civil rights in the Democratic Party Platform of 1948
 (D) The endorsement of the "Jim Crow" system by the Democrats

For Questions 52-55 refer to the two excerpts below:

"...overgrown military establishments, which, under any form of government, are inauspicious to liberty, and which are to be regarded as particularly hostile to Republican Liberty."

George Washington, "George Washington's Farewell Address," 1796

"In the councils of government, we must guard against the acquisition of unwarranted influence, whether sought or unsought, by the military industrial complex. The potential for the disastrous rise of misplaced power exists and will persist."

Dwight D. Eisenhower, "Eisenhower's Farewell Address to the Nation," 1960

52. The advice given by George Washington was reiterated by Dwight D. Eisenhower in that they both warned against the inherent danger of which powerful U.S. institution?

(A) Supreme Court
(B) Congress
(C) Protestant Churches
(D) Armed forces

53. Which of the following is evidence that Washington and Eisenhowers predictions have taken hold in the 21st century

(A) The military and industry have successfully lobbied Congress and the President for bloated defense budgets
(B) With ever growing budget deficits the nation has practiced fiscal restraint to reign in spending
(C) The peace dividend from the end of the Cold War has scaled back the funds spent on arms and armaments
(D) In order to fight a war on terror conventional military spending has to be increased

54. Which of the following political groups would be most in favor of the advice given by the two Presidents?

(A) Populists
(B) SDS (Students for a Democratic Society)
(C) New Dealers
(D) John Birch Society

55. These two documents written 164 years apart suggest that there is a continuing danger to

(A) liberty by a powerful military establishment and business class
(B) religious thought by a powerful government bureaucracy
(C) persecuted groups who constitute minorities that need special class protection
(D) political democracy by those vested with unlimited finances

TEST THREE

Directions: Read each question carefully and write your responses in the corresponding boxes on the free-response answer sheet.

Use complete sentences; an outline or bulleted list alone is not acceptable. You may plan your answers in this exam booklet, but only your responses in the corresponding boxes on the free-response answer sheet will be scored.

"In truth, the office of President has been altered beyond recognition as Mr. Roosevelt exercised the power of a dictator. The Constitution has been given deep wounds by his procedures...[he] changed not only the direction, but the fabric of American society and had done much to alter the American spirit of self-reliance and faith. Millions of Americans did not like the results. They found themselves committed to attributes of a collectivist state, and certainly to the central point of view of a Socialist philosophy."

> Edgar E. Robinson, *The Roosevelt Leadership*, 1933-1945, 1955

".... The New Deal was socialism?" Cried Norman Thomas [Socialist candidate for President, 1924-1948].... "Emphatically not. Roosevelt had not carried out the Socialist platform—except on a stretcher...." Thomas ticked off New Deal reforms. "The banks? Roosevelt had put them on their feet and turned them back to the bankers. Holding company legislation? True Socialist would nationalize holding companies, not try to break them up. Social Security? The Roosevelt act was a weak imitation of a real program.... The AAA? Essentially a capitalist scheme to subsidize labor. TVA? State capitalism. CCC? Forced labor...." Thomas's answer was beyond dispute.... He [Roosevelt] wanted to reform capitalism, not destroy it...he was a conservative...."

> James MacGregor Burns, *Roosevelt: The Lion and the Fox*, 1956

1. Using the excerpts above, answer parts a, b, and c.

   (a) Briefly explain the basic interpretation made by Robinson.
   (b) Briefly explain the basic interpretation made by Burns.
   (c) Provide ONE piece of evidence from the era of Roosevelt and the New Deal that is not included in the passages, and explain how it supports the interpretation in either passage.

2. Using your knowledge of United States history, answer parts a and b.

    (a) United States historians have proposed events to mark the beginning of an American identity. Choose ONE of the events listed below, and briefly explain why your choice best represents the beginning of an American identity. Provide at least ONE piece of evidence to support your explanation.
- Publication of Thomas Paine's "Common Sense" in 1776
- Ratification of the Articles of Confederation in 1781
- Signing of the Treaty of Paris in 1783

    (b) Contrast your choice against ONE of the other options, demonstrating why that option is not as good as your choice.

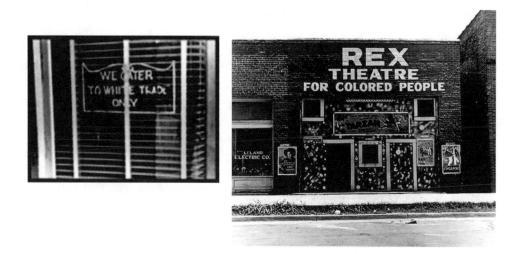

3. Use the image above and your knowledge of United States history to answer parts a, b, c, and d.

   (a) Explain how the photos describe the United States from Reconstruction until the 1960s
   (b) Explain how *Brown v. Board of Education of Topeka, Kansas* decision led to an end to the practices depicted in the two images
   (c) Provide at least one specific piece of evidence from 1954 to 1966 that led to the outlawing of the practice shown in the two images
   (d) Explain how the *Plessy v. Ferguson* decision of 1896 ratified the practice depicted in the photos

4. Using your knowledge of United States history, answer parts a, b, and c.

(a) Progressives attempted to cure the ills of the nation by bringing more democracy into American political life. Analyze and explain how ONE of the following made a contribution to bringing democratic changes into American political life?
   · initiative
   · referendum
   · recall
   · direct primary

(b) Provide at least one specific piece of evidence to support your point of view.

(c) Contrast your choice against one of the other options, demonstrating why that option is not as good as your choice.

TEST THREE

SECTION II, Part B

Total Time—1 hour, 35 minutes

Question 1 (Document-Based Question)
Suggested reading period: 15 minutes
Suggested writing period: 45 minutes

Directions: Question 1 is based on the accompanying documents. The documents have been edited for the purpose of this exercise. You are advised to spend 15 minutes reading and planning and 45 minutes writing your answer.

In your response you should do the following:

- State a relevant thesis that directly addresses all parts of the questions.
- Support the thesis or a relevant argument with evidence from all, or all but one, of the documents.
- Incorporate analysis of all, or all but one, of the documents into your argument.
- Focus your analysis of each document on at least one of the following: intended audience, purpose, historical context, and/or point of view.
- Support your argument with analysis of historical examples outside the documents.
- Connect historical phenomena relevant to your argument to broader events or processes.
- Synthesize the elements above into a persuasive essay.

---

1. Assess the validity of the statement that the U.S. in the 1920s had lost its idealism and was focusing most of its attention on middle-class materialism.

Document 1

> "Here was a new generation, a new generation dedicated more than the last to the fear of poverty and the worship of success, grown up to find all gods dead, all wars fought, all faiths to man shaken."
>
> F. Scott Fitzgerald, *This Side of Paradise*, 1920

Document 2

> "The earth is thirsting for the cup of good will, understanding is its fountain source. I would like to acclaim an era of good feeling …. [American] self-reliant, independent, and ever nobler, stronger, and richer…. Common welfare is the goal of our national endeavor…. We want an America of homes,… where mothers, freed from the necessity for long hours of toil beyond their own doors, may preside as befits the hearthstone of American citizenship. We want the cradle of American childhood rocked under conditions so wholesome and so hopeful that no blight may touch it in its development…. Where genius has made for great possibilities, justice and happiness must be reflected in a greater common welfare…. I accept my part with single-mindedness of purpose and humility of spirit, and implore the favor and guidance of God in His Heaven. With these I am unafraid, and confidently face the future. I have taken the solemn oath of office on that passage of Holy Writ wherein it is asked: "What doth the Lord require of thee but to do justly, and to love mercy, and to walk humbly with thy God?" This I plight to God and country."
>
> Warren G. Harding, "Inaugural Address," March 4, 1921

Document 3

Appliances Owned		
	1920	1930
Indoor Flush Toilets	20%	51%
Central Heating	1%	42%
Electric Home Lighting	35%	68%
Refrigerators	1%	8%
Washing Machines	8%	24%
Vacuum Cleaners	9%	30%
Radios	1%	40%
Automobiles	26%	60%

Document 4

"Just as he was an Elk, a Booster and a member of the Chamber of Commerce, just as the priests of the Presbyterian Church determined his every religious belief and the senators who controlled the Republican Party decided in little smoky rooms in Washington what he should think about disarmament, tariff, and Germany, so did the large national advertisers fix the surface of his life, fix what he believed to be his individuality. These standard advertised wares—toothpastes, socks, tires, cameras, and instantaneous hot water heaters—were his symbols and proofs of excellence; at first the signs, then the substitutes, for joy and passion and wisdom."

Sinclair Lewis, *Babbitt*, 1922

Document 5

"It was only a few years ago that the possibility of over saving occurred to anyone as an idea. Now you may hear it discussed as a problem of the utmost importance…. unless we demand and consume … there will be unemployment. We must be careful not to increase our power of production faster than we increase our power of consumption—careful, not to go on adding to our capital means at the expense of our own buying power…. The anxiety of modern business is how to stimulate effective wanting, how to induce people in the average to exert themselves more in order to be able to have and consume more. Installment selling has that motive. Give a man on credit a better house in a better neighborhood, give him credit on a garage and a motor car to put in it…. Will he give up these things, the house, neighborhood, car and all, because he cannot afford them? Not for that reason. Not for any reason whatever if he can help it. He will think of way to increase his income. This mean only that he will exert himself more to produce other things the equivalent of these, and that will be more than he ever produced before."

Garet Garrett, *The American Omen*, 1928

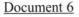

<u>Document 6</u>

"If one judges by appearances, I suppose I am a flapper. I am within the age limit. I wear bobbed hair, the badge of flapperhood. (And, oh, what a comfort it is!). I powder my nose. I wear fringed skirts and bright-colored sweaters, and scarfs, and waists with Peter Pan collars, and low-heeled "finale hopper" shoes. I adore to dance. I spend a large amount of time in automobiles. I attend hops, and proms, and ball-games, and crew races, and other affairs at men's colleges. ...I don't use rouge, or lipstick, or pluck my eyebrows. I don't smoke (I've tried it, and don't like it), or drink, or tell "peppy stories." I don't pet.... I want to beg all you parents, and grandparents, and friends, and teachers, and preachers--you who constitute the "older generation"--to overlook our shortcomings, at least for the present, and to appreciate our virtues. I wonder if it ever occurred to any of you that it required brains to become and remain a successful flapper? ... Attainment of flapperhood is a big and serious undertaking! "Brains?" you repeat, skeptically. "Then why aren't they used to better advantage?" That is exactly it! And do you know who is largely responsible for all this energy being spent in the wrong directions? You! You parents, and grandparents, and friends, and teachers, and preachers--all of you! "The war!" you cry. "It is the effect of the war!" And then you blame prohibition. Yes! Yet it is you who set the example there!.... You must help us. Give us confidence—not distrust. Give us practical aid and advice--not criticism. Praise us when praise is merited. Be patient and understanding when we make mistakes. We are the Younger Generation. The war tore away our spiritual foundations and challenged our faith. We are struggling to regain our equilibrium."

Ellen Welles Page, "A Flapper's Appeal to Parents," *Outlook*, December 6, 1922.

Document 7

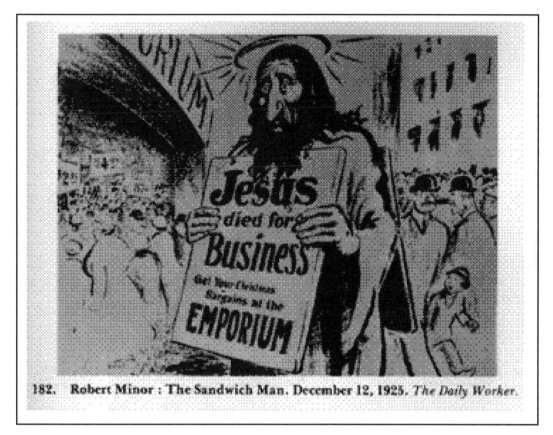

182.   Robert Minor : The Sandwich Man. December 12, 1925. *The Daily Worker.*

TEST THREE

Question 2 or Question 3 (Long Essay)
Suggested writing period: 35 minutes

Directions: Choose EITHER question 2 or question 3. You are advised to spend 35 minutes writing your answer..

In your response you should do the following.

- State a relevant thesis that directly addresses all parts of the question.
- Support your argument with evidence, using specific examples.
- Apply historical thinking skills as directed by the question.
- Synthesize the elements above into a persuasive essay.

2. Some historians have argued that the census report of 1890 announcing the closing of the frontier in the United States could lead to an end to the promotion of democracy and democratic institutions. Support, modify, or refute this contention using specific evidence.

3. Some historians have argued that the publication of Betty Friedan's *Feminine Mystique* in 1963 launched the modern women's movement that would lead to dramatic changes for women in society. Support, modify, or refute this contention using specific evidence.

TEST FOUR

SECTION I, Part A

Time—55 minutes

55 Questions

Directions: Each of the questions or incomplete statements below is followed by either four suggested answers or completions. Select the one that is best in each case and then fill in the appropriate letter in the correspoinding space on the answer sheet.

Questions 1-2 refer to the excerpt below:

"The Flatheads' affinity for the land and its creatures was spiritual. Indians did not conquer earth or bring it under their sway; they regarded earth as a mother, nurturing and sustaining them. The Flatheads thought of their homeland as a broad area they could never use for farming. In early times they did not think of farming the land at all. The unfortunate estimate that each Indian required eighty square miles of wild country to sustain his natural mode of living eventually convinced white men of the impracticality of the Indians concept of land. As earth was eternal, time was the present. Until the advent of white men among them the Flatheads recognized no historical continuity.... The Flathead past, except as expressed in their folk tales, ended with the recollections of the oldest men and women."

John Fahey, *The Flathead Indians*, 1974

1. The biggest conflict between the white men and the Flatheads and other Indians was over

(A) their opposing views of the after life
(B) different concepts of land use and ownership
(C) white men forcing the Indians into sedentary agriculture
(D) the use of history in understanding their culture

2. The natural mode of living for the Flathead before the arrival of the Europeans was

(A) hunting the buffalo on horseback
(B) settled farming of corn, beans, and squash
(C) nomadic wandering amongst the big trees of the Northwest
(D) hunting small game and gathering plants

597

Questions 3-4 refer to the excerpt below:

"Scots-Irish settlements east of the Appalachians marked,... a turning point in American life. They were a field, as the Tidewater was not, in which opposing values found full play, with those who chose the other set going on farther west. Those who stayed showed their belief in stability, viable institutions, community control of morality,... decency and order, the worth of tradition. Those who moved away preferred instead the values of individualism, adventure, independence of action, making their own way in the world, taking risks. The region of Scots-Irish settlement, simply by its geographical location, was both the last bastion of traditional standards and the threshold across which Americans could pass to more egalitarian ways of life,... each new move to the West strengthened the democratic impulse... The memory of Ulster... meant little or nothing to these constant pioneers. They were Americans."

James G. Leyburn, *The Scots-Irish*, 1962

3. The interpretation in the above passage tends to support which view of American history?

   (A) Cultural Diversity theory
   (B) Assimilationist doctrine
   (C) Beard's economic determinism
   (D) Turner thesis

4. Scots-Irish settlements east of the Appalachians marked a turning point in American life and provide evidence to support the Turner thesis because

   (A) these risk taking, adventuresome, egalitarian, individualists strengthened democracy as they moved west
   (B) their belief in stability, viable institutions, and community control would establish the value of tradition in America
   (C) prior to their arrival as immigrants there was little movement west by earlier pioneer groups
   (D) they clung to the Scots-Irish traditions of their native land of Ulster establishing this precedent for later immigrants

To Answer Questions 5-6 refer to the excerpt below:

"Let me... warn you in the most solemn manner against the ruinous effects of the spirit of party.... the alternate domination of one faction over another, sharpened by the spirits of revenge natural to party to dissension... is itself a frightful despotism."

George Washington, "Farewell Address," 1801

5. This statement reflects which of the following political developments?

    (A) Alexander Hamilton's reaction to the almost universal dislike of Jay's Treaty

    (B) James Madison's concern about the economic precedent of Funding and Assumption

    (C) Thomas Jefferson's opposition to the log-rolling deal that put the permanent capital in the South

    (D) George Washington's concerns about the growing division with the administration and the country over policy disagreements

6. The factions that the document is referring to are the

    (A) Federalists and Democratic-Republicans

    (B) Democrats and Whigs

    (C) Republicans and Democrats

    (D) Libertarians and No Nothings

For Questions 7-9 refer to the cartoon below:

7. In the 1823 political cartoon above President Monroe is

   (A) inviting European leaders to a summit meeting to discuss international relations
   (B) opening the door for full scale immigration to the U.S.
   (C) warning Europe that it had stay out of the affairs of North and South America
   (D) showing the world the might of the U.S. Navy against all other military forces

8. Which of the following is the best description of the three main parts of the Monroe Doctrine?

   (A) We hold these truths to be self evident, among them are life, liberty, & the pursuit of happiness....
   (B) Separate spheres of influence for the Americas and Europe, non-colonization, and non-intervention
   (C) ...form a more perfect union, establish justice, and secure the blessings of liberty for ourselves and our posterity...
   (D) Government of the people, by the people, and for the people shall not perish from the earth

9. The basic interpretation in the cartoon above is that President Monroe is

   (A) keeping his hands in his pockets to indicate to Europe the U.S. would not loan them more money
   (B) an indication that the western hemisphere is going to be dominated and controlled by a U.S. that is governed by the doctrine of manifest destiny
   (C) invoking the Declaration of Independence and Constitution in promoting harmony between the U.S. and Europe
   (D) represented by Uncle Sam, the body posture and placement of the hat says no to further European colonization of the Americas

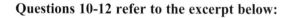

Questions 10-12 refer to the excerpt below:

"... [the U.S. has] equality of condition among the people.... it gives a peculiar direction to public opinion and a peculiar tenor to the laws; it imparts new maxims to the governing authorities and peculiar habits to the governed. I soon perceived that the influence of this fact extends far beyond the political character and the laws of the country, and that it has no less effect on civil society than on the government; it creates opinions, gives birth to new sentiments, founds novel customs, and modifies whatever it does not produce. The more I advanced in the study of American society, the more I perceived that this equality of condition is the fundamental fact from which all others seem to be derived and the central point at which all my observations constantly terminated. I then turned my thoughts to our own hemisphere,... I observed that equality of condition, though it has not there reached the extreme limit which it seems to have attained in the United States, is constantly approaching it; and that the democracy which governs the American communities appears to be rapidly rising into power in Europe."

Alexis de Tocqueville, *Democracy in America*, 1835

10. According to de Tocqueville's observations an idea about the United States that he was concerned about was

(A) economic liberty
(B) adherence to the Constitution
(C) religious diversity of the people
(D) tyranny of the majority

11. De Tocquville concluded that the democracy governing the American communities

(A) would be soon replaced by a more republic form of government
(B) was also present in the other countries of the western hemisphere
(C) was quickly becoming a force in Europe
(D) was regarded by the international community as a blueprint for the future

12. The ideas expressed by de Tocqueville most directly reflect which of the following continuities in United States History?

(A) Patrick Henry—"Give me liberty or give me death."
(B) John Winthrop—"...we shall be a city upon a hill. The eyes of all people are upon us..."
(C) Declaration of Independence—"...that all men are created equal..."
(D) Preamble to the Constitution—"...establish Justice, insure domestic Tranquility, provide for the common defense, promote the general Welfare, and secure the Blessings of Liberty

Questions 13-15 refer to the excerpt below:

"When, in the course of human events, it becomes necessary for one portion of the family of man to assume among the people of the earth a position different from that which they have hitherto occupied, but one to which the laws of nature and of nature's God entitle them,... We hold these truths to be self-evident: that all men and women are created equal; that they are endowed by their Creator with certain inalienable rights; that among these are life, liberty, and the pursuit of happiness; that to secure these rights governments are instituted, deriving their just powers from the consent of the governed. Whenever any form of government becomes destructive of these ends, it is the right of those who suffer from it to refuse allegiance to it, and to insist upon the institution of a new government, laying its foundation on such principles, and organizing its powers in such form, as to them shall seem most likely to effect their safety and happiness...."

Elizabeth Cady Stanton and Lucretia Mott, "Declaration of Sentiments," 1848

13. The document above is an adaptation of which historic document?

   (A) Declaration of Independence
   (B) Articles of Confederation
   (C) Constitution
   (D) Bill of Rights

14. Women pursuing the goals of the "Declaration of Sentiments" were often involved in which other movement during the antebellum era?

   (A) Civil Rights
   (B) Immigration
   (C) Labor Unions
   (D) Abolitionism

15. An attempt to implement the Declaration of Sentiments in the 1970s that failed was the

   (A) Civil Rights Act
   (B) Equal Rights Amendment
   (C) Dayton Accords
   (D) Declaration of Rights

Questions 16 & 17 refer to the chart below:

Number of Slaveholders in the Slaves States that did not leave the Union (1860)					
State	1-9 slaves	10-20 slaves	20-50 slaves	50-100 slaves	100-500
Delaware	562	25			
Kentucky	31,819	5,271	1,485	63	7
Maryland	11,203	1,718	747	99	16
Missouri	21,380	2,400	502	34	4

16. From viewing the chart above which of the following conclusions is most valid?

   (A) A majority of the slaveholders had plantations with at least 10 slaves
   (B) There were nearly as many slaveholders in Kentucky as the other three states combined
   (C) Large plantations of 100 to 500 slaves existed in the four border states that did not leave the union
   (D) A majority of the slaveholders only owned one slave

17. All of the following statements are true about the four slaveholding states that did not leave the Union in 1861 EXCEPT

   (A) the total number of slaveholders in all of Delaware was less than the total number of slaveholders who had at least 20 slaves in the other three states.
   (B) although Maryland had slightly more half the number of slaveholders than Missouri did, it had 60% more slaveholders with more than 20 slaves than Missouri did.
   (C) of the total number of slaveholders in the states that did not leave the Union, Delaware had less than 1%.
   (D) it was most important to the Union cause to keep Maryland in the Union because it because it had the most plantations with at least 50 slaves

Question 18-21 refer to the excerpt below:

"All freedmen, free Negroes, mulattos... found... with no lawful employment... shall be deemed vagrants... [and] shall be fined in the sum not exceeding fifty dollars... and be imprisoned at the discretion of the court.... [It is] the duty of the country police... to levy to levy a poll of capitation tax on each and every freedman, free Negro, or mulatto... not to exceed the sum of one dollar annually,... which tax...shall... constitute a fund to be called the Freedmen's Pauper Fund which shall be applied... for the maintenance of the poor of the freedmen, free Negroes, and mulattoes.... If any freedman, free Negro, or mulatto shall fail or refuse to pay any tax levied... it shall be prima facie evidence of vagrancy, and it shall be the duty of the sheriff to arrest such freedmen, free Negro, or mulatto or such person refusing or neglecting to pay such tax, and proceed at once to hire for the shortest time such delinquent taxpayer to any one who will pay the said tax...."

Laws of Mississippi, "A Black Code," 1865

18. A negative implication of this law regarding capitation or poll taxes is that

(A) it made the citizens more responsible
(B) people were likely to voluntarily perform their civic duty of voting
(C) like any tax this one tended to depress the activity it was intended to encourage
(D) equality before the law was encouraged as everyone was treated equally

19. If freedmen, free Negroes, or mulattos were unemployed they could

(A) apply for welfare from the federal government
(B) be deported back to Africa
(C) turn themselves into the state to get public assistance
(D) be treated like second class citizens just above a condition of slavery

20. Not paying a tax could result in someone else paying and the freedmen, free Negro, or mulatto would be forced to work for whomever paid it in a form of bondage similar to

(A) the peculiar institution
(B) convict labor
(C) involuntary servitude
(D) peonage

21. The 24th Amendment to the Constitution in 1964 declared the poll tax illegal in

(A) state elections
(B) local elections
(C) federal elections
(D) all elections

Questions 22-25 refer to the excerpt below:

"The man of wealth must hold his fortune "in trust" for the community and use it for philanthropic and charitable purposes. The problem of our age is the proper administration of wealth, that the ties of brotherhood may still bind together the rich and poor in harmonious relationship... the duty of the man of wealth;... to set an example of modest...living...to consider all surplus revenues which come to him simply as trust funds, which he is called upon to administer... in the manner which, in his judgment, is best calculated to produce the most beneficial results for the community—the man of wealth thus becomes the mere trustee and agent for his poorer brethren, bringing to their service his superior wisdom, experience, and ability to administer, doing for them better than they would or could do for themselves."

Andrew Carnegie, "The Gospel of Wealth," 1889

22. The advice given in the passage above was intended to

   (A) describe the responsibility of philanthropy by the new upper class of the self- made rich millionaires
   (B) make the poor feel better knowing that excess money being made would be wisely spent on their communities
   (C) advise the poor that the proper way to conduct their lives is through modest living
   (D) to turn the surplus revenue over to the government to have them administer it better than if it was administered by private individuals

23. The ideas in the Gospel of Wealth could be used to justify what kind of taxes?

   (A) Inheritance
   (B) Sales
   (C) Income
   (D) Property

24. As a result of the Gospel of Wealth the millionaires created which institutions to distribute their excess wealth?

   (A) Private Social Clubs
   (B) Lobbying Groups
   (C) Philanthropic Foundation
   (D) Political Action Committees

25. The statement "doing for them better than they would or could do for themselves" seems to be contrary to which American fundamental belief?

   (A) Liberty
   (B) Democracy
   (C) Pursuit of Happiness
   (D) Republicanism

Questions 26-27 refer to the speech below:

"I am tired of fighting.
Our chiefs are killed.
Looking Glass is dead.
Toohulhulsote is dead.
The old men are all dead.
It is the young men who say no and yes.
He who led the young men is dead.
It is cold and we have no blankets.
The little children are freezing to death.
My people, some of them, Have run away to the hills And have no blankets, no food.
No one knows where they are. Perhaps they are freezing to death.
I want to have time to look for my children And see how many of them I can find.
Maybe I shall find them among the dead.
Hear me, my chiefs, I am tired.
My heart is sad and sick.
From where the sun now stands I will fight no more forever."

Chief Joseph of the Nez Perce, "I Will Fight No More Forever," 1877

26. Chief Joseph and the Nez Perce were trying to get to Canada in order to escape from what United States government imposed system?

    (A) Relocation
    (B) Concentration
    (C) Reservation
    (D) Stewardship

27. As a result of what happened to Chief Joseph and other Indians forced from their ancestral homelands, Congress passed the Dawes Severalty Act to

    (A) grant individual ownership of land to make them yeoman farmers
    (B) set up a system of connected villages so Indians could stay in touch with each other
    (C) establish the communal ownership of property under the tribal system
    (D) allow the individual Indian nations to govern themselves according to the treaty system

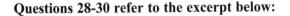

Questions 28-30 refer to the excerpt below:

"….We demand the free and unrestricted coinage of silver and gold at the present rate of 16 to 1…. We demand a graduated income tax…. The Government should own and operate the railroads in the interests of the people…. The telegraph being a necessity for the transmission of news, should be owned by the Government in the interest of the people…. We favor a system of direct legislation, through the initiative and referendum…. We demand the election of President, Vice-President, and United States Senators by a direct vote of the people…."

Political platform adopted in St. Louis, July 14, 1896

28. This political platform represents the stand of which political party or group?

(A) Populist or People's Party
(B) Civil Rights Party
(C) Knights of Columbus
(D) Bull Moose Party

29. Which demand in the political platform above was enacted into law by the 17th Amendment?

(A) Government ownership of the telegraph
(B) Free and unrestricted coinage of silver and gold at the rate of 16-1
(C) U. S. Senators elected by direct vote of the people
(D) Railroads owned and operated by the Government in the interest of the people

30. As a continuity in American history, much of what the political platform of 1896 asked for subsequently came into being as a result of what two later movements?

(A) Social Darwinism and Gospel of Wealth
(B) Progressivism and New Deal
(C) Social Gospel and Settlement Houses
(D) New Frontier and Great Society

Questions 31-32 refer to the excerpt below:

"... thousands of ewes were killed by the sheep raisers because they did not bring enough in the market to pay the freight on them. And while Oregon sheep raisers fed mutton to the buzzards, I saw men picking for meat scraps in the garbage cans in the cities of New York and Chicago... one man... had to kill 3,000 sheep this fall... because it cost $1.10 to ship a sheep, and then he could not afford to feed the sheep, so he just cut their throats and threw them down the canyon.... In Oklahoma, Texas, Arkansas, and Louisiana I saw untold bales of cotton rotting in the fields because the cotton picker could not keep body and soul together on 35 cents paid for picking 100 pounds.... The farmers are being pauperized... as a result of this appalling overproduction on one side and staggering under consumption on the other side."

Oscar Ameringer, "U.S. Congress, House, Committee on Labor," 1932

31. The idea of killing the sheep because they would not bring a high enough price to make it worth while to ship them was emulated by which New Deal alphabet agency?

(A) NRA
(B) AAA
(C) WPA
(D) TVA

32. The economic condition that is being described in the passage above is

(A) too much production leading to low prices
(B) too much consumption leading to high prices
(C) both too little consumption and too much production
(D) an equilibrium between production and consumption leading to stable prices

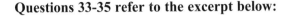

Questions 33-35 refer to the excerpt below:

"In the coming years, our program for peace and freedom will emphasize four major courses of action. First, we will continue to give unfaltering support to the United Nations... Second, we will continue our programs for world economic recovery. This means, first of all, that we must keep our full weight behind the European recovery program.... In addition, we must carry out our plans for reducing the barriers to world trade and increasing its volume.... Third, we will strengthen freedom-loving nations against the dangers of aggression. We are now working out with a number of countries a joint agreement designed to strengthen the security of the North Atlantic area.... Fourth, we must embark on a bold new program for making the benefits of our scientific advances and industrial progress available for... growth in underdeveloped areas."

Harry S. Truman, "Inaugural Address," January, 1949

33. The ideas expressed by Truman in his "Inaugural Address" were primarily

   (A) an attempt to return to the isolationism of the pre-war era
   (B) an economic extension of the containment policy
   (C) designed to support the independence movements in the countries of Africa and Asia
   (D) to help the refuges of Wold War II return to their home countries

34. The European recovery program that Truman is alluding to is commonly known as the

   (A) General Agreement on Trade and Tariffs (GATT)
   (B) North Atlantic Treaty Organization (NATO)
   (C) World Trade Organization (WTO)
   (D) Marshall Plan

35. Later, under President Kennedy, Truman's 4th Point became which program?

   (A) Great Society
   (B) New Federalism
   (C) Alliance for Progress
   (D) North American Free Trade Agreement

Questions 36-38 refer to the excerpt below:

"... Title IX [1972] is a comprehensive federal law that prohibits discrimination on the basis of sex in any federally funded education program or activity. The principal objective of Title IX is to avoid the use of federal money to support sex discrimination in education programs and to provide individual citizens effective protection against those practices. Title IX applies, with a few specific exceptions, to all aspects of federally funded education programs or activities. In addition to traditional educational institutions such as colleges, universities, and elementary and secondary schools, Title IX also applies to any education or training program operated by a recipient of federal financial assistance. The Department of Education has issued regulations on the requirements of Title IX, 34 C.F.R. § 106.*1et seq*. The Title IX common rule published on August 30, 2000 covers education program providers/recipients that are funded by other federal agencies."

U.S. Department of Justice, Civil Rights Division, 2000

36. Title IX's impact on education is most profound in which area?

    (A) Sports
    (B) Academics
    (C) Music
    (D) Research

37. Title IX had a major influence on which of the following?

    (A) Passage of the Equal Rights Amendment
    (B) Expanding the right to vote for all women
    (C) Affirmative action programs
    (D) Educational access for women

38. Title IX is a continuation of the movement for women's rights that begin with the

    (A) Declaration of Independence
    (B) Articles of Confederation
    (C) Declaration of Sentiments
    (D) Bill of Rights

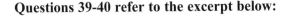

Questions 39-40 refer to the excerpt below:

"Ideas matter, [to] President Obama. He is not a rigid ideologue and is capable of flexible maneuvering. But his interpretation of history, his attitude toward sovereignty, and his confidence in multilateral institutions have shaped his views of American power and of American leadership in ways that distinguish him from previous presidents.... he cares more about restraining America than about accomplishing any particular result in Libya. He views Libya and the whole Arab Spring as relatively small distractions from his broader strategy for breaking with the history of U.S. foreign policy as it developed in the last century. The critics who accuse Obama of being adrift in foreign policy are mistaken. He has clear ideas of where he wants to go. The problem for him is that, if his strategy is set forth plainly, most Americans will not want to follow him."

Douglas J. Feith and Seth Cropsey, "The Obama Doctrine Defined," 2011

39. According to the passage above Obama differs from his predecessors as President as he is not a (an)

(A) cold warrior
(B) pragmatist
(C) realist
(D) ideologue

40. Obama's views of American power have been shaped by all of the following EXCEPT

(A) the brinkmanship policy of John Foster Dulles
(B) his interpretation of history
(C) a confidence in multilateral institutions
(D) an attitude toward sovereignty

For Questions 41-43 refer to the excerpt below:

"... in your time we have the opportunity to move not only toward the rich society and the powerful society, but upward to the Great Society. The Great Society rests on abundance and liberty for all. It demands an end to poverty and racial injustice,... The Great Society is a place where every child can find knowledge to enrich his mind and to enlarge his talents. It is a place where leisure is a welcome chance to build and reflect, not a feared cause of boredom and restlessness.... It is a place where man can renew contact with nature. It is a place which honors creation for its own sake and for what it adds to the understanding of the race. It is a place where men are more concerned with the quality of their goals than the quantity of their goods. But most of all, the Great Society is not a safe harbor, a resting place, a final objective, a finished work. It is a challenge constantly renewed, beckoning us toward a destiny...."

Lyndon Johnson, "Great Society Speech," May 24, 1964

41. Which of the following lines from Johnson's "Great Society" speech delivered at the University of Michigan could have influenced the counterculture's mantra of "do your own thing?"

   (A) It is a place which honors creation for its own sake
   (B) In your time we have the opportunity to move... upward to a Great Society
   (C) The Great Society rests on abundance and liberty for all
   (D) It is a challenge constantly renewed, beckoning us toward a destiny

42. The phrase Great Society is closely associated with which 1960s ideology?

   (A) The moral majority
   (B) Liberal idealism
   (C) Neo-conservatism
   (D) Middle of the road moderation

43. The part of the Great Society ideal that has been almost a complete failure is which of the following?

   (A) War on Poverty
   (B) Civil Rights
   (C) Vietnam War
   (D) Educational Policy

Questions 44-45 refer to the excerpt below:

"Three distinct stages of migration marked the 19th century. The first... began in the 1830's and continued until 1860, reaching its crest in... 1847-1854. To this exodus the adjective "Celtic" may properly be applied. The immigrants came from Ireland, the Highlands of Scotland and the mountains of Wales— regions where the language and blood were predominately Celtic.... Though many came also from the upper Rhine Valley of Germany... these newcomers may in a sense also be regarded as Celtic, for the first peoples to cultivate their hills and valleys had been Celts and, when the conquering German tribes occupied the villages and fields, they took over the divisions and the customs which in primitive times formed such an important feature of the agricultural routine."

Marcus Lee Hansen, *Atlantic Migration 1607-1860*, 1940

44. Of these Celtic people, the only ones who could not be considered to be WASPS (White, Anglo-Saxon, Protestant) were the

(A) Irish
(B) Scots
(C) Welsh
(D) Rhinelanders

45. This Celtic stage of migration from the 1830s to1860 can be contrasted with the 3rd stage of immigrants that lasted from 1890 to 1915 and consisted of immigrants primarily from

(A) China and Japan
(B) East Asia
(C) Northern and Western Europe
(D) Southern and Eastern Europe

Questions 46-48 refer to the documents below:

- Section 1. Equality of rights under the law shall not be denied or abridged by the United States or by any state on account of sex.
- Section 2. The Congress shall have the power to enforce, by appropriate legislation, the provisions of this article.
- Section 3. This amendment shall take effect two years after the date of ratification.

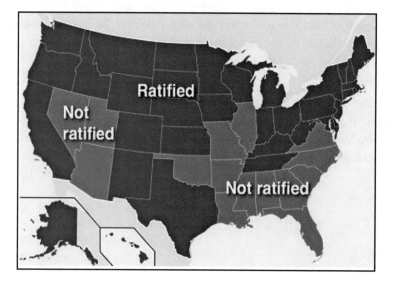

46. This proposed Constitutional Amendment, first proposed by Alice Paul in 1923 is commonly called the

    (A) Equal Rights Amendment
    (B) Equality Before the Law Amendment
    (C) State's Rights Amendment
    (D) Gender Neutral Amendment

47. When it was introduced this Constitutional Amendment was considered the culmination of a long campaign started in 1848 that had resulted in the success of the passage of which Amendment in 1920?

    (A) 16th
    (B) 17th
    (C) 18th
    (D) 19th

48. The Amendment failed to be ratified by the necessary 38 states before its time ran out in which decade?

    (A) 1950s
    (B) 1960s
    (C) 1970s
    (D) 1980s

49. The vast majority of the states who failed to ratify the ERA had which of the following in common historically?

    (A) Sates of the Northwest Ordinance
    (B) States of the Confederacy
    (C) States who had Progressive Legislatures
    (D) States located in New England

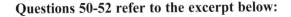

Questions 50-52 refer to the excerpt below:

"I have... signed a request to the Congress for $500 million as a first step in fulfilling the Act of Bogota.... The money will be used to combat illiteracy, improve the productivity and use of their land, wipe out disease, attack archaic tax and land-tenure structures, provide educational opportunities, and offer a broad range of projects designed to make the benefits of increasing abundance available to all.... political freedom must be accompanied by social change. For unless necessary social reforms, including land and tax reform, are freely made,... unless the great mass of Americans share in increasing prosperity, then our alliance, our revolution, our dream, and our freedom will fail. But we call for social change by free men-change in the spirit of Washington and Jefferson, of Bolivar and San Martin and Marti.... Our motto is what it has always been-progress yes, tyranny no—*Progreso si, tirania no!*"

John F. Kennedy, "Alliance for Progress," 1961

50. This John F. Kennedy program was intended to help which region of the world?

(A) Latin America
(B) European Union
(C) Iberian Peninsula
(D) Northern Mexico

51. In some respects this U.S. assistance could be considered a continuation of which earlier program of economic aid in a different region?

(A) Truman Doctrine
(B) Marshall Plan
(C) 14 Points
(D) Great Society

52. The Alliance for Progress was a government program launched to change South America

(A) politically, economically, and socially
(B) diplomatically, militarily, bureaucratically
(C) intellectually, culturally, educationally
(D) scientifically, philosophically, psychologically

Questions 53-55 refer to the song below:

"Come to my door, baby,
Face is clean and shining black as night.
My mother went to answer you know
That you looked so fine.
Now I could understand your tears and your shame,
She called you "boy" instead of your name.
When she wouldn't let you inside,
When she turned and said "But honey, he's not our kind."
She says I can't see you any more, baby,
Can't see you anymore.
Walk me down to school, baby,
Everybody's acting deaf and dumb.
Until they turn and say, "Why don't you stick to your own kind."
My teachers all laugh, the smirking stares,
Cutting deep down in our affairs.
Preachers of equality,
Think they believe it, then why won't they just let us be?
They say I can't see you anymore baby,
Can't see you anymore.
One of these days I'm gonna stop my listening
Gonna raise my head up high.
One of these days I'm gonna raise up my glistening wings and fly.
But that day will have to wait for a while.
Baby I'm only society's child.
When we're older things may change,
But for now this is the way, they must remain.
I say I can't see you anymore baby,
Can't see you anymore. No, I don't want to see you anymore, baby."

Janis Ian, "Society's Child," 1965

53. The theme of this protest song revolved around the issue of

(A) Jim Crowism
(B) anti-integration laws
(C) interracial romance
(D) legal segregation

54. The ideas and sentiments expressed in this song indicate that which movement that had great impetus from its primarily 1950s origins still had a long way to go to accomplish its goals?

(A) Civil rights
(B) Progressivism
(C) Anti-nuclear
(D) Counterculture

55. Songwriter Janis Ian was 13 when she wrote this song that had all of the following elements in it EXCEPT

(A) disdain for her mother who called her date the pejorative term "boy"
(B) her fellow students chastisement for not sticking with "her own kind"
(C) hypocrisy of the laughing and smirking teachers who preach equality but don't practice it
(D) criticism of state laws that forbid race mixing

TEST FOUR

SECTION I, Part B

Time—45 minutes

4 Questions (Short Answer)

Directions: Read each question carefully and write your responses in the corresponding boxes on the free-response answer sheet.

Use complete sentences; an outline or bulleted list alone is not acceptable. You may plan your answers in this exam booklet, but only your responses in the corresponding boxes on the free-response answer sheet will be scored.

"... southern and eastern Europeans are of a very different type from the north European who preceded them. Illiterate, docile, lacking in self-reliance and initiative and not possessing the Anglo-Teutonic conceptions of law, order and government, their coming has served to dilute tremendously our national stock and to corrupt our civic life.... Our task is to break up their groups of settlements, to assimilate and amalgamate these peoples as a part of our American race, and to implant in these children, so far as can be done, the Anglo-Saxon conception of righteousness, law and order and popular government, and to awaken in them a reverence for our democratic institutions...."

E. P. Cubberly, *Changing Conceptions of Education*, 1909

"The idea that the predominate stock of the inhabitants of the United States is Anglo-Saxon is a myth. The composite American is a multi-form hyphenate: Scotch-Irish-English-German-Polish-Jewish-Italian-Russian, etc.... To conceive of America as belonging exclusively to one race, because priority of habitation has given it a divine right to possession of the land, is a notion contrary to democracy.... To say, however, that American institutions ...have...all been fixed by the fathers...and that the newcomers, the majority, must mould themselves into these forms, is itself contradictory to the principle of freedom upon which these forms are built."

Isaac B. Berkson, *Theories of Americanization*, 1920

1. Using the excerpts above, answer parts a, b, and c.

    (a) Briefly explain the basic interpretation of Cubberly.
    (b) Briefly explain the basic interpretation of Berkson.
    (c) Provide ONE piece of evidence from the era of the New Immigrants (1890-1914) that is not included in the passages, and explain how it supports the interpretation in either passage.

617

2. Using your knowledge of United States history, answer parts a and b.

(a) United States historians have proposed events to mark the beginning of an American indentity. Choose ONE of the events listed below, and explain why your choice best represents the beginning of an American identity. Provide at least ONE piece of evidence to support your explanation.
   · Washington's Neutrality Proclamation
   · Battle of New Orleans in 1815
   · Monroe Doctrine

(b) Contrast your choice against ONE of the other options, demonstrating why that option is not as good as your choice.

3. Use the image above and your knowledge of United States history to answer parts a, b, and c.

   (a) Explain the point of view reflected in the image above of one of the following:
- Business
- Labor
- Landlords

   (b) Explain how ONE element of the image expresses the point of view you identified in part a

   (c) Explain how the point of view you identified in part a helped to shape ONE specific United States government action between 1880 and 1914

4. Using your knowledge of United States history, answer parts a, b, and c.

(a) The United States involvement in the Vietnam War from 1959 to 1975 revolved around a number of different controversial issues. Analyze and explain how ONE of the following issues played a role in the U.S. involvement in the Vietnam War.
· Cold War
· Domino Theory
· International Law
· Self Determination

(b) Provide at least one specific piece of evidence to support your point of view.

(c) Contrast your choice against one of the other options, demonstrating why that option is not as good as your choice.

TEST FOUR

SECTION II, Part B

Total Time—1 hour, 35 minutes

Question 1 (Document-Based Question)
Suggested reading period: 15 minutes
Suggested writing period: 45 minutes

Directions: Question 1 is based on the accompanying documents. The documents have been edited for the purpose of this exercise. You are advised to spend 15 minutes reading and planning and 45 minutes writing your answer.

In your response you should do the following:

- State a relevant thesis that directly addresses all parts of the questions.
- Support the thesis or a relevant argument with evidence from all, or all but one, of the documents.
- Incorporate analysis of all, or all but one, of the documents into your argument.
- Focus your analysis of each document on at least one of the following: intended audience, purpose, historical context, and/or point of view.
- Support your argument with analysis of historical examples outside the documents.
- Connect historical phenomena relevant to your argument to broader events or processes.
- Synthesize the elements above into a persuasive essay.

---

1. Analyze the origins, events, and ideology of the beginning years (1946-1962) of the Cold War that dominated American foreign policy from 1946 to 1989.

Document 1

Winston Churchill's "Sinews of Peace," March 5, 1946

"From Stettin in the Baltic to Trieste in the Adriatic, an iron curtain has descended across the Continent. Behind that line lie all of the capitals of the ancient states of central and eastern Europe: Warsaw, Berlin, Prague, Vienna, Budapest, Belgrade, Bucharest and Sofia, all these famous cities and the populations around them lie in what I might call the Soviet sphere, and all are subject, in one form or another, not only to Soviet influence, but to very high, and in some cases, increasing measure of control from Moscow."

Document 2

George F. Kennan, "The Sources of Soviet Conduct," 1947

It must continue to regard the Soviet Union as a rival, not a partner, in the political arena. It must continue to expect that Soviet policies will reflect no abstract love of peace and stability, no real faith in the possibility of a permanent happy coexistence of the Socialist and capitalist worlds... as opposed to the western world in general, [USSR] is still by far the weaker party... This would of itself warrant the United States entering with reasonable confidence upon a policy of firm containment, designed to confront the Russians with unalterable counter-force at every point where they show signs of encroaching....

It would be an exaggeration to say that American behavior unassisted and alone could exercise a power of life and death over the Communist movement and bring about the early fall of Soviet power in Russia. But the United States has it in its power to increase enormously the strains under which Soviet policy must operate, to force upon the Kremlin a far greater degree of moderation and circumspection than it has had to observe in recent years, and in this way to promote tendencies which must eventually find their outlet in either the breakup or the gradual mellowing of Soviet power... the Kremlin – can [not] face frustration indefinitely... The issue of Soviet-American relations is in essence a test of the overall worth of the United States as a nation among nations....

.... the thoughtful observer of Russian-American relations will find no cause for complaint in the Kremlin's challenge to American society. He will rather experience a certain gratitude to a Providence which, by providing the American people with this implacable challenge, has made their entire security as a nation dependent on their pulling themselves together and accepting the responsibilities of moral and political leadership that history plainly intended them to bear.

Document 3

North Atlantic Treaty Organization (NATO) April 4, 1949

"The parties to this Treaty...are determined to safeguard the freedom, common heritage and civilization of their people, founded on the principle of democracy, individual liberty and the rule of law....

Article 3....the Parties, separately and jointly...will maintain and develop their individual and collective capacity to resist armed attack....

Article 5. The Parties agree that an armed attack against one or more of them in Europe or North America shall be considered an attack against them all; and...if such an armed attack occurs, each of them will assist the Party or Parties so attacked...."

Document 4

Glen E. Curtis, ed. *The Warsaw Pact*, 1992

"In May 1955, the Soviet Union institutionalized its East European alliance system when it gathered together representatives from Albania, Bulgaria, Czechoslovakia, Hungary, Poland, and Romania in Warsaw to sign the multilateral Treaty on Friendship, Cooperation, and Mutual Assistance.... Soviets claimed that the Warsaw Pact was a direct response to the inclusion of the Federal Republic of Germany (West Germany) in NATO in 1955.

The formation of a legally defined, multilateral alliance organization also reinforced the Soviet Union's claim to power status as the leader of the world socialist system, enhanced its prestige, and legitimized its presence and influence in Eastern Europe.... At the same time, the Soviet Union also proposed to the Western powers a general treaty on collective security in Europe and the dismantling of existing military blocs (meaning NATO). ... The Soviet Union also used West Germany's membership in NATO for propaganda purposes. The Soviets evoked the threat of a re-armed, "revanchist" West Germany seeking to reverse its defeat in World War II to remind the East European countries of their debt to the Soviet Union for their liberation, their need for Soviet protection against a recent enemy, and their corresponding duty to respect Soviet security interests and join the Warsaw Pact.

As a formal organization, the Warsaw Pact provided the Soviet Union an official counterweight to NATO in East-West diplomacy. The Warsaw Pact gave the Soviet Union an equal status with the United States as the leader of an alliance of ostensibly independent nations supporting its foreign policy initiatives in the international arena."

Document 5

Nikita Khrushchev, "Khrushchev Interprets the Cold War," in Allan O. Kownslar and Donald B. Frizzle, eds., *Discovering American History*, 1967

"Soon after the Second World War ended, the influence of reactionary and militarist groups began to be increasingly evident in the policy of the United States of America, Britain, and France. Their desire to force their will on other countries by economic and political pressure, [by] threats and military provocation prevailed. This..."position of strength" policy...reflects the aspiration of the most aggressive sections of present day imperialism to win world supremacy, to suppress the working class and the democratic and national-liberation movements; it reflects their plans for military adventures against the Socialist camp."

Document 6

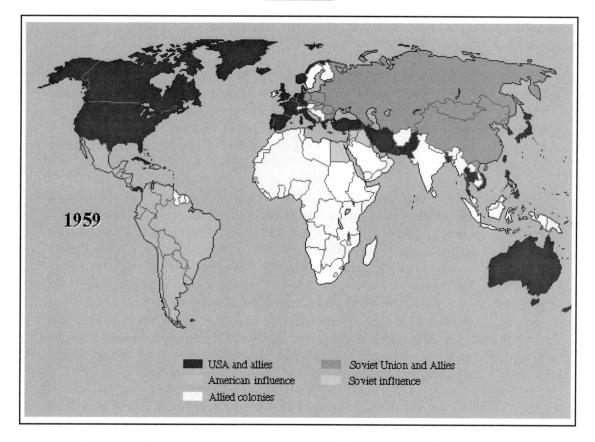

Document 7

John Lewis Gaddis, *The Cold War: A New History*, 2005

"Victory in World War II brought no sense of security, therefore, to the victors. Neither the United States, nor Great Britain, nor the Soviet Union, could regard the lives and treasure they had expended in defeating Germany and Japan as having made them safer: members of the Grand Alliance were now Cold War adversaries. Interests had turned out not to be compatible; ideologies remained at least as polarizing as they had been before the war; fears of surprise attack continued to haunt military establishments in Washington, London, and Moscow. A contest that began over the fate of postwar Europe had now spread to Asia. Stalin's dictatorship remained as harsh—and as reliant on purges—as it had always been, but with the onset of McCarthyism in the United States...it was not at clear that the western democracies themselves could retain the tolerance for dissent and the respect for civil liberties that distinguished them from the dictators, whether of the fascist or the communist variety."

TEST FOUR

Question 2 or Question 3 (Long Essay)
Suggested writing period: 35 minutes

Directions: Choose EITHER question 2 or question 3. You are advised to spend 35 minutes writing your answer..

In your response you should do the following.

- State a relevant thesis that directly addresses all parts of the question.
- Support your argument with evidence, using specific examples.
- Apply historical thinking skills as directed by the question.
- Synthesize the elements above into a persuasive essay.

---

2. Some historians have argued that American trade with the allied belligerent powers in WWI gave the United States a growing economic stake in the war that ultimately prompted U.S. intervention. Support, modify, or refute this contention using specific evidence.

3. Some historians have argued that the 1960s counterculture movement changed American society. Support, modify, or refute this contention using specific evidence.